Corporate Finance and Valuation

Bob Ryan

THOMSON
™

Australia • Canada • Mexico • Singapore • Spain • United Kingdom • United States

Corporate Finance and Valuation
Bob Ryan

Publishing Director	**Publisher**	**Development Editor**
John Yates	Patrick Bond	Laura Priest
Senior Production Editor	**Manufacturing Manager**	**Marketing Manager**
Alissa Chappell	Helen Mason	Katie Thorn
Typesetter	**Production Controller**	**Cover Design**
Integra, India	Maeve Healy	Hannah Dale, HL Studios, Oxford
Text Design	**Printer**	
Design Deluxe, Bath, UK	Canale, Italy	

British Library Cataloguing-in-
Publication Data
A catalogue record for this book is
available from the British Library

CONTENTS

PART III Developments in corporate finance 233

13 Short term finance and the management of interest rate risk 487

14 International financial markets 522

D reaming up novel business strategies or putting together an aggressive marketing plan is much more fun than worrying about a business's finances. We accept that many students and managers see the world that way and regard finance as the 'hard bit' – the subject they acknowledge is pretty important but best avoided or, if that is not possible, left to the professionals. However, even professionals can quail at the thought of keeping up to date with a subject they probably found difficult when they first encountered it some years previously. This book is therefore a complete spectrum antidote to jaded or non-existent financial knowledge. It is designed to give the student, whether academic or professional, or the business manager a thorough introduction to the subject. Indeed, the material in these pages will probably provide over 95 per cent of everything the potential financial manager needs to know. We also hope that this book has the sort of interest and fun which will engage even the wariest reader.

This book is for the reader who is prepared to take on the challenge of learning finance seriously. It is equally useful as a self-study book or as an adopted text on a course in financial management or corporate finance. We envisage that it will be of great interest to the following: students pursuing advanced undergraduate work in corporate finance or financial management. Postgraduate students on MBA or diploma programmes and professional students undertaking advanced level courses in financial management. We hope too that it will be of interest to financial managers and accountants who need to update their knowledge and who may be looking for inspiration about how to deal with the current preoccupations of business: the management of risk and value creation.

This book takes a thematic approach to the subject focusing on how the manager can add financial value to his or her business. In this book there are three themes: value, return and risk. The word value, like profit or strategy, has different meanings to different people. In this book we develop some precise definitions of value and describe how it can be measured and enhanced. Value can be viewed as a 'stock' concept and in this book ways are described of valuing business entities whether they are individual investment projects or a whole firm. Value can also be viewed as a 'flow' concept and the measurement and estimation of value flow or 'return' is also a key feature of this book. However, even though it may be possible to define value precisely, its estimation is an uncertain art. So along with value and return we add the concept of risk. Value, return and risk are the three building blocks of our subject and they form a unifying thread throughout this book.

Because value, return and risk are conceptual terms we need to be able to discuss them in both in a theoretical and a practical way. The theory of finance has developed rapidly over the last 50 years and in many areas of the subject there is a tight correspondence between theory and practice. In this book we have had to make some compromises at the theoretical level. We cannot expect the typical student or manager to handle some of the mathematics which is used in the research literature for example. However, in most cases we have been able to provide an intuitive insight into the 'deep theory' of the subject using the minimum of mathematical argument. However, in some areas of discussion it would not be doing the reader or the subject justice to ignore the formal bits. Where the mathematics is absolutely vital to understanding we have included it within the chapter as part of the running narrative of the subject. Where it is important but not vital we have put it in an appendix and where it is neither vital nor important we have left it out.

How to use the book

The book develops its themes in a progressive way and offers a managerial perspective on the subject. What this means is that the material is 'ready for use'. Throughout the book we give the practical tools and techniques for identifying and solving financial problems in the real world. So for every problem, from estimating a business' cost of capital through to the valuation of its intangible assets, we show how the job can be done using readily available tools and freely available data. Apart from pen and paper these are the most important adjuncts to the study of this subject:

A good calculator which has scientific functionality. 'Financial calculators' can be a waste of time but one that has the ability to calculate powers and roots to any order is a vital addition to the briefcase. Look for a y^x x^y or $\wedge$ key – this tells you that it will calculate power terms. If it does that then it will do most other things you will require of it. After that, all that matters is whether it is easy to use and has a clear display.

Access to a PC or laptop running a good spreadsheet program. Microsoft Excel is the market leader and it is a very good package which is remarkably easy to use. We have used Excel throughout this book. There are very good and cheaper alternatives such as Star Office which have similar functionality to Excel.

Access to the data sources on the World Wide Web. With this book there is free access to Thomson One which provides company specific data and relevant market information. This information is very reliable and continuously updated. Yahoo-finance at http://uk.finance.yahoo.com/ is also an extremely valuable data source. Both Thomson One and Yahoo Finance give access to news reports and summaries. The Financial Times website at FT.com is also a useful source of news and articles. However, the best material on FT.com is on a subscription basis and in this book we have endeavoured to avoid sources that cost money.

We strongly recommend that those new to the subject follow the book through from the beginning to end. There is a narrative to the subject which can be missed by a more haphazard reading approach. For the more financially experienced reader the chapters can be taken individually – we have tried to minimize the amount of back referencing that is required to understand each topic.

Friendly Grinders plc and Cobham plc

Two companies dominate our discussion of corporate finance and valuation. The first is Friendly Grinders plc where we have been granted unprecedented access to the company's internal discussions and data. Friendly Grinders was founded by Fred Grinder and his grandson Jack, the company's current Chief Executive Officer, has been most supportive of this project and has our particular thanks. Friendly Grinders appear throughout the book in numerous worked examples and case studies. However, we also felt it would be useful to feature another company where we restricted ourselves to information that is purely in the public domain. We chose Cobham plc which is a UK aerospace company based in Dorset. Cobham sits within a small cluster of UK aerospace businesses and this, as well as the clarity of its published financial information, makes it an excellent subject for analysis.

For the teacher

There is also one other important class of readership for this book – the tutor or teacher. Throughout my career I have always enjoyed books that give me a challenging perspective on the subject I am trying to teach. I hope that there is much in this book that will appeal to you and which, with your expertise, can offer you a programme which is fresh and original and will be valued by your students. I do recognize that there are substantial costs when adopting and recommending a new book. Lecture notes need to be rewritten and course materials updated. I have great sympathy with this problem and we have tried to make your job as easy as possible by providing you with a wide range of supplementary material including a teacher's manual, student study guide (which with minimum adaptation can be used as a distance learning manual) and an array of other useful stuff such as additional questions and answers and a collection of PowerPoint slides ready to go. In addition adopting teachers can make contact with me through the publisher. I would be delighted to receive your feedback and also, where I can, to help you get the most out of the book with advice and solutions to any queries you may have.

ACKNOWLEDGEMENTS

T his book has been developed over many years teaching corporate finance at different academic levels and presenting short courses delivered to professional managers. In recent years my association with the distance learning programmes operated by Manchester Business School (Worldwide) and the University of London External Programmes has brought me into contact with many students from different educational, cultural and business backgrounds. There is nothing as inspiring as good students and they have my deepest thanks.

I persuaded Pat Bond at Thomson Learning that this was a book that needed writing. He has been a great source of encouragement (and criticism from time to time) as the book has been transformed from outline idea to finished product. I would also like to thank my development editor Laura Priest and the production team for their hard work and commitment to this project. A word of thanks is also due to my agent Frances Kelly whose skills in negotiation and persuasion finalized my contract with Thomson Press and then ensured that I stuck to it.

Some academics argue that book publishing is not as worthwhile as contributing to the peer reviewed academic literature. That view is, in my opinion, of great detriment to our subject and its development. It also misses the point that books like this are also subject to stringent peer review. I would like to give my special thanks to all the reviewers who have come out blinking in the light and agreed to have the veil of anonymity lifted. They all did a magnificent job under tight time pressures and I am very grateful for the generosity of their insights and their time.

My special thanks also to Margaret Greenwood who has provided me with a very careful and detailed review of all the chapters and to Martin Bennett, Rhian Dow and Angela Lorenz at the University of Gloucestershire who gave me comments on sections of the text as it progressed.

Finally there has to be a real motive behind writing a book like this apart from the love of the subject. Mine is Alison who makes it all worthwhile.

The publisher would like to thank the following reviewers for their comments:
Abe de Jong, Erasmus University, Rotterdam
Peter Oliver, University of Nottingham
Marco Mongiello, University of Westminster
Sophie Manigart, Ghent University and Vlerick Leuven Gent Management School
Chen-Yu Chang, University College London
Suzette Viviers, University of Port Elizabeth, South Africa
Ciaran mac an Bhaird, Dublin City University
Bob Davidson, Glasgow Caledonian University
J. Marx, University of South Africa
Chin-Bun Tse, University of Leicester
Mike Adams, University of Swansea
Simon Gao, Napier University

WALK THROUGH TOUR

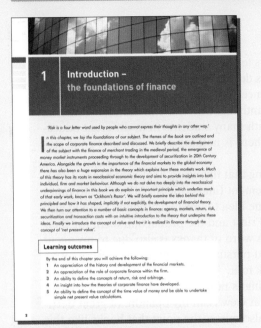

Learning outcomes

By the end of this chapter you will achieve the following:

1 An appreciation of the history and development of the financial markets.
2 An appreciation of the role of corporate finance within the firm.
3 An ability to define the concepts of return, risk and arbitrage.
4 An insight into how the theories of corporate finance have developed.
5 An ability to define the concept of the time value of money and be able to undertake simple net present value calculations.

Learning outcomes These define what the student can expect to achieve as they read the chapter and what will be assessed by the exercises and other assessments as the chapter proceeds.

Theoretical note Highlight important theoretical concepts to help students to remember them as they read through the chapters.

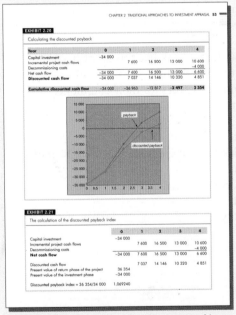

Exhibits These give a visual representation of key concepts or data.

Financial case These are exercises culled from real life situations using publicly available data. Most of them discuss the financial problems and issues faced by Cobham plc – a successful UK aerospace manufacturer.

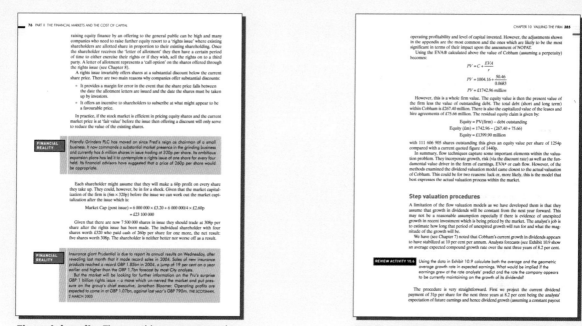

Financial reality These problems are reviewed in the text and are a key part of the learning process. Most of these feature the financial activities of Friendly Grinders Ltd.

Review activity These short questions allow students to explore the learning gained so far. They include challenging issues which can be used as a basis of further discussion or reading.

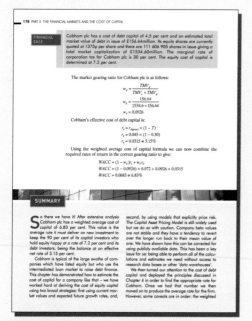

Summary Found at the end of each chapter, the summary offers a useful method of reviewing knowledge for exams by reminding students of what they have learned so far.

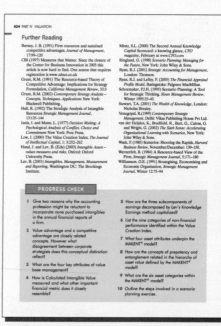

Further reading A wide variety of some of the best literature available on the subject.

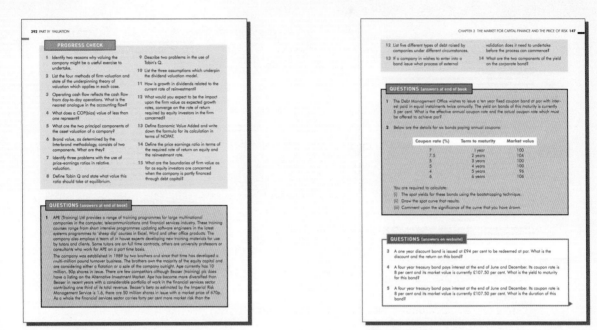

Progress check These brief end of chapter questions are designed to test students' memory and understanding of the text.

Questions A variety of questions and short cases designed to give students a thorough familiarity with the chapter material and to open up areas of further discovery.

SUPPLEMENTARY RESOURCES

Visit the Corporate Finance and Valuation accompanying website at www.thomsonlearning.co.uk/ryan_cfv to find further teaching and learning material including:

For the reader:
- Information about the book to help guide you through your studies.
- Chapter overviews to give you an idea of the book's coverage.
- Multiple choice questions designed to test your understanding of key points in the text.
- Additional cases, questions and answers to further your knowledge.
- Answers to more of the review activities and end of chapter questions in the book.
- A self-study manual which will give you the opportunity to study the whole book on your own. This manual contains study plans, overviews and further reading.
- Excel templates for set exercises and algorithms.

For the lecturer
A downloadable lecturer's manual including:
- Answers to reserved questions in the book.
- Some longer additional cases, questions and suggested answers.
- PowerPoint slides prepared in 14 lecture sets.
- Teaching notes for each chapter.
- Additional multiple choice questions.

ExamView®
This testbank and test generator provides a huge amount of different types of questions, allowing lecturers to create online, paper and local area network (LAN) tests. This CD-based product is only available from your Thomson Learning sales representative.

I | Introduction to Corporate Finance and Valuation

1 Introduction – the foundations of finance

'Risk is a four letter word used by people who cannot express their thoughts in any other way.'

I n this chapter, we lay the foundations of our subject. The themes of the book are outlined and the scope of corporate finance described and discussed. We briefly describe the development of the subject with the finance of merchant trading in the medieval period, the emergence of money market instruments proceeding through to the development of securitization in 20th Century America. Alongside the growth in the importance of the financial markets to the global economy there has also been a huge expansion in the theory which explains how these markets work. Much of this theory has its roots in neoclassical economic theory and aims to provide insights into both individual, firm and market behaviour. Although we do not delve too deeply into the neoclassical underpinnings of finance in this book we do explain an important principle which underlies much of that early work, known as 'Ockham's Razor'. We will briefly examine the idea behind this principle and how it has shaped, implicitly if not explicitly, the development of financial theory. We then turn our attention to a number of basic concepts in finance: agency, markets, return, risk, securitization and transaction costs with an intuitive introduction to the theory that underpins these ideas. Finally we introduce the concept of value and how it is realized in finance through the concept of 'Net Present Value'.

Learning outcomes

By the end of this chapter you will achieve the following:
1   An appreciation of the history and development of the financial markets.
2   An appreciation of the role of corporate finance within the firm.
3   An ability to define the concepts of return, risk and arbitrage.
4   An insight into how the theories of corporate finance have developed.
5   An ability to define the concept of the time value of money and be able to undertake simple Net Present Value calculations.

The origins of financial markets

The development of markets is as long as human history – within every settled community some form of exchange has taken place. Economic historians suggest that independent merchants, buying and selling goods and even land, can be traced back to the third millennium before Christ. We also know that at this time loans were used to finance trade, that there were street markets and that silver was a common form of money.

The Ancient Greeks were the first to generalize the concept of money, but although borrowing and lending for interest was well established there is scant evidence of a money market, where rights to indebtedness or shares in a business venture were bought and sold.

Roman times saw the establishment of the legal principles upon which western law, and in particular the law of property and contract, were established. During this era the concept of a separate legal entity in the form of a company first emerged (the word company comes from the Latin *cum panis* meaning to 'share bread', representing the sharing of common interests within a legal framework of co-ownership).

The growing influence of Christianity and Islam following the fall of Rome slowed the development of financial markets as both religions forbade the charging of interest on loans. After AD 1150 trade fairs were established in France and it was here that letters of credit were issued and the first European banking system began to emerge. It was at these fairs that letters of credit (a guarantee of payment to the holder of the letter) could be both cashed and exchanged. However, another key factor in the development of the financial markets, the concept of the limited liability company, did not arise until the end of the 15th Century, when the city state of Florence dominated European trade. These early Florentine companies were largely financed through private subscription or by the Italian banking houses. It was another three centuries before a 'capital market' for the trading of securities began to emerge.

In Britain in the 18th and 19th Centuries the Industrial Revolution rapidly expanded the need for capital which could no longer be financed privately or through the banking system. This demand for capital finance led to the creation of a number of regional stock exchanges in Britain and other European countries, and later in their colonies.

However, the emerging capital markets created almost as many problems as they solved with spectacular gyrations in stock prices fueled by uncontrolled speculation and the burgeoning capital requirements of industry and commerce. One dramatic example involved the South Sea Company. This company was one of a number of merchant enterprises given the right, by the Crown, to trade in the South Seas and, in particular in South America.

Inspired by a speculative rush for stock in the American colonies and elsewhere, the directors of the South Sea Company attempted to recreate the same effect in Britain by announcing ventures which had no real substance. One bizarre example was a 'company for carrying on an undertaking of great advantage, but nobody to know what it is'. In one day of trading in the new issue, the proposer of this venture cleared £2000 in investor deposits and promptly disappeared. The South Sea Bubble, as it became known, burst in 1720 leading to wide scale bankruptcies and the recall of Parliament.

Michael Roach/mapshotz.com

These booms and crashes made the concept of risk much more tangible and an issue for the investors of the day. Mathematicians had been developing a theory of risk through their discovery of the laws of probability. They discovered that 'risk' could be measured and priced using probabilities and these measurements manipulated using simple rules. These important ideas shaped the development of the insurance industry and business in general, the most noticeable result being the development of securitization, where the risk of capital investment is shared among as many investors as possible.

Trading in stocks and shares was nevertheless just one part of the developing capital market. The merchant banks of Europe that had originally developed as a means of financing trade were also an important source of finance for new business ventures. Merchant banks traditionally organized private equity finance but as they matured many also began to act as conventional commercial banks, receiving deposits from savers and lending funds either within the banking sector or more broadly to high quality companies seeking short to medium term loan finance.

Following the Wall Street Crash and the resulting collapse in confidence in the US banking sector in the 1920s, a process of financial disintermediation began to develop, first in America and then elsewhere. Companies, like governments, began to issue debt in the form of securities rather than following the European model of borrowing directly from banks.

The US financial model of disintermediated markets has become pivotal in the development of the global financial markets as securitization and the 'spreading' of risk has permitted the creation of a well regulated system for the management of capital flows. The success of the US financial system is a relatively recent phenomenon, reflecting the growing strength of its wider economy and the universal adoption of the dollar as the world's principal reserve currency. However, markets and world events are unpredictable. It is salutary to note that in 1900 the US economy was the same size as that of Argentina, and that Great Britain was the dominant world economy.

The modern financial markets

What we refer to as the financial markets are a number of trading exchanges such as the London and New York Stock Exchange which deal principally in capital securities as well as a variety of specialized exchanges dealing with other types of financial security. Alongside these there are a number of banks and other financial houses whose trading desks buy and sell securities with one another and with the public. The various exchanges, brokerage houses and financial institutions are now connected into what has in recent years become a global financial market. This market is not a single entity but a networked series of institutional relationships which apart from a very small number of countries that choose to remain outside it, spans the globe.

The modern financial markets are separated into three:

1 The money markets which exist for the purchase and sale of money in the form of foreign exchange (FOREX) and financial securities that have less than one year until maturity. Money market securities are generally referred to as 'bills'.

2 The capital markets which exist for the purchase and sale of financial claims which have a term to maturity, when issued, of greater than one year. The capital market is divided into a number of subordinate markets the most important being the market for fixed interest securities (bonds) and equities. Within each market there is a 'primary market' where the user of capital (government, firms or other institutions) issues securities to the market to

be taken up by either private or institutional investors and a secondary market, where issued securities are subsequently traded.

3 The derivatives market which exists for the purchase and sale of securities 'derived' from, in the sense that they depend upon, the value of other financial securities. Such derivatives include swaps, futures and options upon both capital market and money market securities. The derivatives markets are important for two reasons: First they allow investors to manage the risk associated with their holdings of securities. Second, in perfectly competitive markets, the prices of the derivative securities should exist in a clear relationship to the price of the principal securities concerned. This allows us to develop pricing models both for derivatives and for their underlying securities based upon the law of 'one price'.

The nature of financial securities and the law of one price

A financial security is a legally binding claim upon the current monetary value of an asset or assets held by another which is freely tradable without any loss in the value of the claim to which the asset relates. The idea of tradability (or 'negotiability' as it is more formally known) means that the property rights under the claim are freely transferable from one person to another. Here are some examples of financial securities:

- A company wishes to borrow some money from the public. It issues certificates binding it to pay interest and repay the capital to the owner of the 'bond'. The borrowing is denominated in set units of say £100 each and the firm issues as many £100 bonds as it requires to raise the finance it needs. The holders of each bond certificate have a claim against £100 held by the firm which will be repaid to them at the due time. Furthermore, the holders of the bonds, provided they have been issued in the correct way, can sell them on in the 'bond market' and the price they get will depend upon how potential purchasers value the promise of the future interest payments and the redemption value that the bond represents.

- A business wishes to expand and its directors decide to issue further 'shares' in the ownership of the firm. A share such as this is referred to as an 'equity' share and it represents a claim upon the value of the business as a whole. The business as a whole is the 'asset' and the share is a claim to one of a number of equal parts of the net value of the firm. When the share is issued its value to its subscriber will be based upon the current value of the company concerned. However, as the fortunes of the enterprise fluctuate the value at which the share can be exchanged in the 'equity market' will change. It is important to note that an equity share is a claim against the value of the business and not against any particular assets that the firm may own at any one time.

- A bank has granted its customer credit under a trade credit agreement and creates a security against the value of that credit. The asset is the debt receivable by the bank and its guarantee creates a 'banker's acceptance' which it can sell into the money market at a discount. What this means is that the bank offers the guarantee document in a standard form to the market at a small discount on its face value and promises to pay the eventual holder the full amount at the end of the credit period when the banker's acceptance matures. The banker's acceptance is a money market security which is tradable between individuals and firms who are interested in this type of investment.

EXHIBIT 1.1

An ordinary share certificate issued by Friendly Grinders Ltd in 1966

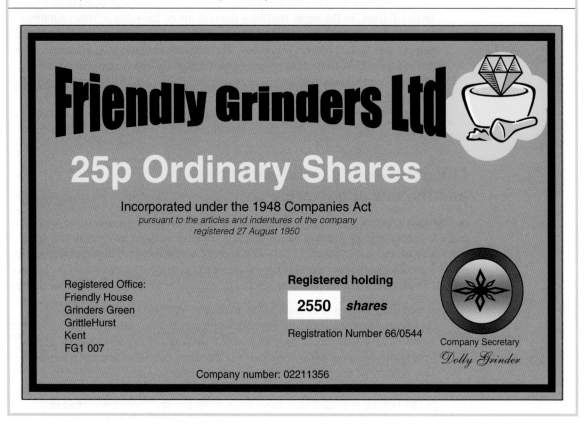

The ability of the financial markets to create novel financial securities is almost boundless. One hundred years ago most firms were financed through equity shares, borrowing from banks and internally generated finance. In the 1950s and 60s new types of 'hybrid' financial security became popular and were issued by rapidly growing companies willing to offer future equity participation to individuals and institutions who in their turn were willing to lend them the money they needed to expand. These securities had some of the characteristics of debt and equity as well as granting the option to convert from one to the other at some future stage. Then in the early 1970s derivative securities such as futures contracts and options started to emerge as investors sought different ways of 'bundling' and 'unbundling' the risk which the more fundamental securities represented.

Now, in the large western style economies, virtually any financial claim from the mortgages granted to homeowners to the receivables balances of large corporations is 'securitized', sold on and then actively traded in what have become multi-trillion dollar markets.

Financial securities offer a specified set of financial rights over the underlying asset that they represent. The value of a financial security is measured in terms of the cash flow that it offers to the investor. With some securities those cash flows are highly certain; with others the cash flows may be highly unpredictable. However, financial securities of all types present some risk to the investor in terms of the uncertainty attaching to the future cash flows they represent. As a result the prices at which financial securities trade in the market place are volatile. So we can make the following generalized statements about all financial securities:

1 They represent a financial claim upon some underlying asset even though the asset concerned may be another security.

2 They are negotiable in that they can be transferred from one party to another through sale without any loss in the value of the legal claim that they represent.

3 They are fungible in that securities of a particular type are perfect substitutes for one another.

4 They are risky in that future financial returns are always uncertain.

The law of one price

Because the value of a financial security rests solely in the future cash flows it promises to the holder then two securities which in all respects offer identical future cash flows must have the same value. This is the idea, which is central to economics, that in free markets identical assets and hence the claims on those assets should have identical value. If the equity shares in one company are trading at two different prices in different markets savvy investors will simply buy them in the low price market and sell them in the high price market and make a profit. Indeed with modern electronic trading systems traders should be able to make their deals simultaneously with one another and hence earn, what is known as an arbitrage profit. Such profit opportunities will not last for long as buyers in the 'cheap market' bring up the price of the security concerned through the pressure of their demand and then their selling in the 'dear market' pushes the price down through the pressure of excess supply. In perfectly competitive markets such mispricing should be instantaneously eliminated. In real markets it does occur but as we shall see later in this book we would expect it to be no more than a transient phenomenon and for the law that identical securities should be identically priced to hold in all but the very short run.

Corporate finance and the modern firm

Modern companies need to raise finance from the capital market in order to invest in the real and intangible assets they need to earn profits. Their first priority is to ensure that they can source finance for both their short run and their long run needs in the most economical way possible. Corporate investment is by its nature risky and often capital intensive. It usually means that the finance needed will be tied up in assets for the long run and which are depreciating in value as they age. Potential investors will need to be compensated for the level of risk to which they will be exposed. However, the firm will want to make sure that the returns it offers in the way of dividends and interest payments (the cost of the capital it uses) are fairly set given its risk. A primary concern in corporate finance is how firms raise capital and the potential cost of that capital that it will, as a result, be expected to bear.

In order to justify the use of other people's money a firm needs to ensure that the investment decisions it makes, taking into account its cost of capital, lead to an overall increase in the value of the firm and hence its investors' wealth. Alongside the problem of sourcing finance at the cheapest cost, the firm has to make sure that all the investment decisions it undertakes are 'value adding'. If they are not the firm will not be able to justify its existence for very long and will find itself out of business.

Within these 'financing' and 'investment' decisions a firm will have to make a number of related decisions: what is the optimal source of capital, how can the effect of tax be mitigated, should all of the profits each year be returned to investors or should they be reinvested and so on. It is these questions which the modern firm has to address because getting the right answers is probably the most important thing a firm has to do. Modern firms exist in a 'sea of markets'. The analogy of the sea is quite apposite, generally the sea supports the existence of those who use it and respect its power. However, once it turns it finds any weakness and destroys its hapless victim. This is no truer than in the case of the capital markets. A firm can have the most carefully thought out strategy, the most effective marketing operation and the most benign human resource management policies. However, if it fails to satisfy the requirements of the capital market then its failure will be swift and brutal.

Part of our understanding of corporate finance is understanding the way the capital and other financial markets operate. To this end we will in this book be exploring the phenomenon which has given the modern markets much of their current force – securitization. The ability to trade the financial claims of business ventures has been known about and practised for centuries. In the modern era the standardization of financial claims into homogenous trading units has transformed the way markets operate. Until the 1930s companies, for example, borrowed money from banks – but following the Wall Street Crash in the United States there was a sudden loss of confidence in the banking sector. As a result, companies started to practise what governments had been doing for some time and sidestepped the banks going directly to lenders and offering them securitized debt in the form of bonds. As we shall see in Chapter 4 this transformed the way in which large (and not so large) companies raised finance and immediately created a secondary market as investors bought and sold their bonds. More recently, more complex financial securities have been created which bundle financial claims in ways which give investors and firms greater flexibility in the way they manage their finance and their exposure to risk.

In seeking to understand how the capital markets operate and how firms can optimize their financial decision making we need to be able to build theories and test those theories against practice. It has been said that 'there is nothing as useful as a good theory' and conversely 'a practical man (or woman) is someone who is wedded to out of date theories'. Whichever way you put it theory and practice go hand in hand so with this in mind we will turn aside to review briefly the approach taken in the development of the early theory of finance and which still dominates today.

Theoretical development in finance

The modern theory of finance began to emerge in the 1950s with important contributions from a number of American economists, many of whom went on to win Nobel prizes for their work. Of these Milton Friedman in the 1950s and 1960s at Chicago and Paul Samuelson at Harvard and MIT were highly influential. These early scholars were heavily influenced by a philosophical approach to theory development and testing which owed much to the empiricist tradition within Western philosophy. They took the view that a theory only had meaning if there was some way in which it could be tested. This emphasis upon testability and the formal verification of theories through experiment is often referred to as a 'Positive' approach to economic and financial research. Although even within this tradition there were sharp disagreements. Friedman for example advocated a form of 'instrumentalism' in the development of theory. He argued that the 'acid test' of a good theory was not the realism of the underlying assumptions but rather whether it worked in the sense that it generated results that could be tested. For Friedman, the ultimate test of a good theory is its predictive power rather than congruence between the theory and what may be described as reality.

Samuelson's philosophy, on the other hand, influenced by his mentor Joseph Schumpeter (1883–1950) at Harvard, believed that the realism of a theory's assumptions do matter and that although predictive success is an important consideration the use of assumptions that are demonstrably untrue only serve to undermine its credibility. In addition to this Samuelson employed a strict rule in theory development in that he always sought to reduce the number of variables in a theory to the minimum number possible. In this both he and Friedman would have been on common ground in that both accepted and utilized a philosophical approach to deciding between competing theories first advanced by a 13th Century English philosopher William of Ockham.

Ockham argued that the explanation of general and quite complex things (such as in our terms society, markets, firms) can be *reduced* to explanations in terms of simpler things which do not make reference to these higher order terms.

Ockham's reductionism led him to formulate a principle which has become known as Ockham's Razor or more technically the Law of 'Parsimony of Inference':

'... *what can happen through fewer principles happens in vain through more'.*

In more modern terms Ockham's Razor asserts that all theories should be simplified so that they contain the minimum number of assumptions required for them to work.

What does this mean for scholars in general and did it mean for the early pioneers in the theory of finance in particular? If there are two or more competing theoretical explanations of a market or corporate phenomena the simplest, in terms of the number of assumptions involved, is to be preferred. In modelling market behaviour for example, the simplest model which explains the data with which are presented is the one to be preferred. Take, for example, scatter of data points relating the returns on a share against the returns on the index (see Chapter 3) as shown in Exhibit 1.2.

EXHIBIT 1.2

Alternative interpretations of data

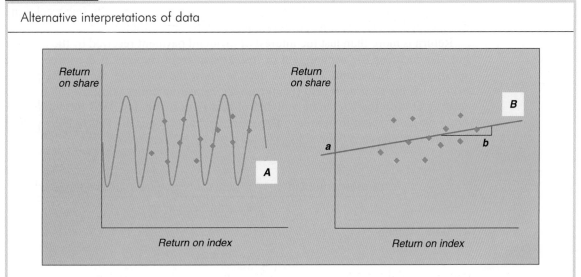

The question we have to resolve when looking at these two graphs is which explanation of the data points is likely to be most useful: the sinusoidal function shown in (A) or the straight line shown in (B). Using Ockham's Razor we can make our decision: we would choose (B) because a straight line is defined by two parameters (the slope of the line (b) and the point it cuts the share return axis at (a)) whereas the sinusoidal function requires four: its amplitude, its period, the phase shift and the vertical shift. So unless we had a positive reason for rejecting the straight-line as the best explanation of the data the interpretation (B) is what we would prefer.

The caveat we should enter about Ockham's Razor is this: the simplest explanation is not always the truth. It is not always the case that the theory which is based upon the fewest assumptions turns out to be the most successful in explaining and predicting the phenomena we are interested in. Ockham's Razor is a strategy we can use in our thinking to help us derive theories efficiently. Invariably, the simpler a theory the easier it is to test and possibly to refute. Once a theory is refuted we can then start adding in complexity. The theory of capital asset pricing discussed in Chapter 3 is a very good example of this.

There are many who would argue that this philosophical approach is wrong. What is undeniable is that it has been remarkably efficient at producing theories about the way the financial world works and many of these theories have shown themselves to be both useful to practitioners and reliable in explaining and predicting financial phenomena. So with that brief introduction to the theory of finance we now turn to two of the most basic theoretical concepts which underpin the subject.

Risk and return

The formal measurement of the performance of a financial security is dominated by two important and interrelated parameters: its 'return' and the 'risk' associated with that return.

The concept of a security's return is easily misunderstood. In principle it represents the financial reward achieved by the investor who holds that security over a specified period of time. This period of time may be any of our choosing although conventionally for comparison purposes annual returns are commonly quoted. However, in different applications returns of a quarter, one month, one week, one day and, indeed, of any time period we like may be appropriate.

Return is more than just the interest or dividend payment received by the investor but also includes the capital gain or loss arising from changes in the value of the security held. To measure return we need to know the following: the holding period over which the security is held (i.e. the return measurement period), the value of the security at both the beginning and end of that period and any dividend, interest or other payment made in between. Therefore the return over the first holding period in a given sequence is defined as:

Return

$$= \frac{\text{price at period end}\,(p_1) - \text{price at the beginning}\,(p_0) + \text{dividend paid}\,(D_0)}{\text{price at the beginning}\,(p_0)}$$

or more formally:

$$r_1 = \frac{p_1 - p_0 + D_0}{p_0}$$

This measure of return can be split into two components:

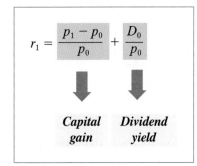

$$r_1 = \frac{p_1 - p_0}{p_0} + \frac{D_0}{p_0}$$

Capital gain   Dividend yield

1 The capital gain component arising from an increase in the security price or a loss following a decrease in price.

2 The dividend yield which is the dividend or interest received, in cash, during that period.

In Exhibit 1.3 we have collected monthly share prices for Tesco plc and the dividends paid during the year. Notice that the dividend component of return only materializes in the period in which it is paid to and received by investors. A similar data series could have been retrieved for a government or corporate bond. Again, monthly prices could have been recovered but the 'dividend' would have been replaced by the interest payment made on the 'nominal value' of the bond when it was paid to the investor.

EXHIBIT 1.3

Monthly share prices and dividends for Tesco plc

date	share price	dividend	gain	Yld	return
03/11/03	249.00				
28/11/03		2.07			
01/12/03	257.25		0.0331	0.0083	0.0414
02/01/04	240.41		−0.0655		−0.0655
02/02/04	257.50		0.0711		0.0711
01/03/04	245.75		−0.0456		−0.0456
01/04/04	248.75		0.0122		0.0122
04/05/04	249.00		0.0010		0.0010
01/06/04	266.25		0.0693		0.0693
26/06/04		4.77			
01/07/04	254.75		−0.0432	0.0179	−0.0253
02/08/04	266.61		0.0466		0.0466
01/09/04	285.88		0.0723		0.0723
01/10/04	288.33		0.0086		0.0086
01/11/04	297.89		0.0332		0.0332

$$= \frac{257.25 - 249.00}{249.00}$$

$$= 0.0331$$

$$= \frac{2.07}{249.00}$$

$$= 0.0083$$

We can express the return formula above in a number of ways:

$$r_1 = \frac{p_1 - p_0 + D_0}{p_0}$$

$$r_1 = \frac{p_1}{p_0} - 1 + \frac{D_0}{p_0}$$

$$1 + r_1 = \frac{p_1 + D_0}{p_0}$$

Or, to put it another way, the period return is the ratio of the end price to the beginning price plus the dividend yield. We will use this very important result in Chapter 10 to derive one of the principal valuation models for the firm.

It is important to note that the return interval chosen is largely a matter of choice although in finance many research studies use data with monthly intervals. Note also that we have shown the returns as decimals rather than percentages which again is a matter of taste!

Geometric and arithmetic average return

Once a series of returns have been calculated it is then possible to average the returns either arithmetically or geometrically. Using the Tesco example and the 12 monthly return observations we can calculate the arithmetic average return by simply summing the 12 monthly returns and dividing by 12:

$$Average\ return = \frac{\begin{array}{l}0.0414 + (-0.0655) + 0.0711 + (-0.0456) + 0.0122 + 0.0010 \\ + 0.0693 + (-0.0253) + 0.0466 + 0.0723 + 0.0086 + 0.0332\end{array}}{12}$$

$$average\ return = 0.0183 \equiv 1.83\%\ per\ month$$

The geometric return is more complicated. Again using the 12 months of data for Tesco, we calculate one plus the return for each month and then all the months are multiplied together to give a 12 monthly compound return which will be the total return earned on a pound invested at the beginning and reinvested each month for the year.

Over the 12 month period the reinvestment of the £1 will accumulate to £1.2286 which is a 22.86 per cent return. The monthly geometric average return can be calculated by taking the twelfth root of the accumulated value as follows:

$$Geometric\ return\ (monthly) = \sqrt[12]{1.2286} - 1 = 0.0173 \equiv 1.73\%$$

The obvious question is why is there a difference? The arithmetic average (or mean) reveals the percentage return we are most likely to make in any given month. The arithmetic average is usually taken as our best guess of what the future return might be in any given month on the basis of past evidence. Thus in any one month we would expect a return of 1.83 per cent. However, if we wanted to discover the constant monthly rate of return we would need to apply to achieve the same overall return over the sequence of 12 months as given by the actual monthly returns then we would use the geometric average return of 1.73 per cent. Thus £100 invested for one

EXHIBIT 1.4

Tesco's return reinvested monthly

date	return	(1+r)	product(1+r)
03/11/03			
28/11/03			
01/12/03	0.0414	1.0414	1.0414
02/01/04	−0.0655	0.9345	0.9733
02/02/04	0.0711	1.0711	1.0425
01/03/04	−0.0456	0.9544	0.9949
01/04/04	0.0122	1.0122	1.0070
04/05/04	0.0010	1.0010	1.0080
01/06/04	0.0693	1.0693	1.0779
26/06/04		1.0000	1.0779
01/07/04	−0.0253	0.9747	1.0506
02/08/04	0.0466	1.0466	1.0995
01/09/04	0.0723	1.0723	1.1790
01/10/04	0.0086	1.0086	1.1891
01/11/04	0.0332	1.0332	1.2286

month will grow to £101.73 at the end of one month, to £103.50 (i.e. £100 × 1.0173²) at the end of the second month and so on.

The key to understanding the difference is this: given a series of 'n' different return measures what constant value if multiplied by 'n' would be equal to the sum total of the individual returns? This constant value is the arithmetic mean. Now, given the same series of 'n' different return measures what constant value if multiplied by one plus itself 'n' times would give the product of one plus the individual returns? This value is the geometric mean.

So, we use the arithmetic average whenever we are describing our beliefs about the likely return which we would expect to arise in any given period of time. We use the geometric return when we are describing the average that will be realized over a sequence of returns where those returns are compounded. The arithmetic average return is sometimes referred to as the 'simple' average return and the geometric average return is referred to as the 'compound' average return.

REVIEW ACTIVITY 1.1 Calculate the quarterly returns for Tesco plc using the above data. Calculate the average quarterly return, the quarterly geometric return and the equivalent annual return.

The development of the theory of risk

Much of the financial theory of risk has been developed on the basis that returns can best be described using the normal distribution. The normal distribution is important because it represents that distribution which occurs in many natural processes. We also know that if we take the average from a sample of observations of data and repeat many times that the distribution of the averages will be normal irrespective of the shape of the distributions from which we took the samples.

For example, in the UK National Lottery players are required to select six numbers from the set 0 to 49. Each number is equally likely to be drawn so the underlying distribution is 'rectangular' in shape because it is equally likely (unless there is some bias in the lottery machines) that any number in the range will be drawn. However, when the averages of each set of six numbers are drawn these averages cluster in the approximate shape of the normal distribution – and the more averages you calculate the closer the final approximation will be to the ideal 'bell shaped' curve. The averages will never perfectly reflect a normal distribution although they may come very close because a normal distribution has 'infinite tails' (this means that there is a tiny probability of averages both smaller than 3.5 and greater than 46.5 which is the smallest and largest average that can be drawn using lottery numbers).

The tendency of sample means to approach a normal distribution is known as the Central Limit Theorem. This theorem provides a rationale for why many economic processes appear to be normally distributed. To give one case in point, studies of share returns have been shown to be normally distributed using many years of stock-market data. The actual share returns generated by share prices (and dividends) are what we refer to as a revealed average. The underlying reason for this is that if we sampled a group of individuals in the population of actual or potential investors and asked them what return they would require and hence the price at which they were willing to trade the shares of a given security then the actual return and the actual price delivered in the market would be at, or very close to, the average of their responses.

The price of a share and its return as it is traded in the market place represents the consensus belief of all those individuals trading in the marketplace at a given point in time. Because returns generated over time arise from a compounding process there is a somewhat complex relationship between the average of the pricing process and

EXHIBIT 1.5

The distribution of averages drawn from a random number generator selecting six numbers with equal probability of being chosen in the range 0–49

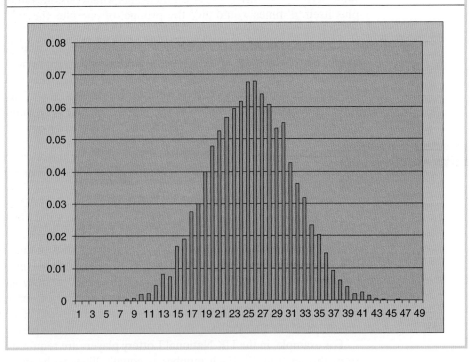

the average of the return generating process. Simply, however, the action of the central limit theorem is such that, other things being equal:

1 Returns will appear to be best described by a normal distribution, and

2 Share prices will appear to be best described by a log normal distribution. We return to the nature of the log normal distribution in Chapter 3 but it is one where the logarithm of the variable concerned (prices in this case) is normally distributed.

In Exhibit 1.6, for example, we show the weekly return distribution for Tesco plc taken using 200 weeks from April 2001 to February 2005.

Considering security returns for a moment we can note that the normal distribution is defined by just two variables:

- The average or mean value of the distribution, and

- The spread of the distribution as measured by its standard deviation.

These two variables allow us to 'reduce' a complex array of data (such as the 200 weekly return observations from Tesco) into a 'normal distribution' defined uniquely by its mean and standard deviation.

The mean of the distribution gives us our best estimate of the expected return (which is the mid point value on the curve) and the standard deviation gives an

EXHIBIT 1.6

The weekly return distribution for Tesco plc (200 observations from April 2001 to February 2005)

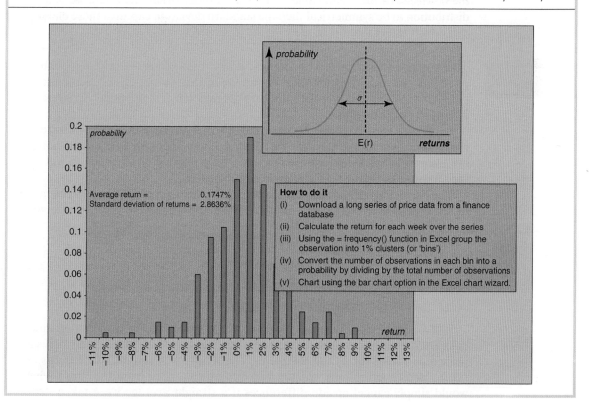

EXHIBIT 1.7

The normal distributed returns of two securities (A) and (B)

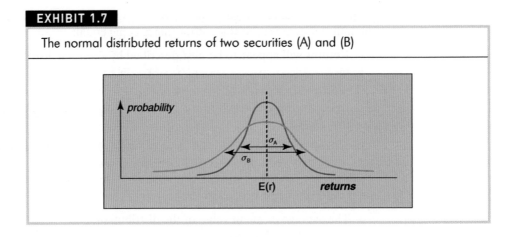

indication of the variability of the returns. It is this measure of variability which has become synonymous in the finance literature with the concept of risk. Generally speaking, the greater the standard deviation the greater the risk which attaches to the distribution of outcomes and in particular the greater the standard deviation the greater the probability that extreme values will be obtained.

To make the point clear consider the two distributions in Exhibit 1.7. Note how distribution B, which has the larger standard deviation, is the one which presents the greater likelihood of an extreme outcome occurring. It might be objected however that the real measure of risk should be just that part of the distribution which lies on the downside of the mean value. However, in those situations where we believe the distribution to be symmetrical then the standard deviation captures those elements of risk, which are of interest to us.

THEORETICAL NOTE

The normal distribution is a 'theoretical' distribution which relates the probability of an outcome occurring with the magnitude of that outcome. The distribution is symmetrical about the average value and has tails which mathematically stretch to infinity in either direction.

In practice, data resulting from natural or social processes may approximate the distribution. We also know that the Central Limit Theorem guarantees that the averages of samples drawn from any underlying population distribution will also tend towards normality as the sample size increases.

The mean of a normal distribution is given by the weighted average of the range of outcomes where the weights are the probabilities of given outcomes occurring.

$$E(x_i) = \sum_{i=1}^{i=n} p_i X_i$$

Where: $E()$ signifies the expected value of the variable in the bracket
p_i is the probability of X_i occurring.

The standard deviation is a measure of the spread of the distribution and is calculated from the weighted average of the square of the differences between individual values for X_i and the mean. The reason why squared differences are taken used to bring into account downside differences from the mean which would simply cancel upside differences if a straight average were taken. Once the weighted average of the squared differences has been taken, the square root of the result provide gives the standard deviation:

$$\sigma_i = \sqrt{\sum_{i=1}^{i=n} p_i [X_i - E(X_i)]^2}$$

The standard deviation also has the property that it encloses approximately 68 per cent of the normal distribution. Two standard deviations capture 95 per cent and three standard deviations capture approximately 99 per cent. What this means is that there is a 68 per cent chance that the weekly returns on Tesco shares fell between −2.6889 and +3.0383 per cent. There was also less than a 1 per cent chance that the returns would fall more than three standard deviations from the mean value:

$$Range(3\sigma) = [0.1747 \pm (3 \times 2.8636)] = 8.4161 - 8.7655\%$$

Putting it another way, if you observed a weekly price gain for Tesco giving a return of (say) 10 per cent then you could infer that there was a less than a one in one hundred chance of that occurring.

The standard deviation may in certain situations be replaced by the 'variance' of the distribution which is simply the standard deviation squared:

$$Variance = \sigma^2$$

The variability as measured by the standard deviation has many names in the finance literature: risk being the most common but you will also come across terms such as 'variability' and 'volatility' and most problematic of all 'uncertainty'. Uncertainty is normally taken to imply that the probability estimates in forming the distribution are subjective where in the case of risk those probabilities are derived from empirical data. However, in the finance literature we hover on the borderline between the two in that we are using past data to inform beliefs about the future. In this book we will only use the term 'uncertainty' when we are dealing with beliefs which are only weakly supported by evidence and risk we will use for virtually everything else.

As our study of corporate finance develops we will explore the concept of risk in much greater detail. In particular, in Chapter 3 we will explore what happens to the distribution of a group of securities held together (a portfolio) given that we know the standard deviations of each share's returns. In that chapter we begin our exploration of market risk and the way that securities are 'priced' in markets to compensate for the risk that they carry. Indeed, much of what we refer to as the financial markets is about the bundling and unbundling of risk into financial products which are then bought and sold.

Arbitrage

Good levels of return are regarded as a desirable property of any investment whereas risk is undesirable. The question that haunts many able minds in the financial centres of the world is whether it is possible to have the one without the other. Is it possible, in any market, to enter into instantaneous buy/sell transactions which would allow you to make money (i.e. earn a return) on the price difference. This process of making simultaneous buy/sell deals in the hope of capturing profit is called 'arbitrage' after the Latin word *arbitrare* which means 'to give judgement'. It also sometimes called taking 'a free lunch' or exploiting 'a cash machine'.

Suppose a company security was trading in New York at 105p and in the UK for 100p. The savvy trader would immediately buy in the UK and sell in New York and indeed we would expect the buying pressure in the UK to build up and the pressure of demand lead to an increase in the price. In New York, the trading pressure would be the other way around as traders sold to make their profit thus increasing the supply of the security in the New York market and taking the price down. Presumably, when the price had risen in the UK to about 102.5p and fallen in the United States to 102.5p the buying and selling to make an arbitrage profit would stop.

Arbitrageurs, or 'arbs', as these types of traders are called, fulfil a very important function in any free market in that they work to eliminate mispricing between markets. In so doing they ensure that the Law of One Price holds as discussed earlier.

Interest – simple and compound

The price of money or capital is expressed as an interest rate. Interest accumulation on an invested sum can be either simple or compound. In the first case it is assumed that the interest is withdrawn as soon as it is earned. The *coupon* payment on a government savings bond is paid to the investor in regular instalments and is not reinvested with the capital sum involved.

For example an investor purchases a four year £1000 savings bond at the beginning of the year (time 0) and at the end of the year interest is paid at a rate of 6 per cent. She can elect whether to take the interest each year or add it to her original investment thus earning interest on interest. Exhibit 1.8 shows the result in either case.

EXHIBIT 1.8

Simple and compound interest on a savings bond

Election 1: simple interest – choose to take interest as it arises

	0	1	2	3	4	Total
Investment / balance brought forward	1000	1000	1000	1000	1000	1000
add interest at 6%		60	60	60	60	240
		1060	1060	1060	1060	1240
withdrawal		–60	–60	–60	–60	–240
Balance carried forward	1000	1000	1000	1000	1000	1000

Election 2: compound interest – choose to reinvest interest payments along with the accumulated sum

	0	1	2	3	4	Total
Investment / balance brought forward	1000.00	1000.00	1060.00	1123.60	1191.02	1000.00
add interest at 6%		60.00	63.60	67.42	71.46	262.48
		1060.00	1123.60	1191.02	1262.48	1262.48
withdrawal		0.00	0.00	0.00	0.00	0.00
Balance carried forward	1000.00	1060.00	1123.60	1191.02	1262.48	1262.48

Compound interest can be calculated using the following equation:

$$FV_n = PV(1 + i)^n$$

Where:

FV_n is the future value of the fund accumulated 'n' periods of time from now.

PV is the present value invested.

i is the rate of interest.

Therefore at year four in the above example:

$$FV_4 = 1000 \times (1 + 6\%)^4$$

$$FV_4 = 1000 \times 1.06^4 = 1262.48$$

TECHNICAL NOTE

To do this sum on your calculator use the $^\wedge$ or y^x key to find the 'power':

And your calculator should return the answer above.

Exhibit 1.9 shows the dramatic effect of compounding upon future values: as a rule of thumb the initial sum invested is doubled when compounded at 10 per cent for seven years or compounded at 7 per cent for ten years.

EXHIBIT 1.9

The change in future value with time at different interest rates

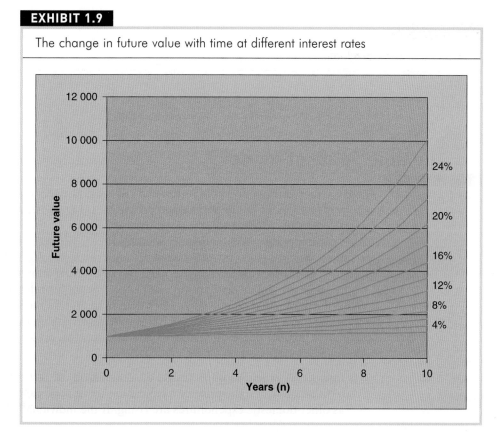

Equivalent rates

The idea of an equivalent rate is straightforward: if an interest rate is calculated on the basis of one time period, what is the equivalent rate of interest if the rate is compounded to a different time period? So, if a monthly rate is quoted, what is the equivalent annual rate assuming that the monthly rate is compounded over the 12 monthly periods of the year? The answer is given by the following formula:

$$(1 + i_a) = (1 + i_m)^{12}$$

If the monthly rate (i_m) is 1.5 per cent the annual equivalent rate (i_a) would be:

$$(1 + i_a) = (1.015)^{12}$$

$$i_a = 1.19562 - 1 = 0.19562 \equiv 19.562\%$$

A daily rate can be similarly converted to an equivalent annual rate by compounding over 365 periods as follows. Assume a daily rate of interest is 0.1 per cent the annual rate would be:

$$(1 + i_a) = (1.001)^{365}$$

$$i_a = 1.44025 - 1 = 0.44025 \equiv 44.025\%$$

It is possible to convert an annual rate to a shorter time period by rearranging the annual equivalent rate formula in terms of the shorter time period. Thus an annual rate of 20 per cent equates to a monthly equivalent rate as follows:

$$(1 + i_a) = (1 + i_m)^{12}$$

rearranging:

$$(1 + i_m) = \sqrt[12]{(1 + i_a)}$$

therefore

$$i_m = \sqrt[12]{(1 + i_a)} - 1$$

$$i_m = \sqrt[12]{(1.2)} = 0.0153 \equiv 1.53\%$$

The time value of money

Having explored the concepts of return and risk we now need to address the question as to why investment of any sort should promise a reward whether in the form of an interest payment, a dividend or a potential capital gain to the investor. Investment entails surrendering current monetary wealth with the promise of more given back in the future. Why shouldn't investors be happy with getting back exactly what they have given up? To answer this problem we need to explore why money has 'time value'.

If we make the simple observation that people generally prefer, if given the choice, to have the power to consume now rather than in the future then £100 is worth more if its in the hand rather than if that £100 is only receivable in (say) one year's time. There are a number of factors which we can influence this preference for money now rather than money later:

- *Inflation/deflation*: most successful economies are characterized by mild levels of inflation where the price of a typical basket of goods and services as well as other domestic expenditures are rising. If the individual expects those prices to continue rising he or she will expect to get less goods for the same amount of money in the future as now. This creates an incentive towards immediate consumption leading to greater demand for goods which in turn provide incentives for producers and suppliers of goods and services across the economy. Thus mild inflation has an invigorating effect upon an economy. In some economies prices are falling and this will lead to the reverse effect where individuals switch from consumption to saving, demand and production falls and the economy begins to stagnate.

- *Risk*: if the future is uncertain and there is some concern whether or not the future cash sum will arise or not, or if there is uncertainty about the level of future inflation, then the individual will put even less value on the future sum compared with the situation where no uncertainty is present.

- *Liquidity*: even in the absence of inflation and risk we would presume that most people would prefer their money now rather than in the future. The less the individual's current wealth the less willing an individual will be to defer consumption.

These three factors combine together for the individual to give their 'marginal rate of time preference for money' that is: the rate of return they would require to justify the sacrifice of a marginal amount of their current wealth in exchange for an increase in their wealth at some specified time in the future. Every individual will have a slightly different percentage rate given their own beliefs about the risk they are facing in the given investment, their expectations of future inflation and their current need for cash to finance their immediate as opposed to their future consumption needs.

Pat has been offered an investment requiring an outlay of £5000. It is likely to return £6600 in one year's time. When considering whether to invest Pat decides that he has a marginal rate of time preference of 20 per cent reflecting his current impoverished state, the expected levels of inflation over the next year and the risk which he believes it will be exposed to.

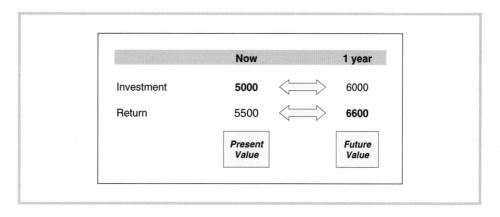

When Pat considers the investment he will automatically equate £5000 now with £6000 in one year's time.

$$\text{Future Value} = \text{Present value} + 20\% \times \text{present value}$$

$$= 5000 + 20\% \times 5000$$

$$= 5000 \times 1.2 = 6000$$

Pat immediately realizes that in one year's time he will obtain £600 more than the future value of his current investment. Alternatively, he might think of it the other way around: the present value of the promised return is £5500 which he calculated as follows:

$$\text{Present value} = \text{Future value} / (1 + 20\%)$$
$$= 6600 / 1.2$$
$$= 5500$$

This technique of 'undoing' the compounding by calculating the present value of a future cash flow is known as 'discounting'. For Pat, the present value sum of £5500 calculated by discounting the future value sum of £6600, is worth more than his present value sacrifice of £5000 – so Pat writes the cheque!

So the investor's marginal rate of time preference allows them to equate present values with future values and thus determine whether any sacrifice of cash is going to be worthwhile. This concept is both straightforward and fundamental to our understanding of how investment decisions can be made.

Net Present Value – a first look

The 'time value of money' concept allows us to make comparisons between cash payments and receipts which occur at different points in time. Pat, in the example above was not able to make an immediate comparison between an investment of cash today of £5000 and a receipt in one year's time of £6600. It certainly looked a good deal but he could not be sure how good it was until he converted the future cash receipt to its present value of £5500 and realized how much better off he would be.

To take a somewhat more complex example: let us assume that Pat realized that the deal is not quite what he thought. He would have to make an investment of £5000 but the cash flows he would receive would be £2400 in year 1 and £4200 in year 2. Note that the 'nominal' value of the cash to be returned to Pat is still £6600 but now it is split over two years rather than receivable in one.

Taking the first year's receipt of £2400 and using his 20 per cent rate of time preference, Pat figures out, by rearranging the compound interest formula:

$$FV_n = PV(1 + i)^n$$

therefore

$$PV = \frac{FV_n}{(1+i)^n}$$

that £2400 is worth £2000 to him currently:

$$PV = \frac{FV_1}{(1+i)^1}$$

$$PV = \frac{£2400}{1.2}$$

$$PV = £2000$$

Likewise, the cash receipt of £4200 in the second year would be worth just £2917 to him currently:

$$PV = \frac{FV_2}{(1+i)^2}$$

$$PV = \frac{£4200}{(1.2)^2}$$

$$PV = £2917$$

When he adds up the present values of the two cash flows he will receive he realizes that they total £5917 which is considerably less attractive than receiving the whole £6600 in one year and is now worth less than the outlay of £5000.

The Net Present Value is a very sensitive measure of the value of a given investment opportunity. As we shall see in Chapter 2 it represents, under ideal conditions, the change in the wealth of the investor decision maker. From a financial point of view an investment yielding a positive Net Present Value is worthwhile while one yielding a negative Net Present Value is to be avoided. There are many operational difficulties to overcome in implementing the Net Present Value concept in practice. We need to know the appropriate discount rate for an individual or a company – this we refer to as the individual or firm's 'cost of capital' – and we need to be able to predict the future cash flows that a given investment will generate. It may also be that we cannot discover the cost of capital until we know how much the project has added to the value of the firm, but we cannot know the value added to the firm by an investment project until we know its cost of capital – this is the quintessential chicken and egg problem which bedevils much of corporate finance especially when we consider large projects in relation to the individual's existing wealth or the firm's existing value.

However, the Net Present Value method is the most important method for determining the amount by which the value of an individual or a firm is likely to increase as a result of a capital investment decision. Thus, if we are confident of the inputs into the Net Present Value model we have the following rule:

> A capital investment decisions is only worthwhile if it adds value to the individual or the firm. This means that the Net Present Value of an investment must be greater than zero for the decision to proceed and the project to be financially worthwhile to the investors.

This is the 'iron law' of corporate finance but like all laws, ferrous or otherwise, there are problems with its implementation which we will discuss in the ensuing chapters.

REVIEW ACTIVITY 1.2 What would be the Net Present Value of Pat's investment if he took the view that a rate of time preference of 20 per cent was too high and that 15 per cent was more appropriate? Do both examples where he receives in (i) the return of £6600 in one year and (ii) the return split between £2400 in year 1 and £4200 in year 2.

What general conclusions can you come to about (a) the impact of delaying cash flows and (b) reducing the rate of time preference in discounting?

In this chapter we have introduced some basic concepts in corporate finance. Our focus has been on exploring the role that corporate finance plays within the business firm and some of the ideas that have shaped the development of the subject. In particular we examined Ockham's Razor which is fundamental to the way that theories are built within finance generally and then subjected to testing in the real world. We then turned our attention to two interconnected ideas: return and risk. We emphasized that return is the sum of two components: capital gain on holding a security and any dividend or interest that may be received. Risk is the extent to which returns are likely to vary around their average value. Central to the story of risk is the 'normal distribution' and its importance in any system where average values are being generated from a sampling process. The central limit theorem is a statistical law with far reaching consequences and we will be returning to it in later chapters.

Finally we got down to some numbers and reviewed how to calculate interest rates, how to compound and discount and, most importantly, how to calculate the Net Present Value of a simple investment opportunity.

Further Reading

Bernstein, P.L. (1996) *Against the Gods – the remarkable story of risk*, New York: Wiley. This is an excellent and readable account of the development of the theory of risk. There is barely an equation is sight and the wealth of historical anecdotes makes what might appear to be a mundane subject enthralling.

Kay, J. (2003) *The Truth about Markets – their genius, their limits, their follies*, London: Penguin. This book contains 'what it says on the tin'. It offers a fair but critical view of the operation of markets and their impact upon modern society.

Levinson, M. (2002) *Guide to the Financial Markets* (3rd Ed.) London: The Economist Publications. This is a very useful reference book to have to hand when reading this book.

Ryan, B., Scapens, R.W. and Theobald, M. (2002) *Research Methods and Methodology in Finance and Accounting* (2nd Ed.) London: Thomson. Chapters 1 and 3 give a very clear introduction to the philosophical underpinnings of financial theory.

Sapori, A. (1999) *The World of Renaissance Florence*, Florence: Giunti Press.

Silver, M. (1995) *Economic Structures of Antiquity*, Westport, Connecticut: Greenwood Press. This is an interesting and authoritative account of early markets and how they emerged in the ancient world.

Spade, P.V. (ed) (1999) *The Cambridge Companion to Ockham*, Cambridge (UK): Cambridge University Press. Not for the philosophically faint hearted but Chapters 1 and 5 provide a useful introduction to Ockham's life and work.

PROGRESS CHECK

1 Where did the first banking system emerge in Europe?

2 How are the financial markets subdivided?

3 What are the two most important decisions in corporate finance?

4 Briefly state what is meant by Ockham's Razor.

5 Define return for a security that generates dividends for its investors.

6 How does average mean return differ from geometric mean return?

7 How is the risk of a series of returns measured?

8 What is the difference (if any) between the term risk and the term uncertainty?

9   If the average of a series of samples of returns are drawn as a frequency distribution. To what distribution would the sample averages approximate?

10 State the formula that links the present value of a cash sum to its future value.

11 What is the formula for converting a monthly return to an annual return and an annual return to a monthly return?

12 What is the name of the process which is used (a) to calculate a future value from a present value and (b) a present value from a future value?

13 What three factors influence an individual or a firm's time value of money?

14 Under what financial circumstances is an investment worthwhile: (a) when the present value of the future cash flows is less than the sum invested or (b) when the present value of the future cash flows is greater than the sum invested.

QUESTIONS (answers at end of book)

1   An investment of 10 000 offers a return of 6 per cent per annum. What will be the value of that investment after (i) one year (ii) five years and (iii) seven years?

2   An investment offers a cash flow of £50 000 in six years' time. What is the present value of that investment if the rate of interest to be used in compounding and discounting is 10 per cent?

3   An investment offers a monthly return of 2 per cent. What is the equivalent annual return?

4   An investment offers an annual return of 24 per cent. What is the equivalent (i) monthly and (ii) weekly return?

5   A financial investment of £16 000 offers a fixed repayment over the following four years of £5000 per annum. An investor requires a rate of return of 7 per cent. Is this investment worthwhile?

QUESTIONS (answers on website)

6   Using available internet resources (such as Google) look up the following four terms:
    (i)   ancient money markets,
    (ii) ancient capital markets,
    (iii) shares on ventures,
    (iv) the Champagne fairs.

7   Using the resources of the world wide web discover the means by which the East India Company financed its trade.

8 Using the resources of www.bankofengland.com discover the level of new capital raised in the UK by British firms.

9 For an equity share traded on the UK stock market download the last six years' monthly share price data from www.yahoo.co.uk/finance.

10 Using the share price data collected from Yahoo! for the company of your choice calculate the monthly return, the average monthly return and the standard deviation of monthly returns. Note the extent to which the return distribution appears to be normal.

11 Using the share price data collected from Yahoo! calculate the mean geometric return and explain why it is different from the arithmetic mean return.

Traditional approaches to investment appraisal

2

I n this chapter we explain what we mean by a capital investment 'project' and describe and
evaluate a range of techniques for their appraisal: including the Net Present Value, Internal
Rate of Return, Accounting Rate of Return, and payback methods as well as a range of other
metrics. A substantial issue in this chapter is the justification of the technical supremacy of the Net
Present Value model. However, notwithstanding the importance of that model we also discuss the
complementary nature of the more traditional techniques employed in investment decision making
in practice. In particular we show how methods such as the Internal Rate of Return (conventional
and modified), payback (simple and discounted) and rates of return measures complement the use
of Net Present Value in practice.

In the appendix to this chapter we describe the mathematics of discounting and compounding,
the calculation of annuities, perpetuities and terminal fund values. We also review how
compounding and discounting work when we apply shorter and shorter time intervals leading
ultimately to the methods of continuous time analysis.

Learning outcomes

By the end of this chapter you will achieve the following:

1 Define what is meant by the term 'project'.
2 Specify the objective of investment appraisal for the business organization.
3 Calculate a project's promised 'value added' to the firm using the Net Present
   Value rule.
4 Calculate other project metrics understanding their significance in investment
   decision making.
5 Employ a range of techniques for converting interest rates to different time scales
   and evaluating unusual patterns of cash flow.

The investment project

A capital investment project is the term we give to any business decision that entails the expenditure of a significant cash sum and where the future benefits (and costs) arising from that expenditure continues for more than one year in the future.

Using one year as the lower time limit is somewhat arbitrary but reflects the distinction between the capital market and the money market outlined in Chapter 1. The word *project* is now customary but very apposite in this context as it comes from the Latin word *projectum* which means 'something prominent' but which in its turn was derived from *proicere* which means to 'throw forth'. As you will see as our discussion proceeds there is a lot of 'throwing forth' in capital investment appraisal.

Here are some examples of capital investment projects:

1 Investment by an individual or a firm in a completely new business venture. In this case the investment is the capital stake and the benefits are the net cash flows arising as surplus over the expected lifetime of that business.

2 Investment by an individual or firm in a new product or product range. The investment is the costs of establishing the capacity to produce and in gaining entry to the new market. The benefits that will flow are the additional net cash flows that arise in the future that contribute to the overall cash flows of the individual or firm concerned.

3 Investment in a new business process which enhances the firm's existing activity. The Bernie Flower case discussed later in this chapter is a good example where new capital expenditure is considered in order to achieve an improvement in revenue, a saving in cost or indeed both. The net benefit attaching to this type of capital investment project is the incremental gain in revenue or the incremental saving in cost that result.

4 The replacement of existing capital equipment where the benefit that accrues is usually cost savings and improved capacity or efficiency of production.

In making these sorts of business decisions there are three critical issues for the decision maker to resolve: first the projection of the capital expenditure and the future cash flows that will arise if the decision to proceed is made; second the estimation of the risk involved and third the estimation of the value which is added to the individual or firm as a result of the investment.

This brings us to two key issues affecting most capital investment decision making: differentiability and contingency. Capital investment decision making assumes that we can isolate and identify the impact of the project on the overall cash flows of the firm. This issue of differentiability is not a problem with 1 above but exists, to a certain extent in all other capital investment decisions 2 to 4. Contingency occurs when a decision made now gives us the option to make further value enhancing decisions in the future. However, the nature of those future decisions, and their outcomes, will all be dependent on future states of the world and which are not knowable now. Where a current decision entails contingencies of this type the nature of the choice now can profoundly influence our future degrees of freedom. Contingencies and the options they offer are discussed in Chapter 9.

FINANCIAL CASE

Bernie Flower was pondering his choice between a Digemup Model 007 and the model 005 minidigger for his garden business. He believed he could identify the net cash benefits that would accrue to his current business if he invested in a minidigger. However, the 007 had attachments and fittings that would allow him to enter the groundworks side of house building which entailed cutting and clearing. He did not know if that was a business he wanted to get into just yet but it might well be an option worth considering over the next three to four years. His wife, Pettle, had worked on this during her MBA and recognized that the first problem was one of differentiating the net benefits of the new investment from Bernie's existing business cash flows. The second problem was that one of the alternatives presented a real option for the future.

The objectives of business decision making

The central objective of all business enterprise is to maximize the value invested by its owners. In the most general terms this means the value of all the future cash income less expenditures over the foreseeable life of the business. The way we use the concept of value in practice is through the Net Present Value rule outlined in Chapter 1. The NPV of an investment project, if the inputs to the model are correctly estimated, measures the value that project will add to the firm overall. It therefore follows that:

1 A business firm should invest in all projects which have a positive Net Present Value.

2 Where more than one project are available which have positive Net Present Values but which are mutually exclusive (e.g. a firm is deciding whether to use a patch of land to build a hotel or a housing development), then the project with the highest Net Present Value should be chosen.

3 If the capital markets are perfectly efficient in the way that securities are priced then the increase in value represented by a given project will lead to the value of the firm being 'marked up' in the market. This marking up will occur as soon as the market recognizes:

   (a) that a decision to invest has been made by the firm, or

   (b) anticipates that such a decision is likely to be made.

It follows from the above that a firm can only grow in value by identifying and investing in positive Net Present Value projects. However, in competitive markets positive Net Present Value projects become progressively more and more difficult to discover and in the limiting case of a perfectly competitive market the Net Present Value of all firms will be driven to zero.

REVIEW ACTIVITY 2.1 Summarize the importance of the NPV rule in setting financial policy for the firm.

In practice the financial injunction to maximize Net Present Value above all else is conditional: we know from the theory of agency that directors and managers are often more concerned with measures of their firm's (and hence their) performance even though, as we shall see later, performance measures may give ambiguous messages about the value of different investment projects. Also, although directors and managers may acknowledge the importance of maximizing the whole value of the firm they may be more concerned with short term performance. Managers do not get fired for decisions that lead to an immediate boost in their firm's reported profits even though the long term effect of those decisions may be to destroy firm value.

We will take it as axiomatic that the directors and managers of a firm will seek to maximize the economic value of the business. However, we do need to express a note of caution. Value maximization represents a normative objective: it states what a firm and its management ought to do rather than what they actually do. The neoclassical description of the firm as driven by the principles of value maximization was undermined in the 1930s by Berle and Means (1932) who argued that the shareholders in modern public corporations enjoy few rights and that effective control lies in the hands of management who may well subvert the firm to meet their own demands for high salaries and perks. This rather provocative idea was extended by agency theorists such as Jensen and Meckling (1976) who described firms as a series of contractual relationships between a principal (the shareholder or owner) and their agent (the directors); who in their turn act as principals to more junior managers who operate as their agents and so on down the hierarchy of the firm. Jensen and Meckling's analysis leads to the concept of 'agency loss' that is the loss from the optimum achieved by a profit maximizing firm as the agent gains advantage either through contractual weaknesses or through access to information which is unavailable to the principals in the relationship or both.

Jensen and Meckling have been criticized on a number of grounds: first in as far as their argument extends to the relationship between shareholder and manager they ignore the fact that the directors are, in law, responsible to the company which is a legal entity distinct from the owners of the firm. Second, although theoretically appealing their analysis makes some strong assumptions about the rationality of both principals and agents as they attempt to construct risk sharing contracts. A more satisfactory description of the driving motivation of firms was provided by Ronald Coase who in 1937 suggested that firms come into existence because they offer a superior mode of transacting than can be achieved through open markets.

Coase's insight is that transacting either within firms or within markets carries a cost. However, he is not referring to the agreed price for the resources being transferred but rather the collateral costs of engaging the particular transaction. For example, buying a car involves the purchaser in a number of incidental costs: the costs of evaluating the various alternatives, determining the prices of the choices on offer, the costs of getting to and from the showroom and so on. These side costs can be very important and in certain circumstances and with certain sorts of resource transfers it may be sensible to organize (i.e. create a firm) to minimize them.

Transaction cost economists identified three reasons why organizing through firms might be preferred to organizing through markets:

1 The frequency of transacting.

2 Uncertainty.

3 The degree to which the asset involved (labour, plant, machinery) has a specific use. The more flexible an asset is, paradoxically the more attractive it

will be to a firm to hire that asset on a job by job basis rather than contract it on a permanent basis if it is labour or purchase it outright in the case of any other asset.

Finally governments do treat firms differently to individuals in the way that they levy tax and impose other legislation. These differences of themselves may be sufficient to warrant the formation of a firm.

Once having identified the fundamental economic rationale for why firms exist, Coase offered an important criterion for determining the maximum size which a firm would achieve:

> '*a firm will tend to expand until the costs of organising an extra transaction within the firm becomes equal to the costs of carrying out the same transaction by means of an exchange on the open market of the costs of organising in another firm.*' COASE, R.H. (1937) P. 24

This theorem balances the cost of conducting transactions within a firm setting (the costs of 'managing') with the costs of coordinating those same market transactions in an open market. Only when the marginal cost of the former is equal to the marginal cost of the latter will the process of firm growth cease.

Coase's work is important because it demonstrates the limits on the growth of the firm. Firms do not have an inexhaustible supply of new investment opportunities in any event. However, even given that because the costs of managing each new investment opportunity are cumulative, the time will come where even though new opportunities appear valuable in their own terms the incremental cost of adding them into the firm will result in a loss of value overall.

The modern theory of the firm raises a number of question marks against the 'simple' view of the firm described by the neoclassical approach. However, in this book we adopt the normative strategy of assuming that directors and managers should make decisions with the objective of maximizing the firm's value. When we discuss how firms actually behave we will normally take a transactions cost framework and assume that they will seek cost efficiency by choosing that mode or organization which minimize their exposure to transaction costs.

FINANCIAL CASE

Part of Bernie's reasoning for seeking to purchase a minidigger was the time and effort involved in hiring one. The vagaries of the weather and the progress of each job made it difficult to forecast exactly when he would need one which meant that he always seemed to be on the phone trying to get one and having to take whatever price the hirer liked to charge. He also found himself needing one more frequently as his business expanded and there were many occasions upon which it would have been useful but he and his men had to undertake days of back-breaking work because none were available to hire. He also felt that he needed a machine with a greater range of cutting tools and shovels than came with the hired machine. This rationale presented by Bernie to Pettle focused on the uncertainty of transacting for a minidigger, the frequency with which he hired the machine and his demand for a machine of greater asset specificity. This would suggest buying a machine (i.e. internalizing the asset within the firm) rather than hiring one (an open market transaction).

Calculating the Net Present Value

In the last chapter we introduced the Net Present Value method for evaluating capital investment decisions. It is hard to overstate the importance of the Net Present Value method in business decision making. It is the formalization of what corporate strategists refer to as 'value added'. Net Present Value allows us to estimate the value added to the firm as a result of a given investment decision. If an investment decision does not promise a positive Net Present Value then by implication it does promise to destroy firm value. It is important therefore that we return to the basic ideas that underpin this method.

To calculate the Net Present Value for a given project we need to know the following:

1 The magnitude and the timing of the capital investment. This will normally be the total expenditure during the investment phase of the project including the acquisition of current as well as fixed and intangible assets.

2 The operating cash flows which will arise *in addition* to the firm's existing cash flows as a necessary result of the project investment decision.

3 Any cessation costs or receipts as the project is terminated. Most projects when they are terminated will involve either a recovery of some scrap value or sale proceeds on the exhausted plant or other fixed assets. It may be that there will also be decommissioning costs.

4 A rate of discount, which we refer to as the 'hurdle rate', that allows the firm to equate the future cash receipts and expenditures with the current outlay.

FINANCIAL CASE

Jack Cox - Travel Pics Pro/Alamy

Fred was the sole owner of Friendly Grinders Ltd a small company in Monkley Barley in the depths of Wiltshire. Fred had, in recent years, taken a more passive role in the management of the business. This year the board had given him an indication of the dividend they thought they could pay which would be in the region of £34 000. Fred was very pleased as this was his eightieth year and he fancied a very long holiday on the Costa del Sol, accompanied by his personal assistant. Fred was being realistic and anticipated, given his prodigious consumption of the finest malt whisky and a serious tobacco habit, that this could be his last opportunity for some high life. When Fred arrived at the Board meeting his fellow directors looked rather worried: 'Fred', they said 'we have some good news and some bad news'. 'Give me the good news' he replied, not liking the sound of this at all. His CEO explained that they had identified a new investment project which at the company's hurdle rate of 8 per cent would add value to the firm. Unfortunately the capital outlay would be £34 000 but here is the table of projected cash flows.

EXHIBIT 2.1

Projection of the net cash flows for Friendly Grinders Project

	0	1	2	3	4
Capital investment	−34 000				
Incremental project cash flows		7 600	16 500	13 000	10 600
Decommissioning costs					−4 000
Net cash flow	**−34 000**	**7 600**	**16 500**	**13 000**	**6 600**

In order to assess the Net Present Value of Friendly Grinders project each of the future cash flows needs to be discounted at the rate of 8 per cent to give its corresponding value at the decision point.

For year 1 and 2 of the investment we get using the formula shown in the last chapter:

$$PV_0 = \frac{FV_n}{(1+i)^n}$$

For year 1:

$$PV_0 = \frac{7600}{(1.08)^1} = 7037$$

For year 2:

$$PV_0 = \frac{16500}{(1.08)^2} = 14\,146$$

Doing the same for the subsequent years our analysis of Fred's cash flows looks like this:

EXHIBIT 2.2

Calculating the Net Present Value for Friendly Grinders Project

Net Present Value using 8 per cent

	0	1	2	3	4
Capital investment	−34 000				
Incremental project cash flows		7 600	16 500	13 000	10 600
Decommissioning costs					−4 000
Net cash flow	**−34 000**	**7 600**	**16 500**	**13 000**	**6 600**
Present value of first year cash flow	7 037				
Present value of second year cash flow	14 146				
Present value of third year cash flow	10 320				
Present value of fourth year cash flow	4 851				
Net Present Value	**2 354**				

There are two ways of interpreting these present values, both of which are equally valid:

1   The present value is the sum which invested at the start of the project at 8 per cent would yield the future value concerned. So, if £7037 were invested at 8 per cent for one year it would result in a cash return of £7600 one year later. £14 146, if invested for two years would return £16 500 and so on.

2   The firm or more accurately in this case Fred, as he is the sole owner, should be strictly indifferent between a current sum of £7037 in his hand and £7600 in one year's time. This relates back to the time preference of money concept discussed in Chapter 1.

REVIEW ACTIVITY 2.2   Project the cash flows as shown above for Friendly Grinders Ltd but assuming the decommissioning costs are zero and recalculate the Net Present Value of their project.

FINANCIAL CASE   Now Fred is not very happy – for the obvious reason that he would like his cash now rather than spread out over four years. When he heard that his directors were contemplating retaining the proposed dividend of £34 000 to finance the new project (that was the bad news) he erupted. Well what could he do about it?

Assuming that the directors have done their job well and this is truly a value adding project for the firm then there are some options open to Fred which will allow him to resolve his dilemma. First, in an ideal world either Fred or his company would be able to borrow or lend against this project and in that way Fred could realize his dream of a long holiday on the Costa. Unfortunately, ideal worlds do not exist and Fred could be forced to borrow at possibly very unattractive rates of interest. Alternatively Fred could override his directors (although his thoughts were more in terms of walls and firing squads) or he could sell at least part of his stake in the company. Let us at this stage examine the ideal case and consider what would happen if borrowing or lending is allowed, for any amount at a standard market rate of 8 per cent, free of transactions costs and taxes and on the assumption that the future is known for certain. These conditions create what is known as a 'perfect capital market'.

Given the project described above, Fred could borrow £36 354 being the dividend foregone of £34 000 and the Net Present Value of £2354 assured by the project.

Note from Exhibit 2.3 that the project has repaid his borrowing so Fred has been able to use the capital market to borrow against the value of his dividend plus the Net Present Value of the project. Of course, in these circumstances, a considerate board of directors would not have exposed Fred to the risk of a heart attack but would have borrowed the money on the company's behalf and given Fred his dividend plus a modest present of £2354 to speed him on his way.

The point about this case is that under these rather exceptional economic circumstances the Net Present Value model accurately measures the increase in the present cash wealth of the investor at the point the decision is made to proceed. This result is known as the Fisher Hirshliefer Separation Theorem.

Under perfect capital market conditions (certainty, no transaction costs and taxes, and a single market rate for borrowing or lending in any amount):

1   The Net Present Value of an investment, when discounted at the prevailing market rate of interest on borrowing or lending, represents the increase in the net disposable cash wealth of the owner.

EXHIBIT 2.3

Fred's application of the Fisher Hirshliefer Separation Theorem

	0	1	2	3	4
Capital investment	−34 000				
Incremental project cash flows		7 600	16 500	13 000	10 600
Decommissioning costs					−4 000
Net cash flow	**−34 000**	**7 600**	**16 500**	**13 000**	**6 600**
Fred's borrowing carried forward	−36 354	−36 354	−31 662	−17 695	−6 111
Interest accumulated at 8%		−2 908	−2 533	−1 416	−489
Project repayment		**7 600**	**16 500**	**13 000**	**6 600**
Outstanding borrowing	−36 354	−31 662	−17 695	−6 111	0

2 The evaluation of the project is independent of the means by which it is financed (retained earnings or borrowing).

A moment's thought reveals one consequence of the perfect capital market assumption. At the point Fred walked into the meeting his marginal rate of time preference was presumably much higher than 8 per cent. Indeed, we can assume that it was extremely high reflecting his desire to have his holiday money in his pocket. However, in a situation of perfect capital markets the ruling market rate of interest takes over from the individual decision maker's marginal rate of time preference as the hurdle rate he or she should use in evaluating capital investment projects.

With a perfect capital market the Net Present Value model works perfectly. In reality, the presence of uncertainty means that borrowing and lending rates will diverge, transactions costs will come into the equation and there may be limits on the borrowing or lending any individual or firm will be allowed to undertake. There are also bound to be taxes!

REVIEW ACTIVITY 2.3   What would be the outcome if the firm could borrow at 8 per cent but Fred could only borrow at 9 per cent?

THEORETICAL NOTE   Operating the Net Present Value rule relies upon a prediction of the future cash flows arising to the business as a consequence of the investment decision being undertaken and for no other reason. Here are five useful rules to remember when projecting a net cash flow for an investment project:

Rule 1: You are dealing with the changes to the net cash flow of the firm if the project is accepted. You are not forecasting 'profits' and hence should not include any costs in the projection which can be classified as accounting costs and which do not affect the cash flows of the firm. Depreciation and amortization are the most common examples. However, do note that a form of depreciation used for tax purposes called capital allowances may have an impact upon the change in the firm's tax liability brought about by the project. The change in the firm's tax liability will create a cash flow which is incremental upon the decision to invest and thus should be included. We will consider this problem in greater depth in Chapter 7.

Rule 2: Following rule 1 do not include any costs or revenues in the cash flow which will not be incurred if the project does not go ahead. The company's fixed costs, whether or not 'allocated' to projects by the firm's accounting practices, should be excluded from the analysis unless they can be identified as changing as a result of the investment decision – and then they should only be included to the extent that they are expected to change.

Rule 3: On the same principles costs which have been incurred in the past, whether or not they were directly incurred in setting up the project should be excluded. The reason is that such 'sunk' costs will be incurred whatever the outcome of the decision and will not influence the project's value, at that point in time.

Rule 4: Do not include any new capital raised (e.g. by borrowing or otherwise) as a positive cash inflow when forecasting the project's cash flows. The decision we are making is whether the investment of a certain amount of money is justified irrespective of the method of finance.

Rule 5: Do not include any costs of financing (such as interest payments) as expenditures before arriving at the project's net cash flow. The rate of interest used in discounting the cash flows will compensate for the cost of using the firm's capital.

Like all rules they work nearly all the time.

Net Present Value and the hurdle rate

The Net Present Value of any investment project will increase as the chosen hurdle rate decreases and vice versa. Therefore the greater the rate of return required by the investor the lower will be the Net Present Value of any project. There are a number of reasons why investors may raise the rate of return they require and hence the rate of discount that they or their firm should apply when calculating the Net Present Value of a given investment:

1 *Risk:* The level of uncertainty attaching to the investment's cash flows may be high and the investors require a correspondingly high rate of return to compensate them for the higher level of risk attaching to the project's Net Present Value.

2 *Inflation:* The rate of inflation may increase forcing the investors to demand a higher rate of return to compensate for the loss in spending power attached to future as opposed to current cash flows.

3 *Liquidity preference:* The investors' circumstances may change: there may be other attractive opportunities for the use of their cash or they may simply not feel as wealthy as they once did. Many subtle effects can bring this about. Falling property prices, for example, tend to make homeowners feel less wealthy; to compensate their preference for current as opposed to future liquidity will rise and thus their required rate of return will also increase.

There are other influences on the hurdle rate a firm may choose, many of which will be discussed later in this book. The key point to remember at this stage is the inverse relationship which exists between value generation (as measured by the Net Present Value method) and the rate of return required by investors.

Other methods of investment appraisal

There are a number of other methods for appraising capital projects. Unfortunately, none offer the technical validity of the Net Present Value rule to the decision maker but do however offer additional insights which managers might find useful in certain circumstances. For obvious reasons managers tend to be interested in performance and measures of improvement in those areas for which they are responsible. For this reason they tend to favour percentage measures of return against which comparisons between different areas of activity can be made (we discuss some of the empirical evidence for this in Chapter 7). We will now consider a number of investment techniques which focus on project return and liquidity.

Return based measures of investment performance

Percentage based measures of investment performance are popular with managers for the straightforward reason that they can be compared with agreed benchmarks. Unfortunately, there are a number of methods of greater or lesser sophistication, which do not always carry the significance that managers expect. They are also based upon a number of assumptions in each case which vary in their validity. We will discuss four measures here:

(i)   the Internal Rate of Return which measures the economic yield of an investment project,

(ii) the modified Internal Rate of Return which makes weaker assumptions than the Internal Rate of Return, and two measures of accounting performance,

(iii) the Accounting Rate of Return, and

(iv) the differential return on capital employed.

Internal Rate of Return (IRR)

This superficially simple metric measures the rate of discount at which a given project's cash flows will just give a Net Present Value of zero. It is therefore the 'breakeven' rate or return that is required. It is sometimes known as the economic yield on a project and for the mathematically minded here is the formula we need to solve to get this breakeven rate:

$$-I_0 + \frac{CF_1}{(1+irr)} + \frac{CF_2}{(1+irr)^2} \cdots\cdots\cdots \frac{CF_n}{(1+irr)^n} = 0$$

Entering the values for Friendly Grinders Ltd:

$$-34\,000 + \frac{7\,600}{(1+irr)} + \frac{16\,500}{(1+irr)^2} + \frac{13\,000}{(1+irr)^3} + \frac{6\,600}{(1+irr)^4} = 0$$

This is a mathematical polynomial and it is difficult to solve for the value of the Internal Rate of Return especially when the number of terms in the model is large.

Graphical solution of the Internal Rate of Return One way of discovering the Internal Rate of Return is to calculate the Net Present Value of the project for different interest rates and graph the result. The cutover point on the interest axis of the graph is the Internal Rate of Return.

A careful examination of the curve shows that it cuts the discount rate axis at approximately 11.25 per cent. Although useful for demonstrating the principles of measurement this method is time consuming and prone to inaccuracy.

The graphical interpretation of the Internal Rate of Return (IRR) for a project

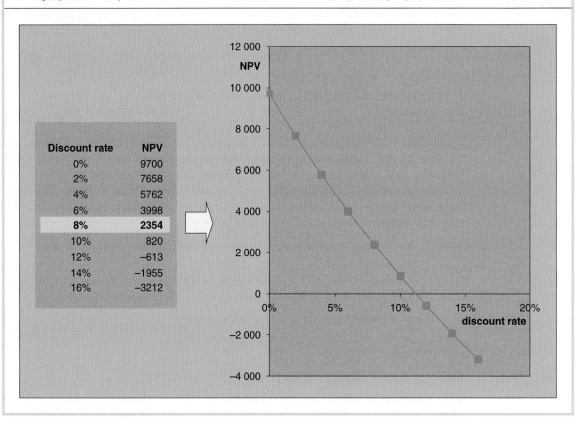

Discount rate	NPV
0%	9700
2%	7658
4%	5762
6%	3998
8%	2354
10%	820
12%	−613
14%	−1955
16%	−3212

Arithmetic solution to the Internal Rate of Return An alternative method is to calculate the Net Present Value at different discount rates as we have done above searching for two rates which 'straddle the zero'. Here we can see that with 2 per cent increments at 10 per cent the NPV is positive and at 12 per cent it is negative. Clearly, the Internal Rate of Return lies between the two and by assuming that the NPV function is linear between these two points we can 'interpolate' the result.

If we examine the graph in Exhibit 2.5 in more detail at the cross over point we recognize that an increase in the discount rate of 2 per cent brings a fall of 1433 in the Net Present Value (from +820 to −613). We note the drop to zero was 820 from 10 per cent therefore our estimate of the Internal Rate of Return is:

$$IRR = i^+ + \frac{NPV^+}{NPV^+ - NPV^-} \times (i^- - i^+)$$

or

$$IRR = 10\% + \frac{820}{820 - (-613)} \times (12\% - 10\%)$$

$$IRR = 11.14\%$$

EXHIBIT 2.5

The linear interpolation method for finding the Internal Rate of Return

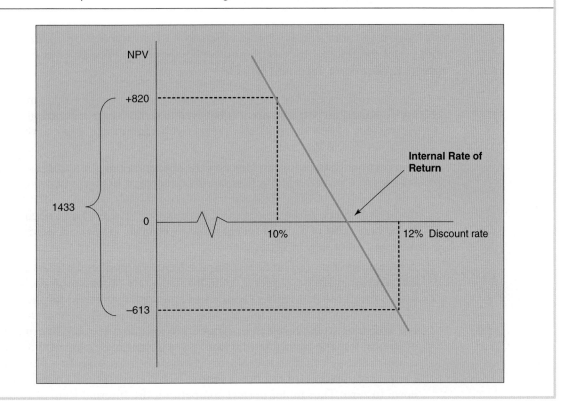

The problem with this method of course is that it does assume linearity in the relationship between interest rate and Net Present Value over the range of the interpolation.

Excel solution to the Internal Rate of Return In practice you would not bother with either of the above techniques. Spreadsheet packages like Excel can do the trick with the IRR function:

$$= \text{IRR(values,guess)}$$

In this case, the values are the range of cells containing the net cash flows from the project. The 'guess' can be ignored or a percentage that you think is likely to be close to the final result can also be included. If you do not include it Excel assumes a value of 10 per cent.

It is also possible to use the 'goal seek' procedure to obtain a zero value for the Net Present Value by varying the discount rate chosen.

For this project Excel returns a discount rate of 11.13 per cent.

The Internal Rate of Return rule (IRR) Generally any project is acceptable if it has an Internal Rate of Return that is greater than the company's chosen hurdle rate. Friendly Grinders Ltd required an 8 per cent return on investment. This project has an Internal Rate of Return of 11.13 per cent and so the project is acceptable. The Internal

Rate of Return will be positive if the project has a positive Net Present Value so using the Internal Rate of Return as a test for project acceptability will ensure that only value enhancing investment decisions are made.

The advantages and disadvantages of using the Internal Rate of Return Many firms prefer the Internal Rate of Return to the use of Net Present Value because it appears to offer three important benefits:

1 The Internal Rate of Return is a percentage measure and given that managers are appraised on performance it is believed that this return measure gives a clearer idea of how one project compares with another in the rate at which it will add value to the firm.

2 The Internal Rate of Return indicates the maximum rate for acquiring finance for the given project which a firm would be prepared to accept in negotiations with its bankers or other financial institution. However, a number of other factors will intervene in these sorts of negotiations. The problems of changes in the firm's cost of capital brought about by changes in financial gearing are discussed more fully in Chapter 6.

3 A percentage rate can be decomposed into its component parts. As you will remember from Chapter 1, an individual's rate of time preference (and a firm's for that matter) consists of a percentage reward for the loss of liquidity, compensation for inflation and an additional element for the risk attaching to the investment. The return premium (i.e. the Internal Rate of Return less the chosen hurdle rate) gives a clear indication of the extent to which the new project is capturing *competitive advantage*. In a perfectly competitive market for the firm's output Net Present Values are driven down to zero. Thus under perfect competition the Internal Rate of Return on a firm's investment will be driven down to its market determined hurdle rate. Thus the return premium is generated by the firm's ability to capture the benefits of market imperfection perhaps by gaining some monopoly power through branding or other forms of product differentiation or by exploiting some contractual or regulatory advantage it may possess. The different components of the Internal Rate of Return are shown in Exhibit 2.6.

At first sight it might appear that the Internal Rate of Return measure should always give the same advice on the merits of an investment project as Net Present Value. If a project has a positive Net Present Value then it will have an Internal Rate of Return greater than the hurdle rate. Furthermore it would appear to measure a project's potential in terms of the return it promises. This should make comparison between different investment opportunities more straightforward than is the case when comparing the absolute value sums generated by the Net Present Value method. Although both Net Present Value and Internal Rate of Return enable a firm to identify positive value adding projects there are a number of problems with the latter method that we will now explore.

1 Although any project that has a positive Net Present Value will also have an Internal Rate of Return greater than the firm's hurdle rate, the two techniques can conflict when a firm is forced to make a choice between two or more mutually exclusive projects.

EXHIBIT 2.6

The components of the Internal Rate of Return

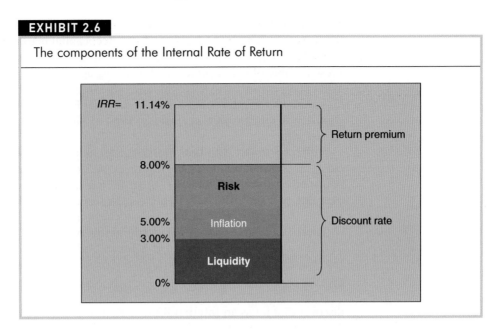

FINANCIAL CASE

The directors of Friendly Grinders Ltd had another problem to wrestle with before they confronted Fred. The new project they were considering could only be conducted in the principal factory in Monkly Barley. There was an alternative project which could utilize the capacity which promised a cash flow as shown under the cash flows from project 1 which we have already considered. The discussion had arisen because the Net Present Value and Internal Rate of Return did not lead to the same conclusion about which to pursue.

EXHIBIT 2.7

NPV and IRR compared for mutually exclusive projects

	0	1	2	3	4	NPV	IRR
Net cash flow (project 1)	−34 000	7 600	16 500	13 000	6 600	2 354	11.128%
Net cash flow (project 2)	−10 000	4 000	6 000	2 000	1 000	1 170	14.405%

Although the second project would give a lower NPV the directors also thought that Fred might be willing to consider the smaller project which would give them some room to pay him a dividend albeit not of the same amount as had already been suggested. What should they do and why do the two methods of investment appraisal conflict?

REVIEW ACTIVITY 2.4 Calculate the Net Present Value and Internal Rate of Return for a third alternative which involves an outlay of £20 000 and two annual cash flows in the two years following of £13 000 each year. This project will also be used in subsequent review activities.

The first point to note here is that the size of the project is irrelevant. Because the firm is working in the context of a perfect capital market the size of the investment outlay is irrelevant. Friendly Grinders can 'capture' the Net Present Value of either project by borrowing against its future cash flows. What matters to Fred as the company's sole owner is which one will increase his wealth by the greater amount. The Internal Rate of Return does not consistently rank projects against Net Present Value and Exhibit 2.7 shows the reason why.

Different project cash flow profiles generate different Net Present Value curves as shown in Exhibit 2.8. Different cash flows' profiles normally cross one another at some point and if the firm's hurdle rate is less than this cross over rate (it's approximately 10 per cent in this example) the Internal Rate of Return will conflict with the Net Present Value rule.

There is a simple way to work around this problem. If we deduct the cash flows of project 2 from project 1 we obtain a 'differential cash flow' representing the opportunity foregone if project 2 is chosen instead of project 1.

If we calculate the Internal Rate of Return of this opportunity foregone we discover that it has an Internal Rate of Return of 10.072 per cent and a

EXHIBIT 2.8

Graphical representation of the conflict between NPV and IRR

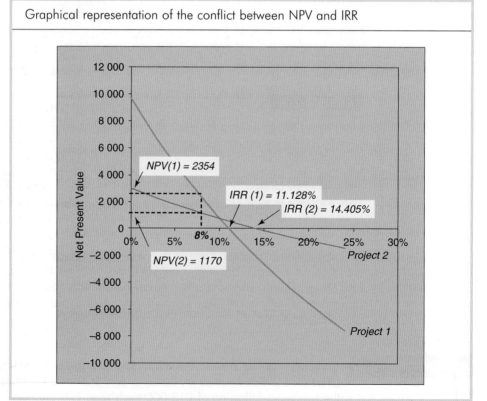

EXHIBIT 2.9

The differential cash flow from two mutually exclusive projects

	0	1	2	3	4
Net cash flow (project 1)	−34 000	7 600	16 500	13 000	6 600
Net cash flow (project 2)	−10 000	4 000	6 000	2 000	1 000
differential cash flow	−24 000	3 600	10 500	11 000	5 600

---

positive Net Present Value of 1184. This strongly suggests that we should not forego that opportunity. There is another way that we can view this situation: project 1 is equivalent to project 2 plus the differential cash flow. Project 2 has an NPV of 1170 and an Internal Rate of Return of 14.405 per cent. The differential cash flow has an NPV of 1184 and an Internal Rate of Return of 10.072 per cent. So why not do both and get the benefits of project 2 and the differential cash flow in one bundle by doing project 1?

2 Sometimes projects with unusual cash flow profiles can create the most unusual Net Present Value curves, indeed even producing multiple rates of return. This is because the Internal Rate of Return function is, mathematically of the form of a polynomial the solution of which can have multiple roots.

$$-I_0 + \frac{CF_1}{(1+irr)} + \frac{CF_2}{(1+irr)^2} \cdots\cdots\cdots \frac{CF_n}{(1+irr)^n} = 0$$

In practical application this is rarely a problem and usually the lowest value derived is the Internal Rate of Return.

3 A much deeper problem lies within the Internal Rate of Return rule. When we considered the concept of present value we described it as the current sum, which if invested at the chosen hurdle rate would lead to the nominal cash sum in the year in question. Where more than one year is involved it is assumed that the rate of return represented by the hurdle rate is *reinvested* annually until the relevant future value is achieved. With the Internal Rate of Return it is implicitly assumed that the cash flows are reinvested at the Internal Rate of Return. However, the firm may not be able to secure the Internal Rate of Return on reinvestment especially when the rate is considerably higher than the firm's chosen hurdle rate. We now turn to a technique which defeats this particular problem and is somewhat easier to calculate.

Modified Internal Rate of Return (MIRR)

The Modified Internal Rate of Return or MIRR assumes that the cash flows arising from a project (but excluding the initial investment) are reinvested at the firm's chosen hurdle rate. Using Friendly Grinders' first project as an example each of the annual net cash flows are projected forward using the company's hurdle rate of 8 per cent to obtain terminal values for each cash flow at the end of the project.

This will create a modified cash flow consisting of an outlay of 34 000 and a future inflow of 49 459. The Net Present Value of this modified cash flow is 2354 which is identical to that of the original cash flow:

$$NPV = -34\,000 + \frac{49\,459}{1.08^4}$$

$$NPV = 2354$$

EXHIBIT 2.10

Calculating the Modified Internal Rate of Return

Calculating the Modified Internal Rate of Return

	0	1	2	3	4
Capital investment	−34 000				
Incremental project cash flows		7 600	16 500	13 000	10 600
Decommissioning costs					−4 000
Net cash flow	**−34 000**	**7 600**	**16 500**	**13 000**	**6 600**
Future value of first year cash flow					9 574
Future value of second year cash flow					19 245
Future value of third year cash flow					14 040
Modified cash flow	**−34 000**				**49 459**
	36 354				
NPV of modified cash flow	**2 354**				

We can now use this modified cash flow to calculate the Internal Rate of Return which we achieve as follows:

$$-34\,000 + \frac{49\,459}{(1 + MIRR)^4} = 0$$

$$MIRR = \sqrt[4]{\frac{49\,459}{34\,000}} - 1$$

$$MIRR = 9.82\%$$

The MIRR certainly gets around the problem of multiple rates of return as the formula required for its solution leads to a single value answer:

$$MIRR = \sqrt[n]{\frac{\text{Terminal value of project cash flows}}{\text{investment outlay}}} - 1$$

Where n is the number of years to the conclusion of the project. MIRR also surmounts the reinvestment rate problem and indeed the firm can choose any rate of reinvestment it thinks appropriate to calculate the terminal value of the project's operating cash flows. However, it does not get around the scaling problem and may still give a contradictory signal when compared with Net Present Value. In the case of projects 1 and 2 we see that MIRR still favours project 2:

EXHIBIT 2.11

NPV, IRR and MIRR compared

	0	1	2	3	4	NPV	IRR	MIRR
Net cash flow (project 1)	−34 000	7 600	16 500	13 000	6 600	2 354	11.128%	9.823%
Net cash flow (project 2)	−10 000	4 000	6 000	2 000	1 000	1 170	14.405%	11.030%

The MIRR can also be adapted to situations where the investment phase of a project is greater than one year. In Exhibit 2.12 we show such a project.

EXHIBIT 2.12

Project with an investment phase of greater than one year

	0	1	2	3	4	5
	investment phase			**return phase**		
Project net cash flows	−30 000	−20 000	14 000	25 000	20 000	5 000

The MIRR can be calculated in one of two ways:

(i) As we have done previously calculating all project cash flows from year 1 forward to year 5 (in this case):

EXHIBIT 2.13

Project with extended investment phase (MIRR calculation method (i))

	0	1	2	3	4	5
	investment phase			**return phase**		
Project net cash flows	−30 000	−20 000	14 000	25 000	20 000	5 000
year 4						21 600
year 3						29 160
year 2						17 636
year 1						−27 210
Modified cash flow	**−30 000**					**46 186**

The MIRR is then given using the formula above:

$$MIRR = \sqrt[n]{\frac{\text{Terminal value of project cash flows}}{\text{investment outlay}}} - 1$$

$$MIRR = \sqrt[5]{\frac{46\,186}{30\,000}} - 1$$

$$MIRR = 9.013\%$$

(ii) In this case we calculate the Net Present Value of the investment phase cash flows and the future value of the return phase cash flows as shown in Exhibit 2.14.

EXHIBIT 2.14

Project with extended investment phase (MIRR calculation method (ii))

	0	**1**	**2**	**3**	**4**	**5**
	investment phase			**return phase**		
Project net cash flows	−30 000	−20 000	14 000	25 000	20 000	5 000
year 4						21 600
year 3						29 160
year 2						17 636
	−18 518.5					
Modified cash flow	**−48 518.5**					**73 396**

The MIRR is then given by the formula as shown below:

$$MIRR = \sqrt[n]{\frac{\text{Terminal value of project cash flows}}{\text{present value of investment outlay}}} - 1$$

$$MIRR = \sqrt[5]{\frac{73\,396}{48\,518.5}} - 1$$

$$MIRR = 8.63\%$$

Which of the two methods is to be preferred? The answer is somewhat more complex than it might appear. The difference between the two answers arises because the second cash flow in the investment phase has not been reinvested at the hurdle rate of 8 per cent in method (ii) whereas it has in method (i). Now if the second investment outlay of £20 000 is to be financed from external sources then method (ii) is arguably correct, whereas if the project is financed through the use of retained capital then the firm is foregoing the reinvestment opportunity and method (i) is correct.

In addition, the second method does have the advantage that it keeps all of the outlay cash flows on the investment side of the project and the future cash benefits of the project on the return phase. Overall however, the MIRR is preferable to the standard form of the Internal Rate of Return as it makes stronger assumptions about the reinvestment rate. It also, necessarily, returns a more pessimistic value than Internal Rate of Return reflecting more realistic assumptions about the rate of return the firm can earn as it reinvests the project cash flows, as they arise, within the business.

REVIEW ACTIVITY 2.5 Calculate the Modified Internal Rate of Return for project 3.

The Accounting Rate of Return (ARR)

Managers invariably worry about how good they are going to look in the eyes of investors as a new capital investment project comes on stream. This is where, from a theoretical point of view, we might shrug our shoulders at the irrationality of managerial behaviour and move on. However, in the real world managers are acutely concerned about how their new project will impact upon the financial performance of the business and the primary measure of financial performance is the rate of return on capital employed. The Accounting Rate of Return (ARR) is a rather weak measure which, like the Internal Rate of Return, is influenced by scale effects. It is measured by taking the average contribution to each year's operating profit generated by the project as a percentage of the average invested capital in the project.

$$ARR = \frac{average\ contribution\ to\ operating\ profit}{average\ capital\ invested} \times 100$$

Taking the Friendly Grinders project again we can see how the relevant figures are derived for the project's contribution to operating profit:

EXHIBIT 2.15

Calculating the project contribution to operating profits for the Accounting Rate of Return

	0	1	2	3	4
Capital investment	−34 000				
Incremental project cash flows		7 600	16 500	13 000	10 600
Decommissioning costs					−4 000
Net cash flow	−34 000	7 600	16 500	13 000	6 600
Depreciation on the basis of complete write off (straight line)		−8 500	−8 500	−8 500	−8 500
Project contribution to operating profit		−900	8 000	4 500	−1 900

The first step is to convert the project cash flows to profit figures by deducting from each year an appropriate charge for depreciation. The depreciation method is calculated on a straight line basis:

$$Depreciation\ charge = \frac{initial\ investment - residual\ value}{project\ term}$$

In this example there is no residual value on the capital investment so given that the initial investment is 34 000, the term of the project is four years then the annual depreciation charge is 8500. If there had been a residual value this would have been excluded from the calculation of the operating profit in the final year.

Once we have the sequence of contributions to operating profit the average can then be calculated:

$$Average\ contribution\ to\ operating\ profit = \frac{-900 + 8000 + 4500 - 1900}{4} = 2425$$

The next step in the Accounting Rate of Return calculation is to calculate the average capital invested in the business. What this means is that we find the capital invested halfway through the project's term. We can see this from the decline in the value of the invested capital year by year as shown in Exhibit 2.16, with the annual depreciation of 8500 deducted each year. The mid point is at the end of year (2) which is 17 000.

EXHIBIT 2.16

The decline in invested capital employed over the life of a project

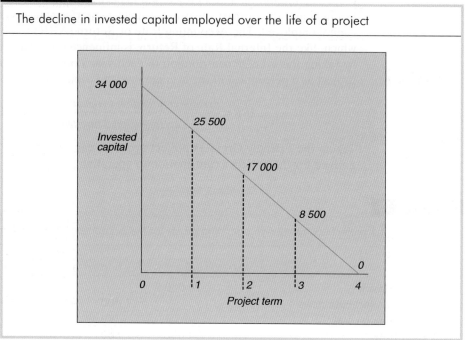

An easier approach is to take the following formula:

$$Average\ invested\ capital = \frac{capital\ invested + residual\ capital\ at\ end}{2}$$

$$Average\ capital\ invested = \frac{34\,000 + 0}{2} = 17\,000$$

The Accounting Rate of Return is then as follows:

$$ARR = \frac{average\ contribution\ to\ operating\ profit}{average\ capital\ invested}\%$$

$$ARR = \frac{2425}{17\,000} \times 100 = 14.26\%$$

The problems with the Accounting Rate of Return from the technical point of view is that it ignores the time value of money, and thus the cost of the finance used by the firm in establishing the project. It assumes that the depreciation charge is a good approximation for the cost of maintaining the firm's capital. The Accounting Rate of

Return measures the impact of a project on a firm's return on fixed capital employed (ROFCE) rather than its return on capital employed (ROCE).

REVIEW ACTIVITY 2.6 Calculate the Accounting Rate of Return for project 3

Differential return on capital employed (ΔROCE)

This measure is similar to the Accounting Rate of Return except that the total capital employed by the project is used rather than the capital invested. To calculate it we draw up a simple project balance sheet accumulating the profits (from Exhibit 2.15) as part of the capital invested as shown in Exhibit 2.17.

EXHIBIT 2.17

Calculating the average differential return on capital employed

Project balance sheet		0	1	2	3	4
Capital investment		34 000	34 000	34 000	34 000	34 000
Accumulated depreciation			−8 500	−17 000	−25 500	−34 000
		34 000	25 500	17 000	8 500	0
Cash account			7 600	24 100	37 100	43 700
		34 000	33 100	41 100	45 600	43 700
Capital invested		34 000	34 000	34 000	34 000	34 000
Accumulated profit			−900	7 100	11 600	9 700
		34 000	33 100	41 100	45 600	43 700
Mid year value of capital employed			33 550	37 100	43 350	44 650
Project contribution to operating profit			−900	8 000	4 500	−1 900
Differential return on capital employed			−2.68%	21.56%	10.38%	−4.26%
Average differential return on capital employed	6.252%					

Now, we can take two approaches:

(i)   Calculate the project average capital employed which in this case will be (33 550 + 44 650)/2 = 39 100. This combined with an average project contribution to operating profit of 2425 gives a differential return on capital employed of 6.202 per cent.

(ii) Alternatively, calculate the average capital employed each year as shown in Exhibit 2.17 and calculate the differential return on capital employed each year. The average of the annual rates can then be calculated which will be very close to that calculated directly under method (i). A project performance profile can then be drawn showing the relative impact of the project upon the firm's overall return on capital employed. If we assume Friendly Grinders Ltd has a target rate of return on capital employed of 11 per cent then this project will have a negative impact upon its reported performance in three out of the four years of the project's operation.

The virtue of this differential return measure is that it is calculated on the same basis as the most commonly used performance ratio in business: return on capital

EXHIBIT 2.18

The variation of annual differential return on capital employed compared with
the average and the target rates

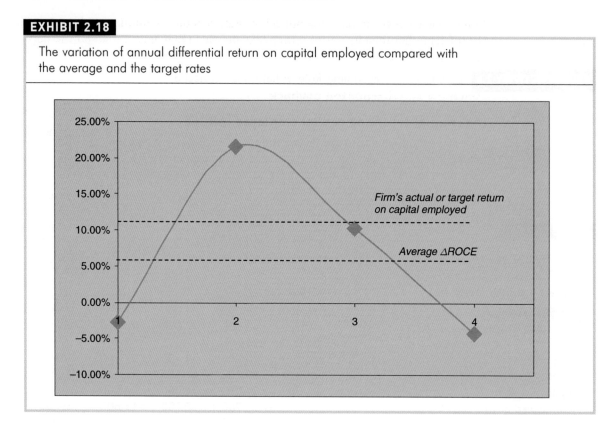

employed. The method assumes that the project can be regarded as a discrete contribution to the overall business and that the capital, once invested, is not exhausted but
is converted into cash as the project proceeds.

The problem with this method of capital investment appraisal is that it does not
focus on the process of wealth generation directly. Rather, it focuses on the reported
performance of managers and directors which is the primary mechanism by which
shareholders can assess the actual returns and the potential for growth in their investment. In the longer run, if managers choose investments which do not have the highest possible Net Present Values then, on the assumption that their investment cash
flows turn out as forecast, the return generating 'engine' of the business will begin to
fail. In the long run, the market should 'notice' that the company is not doing as well
as it might. This is an issue we will return to later after having a look at a range of
investment appraisal techniques which focus, in different ways, on the liquidity of the
business.

Investment appraisal techniques that focus on liquidity

Investment appraisal techniques that focus on the liquidity implications of a capital investment project are of two types: payback and duration. Payback considers
the time taken to recover the investment outlay and duration measures the time

over which a project can be expected to yield a superior rate of return above its hurdle rate. Both measures give different signals to management about the implications of a given project upon the liquidity of the business.

Payback and discounted payback

This is the simplest appraisal technique in the analyst's armoury. It is also very popular, especially with small- and medium-sized businesses, but it is also the one measure that receives the most criticism from a theoretical perspective.

The idea behind payback is to calculate the number of years, months and possibly days that a given capital investment takes to be repaid by the resulting cash flows. Taking the case of Friendly Grinders project we convert the cash flow from the project into a cumulative cash flow as shown in Exhibit 2.19.

Take the investment outlay at time 0, and add the positive cash flow in year 1 to give an outstanding balance of −26 400. Take this balance for the next year and add

---

EXHIBIT 2.19

Calculating the payback

Year	0	1	2	3	4
Capital investment	−34 000				
Incremental project cash flows		7 600	16 500	13 000	10 600
Decommissioning costs					−4 000
Net cash flow	−34 000	7 600	16 500	13 000	6 600
Cumulative cash flow	−34 000	−26 400	−9 900	**3 100**	**9 700**

the net cash flow in year 2 to get an outstanding balance at the end of the second year of the project of –9900 and so on. You will notice that the project goes from an outstanding balance of –9900 at the end of year 2 to a positive balance of 3100 at the end of year 3. During that third year cash was received of 13 000 which, on the assumption that the cash accumulates evenly during the year, implies that the project went through cash recovery at:

$$Payback = 2 + \frac{9\,900}{13\,000} = 2.76 \; years$$

or two years and nine months after the investment was undertaken.

The problem managers have when using this technique is to know what significance to give to a particular payback period. In some businesses such as fashion or consumer electronics a payback of this length would be unacceptable. For a pharmaceutical company, where payback on investment is often greater than ten years, a project with payback in two and three quarter years would be seen as very attractive. So what is an attractive payback period, and what is not, is very much an industry specific and almost product specific decision.

The other obvious disadvantages are that payback ignores the magnitude and indeed the sign of cash flows beyond the payback date. The payback on a project with very heavy disinvestment costs, such a nuclear power station, would not reveal the magnitude of those costs in the result. Payback also ignores the cost of the money involved in financing the project. This last objection is easily surmounted by calculating the payback on the basis of the discounted cash flows rather than the raw cash flow figures. In this case the discounted payback occurs not in year 2 but in year 3 and the 'exact' figure is:

$$Discounted \; payback = 3 + \frac{2497}{4851} = 3.51 \; years$$

There are three points worth noting here: as the chart in Exhibit 2.20 shows, the discounted payback lags the conventional payback and this will invariably be the case. The second point is that the cumulative discounted cash flow reveals as its final figure the original Net Present Value of the project. At this stage the only significance of this point is that it provides a cross check on the calculation. The third point is that the discounted payback still does not get us around the problem that cash flows beyond the payback point are ignored. However, for firms wedded to idea of knowing how long it will take to recover their money there are alternatives.

REVIEW ACTIVITY 2.7 Calculate the payback and discounted payback for project 3.

The discounted payback index and project recovery

The discounted payback index (DPBI) is a simple technique for overcoming the problem of post-payback cash flows. The discounted payback index is calculated by taking the present value of the return phase of the project and dividing by the present value of investment phase.

Taking the project cash flows as before the discounted payback index is shown as 1.06924 in Exhibit 2.21 which shows the number of times the capital investment is 'covered' by the subsequent project cash flows. Any value greater than one indicates that a project has a positive Net Present Value which is equal, in this case, to 6.924 per cent

EXHIBIT 2.20

Calculating the discounted payback

Year	0	1	2	3	4
Capital investment	−34 000				
Incremental project cash flows		7 600	16 500	13 000	10 600
Decommissioning costs					−4 000
Net cash flow	−34 000	7 600	16 500	13 000	6 600
Discounted cash flow	−34 000	7 037	14 146	10 320	4 851
Cumulative discounted cash flow	−34 000	−26 963	−12 817	**−2 497**	**2 354**

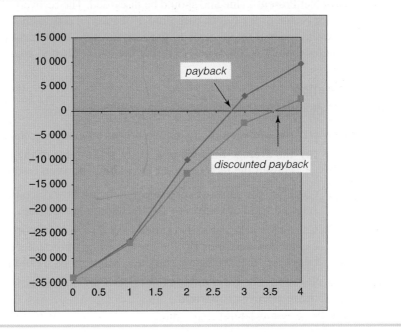

EXHIBIT 2.21

The calculation of the discounted payback index

	0	1	2	3	4
Capital investment	−34 000				
Incremental project cash flows		7 600	16 500	13 000	10 600
Decommissioning costs					−4 000
Net cash flow	−34 000	7 600	16 500	13 000	6 600
Discounted cash flow		7 037	14 146	10 320	4 851
Present value of return phase of the project	36 354				
Present value of the investment phase	−34 000				
Discounted payback index = 36 354/34 000	1.069240				

of the capital outlay ($0.06924 \times £34\,000 = £2354$. The discounted payback index can also be used to calculate the number of years required to recover the initial cash flow from the project including the cost of finance:

$$Recovery = \frac{1}{DPBI} \times project\ life$$

$$Recovery = \frac{1}{1.06924} \times 4$$

$$Recovery = 3.74\ years$$

Clearly, the greater the value of the index above one the more valuable a project is to the firm. A value of less than one simply signals that the project concerned has a negative Net Present Value and should be discarded. The recovery period assumes that the present value of the future cash flows is recovered continuously which will tend to put a pessimistic bias on the time to payback for most investment projects where the discounted cash flow comes before rather than after the mid point of the return phase.

Duration

The duration of a project can be calculated in two ways:

(i) the average time taken to recover the initial capital investment or

(ii) the average time taken to recover the value of the project. Whichever is chosen the technique for calculating duration is straightforward:

1 Calculate the value of each future net cash flow discounted at (i) the project's Internal Rate of Return or (ii) the chosen hurdle rate.

2 Calculate each year's discounted cash flow as a proportion of (i) the original capital investment or (ii) the present value of the future cash flows (check in both cases that the sum of all these proportions should total 100 per cent).

3 Take the time from investment to each discounted cash flow and multiply by the respective proportion.

4 Sum the weighted year values.

Using the previous example we show these alternative calculations in exhibit 2.22.

What the duration reveals is that *on average* this company will take 2.332 years to recover the investment or 2.52 years to recover half the present value of the project. However, there is another side to duration. As we will discover later when we consider fixed income securities such as government and corporate bonds, duration is a measure of the risk attaching to the future cash flow. Generally, the longer the duration the greater the uncertainty attaching to future returns and thus duration not only reveals the time taken on average to recover the value or the investment associated with a capital project, it also tells us something about the risk associated with it as well. We will discuss the use of duration in the measurement of project risk more fully in Chapter 7.

Measuring growth in investment value

The final technique to be discussed in this chapter focuses on the rate of growth in value arising from a capital investment project. We know that the Net Present Value of a project is related to its investment outlay through the discounted payback index. More simply, it is also related by another appraisal technique called the 'profitability

EXHIBIT 2.22

The calculation of project duration

	0	1	2	3	4
Capital investment	−34 000				
Incremental project cash flows		7 600	16 500	13 000	10 600
Decommissioning costs					−4 000
Net cash flow	−34 000	7 600	16 500	13 000	6 600

Method (i) duration to recover original investment

Internal Rate of Return	11.13%				
1. discount all future cash flows by the IRR		6 839	13 361	9 473	4 328
2. proportion of initial investment		0.201	0.393	0.279	0.127
3. weight each year by proportion		$= 1 \times 0.201$	$= 2 \times 0.393$	$= 3 \times 0.279$	$= 4 \times 0.127$
=		0.201	0.786	0.837	0.508
4. sum to give duration	2.332				

Method (ii) duration to recover present value of the project

1. discount all future cash flows at the chosen hurdle rate	7 037	14 146	10 320	4 851
2. proportion of initial investment	0.207	0.416	0.304	0.143
3. weight each year by proportion	$= 1 \times 0.207$	$= 2 \times 0.416$	$= 3 \times 0.304$	$= 4 \times 0.143$
=	0.207	0.832	0.912	0.572
4. sum to give duration	2.523			

index' which we discuss more fully in Chapter 7. Although the profitability index has wider significance which we will defer until later its measurement is straightforward:

$$\text{Profitability Index (PI)} = \frac{\text{Project NPV}}{\text{Present value of project outlay}}$$

Returning to the example above but this time calculating the profitability index as shown in Exhibit 2.23 we obtain the figure of 0.06924 or 6.924 per cent again. This

EXHIBIT 2.23

Calculation of the profitability index for project 1

	0	1	2	3	4
Capital investment	−34 000				
Incremental project cash flows		7 600	16 500	13 000	10 600
Decommissioning costs					−4 000
Net cash flow	−34 000	7 600	16 500	13 000	6 600
Discounted cash flow	−34 000	7 037	14 146	10 320	4 851
Net Present Value	2 354				
Profitability index = 2 354/34 000	0.06924				

tells us that upon acceptance the project will 'grow' the capital investment of £34 000 and hence the value of the business to £36 354 in present value terms.

Using the equivalent value techniques discussed in Chapter 1 we can work out the annual equivalent growth rate, which we refer to as the 'marginal growth rate' (MGR) as follows:

$$MGR = \sqrt[4]{(1 + PI)} - 1$$

$$MGR = \sqrt[4]{(1.06924)} - 1$$

$$MGR = 0.0169 \equiv 1.69\%$$

Alternatively the formula:

$$MGR = \sqrt[4]{DPBI} - 1$$

Can be used which gives exactly the same answer.

A figure of 1.69 per cent may not seem high but this is the rate of value addition to the firm brought about by the discovery of a positive Net Present Value project. If any project offers a marginal growth rate that is positive then the project is value generating at the firm's current hurdle rate. However, in compiling this figure we have already assumed a discount rate of 8 per cent so we are requiring that any project grows at a minimum of 8 per cent to be acceptable. The overall growth rate for a project (annualized) is therefore:

Project Growth Rate = hurdle rate + marginal growth rate

Project Growth Rate = 8 per cent + 1.6924 per cent

Project Growth Rate = 9.6924 per cent per annum

There is one final twist in this which is worthy of note. The marginal growth rate is directly related to the modified Internal Rate of Return. We know that the modified Internal Rate of Return is given as follows (for convenience we now show 'root to the power' as the power of the reciprocal of the number of periods concerned):

$$MIRR = \left[\frac{FV_n}{A_0} \right]^{\frac{1}{n}} - 1$$

therefore

$$1 + MIRR = \left[\frac{FV_n}{A_0} \right]^{\frac{1}{n}} \cdots\cdots\cdots (i)$$

Where FV_n and A_0 are the future value of the project cash flows and the investment outlay respectively.

The marginal growth rate is defined as follows:

$$MGR = (1 + PI)^{\frac{1}{n}} - 1$$

$$1 + MGR = \left[1 + \frac{PV - A_0}{A_0} \right]^{\frac{1}{n}}$$

$$1 + MGR = \left[\frac{PV}{A_0} \right]^{\frac{1}{n}}$$

But the future value (FV_n) is related to the present value (PV) as follows

$$FV_n = PV(1+i)^n$$

Substituting this in the formula for the modified Internal Rate of Return (i) gives:

$$1 + MIRR = \left[\frac{FV_n}{A_0} \right]^{\frac{1}{n}}$$

$$1 + MIRR = \left[\frac{PV(1+i)^n}{A_0} \right]^{\frac{1}{n}}$$

$$1 + MIRR = \left[\frac{PV}{A_0} \right]^{\frac{1}{n}} (1+i)$$

$$(1 + MIRR) = (1 + MGR)(1 + i)$$

Our calculation of the marginal growth rate is designed to show its relationship to the value added to an initial capital investment by a project. However, its close relationship to the modified Internal Rate of Return gives an alternative method for its calculation. More pertinently it also gives a very simple means of calculating the modified Internal Rate of Return and avoiding the tedious part of estimating the future value of the project's cash flows.

For example, we take again the two projects being considered by Friendly Grinders in Exhibit 2.24. The Net Present Value of these two projects is £2354 and £1170 respectively. The marginal growth rate of both projects is easily calculated and from that the MIRR is produced at the top of the following page.

When we compare the investment metrics for these two projects we can now begin to make sense of the conflict between modified Internal Rate of Return (and indeed Internal Rate of Return itself) and the Net Present Value rule.

EXHIBIT 2.24

Projects 1 and 2 – cash flows

	0	1	2	3	4
Net cash flow (project 1)	−34 000	7 600	16 500	13 000	6 600
Net cash flow (project 2)	−10 000	4 000	6 000	2 000	1 000

Exhibit 2.24   continued

	Project 1	Project 2
Net Present Value	£2 354	£1 170
Outlay	£34 000	£10 000
PV/outlay	= (2 354 + 34 000)/34 000 = 1.06924	= (1 170 + 10 000)/10 000 1.1170
$1+MGR = \left[\dfrac{PV}{A_0}\right]^{\frac{1}{n}}$	$1+MGR = 1.06924^{\frac{1}{4}}$ $(1+MGR) = 1.01688$	$1+MGR = 1.1170^{\frac{1}{4}}$ $(1+MGR) = 1.02805$
$(1+MIRR) = (1+MGR)(1+i)$	$(1+MIRR) = 1.01688 \times 1.08$ $(1+MIRR) = 1.09823$ $MIRR = 0.09823\ (9.823\%)$	$(1+MIRR) = 1.02805 \times 1.08$ $(1+MIRR) = 1.11029$ $MIRR = 0.11029\ (11.029\%)$

The conventional argument is that we should always take the project which offers the highest Net Present Value irrespective of the rates of return. What our analysis has now shown is that the modified Internal Rate of Return is closely related to the marginal growth rate and hence the overall rate of growth in the firm's value that a project is likely to bring about (the project growth rate). Many managers would argue that this is what is important and not just the absolute Net Present Value of a given capital project. In the restricted world of a corporate finance book we can set up innumerable examples that demonstrate the superiority of Net Present Value over Internal Rate of Return and the measures of project growth that we have now derived. However, corporate managers might well point out that when comparing projects 1 and 2. For example, with project 2 they get both a higher growth rate and they avoid spending £24 000 which might be better put to another use. The Net Present Value rule does assume perfect capital markets where capital is freely available. If that assumption is valid then the value maximizing firm would choose project 1. However, capital finance is often constrained and as we shall see in Chapter 7 it is in these circumstances that project growth rates become critically important in deciding between alternative investment opportunities.

EXHIBIT 2.25

The Net Present Value, rate of return and growth measures for projects 1 and 2

	NPV	IRR	MIRR	PI	MGR	PGR
Project 1	2354	11.13%	9.82%	6.92%	1.69%	9.69%
Project 2	1170	14.40%	11.03%	11.70%	2.81%	10.81%

The investment techniques discussed in this chapter focus on different aspects of the capital investment appraisal problem. Net Present Value focuses on the added value to the investor and under conditions of perfect capital markets and complete certainty about the future cash flows it works perfectly. Once Friendly Grinders knew that the Net Present Value of the project when discounted at their chosen hurdle rate (under these conditions the ruling market rate of interest) was £2354 then they had no choice but to proceed if they were attempting to maximize the value of Fred's wealth.

However, in practice, managerial incentives come into play and in a world where impressions often count as much as reality, the management may be more concerned that their investment choices look good from a return perspective. The economic return as measured by the Internal Rate of Return criterion will, like Net Present Value, signal that a given investment is wealth generating if the return is greater than the chosen hurdle rate. That is providing that the cash flows are well behaved and multiple solutions do not emerge as the Internal Rate of Return is calculated. We also noted that Internal Rate of Return makes some strong assumptions about the implied reinvestment rate of cash flows and suggested one way of defeating this problem by modifying the measure to assume reinvestment at the hurdle rate rather than the Internal Rate of Return itself. Internal Rate of Return can lead to conflicting advice to Net Present Value when mutually exclusive projects are considered even though there is a relatively straightforward 'work around' to this problem. This is a significant disadvantage with the technique although as we shall see later in this book points to a much deeper issue within the application of the Net Present Value concept.

In the real world of capital markets and director accountability the presentation of investment decisions through the financial reporting system is opaque to say the least. Management will therefore be interested in the likely impact of new investment on the reported figures particularly for earnings and return on capital employed. For this reason, many firms use the Accounting Rate of Return as a measure of investment performance. Unfortunately, the Accounting Rate of Return does not bear any resemblance to the economic performance of a project which says more about the conventions of accrual based accounting than the technique itself.

We then considered a range of measures which focus on a project's ability to repay its investment: payback, discounted payback, the discounted payback index and duration. The conventional textbook wisdom is that payback is deeply flawed as a technique even though it is widely used in practice. This would suggest either that the technique is flawed and management are behaving in an irrational way or the technique reveals more at a deeper level of analysis than is normally found in simple textbooks. We take the latter view and later in this book payback will make a comeback as we probe more deeply into the economics of real investment decision making.

Finally we explored the concept of project growth. Project growth is the instantaneous change in the value of the firm once a capital investment is recognized and is calculated as an equivalent annual rate based upon the life of the project. We demonstrate that the project growth rate and the modified Internal Rate of Return are closely connected and later in this book we will return to the problem of the measurement of capital growth in greater detail.

Further Reading

Barney, L.D. (2004) Ranking Mutually Exclusive Projects: the role of duration, *The Engineering Economist*, 49:43–61.

Berle, A.A. and Means, G.C. (1932) *The Modern Corporation and Private Property*, New York: The Macmillan Company. (Reprint, 1991, Transaction Publishers, New Brunswick, N.J.)

Beaves, R.G. (1988) Net Present Value and Rate of Return: implicit and explicit reinvestment assumptions, *The Engineering Economist*, 33,4:275–302.

Bernhard, R.H. (1979) Modified Rates of Return for Investment Project Evaluation – a comparison and critique, *The Engineering Economist*, 24,3:161–167.

Binder, J.L. and Chaputt, J.S. (1996) A Positive Analysis of Corporate Capital Budgeting Practices, *Review of Quantitative Finance and Accounting*, 6:245–257.

Coase, R.H. (1937) *The Nature of the Firm*, reproduced in Williamson, O.E. and Winter, S.G. (1991) *The Nature of the Firm – origin, evolution and development*, New York: Oxford University Press. Coase's classic work can be found in this book of readings – which is an excellent place to start in getting to grips with Transaction Cost Economics.

Cornell, B. (1999) Risk, Duration and Capital Budgeting: New Evidence on Some Old Questions, *Journal of Business*, 72,2:183–208.

Demsetz, H. (1988) *Ownership, Control and the Firm*, Oxford: Blackwell. This brilliant and highly cited overview of the problems of the separation of ownership and control is well worth reading.

Fisher, I. (1930) *The Theory of Interest*, New York: Macmillan. This is the source document for much of our modern understanding of the role of the present value rule in investment decision making.

Hirshliefer, J. (1965) Investment Decisions under Uncertainty: choice-theoretic approaches, *The Quarterly Journal of Economics*, LXXIX, 4:509–536.

Hirshliefer, J. (1966) On the Theory of Optimal Investment Decisions, *The Journal of Political Economy*, 66,4:329–352. This article explores the economics of the separation theorem and its extension into the problem of uncertainty.

Jensen, M.C. and Meckling, W.H. (1976) Theory of the Firm: Managerial Behaviour, Agency Costs and Ownership Structure, *Journal of Financial Economics* 3:305–360. This is not an article for the faint hearted. However, if you want to find out how the economic theory of agency arose this is the place to start.

Pike, R. (1996) A Longitudinal Survey on Capital Budgeting Practices, *Journal of Business Finance and Accounting*, 23(1):79–92.

PROGRESS CHECK

1 What are the likely cash flows which will arise from the replacement of existing capital equipment?

2 What are the three critical issues that the decision maker must resolve when making a capital investment decision?

3 Explain the concepts diffentiability and contingency in investment decision making.

4 Outline the Net Present Value rule and the circumstances where capital investment decision will lead to an increase in the market value of the firm.

5 Outline why the agency problem might lead to managers investing in projects that do not maximize shareholder value.

6 To what extent does transaction cost economics extend our understanding about how managers behave?

7 When undertaking capital investment appraisal what condition is imposed upon our estimation of the operating cash flows from the new project?

8 List the conditions required for a perfect capital market.

9 Explain what you understand by the Fisher Hirshliefer Separation Theorem.

10 List the three factors which are likely to influence the level of the discount rate chosen by investors.

11 Define the Internal Rate of Return and the condition under which the IRR of a project is acceptable.

12 Under what circumstances could the Internal Rate of Return conflict with the Net Present Value of an investment project?

13 Describe the change in assumption required to calculate the modified Internal Rate of Return compared with the Internal Rate of Return itself.

14 What are the perceived benefits of the Accounting Rate of Return for managers and how are the deficiencies of the measure overcome by the differential return on capital employed?

15 What information does the payback or discounted payback convey to the decision maker?

16 Define the duration of capital investment project.

QUESTIONS (answers at end of book)

1 You are reviewing a capital investment bid in your firm which has been costed by the firm's accountant who is a little hazy on the principles of finance. The company, he tells you demands a rate of return of 10 per cent on all capital investment and they currently have to pay the bank 6 per cent on all funds borrowed at the beginning of the financial year. On the basis of his calculations he does not believe that the investment is worthwhile. Below is the working sheet he has prepared:

NOIDEA LTD

	01-Jan 2004	31-Dec 2004	31-Dec 2005	31-Dec 2006	31-Dec 2007	31-Dec 2008	31-Dec 2009
Capital investment	860 000						
Expected scrap and resale							20 000
Annual depreciation (straight line)		(140 000)	(140 000)	(140 000)	(140 000)	(140 000)	(140 000)
Book Value	860 000	720 000	580 000	440 000	300 000	160 000	20 000
Preincurred design and development costs	(42 000)						
Sales revenue		520 000	650 000	600 000	600 000	500 000	350 000
Direct project operating costs		156 000	195 000	180 000	180 000	150 000	105 000
Annual project operating profit		364 000	455 000	420 000	420 000	350 000	245 000
Allocated company overheads		(117 000)	(146 250)	(135 000)	(135 000)	(112 500)	(78 750)
Depreciation		(140 000)	(140 000)	(140 000)	(140 000)	(140 000)	(140 000)
Annual project profit before interest		107 000	168 750	145 000	145 000	97 500	26 250
Interest charge on capital invested		(51 600)	(43 200)	(34 800)	(26 400)	(18 000)	(9 600)
Annual project profit		55 400	125 550	110 200	118 600	79 500	16 650
Average project profit	84 317						
Less required return	86 000						
Average annual surplus/(deficit)	(1 683)						

You are required to:

(i) Identify, giving reasons, which elements of the above analysis should be excluded in the assessment of the value of this project to the firm.

(ii) Calculate the Net Present Value of the project to the firm assuming that the firm's required rate of return is the discount rate that should be applied.

2 Burco plc is considering what to do with a piece of land it owns on the outskirts of town. It has planning permission for a warehouse but is reviewing the possibility of building an office block instead. The warehouse would cost £2.5 million and the office block £6.5 million to construct. The warehouse would create substantial savings to the firm's current storage solutions and allow it to be much more flexible in its inventory holdings. The firm only plans on a seven-year time horizon and assumes a future break up value based upon a 30 per cent per annum write down of its assets. The land would have a residual value based upon its current value of £300 000 plus 5 per cent appreciation in value each year. The company's required rate of return is 10 per cent.

After careful analysis the net cash flows for each proposal are as below.

You are required to fill in all of the shaded boxes and then answer the following questions:

(i) What is the relevance of the value of the land committed to the project to the decision? Would it change your decision if you knew the value of the land was worth £750 000?

	0	1	2	3	4	5	6		
Value of land committed to project	☐						☐		
Warehouse project – capital spend	☐								
Estimated break up value							☐		
Estimated net cash savings		500 000	600 000	700 000	800 000	900 000	1 000 000	NPV	IRR
Warehouse project net cash flow	☐	500 000	600 000	700 000	800 000	900 000	☐	☐	☐
Office block project – capital spend	☐								
Estimated break up value							☐		
Annual rental income		1 000 000	1 200 000	1 800 000	2 200 000	2 400 000	2 400 000		
Warehouse project net cash flow	☐	1 000 000	1 200 000	1 800 000	2 200 000	2 400 000	☐	☐	☐

(ii) Explain the significance of the Net Present Value and Internal Rate of Return figures you have calculated for each project.

(iii) Calculate the modified Internal Rate of Return for each project and each project's marginal growth rate.

QUESTIONS (answers on website)

3 You plan to invest £10 000 for five years earning 7.5 per cent (complete the table).

	0	1	2	3	4	5
Initial investment	10 000	10 000	10 500			
Add interest at 5% for one year		500	525			
Balance invested for the year	10 000	10 500	11 025			

4 You plan to invest £10 000 per annum at 10 per cent for seven years. Calculate the accumulated value assuming interest is reinvested annually.

5 You are due to receive a cash sum of £80 000 in five years' time. What is the present value to you of this cash sum assuming an interest rate of 8 per cent per annum?

6 An investment of $60 000 offers a return of $100 000 in 12 months. The investor requires a rate of return of 6 per cent per annum. What is the Net Present Value and the Internal Rate of Return of this investment?

7 An investment of $60 000 promises to yield a net cash return of £50 000 within the following 12 months and £50 000 the year after. The investor has a required rate of return of 8 per cent. Calculate the Net Present Value and the Internal Rate of Return of this investment and explain why your result is different to that from question 6.

8 A company is considering moving from its current head office premises to a new 'intelligent design building' which although more expensive to rent would offer considerable savings in annual operating costs. Its location would also mean that there would be a saving in local business taxes. Its annual rental for the current property is £450 000 per annum. The rental for the new property would be £475 000 for the first three years and £500 000 thereafter. The estimated cost savings with the new property are: £75 000 in operating costs and £50 000 in local taxes. The fitting out of the new premises and the costs of the removal is estimated to be £500 000. The current lease has ten years to run and the new lease would also be taken out for ten years. The company has a required rate of return of 8 per cent.

You are required to estimate for this move:

(i) The Net Present Value.

(ii) The Internal Rate of Return and the modified Internal Rate of Return.

(iii) The payback and discounted payback.

(iv) The discounted payback index and the marginal growth rate of the project.

9 Bernie Flower runs a garden landscaping service and is considering purchasing a Digemup Mini Digger.

- He currently hires a minidigger from the local building merchants at a daily hire rate of £75.

- During the previous year he hired a digger for 65 days although he could have used one for 75 days saving himself 30 days of labourer time at £50 per day.

- A new minidigger would cost £24 000 and would last six years at which time he expects to be able to sell it on for £4000. He would provide depreciation on a straight-line basis.

- He estimates that its current running costs including diesel, servicing and insurance would be £480 per annum. Hire charges and costs are rising in his business at approximately 4 per cent per annum.

- If Bernie bought the new machine he would need to invest in a trailer and trailer bar for his flatbed truck which would cost an additional £6000 and which would be written off over the life of the minidigger.

- Bernie has a cost of finance of 8 per cent per annum.

Find the Net Present Value, Internal Rate of Return, payback and discounted payback for this project.

Perpetuities, annuities and future fund values

In this appendix we deal with the maths (and some practical examples) of how to deal with compounding and discounting problems where the cash flows are a constant annual sum. Many financial products are of this type including pensions, bonds, and mortgage funds. In this part of the appendix we will deal with the present value of a perpetual future cash sum and with both the present value and the future value of a predictable annual cash flow of fixed duration. Note the definitions:

- a perpetuity is a constant cash flow which is assumed to occur annually into the indefinite future.
- an annuity is a constant cash flow which is assumed to occur annually for a given period of time.

The present value of a perpetuity

Assume that a constant cash flow (C) will arise annually into the indefinite future then, using an annual rate (i) its present value is given by the infinite progression:

$$PV = \frac{C}{(1+i)} + \frac{C}{(1+i)^2} + \frac{C}{(1+i)^3} + \cdots\cdots\infty \qquad \text{equation 1}$$

We can sum this progression to find the present value by multiplying both sides by $(1+i)$:

$$PV(1+i) = \frac{C(1+i)}{(1+i)} + \frac{C(1+i)}{(1+i)^2} + \frac{C(1+i)}{(1+i)^3} + \cdots\cdots\infty$$

$$PV(1+i) = C + \frac{C}{(1+i)} + \frac{C}{(1+i)^2} + \frac{C}{(1+i)^3} + \cdots\cdots\infty \qquad \text{equation 2}$$

Deduct equation 1 from equation 2:

$$PV(1+i) - PV = C + \left\{ \frac{C}{(1+i)} + \frac{C}{(1+i)^2} + \frac{C}{(1+i)^3} + \cdots\cdots\infty \right\}$$

$$- \left\{ \frac{C}{(1+i)} + \frac{C}{(1+i)^2} + \frac{C}{(1+i)^3} + \cdots\cdots\infty \right\}$$

which reduces to:

$$PV(1+i) - PV = C$$

or

$$PV = \frac{C}{i}$$

For example, a Government perpetual bond pays 4 per cent per annum on each £100 unit. Assuming that an investor has a marginal rate of time preference of 10 per cent what is the value of the bond to that individual?

As the unit pays £4 per annum its present value at 10 per cent is:

$$PV = \frac{4}{0.1} = £40$$

The present value of an annuity

An annuity is similar to a perpetuity except that the sequence of cash flows end after a specified number of years (n). Its present value can be expressed by the general formula:

$$PV = \frac{C}{(1+i)^1} + \frac{C}{(1+i)^2} + \frac{C}{(1+i)^3} + \cdots\cdots + \frac{C}{(1+i)^{n-1}} + \frac{C}{(1+i)^n} \qquad \text{equation 3}$$

To sum this progression again multiply both sides by $(1+i)$:

$$PV(1+i) = \frac{C(1+i)}{(1+i)^1} + \frac{C(1+i)}{(1+i)^2} + \frac{C(1+i)}{(1+i)^3} + \cdots\cdots + \frac{C(1+i)}{(1+i)^{n-1}} + \frac{C(1+i)}{(1+i)^n}$$

$$PV(1+i) = C + \frac{C}{(1+i)^1} + \frac{C}{(1+i)^2} + \cdots\cdots + \frac{C}{(1+i)^{n-2}} + \frac{C}{(1+i)^{n-1}} \qquad \text{equation 4}$$

Deducting equation 4 from equation 3:

$$PV - PV(1+i) = \left\{ \frac{C}{(1+i)^1} + \frac{C}{(1+i)^2} + \frac{C}{(1+i)^3} + \cdots\cdots + \frac{C}{(1+i)^{n-1}} + \frac{C}{(1+i)^n} \right\}$$

$$- \left\{ C + \frac{C}{(1+i)^1} + \frac{C}{(1+i)^2} + \cdots\cdots + \frac{C}{(1+i)^{n-2}} + \frac{C}{(1+i)^{n-1}} \right\}$$

which on simplifying gives:

$$PV - PV(1+i) = \frac{C}{(1+i)^n} - C$$

Rearranging this formula produces the expression for an annuity of n years at 'i' per cent:

$$PV = C \times \overline{A}|_n^i = C \left[\frac{1 - \dfrac{1}{(1+i)^n}}{i} \right]$$

Where $\overline{A}|_n^t$ is the actuarial symbol for the present value of £1 discounted in each of 'n' years at i per cent.

So for example, a pension fund promises to pay a 60-year-old woman a pension of £15 000 per annum. She expects to live for ten years and has a marginal rate of time preference of 8 per cent. What is the present value of the fund to her?

$$PV = £15\,000 \times \overline{A}|_{10}^{0.08}$$

$$PV = £15\,000 \times \left[\dfrac{1 - \dfrac{1}{(1.08)^{10}}}{0.08} \right]$$

$$PV = £15\,000 \times 6.71008$$

$$PV = £10\,0651.20$$

The future value of an annuity

With a future value of an annuity, the constant annual cash flows are compounded over the period which remains until their maturity, i.e. the point at which the future value is to be calculated. The first cash flow will be held for n years, the second for $n-1$ and the final for one year only. Thus:

$$FV = C(1+i)^n + C(1+i)^{n-1} + C(1+i)^{n-2} + \ldots + C(1+i)^2 + C(1+i)^1 \quad \text{equation 5}$$

To sum the future value divide throughout by $(1+i)$

$$\dfrac{FV}{(1+i)} = \dfrac{C(1+i)^n}{(1+i)} + \dfrac{C(1+i)^{n-1}}{(1+i)} + \dfrac{C(1+i)^{n-2}}{(1+i)} + \ldots + \dfrac{C(1+i)^2}{(1+i)} + \dfrac{C(1+i)^1}{(1+i)}$$

Which simplifies to:

$$\dfrac{FV}{(1+i)} = C(1+i)^{n-1} + C(1+i)^{n-2} + C(1+i)^{n-3} + \ldots + C(1+i)^1 + C \quad \text{equation 6}$$

Deducting equation 6 from equation 5:

$$FV - \dfrac{FV}{(1+i)} = \left\{ C(1+i)^n + C(1+i)^{n-1} + C(1+i)^{n-2} + \ldots + C(1+i)^2 + C\,(1+i)^1 \right\}$$

$$- \left\{ C(1+i)^{n-1} + C(1+i)^{n-2} + C(1+i)^{n-3} + \ldots + C(1+i)^1 + C \right\}$$

$$FV - \dfrac{FV}{(1+i)} = C\left[(1+i)^n - 1 \right]$$

Rearranging the future value of the constant cash sum is given by:

$$FV = C \times \overline{F}|_n^i = C \times \left| \dfrac{(1+i)^{n+1} - (1+i)}{i} \right|$$

Where $\overline{F}\rvert_n^i$ is the future value of £1 invested annually at the end of each of n years at i per cent interest.

For example, an executive plans to put £5000 away each year for 15 years. What will its value be at the end of that period if she can invest at a rate of 8 per cent per annum?

$$FV = C \times \overline{F}\rvert_n^i = C \times \left[\frac{(1+i)^{n+1} - (1+i)}{i} \right]$$

$$FV = C \times \overline{F}\rvert_n^i$$

$$FV = £5000 \times \left[\frac{(1.08)^{15+1} - (1.08)}{0.08} \right]$$

$$FV = £5000 \times 29.324$$

$$FV = £146\ 621.41$$

Compounding and discounting in continuous time

One important limitation of conventional methods of compounding and discounting is that they assume that interest or return accrues at discrete points in time. The conventional method described so far is fine for calculating future or present values of annual, monthly or indeed weekly cash flows. Many processes create return on a continuing basis: shares change value moment by moment, inventories in warehouses change value continuously. Therefore it is important to know how to compound or discount when the return generating process is continuous. This method is also very useful as an approximation when we are required to compound or discount over an unusual period of time.

In the Exhibit A2.1 below we work out the implications for a £1000 investment where compounding and discounting is conducted over shorter and shorter periods. In the first column of the table, compounding is assumed to be annual, this is then progressively reduced in successive columns until in the penultimate column we assume that compounding and reinvestment is conducted on an hourly basis.

EXHIBIT A2.1

Compounding and discounting over contracting intervals of time

Compounding/discounting interval	annual	quarterly	monthly	weekly	daily	hourly	continuous
Number of intervals	1	4	12	52	365	8760	infinite
Rate of interest	=0.12	=0.12/4	=0.12/12	=0.12/52	=0.12/365	=0.12/8760	*
equals (per period)	0.12	0.03	0.01	0.00230769	0.00032877	1.3699E-05	*
Present value sum	1000	1000	1000	1000	1000	1000	1000
Future value sum	1120.000	1125.509	1126.825	1127.341	1127.475	1127.496	1127.497
Future value sum	1000	1000	1000	1000	1000	1000	1000
Present value sum	892.857	888.487	887.449	887.043	886.938	886.921	886.920

Note: (* the rate of interest divided by the frequency of compounding or discounting in a given period) will tend towards zero as the frequency tends towards infinity.

In each case the rate of interest we will use for compounding and discounting is found by dividing the annual rate by the number of time intervals.

As you can see from Exhibit A2.1 both the compounded values and the discounted value approach a limit. To find this limiting value, which represents the position where compounding or discounting is conducted on a continuous basis we must find the limiting value of the following expression:

$$FV_c = PV_c \times \lim_{m \to \infty} \left(1 + \frac{i}{m}\right)^{\frac{t}{m}}$$

as m tends towards infinity.

Lim = the limit operator

$\quad i$ = the period rate of interest

$\quad m$ = the frequency of compounding or discounting within the period,
$\qquad$ If compounding is annual, $m = 1$, monthly m is 12, weekly 52 and so on.

$\quad t$ = the time period over which compounding will take place expressed in terms
$\qquad$ of the period controlling the interest rate applied.

If, (i) is an annual interest rate (as it is in the example in the figure below), then t will be expressed in multiples or parts of a year.

The mathematical limit of this equation is given as:

$$FV_c = PV_c \times e^{it}$$

where:

$\qquad e$ = the exponential constant = 2.718281828 ... (a standard constant)

Assuming a present value sum of £1000, an annual rate of interest of 12 per cent and continuous compounding then the future value at the end of one year will be:

$$FV_c = £1000 \times e^{0.12 \times 1}$$
$$= £1127.50$$

This is how you would do this on a standard calculator:

1000	x	2nd	e^x	(	.12	x	1	)	=

The present value formula, assuming continuous time discounting is very similar. Because

$$FV_c = PV_c \times e^{it}$$
$$PV_c = \frac{FV_c}{e^{it}} = FV_c \times e^{-it}$$

Using the example in the table the present value of £1000 using continuous time discounting is given by:

$$PV_c = FV_c \times e^{-it}$$
$$= £1000 \times e^{-0.12 \times 1}$$
$$= 886.92$$

It is important to note that this is a limiting value in both cases and indeed, compounding or discounting using a reinvestment interval of less than one month is very closely approximated by the continuous time formula.

These formulas have two useful applications:

- As an accurate measure of future or present values when the returns are being earned on a continuous basis (as with holdings of shares for example).
- As a close approximation when short period compounding or discounting is entailed.

You will come across important applications of the use of continuous time discounting when we discuss the pricing of options in Chapter 8.

A University has implemented a strict credit control policy in collecting rents from its students in their halls of residence. At any one point of time, its average outstanding rents stood at £350 000 which was recovered over an average of 65 days. It now recovers its outstanding debts over 30 days and the outstanding rent bill has fallen to £200 000. What is the benefit of this tightening of policy assuming that the University has an effective rate of borrowing of 10 per cent per annum?

The present value of the outstanding rents to the University prior to the change was:

$$PV = £350\ 000 \times e^{-0.1 \times 65/365}$$
$$= £350\ 000 \times 0.982349$$
$$= £343\ 823$$

Clearly, if the University could obtain this rent immediately it would be worth £350 000 so the annual loss to the University because of the credit given is:

$$\text{Loss} = £350\ 000 - £343\ 823$$
$$= £6177$$

The present value of the rents after the change was:

$$PV' = £200\ 000 \times e^{-0.1 \times 30/365}$$
$$= £200\ 000 \times 0.991814$$
$$= £198\ 363$$

The annual loss to the University is now reduced to:

$$\text{Loss}' = £200\ 000 - £198\ 363$$
$$= £1637$$

The net benefit to the University is thus the difference between these two losses, i.e. £4540 as well as the fact that it will gain a one-off 'surge' of cash through its system of £150 000 as its tenants pay up more quickly.

The University has reduced the present value of its rents outstanding by £145 460.

II

The Financial Markets and the Cost of Capital

3 The market for capital finance and the price of risk

I n this chapter we review the practice and theory of the equity markets. Equity finance is the primary source of finance for business – it represents the capital subscribed by the owners of the firm. For managers and investors it is important to understand how the market for equity finance operates and how we can determine the cost of raising new equity, or the opportunity cost of using existing equity retained within the firm. First we explore how firms raise equity capital through their life cycle commencing with the unincorporated owner-manager business through to the public limited company. The process of raising finance through the equity market is discussed focusing on the different types of issues that can be made. Following this preliminary discussion we explore the issue of market efficiency and the importance of efficiency arguments in theory and model building. The arguments for and against efficiency are discussed informally and the potential impact of systematic inefficiencies signposted for further discussion in later chapters. The final part of this chapter is devoted to a treatment of modern portfolio theory and capital asset pricing.

Learning outcomes

By the end of this chapter you will achieve the following:

1 Distinguish between the primary and secondary capital market.

2 Characterize different types of equity finance and have an outline understanding of the mechanisms by which they are issued.

3 Define what is meant by the Efficient Market Hypothesis and be able to describe the hypothesis in its three forms.

4 A good understanding of the theory of risk, the concept of mean-variance efficiency, the Markowitz/Tobin Separation Theorem and be able to make simple asset allocation decisions.

5 A good understanding of the Capital Asset Pricing Model and know how to source the necessary information for calculating the rate of return required by equity investors.

6 An outline understanding of the Arbitrage Pricing Theory model and be able to identify its relative advantages to the Capital Asset Pricing Model.

The structure of the capital market

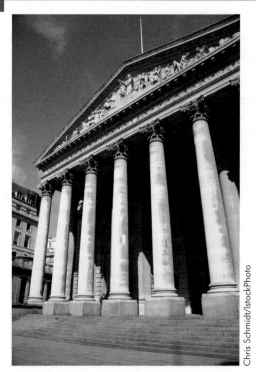

The Royal Exchange home of the first London Stock Market

The modern equity markets exist so that firms can raise new risk finance and allow investors to trade their ownership shares. The market can be separated into two sub-markets: a primary market in which companies raise new funds from investors and a secondary market where investors can trade their shares with one another. The equity market is organized through stock exchanges (such as those in New York, London, Tokyo and elsewhere), although, as we shall see later, much of the dealing is now done on-line through the offices and computer systems of member firms.

What most people know of as the 'stock exchange' is the spot market for buying and selling shares. The term 'spot market' is used to describe any market where financial securities are traded for immediate delivery and settlement and the price quoted by the market makers (licensed traders) is the current price at which they are prepared to buy or to sell the security concerned. A third market has also emerged in recent years which allows investors to trade commitments to buy or sell securities in the future in the form of futures and option agreements and for firms and investors to swap their capital commitments with one another. We will return to this third or derivative market in Chapter 8.

EXHIBIT 3.1

The three components of the capital markets

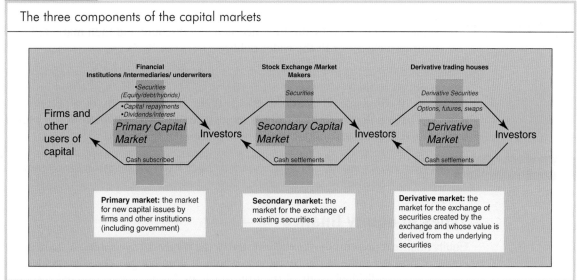

Chris Schmidt/IstockPhoto

In Exhibit 3.1 we outline the basic structure of the capital markets. In this chapter we are principally concerned with market for equity, in the next chapter we will turn our attention to the debt market.

The role of financial institutions (FIs)

You will note in Exhibit 3.1 that between each party sits a financial institution. These institutions include banks, merchant banks, financial services firms, insurance companies, pension funds and a wide range of smaller organizations offering specialist services to their commercial clients and to investors.

Some FIs facilitate the issue of capital market securities on behalf of client companies. In the primary capital market firms that have the right to issue shares to the public (in the UK they are termed 'public limited companies' or 'plcs' and have a 'listing' on the stock exchange) can seek to raise new equity through a range of methods. Invariably they will need to acquire the services of a financial institution to organize the issue on their behalf. Because individual firms rarely go to the capital market to seek new equity finance they are unlikely to have the in-house expertise to handle the complexities of a new issue. There are a number of reasons why financial institutions have such a large role to play in the organization of the capital market:

1 Individual firms do not have the skills nor the administrative mechanisms necessary to organize a capital issue on their own behalf. This is a transactions cost argument as outlined in Chapter 1 in that it is cheaper to 'outsource' the management of a capital issue given its low level of frequency in the life of the business and the high levels of skill (in the jargon of transaction cost economics – high human asset specificity) required.

2 Given the high burden of regulation and compliance, FIs can arrange issues which have relatively low compliance burdens and offer more stable returns for all the parties involved.

3 In the debt and derivative markets the FI may bring together a number of lenders or, in the case of the latter, writers of derivative contracts and 'securitize' the issue. We will meet this more when we discuss corporate bond issues in Chapter 4.

4 They may also act as, or organize underwriting facilities where new issues of capital are taken up by the FI concerned at a discount and then marketed to their own clients or to the wider public.

Some FIs also act as intermediaries in that they offer their own savings and investment products to their private and other clients and then in their turn either invest in the equity of companies or lend directly to them. As we will discuss in Chapter 4, there has been a decline in the relative importance of intermediation in the capital markets and in particular in the supply of debt through the banks.

REVIEW ACTIVITY 3.1 Why do you think that the capital markets have been organized the way they are? What alternative systems could have emerged?

Types of equity finance

Equity finance represents the capital invested by the owners of a business. A share in the equity of firm is a share in the business as whole. It does not give the shareholder any claim over the individual assets of the firm which are 'owned' by the limited company as a separate legal entity from its owners. As outlined in Chapter 1, this separation of shareholders from the management of their firms is an important feature of the way in which modern capital economies operate.

Equity finance is available to firms from two principal sources: direct investment of capital subscribed by investors in exchange for shares or indirect investment as profits that are potentially distributable to shareholders are retained within the business.

'Ordinary shareholders' gain certain rights in exchange for their ownership stake within the business. They have the right to dividends, if a dividend is declared by the directors; they have the right to elect their Board of Directors and to vote at company meetings. They do not have any right to repayment of share capital unless it is (a) repurchased by the company, or (b) the company is liquidated or sold at which point they will be entitled to their proportionate share of the proceeds after all other claims upon the assets of the business have been settled. Equity shareholders are, if you like, the 'tail enders' – they get what is left, whether it be profits or capital repayment, after everybody else has been repaid. They do have certain rights in law: it is illegal to discriminate in favour of one group of shareholders at the expense of the others. A company, for example, cannot give a higher dividend to those shareholders who are also its employees. Shareholders are also entitled to be treated equally with respect to information, in that a company should not issue information selectively to certain shareholders rather than to others.

Limited liability companies (that are not plcs) can raise finance privately from family, friends or through a private equity finance firm or 'venture capitalist'. Venture capitalists are individuals or organizations that can offer to finance the start up phase of a new business in exchange for an equity stake. The venture capitalist's equity stake which may have 'preferred terms' granting the investor prior rights over the company's founders if the business is liquidated or sold. The venture capitalist invests with an 'exit strategy' in mind which will normally be via a management buyout or a listing on the Alternative Investment Market (see below) or, if the company is big enough, via a full listing on the main market.

There are two broad types of equity share that can be issued:

- *Ordinary shares* these carry voting rights at company meetings, dividends (if distributed) and the residue of any capital on winding up. Occasionally, ordinary shares may be classed as 'A' or 'B' shares by the company. What this usually means is that one or other does not have full voting rights.

- *Preference shares* these carry a set dividend calculated as a percentage of the nominal value of the share. So, a 7 per cent, £1 preference share would carry a 7p per share dividend which would be paid if the directors decide to make a dividend payment. If they do decide to make a dividend payment then the preference shareholders must be paid in preference to the ordinary shareholders. Preference shares can be cumulative (in that any dividend not paid in one year must be rolled forward for payment when the directors do decide to pay a dividend) and they may be convertible in that they can be exchanged for ordinary shares at a future date specified when they are issued.

When a company issues new shares to the public via an Initial Public Offering (IPO) or a further issue it is required to produce a 'prospectus' which details the nature of the issue and its purpose, and provide a forecast of its future profitability. Invariably an underwriter will be involved with a large issue as well. The underwriter enters into an agreement with the company to take the entire issue (at a discount) and then organizes the issue of those shares to the public. The cost of raising equity finance by an offering to the general public can be high and many companies who need to raise further equity resort to a 'rights issue' where existing shareholders are allotted shares in proportion to their existing shareholding. Once the shareholder receives the 'letter of allotment' they then have a certain period of time to either exercise their rights or if they wish, sell the rights on to a third party. A letter of allotment represents a 'call option' on the shares offered through the rights issue (see Chapter 8).

A rights issue invariably offers shares at a substantial discount below the current share price. There are two main reasons why companies offer substantial discounts:

- It provides a margin for error in the event that the share price falls between the date the allotment letters are issued and the date the shares must be taken up by investors.
- It offers an incentive to shareholders to subscribe at what might appear to be a favourable price.

In practice, if the stock market is efficient in pricing equity shares and the current market price is at 'fair value' before the issue then offering a discount will only serve to reduce the value of the existing shares.

FINANCIAL REALITY

Friendly Grinders PLC has moved on since Fred's reign as chairman of a small business. It now commands a substantial market presence in the grinding business and currently has 6 million shares in issue trading at 320p per share. Its ambitious expansion plans has led it to contemplate a rights issue of one share for every four held. Its financial advisors have suggested that a price of 260p per share would be appropriate.

Each shareholder might assume that they will make a 60p profit on every share they take up. They could, however, be in for a shock. Given that the market capitalization of the firm is (6m × 320p) before the issue we can work out the market capitalization after the issue which is:

$$\text{Market Cap (post issue)} = 6\ 000\ 000 \times £3.20 + 6\ 000\ 000/4 \times £2.60\text{p}$$
$$= £23\ 100\ 000$$

Given that there are now 7 500 000 shares in issue they should trade at 308p per share after the rights issue has been made. The individual shareholder with four shares worth £320 who paid cash of 260p per share for one more, the net result: five shares worth 308p. The shareholder is neither better nor worse off as a result.

FINANCIAL REALITY

Insurance giant Prudential is due to report its annual results on Wednesday, after revealing last month that it made record sales in 2004. Sales of new insurance products reached a record GBP 1.85bn in 2004, a jump of 19 per cent on a year earlier and higher than the GBP 1.7bn forecast by most City analysts.

But the market will be looking for further information on the Pru's surprise GBP 1 billion rights issue – a move which unnerved the market and put pressure on the group's chief executive, Jonathan Bloomer. Operating profits are expected to come in at GBP 1.07bn, against last year's GBP 790m. *THE SCOTSMAN*, 2 MARCH 2005

A key issue here is how well the market 'values' the underlying value of the company and can it be hoodwinked into believing that the discount being offered is a real gain in value to the investor. Indeed, as the following news extract from the financial press suggests, rights issues can undermine market confidence in a company.

REVIEW ACTIVITY 3.2 From an up to date copy of the *Financial Times,* Yahoo Finance and Thomson One, discover all that you can about Prudential's shares. How many are there in issue? What is the value of each share? What is the company's P/E (price per share to earnings per share) ratio? These are just some of the questions you may wish to ask and get answered.

Stock market efficiency

The western model of capitalism as it has developed over the last 400 years relies upon financial capital as the primary means for storing and distributing wealth throughout the economy. If the capital markets are to fulfil their function effectively, users or suppliers of capital must have confidence that the market price of a security is an efficient estimate of the intrinsic value of the underlying assets that capital represents. So, for example, if the directors of Friendly Grinders plc are contemplating making a new share issue they, and all potential investors, need to be confident that the current market price for their shares is a fair representation of the value of the company. If the price is too high relative to the underlying value then investors are likely to pay too high a price for their shares resulting in a return to them and a cost of capital to the company which is too low. On the other hand if the price is too low, then Friendly Grinders will be at a disadvantage in the capital market and as a consequence will be paying a cost of capital which is greater than what they should be paying given the nature of its business and the opportunities available to it. Thus:

- Equity which is overpriced leads to a cost of capital which is lower than what it should be given the nature of the business. This will lead to the company accepting investment opportunities internally which they should not be accepting as the investment hurdle rate is set too low.
- Equity which is underpriced leads to a cost of capital which is higher than it should be. This will lead to underinvestment where the company rejects opportunities which it should accept.

The prerequisite for any market to operate efficiently in pricing the resources traded within it is that it should be perfectly competitive. What this means is that there are so many buyers and sellers that no individual or group can, on their own, influence the price. Ideally, the market should be free of transactions costs, taxes and other impediments to trading, there must be complete and free access to information pertinent to the pricing of securities and there should be no uncertainty in the pricing process. The perfectly competitive market is a limiting or ideal case situation which will never be fully realized in practice. However, as a matter of public policy in the capital economies, the capital markets should be as free as possible from distortion and anti-competitive practices outlawed. In the UK, as in most western economies the capital markets are regulated by government to ensure that the pricing process is as fair as possible.

FINANCIAL REALITY

'We believe that efficient markets are the best means of providing benefits to both industry participants and their customers. That's why, where we have discretion, which is limited where we are required to implement European legislation, we intervene only where there is a market failure and where regulatory intervention is likely to be cost-effective. We strongly support the call for regulation to be based on principles rather than prescriptive rules.' JOHN TINER, CHIEF EXECUTIVE OF THE UK FINANCIAL SERVICES AUTHORITY, QUOTED IN *THE DAILY TELEGRAPH*, 7 MARCH 2005

If the capital market is perfectly competitive then we would normally expect the price to react perfectly to changes in the beliefs of individuals about the underlying or intrinsic value of the financial securities being traded. A perfectly efficient capital market also relies upon an adjustment process whereby participants in the market instantly and without bias alter their beliefs as they become aware of any new information. If this is true then the market is perfectly information efficient.

As the capital market is a human contrivance we would not expect it to be perfectly efficient under all conditions. But, invoking Ockham's Razor, the question we should ask is; is efficiency the simplest assumption we can make concerning the expected behaviour of the markets? Any other model of market behaviour would require more assumptions about individual rationality, the nature or availability of information or the conditions and constraints that control the market. If we accept that future market behaviour is most likely to be efficient then we can use the concept of efficiency to deduce how markets price financial securities. If it isn't then not only will our resulting theories be suspect we will also have a serious economic and social problem on our hands in that the capital market is not doing its job properly in allocating scarce financial resources throughout the economy.

The Efficient Markets Hypothesis (or EMH) has been intensively investigated in three forms originally defined by Eugene Fama (1970). If it is impossible for any individual to systematically 'beat the market' by making an excess return over the average return offered by the market for investment of a given risk then:

- The market is weak form efficient if traders cannot make an excess return relying upon the information contained within past share prices.
- The market is semi strong form efficient if traders cannot make an excess return relying upon any information in the public domain.
- The market is strong form efficient if traders cannot make an excess return relying upon all knowable information whether public or private.

Before we take a more detailed look at these three versions of the EMH it is worth noting that if the hypothesis is valid then it implies that the capital market is more efficient in valuing financial securities than any trader no matter what their level of expertise. Later in this chapter we give a more formal explanation of why this may be the case. For the moment it is worth reflecting upon why it may be that the market can get the value of a financial security right even though the beliefs of individual traders may not be perfectly formed and indeed might, in some cases, be quite barmy.

In 1906 the eminent social scientist and statistician Francis Galton attempted to confirm his long held belief that in any social situation only a few well bred and well educated individuals influence events. Galton is famous, among other things, for his work on the concept of the normal probability distribution. However, on this occasion

EXHIBIT 3.2

The three forms of the Efficient Market Hypothesis covering the three levels of information

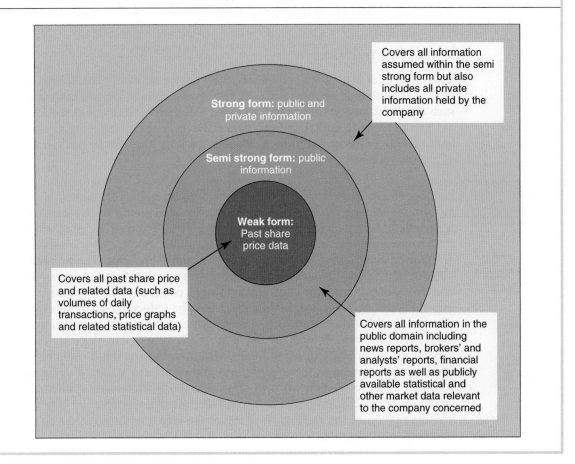

his interest was aroused at a county fair in Plymouth where a competition was being held where people were invited to guess the weight of an ox after it had been slaughtered and butchered for sale. Individuals paid a silver sixpence (now 2.5p) to make their guess and the closest would get a prize. Galton borrowed the 800 tickets that competitors had entered and noted that even the winning guesses were wide of the mark. However, what changed his mind about the 'wisdom of the crowd' was that the average weight as guessed by the competitors was 1197lbs. The actual weight was 1198lbs!

Undoubtedly there were many butchers, slaughtermen, housewives and other 'experts' who tried their hand at guessing the weight of the ox but the crowd beat the individuals. Why? The reason is that the decision making across the crowd was mostly independent. There may have been some gossiping in the queue to buy the tickets or in the beer tent but essentially each person who played made up their own mind. There was a significant sacrifice involved in that sixpence then would be worth approximately £5 today, and everybody could play. When these conditions hold a process occurs where justified beliefs (that is beliefs which are well correlated with the information available) dominate and 'irrational' or uncorrelated beliefs tend to be self cancelling. We will come across this phenomenon again when we consider the problem of portfolio selection.

A stock market, like any efficient market, is a system for averaging beliefs whereby at market equilibrium prices represent the consensus of market traders about the true value of the securities concerned. The question is to what extent the evidence supports the EMH in any of its three forms.

Weak form efficiency

Louis Bechelier in 1906 was the pioneer of what we now call the Efficient Markets Hypothesis although his ideas were not fully exploited until the 1950s when scholars such as Paul Samuelson, Eugene Fama, Harry Roberts and others at the University of Chicago began to explore its implications. Bechelier proposed that share price followed a form of 'Brownian Motion' which is the term given to the random vibration of particles in a box.

THEORETICAL NOTE

Bechelier's idea that share prices follow a random walk is fundamental in the modern modelling of share prices and other financial securities. A random walk is sometimes likened to the chaotic movements of a drunk. The drunk will start from some point (presumably the door of the public house or bar) and stagger off into the night taking very small steps to avoid falling over. The point of the random walk is that the next step could be, with equal probability, in any direction. In market theory, the short discrete steps of the security price, as it staggers along through time, can (unlike the drunk) be reduced to an infinitely short step length. What this means is that security price movements can be assumed to change continuously and, at the limit, each subsequent price movement appears to be drawn from a normal distribution where the last share price observed is the mean of that distribution and where the standard deviation is constant. For the moment we will stay with short discrete time intervals to model share price behaviour. Later in the text we will consider the case of the limiting version of the random walk where the step lengths are reduced to an infinitely short duration.

The discrete model of share price movement can be described by the formula:

$$\frac{\Delta P}{P} = E(r_i)\Delta t + \xi \sigma \sqrt{\Delta t}$$

where:
Δt is the time step where the delta sign means 'change in' and t is time.
P is the price at the beginning of the time interval
$E(r_i)$ is the expected return on the stock (the subscript 'i' denotes the security concerned).
σ is the standard deviation of that stocks return
ξ is a number selected using a random drawing from a normal distribution of mean zero and standard deviation 1

Although it looks somewhat formidable this formula is quite straightforward. The left hand side says that the return over a given period of time (excluding dividends) is equal to the two terms on the right hand side. The first term (sometimes referred to as the 'drift rate') gives the expected rate of return over the interval of time measured by the time step. The second term, known as the 'volatility rate' is the element of return brought about by random movements away from the average and is controlled by the standard deviation of returns over the time step.

Example: British Petroleum has a current value of 248p, has an average quarterly return of 3.21 per cent and a standard deviation of quarterly returns of 25.44% then the change in the share price over a day can be modelled as:

$$\frac{\Delta P}{P} = 0.0321 \times \frac{1}{90} + 0.2544 \times \sqrt{\frac{1}{90}} \xi$$

$$\Delta P = 248(0.0321 \times \frac{1}{90} + 0.2544 \times \sqrt{\frac{1}{90}} \xi)$$

$$\Delta P = 248(0.000357 + 0.02682\xi)$$

We can use this formula to produce a time series of how BP share prices might move on a daily basis if they followed a random walk.

Bechelier could not see any difference in the statistical properties of this type of randomly generated prices and a 'real' track of share prices. Indeed, in studies where this type of graph has been presented to Technical Analysts they have been unable to differentiate the random from the real.

REVIEW ACTIVITY 3.3 Using the =RAND() and =NORMSINV() functions in Excel set up the model as shown above. By hitting the recalculate key (F9) it is possible to create endless different patterns of share prices – just like the real thing!

EXHIBIT 3.3

A stochastically generated share price chart for British Petroleum plc (using the =NORMSINV function in Excel to create random numbers ξ)

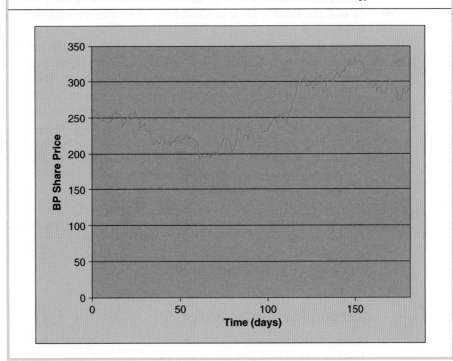

The early studies at the University of Chicago School of Business and elsewhere in the 1950s appeared to confirm Bechelier's observation. If true it would render obsolete the idea that past share price movements could be used to predict future share price movements. As a result 'Technical Analysis' which is concerned with identifying trends and turning points in price charts is unlikely to be profitable except by chance.

The readings at the end of this chapter will provide you with further evidence for and against the 'random walk' theory of share price movement. However, there is evidence which suggests that share prices are not purely random. Studies confirm that share prices show zero serial correlation over time irrespective of the time intervals used although there is some persistence in the direction that share prices move in that there is a slightly greater chance that a positive change will follow a positive change and vice versa. Many of the anomalies that have been discovered have turned out to be due to poor research design but where they have been shown to be real they do not generally overcome transaction costs and so are not profitable for investors.

The empirical evidence is still strongly weighted in support of the EMH in its weak form although the counter-evidence does suggest that at least transiently share prices depart from randomness. But the question is: what is the most reasonable view to take concerning future share price movements? In our view the logic of the pricing process, the force of the central limit theorem and the high degree of market perfection suggests that the simplest belief is that the market will exhibit the properties of a random walk in the way that future price movements occur.

Semi strong form efficiency

The testing of this form of efficiency has focused on how the market reacts to 'news events' such as the publication of earnings announcements, rights issues, economic events and so forth. The original design for this type of study was developed in the 1960s by Ball and Brown. Their methodology, which has been adapted and extended over the years, involves calculating an 'abnormal return figure' being the difference between the observed return over a given period less the return predicted by a 'return generating model' such as the Capital Asset Pricing Model or similar. A sample of firms who have been impacted by the 'news announcement' are then analyzed and the cumulative abnormal returns averaged across the sample for the periods prior to and following the announcement dates for each firm. Indeed, Ball and Brown discovered (see Exhibit 3.4) a large anticipatory effect as the abnormal returns of firms that went on to declare increases in earnings over the previous year showed positive abnormal returns up to 12 months ahead of the announcement of the financial figures to the market.

However, as was the case with weak form testing a number of anomalies have been detected. Indeed, even Ball and Brown discovered what appeared to be an underreaction to earnings surprises. Others discovered overreactions which was taken as evidence that the EMH did not hold in the semi strong form. However, as Fama (1998) in a thorough critique of the anomalous evidence pointed out, if the EMH holds then just as many underreactions should be detected as overreactions – and that is exactly what has been found.

Strong form efficiency

Strong form efficiency requires that no investor can systematically make a gain on the basis of private as well as public information. Testing this is difficult because few

EXHIBIT 3.4

A replication of the association of annual earnings changes and abnormal returns
Source: Ball and Brown (1968)

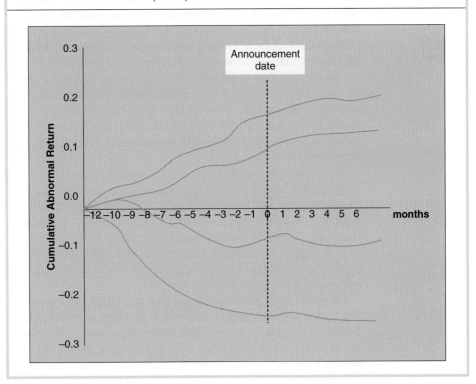

investors are likely to own up to what amounts to 'insider trading' which is illegal. Nevertheless indirect studies have been conducted which focus on the performance of that subset of investors who we would expect by virtue of their expertise to be able to earn systematically superior returns. Fund managers and other investment specialists are employed by their financial institutions to research the performance of their 'list' of companies and build funds which can be used either as direct retail product or to support pension schemes.

In 1968 Michael Jensen studied the performance of mutual fund managers and came to the conclusion that after risk adjustment their performance was significantly less than would be expected by a random stock selection policy. This study was extended by Mark Carhart in 1997 in what is regarded as the most authoritative empirical study of persistence in mutual fund performance. Using data from Carhart's analysis, Kettell (2001) replicated Jensen's approach and came to the conclusion:

> 'active management does not generate superior performance, especially after transaction costs and fees . . . Even if entry into the industry is so easy that the average fund does not outperform simple indices one would expect a few stars to outperform year after year . . . Alas the contrary fact is the result of practically every investigation . . .'. KETTELL (2001) *FINANCIAL ECONOMICS*, 422–423.

The empirical evidence is absolutely solid, fund managers cannot outperform the market, in fact they appear as a group to under perform a random stock selection policy by between 1.5 and 2 per cent. The weak persistence in the performance of funds Carhart noted could only be attributed to the underlying persistence in the price movements of the constituent securities and not down to the skill of the fund managers.

The result of these studies and the many others which have replicated the results in different markets strongly suggest that fund managers cannot convincingly capitalize on their skills and knowledge and beat the market by earning a superior rate of return to that predicted as the average given the risk of the fund. This is regarded as indirect evidence that the market is strong form efficient. Other studies have been conducted looking at this level of efficiency but it has proved very difficult to construct well targeted tests which demonstrate the validity of the Efficient Market Hypothesis at this level.

There is evidence that the market does not always revise its beliefs as rapidly as the EMH would predict and that there is persistence. This we would not take as refuting the EMH as such but it does put a question mark against the explanation of the process that drives efficiency. Most academics take the view that there are some 'savvy' investors who when hearing a news announcement are able to capitalize on its significance by placing buy or sell orders quickly enough to seize a profit and by so doing correct the price to reflect the value in the new information.

However, they also then argue that no trader can expect to consistently achieve this feat (except through luck). An alternative view takes us back to Galton's Ox. Investors as a whole absorb new information and on that basis adjust their beliefs about market prices. Those beliefs can only be partial as no investor (indeed no one) can be in possession of a complete understanding of the economic and other forces acting upon the firm, and which the news announcement reflects. The market, in the price formation process, 'distills' those beliefs into a price which is (almost) always a truer reflection of the underlying reality than can ever be guessed by a single market trader working alone. Hence, we see persistence in beliefs in the historical evidence, but we cannot expect any individual to capitalize on the time lag caused by the market adjusting to new information in the future.

THEORETICAL NOTE

William Beaver an eminent US accounting academic who has also been heavily involved in testing the EMH made the same point:

The crux of a theory of market efficiency which does not rely upon the existence of a set of 'experts' is that the level of knowledge reflected in prices is greater than merely the 'average' level of knowledge in the market. Some simple analogies illustrate this point. Consider each individual containing a 'small' amount of knowledge and a considerable amount of idiosyncratic behaviour. This can be modeled as each individual receiving a garbled signal from an information system that provides an ungarbled signal disguised by a 'noise' component. The garbling is so large that any inspection of that individual's behaviour provides little indication that such an individual is contributing to the efficiency of the market with respect to the ungarbled information system. Moreover, assume that this is true for every individual who

*comprises the market. However, the idiosyncratic behaviour, by definition, is
essentially uncorrelated among individuals. As a result, security price, which can be
viewed as a 'consensus' across investors, is effectively able to diversify away the large
idiosyncratic component, such that only the knowledge (i.e. the ungarbled signal)
persists in terms of explaining the security price.* BEAVER (1981) *FINANCIAL
REPORTING: AN ACCOUNTING REVOLUTION* (3RD ED)

In summary, the Efficient Market Hypothesis has always been controversial and a
source of disagreement between professionals (who are often paid large sums on
the basis that the market is inefficient) and academics (who are paid more modest
sums for collecting the hard evidence). A safe position is that there have been doc-
umented departures from efficiency in the past although none are strong enough to
abandon the belief that the market will be efficient in the way that it prices information in the future (for a defence of this position see the excellent paper by Mark
Rubinstein (2001)). However, if you do believe the market to be absolutely efficient
it is probably best to keep it to yourself. If everyone believed in the Efficient
Markets Hypothesis then there would be no incentive for traders to look for new
information – which is a pretty good way of making sure that the markets became
inefficient.

> *'The market can be likened to an almost exhausted goldmine. A few nuggets
> remain and are occasionally found, which encourages further efforts by the over
> confident, but no miner can reasonably expect continued mining to be worthwhile.
> As a result, there is a sense that asset prices become hyper-rational; that is, they
> reflect not only the information that was cost effective to learn and impound into
> prices but also information that was not worthwhile to gather and impound. Over
> spending on research is not in one's self interest, but it does create an externality
> for passive investors who now find that price embed more information and
> markets are deeper than they should be.'* RUBINSTEIN (2001) *FINANCIAL ANALYSTS
> JOURNAL*, MAY/JUNE, 20

A portfolio theory of risk

In 1952 an America academic, Harry Markowitz, produced a seminal paper on portfolio selection. Markowitz was concerned with the problem of diversification. His
insight was that investors when deciding upon the 'pros' and 'cons' of an investment
make a trade-off between the average return they expect to get (that's the 'pro') and
the variance (or standard deviation of those returns) that's the 'con'.

Markowitz's portfolio model is derived deductively from a set of assumptions about
the way individual investors behave when they are faced with risk and the nature and
operation of the capital market. It is assumed that all investors are strictly rational in
that they seek to maximize their own utility and have the ability to do so in a consistent and transitive way. It is also assumed that investors are 'risk averse'. What this
means is that if an individual is faced with two securities of identical risk than the one
with the higher return will be chosen. Conversely if the two securities offer identical
returns then the one with the lowest risk will be chosen. Markowitz also assumed that
there are no transaction costs and that there are no taxes (these we refer to technically
as market 'frictions').

Markowitz argued, that risky investments do not exist in isolation and that the rational investor will hold a number of different securities all of which respond to changing conditions in different but statistically measurable ways. For this reason, the risk of an individual security should not be measured in isolation but must be taken in the context of all other securities held by the investor. The Markowitz concept of risk introduces us to the problems of measuring the standard deviation of a combined distribution of two or more risky assets or investments.

Markowitz's portfolio theory therefore relies upon an understanding of how individual return distributions combine together to create combined (or multivariate) distributions. When combining risky investments the following simple (and often repeated story) should make the point:

FINANCIAL REALITY

Goldi Locke decided to set herself up in business selling ice cream from a small outlet on a beach in Southern Spain. Her business was a great success generating high average returns which she measured on a daily basis. However, she did notice that those returns were very volatile and it didn't take her long to figure out that sales were down when it rained and were up when the sun shone. Goldi hit on a brilliant idea. She purchased a large terracotta pot, filled it with umbrellas and started to sell them alongside her ice creams. When she did her accounts she noticed that the daily returns from selling umbrellas were, on average quite high – just like the ice creams – but they were also highly volatile – just like the ice creams. When she put the two selling operations together she was delighted to see that she still earned an average return which was just as good as selling either ice creams or umbrellas on their own but that the volatility or riskiness of those returns had completely disappeared. It is not hard to see why. These two activities have returns which are perfectly negatively correlated with one another. As the returns on one rose as the sun shone the other fell and vice versa when the storm clouds blew in. Goldi had discovered the Markowitz portfolio effect.

Introducing the correlation coefficient as the linking factor is achieved through what we call the 'covariance' of two variables. The covariance ($\sigma_{A,B}$) is given as:

$$\sigma_{AB} = \rho_{AB}\sigma_A\sigma_B$$

where $\rho_{A,B}$ is the correlation coefficient which takes a range from -1 where the return series (as in Goldi Locke's case) are perfectly negatively related and $+1$ where they move together. σ_A denotes the standard deviation of security A's returns and σ_B the standard deviation of security B's returns.

FINANCIAL CASE

Goldi Locke discovers that her average daily returns from selling ice creams are a stunning 14 per cent but there is also a standard deviation of 12 per cent above and below the average value. For umbrellas she averages 10 per cent return with a standard deviation of 8 per cent. She originally invested approximately 50 per cent of her resources into each activity. She carefully monitored her daily returns and using the (=CORREL) function on her Excel spreadsheet discovered that they are perfectly negatively correlated.

Therefore the risk formula for a two security portfolio consists of the following elements:

- The standard deviation (σ) of each individual security's returns.
- The weights by value (w) of each individual security in the portfolio.
- The covariance term which measures the degree of interdependence between the two securities and where the covariance is related to the correlation coefficient by $\sigma_{AB} = \rho_{AB}\sigma_A\sigma_B$ to give:

$$\sigma_p = \sqrt{w_A^2\sigma_A^2 + w_B^2\sigma_B^2 + 2w_A w_B \sigma_{AB}}$$

On the basis of this, the overall risk as measured by the standard deviation of returns is as follows:

$$\sigma_p = \sqrt{w_A^2\sigma_A^2 + w_B^2\sigma_B^2 + 2w_A w_B \rho_{AB}\sigma_A\sigma_B}$$

$$\sigma_p = \sqrt{0.5^2 \times 0.12^2 + 0.5^2 \times 0.08^2 + 2 \times 0.5 \times 0.5 \times (-1.0 \times 0.12 \times 0.08)}$$

$$\sigma_p = 0.02 (= 2\%)$$

Note how the negative correlation has created a negative covariance which effectively eliminates much of the risk donated by the standard deviations of the individual returns.

Let us now consider a real world example of two ordinary shares traded on the London exchange: the oil giant British Petroleum and the national carrier British

---

EXHIBIT 3.5

Quarterly data for British Airways plc and British Petroleum plc

quarter	FTSE ASI	BA Close	BP Close	BP Dividend	BA return	BP return
1	2512.00	236.25	588.77	5.75		
2	2050.80	159.82	497.00	5.75	−32.35%	−14.61%
3	1938.70	126.00	410.00	6.00	−21.16%	−16.30%
4	1722.30	114.25	379.51	6.00	−9.33%	−5.97%
5	1891.50	124.29	397.10	6.25	8.79%	6.28%
6	2045.80	172.79	425.05	6.25	39.02%	8.61%
7	2125.40	207.72	408.15	6.50	20.22%	−2.45%
8	2187.10	308.19	428.25	6.50	48.37%	6.52%
9	2237.30	285.85	487.62	6.75	−7.25%	15.44%
10	2192.22	230.75	516.00	6.75	−19.28%	7.20%
11	2297.66	217.44	528.02	7.10	−5.77%	3.71%
12	2430.05	248.00	513.26	7.10	14.05%	−1.45%
			average return		3.21%	0.63%
			standard deviation		25.44%	9.89%
			correlation		0.48	

Source: Downloaded from Yahoo Finance for the three year period to February 2005

Airways. The prices and dividends from these two companies were collected for three years on a quarterly basis ending on 31 January 2005.

We have included data for the FTSE All Share Index which we will return to later. Note that BA did not pay a dividend whereas BP did throughout this period. BA's return is the price difference over each quarter divided by the price at the beginning. In the case of BP the return also includes the dividend paid in the month. Using the =average(), =stdev() and =correl() functions in Excel we produce the statistics for these two shares as shown. You will note that BA generated the higher average return of the two but was considerable more risky. Consider now an investor who wished to put half of their capital available into BP and half into BA. The return and risk of the portfolio would be as follows:

$$r_p = 0.5 \times 3.21\% + 0.5 \times 0.63\% = 1.92\%$$

This is equivalent to 7.9 per cent per annum (see how to calculate equivalent annual rates in Chapter 1).

The standard deviation of the portfolio is:

$$\sigma_p = \sqrt{0.5^2 \times .2544^2 + 0.5^2 \times .0989^2 + 2 \times .5 \times .5 \times .48 \times .2544 \times .0989)} = 15.70\%$$

Let us now calculate what happens to the portfolio return and risk for different weightings by value of the investment in each security. A spreadsheet of the return and risk calculations produces a result which we can graph as shown in Exhibit 3.6.

Note that the risk of the portfolio does not increase linearly as the balance of the investment in the portfolio is switched from the limiting case of 100 per cent investment in BP shares to a combination of BA and BP shares. The curvature of the risk curve has been caused by the less than perfect correlation between the two securities. If we experiment with the diagram by varying the correlation between the two securities the effect becomes rather dramatic once we move towards a correlation of –1. Indeed, if the returns between these two securities were perfectly

---

EXHIBIT 3.6

The return and risk for combinations of British Petroleum plc and British Airways plc

w(BA)	w(BP)	PORTRET	PORTRISK
0.00	1.00	0.63%	9.89%
0.10	0.90	0.89%	10.37%
0.20	0.80	1.15%	11.29%
0.28	0.72	1.36%	12.27%
0.30	0.70	1.41%	12.54%
0.40	0.60	1.67%	14.04%
0.50	0.50	1.92%	15.72%
0.60	0.40	2.18%	17.52%
0.70	0.30	2.44%	19.41%
0.80	0.20	2.70%	21.38%
0.90	0.10	2.95%	23.39%
1.00	0.00	3.21%	25.44%

EXHIBIT 3.7

The risk return mapping for British Airways plc and British Petroleum plc assuming different return correlations

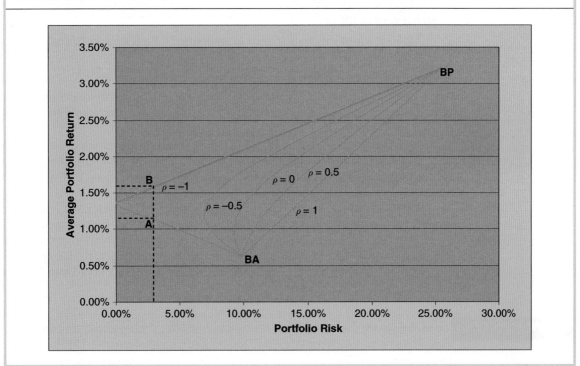

negatively correlated then by putting 28 per cent of our investment into BA and 72 per cent into BP we could eliminate risk altogether and earn a quarterly return of 1.36 per cent.

THEORETICAL NOTE

You may be wondering how we determined the portfolio combination which gives the minimum risk in each case (and in the case of perfect negative correlation a risk of zero). There are three ways of doing it:

1 draw a graph (not very accurate),

2 use the goal seek function in Excel, or

3 solve the problem analytically.

In the appendix we give further guidance on how to do 2 and 3.

The efficient frontier

For any portfolio of securities it is possible to vary the risk of the portfolio by adjusting the weights of the individual components. Now consider an investor who would like some risk providing they can earn a commensurately greater return and let us assume that they are willing to accept a variability of 3 per cent in their returns. Consider the case where the two securities in Exhibit 3.7 happen to be perfectly negatively correlated. There are two possible portfolios which give a risk of this level:

1 portfolio A which can be achieved by investing 20 per cent in BA and 80 per cent in BP, or

2 portfolio B which can be achieved by investing 36.5 per cent in BA and 63.5 per cent in BP.

Which would you choose? The answer is obvious, portfolio B because it offers the higher level of return for that given level of risk. Indeed, all portfolio combinations on the top side of the V shaped curve offer higher levels of returns than the combinations on the bottom side. Thus the top side of the curve offers more risk/return efficient portfolios than the bottom side and thus, is known as the efficient frontier. In Exhibit 3.7 the efficient frontier or, as it sometimes called the 'efficient set', is shown in bold and any rational, risk averse investor, will choose portfolios on that side of the V shaped curve rather than on the other.

In reality, security returns are invariably imperfectly correlated with one another. The true result for BA/BP of 0.48 per cent is more likely to be typical and the maths of the risk formula suggests that any combination of the two securities (see Exhibit 3.6) will be efficient. However, an efficient set begins to emerge when the correlation between the two returns approaches zero and is sharply defined when the correlation is negative.

REVIEW ACTIVITY 3.4 Find the site for the Nobel Prize in economics at http://nobelprize.org/economics/ laureates/ and read the citation and lecture given by Markowitz in 1990.

Markowitz portfolio analysis with more than two securities

In principle we could discover how every security in the market place correlates with every other possible security and indeed how every security correlates with every other possible combination of securities. The calculations become complex very quickly. In the appendix we show how to build the risk formula for portfolios of more than two securities. In principle the maths for optimizing a large portfolio is straightforward (assuming that you are happy with Lagrangian optimization and solution of sets of equations using matrix algebra), but the data analysis to obtain all of the correlations and standard deviations is much more demanding. Indeed, a simple formula tells us the number of data items (standard deviations and correlations) required to deliver an efficient set from a portfolio of N securities.

$$Z = \frac{N^2 + N}{2}$$

So, if you are analyzing the efficient set for a portfolio of (say) ten shares you will need 55 data elements consisting of ten individual standard deviations and 45 correlations that being the number of pairwise combinations that can be constructed.

Markowitz conceived of the possibility that all securities in the capital market could be analyzed in the way he had described and an efficient set drawn. The near infinite number of combinations creates a set of all global securities and ultimately, using the mathematics of portfolio theory, an efficient set of portfolios (shown as E1 to E2 in Exhibit 3.8) which offer the highest level of return available for a given level of risk or the lowest level of risk available for a given level of return. A rational investor who (say) holds a portfolio P should immediately adjust their portfolio of shares until they reach the efficient set because at P^* they can get the same return as at P with less risk, or at P^{**} get a higher level of return for the same risk.

The emboldened region of the set represents those portfolios that a rational investor would be interested in. Clearly, any of the other portfolios would not be preferred because they offer a higher level of risk for the same return as a portfolio in the preferred group. We are assuming here, of course, that other things being equal, a rational individual would prefer an investment of lower risk rather than higher risk if the level of expected return (remember this is the average return offered by the investment) is the same for both alternatives. Correspondingly, a rational investor faced with two alternative investments of identical risk would automatically choose the investment with the higher average return. This is the concept of risk aversion which is normally assumed in all theoretical work concerning portfolio management.

For a portfolio of many securities, the range of possible portfolios will be much extended and indeed, it is possible to construct the most efficient set of portfolios from any set of individual securities providing of course that their return, standard deviation of returns and covariance of returns can all be measured. This sector of efficient portfolios is referred to as the Markowitz efficient set or, sometimes, as the Markowitz Efficient Frontier.

EXHIBIT 3.8

The definition of the Markowitz Efficient Set bounding the set of all securities in the market place (A, B, C. . . .) and all portfolio combinations of those securities

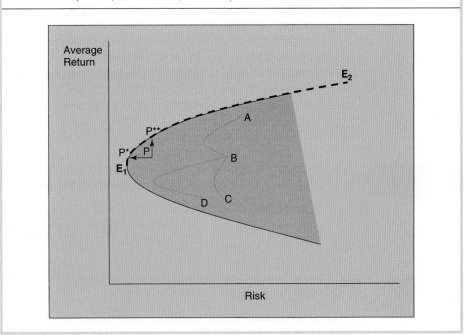

The Tobin/Markowitz separation theorem

In 1959, James Tobin extended the logic of Markowitz portfolio theory. On the basis that investors are rational, risk averse, two parameter utility maximizers they will seek out the efficient frontier. An underlying assumption here is that investors can form an expectation of the future average return and risk of every security available to them in the global capital market and through the expected correlations between securities determine the characteristics of every possible portfolio and ultimately the efficient set. This relies upon the idea that from the evidence of past share returns we can assume that future returns are adequately described by the mean and the standard deviation of a normal return distribution. It is also assumed that there are no transactions costs or taxes preventing investors fine tuning their portfolios to stay on the efficient set.

Markowitz argued that the exact position any investor will take along the curve of the efficient set is solely down to their personal tolerance for risk. Tobin took this one stage further with theoretically dramatic results. Tobin proposed that investors could also borrow or lend at a 'pure rate of interest'. What he meant here was that investors, as well as buying a risky portfolio located on the efficient set, could also invest in a risk free investment at a risk free rate of return (R_f). Further, he assumed that they could borrow at that rate as well. As a result investors could choose to invest in a combination of risk free investment and the tangency portfolio (M) which lies on the efficient set at a point that just touches a line extended from the risk free rate of return.

Take, for example, an investor in portfolio P as shown in Exhibit 3.9, she can obtain the same level of return at lower risk by ignoring the portfolio on the efficient set and investing in a combination of the tangency portfolio and risk free deposit at point P^*. Alternatively, if she was happy with the level of risk she was carrying she could reach the level of return at point P^{**} by borrowing at the risk free rate and investing all, including her own cash again in the tangency portfolio. Indeed, her best position is always to hold an investment portfolio which lies on the capital market line in Exhibit 3.9 consisting of deposit or borrowing at the risk free rate and the tangency portfolio (M).

Presumably, the statistical properties of all securities in the capital market can be established by all investors and it is reasonable to assume that all investors will form the simplest beliefs about the future expected returns from their investment. The simplest belief is that security returns are represented by a normal distribution which can be described by just two parameters: their mean and their standard deviation – both

| **THEORETICAL NOTE** | It is not strictly necessary, in Markowitz portfolio theory, to assume that security return distributions are normal. However, there are two reasons why we stick with it: |

1 as we noted in Chapter 1 the normal distribution requires just two parameters and has a (relatively) simple mathematical structure, and

2 if we do not assume normality then we must, in order to make Markowitz portfolio theory work, invoke an additional assumption about the way that individuals form their preferences (technically: that they have quadratic utility functions).

So the simplest assumption required to support the model is that return distributions are normal and this, using Ockham's Razor, is the position we should take.

EXHIBIT 3.9

The introduction of a risk free asset into the Markowitz portfolio model

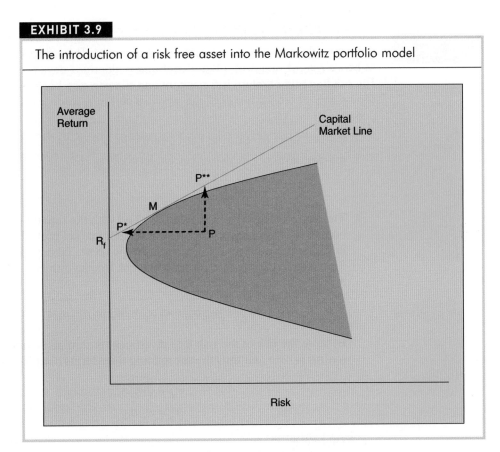

of which can be estimated from the historical data. If all investors 'reduce' their beliefs in this way then all investors will see the same efficient set, the same risk free rate and hence, will identify the same tangency portfolio *M*.

Given that all rational investors hold only the portfolio *M* as the 'risky' part of their strategy for getting to their most favoured position on the capital market line, *M* must in some part consist of all shares traded in the capital market. As this is the only risky investment the rational individual will hold, no security can lie outside *M* in the sense that its price is determined by investors holding it within the context of their holding of portfolio *M*. It follows that the decision about how to invest narrows down to:

1 the acquisition of a single portfolio *M* which perfectly represents the total market for risk, and

2 the level of risk exposure which is not determined by the construction of that portfolio but by the proportion of the investor's funds it occupies compared with the risk free security.

It is in that sense that the fund selection problem is separated from the asset allocation decision, i.e. how much of the investor's wealth should go into the market portfolio as opposed to the risk free investment.

Goldi Locke has a portfolio which returns on average 10 per cent per annum with a standard deviation of returns of 18 per cent. The efficient market portfolio M has a rate of return of 11 per cent and a standard deviation of 12 per cent. The risk free rate of return is 5 per cent and she can also borrow at that rate. How should she rebalance her portfolio which is currently worth £100 000 in order to achieve:

1 the best level of return at her current level of risk, or

2 the best level of risk at her current level of return?

1 The key issue here is the level of risk and with the separation theorem the only issue is the proportions of the efficient market portfolio and the risk free investment required to give a risk of 18 per cent. Taking the two security risk formula and casting it in terms of the risk free investment and the efficient market portfolio:

$$\sigma_p = \sqrt{w_m^2 \sigma_m^2 + w_f^2 \sigma_f^2 + 2 w_m w_f \rho_{m,f} \sigma_m \sigma_f}$$

Because the risk of the risk free investment is zero, its standard deviation of returns is zero and thus the second and third terms disappear to give:

$$\sigma_p = \sqrt{w_m^2 \sigma_m^2}$$
$$\sigma_p = w_m \sigma_m$$

Therefore:

$$0.18 = w_m \times 0.12$$
$$w_m = 0.18/0.12 = 1.5$$

Because this level of risk entails that 150 per cent of Goldi's investment should be in M, this means that she must borrow £50 000 to add to the £100 000 she currently has from the sale of portfolio P. The return she will earn is then easy to calculate from the return formula for a two security portfolio:

$$r_p = w_m r_m + w_f R_f$$
$$r_p = 1.5 \times 11\% + (-.5) \times 5\%$$
$$r_p = 14\%$$

This return is considerably better than Goldi was earning with her inferior portfolio.

2 In this case Goldi wants to seek a holding with the minimum risk commensurate with a return of 10 per cent. Note that this rate of return is lower than that offered by the efficient market portfolio so we can see that to obtain her desired level of return Goldi will need the appropriate mix of M and deposit (rather than borrowing) at 5 per cent. Using the return formula we can recast it purely in terms of the weight of the efficient market portfolio as:

$$w_f = 1 - w_m$$

and,

$$r_p = w_m r_m + (1 - w_m) R_f$$
$$r_p = w_m r_m + R_f - w_m R_f$$
$$w_m = \frac{r_p - R_f}{r_m - R_f}$$

Therefore, substituting our known values:

$$w_m = \frac{10\% - 5\%}{11\% - 5\%} = 83.3\%$$

and

$$w_f = 1 - w_m = 1 - 83.3\% = 16.7\%$$

Goldi's risk is found using the risk formula:

$$\sigma_p = w_m \sigma_m$$
$$\sigma_p = 83.3\% \times 12\% = 10\%$$

which is considerably better than the 18 per cent she was carrying in her original portfolio.

The implications of the Markowitz/Tobin separation theorem

The Markowitz/Tobin separation theorem implies that all investors in the capital market will actively seek the efficient market portfolio as their sole vehicle for risky investment. They should then leverage their portfolio by borrowing if they are more risk tolerant than the average, or depress the risk of their holding by depositing at the risk free rate if they are less tolerant of risk than the average.

The optimality of this investment strategy depends of course on the validity of the assumptions supporting the Markowitz/Tobin theorems. In practice, all of the assumptions will be violated to a certain degree but what matters for investors is whether it would be rational to do anything else given the simplicity of the advice generated by the separation theorem. In practice, it may appear unrealistic to expect investors to scrutinize and evaluate all securities in the market place. However, if each investor makes the assumption that other investors are also acting rationally, then they could further assume that actual share prices are formed in accordance with the contribution each security makes to the efficient market portfolio. The efficient market portfolio will then be revealed by the performance of all securities when combined into an overall stock market index weighted by their capital values.

This would suggest that rational investors eschew 'stock picking' as an investment strategy and purchase a fund of shares and other securities which reflects the most widely drawn global index of securities available.

The efficient market portfolio

The Markowitz/Tobin separation theorem emphasizes the role of the efficient market portfolio (*M*). In principle, this is a portfolio of all risky investments available in the global market for investments of this type. Thus this portfolio does not consist simply of shares but also bonds, derivatives, investment in real assets such as works of art, land, fine wine and indeed virtually anything which could be used as an investment as opposed to being just used for consumption. In practice, we narrow the field to consist of readily traded securities in the capital market – but even there we should consider the global as opposed to national markets for shares and other risky investments. As we will see shortly, the use of value weighted equity indexes such as the S&P500 or the FTSE All Share Index are often used as surrogates for the efficient market portfolio. However, it is worth bearing in mind that these indexes are always likely to underspecify the efficient market portfolio as prescribed by theory.

REVIEW ACTIVITY 3.5 What do you understand by the 'Capital Market Line'? How can an investor use this line to determine their optimum investment/asset allocation strategy?

Capital asset pricing theory

Markowitz portfolio selection and the application of the separation theorem proved very difficult to test in the early 1950s. Indeed, the first mainframe computer had only become operational at the University of Manchester in 1948. In order to overcome the operational difficulties William Sharpe proposed a simplification whereby the returns of individual securities are correlated, not against one another, but against the returns of a single benchmark portfolio. This benchmark is the 'efficient market portfolio'. Sharpe's model is based upon the Markowitz/Tobin assumptions:

1 Investors are risk averse; single period, two parameter utility maximizers. What this means is that investors make their investment decisions solely in terms of their expectation of returns over a single holding period and the risk of those returns as measured by their standard deviation or variance.

2 Security markets are frictionless in that there are no transactions costs or taxes.

3 There is a pure rate of interest reflecting the returns on risk free investment and investors have an unlimited borrowing or lending opportunity at this rate.

4 All investors form common beliefs about the expected returns and risk from all securities.

The formal derivation of Sharpe's model is shown in the appendix and it is known as the Capital Asset Pricing Model or 'CAPM'.

The CAPM links the expected return on any given risky investment with the risk free rate of return plus a risk premium. The risk premium is the reward to the investor for carrying market driven risk, that is risk which is created through exposure to market wide forces rather than more firm specific risk factors. Within the context of the portfolio model, it is easy to demonstrate that the total risk consists of two parts: a part which is governed by the correlation of a given security's return with the efficient market portfolio and a part which is independent of the market. This second part mathematically tends towards zero as we create larger and larger portfolios. This is in effect the cancelling out of idiosyncratic performance between different shares leaving a situation where only the systematic or market correlated risk dominates.

EXHIBIT 3.10

Risk reduction against portfolio size (number of randomly drawn securities weighted equally by value)

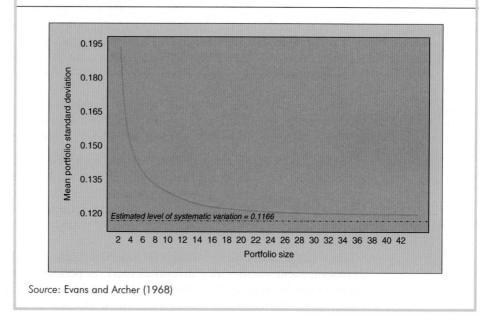

Source: Evans and Archer (1968)

The implications of the Capital Asset Pricing Model can be summarized as follows:

1 Investors are only rewarded in the pricing process for carrying 'market driven' or 'systematic risk'. The assumptions of the CAPM imply that all investors are fully diversified (in that they hold only the efficient market portfolio) and the return they can expect for holding any security is found solely within the context of that portfolio. As they are fully diversified and lying on the efficient set they will not be carrying any firm specific risk (i.e. non-market risk as this will have been diversified away). In a classic study, Evans and Archer demonstrated this diversification effect as shown in Exhibit 3.10.

Exhibit 3.9 shows that as the number of individual securities in a portfolio are increased the standard deviation of the portfolio as a whole comes down and approaches a limiting value which is the standard deviation of the 'market' which, theoretically, is reflected by the efficient market portfolio.

THEORETICAL NOTE

The curve shown by Evans and Archer can be derived by simulating share returns using Excel or some other spreadsheet package. If we assume zero correlation between individual securities then the above curve results but it drops towards zero rather than a constant value. What Evans and Archer had demonstrated is that the diversification effect is another example of the law of large numbers in that as we go above about a dozen randomly drawn variables in a group, the variability of the whole diminishes to a constant level which will be zero if the variables are uncorrelated with one another.

2 The trade-off between expected return and market risk is linear. This is the principal prediction of the Capital Asset Pricing Model. A straight line can be represented algebraically by the following equation:

$$y = a + bx$$

where y and x are the dependent and independent variables respectively, a is the point that the line cuts the horizontal axis and b is the slope of the line. With the Capital Asset Pricing Model, the 'x' variable in the linear equation is the beta coefficient, the y variable is the return on the security concerned, a is the risk free rate of return and b is the equity risk premium. Exhibit 3.11 shows this straight line relationship between the expected return on a given security and its market risk as measured by its beta. Note that the efficient market portfolio has a beta of one.

If the Capital Asset Pricing Model can be operationalized, and if it correctly represents a real underlying relationship between return and risk then it will be very useful. It would allow investors to build portfolios of any given risk (as measured by β_i) and it would allow firms to determine the rate of return the equity market expects for carrying the level of market risk to which the firm is exposed.

The Capital Asset Pricing Model is an expectations model and there will always be a question about whether what investors expect (or perhaps should expect if they are acting rationally) is perfectly reflected in the revealed behaviour of share prices and returns in the market. The Capital Asset Pricing Model is an equilibrium model and within the structure of rational expectations upon which it is built it would not be surprising if it failed to predict perfectly the observed risk return relationships in the market. However, the first step in testing the model is to find approximations (proxies) for the variables in the model.

EXHIBIT 3.11

The Capital Asset Pricing Model

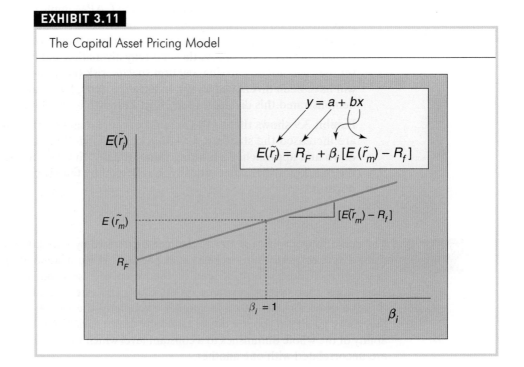

Estimating the risk free rate of return

In theory, the risk free rate is the pure rate of interest which an investor can borrow or lend in any amount in order to optimize their risk return preferences. In practical terms this means that we need to find the lowest money market rate for buying very short dated government bills. Why short dated? The reason is that we wish to remove as much uncertainty as we can and the longer a bill has to come to maturity the more exposed it will be to volatility in the inflation rate. You may also remember that the logic of the CAPM is that the investor is deemed to hold their investment for a single holding period. If the term to maturity of the Treasury Bill is less than the assumed holding period it is assumed that on redemption the investor can refinance their borrowing by rescheduling their holding of the risk free security. Thus the best estimate of the risk free rate of return is the return on a short term government bill. In the UK this will be a one month Treasury Bill or the equivalent in the US.

In the *Financial Times* we see quoted a one month Treasury Bill at 4.72 per cent being the mid selling and buying price for a one month Treasury Bill (see Exhibit 3.12).

Estimating beta

The beta coefficient measures the sensitivity of a given security to market risk. Securities that are more volatile than the market have a beta value greater than one, those that are less responsive to market shocks than the average have a beta of less than one. By definition, the average beta for all shares is one. The beta coefficient is the ratio of the security's covariance with the returns of the market portfolio to the variance of the market portfolio's returns. More formally, the beta coefficient (see appendix) is defined in terms of the correlation coefficient and standard deviations of the security and the index as follows:

$$\beta_i = \frac{\rho_{im}\sigma_i}{\sigma_m}$$

EXHIBIT 3.12

Extract of UK interest rate data

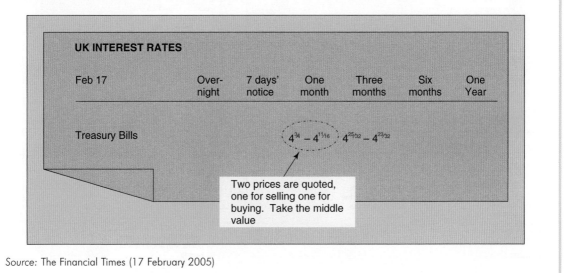

Source: The Financial Times (17 February 2005)

REVIEW ACTIVITY 3.6 If a security has a standard deviation of returns of 16 per cent and the standard deviation of market returns is 18 per cent what is the beta value for the security if (a) its correlation with the market is +1, (b) zero and (c) −1?

Estimating beta relies upon being able to find an appropriate proxy for the efficient market portfolio. In the UK context that is usually taken to be the Financial Times Actuaries All Share Index. If we regress the returns of the security we are interested in, the slope of the best fit line is the estimate of beta. In Exhibit 3.13 we have calculated the returns on British Airways against the returns on a holding of the All Share Index. We have chosen quarterly returns over a three year period to illustrate the general method.

The steps for obtaining a 'raw' estimate of beta are straightforward:

1 Collect share prices and dividend payments for as long a time series as possible on preferably a monthly basis although quarterly can also produce a reasonably reliable estimate.

2 Collect the equivalent index values using a broadly based all market index.

3 Calculate the returns for each month/quarter using the formula described in Chapter 1 for both the security and the index.

4 Using the (=slope()) and (=intercept()) functions in Excel calculate the intercept and the slope of the regression line which best fits the data points generated by the returns on the security (the y variable) and the index (the x variable).

EXHIBIT 3.13

The steps towards the estimation of beta using ordinary least squares regression

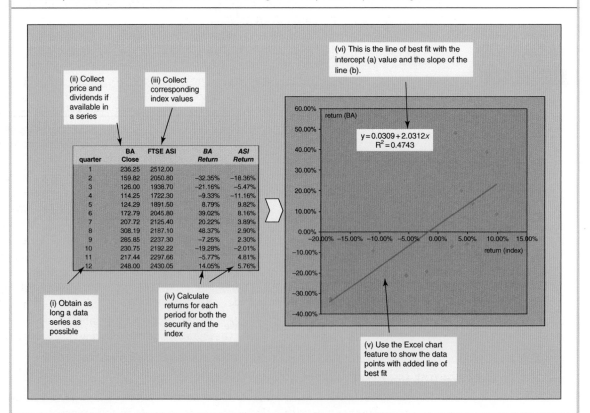

It is also useful to calculate the R^2 coefficient which is given by the square of the correlation between the security and index returns. In the BA example the R^2 value of 0.4743 suggests that 47.43 per cent of the variability (or riskiness) of the securities returns can be explained by variability in the index. This suggests that 47.43 per cent of the risk is driven by market factors and 52.57 per cent comes from other sources.

Estimates of beta suffer from a number of problems:

1 *Non-stationarity*. Beta values change with the data and they do vary over time. Individual company betas are less reliable than the beta of a portfolio of shares where idiosyncratic variability in the beta estimates tends to cancel out.

2 *Beta values can be influenced by alterations in the company's fundamentals*. As a company changes the proportion of debt to equity in its capital structure (its gearing) we would expect the equity to become more risky and the beta to corresponding increase. If we use return data over a period of time the beta we estimate will only reflect the average gearing over the period and not the gearing of the firm at the present day.

3 *Non-trading bias*. Sometimes share prices do not change because of a lack of trading. This happens in thin markets and particularly with smaller firms. Non-trading bias can distort a firm's beta by reducing its apparent volatility when compared with the market.

4 *Beta tends to be mean reverting over a period of time*. What this means is that there is a tendency for beta to tend towards one over the longer run.

Commercial beta providers do make adjustments to the 'raw betas' derived from ordinary least squares regression techniques. However, this is a topic to which we will return in greater detail in Chapter 5 when we look at the empirical problems of estimating the cost of equity capital for a firm.

Estimating the equity risk premium

The equity risk premium is the additional return we expect to get for holding 'the market' rather than the risk free security. There are sound arguments that this risk premium should be relatively stable reflecting an average degree of risk aversion between consumer/investors. The problem is that the historical evidence suggests that the equity risk premium is much higher than we would anticipate on theoretical grounds. This is what is known as the equity risk premium puzzle.

There are a number of problems with using the historical average of market returns to calculate the premium. The most important of these is 'non-survivor' bias in the data. If we compare the all share index now with the index some years ago we have a problem in that the current index does not include the firms that have failed in the intervening period. A range of other biases also make it difficult to predict expected risk premia on the basis of historical data. In a series of studies Fama and French (1992) and Dimson, Marsh and Staunton (2002) have questioned the conventional interpretation of the past evidence suggesting that the equity risk premium is of the order of 6–8 per cent. Their studies put the equity risk premium significantly lower and suggest that approximately 4 per cent is an appropriate figure for the US market and 3.5 per cent for the United Kingdom. It is this figure we will use throughout this book.

Putting the Capital Asset Pricing Model together

The Capital Asset Pricing Model should allow us to 'estimate' the expected returns on our sample company, British Airways plc, using the data so far collected.

The UK risk free rate of return = 4.75 per cent (Treasury Bills).
The UK equity risk premium (over the T-Bill rate) = 3.5 per cent.
British Airway's beta = 2.03 (see Exhibit 3.13).

$$E(\tilde{r}_i) = R_F + \beta_i[E(\tilde{r}_m) - R_f]$$
$$E(\tilde{r}_{BA}) = 4.75\% + 2.03 \times 3.5\%$$
$$E(\tilde{r}_{BA}) = 11.855\%$$

In Exhibit 3.14 we have drawn the security market line predicted by the Capital Asset Pricing Model. This line represents the return we should expect from a holding of any security and assuming a risk free rate of 4.75 per cent and an equity risk premium of 3.5 per cent. The beta for British Airways implies an expected return of 11.855 per cent. However, the observed historical return is slightly higher at 13.5 per cent. You will remember that return is inversely related to price. The slightly higher return than expected suggests that the share is undervalued in the market and that its price should rise until the return drops to the level we expect given the company's exposure to market risk.

When we turn to British Petroleum this company has a beta of 0.8 which implies an expected rate of return of 7.55 per cent given its exposure to market risk. In fact its actual return was 2.56 per cent. This suggests that British Petroleum is significantly overvalued. In later chapters we will discuss the problem of valuation of equities in more detail but for the moment it is worth reflecting how this over and undervaluation may have come about.

EXHIBIT 3.14

The security market line

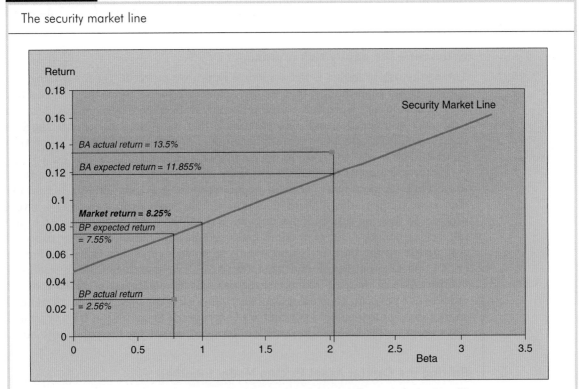

1 The market is correctly valuing the two firms and the Capital Asset Pricing Model is misspecified. It may be that return is not simply a function of a security's exposure to market risk but other factors need to be taken into account. This approach has been adopted by (among others) Fama and French who have developed a three-factor model which we discuss in Chapter 5.

2 The Capital Asset Pricing Model is correctly modelling expectations but the market is not perfectly translating those expectations into realized returns. The problem with this approach is that the proposition is untestable.

3 Both the model and the market are working just fine but that our estimation of beta, the risk free rate and the equity risk premium are not reliable. In particular, Richard Roll in a landmark paper in 1977 argued that the efficient market portfolio is unobservable unless we could identify all tradable securities in the global market place which is clearly impossible. If the proxies we choose are not efficient we cannot empirically confirm or refute the validity of the Capital Asset Pricing Model.

As the pricing of equity and estimating the returns required by investors will form a dominant part of our discussion throughout this book we will return to the issue of the validity of the Capital Asset Pricing Model in later chapters. The great virtue of the model is its simplicity. As Fama and French (2003) say:

> 'The CAPM . . . is a theoretical tour de force . . . but we also warn . . . that despite its seductive simplicity, the CAPM's empirical problems probably invalidate its use in applications.'

However, even though there is considerable doubt about the validity of the model in simplest form it does appear as the core of more sophisticated models to be discussed later in this book.

Portfolio betas

Our analysis of the shares of British Airways suggests that with a beta twice the market average they should only be purchased by highly risk aggressive investors. Well, not necessarily, because combined with other companies that are less exposed to market risk we can create a portfolio of any market risk level that we wish. The mechanics of this are straightforward. Because of the linearity of the security market line two or more securities can be combined weighted in proportion to their market values. For example, the beta coefficient for BP is 0.8. Using this we can calculate the beta for a portfolio containing equal proportions by value of these two securities as follows (where 'w' is the weight of the security concerned):

$$\beta_p = w_1\beta_1 + w_2\beta_2$$
$$\beta_p = 0.5 \times 2.03 + 0.5 \times 0.8$$
$$\beta_p = 1.415$$

The beta of more highly diversified portfolios is given by:

$$\beta_p = w_1\beta_1 + w_2\beta_2 + w_3\beta_3 \cdots\cdots w_n\beta_n$$

Thus it is possible to engineer a portfolio of any size with a given degree of exposure to market risk.

REVIEW ACTIVITY 3.7 Three securities have betas of 1.15, 0.98 and 0.43. An investor holding these three securities has £50 000, £24 000 and £90 000 in each respectively. What is the investor's exposure to market risk and how would you rebalance the portfolio to achieve an exposure closer to the market average?

Arbitrage Pricing Theory (APT)

The central prediction of the Capital Asset Pricing Model is that only market risk is priced at equilibrium as firm specific risk can be 'traded' away by the rational investor. However, the CAPM is based upon a set of assumptions that may not fully reflect actual investor and market behaviour. The principal one being that investors are mean-variance efficient and will naturally gravitate towards a holding of the efficient market portfolio. The limitations of this approach led to the development of Arbitrage Pricing Theory by Stephen Ross (1976). The idea behind APT is that for any given security or portfolio it is possible to create another 'synthetic' portfolio of identical risk. The law of one price says that in competitive markets where traders are not hindered by transactions costs, securities of identical risk should offer an identical return. To give a simple example supposing an investor holds shares in company C and it is possible to create a portfolio (P) of shares A and B as shown in Exhibit 3.15. What should happen is that the investor will seize the opportunity and sell their investment in C (which is overpriced relative to portfolio P) and use the proceeds to

EXHIBIT 3.15

Arbitrage drivers and the linearity of the security market line

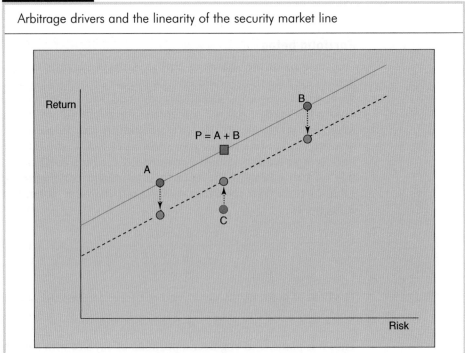

buy P. As a result of the proceeds the selling pressure on C will tend to reduce its price (and hence increase its return) and the buying pressure on A and B will tend to increase their price (and hence reduce their returns) until the returns offered by all three securities lie along a straight line.

This simple arbitrage argument leads us to two conclusions:

1 All security returns should be linear with respect to the factors which capture the risk of those securities, otherwise arbitrage opportunities will occur.

2 By extension, it should be possible to create a risk free portfolio which consists of a number of securities which taken together have zero risk relative to the factors which drive risk in the market and where firm specific risk has been diversified away.

To see how this works let us assume the more complex situation where the returns on a given security are 'explained' by two macroeconomic indices, I_1 and I_2. It doesn't matter what these indices are, but the first could be some measure of the level of Gross Domestic Product in the economy and the second interest rates.

By the logic outlined above APT assumes that the returns on any given security are linear with respect to a certain number of indices which capture the 'systematic' risk of holding that investment. In this case the basic APT model would be as follows:

$$r_i = \hat{a}_i + \hat{b}_{i1} I_1 + \hat{b}_{i2} I_2 + e_i$$

where:
a_i is the return which will be earned if both the index values are zero,
b_{i1} is the sensitivity of the security i to the first index and b_{i2} is its sensitivity to the second,
I_1 and I_2 the value of the first and second index respectively which influences the value of the security,
e_i is a random error term.

This model, as it stands is simply a multi-variable linear model. Now, we have used just two index terms above but in principle any number of terms can be used to explain security returns. However, what is new about APT is it gives a theoretical logic for translating a statistical relationship between certain macro indicators (the index values) and security prices at equilibrium.

The way this is achieved is by the following steps:

1 The well diversified investor will be interested in the return on their investment $E(r_i)$, and the factors b_1 and b_2, which measure their exposure to variability (risk) from the source measured by the index (in this case economic risk and interest rate risk). As we assumed with the Markowitz/Tobin approach non-systematic or firm specific risk is diversified away.

2 For the two factor model we have described then the return of any investment should lie on the plane which is defined by two slopes, λ_1 which relates to the first sensitivity factor b_1 and λ_2 which relates to the second sensitivity factor b_2.

3 If a portfolio is not located on this plane then the implication is that it is offering an expected return which is either above or below that for a portfolio of identical risk which lies on the plane. In that case, an arbitrage opportunity exists where the investor can go either long or short in the mis-priced portfolio and hence generate a risk free profit.

EXHIBIT 3.16

The Arbitrage Pricing Model (two factor case)

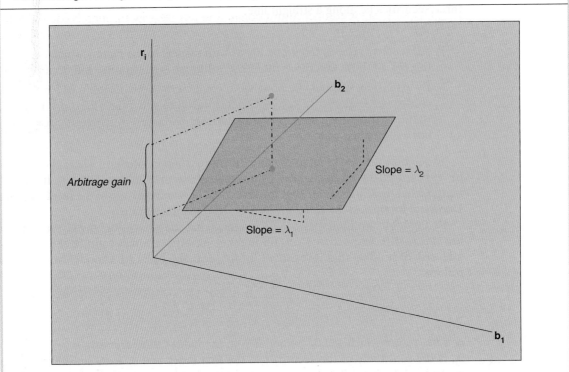

4 The equation of the plane is given by the following formula:

$$\bar{R}_i = \lambda_0 + \lambda_1 b_{i1} + \lambda_2 b_{i2}$$

where:

λ_1 is the additional return in the security created by a unit increase in the level of the index b_{i1} and λ_2 is the additional return in the security created by a unit increase in the level of the index b_{i2}.

This model for the expected return on an individual security is the basic equilibrium model generated by Arbitrage Pricing Theory. Now suppose that all the index terms b_{i1}, b_{i2} are zero then:

$$\bar{R}_i = \lambda_0 = R_F$$

Now if, b_{i1}, is one and b_{i2} is zero and substituting the risk free rate then the expected return generated by a unit increase in the first index b_{i1} is given by:

$$\bar{R}_1 = R_F + \lambda_1 1$$

or

$$\lambda_1 = \bar{R}_1 - R_F$$

Similarly,

$$\lambda_2 = \bar{R}_2 - R_F$$

Thus λ_1 is the additional return donated to any security through holding the risk as measured by the first index term, and λ_2 is the additional return donated by the second index term and so on.

Our simple geometrical analysis has been in terms of just two indices controlling the systematic risk impacting upon a security or portfolio. The proof is alarmingly more complex but the model can be generalized up to any number of terms.

To summarize:

The empirical multi-factor model which can be used to generate the 'b' values for given levels of the specified index (the factor) is as follows:

$$R_i = a_i + b_{i1}I_1 + b_{i2}I_2 + b_{i3}I_3 + \cdots\cdots + b_{ij}I_j + e_i$$

and this can be interpreted in terms of a number of 'slopes' which measure the sensitivity of expected return to each 'b' term:

$$\bar{R}_i = \lambda_0 + \lambda_1 b_{i1} + \lambda_2 b_{i2} + \lambda_3 b_{i3} + \cdots\cdots + \lambda_j b_{ij}$$

where:

$$\lambda_0 = R_F$$
$$\lambda_j = \bar{R}_j - R_F$$

THEORETICAL NOTE

Three terms are of importance in the APT. The 'factor' or index (I_j) terms which control the return earned by all securities and portfolios in the market place. The b_{ij} terms measure the sensitivity of a given security (i) to the market-wide risk factor measured by I_j. The λ_j terms measure the additional return which accrues to security (i) if there is an increase of one additional unit of the risk factor.

This model is much more robust than the CAPM which can be demonstrated to be a special case of the APT where only one index controls all of the non-systematic or diversifiable risk in the market i.e.:

$$\bar{R}_i = \lambda_0 + \lambda_1 b_{i1}$$

and if the index is the entire market then:

$$\bar{R}_i = \lambda_0 + \lambda_m b_{im}$$

and given that:

$$\lambda_0 = R_F$$
$$\lambda_m = \bar{R}_m - R_F$$

then:

$$\bar{R}_i = R_F + \left[\bar{R}_m - R_F\right]b_{im}$$

which is the Capital Asset Pricing Model.

We will not go into all of the testing of the APT which has required considerable ingenuity as unlike the CAPM where the Index term is defined theoretically as the efficient market portfolio, the various index terms in the APT are not so defined. The most common form of testing of the APT uses a statistical technique called factor analysis to simultaneously generate the index factors (Ij) and the sensitivity terms (*bj*). Other methods hypothesize certain index factors and use these to generate the corresponding sensitivities.

A range of risk factors have been hypothesized in various studies. For example, Chen, Roll and Ross, Economic Forces and the Stock Market, *Journal of Business*, 59 (July 1986) hypothesized that the following factors are important:

- inflation
- the term structure of interest rates
- risk premia (the difference between Aaa and Baa bonds)
- industrial production.

Burmeister and Elroy (1988) used factors measuring:

- Default risk (return on long term government bonds less the return on equivalent corporate bonds).
- Time premia (return on long term government bonds less the one month Treasury Bill rate one month ahead).
- Deflation (expected inflation at the beginning of the month less the actual rate during the month).
- Changes in expected sales.
- Market return excluding the effect of the first four variables.

SUMMARY

In this chapter we have tackled one of the central themes of the capital market – the pricing of risk. To underpin the theory and practice discussed in this chapter we have explored the efficiency of the capital markets in order to form a judgement whether any formal models of investment behaviour are likely to succeed. We argue that the evidence strongly supports the Efficient Market Hypothesis and while there are anomalies it still offers a superior mechanism for collecting judgements about the value of companies than any individual can reasonably expect to achieve on their own.

On reasonably sound efficiency ground we then describe the development of the theory of risk and the way in which capital securities can be priced. The centrepiece of our discussion has been the Capital Asset Pricing Model while not as empirically robust as some other approaches has the virtue of simplicity. Our brief look at Arbitrage Pricing Theory closes our discussion of this important subject for the moment as we turn our attention to the debt market and the pricing of fixed income securities.

Further Reading

Ball, R. and Brown, P. (1968) An empirical evaluation of accounting income numbers, *Journal of Accounting Research* 6:159–178. This is the study that started the events literature and began to build the case for semi strong form market efficiency.

Beaver, W. (1981) *Financial Reporting: an Accounting Revolution*, Englewood Cliffs, NJ: Prentice Hall. An excellent book integrating financial reporting with financial market research. Beaver's book is in its third edition but the quote in the text is taken from the first.

Burmeister, E. and Elroy, M.B. (1988) Joint Estimation of Factor Sensitivities and Risk Premia for the Arbitrage Pricing Theory, *Journal of Finance*, 43:3 (July).

Carhart, M., On Persistence in Mutual Fund Performance, *Journal of Finance*, 52:1. This article did a lot of damage to the active fund management industry. Persistently good performance occurs only by chance – a fund manager might get lucky, but luck is all it is.

DeBondt, W.F.M. and Thaler, R. (1985) Does the stock market overreact? *Journal of Finance*, 40. This paper started the hare running that systematic irrationalities in human decision making could explain some anomalous stock market behaviour. The problem was they never counted how many times markets under-react.

Dimson, E., Marsh, P. and Staunton, M. (2002) *Triumph of the Optimists – 101 years of Global Investment Returns*, Princeton: Princeton University Press. This is an exhaustive study of the global financial markets which makes the case that equity risk premiums have been overstated in the literature.

Elton, E.J. and Gruber, M.J. (1995) *Modern Portfolio Theory and Investment Analysis*, New York: Wiley. This is an excellent follow-on book for this text if you wish to explore portfolio management and investment in more detail.

Evans, J.L. and Archer, S.H. (1968) Diversification and the Reduction of Dispersion – an Empirical Analysis, *Journal of Finance*, December 1968. This famous study shows how portfolio risk decreases as diversification increases. An accessible paper.

Fama, E.F. (1970) Efficient capital markets: a review of theory and empirical work. *Journal of Finance*, 25. This is where our tip for a future Nobel Prize came up with the three forms of the EMH.

Fama, E. (1991), Efficient capital markets: II, *Journal of Finance*, 46:1575–1617. In this paper Fama reviews the 20 years of research since his first paper.

Fama, E. (1998) Market efficiency, long term returns and behavioural finance, *Journal of Financial Economics*, 49:283–306. This classic is where our two heroes take apart the 'research' in behavioural finance.

Fama, E. and French, K. (1992) The cross-section of expected stock returns, *Journal of Finance*, 47:427–465. In this paper the authors provide evidence which appears to undermine the validity of the Capital Asset Pricing Model. They also started to question prevailing orthodoxy about the equity risk premium.

Fama, E. and French, K. (2003) The Capital Asset Pricing Model: Theory and Evidence, *CRSP Working Paper* 550; *Tuck Business School Working Paper* 03–26. This paper, which was not published at the time of writing, is a very useful critique of the Capital Asset Pricing Model.

Jensen, M.C. (1968) The Performance of Mutual Funds in the Period 1945–64 *Journal of Finance*, 23:2:389–415. A classic paper which suggests that mutual fund managers are no better at picking stocks than monkeys.

Kettell, B. (2001) *Financial Economics*, London: FT Prentice Hall. This is a first class overview of financial economics for the non-technical reader.

Malkiel, B.G. (2004) *A Random Walk Down Wall Street: The Time-tested Strategy for Successful Investing*, New York: Norton & Company Ltd. If you think you can pick shares and make money read this book first.

Markowitz, H. (1953) Portfolio selection, *Journal of Finance* 7:1:77–91. The one that started it all and gave birth to the modern theory of risk and portfolio selection.

Nichols, D.C. and Wahlen, J.M. (2004) How do Earnings Numbers Relate to Stock Returns? *A Review of Classic Accounting Research with Updated Evidence*, 18:4:263–286. An interesting and up to date study of the events literature.

Roll, R. (1977) A Critique of the Asset Pricing Theory Test: Part 1: On past and potential testability of the Theory, *Journal of Financial Economics*, 2:129–176. This was a very important paper which highlighted many of the problems of testing the Capital Asset Pricing Model.

Ross, S.A. (1976) The arbitrage theory of capital asset pricing. *Journal of Economic Theory* 13. Very difficult paper, but one which makes more sense the more you read it.

Rubinstein, M. (2001) Rational Markets: Yes or No? The Affirmative Case, *Financial Analysts Journal*, May/June 2001. One of the most vigorous and compelling papers in recent years summarizing the arguments in favour of rational (efficient) markets.

Sharpe, W. (1964) Capital asset pricing: a theory of market equilibrium under conditions of risk. *Journal of Finance* 19:3:425–442. A brilliant article that gave us the Capital Asset Pricing Model. But did he derive it first? There is in existence a draft paper prepared by Jack Treynor written earlier which gives a version of the model. However, Treynor never published, Sharpe did and he got the credit and the Nobel Prize.

Tobin, J. (1958) Liquidity Preference as Behaviour Towards Risk, *The Review of Economic Studies*, XXVI:1:65–86. Another classic which along with Markowitz's 1953 paper gave us modern portfolio theory.

PROGRESS CHECK

1 Name the three different types of sub-market which exist within the capital market and outline their function.

2 Name two types of equity finance and describe the principal differences between them.

3 Why is it unlikely that a rights issue of equity shares, even when offered at a discount, is unlikely to offer a financial advantage to the company shareholders?

4 Which form of the efficient markets hypothesis is concerned with publicly available information?

5 There are three factors which contribute to portfolio risk. What are they?

6 What is the lowest risk that can be achieved between two securities whose returns are perfectly negatively correlated?

7 Explain what you understand by the term 'risk aversion'.

8 If an investor wishes to satisfy their own preferences for risk and return what should they do apart from investing in the efficient market portfolio?

9 List the assumptions which are required to derive the Capital Asset Pricing Model.

10 What would you expect the risk of a portfolio to do as the degree of diversification is increased?

11 What three variables are required to implement the Capital Asset Pricing Model?

12 List four factors which are likely to bias the estimation of beta?

13 How many risk factors can be incorporated into the Arbitrage Pricing Model?

QUESTIONS (answers at end of book)

1 Two securities (a) and (b) generate the following return data (Ra) and (Rb) and portfolio return (Rp) and standard deviation of returns (SDp) assuming different portfolio weights (Wa) and (Wb).

Wa	Wb	Ra	Rb	Rp	SDp
0.000	1.000	0.000	15.000	15.000	0.150
0.050	0.950	0.500	14.250	14.750	0.139
0.100	0.900	1.000	13.500	14.500	0.129
0.150	0.850	1.500	12.750	14.250	0.118
0.200	0.800	2.000	12.000	14.000	0.108
0.250	0.750	2.500	11.250	13.750	0.097
0.300	0.700	3.000	10.500	13.500	0.087
0.350	0.650	3.500	9.750	13.250	0.077
0.400	0.600	4.000	9.000	13.000	0.067
0.450	0.550	4.500	8.250	12.750	0.058
0.500	0.500	5.000	7.500	12.500	0.049
0.550	0.450	5.500	6.750	12.250	0.042
0.600	0.400	6.000	6.000	12.000	0.036
0.650	0.350	6.500	5.250	11.750	0.033
0.700	0.300	7.000	4.500	11.500	0.034
0.750	0.250	7.500	3.750	11.250	0.038
0.800	0.200	8.000	3.000	11.000	0.044
0.850	0.150	8.500	2.250	10.750	0.052
0.900	0.100	9.000	1.500	10.500	0.061
0.950	0.050	9.500	0.750	10.250	0.070
1.000	0.000	10.000	0.000	10.000	0.080

You are required to:

(i) Draw the permissible portfolio combinations on a graph of risk and return and identify (a) the minimum risk portfolio and (b) the efficient set.

(ii) Discuss the validity of the assumptions which underpin Markowitz portfolio theory and the significance of the model for investor choice.

2 On the basis of the data below for BT Group plc:

	BT Group		FTSE ASI
Mar-05		202.25	2492.84
Dec-04		203.00	2410.75
06-Sep-04	5.30 pence Cash Dividend		
Sep-04		180.17	2271.67
Jun-04		198.50	2228.70
Mar-04		177.00	2197.00
09-Feb-04	3.20 pence Cash Dividend		
Dec-03		188.00	2207.40
Sep-03		180.00	2027.70
Jun-03		203.47	1971.30
Mar-03		159.22	1735.70
10-Feb-03	2.25 pence Cash Dividend		
Dec-02		195.00	1893.70
09-Sep-02	2.00 pence Cash Dividend		
Sep-02		164.50	1801.50
Jun-02		251.14	2263.10
Mar-02		280.00	2557.40
Dec-01		253.07	2523.90
Sep-01		340.00	2340.50
Jun-01		447.00	2728.12
Mar-01		510.00	2711.40
Dec-00		561.84	2983.81
Sep-00		711.00	3029.36
Jun-00		866.00	3029.74
Mar-00		1169.00	3110.56

You are required to:

(i) Calculate the equity beta for BT Group plc using the quarterly prices and index values as shown.

(ii) On the basis that the rate of return on a short dated government bill is 4.7 per cent per annum and the UK equity risk premium is 3.5 per cent annum determine whether the shares in BT group are over or undervalued.

QUESTIONS (answers on website)

3 The capital markets exhibit a considerable degree of efficiency in both their competitive characteristics and their ability to rapidly impound information into the prices of securities. Discuss the validity of this statement and evaluate the empirical evidence which supports this claim.

4 Security A offers an average return of 16 per cent with a standard deviation of returns of 24 per cent. Security B has an average return of 10 per cent and a standard deviation of 10 per cent. The returns of the two securities have a correlation coefficient of –0.2.

You are required to:

(i)   Find the proportions of each security which give a minimum risk portfolio.

(ii) Calculate the average return which can be expected from the minimum risk portfolio.

(iii) Find the optimum return which can be achieved if a standard deviation of returns of 8 per cent is required.

5 The rate of return on the efficient market portfolio is 7.5 per cent and the risk free rate is 4 per cent. The standard deviation of returns on the efficient market portfolio is 15 per cent.

You are required to calculate the allocation of a fund of £100 000 such that:

(a) The investor carries two thirds market risk.

(b) The investor carries double market risk.

6 The risk free rate of return is 4 per cent and the rate of return on a broadly based market index is 7.5 per cent.

You are required to calculate:

(i) The expected return for a security with a beta of 0.9.

(ii) The beta for a security which offers a return of 9 per cent.

7 Security A offers an average return of 16 per cent with a standard deviation of returns of 24 per cent. Security B has an average return of 10 per cent and a standard deviation of 10 per cent. Security A has a correlation with the all share index of 0.7 and security B has a correlation with the index of 0.2. The standard deviation of market returns is 18 per cent.

You are required to:

(a) Calculate the beta for each security.

(b) Calculate the beta of a portfolio resulting from an investment of £20 000 in each.

This appendix explores some of the more formal aspects of portfolio risk optimization and also show the derivation of the Capital Asset Pricing Model.

In the example below we show how risk can be minimized in a very simple two security case. We demonstrate two methods using an example:

Two investments offer a 10 per cent and a 15 per cent rate of return with an 8 per cent and 15 per cent standard deviation attached to each. The two investments are expected to vary counter-cyclically with one another with a return correlation of –0.8. An individual has £600 000 to invest in each. What would be the minimum risk combination of investment in the two securities?

Exhibit A3.1 shows a spreadsheet solution to this problem using the two formulas for return:

$$r_p = w_a r_a + w_b r_b$$

and risk:

$$\sigma_p = \sqrt{w_a^2 \sigma_a^2 + w_b^2 \sigma_b^2 + 2 w_a w_b \rho_{ab} \sigma_a \sigma_b}$$

This problem can be solved in two ways: the first is analytically as the first derivative of risk (expressed as the variance) with respect to the weight of either component will give us a minimum when set to zero given that the sum of the two weights must be equal to one.

$$\sigma_p^2 = w_a^2 \sigma_a^2 + w_b^2 \sigma_b^2 + 2 w_a w_b \rho_{ab} \sigma_a \sigma_b$$
$$\sigma_p^2 = w_a^2 \sigma_a^2 + (1 - w_a)^2 \sigma_b^2 + 2 w_a (1 - w_a) \rho_{ab} \sigma_a \sigma_b$$
$$\sigma_p^2 = w_a^2 0.08^2 + (1 - w_a)^2 0.15^2 + 2 w_a (1 - w_a)(-0.8) \times 0.08 \times 0.15$$

simplifying

$$\sigma_p^2 = 0.0481 w_a^2 + .0225 - 0.0642 w_a$$
$$\frac{d\sigma_p^2}{dw_a} = 0.0926 w_a - 0.0642 = 0$$
$$w_a = 0.6933$$
$$w_b = 0.3067$$

This tells us that with £600 000 to invest the minimum risk portfolio would entail an investment of 69.33 per cent in (a) and 30.67 per cent in (b) or £415 980 and £184 020 respectively.

Once we have the weights they can be put back into the risk formula to give the risk of the minimum risk portfolio.

$$\sigma_p = \sqrt{w_a^2 0.08^2 + w_b^2 0.15^2 + 2 w_a w_b (-0.8) \times 0.08 \times 0.15}$$
$$\sigma_p = 0.03332 = 3.332\%$$

The portfolio return can also be calculated:

$$r_p = w_a r_a + w_b r_b$$

$$r_p = 0.6933 \times 10\% + 0.3067 \times 15\%$$

$$r_p = .11534 = 11.534\%$$

The second method is to put the return and risk formula into a spreadsheet and find the minimum value by constructing a table as shown in Exhibit A3.1 or by using the goal seek function.

EXHIBIT A3.1

The return and risk formula put into a spreadsheet

Wa	Wb	Ra	Rb	Rp	SDp
0.000	1.000	0.000	15.000	15.000	0.150
0.050	0.950	0.500	14.250	14.750	0.139
0.100	0.900	1.000	13.500	14.500	0.129
0.150	0.850	1.500	12.750	14.250	0.118
0.200	0.800	2.000	12.000	14.000	0.108
0.250	0.750	2.500	11.250	13.750	0.097
0.300	0.700	3.000	10.500	13.500	0.087
0.350	0.650	3.500	9.750	13.250	0.077
0.400	0.600	4.000	9.000	13.000	0.067
0.450	0.550	4.500	8.250	12.750	0.058
0.500	0.500	5.000	7.500	12.500	0.049
0.550	0.450	5.500	6.750	12.250	0.042
0.600	0.400	6.000	6.000	12.000	0.036
0.650	0.350	6.500	5.250	11.750	0.033
0.700	0.300	7.000	4.500	11.500	0.034
0.750	0.250	7.500	3.750	11.250	0.038
0.800	0.200	8.000	3.000	11.000	0.044
0.850	0.150	8.500	2.250	10.750	0.052
0.900	0.100	9.000	1.500	10.500	0.061
0.950	0.050	9.500	0.750	10.250	0.070
1.000	0.000	10.000	0.000	10.000	0.080

Portfolio risk with more than two securities

The risk formula for a portfolio of more than two securities can best be represented by a matrix of terms consisting of the variances (the squares) of the individual securities and the covariance between all conceivable combinations of securities.

Our first formulation in the matrix layout is for the two security portfolio considered in the chapter:

$$\sigma_p = \sqrt{\begin{bmatrix} w_1 w_1 \sigma_{11} & w_1 w_2 \sigma_{12} \\ w_2 w_1 \sigma_{21} & w_2 w_2 \sigma_{22} \end{bmatrix}}$$

Note that in matrix notation we do not show the addition signs between each term and for ease of layout we show the variances (square of the standard deviations) as

σ_{11} and we have numbered the securities 1 and 2 rather than using letters. Note also that with the covariance terms:

$$\sigma_{12} = \sigma_{21}$$

The reason for this should be straightforward if you review the formula for the covariance above.

We can expand the formula to look at larger portfolios. Below is the four security case:

$$\sigma_p = \sqrt{\begin{bmatrix} w_1 w_1 \sigma_{11} & w_1 w_2 \sigma_{12} & w_1 w_3 \sigma_{13} & w_1 w_4 \sigma_{14} \\ w_2 w_1 \sigma_{21} & w_2 w_2 \sigma_{22} & w_2 w_3 \sigma_{23} & w_2 w_4 \sigma_{24} \\ w_3 w_1 \sigma_{31} & w_3 w_2 \sigma_{32} & w_3 w_3 \sigma_{33} & w_3 w_4 \sigma_{34} \\ w_4 w_1 \sigma_{41} & w_4 w_2 \sigma_{42} & w_4 w_3 \sigma_{43} & w_4 w_4 \sigma_{44} \end{bmatrix}}$$

Note how the pairwise combinations of securities are built up from left to right and from top to bottom to give a resulting equation which like the two security case contains a variance term for each of the securities and then a covariance term for every pairwise combination.

$$\sigma_p = \sqrt{w_1 w_1 \sigma_{11} + w_2 w_2 \sigma_{22} + w_3 w_3 \sigma_{33} + w_4 w_4 \sigma_{44} + 2w_1 w_2 \sigma_{12} + 2w_1 w_3 \sigma_{13} + 2w_1 w_4 \sigma_{14} + 2w_2 w_3 \sigma_{23} + 2w_2 w_4 \sigma_{24} + 2w_3 w_4 \sigma_{34}}$$

The efficient frontier with more than two securities

It is possible to define the efficient frontier of a portfolio of any size using either proprietary software or analytically using the calculus. In outline the technique involves partially differentiating the combined return/risk equations with respect to each weight and a Lagrangian operator. The resulting structure of differentials can be organized as a Jacobian matrix and solved for any defined level of risk. For those who are familiar with the maths it is relatively straightforward but is tedious as the number of securities rises above three or four.

The formal derivation of the Capital Asset Pricing Model

Consider a hypothetical portfolio consisting of the market portfolio (M) and a security i with weights (w) by value:

$$\sigma_p = \sqrt{w_m^2 \sigma_m^2 + w_i^2 \sigma_i^2 + 2w_m w_i \rho_{im} \sigma_i \sigma_m}$$
$$as : w_i + w_m = 1$$

$$\sigma_p = \sqrt{(1-w_i)^2 \sigma_m^2 + w_i^2 \sigma_i^2 + 2(1-w_i) w_i \rho_{im} \sigma_i \sigma_m}$$

where *sigma* is the risk of M or i respectively and *rho* is the correlation coefficient.

Taking the first differential of the portfolio risk *wrt* to the weight of the *ith* security

$$\frac{d\sigma_p}{dw_i} = -\frac{(\sigma_m^2 - \rho_{im} \sigma_i \sigma_m)}{\sigma_p}$$

As the weight of the *ith* security tends towards zero the risk of the portfolio tends towards the risk of the market portfolio M, so this differential at the limit becomes:

$$\frac{d\sigma_p}{dw_i} = -(\sigma_m - \rho_{im}\sigma_i)$$

The return of this hypothetical portfolio is:

$$R_p = w_m R_m + w_i R_i$$
$$R_p = (1 - w_i)R_m + w_i R_i$$
$$\frac{dR_p}{dw_i} = -(R_m - R_i)$$

We are interested in the slope of the efficient set at the point of tangency with the capital market line which has a slope:

EXHIBIT A3.2

The efficient set at the point of tangency with the capital market line

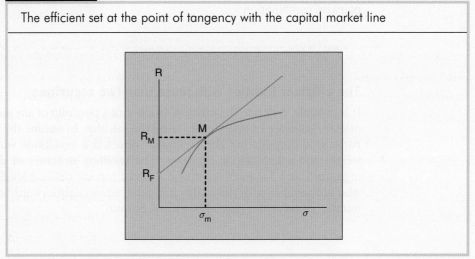

$$\lambda = \frac{R_m - R_F}{\sigma_M}$$

At the limit $\sigma_p \to \sigma_m$ and this, plus the equation for the slope, gives:

$$\lambda = \frac{dR_p}{d\sigma_p} = \frac{-(R_m - R_i)}{-(\sigma_m - \rho_{im}\sigma_i)} = \frac{R_m - R_F}{\sigma_M}$$

$$R_i = R_F + \frac{\rho_{im}\sigma_i}{\sigma_M}(R_M - R_F)$$

$$R_i = R_F + \beta_i(R_M - R_F)$$

which is of course the Capital Asset Pricing Model.

The fixed interest market

4

I n the last chapter we considered the equity market and the pricing theory of capital assets pricing. However, equity capital is only one way in which companies raise capital so now we turn our attention to the second way: through borrowing.

The most direct way for companies and public sector organizations to borrow money is to find a lender, usually a bank, and request a loan. That loan may be from a bank on either fixed or variable terms depending upon the amount to be borrowed and the degree of credit risk the lender perceives in the arrangement. The lender may make the loan on their own account or, in the case of a bank, standing as an intermediary between its own depositors and the firm seeking the loan.

Since the 1930s in the United States and more recently elsewhere 'disintermediation' has occurred where companies sidestep the banks and lend directly to individual investors by issuing bonds. Government and corporate bonds are now one of the most important sources of finance in Europe and are of growing importance in the United States and the United Kingdom.

In this chapter we explore the ways in which governments raise finance through the debt market. First we will review the process by which government's raise debt finance. This, for the major economies allows us to establish the risk free rate of borrowing in the countries concerned. Armed with that knowledge we can then proceed to consider how companies raise debt finance using that risk free rate as the basis for estimating the rate of return they will need to offer to the market. The chapter concludes with a discussion of the nature and problems of the valuation of bonds, hybrid debt and other borrowing instruments.

Learning outcomes

By the end of this chapter you will be able to achieve the following:

1 Describe the difference between debt and equity finance and the methods governments and companies use to raise debt finance.
2 Calculate the discount or the yield on debt.

▶

3 Recognize how government bonds can be stripped into a zero coupon and a coupon only element.

4 Know how to build the yield curve in terms of the term to maturity and the duration of a bond.

5 Know how to bootstrap a spot curve to obtain the expected future rate of return required by the debt market.

6 Calculate the duration, volatility and convexity of a bond and know what these terms mean.

7 Understand the role of the credit assessment agencies in determining the credit rating of a company.

8 Recognize the significance of the bond spread and the factors which determine its magnitude.

The nature of debt and the equity finance

The key difference between the equity and the debt market is that the equity investor is purchasing a share in a business and cannot expect to get his or her capital back until the business comes to the end of its life. With debt capital the finance is lent by the investor to the business concerned and must be repaid at or before a specified date. Of course, like everything else in the capital markets there are oddities. Sometimes debt is irredeemable and sometimes equity can be repurchased by a company and cancelled. However, the norm is that equity finance is for life (of the company) and debt is only for as long as it has been agreed that the company can take before it must repay.

For most large organizations there are two ways of raising debt finance:

- *Intermediated*: which means that the borrowing is raised from a bank or other financial institution. Intermediated borrowing may be on fixed or variable terms. Usually, shorter term borrowing carries a variable rate and longer term borrowing is obtained at a fixed rate.

- *Disintermediated*: where the borrowing is achieved by a direct offer to the capital market in the form of a bond issue. Bonds are negotiable certificates of indebtedness for a term greater than one year. There are a number of mechanisms for a bond issue. With government a form of auction is undertaken by an agency of the Treasury, with corporate debt the issue will normally be arranged through a large merchant bank or other institution and it may be underwritten.

The great virtue of the bond market is the relative speed and cheapness with which finance can be obtained compared with raising equity. Also, government and other public sector organizations do not have equity to issue and borrowing via a bond issue is the only practical way of raising finance. In the case of companies they may wish to match their capital source to a given project and do not want to dilute their equity base by issuing more shares. As a result companies have found this an increasingly attractive way of raising capital.

Bond basics

At one level, fixed interest securities appear simple. They offer the bond investor the following in exchange for the investment of a set sum (the 'par value'):

1 A promise to repay (redeem) the sum originally invested – for most retail bonds in the UK this will be £100 although larger denominations are quite common.

2 A fixed interest payment (the 'coupon') which is paid either annually or semi-annually and is paid on the bond's par value.

3 A term to redemption which is the number of years before the bond is redeemed. In some cases a bond may be dual dated. This gives the issuer the option to redeem anytime between the two dates.

For example, the *Financial Times* quotes (1 January 2005) under UK gilts – cash market:

> price
> Tr 5pc 08............101.37

What this means is that the UK government has borrowed money through the bond market, which is part of the fixed interest debt market, in £100 units. The term 'Tr' signifies that this is a Treasury Bond and each bond certificate carries the commitment from the government to repay to the investor the principal sum, the bond's 'par' value, in 2008. At the start of 2005, the term to redemption is four years. The coupon rate is 5 per cent.

In Exhibit 4.1 we show the pattern of payments and receipts that an investor in UK Treasury Bonds would receive over the period until the bond is redeemed by the government.

REVIEW ACTIVITY 4.1 Find the details of a medium term Treasury Bond including the exact timing of interest payments and redemption.

This bond like all government or corporate bonds is a 'negotiable' instrument in that it can be traded on a secondary market. The current price of this bond is £101.37 per cent where the per cent in this case simply means 'per hundred pound par value'. At first sight, from an investor's point of view, this looks to be a risk free investment. However, risk comes in a variety of disguises:

- *Default risk*: this is the risk that the borrower will default on the payment of interest or the repayment of capital. This default risk is mitigated to a certain extent in that if default occurs the bond holders will normally have the right, in the case of a corporation, to put the company into the hands of 'receivers'. Receivership is the first stage of corporate bankruptcy. The extent to which bond investors face default risk is measured through a credit rating exercise conducted on the company or government concerned by a rating agency. Credit rating is discussed later in this chapter.

- *Interest rate risk*: following a subscription to a newly issued bond, or following the purchase of a bond on the secondary market, interest rates within the wider economy may either rise or fall. If interest rates rise, the fixed rate attaching to the bond will appear less attractive and the market price of the bond will fall. If interest rates fall the reverse will occur and

EXHIBIT 4.1

The cash flows associated with the purchase and retention of Treasury 5 per cent stock, 2008

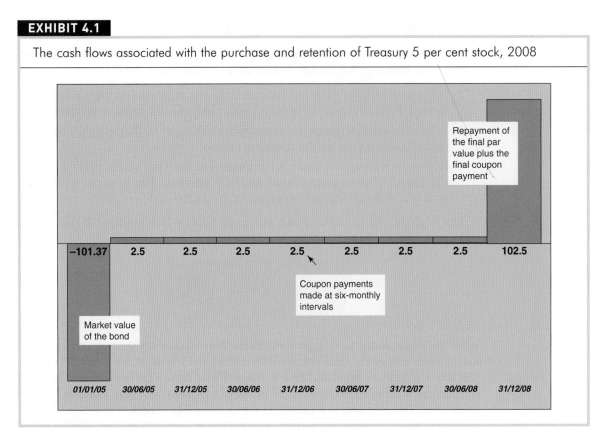

bond prices will rise. From the issuer's point of view, a fall in rates will mean that they are paying a coupon rate which is higher than would currently attach to a loan of that type. If rates rise, the company will find that servicing its debt is cheaper than prevailing rates would suggest. From the company's point of view interest rate risk can be managed as we will see in Chapter 13 which deals with interest rates swaps and other risk management techniques.

- *Inflation risk*: an investor in a government or high quality corporate bond can reasonably expect to receive their investment returned at the due date. They can also reasonably expect to receive their interest at the due time. What they cannot foresee precisely is the spending power that future return will offer. This is not so much a problem of inflation but rather the uncertainty which attaches to future inflation rates. Inflation risk is connected to interest rate risk in that there is a connection between the two. High inflation rates are linked with high interest rates and low inflation with low interest rates. High levels of interest and inflation can lead to corporate (and indeed government) distress increasing the risk of default.

- *Reinvestment rate risk*: as we shall see later the rate at which investors wish to reinvest their receipts from a bond as it passes through its life may vary from time to time. It is possible, as we shall see later, to calculate the 'internal rate of return' or 'yield' from a bond. But the reinvestment rate assumed in calculating the yield may vary and that variation is uncertain. This is what we call 'reinvestment risk'.

How government raises bond finance

As far as investors are concerned the most significant difference between government and corporate bonds is the level of default risk to which they are exposed. The major western economies have never defaulted on their debt and the United States and United Kingdom Treasury Bonds are essentially default risk free. By comparison, even the largest corporation presents some risk of default. Later in this chapter we will explore the difference between the return on a corporate bond and a risk free government bond of the same term to maturity. This difference in return is the 'bond spread'.

Governments borrow money from their own populations and from the rest of the world. They do this primarily to make good the shortfall between what they spend and what they receive from their population through taxes. Government, like companies needs to finance capital investment projects where the benefits in enhanced economic activity will accrue over a number of years. In order to finance these projects, government will raise finance through the bond market, servicing the debt from its taxation receipts. Eventually, when the debt needs to be redeemed government will finance the repayment either out of its current surpluses or by the issue of further debt.

The term gilt-edged security, which is widely used across Europe, was first established in the United Kingdom as the British government started to print its official IOUs on gilt (gold)-edged paper in exchange for the funds required. These funds were used for operational purchases such as building hospitals, paying off national debt and compensating the foreign trade deficit. In the US, traders use a different term for their government bonds which are known as 'Guvies'.

In the UK, government bonds are described as 'shorts' which have a term to redemption of less than five years, 'mediums' which have a term to redemption of between 5 and 15 years and 'longs' which have terms in excess of 15 years. In the United States, government securities are differentiated into three major categories: Treasury bills, Treasury notes, and Treasury bonds. In the US Treasury bills are defined as pure discount obligations of the US Treasury with a maturity period of one year (360 days) or less. Mid- and long-term financial contracts such as US Treasury notes have their period to maturity set otherwise. A common maturity period for US Treasury notes is between 2 and 7 years with semi-annual coupons attached to the contracts. US Treasury bonds are the third type of securities and are issued with maturities ranging from 10 to 30 years with semi-annual coupon payments attached. Unlike US Treasury bills, both Treasury notes and Treasury bonds yield on a 365 days per year maturity basis.

TECHNICAL NOTE

In the United States, unlike the British and European financial systems, a financial year is deemed to be 360 days for calculating interest and maturities on financial securities. The use of a 360 day accounting convention is purely for convenience. It has nothing to do with the number of public holidays enjoyed in the United States, nor that their day is somewhat longer than 24 hours, nor that they have accidentally mislaid five days (or six days if you count leap years). It is simply a convention. In the UK the convention is 365/366 days.

The primary market for government bonds

The primary market for government securities in the major economies is normally conducted through an auction system where institutions and individuals bid for the stock offered. Occasionally the government concerned may attempt a direct placement of

Michael Pearcy/Alamy

stock with a specific institution (the so-called 'tap' mechanism). Once those stocks are in the hands of the institutions or private individuals they can be traded on a secondary market. The secondary market is usually conducted by the stock exchange in the country concerned.

During each year the government will, as part of its budgetary process, forecast its borrowing requirements and on the basis of that calculate the number of auctions it needs to hold, their dates and the type of stock which will be issued. In the UK the auctioning process is conducted by the Debt Management Office which is an agency of the Treasury.

Anyone can bid at auction and bidding is of two types: competitive and non-competitive. All gilt edged market-makers (known as GEMMs), are expected to make at least one competitive bid as a demonstration of their commitment to the

FINANCIAL CASE

Below is the remit of the UK Debt Management Office:

The Debt Management Office (DMO), an Executive Agency of HM Treasury, has been given the following objectives in respect of Government debt management:

- to meet the annual remit set by HM Treasury Ministers for the sale of gilts, with high regard to long-term cost minimization taking account of risk;

- to advise Ministers on setting the remit to meet the Government's debt management objectives and to report to Ministers on the DMO's performance against its remit, objectives and targets;

- to develop policy on and promote advances in new instruments, issuance techniques and structural changes to the debt markets that will help to lower the cost of debt financing, liaising as appropriate with the Bank of England, Financial Services Authority, London Stock Exchange, and other bodies; and to provide policy advice to HM Treasury Ministers and senior officials accordingly;

- to conduct its market operations, liaising as necessary with regulatory and other bodies, with a view to maintaining orderly and efficient markets and promoting a liquid market for gilts;

- to provide, including in liaison with the Bank of England and CREST Co, a high quality efficient service to investors in government debt, and to deal fairly and professionally with market participants in the gilt and money markets, consistent with achieving low cost issuance;

- to contribute to HM Treasury's work on the development of the strategy for the debt portfolio; and

- to make information publicly available on the debt markets and DMO policies where that contributes through openness and predictability to efficient markets and lower costs of debt issuance.

market, and they are required to bid a price for at least £500 000 of stock. The process in bidding is as follows: the GEMMs contact the DMO dealing room to place their bids. GEMMs may be bidding on their own account or on behalf of their clients. Other applicants are required to bid in writing direct to the DMO. In competitive bidding, the DMO will determine the amount of stock that it intends to issue through this mechanism and will allocate stock in one thousand pound units to the highest bidder. In non-competitive bidding, the DMO will issue stock at the average bid price determined from the competitive bidding process.

Other types of government bond

So far we have described the standard capital market bond which is the most popular vehicle for governments and companies to raise finance. There are other variants on the theme however.

Zero-coupon bonds These tend to be short dated and carry no interest payment. They are offered at a discount below their par value, so a bond with a face value of £100 000 may be issued at (say) £95 000. The discount is easily calculated as:

$$\text{Discount} = \frac{\text{par value} - \text{issue price}}{\text{par value}} \times 100$$

$$= \frac{100\ 000 - 95\ 000}{100\ 000} \times 100 = 5\%$$

Note that the discount is not calculated relative to the issue price (that would be the 'return') but to the eventual redemption value. This is like purchasing a car at a discount where the percentage is calculated relative to the vehicle's list price. The virtue of zero coupon bonds is their simplicity and they are particularly useful for institutional investors who need to have access to their capital sums at particular times and are not interested in receiving interest payments between times.

Index linked bonds These are bonds whose coupon and eventual redemption payments are linked to the rate of inflation. When inflation was particularly high in the UK, these bonds were particularly attractive to investors who were keen to maintain the real value of their investment. As inflation rates in the western economies have declined over the last 20 years this type of bond has been less popular. However, they are still attractive to pension funds and other institutions that are required to make payments to their members or investors that are linked to the rate of inflation.

Convertible bonds These are where the government offers the holder the option to convert what is usually a short dated bond into a longer dated bond at a specified date.

Calculating the yield on bonds

The yield on a bond is the discount rate that equates the issue price of the bond, or its current market value if different, with the cash flows received by the investor over the lifetime of the bond. The general formula for this is:

$$V_0 = \frac{I}{(1+r)} + \frac{I}{(1+r)^2} + \frac{I}{(1+r)^3} + \cdots + \frac{Par+I}{(1+r)^n}$$

EXHIBIT 4.2

Gross and net gilt issuance (including illustrative projections)

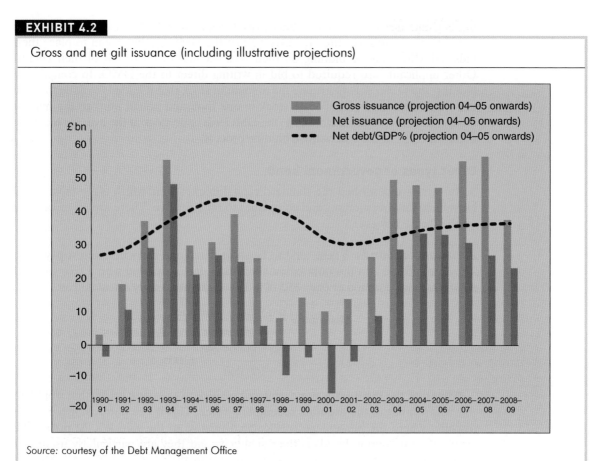

Source: courtesy of the Debt Management Office

where *I* is the fixed coupon payment paid each period, V_0 is the issue or current price of the bond and *Par* is its face or nominal value. '*r*' is what we are after which is the yield on the bond.

For most retail bonds, that is bonds available for the general public, the annual coupon payment on the face of the bond is paid twice annually and thus '*r*' will be a semi-annual yield. We will need to convert that semi-annual yield to its annual equivalent.

Our first example is the rather simple case where the present value of the bond is at its par value.

FINANCIAL REALITY

A Treasury Bond has a coupon rate of 10 per cent, paid in two equal instalments annually. The current price of the bond is £100 and it will be repaid in full at the end of three years.

This means that the investor will receive six, six-monthly instalments of £5 per bond held and a final payment of £100 being its par value. If we discount the bond's value at 5 per cent this gives us the current price of the bond. Thus 5 per cent is the semi-annual yield.

EXHIBIT 4.3

Calculation of the present value of a bond where the discount rate and coupon rate are the same

Instalment number	1	2	3	4	5	6
Cash flow to the investor	5	5	5	5	5	105
Discount by 5 per cent: discount factor	0.9524	0.9070	0.8638	0.8227	0.7835	0.7462
Discounted cash flow to the investor	4.76	4.54	4.32	4.11	3.92	78.35
Present value of the bond	100.00					

To convert to the equivalent annual yield we proceed as follows (see Chapter 1 for the method for calculating equivalent rates):

$$r_a = (1+r)^2 - 1$$
$$r_a = 1.05^2 - 1$$
$$r_a = 0.1025$$

Note that in this neutral case, where the value of the bond is equal to its par value the yield will be slightly higher than the annual coupon. The reason is that the coupon rate of 10 per cent is split into two equal components of 5 per cent of the par value each. The half-yearly payment will however be slightly more valuable to the investor than the end-year payment because it is received earlier and this is reflected in the higher effective value placed upon it in the discounting process.

Now consider the more complex case where the current value is different to the par value:

FINANCIAL REALITY

A Treasury Bond has a coupon rate of 10 per cent, paid in two equal instalments annually. The current price of the bond is £110 and it will be repaid in full at the end of three years.

This yield calculation is, in effect, the same as the internal rate of return calculation discussed in Chapter 2. To see this rearrange the equation for the cash flow to the investor as follows:

$$110 = \frac{5}{(1+r)^1} + \frac{5}{(1+r)^2} + \frac{5}{(1+r)^3} + \frac{5}{(1+r)^4} + \frac{5}{(1+r)^5} + \frac{105}{(1+r)^6}$$

$$-110 + \frac{5}{(1+r)^1} + \frac{5}{(1+r)^2} + \frac{5}{(1+r)^3} + \frac{5}{(1+r)^4} + \frac{5}{(1+r)^5} + \frac{105}{(1+r)^6} = 0$$

As 5 per cent will discount to £100 we know, therefore, that the rate is too high and that a lower rate is required based upon the inverse relationship which exists between yield (or return) and price.

If we put a slightly lower value for 'r' (say 4 per cent) into this equation and rework the table above:

EXHIBIT 4.4

Revised bond calculation where the discount rate is 4 per cent

Instalment number	1	2	3	4	5	6
Cash flow to the investor	5	5	5	5	5	105
Discount by 4 per cent: discount factor	0.9615	0.9246	0.8890	0.8548	0.8219	0.7903
Discounted cash flow to the investor	4.81	4.62	4.44	4.27	4.11	82.98
Present value of the bond	105.24					

then the present value is £105.242 which still understates the current price. Repeating with 3 per cent:

EXHIBIT 4.5

Revised bond calculation where the discount rate is 3 per cent

Instalment number	1	2	3	4	5	6
Cash flow to the investor	5	5	5	5	5	105
Discount by 3 per cent: discount factor	0.9709	0.9426	0.9151	0.8885	0.8626	0.8375
Discounted cash flow to the investor	4.85	4.71	4.58	4.44	4.31	87.94
Present value of the bond	110.83					

with 3 per cent, the discounted value generated is greater than £110 and the true yield lies somewhere between the two values of 4 per cent and 3 per cent. We can approximate the true value to a good degree of accuracy by linear interpolation:

$$r = 3\% + \frac{(110.83 - 110.00)}{(110.83 - 105.24)} \times 1\%$$

$$r = 3.148\%$$

What we have done is to calculate the difference between the market value of the bond given its yield less the market value at 3 per cent in this case. This difference in market value as a proportion of increase in value caused by a 1 per cent fall in yield gives us the proportion of that percentage point that we need to add to the 3 per cent to get our answer. However, if that explanation doesn't make much sense then refer back to Chapter 2 where the interpolation method for calculating the internal rate of return is discussed more fully.

The easiest way to do this, however, is to employ the Excel function for IRR. With Excel, set up a linear array of values:

	A	B	C	D	E	F	G
1	−110	5	5	5	5	5	105
2							

and then use:

$$= \text{IRR}(A1:G1, \text{guess})$$

(the guess is not usually necessary and need only be included if the program reports a number error).

The reported result is 3.145 per cent which is a slightly more accurate figure than that calculated using the interpolation method.

Now we can convert this value to an equivalent annual rate as before to give 6.39 per cent.

$$r = 1.03145^2 - 1$$
$$r = 6.39\%$$

REVIEW ACTIVITY 4.2 A fixed rate British government bond pays interest annually at a coupon rate of 5 per cent, its current market value is £90.15 and it has exactly two years to redemption. Use an Excel spreadsheet to calculate the yield on the bond.

TECHNICAL NOTE

There are two important points to note about the pricing of bonds:

1 Interest is paid on bonds semi-annually but it accrues to the investor on a daily basis. So, if a bond paying half yearly interest on the 30 June and 31 December is sold on 31 January then the seller would be entitled to 31 days interest. The 'clean' price is the price we would calculate by discounting the future coupon payments and redemption value at the yield appropriate for the bond. The actual market price will be a little different because it will be quoted with the accrued interest included so that the buyer, at that price, will be entitled to the next coupon payment in full. The market price is sometimes referred to as the 'dirty' price. Accrued interest is simple to calculate. In the UK a bond paying 10 per cent per annum would accrue interest on the 31 January as follows:

$$\text{Accrued interest} = 10\% \times \frac{31}{365} \times £100 = 84.93p$$

2 Normally a bond trades *cum div*. This means that the investor expects to get the next coupon payment at the half yearly interval. However, a few days before the payment of the coupon the 'books' are closed at the Bank of England and the interest about to be paid goes to the registered holder of the bond at that date even if it is sold before the coupon is paid. During the interval the bond will go *ex-div* reflecting the fact that the purchaser of the bond will not be collecting the next interest payment. Therefore when a bond is trading *cum div* the market price will be the clean price plus the element of interest accruing to the seller up to the date of sale.

Dirty price = clean price + accrued interest

Once the bond goes *ex-div*, the seller will still receive the next coupon payment in full and so the market price will drop recognizing that the seller will get part of the 'clean price' as a coupon payment some days later. So on the day the bond goes *ex-div*:

Dirty price = clean price − present value of the coupon payment

What this means is that after the *ex-div* date the purchaser of the bond will get the present value of the bond (which includes the next coupon payment) less the present value of the coupon payment they will not receive.

The difficulty with the yield concept, as with the internal rate of return discussed in Chapter 2 is the assumption that bond proceeds are reinvested each period at the yield percentage. In reality, this may not be true as investors may not assume a constant reinvestment rate over the longer term. However, before we explore how yields vary over time we turn our attention to what may appear at first sight to be a somewhat bizarre activity: 'stripping'.

The separate trading of interest and principal (STRIPS)

The idea of stripping first arose in the United States in 1984. STRIPS were conceived and manufactured by private financial institutions who realized the opportunity in stripping the coupon payments from the principal to give a pure, time limited coupon bond and a redemption only or 'zero coupon' bond. These two stripped components of the original bond can then be traded separately. Indeed, it is then possible to split the individual coupon payments and in principle an investor would be able to reconstitute a risk free bond from the discount coupons of different amounts and with a par repayment of any maturity. Thus, it is possible to 'engineer' a risk free cash flow to meet any future expected cash flow requirements the investor may have. Since 1998 there has been a small but growing market for strips in the UK. Only GEMMS, the Debt Management Office or the Bank of England are allowed to make strips from a small set of Treasury Bonds which are deemed 'strippable'.

EXHIBIT 4.6

Stripping a bond into its component parts

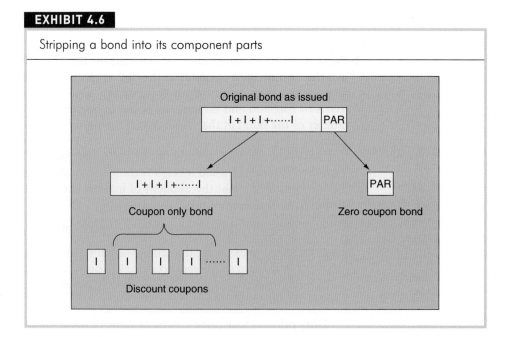

There are two benefits attaching to the practice of stripping: first, it is possible for investors with different cash flow requirements to match the receipts from their investment to their exact needs. A pension fund requiring a secure and regular cash flow to fund its ongoing payments could find the coupon only part of a stripped bond attractive. Another organization that expects to make a lump sum payment may find the zero coupon bond more suited to their needs. The second advantage is investment in strips can help mitigate re-investment risk. Strips thus find their place in the range of securities that individuals and firms can use to minimize the risk of their portfolios. The downside of stripping is that the market value of the individual components will be slightly more than the market value of the original bond. This is the price the investor bears for creating flexibility in the management of future returns from his or her investment.

The yield curve

The yield curve is designed to reveal the rate of return that investors in the debt market require on cash receipts at different points of time in the future. The yield curve is calculated using risk free investments such as Treasury Bonds (in the UK) and is a vital piece of information for analysts seeking out arbitrage gains in the bond market and for companies who need to know the rate of return they need to offer on debt of given maturity. Companies can build up from the risk free curve to a risk adjusted figure as we will discuss later in this chapter. In this section we will deal with two types of yield curve: first a curve showing the yield on a risk free bond against its term to maturity (the yield to maturity curve) and, second a curve showing the interest rate required to discount risk free cash flows arising at any given time in the future (the 'spot' curve).

If the reinvestment rate on bonds was expected to be constant irrespective of the term to maturity we would obtain a yield curve as shown in Exhibit 4.7.

EXHIBIT 4.7

The flat yield curve

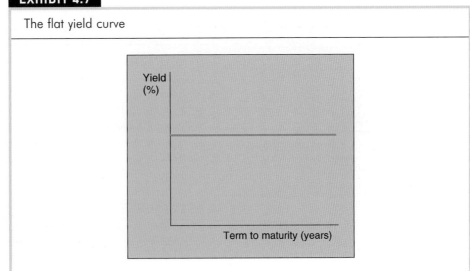

However, expectations of different yields in the future are not constant and in Exhibit 4.8 we plot the yields for Treasury bonds against their term to maturity over the next 35 years using a sequence of gilts of varying coupon and maturity from the *Financial Times*. This version of the yield curve suffers from two problems. First, there is a difficulty in comparing the term to maturity of both short- and long-term bonds. Second, there is a problem with the underlying reinvestment assumption within the mechanics of the calculation of the yield to maturity. This is a similar problem to that discussed in Chapter 2 with respect to the internal rate of return method in capital investment appraisal. The yield to maturity assumes that cash flows are being continuously reinvested at the yield during the life of the bond. In some applications this may be a perfectly reasonable assumption, in others it will not.

Converting from term to maturity to duration

In Chapter 2 we introduced the concept of 'duration' which is the average time taken to recover the cash flow from an investment. With bonds, the average time is governed by the magnitude of the coupon payments as well as the redemption value at the end of the bond's life. Making comparisons purely in terms of the length of time to the final redemption does not reflect the fact that holders of high coupon bonds will, on average, recover their cash more quickly than those on low coupon bonds.

To surmount this problem a yield curve can be constructed which gives the yields to maturity against duration. Duration is the weighted average of the number of years to redemption where the weights are the proportion of the market value recovered by the investor in each year.

The formula for duration is based on the general bond formula given above:

$$V_0 = \frac{I}{(1+r)} + \frac{I}{(1+r)^2} + \frac{I}{(1+r)^3} + \cdots + \frac{Par + I}{(1+r)^n}$$

EXHIBIT 4.8

Plotting yield against term to maturity

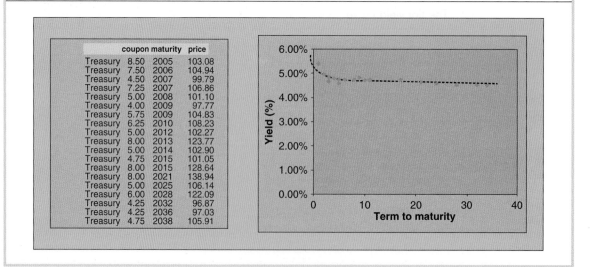

therefore

$$Duration = \left[1 \times \frac{I}{V_0(1+r)} + 2 \times \frac{I}{V_0(1+r)^2} + \cdots n \times \frac{Par+I}{V_0(1+r)^2} \right]$$

FINANCIAL REALITY

Calculate the duration for Tr 4 pc 2009 which has a current market value of £97.77.

Duration is calculated by the following steps:

EXHIBIT 4.9

The calculation of duration on a bond

		01-Jan-05	Jun-05	Dec-05	Jun-06	Dec-06	Jun-07	Dec-07	Jun-08	Dec-08	Jun-09	Dec-09
(i)	Period number		1	2	3	4	5	6	7	8	9	10
(ii)	Cash flow to investor	−97.77	2	2	2	2	2	2	2	2	2	102
(iii)	Yield (= IRR(range)) =	0.0225										
(iv)	Discounted value of cash receipts		1.9560	1.9129	1.8708	1.8296	1.7893	1.7499	1.7114	1.6737	1.6368	81.6398
(v)	Proportion of market value		0.0200	0.0196	0.0191	0.0187	0.0183	0.0179	0.0175	0.0171	0.0167	0.8350
(vi)	Weighted value of period number		0.0200	0.0391	0.0574	0.0749	0.0915	0.1074	0.1225	0.1369	0.1507	8.3502
(vii)	Duration in periods	9.1506										
(viii)	Duration in years	4.5753										

1 List the period numbers for each coupon payment and the combined coupon and redemption value. In this case with a five year bond paying its coupon every six months there will be ten periods.

2 Lay out the market value of the bond and the cash receipts to the investor.

3 Calculate the yield using the (= IRR) function which gives 2.252 per cent in this case.

4 Discount the cash receipts to the investor using the yield as shown.

5 Work out in each period the proportion of the market value received in that period.

6 Multiply each period number (step 1) by its weight from 5.

7 Sum those weighted period values to give the duration in periods. If the coupon is paid annually this will be the duration in years.

8 In this case the duration is in six month periods so divide by two to get the duration in years.

This bond which has a five year term to maturity has duration of 4.575 years. This duration figures is more useful for making comparisons between different bonds as duration is a function of both the term to maturity and the magnitude of the coupon payment on the bond.

REVIEW ACTIVITY 4.3 Calculate the duration for Treasury 5pc 2008 shown in Exhibit 4.1.

Now all we have to do is repeat this for all of the bonds shown in Exhibit 4.8 and produce the same yield curve but plotted against duration as shown in Exhibit 4.10.

This version of the yield curve is particularly useful in the valuation of bonds and in the estimation of the cost of debt capital to be discussed in the next chapter.

Deriving the spot curve

Because the yield curve described above is a composite of coupon and redemption payments on each bond it does not quite answer the question as to the rate of return investors require for investment where the return comes at a specific time in the future. The spot curve is particularly useful in the management of future interest rate risk.

To deal with this issue we need to calculate the return on bonds which promise a single future cash flow only. A U.K. 200 coupon yield curve is shown in Exhibit 4.11. The technique used in producing curves such as this involves calculating the yield on zero coupon bonds of different maturities. The strip market provides the bonds we need. Now that all Treasury securities are deemed strippable there is a small market in zero coupon bonds of widely different maturities. However, there are gaps in what can be achieved given the thinness of the market.

EXHIBIT 4.10

Plotting yield to maturity against duration

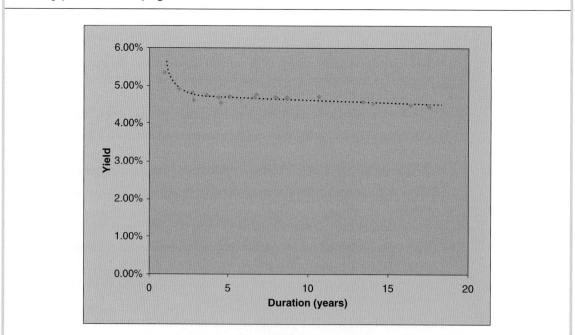

EXHIBIT 4.11

Term structure of interest rates for UK Treasury strips (31 December 2004)

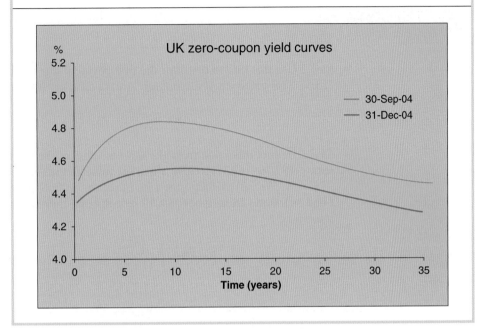

An alternative to using zero coupon bonds is a process known as 'bootstrapping'. Bootstrapping is a technique where the discount rate (the investor's required rate of return) is calculated from a series of bonds with known maturities incrementing (for Treasury Stocks) in six month intervals.

The bootstrapping method proceeds through the following steps:

- *Step 1* Find the yield on the first bond in the series which is returning £103 to the investor in six months:

FINANCIAL REALITY

Five bonds have the following terms to maturity:

EXHIBIT 4.12

The term to maturity of five bonds

Coupon Rate (%)	Term to maturity	Market value
6	6 months	£99.04
7	12 months	£97.76
6	18 months	£94.25
5.5	24 months	£91.30
5	30 months	£88.50

Derive the 'spot curve' using the bootstrapping technique.

$$99.04 = \frac{103}{(1+r)}$$

$$r = \frac{103}{99.04} - 1$$

$$r = 4\%$$

- *Step 2* Use this rate to discount the first payment due on the second bond (£3.5). This value when discounted at a six monthly rate of 4 per cent gives:

$$PV = \frac{3.5}{1.04} = £3.37$$

- *Step 3* Deduct this value from the market value of the second bond in the series (£97.76 – £3.37) to give a market value of the final payment of this bond of £94.39. We can calculate the rate of return on final payment of the second bond as follows (remember as a 12 month bond there are two discounting intervals):

$$94.39 = \frac{103.5}{(1+r)^2}$$

$$r = \sqrt{\frac{103.5}{94.39}} - 1$$

$$r = 4.71\%$$

- *Step 4* Repeat this process with the next bond in the series using 4 per cent to discount the first payment, 4.71 per cent to discount the second payment and then calculate the market value of the bond less these interim payments. This reduced market value is used to calculate the yield on the final payment.

The reduced market value for the third bond is:

$$MV' = 94.25 - \frac{3}{1.04} - \frac{3}{1.0471^2}$$

$$MV' = 88.63$$

The rate of return which equates this market value with the final payment on this bond is given by:

$$r = \sqrt[3]{\frac{103}{88.63}} - 1$$

$$r = 5.14\%$$

REVIEW ACTIVITY 4.4 Repeat step 4 for the 4th bond in the series by discounting the first interim payment (£2.75) at 4 per cent, the second interim payment by 4.71 per cent, the third by 5.14 per cent and deducting these discounted interim payments to get the reduced market value. Then calculate the yield required to equalize the fourth payment of £102.75 with your reduced market value. Remember it is four discounting periods for this calculation. Repeat for the fifth bond in the series.

- *Step 5* Convert each six monthly yield (4%, 4.71%, 5.14% etc.) to its annual equivalent and plot as a function of time (Exhibit 4.13).

EXHIBIT 4.13

Spot curve derived using the bootstrapping procedure

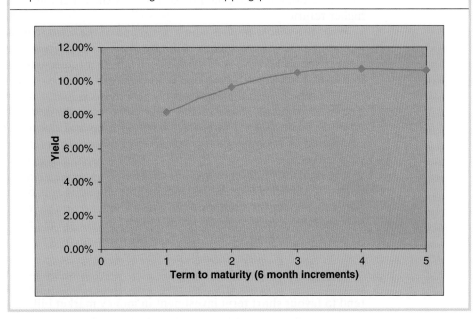

The problem with the bootstrapping technique is that it relies upon finding a series of actively traded bonds maturing in six monthly intervals. In practice this may be difficult but a reasonable approximation can be made by assuming that the cash flows from Treasury Bonds arise at annual intervals (rather than six monthly) and using the bootstrapping technique to find a spot rate.

Factors influencing the yield curve

There are a number of theories that attempt to explain the shape of the yield curve and hence interest rates over future time periods. The most important of these are:

- the expectations hypothesis
- the liquidity preference hypothesis
- the market segmentation hypothesis.

Of these, the expectations hypothesis is regarded as the most fundamental. Fisher, whose 'separation theorem' we have already met in Chapter 2, assumed that bond investors are strictly rational in their efforts to maximize the return from their investment and the bond markets are efficient in that prices, and hence yields will adjust rapidly to altering expectations about future yields. He also assumed that new information is costless and that the markets are frictionless. If these conditions hold, then the yield curve should be a perfect reflection of expectations about future interest rates. In such a perfect world, the period yield will be the same irrespective of the term to maturity of the individual bond or the way in which different bonds are combined together to create that yield.

To see this consider an investor seeking to invest in a bond with a three-year term. He or she could achieve that holding in one of two ways: they could simply purchase a bond maturing in three years or, they could purchase a one year bond then reinvest at the end of the term in a further bond and so on for three years.

Either of these strategies should yield an identical rate of return or the investor would be able make a profit by selling out of the alternative which offers the lower overall return and using the proceeds to buy the other alternative which offers the higher return.

What this theory implies is that the shape of the term structure is determined by period by period expectations of future short term interest rates. Therefore, if the slope of the yield curve is upwards this means that future interest rates are expected to rise, and vice versa if the slope is downwards.

The problem with the expectations hypothesis is that it is not empirically strong. The most common shape of the yield curve over the last half century has been upwards, while interest rates have been both up and down (several times) during that period. Some other factors appear to be at work in determining the shape of the yield curve.

The liquidity preference hypothesis is based upon the idea that borrowers tend to borrow for the long term, while lenders prefer liquidity and, other things being equal, prefer to lend for the short term. As a result, longer term yields are likely to be higher than short term yields (the so called 'liquidity premium') in order to persuade lenders to invest for the longer term. This liquidity premium may be sufficient to explain the predominant upward slope in future bond yields.

Finally, it has also been suggested that certain segments of the yield curve are favoured by different types of investors. Banks and other financial institutions tend to favour short term investment in money market bills and short term bonds, whereas other investors, such as investment and pension funds, may be more interested in longer dated stocks. As a result different markets exist for bonds of different maturities and as a result differences in the shape of the yield curve will result.

Duration, modified duration, convexity and bond risk

The concept of duration and convexity are important in order to measure a security's price risk. The price risk is the sensitivity of the price to unexpected changes in interest rates. To understand the relationship between duration and a bonds risk take the basic bond formula discussed earlier in this chapter:

$$V_0 = \frac{I}{(1+r)} + \frac{I}{(1+r)^2} + \frac{I}{(1+r)^3} + \cdots + \frac{Par+I}{(1+r)^n}$$

Our concern in assessing the riskiness of a bond is how its value varies with changes in its yield to maturity. This sensitivity of the value of a bond to changes in yield we can describe mathematically as the first derivative of the value of the bond with respect to the yield.

$$\frac{dV_0}{dr}$$

Thus decoding this expression we get the 'rate of change in bond value caused by a very small change in yield'. The formula for this differential is given by the formula:

$$\frac{dV_0}{dr} = -\frac{1I}{(1+r)^2} - \frac{2I}{(1+r)^3} - \frac{3I}{(1+r)^4} \cdots \cdots - \frac{nI}{(1+r)^{n+1}}$$

Which simplifies to:

$$\frac{dV_0}{dr} = -\frac{1}{(1+r)}\left[\frac{1I}{(1+r)^1} + \frac{2I}{(1+r)^2} + \frac{3I}{(1+r)^3} \cdots\cdots + \frac{nI}{(1+r)^n}\right]$$

Multiplying both sides by $1/V_0$

$$\frac{dV_0}{dr}\frac{1}{V_0} = -\frac{1}{(1+r)}\left[\frac{\dfrac{1I}{(1+r)^1} + \dfrac{2I}{(1+r)^2} + \dfrac{3I}{(1+r)^3} \cdots\cdots + \dfrac{nI}{(1+r)^n}}{V_0}\right]$$

$$\frac{dV_0}{dr}\frac{1}{V_0} = -\frac{1}{(1+r)}\left[\left[1\frac{I}{V_0(1+r)} + 2\frac{I}{V_0(1+r)^2} + \cdots\cdots n\frac{PAR+I}{V_0(1+r)^n}\right]\right]$$

The term in the right hand bracket is the duration and so the above equation can be simplified to:

$$\frac{dV_0}{dr} = -\frac{D}{(1+r)}V_0$$

The expression on the right contains a term which is known as the modified duration (M):

$$M = \frac{D}{(1+r)}$$

And so the above expression can be simplified to:

$$\frac{dV_0}{dr} = -MV_0$$

Now to a practical example of the use of this formula.

FINANCIAL REALITY

Calculate the likely change in the value of Tr 4 pc 2009 following a 1 per cent change in yield. This bond has a current market value of £97.77 per cent, a duration (see above) of 4.575 years and a yield of 4.5547 per cent per annum.

Rearranging the formula above to express the change in value on the left hand side against the change in yield on the right hand side and substituting:

$$\frac{dV_0}{dr} = -\frac{D}{(1+r)}V_0$$

$$dV_0 = -\frac{D}{(1+r)}V_0 dr$$

$$dV_0 = -\frac{4.575}{(1.045547)} \times £97.77 \times 0.01$$

$$dV_0 = -£4.28$$

This means that if the yield rises by 1 per cent the market value falls by £4.28 or, in percentage terms, by 4.377 per cent of the current market value.

TECHNICAL NOTE

Interest rate changes are measured in terms of 'basis points'. A basis point is .01 of 1 per cent or, if you prefer .0001 of the original. In the example above 1 per cent change in yield would be a change of 100 basis points. The fall in value for the bond discussed above caused by one basis point change in yield is therefore £0.0428 or 4.28p. This is known as the basis point value (BPV) for the bond.

Of course, like all formulas the one above is also very useful when applied the other way round. If we want to know the change in yield that would be brought about by a small change in the price of the bond, a simple method when you know the basis point value is to use that instead of the formula. Given a basis point value of 4.28p a fall of 50p in the value of the bond would give rise to a rise to an increase in the yield of 11.68 basis points or 0.1168 per cent.

Duration is a useful method for quickly identifying the sensitivity of a bond and as such it is just as much a measure of the riskiness of a bond to changes in interest rates and hence yields as it is a measure of the average time taken for the investor to receive their cash flow from their investment. However, it is only accurate as a measure of risk for relatively small changes around the current quoted market price or the yield. The reason for this is that the present value of a bond is not linearly related to the yield. This is the same problem we had when calculating the internal rate of return in Chapter 2.

We can solve this problem of the 'curvature' of the price/yield relationship by introducing the notion of 'convexity'. Technically, convexity represents the second term of a Taylor expansion giving the second derivative of price to yield. However, for our purposes we can simply take it to be the difference in price calculated using the modified duration rather than using the bond pricing formula equating the value of the bond to the discounted coupon payments and redemption value.

REVIEW ACTIVITY 4.5

Using the bond formula and the method using the duration described above calculate the price of Tr 4 pc 2009 following a change in yield from that implied at its current market value of £97.77 per cent to that when the yield is 7 per cent. The duration of the bond is 4.575 years.

Using the two formula for different assumed yields in the example above we can draw up the price/yield curves as shown is Exhibit 4.14. The difference which emerges between the two is the convexity attaching to this particular bond.

The question now remains as to what is the use of the convexity concept. What convexity measures is the rate of change in a security's sensitivity to interest rate movement. Securities that pay a fixed coupon tend to have positive convexity. What this means is that as interest rates and yields fall the price rises and the duration lengthens. This effect is more pronounced the more positive the convexity. Securities with high positive convexity exhibit more rapidly rising prices as interest rates fall than those with low or negative convexity. Similarly, the prices of such securities will fall more slowly under rising interest rates. Measuring the convexity therefore tells us how sensitive a security's price is to changing interest rates.

However, for most of the practical applications in corporate finance convexity does not generate a sufficiently large error to cause concern. For large scale bond investors such as pension funds and other financial institutions minor variations in price can amount to significant differences in the value of their holding. For these investors the convexity of a bond can be highly significant.

EXHIBIT 4.14

Convexity: the differences between the predicted prices using the bond formula and the modified duration

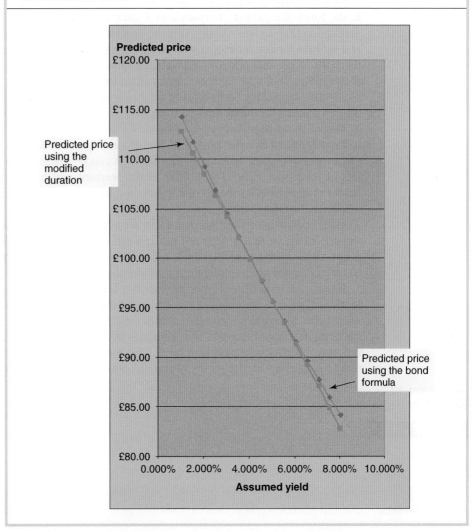

Raising corporate debt

A company seeking to raise long term debt finance will be constrained by its size, its debt capacity and its credit rating. Small- to medium-sized enterprises (SMEs) may make use of private lending through family, friends and other small business investors. For most companies the common route is through a bank who on the basis of a business plan will make a 'lending decision' depending upon its assessment of the credit worthiness of its client supported by any 'collateral security' which can be provided by the owners of the business. For a well established firm with substantial and easily marketable assets the bank may lend on the basis of a 'fixed charge' against specific assets or a 'floating charge' over all its assets. In the absence of such security, the bank may require the directors to secure the loan by offering a second charge against their personal assets such as their homes. Chapter 7 of the author's *Finance and Accounting for Business* gives details of how a business plan can be prepared to support an application for a small business loan.

When raising debt capital a company may decide to add an incentive to the lender in the form of equity participation at a later stage. Such debt is referred to as 'convertible' in that it gives the investor the option to exchange the debt for equity shares at a set rate for conversion at a given point in time. If the company is successful then the right to convert may be very valuable and convertible debt holders will exercise their 'option' and take up their equity entitlement.

A more aggressive form of debt financing is where an option to take up equity is offered along with the debt. So a company can borrow money from lenders who take as part of the agreement rights to subscribe to the equity of the business in addition to their rights to interest payments and the repayment of their capital. These rights are a form of option called a 'warrant' which can be independently traded as securities in their own right. The holder of the warrant will have the right to purchase shares at a specified price up to a specified date unless the warrant is a 'perpetual' in which case no time limit is set.

With both convertibles and warrants attaching to debt, the debt will normally be 'subordinated' in that it does not rank as highly as 'senior' debt for repayment in the event of the company being liquidated. As a result the company may also be required to offer a higher coupon payment to make the debt attractive to investors.

Raising finance of this type represents a level between debt and equity is, in the inexhaustible and imaginative vocabulary of the financial markets, known as 'mezzanine' debt. Mezzanine debt emerged strongly in the 1990s as a favoured means of financing leveraged buyouts of companies by their management. The lender gained not only a higher rate of return (with a greater risk of default) but also an opportunity to participate in the equity of the business if it was eventually successful.

EXHIBIT 4.15

Different types of debt in normal order of seniority

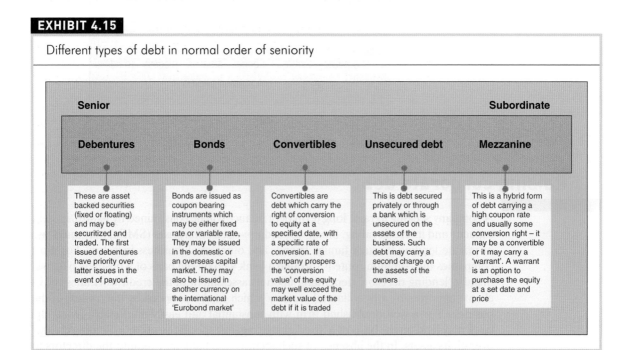

Senior				Subordinate
Debentures	**Bonds**	**Convertibles**	**Unsecured debt**	**Mezzanine**
These are asset backed securities (fixed or floating) and may be securitized and traded. The first issued debentures have priority over latter issues in the event of payout	Bonds are issued as coupon bearing instruments which may be either fixed rate or variable rate, They may be issued in the domestic or an overseas capital market. They may also be issued in another currency on the international 'Eurobond market'	Convertibles are debt which carry the right of conversion to equity at a specified date, with a specific rate of conversion. If a company prospers the 'conversion value' of the equity may well exceed the market value of the debt if it is traded	This is debt secured privately or through a bank which is unsecured on the assets of the business. Such debt may carry a second charge on the assets of the owners	This is a hybrid form of debt carrying a high coupon rate and usually some conversion right – it may be a convertible or it may carry a 'warrant'. A warrant is an option to purchase the equity at a set date and price

Note that the seniority of debt refers to the order in which debt holders are entitled to recover their cash in the event of a liquidation of the firm. The exact order of seniority will depend upon the specific terms of each debt agreement.

A larger company may use any of the above forms of debt although they also have the opportunity of avoiding intermediaries and going directly to investors with an issue of securitized debt. Securitized debt takes the form of the issue of certificates binding the company to pay interest and repay the borrowing denoted on the certificate to the bearer at a specified date.

Corporate bonds

Corporate bond issues may be made purely to the domestic market (as a sterling issue in the UK), or in an overseas market. A large British company, wishing to raise finance for substantial investment in the United States may raise debt finance in that country. Another alternative is for the company to raise debt finance on the international money market using an international syndicate of banks and other finance houses. 'Eurobonds' as they are called, represent debt denominated in any currency (dollars, yen, euro(s) etc.) which are traded on the international capital markets. Initially, Eurobonds cannot be sold to investors who are resident in the country in which the bond is denominated. However, after a short period (usually 90 days) they can be freely traded.

The process of issuing corporate bonds is relatively straightforward. The first step is the appointment, by the company concerned of an issuing house who will act as the 'lead manager' in making the issue. These issuing houses are large merchant banks that have many years of experience in floating debt in the primary market. Such issuing houses are Merrill Lynch, Morgan Stanley, SBC Warburg, Goldman Sachs and numerous others. If the issue is relatively small the issuing house may consolidate the bond issue with a number of others from businesses of similar credit risk.

For a large debt issue, the lead manager may put together a team of co-lead managers (so if Morgan Stanley is leading it may appoint (say) Nomura and Goldman Sachs as it co-leads) who may specialize in handling part of the issue in another country. The lead manager will then put together with its co-lead other members of an underwriting syndicate who together with the lead managers purchase the whole issue and agree the interest rate and other terms upon which the bond will be issued. It is at this point that the credit rating that will attach to the issue is determined. As the credit rating process is so important it will be dealt with separately below.

As part of the process of putting together the underwriting syndicate the lead manager will prepare a sequence of documents which are exhaustively verified by teams of accountants and lawyers. First, an invitation to underwrite is prepared giving details of the issue, then a prospectus is prepared giving details of the borrower and nature of the issue and finally agreement documents are drawn up which will eventually be signed by all the parties.

The underwriting syndicate will commit to pay the full value of the issue to the issuing company and they therefore have an incentive to sell the issue as quickly as possible. Each underwriter will have a list of potential buyers (often other banks not involved in the original syndicate) and an initial or 'grey market' will be established before a public notice is issued to the press announcing the issue to the wider world.

Credit risk assessment

The credit-rating business was the creation of a young man who got his start at a Wall Street bank in 1890 as an errand boy for $20 a month.

Dreaming of becoming a millionaire, John Moody had an epiphany one morning while reading the newspaper. With so little known about a growing number of corporate securities, someone was bound to publish an industrial manual offering financial information to investors. 'When it comes,' he recalled thinking in his autobiography, 'it will be a gold mine.' In 1909, Moody started mining. He published a book about railroad securities, using letter grades to assess their risk. Investors looking for more certainty liked the idea, and the Moody business took off. So did Poors Publishing Co., which began rating corporate debt in 1916, according to its successor company, Standard & Poors. Standard Statistics Co. followed suit in 1922. Fitch entered the rating business in 1924. THE WASHINGTON POST TUESDAY, NOVEMBER 23, 2004

Before making a loan any lender will attempt to measure the credit-worthiness of the company concerned. In large measure this is an issue of assessing the likelihood of corporate failure but in the particular instance of the issue of new debt in establishing the debt carrying capacity of the firm concerned. For small firms credit assessment is carried out by a number of agencies on the basis of the company accounts, a check of the credit worthiness of the owners and a number of other issues which are less relevant in the context of the larger, publicly quoted corporation. Those issues are discussed in detail in *Finance and Accounting for Business*.

With governments, public sector organizations and large firms a credit assessment will normally be carried out by one of the credit rating agencies. The big three agencies are Standard and Poors, Moodys and Fitch. These agencies produce similar rating scales designed to rate debt issues as either 'investment' or 'speculative' (junk) bond status.

EXHIBIT 4.16

Comparative rating scales from Standard and Poors and Moodys. The likelihood of failure is derived from Standard and Poors' submission to the US Securities and Exchange Commission, November 15, 2002.

Standard and Poors	Moodys		Likelihood of default within 15 years
Investment Grade Bonds			
AAA; AA+; AAA–	Aaa; Aaa1; Aaa2; Aaa3	Best quality virtually zero default risk	0.52–1.31 per cent
AA; AA–; A+	Aa; Aa1; Aa2; Aa3	Excellent quality, very little default risk	1.31–2.32 per cent
A; A–; BBB+	A; A1; A2; A3	Rated 'good'; minimal risk	2.32–6.64 per cent
BBB; BBB–; BB+	Baa; Baa1; Baa2; Baa3	Medium rating, low but clear risk	6.64–19.52 per cent
Speculative or 'Junk' Bonds			
BB; BB–, B+	Ba; Ba1; Ba2; Ba3	Marginal grade	19.52–35.76 per cent
B; B–; CCC+	B; B1; B2; B3	Significant exposure to default risk	35.76–54.38 per cent
CCC; CCC–; CCC+	Caa; Caa1; Caa2; Caa3	Considerable exposure to default risk	>54.38 per cent
CC; CC–; C+	Ca; Ca1; Ca2; Ca3	Very high risk	>54.38 per cent
C	C	Very high likelihood of failure	>54.38 per cent

The exact mechanics of the bond rating process vary from company to company. However, the rating will involve a consideration of the firm's business and financial risk. The business risk factors will include an assessment of the firm's industrial and competitive position as well as the quality of its management and its strategic intentions. On the financial side a range of financial metrics are used focusing on profitability, the firm's cash flow generation and its capital structure. The most significant question marks about the process is the effectiveness of the agencies in assessing the strength of a firm's intangible resources including its human capital.

Estimating the yield on a corporate bond

As a result of the bond rating process it is possible to estimate the yield on a corporate bond. As a corporate bond bears some credit risk (unlike Treasury Bonds which can be assumed to be completely risk free) its yield will consist of two components:

The risk free rate of return is derived from the yield curve for a bond of that specified duration. The credit risk premium is established from 'bond spread' data which gives the percentage adjustment to the risk free rate for a security of that given exposure to default risk.

An important issue for us is what determines the magnitude of this 'bond spread'. The most general answer was provided by Robert Merton and his justification must wait until we consider options in Chapter 9. However, in summary, the difference between the risk free rate and the rate of return on a corporate bond is influenced by the following:

1 The value of the firm's assets and in particular the magnitude and relative strength of its annual cash flows. This explains the importance of cash flow ratios such as the ratio of a firm's operating cash flow to its total debt in explaining corporate distress.

2 The term to maturity of the company's debt. The longer debt has to run the more chance there is that the company will hit turbulent trading conditions and thus increase the risk of default.

3 The value of the company's debt in issue. The greater a company's debt value the more difficult it will be for the company to redeem that debt at maturity.

EXHIBIT 4.17

The yield on a corporate bond

| Yield on corporate bond of term to maturity 't' years | = | Risk free rate of return (yield) on a Treasury Bond of term to maturity 't' years | + | Credit risk premium (bond spread) for the rating for the security or company concerned |

4 The volatility of the company's future cash flows. The more volatile the flows the greater the chance that default conditions will occur where the firm cannot pay its ongoing interest liabilities or find the necessary resources to redeem the debt at maturity.

Clearly the stronger a firm's cash flows under 1 above the greater will be the firm's value relative to its debt (it will have a lower gearing ratio) and we would expect the bond spread to be low for a given level of volatility in the firm's cash earnings. However, the lower the equity value of the firm relative to the face value of its debt the greater will be the bond spread and indeed as the equity value of the firm drops towards zero the bond spread will approach infinity.

It is possible, with a reasonable degree of accuracy to predict the likely bond rating for a company using the results of regression studies into debt rating where the explanatory variables are readily observable measures of risk. Kaplan and Urwitz (1979) undertook some of the early work on this from which further studies have developed. Kaplan and Urwitz identified the following measures as important:

- Firm size (F) – measured as total assets in $million.
- Profitability (π) – net income/total assets.
- Debt status (S) – where 0 = unsubordinated debt (i.e. where the debt concerned must be paid before other claims, 1 = subordinated debt).
- Gearing (L) – long term debt to total assets.
- Interest cover (C) – Cash flow before tax and interest/interest payable.
- Systematic risk (β) – measured by the firm's equity beta.
- Unsystematic risk (σ_U) – standard deviation of error term from the market model.
- Risk attaching to earnings (σ_E) – Coefficient of variation (standard deviation/mean) of past five years' earnings.

There are two formulae to apply. The first is for quoted firms where the relevant risk parameters can be obtained from market data. The second relies solely on accounting data but is somewhat less accurate.

$$score(quoted) = 5.67 + 0.0011F + 5.13\pi - 2.36S - 2.85L + 0.007C - 0.87\beta - 2.90\sigma_u$$

or

$$score(unquoted) = 4.41 + 0.0014F + 6.4\pi - 2.56S - 2.72L + 0.006C - 0.53\sigma_E$$

Both of these formulae point to the fact that large, highly profitable firms have lower default risk than small, low profit businesses. Conversely, the status of the debt and the gearing has a high negative impact upon the rating. To convert the score to a rating we use the following:

score	rating
>6.76	AAA
>5.19	AA
>3.28	A
>1.57	BBB
>0	BB

We will return to the issue of bond rating and the use of the Kaplan Urwitz Model in the next chapter when we estimate the cost of capital for Cobham plc.

Given, the theory what is the evidence on bond spreads for given credit ratings of companies? Exhibit 4.18 shows the increasing bond spread against term to maturity for the US industrial sector. Note that the principal theoretical predictions are borne out by the empirical data: bond spread generally increases with term to maturity and this is most noticeable with high credit risk firms.

EXHIBIT 4.18

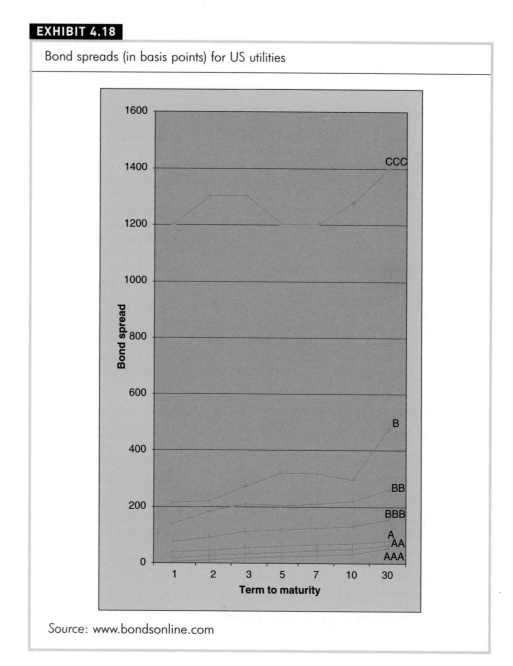

Bond spreads (in basis points) for US utilities

Source: www.bondsonline.com

I n this chapter we have explored the esoteric world of fixed interest securities in some detail. Starting with a basic understanding of fixed interest finance we have explored the role that this type of finance, in its many and varied guises, plays in providing long term funds for government and industry. Much of the analytical tools developed in this chapter such as yield, yield curves, duration and convexity have focused on government debt as archetypes of the type of financial security we are interested in. Top quality government debt is essentially default risk free and as such provides a basis for assessing the premiums that companies will have to pay to secure finance of this type from the capital market. Although technically demanding, much of the work in this and the previous chapter is vital underpinning for our work on the cost of capital. That is the topic to which we now turn in our exploration of corporate finance.

Further Reading

Choudhury, M., Joannes, D., Pereira, R. and Pienaar, R. (2002) *Capital Market Instruments – analysis and valuation*, Harlow: FT Prentice Hall. This is an excellent book and parts 1 and 2 give a thorough if rather technical treatment of this subject.

Cox, J.C., Ingersoll, J.E. and Ross, S.A. (1985) A Theory of the Term Structure of Interest Rates, *Econometrica* 53:385–402.

Dothan, L. Uri (1978) On the Term Structure of Interest Rates, *Journal of Financial Economics* 6:59–69.

Macaulay, F. (1938) *Some theoretical Problems Suggested by the Movements of Interest Rates in the United States since 1865*, New York: National Bureau of Economic Research. This is the work in which Macaulay first defined the concept of duration. It is very difficult to get hold of but can be obtained from the risk classics library at www.riskbooks.com/cluster_riskclassics.shtml

Reuters (1999) *An Introduction to Bond Markets*, Singapore: John Wiley and Sons. This is a comprehensive 'insiders' guide to how the bond markets operate. However, it now a little dated and care should be taken in that practices have changed in the market.

www.bankofengland.co.uk/statistics/yieldcurve/main.htm This is an excellent site with cross references to the Bank of England's review articles on yield curve methodology.

Kaplan, R., and Urwitz, G., (1979) Statistical Models of Bond Ratings: a Methodological enquiry. *Journal of Business,* April, 231–261.

Ryan, B. (2004) *Finance and Accounting for Business*, Thomson Learning, London.

PROGRESS CHECK

1 What are the advantages and disadvantages of debt finance compared with equity?

2 Briefly outline four sources of risk to which the holder of a government bond might be exposed.

3 What is the function of the UK Debt Management Office?

4 What is the nature of a zero coupon bond?

5 How does the dirty price of a bond differ from the clean price?

6 What is the financial benefit of strips to a large institutional investor?

7 How can a spot curve be derived if there are insufficient zero coupon bonds available?

8 How do the expectations hypothesis and liquidity preference hypothesis differ?

9 Typically, how would we expect a yield curve to change over time and why?

10 Apart from the average time that it takes a bond investor to realize their cash flows,

what other important characteristic of a bond does duration measure?

11 Under what situation would duration become an inaccurate measure of a bond's risk and how can it be corrected?

12 List five different types of debt raised by companies under different circumstances.

13 If a company wishes to enter into a bond issue what process of external validation does it need to undertake before the process can commence?

14 What are the two components of the yield on the corporate bond?

QUESTIONS (answers at end of book)

1 The Debt Management Office wishes to issue a ten year fixed coupon bond at par with interest paid in equal instalments twice annually. The yield on bonds of this maturity is currently 5 per cent. What is the effective annual coupon rate and the actual coupon rate which must be offered to achieve par?

2 Below are the details for six bonds paying annual coupons:

Coupon rate (%)	Term to maturity	Market value
7	I year	100
7.5	2 years	104
5	3 years	100
5	4 years	100
4	5 years	96
6	6 years	106

You are required to calculate:

(i) The spot yields for these bonds using the bootstrapping technique.

(ii) Draw the spot curve that results.

(iii) Comment upon the significance of the curve that you have drawn.

QUESTIONS (answers on website)

3 A one year discount bond is issued at £94 per cent to be redeemed at par. What is the discount and the return on this bond?

4 A four year treasury bond pays interest at the end of June and December. Its coupon rate is 8 per cent and its market value is currently £107.50 per cent. What is the yield to maturity for this bond?

5 A four year treasury bond pays interest at the end of June and December. Its coupon rate is 8 per cent and its market value is currently £107.50 per cent. What is the duration of this bond?

6 A five year bond pays interest at the end of June and December. Its coupon rate is 6.5 per cent and its market value is currently £102.50 per cent.

You are required to:

(i) Calculate the yield and duration on this bond.

(ii) Using the data from (i) calculate the impact on the price of the bond of a 1 per cent change in interest rates.

7 You are an assistant finance officer in a large UK company in the electricity supply industry which has a market capitalization in excess of £2.4bn. It is reviewing its sources of finance which until this time has been restricted to equity and borrowing on various terms from its bank and other financial institutions. Its borrowing has an average term of just under four years to maturity. It is considering making a bond issue to support expansion and to reschedule its existing debt finance. Its gearing ratio would however remain below 20 per cent. Preliminary discussions with a bond rating agency suggest that it would have an AA rating. Outline the factors that influence bond rating and describe the steps which the company would have to pursue if it wished to make a bond issue.

The cost of capital 5

I n this chapter we draw together the threads from the previous chapters for an in depth discussion of the cost of capital. Given that capital is a scarce resource, we commence our discussion of its cost from an opportunity costing perspective by posing the question: what rate of return would the firm need to offer the capital market to ensure refinancing in the firm's existing gearing ratio? Our agenda in this chapter is about developing the techniques for determining the 'opportunity cost of capital'. To explain the processes involved we will focus upon two cases: Friendly Grinders plc and Cobham plc. Friendly Grinders is now a well established business which two years previously

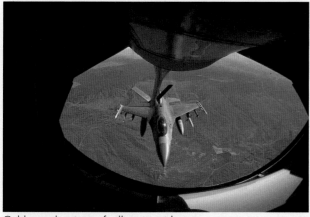

Cobham plc - jets refuelling in mid-air

obtained a public listing. It is run by the young and energetic Jack Grinder who is concerned about strengthening the financial fundamentals of the business. The other company is a much longer established enterprise. Cobham plc is an aerospace manufacturer based in the South of England. It is well diversified and has a history of sound management. Like many mid-sized quoted companies it uses a wide range of sources of capital.

Transtock Inc./Alamy

Learning outcomes

By reading and practising the material in this chapter you will be able to achieve the following:

1   An understanding of the underlying principles in establishing the opportunity cost of capital for a firm.

2   Estimate the cost of equity capital for (a) all firms across the market and (b) individual companies that are quoted.

▶

◄

3   Make reasonable adjustments to the methods of estimating the equity cost of capital for firms that are not traded.

4   Estimate raw betas from price data, making any necessary judgements and corrections to eliminate beta bias.

5   Estimate the firm's cost of debt capital irrespective of whether the firm has traded debt or is financed through loans.

6   Draw the estimates together to calculate the weighted average cost of capital making the necessary adjustments for the impact of tax.

The opportunity cost of capital

Determining a reliable cost of its capital is one of the most important financial problems a firm must resolve. The reason for its central importance is that this is the 'hidden' hurdle which any firm must overcome before it can begin to add value for its investors. In the previous two chapters we have discussed how the market 'prices' the value of a firm's equity and how the yield or return required by debt investors can also be calculated. From the firm's perspective it can use these elements of analysis to work out the effective rate that it has to pay to the capital market for the use of its investors' funds.

As with other aspects of costing what we need to determine is the 'opportunity cost' of the capital used by the firm. Opportunity cost is a straightforward concept in financial terms. For the economist it means the value of the nearest alternative foregone, but in finance it means the net cash loss to the firm as a result of the decision to consume an economic resource (in this case capital). For a moment it is worth rehearsing the general rules for deciding the opportunity cost of a resource.

Exhibit 5.1 shows the general rules that should be applied. If a firm does not have the resources it needs then the cost of acquiring them is simply the cost of purchasing them from the market. The buying in price plus any transactions costs is therefore the cost of the resource concerned. If the firm does have sufficient resources for its purpose then the issue resolves down to what is the best alternative open to it. It is at this point that the economist's definition of opportunity cost and the financial definition converge. If the economic value of the resource is less than its realizable value then the cost of using the resource is the foregone opportunity to dispose of the resource. If, for example, when you have finished this book you decide to keep it on your bookshelves as a memento of your studies then the cost of so doing is the cash you could have received if you had sold it.

We then come to a rather nuanced judgement where (say) you are using this book on a course at your university or college. If you had nearly finished with it then its value to you would be greater than its realizable value so you clearly would not sell it but, given the fact the course is nearly over, if you happened to lose it you would probably not bother to replace it. In this case the opportunity cost of using the book is its remaining economic value to you which will lie somewhere between its realizable value and its replacement cost. If, on the other hand, the course had just started then its economic value to you would be greater than its replacement cost and if some catastrophe befell you and the dog ate it then the opportunity cost of its continued use would be its replacement cost.

EXHIBIT 5.1

Flow chart for estimating the opportunity cost of a resource

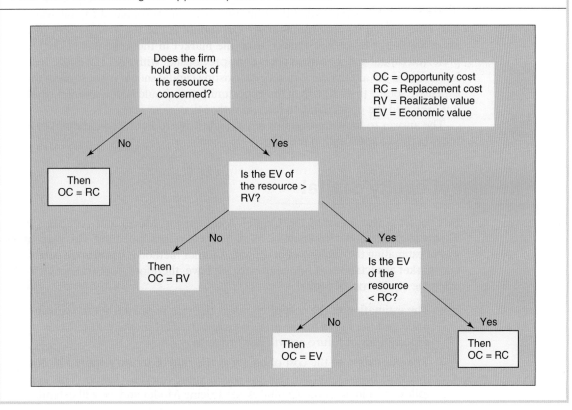

By direct analogy with the above we can establish the opportunity cost of capital for a company:

1 If the company does not have sufficient free capital for its purposes then the company will be required to pay the current market rate of return for new capital which will reflect the risk the market perceives attaching to the return it receives.

2 If the company does have sufficient funds and no alternative uses for those funds then the opportunity cost of capital is the potential saving in the return it has to pay to its investors if the capital is redeemed. So, if the company were to retain that capital for a new investment project then the opportunity cost is the saving in return that is foregone because the capital has not been returned to the investors.

3 If a company does have sufficient capital funds for other value generating uses then the opportunity cost of using those funds is the cost of 'replacing them', i.e. the market rate of return as in 1.

The outcome is that the opportunity cost of capital is under virtually all circumstances the current market rate that the firm either does pay, or would potentially have to pay to acquire new funds. However, as you now know from Chapters 3 and 4, the rate of return required by investors is directly related to the risk they expect to bear so in principle the cost of capital must compensate the investors for the risk of the firm's income flows assuming that the project the firm has in mind is in place.

This leads to another issue: the firm may obtain capital from a variety of sources. For the cases 1 and 3 above should the firm use the cheapest source of capital available to it in determining its opportunity cost? Or, should it use the average cost of capital assuming that it raises new finance from the market in the same mix of debt, equity, preferred capital and so forth as it has done previously? With case 2 an equivalent problem arises: if the alternative is to redeem existing capital should it not redeem the most expensive source first? If so then the opportunity cost should be the return it would save if it exercised the opportunity to redeem rather than reinvest.

The answer to these questions is not straightforward but we will attempt to answer them in this chapter and in the next.

The cost of equity capital

In Chapter 3 we discussed the Capital Asset Pricing Model and Arbitrage Pricing Theory as means of determining the market rate of return for equity. This presents one way of estimating the equity cost of capital. Another method is based upon current data and market expectations of future growth. We have, therefore, two strategies for measuring the equity cost of capital:

1 The estimation of the cost of equity as the rate implied from the current share price and the firm's future growth prospects. This model relies heavily upon expectations of future growth performance.

2 The estimation of the cost of equity as the rate of return required by equity investors based upon the risk and other 'value relevant' factors. This approach follows the logic of the Capital Asset Pricing Model and we will extend it to look at the adjustments that can be made for firm size and other effects.

As we will discover, neither approach gives a completely definitive answer. In much of corporate finance the estimation of firm specific variables such as the cost of capital or the value of the firm as a whole is a rather imprecise science. Partly this is a problem of forming reliable expectations of future performance on the basis of often unreliable evidence but also because the data has arisen at different points in time and under different conditions. It is also partly a problem that even though the models used may capture important aspects of business reality they also miss out much that while not important of itself can in the accumulation of effects degrade their validity. However, given that it is better to be approximately right than hopelessly wrong we will now begin the piecemeal assembly of a firm's cost of capital.

Estimating the cost of equity using a future model of growth

The growth model is one of the simplest and most elegant models in finance. The model relates the value of a firm's equity to the dividend stream that the firm's equity investors can expect from their investment. It is based upon the definition of return described in Chapter 1. Return for any given period of time is simply the sum of the capital gain and the dividend yield. Because of its importance in corporate finance and in valuation we will proceed with a description of how the growth model is derived and the assumptions which support it.

The one period return formula can be stated as:

$$r_1 = \frac{p_1 - p_0 + d_1}{p_0}$$

where p is the price currently (time 0) and one period in the future (time 1) and d_1 is any dividend paid in the first period. A modest amount of algebra leads to this:

$$r_1 p_0 = p_1 - p_0 + d_1$$

and hence

$$p_0 = \frac{d_1 + p_1}{(1 + r_1)}$$

Now let us make a simplifying assumption that the expected rate of return in the future will not change then defining 'r' as the expected annual rate of return in all time periods:

$$p_0 = \frac{d_1 + p_1}{(1 + r)}$$

Now let us skip ahead one year and using the same simplifying assumption about the required rate of return:

$$p_1 = \frac{d_2 + p_2}{(1 + r)}$$

This can then be substituted in the previous equation to deliver:

$$p_0 = \frac{d_1 + \dfrac{d_2 + p_2}{(1 + r)}}{(1 + r)} = \frac{d_1}{(1 + r)} + \frac{d_2 + p_2}{(1 + r)^2}$$

and again we can then skip forward a year and substitute for p_2 and then for p_3 and so on for as long as the firm can be deemed to exist which, under the going concern, assumption is indefinitely. The resultant formula is the dividend valuation model:

$$p_0 = \frac{d_1}{(1 + r)} + \frac{d_2}{(1 + r)^2} + \frac{d_3}{(1 + r)^3} + \frac{d_4}{(1 + r)^4} + \cdots \cdots \infty$$

Which says that: in the absence of the firm being wound up in the foreseeable future the value of the firm is simply the discounted value of all its future dividend payments to its equity investors under the assumption that the firm will continue to exist into perpetuity.

This model makes intuitive sense in that if a firm said to its investors 'thanks for your cash but we will never pay a dividend, nor return your cash' then we could predict their response. The obvious point is that the only value in a perpetual investment such as an equity share (or indeed a perpetual bond) is the dividends that will eventually be paid to the shareholder or the annual interest payments in the case of a bond. You may object that the investor could sell their share and realize the price at some future date. That is true but what does this model say the value of that future price will be? The price at that time would simply be the discounted value of all future dividends from that point forward *ad infinitum*. This point causes so much confusion that we will return to the implications of this model in the next chapter when we discuss dividend policy.

At this stage, the validity of the dividend valuation model depends on just two assumptions: the first is that the firm is a going concern and the second is that the equity rate of return remains constant. The problem in practically implementing this model is that it requires a prediction of all future dividend payments. This is where the difficulty with this model lies and so we are forced to invoke Ockham's Razor again and ask what is the simplest assumption we can make? The simplest assumption is that future dividends are likely to change at a fixed rate of growth (g) over the life of the company. It may be that the estimate of future dividend growth is zero or it may be a positive percentage, but whatever we choose it simplifies the model as next year's dividend is simply the dividend paid in the past year multiplied by one plus the chosen growth rate:

$$d_1 = d_0(1+g)$$

and the second year's dividend will be:

$$d_2 = d_1(1+g) = d_0(1+g)^2$$

Substituting for each future dividend in the growth model we get:

$$p_0 = \frac{d_0(1+g)}{(1+r)} + \frac{d_0(1+g)^2}{(1+r)^2} + \frac{d_0(1+g)^3}{(1+r)^3} + \frac{d_0(1+g)^4}{(1+r)^4} + \ldots \ldots \ldots \quad \text{(i)}$$

This can be simplified by multiplying throughout by $\frac{(1+r)}{(1+g)}$:

$$p_0 \frac{(1+r)}{(1+g)} = d_0 + \frac{d_0(1+g)^1}{(1+r)^1} + \frac{d_0(1+g)^2}{(1+r)^2} + \frac{d_0(1+g)^3}{(1+r)^3} + \frac{d_0(1+g)^4}{(1+r)^4} + \ldots \ldots \ldots \quad \text{(ii)}$$

Which by substituting (i) into (ii) gives:

$$p_0 \frac{(1+r)}{(1+g)} = d_0 + p_0$$

This formula can be rearranged to give a formula in terms of return, market value or implied growth in dividends.

$$r = \frac{d_0}{p_0}(1+g) + g \qquad \text{or} \qquad p_0 = \frac{d_0(1+g)}{(i-g)} \qquad \text{or} \qquad g = \frac{rp_0 - d_0}{p_0 + d_0}$$

We will be reviewing the importance of all three of these relationships throughout this book. For the moment we are interested in the first. What this model says is that the return required by equity investors is a function of the observed dividend yield (d_0/p_0) and dividend growth.

FINANCIAL REALITY	Friendly Grinders plc paid a dividend (interim plus final) of 20p per share in the last financial year. The price of its equity is 420p per share. Dividends have been growing at a geometric average rate of 5 per cent per annum over the last five years.

The equity rate of return suggested by the dividend growth model is:

$$r = \frac{d_0(1+g)}{p_0} + g$$

$$r = \frac{20 \times (1.05)}{420} + .05$$

$$r = 0.1 \equiv 10 \; per \; cent$$

It is often suggested that this model does not account for risk. That is incorrect, because the price which the market puts on the equity shares will be a price that reflects the market's perception of the risk involved – the higher the price of the shares the lower the risk and vice versa. So if, for example the market perceived that the future dividend stream was riskier than before (although the base assumption of a constant rate of 5 per cent was still deemed to be valid) then we would expect the required rate of return to rise.

REVIEW ACTIVITY 5.1 The price of Friendly Grinders plc fell to 380p per share on uncertainties about the future price of industrial grade diamonds. Given that the latest dividend was 20p per share and the long term estimated growth rate is 5 per cent. What is the required rate of return implied by this data?

The weakness of the growth model is the assumption that dividend growth will be constant into the indefinite future. The estimation of the future growth of a company is a separate topic in its own right and will be considered at length in Chapter 10. However, it is worth noting at this stage that the projection of future growth from the most recently observed dividend data is fraught with difficulties especially for the smaller enterprise where there has been considerable recent investment or where the company is going through a period of exceptional growth. Indeed, many companies do not pay dividends for certain periods of time and this too can cause problems in the use of this model.

Estimating growth from past dividends

Cobham plc is a well established company in the aerospace/defence industries. It is technologically advanced and has performed well in what is a particularly competitive business. Its dividend payment history is shown in Exhibit 5.2.

The steps for calculating the average dividend growth follow the procedure for the geometric average described in Chapter 1.

- *Step (i)*: calculate the percentage growth in dividend payment over the previous year as follows:

$$g_{2000} = \frac{d_{2000} - d_{1999}}{d_{1999}}$$

$$g_{2000} = \frac{20.20 - 17.55}{17.55} = 15.10 \; per \; cent$$

EXHIBIT 5.2

Cobham's dividend history for the six years to 31 December 2004

Cobham plc Dividends per ordinary share

	1999	2000	2001	2002	2003	2004
Dividend per ordinary share	17.55	20.20	23.23	25.60	28.16	31.00
(i) Percentage growth over previous year		15.10%	15.00%	10.20%	10.00%	10.09%
(ii) Compound factor		1.1510	1.1500	1.1020	1.1000	1.1009
(iii) Cumulative compound factor	1.0000	1.1510	1.3236	1.4587	1.6046	1.7664
(iv) Average annual growth rate (geometric)						0.1205

And repeat for each year subsequently.

- *Step (ii)*: Calculate the compound factor as one plus the annual growth rate.
- *Step (iii)*: Calculate the product of all the compound factors to give the compound growth over the five year period (=76.64 per cent).
- *Step (iv)*: Calculate the average compound growth as follows:

$$g = \sqrt[5]{(1 + g_{1999})(1 + g_{2000}) \cdots\cdots (1 + g_{2004})} - 1$$

$$g = \sqrt[5]{1.7664} - 1$$

$$g = 12.05 \; per \; cent$$

In general this approach can only be used if it is believed that the dividend history covered is typical and is expected to continue in the future. For reasons we will discuss later Cobham is very unlikely to be able to grow at this sort of compound growth rate indefinitely. However, even taking the figures as they are it may be reasonably objected that the dividend history shows that the company has reduced its annual growth in dividends from 15 per cent to 10 per cent and that the latter is the appropriate figure to take for at least the short term growth in dividends.

Estimating the cost of capital using the growth model

The dividend growth model was first presented by Myron Gordon in 1962. In his paper he suggested the following procedure for estimating the expected growth rate. The current dividends of the firm are related to its earnings (E_0) and its equity capital employed (C_0) as follows:

$$D_0 = E_0(1 - b)$$

and given that:

$$E_0 = rC_0$$

Then the following must also be true:

$$D_0 = rC_0(1 - b)$$

Where:
r is the rate of return on equity shareholder capital
b is the firm's retention ratio being the proportion of retained earnings to earnings.

The next year's dividend will be based upon the equity capital employed in year 0, plus the earnings retained from the year 0:

$$C_1 = C_0 + bE_0$$

The dividend paid will be related to this new capital employed as follows:

$$D_1 = r(C_0 + bE_0)(1 - b)$$

A little mathematics takes us to our conclusion:

$$D_1 = rC_0(1 - b) + rbE_0(1 - b)$$
$$D_1 = D_0 + rbD_0$$
$$D_1 = D_0(1 + rb)$$

The conclusion is that the value of next year's dividend is related to the current year's dividend by the rate of return on equity capital employed times the firm's current retention ratio. Therefore:

$$g = rb$$

REVIEW ACTIVITY 5.2 A company has earnings per share of 160p and a dividend cover of 3. What is its retention ratio?

If we now assume that the current rate of retention will be sustained indefinitely then the growth model can be rearranged in terms of the rate of return required by equity investors:

$$r = \frac{d_0}{P_0}(1+g) + g$$

$$r = \frac{d_0}{P_0}(1+rb) + rb$$

Which can be rearranged to:

$$r = \frac{YLD}{1 - b - bYLD}$$

Where *YLD* is the dividend yield being the dividend per share divided by the price per share.

FINANCIAL REALITY

The *Financial Times* shows the share price of Cobham plc as 1375 and its last quoted dividend is 31p. The *Financial Times* also gives a dividend cover of 3.1. Using this data calculate Cobham's current retention ratio, its yield and the required rate of return on equity.

Cobham's last quoted dividend was 31p per share which on a share price of 1375 gives a dividend yield of 2.254 per cent. The cover ratio (which is earnings per share divided by dividend per share) can be converted to a retention ratio as follows:

$$b = \frac{E_0 - D_0}{E_0}$$

$$b = 1 - \frac{D_0}{E_0} = 1 - \frac{1}{\text{cover}}$$

$$b = 1 - \frac{1}{3.1} = 0.6774$$

With a yield of 2.254 per cent the return on equity is given as follows:

$$r = \frac{YLD}{1 - b - bYLD}$$

$$r = \frac{0.02254}{1 - 0.6774 - 0.6774 \times 0.02254}$$

$$r = 7.33\%$$

Using the Capital Asset Pricing Model to estimate the cost of equity

In Chapter 3 we reviewed the basic components of the Capital Asset Pricing Model. From that chapter you may remember that the CAPM is an equilibrium model which says that in a market of risk/return efficient investors the required rate of return for all securities will lie on a straight line, and that the rate of return on any given security is determined by its exposure to market risk. The Capital Asset Pricing Model is:

$$E(r_i) = R_f + \beta_i[E(r_m) - R_f]$$

The original version of the model does have some deficiencies when tested against the evidence although there is a serious conceptual problem in translating a model of investor expectations into a form which can be tested using long series of past prices and dividends. The theory upon which the model is based assumes that investors form their expectations of risk and return over a single future holding period and thus all of the inputs to the model, the risk free rate, the equity risk premium and the beta, are spot estimates of values which are assumed to hold over that period. The empirical tests of the model cover a long run of past data which gives rise to problems of comparability between time periods, structural changes in the make up of firms and the endemic problem of choosing proxy variables that adequately reflect what the model specifies should be measured.

There is now a considerable body of evidence that the forward equity risk premium, that is the average return that can be expected in the future is somewhat smaller than has been assumed in the past. Dimson, Marsh and Staunton in the *Global Investment Returns Yearbook* (2004) report that the historical equity risk premium based upon 103 years of data is as shown in Exhibit 5.3.

EXHIBIT 5.3

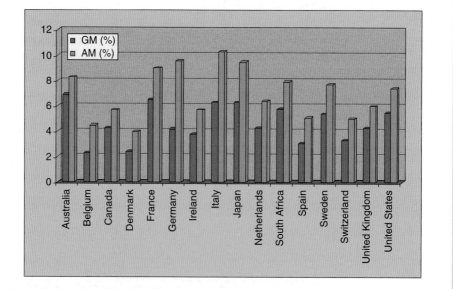

The worldwide equity risk premium (historical) relative to bills (1900–2003)

Source: Dimson, E., Marsh, P., and Staunton, M. (2004)

The data shown in Exhibit 5.3 is relative to the risk free return on short dated government bills which is used as the proxy for the risk free rate of return required by the model. Dimson, Marsh and Staunton argue that these rates are too high for a variety of reasons: first the last 50 years have been characterized by a period of general stability across the global equity markets as well as an increase in the scope of diversification. These factors are unlikely to be repeated and as a result, the forward looking risk premium for the world markets is of the order of 3 per cent (geometric) or 5 per cent (arithmetic).

FINANCIAL REALITY

The dividend yield on the FTSE All Share Index, which is the most broadly based proxy for the UK market as a whole, is 3.08 per cent.

EXHIBIT 5.4

Two key components in estimating the future growth of the economy – growth in Gross Domestic Product and inflationary expectations.

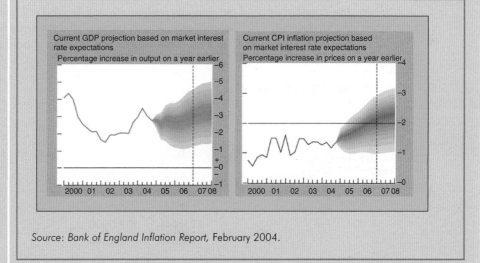

Source: Bank of England Inflation Report, February 2004.

The Bank of England quotes current GDP and inflationary expectations in the UK as 2.8 per cent and 2.0 per cent respectively (see Exhibit 5.4). (The Government's current inflation target is 2 per cent.) The GDP figures are in 'real terms' (more on this in Chapter 7) which means that the impact of inflation has been excluded). Adding the inflation component in (again see Chapter 7) gives a combined 'nominal' rate of 4.86 per cent. Using the dividend growth model expressed in terms of the required rate of return on the market gives the following:

$$r = \frac{d_0}{p_0}(1+g) + g$$
$$r = 0.0308 \times 1.0486 + 0.0486$$
$$r = 0.0809$$

Given that the current Treasury Bill rate is 4.75 per cent this implies that the equity risk premium is 3.3 per cent.

▶

> Throughout this book we will assume that the forward equity risk premium is 3.5 per cent (UK) and 4.1 per cent (US). This rate is consistent with that suggested by Dimson, Marsh and Staunton and also with the spot estimate provided by the dividend growth model.

Given that we now have a reliable estimate of the risk free rate of return and the equity risk premium the question now turns to the estimation of beta. In a publicly quoted firm where there is a reliable series of past share prices and dividends an equity beta can be estimated as described in Chapter 3.

REVIEW ACTIVITY 5.3

Download 61 months of price and index values for Cobham plc and the FTSE All Share Index from an on-line data provider such as http://uk.finance.yahoo.com/. Using this data generate a return series for Cobham plc versus the returns on the index. Then, using the LINEST function in Excel, estimate the slope coefficient, the standard error of the estimate and the R2 statistic. You will need to use the F2 function key and Ctrl-shift-enter to pull out the full data array when using the LINEST function. Our data table was as follows (you should get something like this):

EXHIBIT 5.5

Regression outputs for Cobham plc

	b	a
Coefficients	0.5690	0.0099
Standard errors	0.1613	0.0067
R2/SE(y)	0.1742	0.0520
F/n	12.4441	59.0000
	0.0337	0.1596

The first pair of values is the b and a coefficient respectively and thus our beta estimate was 0.5690. The standard errors of the b and a coefficients are shown on the next row. The R^2 statistic reveals how 'good' our beta value is and that is shown as 0.1742 on the third row alongside the standard error for the 'y' variable which is, in our case, the returns on the security concerned. The R^2 suggests that 17.42 per cent of the variation in the returns of the share can be explained by returns on the Index. The final two rows contain the F statistic (12.4441) and the number of degrees of freedom (the observation less one). This is useful when using the F test to determine the confidence level for the model. The other data is not of particular interest to us at this stage.

Now see if you can replicate this study in order to calculate Cobham's 'raw beta'.

For smaller companies we need to resort to finding suitable comparators and making adjustments for differences in financial structure where they occur. Even for larger companies there can be problems if the shares are not widely traded and there are also problems of bias in the data to be taken care of.

The practical problems inherent in estimating beta

We can classify beta estimation problems into the following categories:

1 Choosing an appropriate return interval and length of data series.
2 Eliminating bias from the raw beta estimate caused by 'thin trading' and 'mean reversion'.
3 Making adjustments for differences in financial structure.
4 Finding suitable comparators for company equity that is not traded.

Choosing an appropriate return interval and length of data series Most empirical work on beta assumes monthly return intervals. The evidence is somewhat mixed but monthly returns are usually regarded as the best compromise between daily or weekly measurements where statistical noise caused by non-trading may disturb the regression and quarterly or annual data where too few data points can be obtained to give meaningful results.

Most data services therefore use five years' of monthly data which gives 60 price observations and hence 59 return measures. The difficulty with extending the historical period over which the data is collected is that it increases the impact of changes within the firm itself which may have disturbed the firm's exposure to market-wide risk.

Eliminating beta bias For very small listed companies the market in their shares may be too thin to make reliable beta estimates. With such companies it may be that the shares are not traded on specific days and thus a zero return is not due to the underlying economic fundamentals but simply to the fact that the share price has been carried forward from day to day unchanged. One solution to the thin trading problem is to ignore those days where the share is not traded and use return intervals of differing periods in the regression. Details of this technique can be found in Dimson and Marsh (1983). An alternative approach as used by Ibbotson Associates, is to undertake a linear regression using both the returns on the index in the current period and the returns in the preceding period as a second (x) variable in the regression.

With large companies non-stationarity of beta can be just as significant. Dimson (1979) proposed a lead/lag approach. The idea behind this method is that the returns on the security concerned is a linear function of the returns observed on the 'market' in the periods before and after as well as in the current period. The multiple regression equation is as follows:

$$r_i = a_i + b_{-1}r_{I,-1} + b_0r_{I,0} + b_{+1}r_{I,+1} + e_i$$

This rather formidable equation says that the return on security (r_i) over a given period is a function of the intercept value (a_i), the return on the index for that period and the returns for the period before and after that. In a sense this model is 'smoothing' the explanatory variable over the three periods. The (b) values are the slope constants with respect to each of the index return variables to which they are attached. The e_i term is an error term which if the regression works properly in finding the line of best fit should have an average value of zero.

Different studies use different numbers of lagged market returns, some use one before and one after, and some do not regress against the returns on the index but the difference between the returns on the index in each period and the return on the risk free security. It might be thought that the more lagged variables that can be bought into the regression the better. Unfortunately this is not the case as the statistical efficiency of the regression in estimating the current beta diminishes rapidly the more terms that are introduced.

To derive the beta for the security concerned simply sum the (b) constants from the linear regression.

$$\beta_i = b_{-1} + b_0 + b_{+1}$$

Multiple regression is a straightforward technique to apply as shown in Exhibit 5.6.

There is evidence that the non-stationarity in beta tends to be mean reverting in that over time betas have a stochastic tendency towards the market average of one.

FINANCIAL CASE

We have downloaded the relevant data for the returns on Cobham's shares and the FTSE All Share Index for 62 months. The table just shows the first four rows of our data table but with one lead and one lag this number of months gives 60 return observations for the linear regression. The LINEST function in Excel does the rest for us giving three slope (b) variables. Our beta is then returned as:

$$\beta_i = 0.0619 + 0.6792 + 0.1629$$
$$\beta_i = 0.904$$

EXHIBIT 5.6

How to advance and lag a return series in Excel, and how to interpret the output from the regression analysis add-in

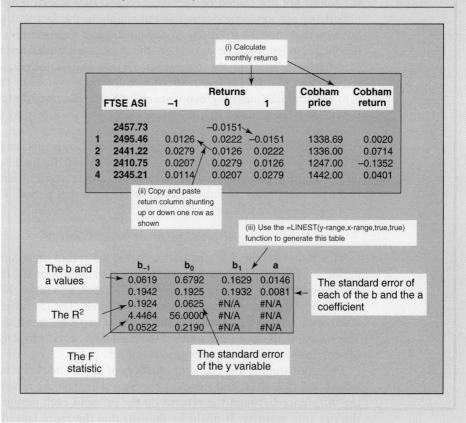

What this means is that a forward looking estimate of beta is always likely to be closer to the market average than the historical estimate of beta acquired from a statistical analysis using ordinary least squares regression. This would suggest that the raw beta calculated for Cobham of 0.5690 is more likely to be closer to one than not in subsequent periods.

There are a number of explanations for the mean regression phenomenon: first, 'shocks' impacting upon a company's share price will lead to an exceptional return measure disturbing the series. As time progresses the effects of such shocks will be lost from the data series and the resulting beta will return progressively towards its trend. Another explanation is that the growth of returns earned by firms tends to revert to zero over the longer run as they use up the readily available investment opportunities open to them. Furthermore they tend to become more diversified as they cast their net wider and wider as they search for positive Net Present Value projects. At the other extreme, where companies are over-diversified we might reasonably expect managers to attempt to focus their business back to what they perceive as their core activities. As a result, for these companies we would expect to see a gradual drift of their beta from a low value (<1) reflecting their over-diversification back to the average for the market. Thus managerial reversal of over- and under-diversification by their companies may be sufficient to explain the mean reversion tendency when we observe how betas behave in the market over time.

Marshall Blume (1971, 1975) developed a simple adjustment technique. Using over four hundred company betas he formed them into small portfolio clusters by beta magnitude (i.e. a portfolio at one extreme consisted of a sample of very high beta stocks and at the other extreme, a sample of low beta stocks). He then calculated the beta of each portfolio using a set historical run of share price data for the years 1948–1954 and a comparable set using data from the period 1955–1961. On the basis of a regression the later time period against the earlier period he was able to determine the degree of correction required to eliminate the mean reversion effect. By so doing he was able to explore the stability of the time series of betas which emerged as he rolled the measurement period forward. The betas of the portfolios which were closest to the mean value of one were significantly more stable than the betas of very high or very low beta portfolios. The variability of the betas of the more extreme portfolios suggested that these were subject to more measurement error and bias than the mainstream portfolios with betas closer to one. To correct out the error and bias of the extreme beta portfolios Blume suggested the following adjustment procedure where β_e and β_o are the adjusted beta and the observed beta respectively:

$$\beta_e = 0.371 + 0.635\beta_o$$

FINANCIAL REALITY

In Chapter 3 we estimated that the beta for British Airways was 2.03 suggesting that this company has a beta value which is over twice the market average. Using the mean reversion adjustment what would be the beta that would result?

Entering the data in to the simplified mean reversion formula serves to take the edge off the value we have derived for the 'raw beta':

$$\beta_e = 0.371 + 0.635\beta_o$$
$$\beta_e = 0.371 + 0.635 \times 2.03$$
$$\beta_e = 1.66$$

REVIEW ACTIVITY 5.4 Use the Blume correction to the beta discovered for Cobham plc using the data from the previous review activity. The figure we obtained was 0.732 – what figure do you obtain using up to date data?

The problem with this adjustment process is that it is takes a rather cavalier approach with the data and although this method is widely used by data providers such as Bloomberg and Value Line we would suggest that an adjustment scale is used which more closely reflects the empirical evidence. Betas that are widely different from one are likely to be most suspect from a bias point of view and demand a more vigorous correction. Those closest to one warrant a lighter degree of correction.

One approach uses a 'Bayesian' modelling technique developed by Vasicek (1973) where the 'prior expectation' that a beta will be at the market value of one is conditionally adjusted by the observed beta (if you knew nothing about a company and were asked to guess its beta the most likely value would be the mean value of one as all betas by definition will be distributed around this value). The advantage of this approach is that it applies the largest adjustment to those betas with the highest standard error and the least adjustment to those with the smallest.

The Vasicek formula is as follows:

$$\beta_i(adj) = \left[\frac{SE(group)^2}{SE(group)^2 + SE(security)^2} \right] \times \beta_i + \left[\frac{SE(security)^2}{SE(group)^2 + SE(security)^2} \right] \times \beta_{group}$$

The terms in brackets are weights which depend for their magnitude upon the standard error of the security concerned and of the group of companies used. Ibbotson Associates for example use a peer group of companies to estimate beta values using this technique. With a sufficiently large database it would be possible to use the standard error of the market as a whole. Clearly if the standard error of the security is high relative to its peer group then the beta of the peer group will be dominant in the model and the correction of the security's beta will be strong. However, if the standard error of the security is low then the model ensures that the impact of the Vasicek correction will also be low.

To illustrate the technique we show the beta of all 11 stocks listed by the *Financial Times* in the Aerospace and Defence industry grouping. We then follow this procedure.

1 Using the market capitalizations for each company calculate the weighted average beta for the peer group.

2 Using this group beta find the difference between each company beta and the average from 1.

3 Take the squared difference and calculate a weighted average of those differences (again using the market capitalizations of each security). This weighted average is the squared value of the standard error of the group.

If we use this data to revise the beta for Cobham plc, using the figures shown in the review activity 5.3 above, and in the data table shown in Exhibit 5.7 we get the result (note that in Exhibit 5.7 we have calculated the square of the standard error for the group):

$$\beta_i(adj) = \frac{0.1378}{0.1378 + 0.1613^2} \times 0.5690 + \frac{0.1613^2}{0.1378 + 0.1613^2} \times 1.1433$$

$$\beta_i(adj) = 0.6602$$

EXHIBIT 5.7

Estimating the standard error of beta for a group of securities

	raw beta	Mkt Cap	w	wxbeta	diff^2	wxdiff^2
Cobham	0.5690	1.5500	0.0705	0.0401	0.3298	0.0233
Rolls Royce	1.7783	4.4400	0.2020	0.3592	0.4033	0.0815
Smiths	0.8561	4.8900	0.2225	0.1904	0.0825	0.0183
BAe	1.1170	8.5900	0.3908	0.4365	0.0007	0.0003
Chemring	0.5459	0.1429	0.0065	0.0035	0.3568	0.0023
Hampson	1.2874	0.0607	0.0028	0.0036	0.0208	0.0001
Meggitt	1.1439	1.1300	0.0514	0.0588	0.0000	0.0000
UMECO	1.2760	0.1383	0.0063	0.0080	0.0176	0.0001
Ultra Elec	0.4452	0.4988	0.0227	0.0101	0.4872	0.0111
VT	1.3388	0.5410	0.0246	0.0329	0.0383	0.0009
			1.0000			
Total Market Cap.=		21.9817	β(group)=	1.1433	SE(Group)^2=	0.1378

We now have four beta values for Cobham plc: a raw beta of 0.5690, a Blume adjusted beta of 0.732, the Vasicek version of 0.6602 and the lead/lag corrected version of 0.904. In reality thin trading is unlikely to be a problem with a company like Cobham which has substantial trading volume every day. However, the raw beta is substantially different from the mean grouping which suggests that some correction for mean reversion would be appropriate. The low standard error of the beta estimate does not indicate that we need a significant correction and for this reason we might elect to choose the Vasicek beta. Whichever we choose it is worthwhile looking at the impact upon the return predicted by the Capital Asset Pricing Model of the various adjustments that have been made (see Exhibit 5.8).

The Capital Asset Pricing Model is given by:

$$E(r_i) = R_F + \beta_i(E(r_m) - R_F)$$

The weight of this evidence strongly suggests that Cobham's equity cost of capital, as predicted by the CAPM is approximately 7.1 per cent. It is worth noting that even accepting that the Capital Asset Pricing Model is valid that the error induced by the beta coefficient is likely to be less significant than the error induced through the

EXHIBIT 5.8

Beta and expected returns for Cobham plc using the Capital Asset Pricing Model (r_f = 4.75 per cent, ERP = 3.5 per cent)

	beta	Exp Return
Raw OLS	0.5690	6.74%
Blume	0.7323	7.31%
Vasicek	0.6602	7.06%
Dimson	0.9039	7.91%

Equity Risk Premium. We might also take reassurance that the growth model discussed in the last section gave a rate of return required by equity shareholders of 7.3 per cent. When two models, derived on the basis of quite different assumptions generate approximately the same answer we are entitled to 'triangulate' the result which is just a fancy way of say we might split the difference. We will therefore settle on a cost of equity capital of 7.2 per cent for Cobham plc.

REVIEW ACTIVITY 5.5   Review the arguments for using the various methods for correcting the bias in beta. Update the figures used in our analysis using the most recent data available.

Making adjustments for differences in financial structure Companies that have different levels of debt in their capital structure will expose their equity investors to different levels of financial risk. What this means in practice is that an investor in a highly geared firm will find that their returns are much more volatile than those of an investor in a lowly geared firm. The formal reasons for this are discussed in the next chapter but for the moment we can put it like this: the equity investor in the highly geared firm will find that the debt interest burden in the profit and loss account will magnify the effect of any downturn, or indeed increase in underlying profitability. It is a relatively straightforward matter to adjust beta for changes in the gearing of the firm. However, the methods for doing so will be dealt with in the next chapter after we have discussed the extent to which a firm's cost of capital will vary with changes in the firm's capital structure.

Estimating the beta for a non-traded company Where a company is not traded the problem of establishing its beta can be solved in one of two ways:

1 Where the company prepares or can prepare using its historical data, monthly or at least quarterly cash flow statements then it should be possible to calculate the free cash flow to equity before capital expenditure in each period. The free cash flow to equity is given by:

> FCFE = operating cash flow less interest paid (net of interest received), tax and any other 'above the line' cash expenditures

A regression of the monthly or quarterly free cash flow figures against the returns on a broadly based market index should also give an indication of the equity beta for the company concerned. The appendix gives an algorithm for deriving the cash flow statement for a company and calculating the free cash flow to equity.

2 By finding a suitable proxy company that is traded, or where the non-traded company is divisionalized and proxy companies can be found for the divisions then a composite beta can be estimated. However, before a proxy beta can be used the gearing effect should be eliminated to establish the underlying asset beta of the proxy company. That beta can then be translated, using the gearing of the non-traded company to obtain a proxy beta.

In choosing a proxy company these are the issues that should be borne in mind:

- Is the company in the same or a closely related line of business with a similar operating gearing (ratio of fixed to total operating costs)?
- Using the usual benchmarks of performance: operating profit margin, return on capital employed, fixed asset and labour turnover etc. are the two companies reasonably similar?

- Does the chosen company trade in similar geographic areas as the non-traded company?
- Is the company's equity actively traded?
- Are the two companies of similar size?

If using these five criteria the two companies are well matched then a reasonable degree of confidence can be placed on the proxy beta.

REVIEW ACTIVITY 5.6 Download the financial information for Rolls Royce plc and Cobham plc – to what extent are they alike?

The problems of using either of these methods is that the beta derived is unlikely to be as reliable as a beta which has been derived in the context of a company which is actively traded in a well organized equity market. However, in the absence of any other route to an estimated cost of equity capital this may be the best the company can achieve.

The Fama and French three factor model

A highly successful derivative of the Capital Asset Pricing Model is the three factor model first proposed by Eugene Fama and Kenneth French in 1993 and amplified in subsequent papers. The early Fama and French studies cast doubt upon the empirical validity of the CAPM. Indeed, in a paper published in 1992 they appeared to demonstrate that there may be no compensation for market risk as far as the returns of the individual firm was concerned. However, Fama and French, working on US data discovered that CAPM's explanatory power could be significantly improved by introducing two further factors apart from market risk. A number of studies had shown the importance of the so called 'size effect' in that compared with what the CAPM would predict, small firms carry a return premium compared with large firms. This tends to suggest that investors find small firms inherently more risky than larger firms and that this is not fully captured within the market risk premium. Further, the equity of smaller firms tends to be less actively traded on the stock markets than larger firms and will incur a (lack of) marketability premium.

The second factor which Fama and French identify as being important is the ratio of book value (the balance on the owners' equity account in the balance sheet) to market value (number of shares in issue times the market price per share). Clearly, as the market value drops towards book value the firm will be perceived to be more exposed to financial distress and this distress factor will lead investors to demand a return premium to compensate. Fama and French's three factor model is as follows:

$$E(r_i) - R_f = \beta_{i,m}[E(r_m) - R_f] + \beta_{i,s}[SMB] + \beta_{i,h}[HML]$$

Where:
$\beta_{i,m}$ is the firm's equity beta measured as described in Chapter 3 and above and $E(r_m) - R_f$ is the equity risk premium.
$\beta_{i,s}$ is the firm's factor loading for the size effect where $[SMB]$ is the difference in return between a portfolio of the smallest stocks in the economy and a portfolio of the largest stocks and,
$\beta_{i,h}$ is the factor loading for the distress effect where $[HML]$ is the difference in return between a portfolio of the highest book to market value stocks and a portfolio of the lowest book to market value stocks.

In order to calculate the additional *SMB* and *HML* premia, Fama and French sort all stocks in the New York Stock Exchange, the American Stock Exchange and the National Association of Dealers Automated Quotation System to produce six representative portfolios:

(i)	Small firms with a low book to market value	(iv)	Large firms with a low book to market value
(ii)	Small firms with an intermediate book to market value	(v)	Large firms with an intermediate book to market value
(iii)	Small firms with a high book to market value	(vi)	Large firms with a high book to market value

The *SMB* and *HML* premiums are calculated using monthly returns as follows:

$$SMB = \text{average return } [(iv)+(v)+(vi)] - \text{average return } [(i)+(ii)+(iii)]$$

$$HML = \text{average return } [(iii) + (vi)] - \text{average return } [(i) + (iv)]$$

Fama and French produce a monthly update of the premiums under each heading for the US market and using multiple regression the slope coefficients for each element of the return model can be found and hence a modified cost of equity capital found. Appendix A to this chapter shows the download of data for the years 1979 to

EXHIBIT 5.9

The three risk factors in Fama and French's three factor model

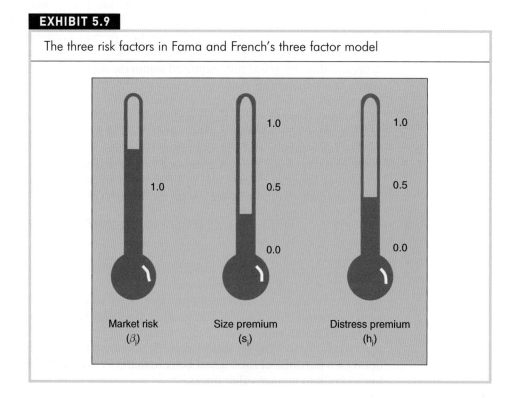

Market risk (β_i) Size premium (s_i) Distress premium (h_i)

EXHIBIT 5.10

Comparative US and UK data for the Fama and French three factors
(as at April 2005)

	ERP	SMB	HML
US mean return (%)	8.09	2.29	4.82
UK mean return (%)	7.84	1.33	3.04

2004 for the United States and Exhibit 5.10 shows the average annual equity risk premium, size premium and distress premium for both the UK and the US.

The early studies conducted by Fama and French using US data suggested that these two additional factors overcame most of the empirical deficiencies of the Capital Asset Pricing Model. They then went on to argue that their model incorporates elements of market risk which are not fully captured by the traditional methods of measuring beta. The fact that investors in small firms require higher returns than when they invest in large firms is not surprising and indeed numerous studies have demonstrated that the market demands an inverse size premium. However, studies that attempt to replicate their results, particularly using UK and Japanese data have not been as successful in explaining actual returns as the original Fama and French studies. However, the overall conclusion Fama and French would suggest is that the Capital Asset Pricing Model is not a reliable way of estimating the cost of equity capital and to use their own words:

'The version of the CAPM developed by Sharpe (1964) and Lintner (1965) has never been an empirical success . . . in the late 1970s, research began to uncover variables like size, various price ratios, and momentum, that add to the explanation of average returns provided by beta. . . . The CAPM . . . is nevertheless a theoretical tour de force . . . but . . . despite its seductive simplicity, the CAPM's empirical problems probably invalidate its assumptions' FAMA AND FRENCH (1992).

That would seem to be that then; the final judgement on the usefulness of the Capital Asset Pricing Model delivered by two eminent theoretical finance academics. However, where there are two against there are inevitably two for and in 2003 Kothari and Shanken produced a vigorous rebuttal of the conventional interpretation of the Fama and French results. The original data, they argued, can be interpreted as suggesting that there was no additional return to the investor in carrying market risk – and this was the interpretation which attracted wide attention. But, as Kothari and Shanken point out the Fama and French data also supports another conclusion:

'What has been neglected, however, is the simple observation that, given the Fama–French evidence, a substantial risk premium of 6 per cent per year (one standard error above the mean) is about as likely as no risk premium. KOTHARI AND SHANKEN (2003) 64.

They went further and discovered using the same time series data as Fama and French that when annual rather than monthly returns are used that the results are highly significant with market risk premium's emerging of between 6 and 12 per cent. The problem with using annual return intervals however is the length of the historical data series required to obtain a meaningful regression.

Estimating the cost of debt capital

In the last chapter we discussed the procedures for calculating the rate of return required by debt investors where a company's debt is in the form of a bond issue. For many large companies the problem is simply one of establishing the current market price of their bonds in issue and finding the rate of return which discounts the future payments on the bond (coupon plus principal) to that market value. With multiple bonds in issue a weighted average rate, by market capitalization may be necessary.

REVIEW ACTIVITY 5.7   A company has five bonds in issue

EXHIBIT 5.11

Bond data for a company whose debt is traded market value as at 31 December 2005

Nominal value (£m)	Coupon*	Redemption	Market value
145	5.0%	2008	£99.65
160	5.5%	2009	£100.86
240	7.0%	2012	£108.83
80	6.3%	2013	£104.85
110	7.0%	2015	£112.14
	* annually paid		

Calculate the required rate of return on each bond using the method shown in Chapter 4, then using the market capitalization of each bond calculate the average rate of return required by debt investors.

The more difficult situation arises when the firm's debt is not traded. Cobham plc is in this situation and we are forced to evaluate the rate of return the firm is expected to pay given its credit rating and the average term to maturity of its debt in issue. This requires a detailed analysis of the redemption terms of their debt outstanding which can, with some difficulty, be found from the accounts. In order to use the cost of debt capital in estimating the overall cost of capital for the firm we need to know, or be able to estimate the following:

1 The average term to maturity of the debt outstanding. Appendix B to this chapter has the relevant notes to Cobham plc's 2004 financial accounts.

2 Using any evidence available (either in the notes or using the interest payable on long term debt) work out the average coupon rate the company pays on its long term borrowings.

3 Given the average term to maturity of the debt outstanding find the nominal yield on an equivalent Treasury Bond of that duration. In this case, we have chosen a US Treasury bond because Cobham plc raises its debt capital in the United States rather than the United Kingdom.

4 The yield spread for a company of Cobham's default risk. Cobham does not have a credit rating and so we have to do the job ourselves looking at a range of ratios which measure the company's exposure to default risk and applying the Kaplan Urwitz model as described in Chapter 4.

5 On the basis of the yield assessed from 1 and 3 we then produce a cash flow to the 'hypothetical holder' of a £100 bond in Cobham plc and discounting by the yield estimate the market value of that bond (the market value equivalent). We calculate the value of an equivalent sterling bond in order to estimate a market value of the debt in issue that is comparable with the firm's equity which is issued and quoted in the UK market.

6 Using the market value equivalent calculate the total market value equivalent of the company's debt. This, with our estimate of the yield from 3 will be combined in the next section of this chapter to give the weighted average cost of capital.

The average term to maturity Few companies are absolutely explicit in their accounts as to the maturities of their debt in issue. Cobham in note 17 (see Appendix B) provides certain information on its borrowing as shown in Exhibit 5.12.

Note we have used the implied sterling dollar exchange rate for converting the senior notes of 1.8000 (i.e. $225/£125) and 1.6129 for the bank loans.

A little forensic accounting suggests that the senior notes referred to at the foot of the note for $55 million and $170 million respectively are the senior notes against borrowing shown at £125 million in the balance sheet. The £15.5 million of bank loan is the second set of senior notes repayable by instalments. We have made an assumption that the loans have been paid off equally and finally the loan notes repayable in two years are those shown as £10.3 million in the balance sheet. Our total is £150.81 million as we have ignored the small element of other borrowing and the finance leases worth 0.5 million in total.

Using the nominal values of each loan and the total we can obtain the weight (as a proportion) of each class of debt within the total. These of course will all add up to one. Multiplying each term by its weight we discover that overall the company's debt has 8.69 years to maturity.

The average interest rate paid (the equivalent coupon rate) Using the weights attaching to the nominal values we determine that this company is paying an average interest rate of 5.48 per cent on its borrowings.

EXHIBIT 5.12

Analysis of the average coupon rate for Cobham's outstanding debt using the weighted average method

Cobham plc Debt in Issue (2004)

Designation in notes to the accounts	Nominal value ($m)	Nominal value (£m)	Term to maturity	Interest rate	Weight	Weight × term	Weight × rate
Senior notes – totalling £125.0m {	55.00	30.6	7	5.14%	0.2026	1.4184	0.0104
	170.00	94.4	10	5.58%	0.6263	6.2629	0.0349
Bank loans – totalling £15.5m {	10.00	6.2	7	6.28%	0.0411	0.2878	0.0026
	15.00	9.3	10	6.42%	0.0617	0.6167	0.0040
Loan notes		10.3	2	4.25%	0.0683	0.1366	0.0029
		150.8			1.0000	8.7224	0.0548

Estimating the current yield Given that Cobham raises a large proportion of its finance in the US$ market it would be most appropriate to use the current US yield curve showing the rate of return required on US Treasury Bonds of differing durations. Exhibit 5.13 shows the current yield curve for US Treasury Bonds.

This yield curve suggests that the risk free rate of return (yield) on debt of the average term to maturity as that held by Cobham plc is 4.2 per cent. This provides a base line for estimating the rate of return required by the market on the company's debt.

The yield spread As discussed in Chapter 4 the yield spread is difficult to measure even when a company's debt is traded and it has a current bond rating. With a company such as Cobham plc we are required to assess the fundamentals of the business and form a view of its likely risk of default. A review of Cobham's accounts shows a relatively large company which has low levels of debt. The Kaplan Urwitz model suggests itself as a good candidate for estimating the firm's default risk and hence its bond rating.

Using the data as derived we can proceed to calculate the score for Cobham plc using the Kaplan Urwitz model as follows:

$$score(quote) = 5.67 + 0.0011F + 5.13\pi - 2.36S - 2.85L + 0.007C - 0.87\beta - 2.90\sigma_u$$
$$\begin{aligned} score(quote) = {} & 5.67 + 0.0011 \times 2038 + 5.13 \times 0.0736 - 2.36 \times 0 \\ & - 2.85 \times 0.1310 + 0.007 \times 12.54 - 0.87 \times 0.57 - 2.90 \times 0.0775 \end{aligned}$$
$$score(quote) = 7.28$$

EXHIBIT 5.13

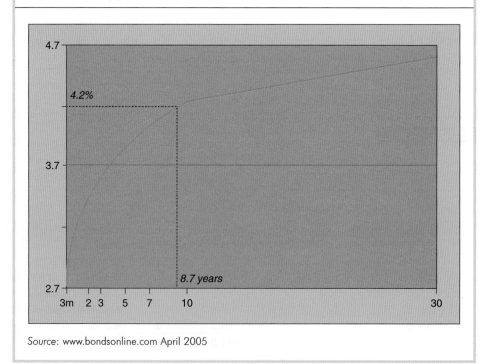

The US Treasury yield curve

Source: www.bondsonline.com April 2005

The following data was extracted from the accounts of Cobham plc for the financial year 2004:

Firm size (F) (total assets in $million) = £1154.60million = $2038.30million (at an exchange rate of $1.7654).

Profitability (π) (net income/total assets) = 7.36 per cent

Debt status (S) = 0 (for unsubordinated debt)

Gearing (L) (long term debt to total assets) = 13.10 per cent

Interest cover (C) (Cash flow before tax and interest/interest payable) = 12.54

Systematic risk (β) (raw equity beta) = 0.57

Unsystematic risk (σ_U) – standard deviation of error term from the market model = 0.0775

The value for the unsystematic risk was estimated using Cobham's alpha and beta values shown in Exhibit 5.5. Using the monthly return data for Cobham the residual return in each month (observed return for Cobham less the return predicted using the regression model) was calculated and the standard deviation produced.

At this level the model would predict that the company is AAA. On the basis of this and interpolating between the 7 and 10 year spreads (see Exhibit 5.14 below), an average term to maturity of 8.7 years suggests a 30 basis point adjustment to the Treasury yield to give a rate of return as follows:

Yield on corporate bond = yield on T-Bond of equivalent term + yield spread

$$= 4.2\% + 0.30\%$$

$$= 4.5 \text{ per cent}$$

Calculate the PV of a notional £100 bond to give the market value equivalent of debt (MV_d) Using the details derived so far we can now proceed to estimate the market value equivalent (MV_d) of the company's debt and hence its total market capitalization. To summarize, we have a bond with approximately 0.7 years

EXHIBIT 5.14

Reuters Corporate Spreads (shown as basis points) for Industrials

Rating	1 yr	2 yr	3 yr	5 yr	7 yr	10 yr	30 yr
Aaa/AAA	5	10	15	20	25	31	59
Aa1/AA+	10	15	20	30	35	40	65
Aa2/AA	15	25	30	35	44	50	70
Aa3/AA–	20	30	35	45	52	55	75
A1/A+	25	35	40	50	55	61	81
A2/A	35	44	55	60	65	69	86

Source: www.bondsonline.com April 2005

EXHIBIT 5.15

Estimating the market value equivalent for Cobham's outstanding debt

Year count	0	0.7	1.7	2.7	3.7	4.7	5.7	6.7	7.7	8.7
Cash flow to investor		5.48	5.48	5.48	5.48	5.48	5.48	5.48	5.48	105.48
Discount to year 0.7 using 4.5 per cent		5.48	6.24	5.02	4.80	4.60	4.40	4.21	4.03	74.17
Value at year 0.7		111.94								
MV_d = PV (discount by 0.7 years)	108.55									

until its first payment of 5.48 per cent and then eight annual payments until the bond is repaid in full. If we try to make the valuation as accurate as possible (so that any inaccuracies are isolated within the data rather than within the model) we can discount the nine future cash flow payments starting with the first arising in 0.7 years to give a (MV_d) at the point the investor receives that interest payment. We can then discount the (MV_d) at that point to a present value by:

$$MV_d = \frac{MV_{d,\,(t=0.7)}}{(1.045)^{0.7}}$$

$$MV_d = \frac{111.94}{(1.045)^{0.7}}$$

$$MV_d = 108.55$$

The total market capitalization of the company's debt is given by:

$$TMV_d = \frac{BV_{debt}}{100} \times MV_d$$

$$TMV_d = \frac{£150.8m}{100} \times 108.55$$

$$TMV_d = £163.68\ million$$

We now have the inputs necessary to calculate the average cost of capital for Cobham plc given that it is financed by both debt and equity.

The weighted average cost of capital

Where a firm is financed entirely through equity then the models discussed in the previous section will generate a rate of return which reflects the equity shareholders' exposure to risk or, in the case of the dividend growth model, risk and the possibility of a growing income stream. However, where a firm is financed partly through debt, its cost of capital will be the average rate it needs to generate from its internal investment to satisfy its different classes of investor. In order to decide the proportion of its capital which must be rewarded at its equity rate, and the proportion at its debt rate the company must use market values to estimate its capitalization under each heading. Using book values will create a balance between the two rates which may have been correct when the capital was originally issued but will not be correct currently.

The weighted average cost of capital (or WACC) calculation relies upon the following inputs.

The effective rate of return the firm must pay to each class of investor (r_n). The proportion of the total market capitalization of the firm held by each class of investor (w_n).

The general formula is as follows:

$$WACC = w_1 r_1 + w_2 r_2 + w_3 r_3 + \cdots + w_n r_n$$

given that:

$$w_1 + w_2 + w_3 + \cdots \cdots w_n = 1$$

Taking the simple case first where a firm is financed solely by ordinary share capital and a single source of debt then the weighted average cost of capital formula reduces to:

$$WACC = w_e r_e + w_d r_d$$

given that:

$$w_e + w_d = 1$$

Simplifying:

$$WACC = (1 - w_d)r_e + w_d r_d$$
$$WACC = r_e - w_d (r_e - r_d)$$

Thus, the debt/equity version of the weighted average cost of capital states that the required rate of return required on internal reinvestment is the return required by the firm's equity investors less the firm's equity premium weighted by its market gearing ratio.

FINANCIAL CASE

Friendly Grinders (2005) plc has two types of capital: debt where there are loans outstanding with an estimated market value of £48million and equity where there are 40 million 25p shares in issue with a market value of 210p each. The equity beta for the company is 1.27 and the average rate of corporation tax on its profits is 30 per cent. The current risk free rate is 4.75 per cent and the current equity risk premium is 3.5 per cent. The cost of debt capital has been worked out using the average duration of its outstanding debt and is currently 5.91 per cent.

Friendly Grinders' gearing ratio is as follows:

$$w_d = \frac{TMV_d}{TMV_e + TMV_d}$$

$$w_d = \frac{48}{84 + 48}$$

$$w_d = 0.364$$

Its cost of equity is given by the Capital Asset Pricing Model (you can probably do this in your head by now):

$$E(r_e) = R_f + \beta_i \left(E(r_m) - R_f\right)$$
$$E(r_e) = 0.0475 + 1.27 \times 0.035$$
$$E(r_e) = 0.09195 \equiv 9.195\%$$

Substituting for this, the cost of equity capital, and the cost of debt capital the weighted average cost of capital (before corporation tax) is:

$$WACC = (1 - w_d)r_e + w_d r_d$$
$$WACC = (1 - 0.364) \times 0.09195 + 0.364 \times 0.0591$$
$$WACC = 0.08 \equiv 8\%$$

The impact of corporation tax is straightforward to incorporate as the effective rate of return payable to the firm's debt investors will be reduced by the tax saving. Thus:

$$r_d = r_{d(gross)} \times (1 - T)$$
$$r_d = 0.0591 \times (1 - 0.30)$$
$$r_d = 0.0414 \equiv 4.14\%$$

Substituting this post tax rate of return on debt into the *WACC* formula produces a lower overall rate of return as follows:

$$WACC = (1 - 0.364) \times 0.09195 + 0.364 \times 0.0414$$
$$WACC = 0.07355 \equiv 7.355\%$$

The components of the weighted average cost of capital

At one level the question of how the weighted average cost of capital is made up is straightforward: it is the returns required on the individual securities weighted by their appropriate proportions in the capital of the firm. However, it is also possible to reconstruct the weighted average cost of capital in terms of the weighted risk premia on each type of capital available to the firm. Our work on the Capital Asset Pricing Model in Chapter 3 and on debt in Chapter 4 suggests that the rate of return on any security is the sum of two components, the risk free rate of return (Rf) and a risk premium. In the case of the Capital Asset Pricing Model the risk premium is of course the equity risk premium multiplied by the firm's beta value measuring its exposure to market wide risk. Given that the CAPM is derived in a single period context, and that the pure risk free rate should exclude uncertainty attaching to future inflation, the risk free rate is most closely approximated by the rate of return on a very short dated Treasury Bill (the T-Bill rate).

As far as debt is concerned the rate of return required is the risk free rate plus a premium for the firm's default risk which will be given by the firm's bond or credit spread over the risk free Treasury Bond rate. Assuming a flat term structure of interest rates (this is as you will remember from Chapter 4 is a simplification) then the required return on debt will be related to the credit spread (δ_d) on the firm's debt as follows:

$$r_d = R_f + \delta_d$$

Substituting this and the formula for the Capital Asset Pricing Model in the *WACC* gives the following intuitively obvious result:

$$WACC = R_f + (1 - w_d)[\beta_i \, ERP] + w_d \delta_d$$

What this version of the model reveals is that the weighted average cost of capital is the weighted average of the individual risk premia attaching to each class of capital held by the firm.

Indeed, we can check that this formula is correct using the data in the previous example:

$$WACC = 0.0475 + (1 - 0.364) \times [1.27 \times 0.035] + 0.364 \times (0.0591 - 0.0475)$$
$$WACC = 0.08 \ (8\%)$$

This approach to defining the model reveals that the cost of capital consists of a risk free rate (which will vary as interest rates move up and down in the firm's economy) and a series of risk premia which are weighted proportionately according the mix of capital which the firm can call upon.

The limitations of the weighted average cost of capital

The most serious limitation in the use of the weighted average cost of capital is when the firm necessarily undertakes an investment which:

1 Alters the magnitude of any of the risk premia to which the firm is exposed. An acquisition of another company may alter (a) the firm's exposure to market risk as measured by its beta value and (b) its exposure to default risk. As a result the weighted average cost of capital will need to be adjusted.

2 Where it proves impossible to finance the project without seeking capital market funds in a different gearing ratio to that currently held.

We need to make two simple computations in order to work out the weighted average cost of capital for Cobham plc: its market gearing ratio and its effective cost of debt capital given a tax rate of 30 per cent.

EXHIBIT 5.16

Weighted average cost of capital formula

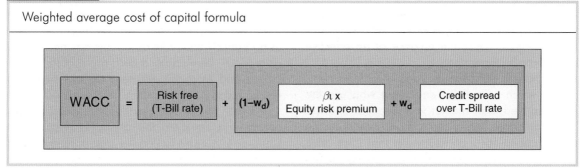

FINANCIAL CASE

Cobham plc has a cost of debt capital of 4.5 per cent and an estimated total market value of debt in issue of £163.68million. Its equity shares are currently quoted at 1375p per share and there are 111 606 905 shares in issue giving a total equity market capitalization of £1534.60million. The marginal rate of corporation tax for Cobham plc is 30 per cent. The equity cost of capital is determined at 7.2 per cent.

The market gearing ratio for Cobham plc is as follows:

$$w_d = \frac{TMV_d}{TMV_e + TMV_d}$$

$$w_d = \frac{163.68}{1534.6 + 163.68}$$

$$w_d = 0.0964$$

Cobham's effective cost of debt capital is:

$$r_d = r_{d(gross)} \times (1 - T)$$
$$r_d = 0.045 \times (1 - 0.30)$$
$$r_d = 0.0315 \equiv 3.15\%$$

Using the weighted average cost of capital formula we can now combine the required rates of return in the correct gearing ratio to give:

$$WACC = (1 - w_d)r_e + w_d r_d$$
$$WACC = (1 - 0.0964) \times 0.072 + 0.0964 \times 0.0315$$
$$WACC = 0.0681 \equiv 6.81\%$$

SUMMARY

So there we have it! After extensive analysis Cobham plc has a weighted average cost of capital of 6.81 per cent. This value is the average rate it must deliver on new investment to keep the 90 per cent of its capital investors who hold equity happy at a rate of 7.2 per cent and its debt investors, being the balance at an effective net rate of 3.15 per cent.

Cobham is typical of the large swathe of companies which have listed equity but who use the intermediated loan market to raise debt finance. This chapter has demonstrated how to estimate the cost of capital for a company like that – we have worked hard at deriving the cost of equity capital using two broad strategies: first using current market values and expected future growth rates, and, second, by using models that explicitly price risk. The Capital Asset Pricing Model is still widely used but we do so with caution. Company beta values are not stable and they have a tendency to revert over the longer run back to their mean value of one. We have shown how this can be corrected for using publicly available data. This has been a key issue for us: being able to perform all of the calculations and estimates we need without access to research databases or other 'data warehouses'.

We then turned our attention to the cost of debt capital and deployed the principles discussed in Chapter 4 in order to find the appropriate rate for Cobham. Once we had that number we then moved on to produce the average rate for the firm. However, some caveats are in order: the weighted average cost of capital assumes that the current level of gearing holds and the company maintains its current level of risk. If either of these change as the result of a new investment then the weighted average cost of capital must be modified to reflect the new financing situation the company would then face. We will return to this issue in Chapter 7 when we consider further extensions of the net present value model in investment appraisal.

However, another danger lurks within the analysis: would it make sense for Cobham to capitalize on its apparently low cost of debt capital by gearing up? Could it not issue new loan notes at an effective rate of 3.15 per cent, buy back and cancel a corresponding portion of its equity shares and at a stroke cut its cost of capital? These and other issues we turn to in the next chapter.

Further Reading

Blume, M. (1971) On the Assessment of Risk, *Journal of Finance*, 26:1–10.

Blume, M. (1975) Betas and the Regression Tendencies, *Journal of Finance*, 30:785–795.

Dimson, E. (1979) Risk Measurement when shares are subject to infrequent trading, *Journal of Financial Economics*, 7: 197–206.

Dimson, E., and Marsh, P. (1983) The Stability of UK risk measures and the problem of thin trading, *Journal of Finance*, 38: 753–783.

Dimson, E., Marsh, P. and Staunton, M. (2004) *Global Investments Year Book 2004*, London Business School and ABN-AMRO.

Fama, E. and French, K.R. (1992) The Cross Section of Expected Returns, *Journal of Finance* 47: 427–465.

Fama, E. and French, K.R. (2001) The Equity Premium, downloadable from: http://papers.ssrn.com/paper.taf?abstract_id = 236590.

Fama, E. and French, K.R. (2004) The Capital Asset Pricing Model: Theory and Evidence CRSP Working Paper No. 550; Tuck Business School Working Paper No. 03–26.

Gordon, M. (1962) *The Investment, Financing and Valuation of Corporations*, Homewood Illinois: Irwin.

Ibbotson Associates (2005) *Stocks, Bonds, Bills and Inflation, 2005 Year Book – valuation edition*, Chicago: Ibbotson Associates.

Kothari, S.P. and Shanken, J. (2003) In Defense of Beta, published in Stern, J.M. and Chew, D.H. (eds) *The Revolution in Corporate Finance*, (4th Ed.), Oxford: Blackwell.

Vasicek, O.A. (1973) A note on using cross sectional information in Bayesian Estimation of betas, *Journal of Finance*, 28:1233–1239.

PROGRESS CHECK

1 How would you define the opportunity cost of capital?

2 What are the two principal approaches to the estimation of the cost of equity capital?

3 How did Myron Gordon suggest that growth could be estimated?

4 Give a definition of the rate of return on equity in terms of dividend yield and the reinvestment rate.

5 List the three inputs to the Capital Asset Pricing Model.

6 What does the R^2 statistic tell us about a beta estimate?

7 List four practical problems associated with the estimation of beta.

8 What does the term 'mean reversion' mean in the context of estimating beta?

9 How are the betas of a company and of its peer group weighted in the Vasicek formula?

10 In choosing a proxy company for the estimation of beta for a non-traded firm what factors are relevant to the decision?

11 What other two factors drive the return on equity apart from the equity risk premium in the Fama and French model?

12 Outline the steps involved in estimating the cost of debt capital for a company whose debt is not traded.

13 Write out the formula for the weighted average cost of capital not taking account the effect of tax and taking account of tax.

QUESTIONS (answers at end of book)

1 If the rate of return on a one month T-Bill is 4.75 per cent what is the equity risk premium for the UK implied from the above data?

2 On the basis of the data below for BT Group plc:

		BT Group	FTSE ASI
Mar-05		202.25	2492.84
Dec-04		203.00	2410.75
06-Sep-04	5.30 pence Cash Dividend		
Sep-04		180.17	2271.67
Jun-04		198.50	2228.70
Mar-04		177.00	2197.00
09-Feb-04	3.20 pence Cash Dividend		
Dec-03		188.00	2207.40
Sep-03		180.00	2027.70
Jun-03		203.47	1971.30
Mar-03		159.22	1735.70

The regression formula for a straight line are as follows:

$$\Sigma y = na + b\Sigma x$$

$$\Sigma xy = a\Sigma x + b\Sigma x^2$$

You are required to:

(i) Calculate the equity beta for BT Group plc using the quarterly prices and index values as shown (12 marks).

(ii) On the basis that the rate of return on a short dated government bill is 4.7 per cent per annum and the UK equity risk premium is 3.5 per cent per annum determine whether the shares in BT group are over- or under-valued (6 marks).

(iii) Describe the possible errors and biases in the estimate of beta that you have produced and how they might be mitigated (7 marks).

3 A company is attempting to evaluate its cost of capital. You are provided with the following information:

(i) The rate of return on a one month government bond is 4 per cent per annum.

(ii) The long term equity risk premium in the UK equity market is 3.5 per cent.

(iii) The correlation of a firm's returns with the FTSE All Share Index is 0.95. The standard deviation of its returns is 18 per cent and the standard deviation of market returns is 15 per cent.

(iv) The market price of a riskless government bond of the same type and average duration as the company's outstanding fixed interest loan stock is £90 per £100 nominal. The company's debt has a duration of four years before redemption at par. The company pays 7 per cent per annum on its loan stock and its credit rating suggests that it should carry a 1 per cent risk premium over and above an equivalent risk free government bond.

(v) Fixed interest is tax deductible at the corporation tax rate of 30 per cent per annum.

(vi) The firm's market gearing is 0.65.

You are required to:

(i) Calculate the firm's cost of equity capital, debt capital and weighted average cost of capital (15 marks).

(ii) Discuss the issues that the firm needs to consider before using the weighted average cost of capital in the appraisal of significant capital investment projects (10 marks).

QUESTIONS (answers on website)

4   What is the rate of return on the market implied by the following data for the FTSE All Share Index:

	£stg	Actual	Cover	P/E
	Mar-29	Yield		ratio
FTSE All Share	2467.63	3.08	2.08	15.61

5   The raw beta for Colotron (UK) plc is 2.04. The standard error of its beta estimate is 24 per cent and that of its peer group is 13.5 per cent. The beta of the peer group is 1.06. What is the adjusted beta for Colotron's beta using (a) the Blume and (b) the Vasicek correction?

6   A company's published accounts show that it has the following debt in issue:

Year of repayment	Coupon	Book value (£m)
2007	5.00%	4.4
2008	5.50%	5.0
2010	7.00%	10.2
2014	7.25%	8.0

It is 1 January 2005 and the scheduled repayment date is the 31 December. The yield curve as published by the Debt Management Office for the UK is as follows:

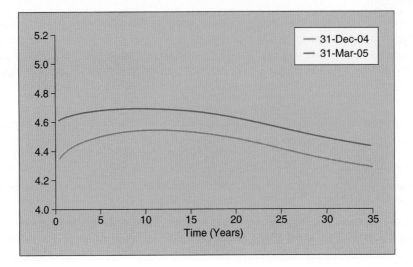

And the yield spread is 65 basis points for a company with this credit rating.

You are required to:

(i) Estimate the implied coupon rate on a £100 bond with the same average redemption period as that offered by this company.

(ii) Calculate the market value equivalent for this company's outstanding debt.

(iii) Calculate its cost of debt capital assuming that it pays corporation tax on its profits of 40 per cent.

7 APE (Training) Ltd provides a range of training programmes for large multinational companies in the computer, telecommunications and financial services industry. These training courses range from short intensive programmes updating software engineers in the latest systems programmes to 'sheep dip' courses in Excel, Word and other office products. The company also employs a team of in house experts developing new training materials for use by tutors and clients. Some tutors are on full time contracts, others are university professors or consultants who work for APE on a part time basis.

The company was established in 1989 by two brothers and since that time has developed a multi-million pound turnover business. The brothers own the majority of the equity capital and are considering either a flotation or a sale of the company outright. Ape currently has 10 million, 50p shares in issue. There are few competitors although Beaser (Training) plc does have a listing on the Alternative Investment Market. Ape has become more diversified than Beaser in recent years with a considerable portfolio of work in the financial services sector contributing one third of its total revenue. Beaser's beta as estimated by the Imperial Risk Management Service is 1.6, there are 50 million shares in issue with a market price of 670p. Other summary statistics for both companies for the year ended 31 December 2004 are as follows:

	Ape	**Beaser**
Net assets at book value (£million)	12	35
EPS (p)	95	40
DPS (p)	40	25
Gearing	5%	12%
Five year historic earnings growth	12%	8%

Analysts forecast revenue growth in computers and telecommunications to be 6 per cent per annum, but the financial services sector is expected to grow at just 4 per cent.

Background information:

The equity risk premium in the UK is 3.5 per cent and the rate of return on short dated government stock is 4.5 per cent.

Both companies can raise debt at 3 per cent above risk free.

Corporation tax is 40 per cent.

You are required to:

(i)   Calculate the equity and weighted average cost of capital for Ape (Training) and explain in which circumstances either rate would be used.

(ii) Advise the principal shareholders in APE (Training) of the likely range of issue price for the company.

(iii) Describe the limitations of the valuation procedure that you have used and the assumptions that you have made.

Download of coefficient data for the US (1979–2004) from http://mba.tuck.dartmouth.edu/pages/faculty/ken.french/data_library.html

	ERP	SMB	HML
1979	13.33	20.4	–2.22
1980	22.1	5.58	–24.57
1981	–18.05	7.3	24.57
1982	10.79	8.79	13.17
1983	14.4	13.94	18.86
1984	–4.76	–8.61	18.63
1985	24.63	–0.92	1.16
1986	10.40	–10.00	10.00
1987	–3.51	–10.39	–2.54
1988	11.55	6.72	13.78
1989	20.50	–12.01	–5.65
1990	–13.84	–14.40	–10.60
1991	29.10	16.50	–15.08
1992	6.41	7.78	23.05
1993	8.36	7.48	16.95
1994	–4.11	0.39	–0.08
1995	31.04	–6.94	–3.46
1996	16.25	–1.86	0.23
1997	26.07	–3.73	11.14
1998	19.42	–23.29	–15.04
1999	20.20	11.66	–39.41
2000	–16.71	–5.69	21.39
2001	–14.78	28.41	27.25
2002	–22.91	4.36	3.72
2003	30.74	28.08	15.14
2004	10.69	6.32	13.21

Notes from the accounts of Cobham plc, y.e. 2004 – Interest Rates and Loans

3 NET INTEREST

£m	2004		2003	
Group				
Interest receivable		4.3		3.4
Interest payable:				
Bank loans and overdrafts	(10.4)		(12.2)	
On finance leases	(1.6)		–	
Other borrowings	(0.8)		(0.5)	
		(12.8)		(12.7)
Net interest		(8.5)		(9.3)
Joint ventures				
Interest receivable		0.5		0.4
Interest payable		(2.5)		(2.6)
		(2.0)		(2.2)

17 CREDITORS: AMOUNTS FALLING DUE AFTER MORE THAN ONE YEAR

	GROUP		PARENT COMPANY	
£m	2004	2003	2004	2003
Borrowings				
Senior notes	125.0	139.7	125.0	139.7
Bank loans	15.5	28.2	–	–
Loan notes	10.3	0.2	–	–
Other borrowings	0.3	12.0	–	–
Finance leases[†]	0.2	0.1	–	–
	151.3	180.2	125.0	139.7

[†]Comprising obligations payable between one and two years.

	GROUP		PARENT COMPANY	
£m	2004	2003	2004	2003
Other creditors				
Other	10.3	11.0	–	–
Amounts owed to subsidiary undertakings (reclassified from investments in group undertakings)	–	–	3.4	–
Accruals and deferred income	0.3	0.7	–	–
	10.6	11.7	3.4	–

£m	GROUP		PARENT COMPANY	
	2004	2003	2004	2003
Borrowings				
Senior notes, debenture loans, bank loans, loan notes and other borrowings are repayable as follows:				
Between one and two years	9.4	19.9	2.6	5.6
Between two and five years	47.3	26.2	33.9	8.4
After five years	94.6	134.1	88.5	125.7
	151.3	180.2	125.0	139.7

Senior notes, repayable on maturity, were issued in October 2002. The facility comprises two series of notes. One for US$55m which has a bullet repayment after seven years and the other for US$170m which has a bullet repayment after ten years. The notes carry a fixed interest rate of 5.14% in respect of the seven year notes and a rate of 5.58% in respect of the ten year notes. These fixed rates have been swapped into rates that vary with LIBOR.

Senior notes, repayable by instalments, were issued in March 1996 and comprise two series of notes for US$25m, one with an average life of seven years and the other an average life of ten years. Repayments totalling US$25m have been made to date. The notes carry a fixed interest rate of 6.28% for the seven year notes and 6.42% for the ten year notes.

Loan notes, repayable in two years, carry a fixed interest rate of 4.25%.

Capital structure and distribution decisions

6

In this chapter we discuss two of the most important financial policy issues: the most appropriate capital structure for the firm and the factors that should influence the level of dividend payout. The early theories of capital structure are discussed focusing on the simple arbitrage arguments of Modigliani and Miller. The continuity of the M&M approach with the separation theorems discussed in Chapter 2 is also explored. The M&M propositions are examined under taxes and from a capital asset pricing perspective. Finally, the more managerial aspects of the capital structure problem are discussed. Turning to dividend policy we explore the theoretical and practical issues involved commencing with M&M's dividend irrelevance hypothesis before going on to consider the range of policy options open to the firm and the likely impact upon the market. The chapter concludes with a discussion of the use of share repurchase schemes.

Learning outcomes

In this chapter you will achieve the following:

1 An understanding of the arbitrage arguments used by Modigliani and Miller to justify their claim that the cost of capital does not change with gearing.

2 The ability to recalculate a firm's cost of equity capital and hence its weighted average cost of capital given a change in its gearing.

3 Be able to regear the firm's beta taking into account changes in financial risk.

4 To understand the managerial issues which influence the decision between different types of finance.

5 To be able to relate the distribution decision to the decision concerning the firm's optimal capital structure.

6 Be able to identify the type of dividend policy adopted by a firm and the likely circumstances favouring share repurchase rather than dividend payment as a means of distributing value back to investors.

Introduction

Two significant financial issues face every business:

- is there some optimal combination of different types of capital which will lead to a lowering of the firm's cost of capital, and
- is it possible to maximize the value of the firm by changing the firm's policy with respect to dividend policy?

The first is what we refer to as the capital structure decision and the second the distribution decision. Underpinning our initial analysis of these two issues are some necessary assumptions:

1 That the financial markets are perfectly competitive in that there are sufficient buyers and sellers of securities such that no individual has power over the price and there are zero transaction costs, taxes or other constraints on the free operation of the markets. This means that, technically there are zero barriers to entry and exit to the market.

2 That individuals and firms can borrow or lend in any amount at a risk free rate of interest free of transaction charges and costs.

3 That buyers and sellers are economically rational and fully informed in their search for personal value.

4 There are no regulatory restrictions on short sales.

5 Information is freely available to all actual and potential market traders.

6 There is no bankruptcy risk.

It follows from this risk free opportunities for financial gain cannot persist in competitive markets. This is the now familiar zero-arbitrage condition or which is sometimes encapsulated in the idea that there is 'no free lunch'.

To a certain extent these assumptions are always violated in real markets. However, our initial analysis starts from these limiting case conditions, and once we have the theoretical answer to the capital structure and distribution decisions we can then explore the extent to which divergence from ideality disturbs the theoretical position.

You may notice that we have not imposed a condition of 'certainty' about future outcomes on our analysis. Indeed, we have already considered the certainty condition when we explored the Fisher Hirshliefer Separation Theorem in Chapter 2. To review the outcome of that theorem for a moment:

- the value of an investment project is determined by the Net Present Value of its future (certain) cash flows when discounted at the market rate of interest, and
- the method of financing is irrelevant in determining the value of the project and hence the value of the firm.

It does not matter whether a firm finances a project out of dividends or retained earnings or out of borrowing or an equity issue. The value of the investment opportunity to the firm is independent of its mode of financing.

Two Nobel Prize winning academics, Franco Modigliani and Merton Miller in 1958 sought to extend the Fisher Hirshliefer Separation Theorem into a world where there is uncertainty (of a very limited form). In a series of important papers they established that under these restricted assumptions:

1 A firm cannot influence its cost of capital by altering its financial structure and thus there is no optimal gearing level for the firm.

2 That dividend policy is irrelevant in determining the value of the firm.

In order to understand the reasoning behind their results we need to review the meaning of the terms: business risk and financial risk.

Business and financial risk

Business risk is the variability in a firm's earnings caused by the uncertainties within its business environment. This can be from a variety of sources both within and outside the firm. This is the primary level of risk to which all investors are exposed although, as we shall see, different classes of investors can share in this risk to a greater or lesser degree.

When a firm alters its mix of finance to include debt investors who want a lower level of risk attaching to their income stream than those who hold equity the burden of the risk that they give up is transferred to the equity investors. The additional burden of risk taken by the equity investors is termed financial risk. To understand the point we can undertake a simple simulation of an earnings stream which has a specified level of variability and see what happens to the residual earnings in the hands of the equity investors as debt capital is introduced.

FINANCIAL REALITY

Friendly Grinders Ltd is considering how to finance their business. Jack Grinder decides to test out some business school theories for himself. He decides to set up two hypothetical companies (Mod Ltd and Mig Ltd) and assume that they are both in the same business and expect to earn £100 000 per annum with volatility in their annual earnings of 10 per cent per annum. Both companies, being subject to the same level of risk, will have exactly the same level of earnings. Mod, Jack assumes will be financed by 1 million equity shares, while Mig is financed by 500 000 equity shares and £500 000 of debt capital at a fixed rate of 5 per cent per annum. He is interested to discover what is the additional risk to Mig's shareholders because of the debt financing.

Using a spreadsheet program we can investigate the impact of the debt charge upon the variability of the net earnings received by the equity investors. Taking a ten-year time sequence and simulating the earnings of both companies using the following function:

$$= \text{NORMINV}(\text{RAND}(), \text{mean}, \text{stdev})$$
$$= \text{NORMINV}(\text{RAND}(), 100000, (10\% * 100\,000))$$

EXHIBIT 6.1

A simulation of earnings for two identical companies but where one is financed by both equity and debt and one is financed by equity alone

Mod Ltd	1	2	3	4	5	6	7	8	9	10	average	st dev	stdev(%)
Earnings (£)	92 115	94 139	100 806	114 920	99 443	90 816	102 088	122 096	98 482	110 710	102 561	10 265.57	10.01%
Earnings per share (p)	9.2115	9.4139	10.081	11.492	9.9443	9.0816	10.209	12.21	9.8482	11.071	10.256	1.027	10.01%

Mig Ltd	1	2	3	4	5	6	7	8	9	10	average	st dev	stdev(%)
Earnings (£)	92 115	94 139	100 806	114 920	99 443	90 816	102 088	122 096	98 482	110 710			
less interest	–25 000	–25 000	–25 000	–25 000	–25 000	–25 000	–25 000	–25 000	–25 000	–25 000			
Net earnings	67 115	69 139	75 806	89 920	74 443	65 816	77 088	97 096	73 482	85 710	77 561	10 265.57	13.24%
Earnings per share (p)	13.423	13.828	15.161	17.984	14.889	13.163	15.418	19.419	14.696	17.142	15.512	2.053	13.24%

Using this function we can create the first row of a spreadsheet showing varying earnings which in each accounting period are assumed to be the same for both companies (Exhibit 6.1).

Note that while the standard deviation of the earnings in the hands of the equity investors in Mod is 10.01 per cent from the simulation of ten years' data, the standard deviation of the earnings available for the shareholders in Mig is 13.24 per cent. The increase in the volatility of their earnings of 3.23 per cent which is exactly what we would expect. Using the two component risk formula, business risk is the combination of the risk attaching to equity and the risk attaching to debt weighted by the magnitude of the earnings going to the holders of each type of finance. If 'w' is the proportion of the earnings stream going to either (w_e) or to debt (w_d) then:

$$\sigma_{bus} = \sqrt{w_e^2\sigma_e^2 + w_d^2\sigma_d^2 + 2w_ew_e\rho_{ed}\sigma_e\sigma_d}$$

However, if the volatility of the return on debt is zero then this above equation simplifies to:

$$\sigma_{bus} = w_e\sigma_e$$

Therefore, using the results from the simulation:

$$10.01\% = \frac{77\,561}{102\,561} \times \sigma_e$$

$$\sigma_e = 13.24\%$$

The key question that Modigliani and Miller attempted to answer is do the equity investors adjust the rate of return they require exactly in line with the increase in their risk, or do they (at least up to a certain point) not appreciate or ignore the higher level of gearing and financial risk to which they are exposed? The traditional view of the gearing problem was that investors do indeed ignore increased gearing, or more accurately, the increased volatility in their earnings brought about by the increased level of debt finance in their capital structure. In Exhibit 6.2 we show the trade-off which the

EXHIBIT 6.2

The traditional perception of how cost of capital varies with gearing

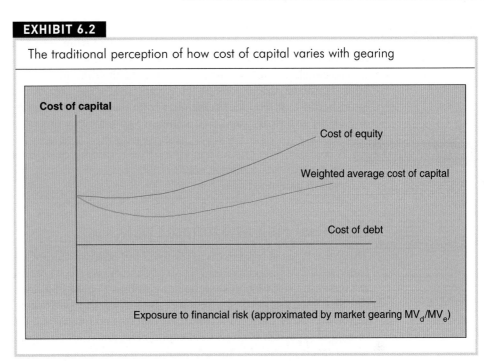

Cost of capital

Cost of equity

Weighted average cost of capital

Cost of debt

Exposure to financial risk (approximated by market gearing MV$_d$/MV$_e$)

traditional perspective proposed. The net effect of a fixed debt cost and a varying equity cost as shown is that the weighted average cost of capital will fall as the firm gains the advantage of cheap debt but without the penalty of a higher rate of return demanded by its equity investors. There comes a point when the financial risk exposure will be noticed and the equity investors will demand a higher rate of return to compensate and at that point the weighted average cost of capital will start to increase.

A note on gearing

The gearing ratio is the principal measure of a firm's capital structure and its exposure to financial risk. Because the returns demanded by investors are measured relative to their personal investment in a given company then their risk exposure is measured with respect to variations in their return based upon the market values of the securities they hold. In all capital structure discussions we therefore refer to 'market gearing' as opposed to 'book gearing' which is based upon accounting measures of outstanding debt and equity in the balance sheet. Market gearing, like book gearing comes in two forms and it is worth remembering which is which (because it causes much confusion) and that many of the assertions you read about how the cost of capital varies is strictly dependent upon the type of gearing being used. The two forms are as follows:

$$\text{Market gearing} = \frac{\text{Total market value of debt in issue}}{\text{Total market value of equity in issue}} = \frac{MV_d}{MV_e}$$

Or

$$\text{Market gearing} = \frac{\text{Total market value of debt in issue}}{\text{Total market value of equity plus debt}} = \frac{MV_d}{MV_e + MV_d}$$

In all practical discussions the latter is the preferable measure as it has a range of 0 to 100 per cent whereas the former has a range from zero to effectively infinity in the case of a firm which is entirely financed by debt.

The classic studies in capital structure use the first measure for reasons we outline later. However, discussions of the weighted average cost of capital tend to use the latter because (as you may remember from the previous chapter) the weights of debt and equity in a firm's capital structure are governed by this ratio.

REVIEW ACTIVITY 6.1 A company has one million equity shares trading at 310p each and £2m of debt which has a market value of £98 per cent. What is the company's market gearing ratio?

Financial risk and default risk

These two types of risk are often confused but reflect different aspects of the risk associated with taking on increased levels of debt. As we have noted above financial risk is the increased volatility of shareholder earnings as debt financing increases the 'above the line' interest payments required to service the borrowing. Default risk is the increased risk of failure if a firm finds that it is no longer in a position to pay interest or capital repayments on its debt capital. Default risk becomes more of a problem at higher levels gearing but the estimation of its magnitude is dependent upon a number of other factors including:

- A firm's level of earnings and the magnitude of its cover ratio (earnings before interest and tax to interest payable).
- The volatility of the firm's earnings (this is the point where default risk intersects with financial risk) in that firms with highly volatile earnings have a higher probability of generating a negative earnings figure in any one year than a firm with the same level of expected earnings but lower volatility.
- The level of operating risk as defined by its ratio of fixed costs (other operating costs to cost of sales).
- The firm's current liquidity and its ability to meet its maturing obligations (operating cash flow to short term liabilities).
- The level of its readily liquidated reserves.
- Its ability to reschedule its maturing debt obligations.

As we will discuss in Chapter 13, there are a number of strategies a company can follow to minimize its exposure to interest rate risk. But this is just one part of a firm's debt management policy.

The Modigliani and Miller analysis of the capital structure problem

Modigliani and Miller's solution to the capital structure problem entails an arbitrage argument which is both simple and elegant.

To develop their argument Modigliani and Miller invoked a model firm which has expected earnings, before financing costs of $£\bar{X}$ per annum. The value of this firm would be these expected earnings (which are assumed to be receivable in perpetuity) capitalized using a risk adjusted rate of return. If that firm is financed purely through equity then:

$$V = \frac{\bar{X}}{r_e}$$

Thus if a firm has expected earnings of £100 000 and its investors require a rate of return of 8 per cent then the value of the firm is simply:

$$V = \frac{100\ 000}{0.08} = £1.25\,million$$

This model shows quite clearly the inverse relationship between the firm's cost of capital (the required rate of return) and firm value. Cut the cost of capital and the value of the firm is increased and vice versa.

In order to bring risk into their analysis, Modigliani and Miller argued that firms could be categorized into identical business risk classes and as a result the only variable that should influence the value of the firm is the magnitude of the expected earnings. For firms of identical business risk the quality of the earnings stream is the same and therefore the 'law of one price' should apply. If two such firms have identical expected earnings they should have an identical value irrespective of the way they are financed.

Modigliani and Miller's three propositions

Building upon their arbitrage argument Modigliani and Miller arrived at three propositions.

Proposition 1

With Proposition 1, Modigliani and Miller demonstrated that if the equity in the two companies are relatively mispriced, then an investor in the overpriced company will sell his or her holding, adjust their personal gearing by borrowing or lending at the market rate of interest, and buy into the other company realizing an arbitrage profit. Because of this, M&M argue that this arbitrage will drive the two market prices of equity to a relative equilibrium such that:

'the average cost of capital to any firm is completely independent of its capital structure and is equal to the capitalisation rate of the pure equity stream of its class.'

Putting this mathematically Modigliani and Millers proposition I can be stated as:

$$\frac{\overline{X}}{(D+E)} = \frac{\overline{X}}{V} = r'_e$$

where $\overline{X}$ is the expected value of the income stream to the firm, E is the market value of its equity, D is the market value of its debt, V is the total market value of equity plus debt and r'_e is the cost of equity capital in a pure equity firm.

Jack Grinder is thinking about Friendly Grinders' capital structure again and in his efforts to understand the principles is looking at Mod and Mig again. Mig earns £100 000 per annum from trading. The business is financed by a £500 000 loan at 5 per cent per annum and by 500 000 equity shares. Mod, has identical net earnings of £100 000 but is financed purely by 1 000 000 equity shares. Jack assumes that the risk of the two companies is identical and that the equity cost of capital in Mod is 8 per cent.

EXHIBIT 6.3

Comparison of the weighted average cost of capital of two firms with identical capital structure but with different levels of gearing

	Mod	Mig
Earnings	100 000	100 000
Interest		25 000
Distributable profit	100 000	75 000
Rate of return on equity	0.08	0.1
Market value of equity	1 250 000	750 000
Market value of debt		500 000
Market value per share	1.25	1.5
WACC	0.08	0.08

On the basis of that Jack can estimate the value of the shares in Mod simply by capitalizing the earnings of £100 000 per annum at the rate of 8 per cent:

$$V_{mod} = \frac{100\,000}{0.08} = £1.25\ million$$

Now if Modigliani and Miller's proposition 1 is correct then the market value of Mig should be £1.25 million but with £750 000 being the equity value and £500 000 being the debt value. If the equity is valued in Mig at £750 000 this means that the rate of return on equity in that company is:

$$r_{e,Mig} = \frac{distributable\ profit}{market\ value\ of\ equity}$$

$$r_{e,Mig} = \frac{75\,000}{750\,000} = 10\%$$

Jack now checks the weighted average cost of capital of Mig and discovers that it equals the equity rate of return in Mod:

$$WACC_{mig} = \frac{MV_d}{MV_d + MV_e}r_d + \frac{MV_e}{MV_d + MV_e}r_e$$

$$WACC_{mig} = \frac{500\,000}{1\,750\,000} \times 5\% + \frac{750\,000}{1\,750\,000} \times 10\%$$

$$WACC_{mig} = 8\%$$

What Jack is interested to discover is: what would happen if Mig's equity was valued at (say) £1.60 per share instead of £1.50 per share? How would the investors react?

Presumably what the rational investor would do is to see whether, by creating a replicating investment in Mod and through personal borrowing, they could earn a profit. Let us assume that an investor has a stake of 10 000 shares in Mig valued at £1.60 per share.

$$\text{Sale proceeds of shares in Mig} = £16\,000$$

Given that the gearing ratio in Mig was (assuming a £1.60 share price):

$$Gearing(Mig) = \frac{MV_d}{MV_e + MV_d}$$

$$Gearing(Mig) = \frac{500\,000}{1.6 \times 500\,000 + 500\,000}$$

$$Gearing(Mig) = 0.3846$$

Our investor would take the proceeds of the sale (£16 000) and borrow a further £10 000 in order to maintain the same exposure to financial risk of 38.46 per cent. To calculate the amount of borrowing required we use the gearing formula:

$$Gearing = \frac{MV_d}{MV_e + MV_d} = 0.3846$$

Therefore:

$$MV_d = 0.3846 \times 16\,000 + 0.3846 MV_d$$

$$MV_d - 0.3846 MV_d = 0.3846 \times 16\,000$$

$$MV_d = 10\,000$$

This gives a total sum to invest in Mod of £26 000. At 8 per cent this will yield £2080 which after deducting the cost of servicing the investor's borrowing of £10 000 at 5 per cent gives a net yield of £1580. If the investor had left their money in Mig Ltd their return would have been £1500 being a 2 per cent stake in the earnings of that firm. The gain of £80 is an arbitrage gain because the investor, by selling Mig at £1.6 per share and buying Mod at £1.25 per share will make an increase in their annual return without altering their exposure to financial risk.

What will be the consequence of this mispricing? According to Modigliani and Miller, investors will sell their equity in the higher priced firm and after readjusting their personal exposure to financial risk by either borrowing or lending at the market rate they will then buy into the relatively low priced firm. The value of the equity in the relatively high priced firm will fall and its return on equity will rise and the equity value of the low price firm will rise and its return fall until both prices and returns are at equilibrium. Of course all of this depends on the investors being able to trade free of transaction costs and taxes and be able to borrow or lend any amount at the same risk free rate as either company.

It is worth reflecting for a moment on what the consequence would be if the company could offset its borrowing for tax purposes but where investors could not get tax relief on the interest payments on their personal borrowing. In this case, the gain through arbitrage would not be at the point where the total market values of the two firms are equal. This is an issue we will return to later.

Proposition 2

Modigliani and Miller's second proposition states that the expected return on a share (r_e) is equal to the rate of return which would be generated by a pure equity company of the same risk class (r_e') with the addition of a financial risk premium equal to the debt to equity ratio times the difference between the pure equity return and the market rate of interest (r_d). Using an equation:

$$r_e = r_e' + (r_e' - r_d)\frac{MV_d}{MV_e}$$

Note here the version of the gearing ratio used by Modligliani and Miller which is the simple ratio of debt to equity. In the example of Mod and Mig the distributable profit of Mig falls to £75 000 compared with Mod because of the impact of interest payments of 5 per cent on the debt of £500 000. Following proposition 1, the value of Mig's equity must be £750 000 which gives a rate of return on equity of

EXHIBIT 6.4

The relationship between return and the gearing ratio (MV_d/MV_e)

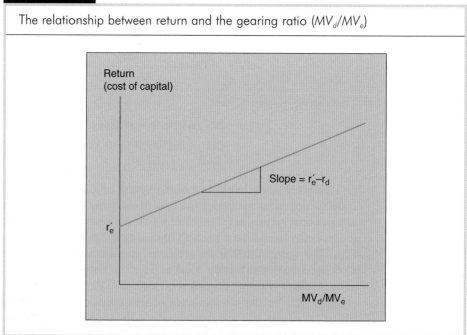

10 per cent compared with 8 per cent in the ungeared firm. The Modigliani and Miller proposition 2 delivers this result:

$$r_e = r_e' + (r_e' - r_d)\frac{MV_d}{MV_e}$$

$$r_e = 0.08 + (0.08 - 0.05) \times \frac{500\ 000}{750\ 000}$$

$$r_e = 0.10$$

REVIEW ACTIVITY 6.2   Assuming that proposition 1 and 2 hold: a company has a weighted average cost of capital of 9 per cent and the rate of return required by its debt investors is 4 per cent. Given its debt equity ratio is 0.5 what is the equity cost of capital?

Given that financial risk is the additional risk which is incurred by the equity shareholders through increased borrowing this implies that Mig, with a nearly 40 per cent gearing level, has added a financial risk premium of 2 per cent to the rate of return required by equity investors compared with that in Mod. The equity return–gearing relationship which this function represents is a restatement of the idea that the risk return trade-off is linear. You may remember from Chapter 1 and Chapter 3 that this fundamental linearity in the risk–return relationship is enforced by arbitrage, but like all arbitrage arguments it is undermined by the presence of transaction costs, taxes and other impediments to so-minded investors capturing the 'risk free profit'.

Proposition 3

In the third and final part of their paper, Modigliani and Miller derived a simple rule for optimal investment policy by firms. Their proposition three states that:

'the cut-off point for investment in the firm will in all cases be the pure rate of return on equity and will be completely unaffected by the type of security used to finance the investment'.

This is a very similar to the Fisher-Hirshleifer separation theorem except that Modigliani and Miller have introduced risk into their analysis, albeit in a very limited form. Proposition 3 implies that the firm should accept an investment opportunity when its Net Present Value, discounted at the pure equity rate, is zero or greater. The term pure equity rate can be replaced by the weighted average cost of capital because the weighted average cost of capital equals the pure equity rate at all levels of gearing if the assumptions underpinning their analysis hold in practice.

The construction of Modigliani and Miller's argument contained many subtleties. Their analysis implied a linear relationship between the income stream received by a firm (its return) and its risk that was later demonstrated by Hamada (1969) within the framework of the Capital Asset Pricing Model. An important aspect of their analysis was that they demonstrated an arbitrage mechanism where equity investors by going long or short in the mispriced security and adjusting their own personal gearing to maintain the same level of financial risk would correct any disequilibria in the prices of the shares in the two firms.

EXHIBIT 6.5

The zero arbitrage relationship between the weighted average cost of capital and market gearing

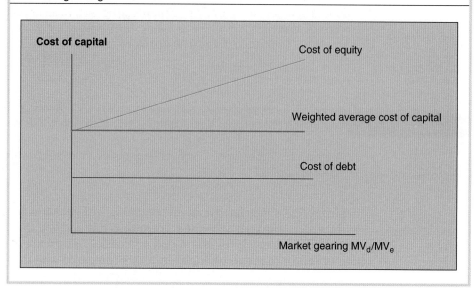

In the second part of their paper, Modigliani and Miller attempted to demonstrate the empirical truth of their propositions by analyzing the cost of capital in a range of companies which would be regarded as being in the same risk class. They chose electrical utility and oil companies. By regressing the cost of capital for these companies against their financial structure as measured by their market gearing ratio, Modigliani and Miller found evidence that supported their conclusion and contradicted the traditional view that there is an optimal level of gearing that value maximizing firms should seek to attain.

For many years the academic and business community debated the truth of the M&M position. In reality, it is clear that the tax advantages attaching to debt (where interest on debt is regarded as a pre-tax expense and is deductible for tax purposes) offers a considerable advantage to gearing. However, this situation is made more complex because of the way in which dividends are treated in the hands of equity shareholders.

The most important challenges to Modigliani and Miller's position arose from the following:

1 Taxation distorts the relative advantage of debt financing as opposed to equity as interest on the former is tax deductible whereas dividends on the latter are not.

2 Default risk which for the reasons outlined above becomes more significant as the gearing level rises.

3 Transaction cost and information signalling effects associated with the use of different types of finance.

4 Agency effects.

Taxation and capital structure

Because interest is an above the line expense for firms (i.e. it is tax deductible), which is not the case for individuals, then a distinct advantage accrues to the firm through the use of debt as opposed to equity finance. Introducing tax into an ungeared firm immediately reduces the market value of the firm as its earnings are reduced. We would not expect the rate of return required by the equity investors to change because the volatility of the earnings stream will not change. However, the impact of tax will work differently when a firm is partly financed by debt.

Modigliani and Miller corrected their original paper in 1963 arguing that the value of a geared firm, where interest is tax deductible, is derived by discounting two income streams:

1   An uncertain net income stream going to the equity investors discounted at the pure equity rate for an ungeared firm that pays corporation tax (T) on its earnings.

2   A certain income stream which flows to the debt holders which will be discounted at the risk free rate.

Mathematically 1 can be expressed in the following way for an ungeared firm:

$$r_e' = \frac{(1-T)\bar{X}}{MV_e'}$$

And

$$r_d = \frac{I}{MV_d}$$

Where I is the annual interest payable by the firm, r_e' is the pure equity rate of return on a net of tax earnings flow and r_d is the rate of return required by debt investors. In a levered firm, the total value of the firm should be equal to the value of an equivalent ungeared firm plus the value of the tax saving which accrues because interest can be offset against earnings:

$$MV_L = \frac{(1-T)\bar{X}}{r_e'} + \frac{T \times I}{r_d} = MV_e' + T \times MV_d$$

Likewise, Modigliani and Miller's proposition 2 also changes

$$r_e = r_e' + (1-T)(r_e' - r_d)\frac{MV_d}{MV_e}$$

This is an intuitively obvious result when you reflect upon it. The impact of taxation will reduce the net earnings available to the equity investor and hence cut the market value of equity. However the ability of the tax shield to reduce the effective cost of debt to the firm reduces the financial risk to which the equity investor is exposed. We can demonstrate the effect with some numbers.

FINANCIAL REALITY

Jack is back at his Mod and Mig case study and beginning to focus on the issues as far as it affects Friendly Grinders Ltd. Friendly Grinders pays tax at an effective rate of 30 per cent and interest payable on loans is fully offset against profits for tax purposes. What would be the effect upon the equity cost of capital of this tax system?

The first thing we notice is that the tax on the earnings of Mod will be £30 000 while the tax on the earnings of Mig is £22 500. The difference is the tax saving because of the interest payment (30 per cent × £25 000 = £7500).

Now this tax saving produces an increase in the value of Mig equal to the tax rate times the market value of debt

$$MV_{Mig} = \frac{(1-T)\bar{X}}{r_{e,Mod}} + \frac{TR}{r_d}$$
$$MV_{Mig} = MV_{e,Mod} + T \times MV_{d,Mig}$$
$$MV_{Mig} = £875\ 000 + 30\% \times £500\ 000$$
$$MV_{Mig} = £1\ 025\ 000$$

Mod's market valuation assuming a 'pure equity' rate of return of 8 per cent is £875 000 as shown in Exhibit 6.6. When we add the additional value generated by the tax saving on the debt interest we obtain a total market value of £1 025 000 for Mig Ltd being split £500 000 of debt and £525 000 of equity. The distributable profits in Mig are £52 500 giving a rate of return of 10 per cent on Mig's equity market value.

The reduction in pretax profit in Mig is matched by an equivalent fall in the value of the firm's equity (and hence an increase in the firm's gearing). The net effect is that its cost of equity is unchanged at 10 per cent, but its gearing has increased from 0.67 to 0.95. Taking Modigliani and Miller's second proposition we can calculate the cost of equity directly:

$$r_e = r'_e + (1-T)(r'_e - r_d)\frac{MV_d}{MV_e}$$
$$r_e = 8\% + (1-30\%)(8\% - 5\%)\frac{500\ 000}{525\ 000}$$
$$r_e = 10\%$$

EXHIBIT 6.6

The impact of tax upon the weighted average cost of capital (shown as a table)

	Mod (without tax)	Mod (with tax)	Mig (without tax)	Mig (with tax)
Earnings	100 000	100 000	100 000	100 000
Interest			25 000	25 000
Pretax profit	100 000	100 000	75 000	75 000
Tax	0	30 000	0	22 500
Distributable profit	100 000	70 000	75 000	52 500
Rate of return on equity	0.08	0.08	0.1	0.1
Market value of equity	1 250 000	875 000	750 000	525 000
Market value of debt			500 000	500 000
Gearing (MV_d/MV_e)	0.00	0.00	0.67	0.95
Market value per share	1.25	0.875	1.5	1.05
WACC	0.08000	0.08000	0.08000	0.06829

However, the overall weighted average cost of capital for the geared firm will no longer be the same as the pure equity rate of return. The reason is that the cost of debt capital is now reduced by the tax saving:

$$r_d' = \frac{25\,000 - 7\,500}{500\,000}$$

$$r_d' = 3.5\%$$

Where r_d' is the effective cost of debt capital which can be more generally stated as:

$$r_d' = (1 - T)r_d$$
$$r_d' = (1 - 0.3) \times 5\% = 3.5\%$$

Thus Mig's weighted average cost of capital is given by the formula you have already met in Chapter 5:

$$WACC_{mig} = \frac{MV_e}{MV_d + MV_e} \times r_e + \frac{MV_d}{MV_d + MV_e} \times r_d \times (1 - T)$$

$$WACC_{mig} = \frac{525\,000}{1\,025\,000} \times 10\% + \frac{500\,000}{1\,025\,000} \times 5\% \times (1 - 30\%)$$

$$WACC_{mig} = 6.829\%$$

We can show the impact of tax on capital structure graphically as in Exhibit 6.7 but if we use the alternative gearing measure a different set of curves emerge as shown in Exhibit 6.8. This exhibit makes clear that the cost of equity capital rises rapidly as we approach 100 per cent gearing, using this gearing measure. The weighted average cost of capital can now be seen to be falling constantly as the proportion of debt in

EXHIBIT 6.7

The impact of tax upon the weighted average cost of capital (shown as a graph)

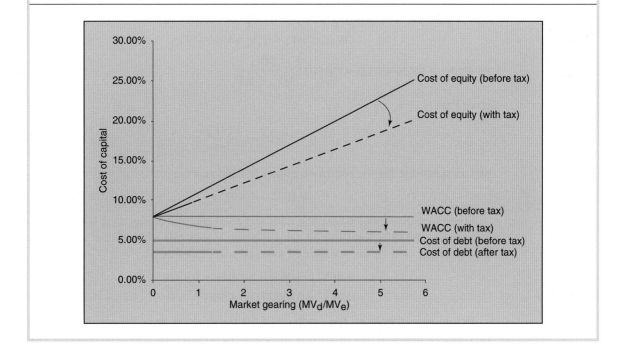

EXHIBIT 6.8

The impact of gearing on the weighted average cost of capital where gearing is defined in terms of the firm's total market capitalization

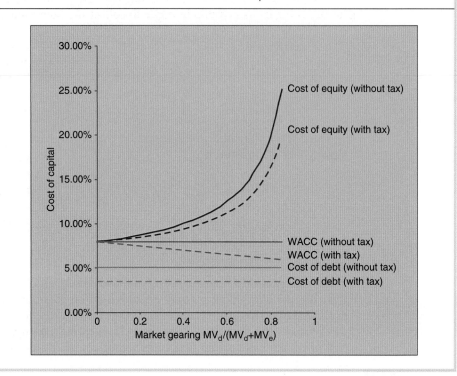

the capital structure is increased and indeed the rate of decline is governed by the tax rate. Taking the weighted average cost of capital formula again:

$$WACC = (1 - w_d)r_e + w_d(1 - T)r_d$$

where w_d is the market gearing ratio $\dfrac{MV_d}{MV_d + MV_e}$

given that:

$$r_e = r'_e + (r'_e - r_d)\frac{MV_d}{MV_e}$$

we can substitute for the return on equity (r_e) and rearrange:

$$WACC = r'_e - Tr'_e w_d$$

In the example above where the debt was £500 000, the equity £525 000 the relative gearing is 0.4878. Substituting using the pure equity rate of 8 per cent and the tax rate of 30 per cent we get a weighted average cost of capital of:

$$WACC = 0.08 - 0.3 \times 0.08 \times 0.4878$$

$$WACC = 0.06829 = 6.829\%$$

In summary, therefore, the presence of the tax shield reduces the equity investor's exposure to financial risk by cutting the effective rate of return to debt holders. This reduces the equity cost of capital at a given level of gearing compared with what it would have been if no tax shield had been in place. The net effect is a reduction in the weighted average cost of capital directly proportional to the tax rate times the cost of equity capital in the equivalent ungeared firm. This suggests that a firm should gear up as highly as possible in order to collect the increasing tax advantage which comes with taking on additional debt.

There are two problems with this analysis: first, in some tax jurisdictions individuals can set interest on their own borrowing against their income before tax is assessed. In that situation there may be little advantage on corporate borrowing over individual borrowing and the possibility for individuals to create 'home made gearing' with the same financial risk exposure of the geared company is re-established. As a result it will be again possible for individuals to arbitrage away any difference in value between differently geared firms. Merton Miller also made the point that any temporary tax advantage in using debt is likely to increase corporate demand for that type of finance over equity. As a consequence of that increase in the macroeconomic demand for debt its cost will rise offsetting any tax advantage. However, that argument is not sustainable in economies such as the UK and elsewhere where the tax shield on corporate interest payments is a permanent feature of the fiscal landscape and where the same benefits are not available to the private investor.

FINANCIAL CASE

Cobham plc has a cost of debt capital of 4.5 per cent and an estimated total market value of debt in issue of £163.68 million. Its equity shares are currently quoted at 1375p per share and have a total market capitalization of £1534.60million. The marginal rate of corporation tax for Cobham plc is 30 per cent. The equity cost of capital is determined at 7.2 per cent. The current weighted average cost of capital (see Chapter 5) is 6.81 per cent. What would be Cobham's cost of equity capital and its weighted average cost of capital if it increased its gearing by a further issue of £400 million in debt at its current cost of debt capital?

Using the Modigliani and Miller proposition 1 the additional debt would add value to the current market value of the firm:

$$MV_{adj} = MV_{orig} + T \times MV_d$$

where MV_{orig} and MV_{adj} are the original market value of Cobham and that as adjusted after the debt issue. Using the data as given:

$$MV_{adj} = £1534.60m + 0.3 \times £563.68m$$
$$MV_{adj} = £1703.70m$$

The pure equity cost of capital for Cobham is found using Modigliani and Miller's proposition 2 as revised for the 30 per cent tax shield:

$$r_e = r_e' + (1 - T)(r_e' - r_d)\frac{MV_d}{MV_e}$$

$$7.2\% = r_{cob}' + (1 - 30\%)(r_{cob}' - 4.5\%)\frac{163.68}{1534.60}$$

$$r'_{cob} = 7.012\%$$

If we now regear the equity rate to reflect the new debt level of £559.5 million the resulting cost of equity is:

$$r_{cob} = 7.012\% + (1 - 30\%)(7.012\% - 4.5\%)\frac{563.68}{1534.60}$$

$$r_{cob} = 7.66\%$$

The weighted average cost of capital is then straightforward:

$$WACC_{cob} = \frac{MV_e}{MV_d + MV_e} r_e + \frac{MV_d}{MV_d + MV_e} r_d(1 - T)$$

$$WACC_{cob} = \frac{1534.6}{1534.6 + 563.68} \times 7.66\% + \frac{563.68}{1534.6 + 563.68} \times 4.5\% \times (1 - 30\%)$$

$$WACC_{cob} = 6.45\%$$

Which is lower than the 6.81 per cent for the firm before the additional capital has been raised.

Capital structure within a capital asset pricing framework

Robert Hamada (1969) demonstrated that the Modigliani and Miller irrelevance theorems could be developed within a capital asset pricing framework rather than the single risk class assumptions originally employed. Hamada used the standard Capital Asset Pricing Model which predicts a linear relationship between expected return and market risk. The no arbitrage condition of Modigliani and Miller's homogenous risk class assumption are easily translated into the linear model where a firm's pure equity beta is a weighted average of the firm's equity beta (i.e. the 'geared' beta) and a beta for the financial component of the firm's risk.

EXHIBIT 6.9

The 'beta' balance sheet showing the relationship between the pure equity (asset) beta and the beta of the securities used to finance the firm

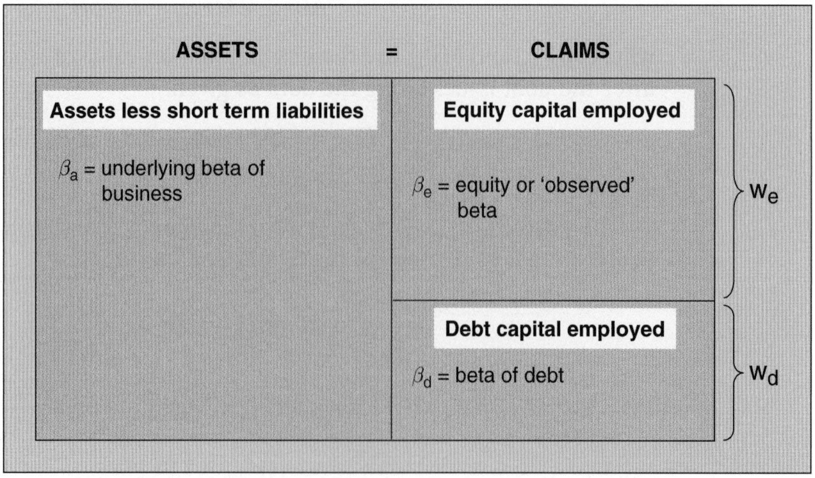

To understand the impact of financial risk on beta consider a diagrammatic representation of a balance sheet (laid out in horizontal format) as shown in Exhibit 6.9.

A firm's 'asset' beta measures the sensitivity of its underlying business to market risk. It is the beta we would expect to observe empirically if the firm was financed solely by equity. Thus for the pure equity firm:

$$\beta_a = \beta_e$$

Where a company has a geared capital structure then the asset beta must equal the beta of the claims on the firm's assets. However, the beta of the claims is the beta of a portfolio consisting of two component securities: the firm's equity and the firm's debt. Thus the beta of the claims (and hence the beta of the firm's assets) equals the value of the two component portfolio as follows:

$$\beta_a = w_e\beta_e + w_d\beta_d$$

The weight of debt (w_d) is the firm's market gearing ratio and is defined by:

$$w_d = \frac{\text{total market value of debt}}{\text{total market value of equity plus debt}} = \frac{MV_d}{MV_e + MV_d}$$

If the company's debt is risk free then the relationship between the firm's equity beta and its asset beta is simplified:

$$\beta_a = w_e\beta_e$$

or

$$\beta_a = (1 - w_d)\beta_e$$

<table>
<tr><td>**FINANCIAL REALITY**</td><td>A company with an AAA credit rating has an equity beta of 0.9. Its total market capitalization contains 30 per cent debt by value. That company is planning to reduce its gearing to 15 per cent by market value. What would its expected beta be after the reduction in gearing level?</td></tr>
</table>

The first step in this exercise is to calculate the firm's asset beta using its current level of gearing:

$$\beta_a = (1 - 0.3) \times 0.9$$
$$\beta_a = 0.63$$

This is the estimate of the beta of the firm if it were financed purely by equity. The equity beta the formula would predict if the company moves to a 15 per cent gearing level is:

$$\beta_e = \frac{\beta_a}{1 - w_d} = \frac{0.63}{0.85} = 0.74$$

Where a company has debt which carries some element of market risk exposure then the calculations are more complex.

<table>
<tr><td>**FINANCIAL REALITY**</td><td>A company has an equity beta of 1.1 and a market gearing ratio of 0.45. Its debt has a beta of 0.05. The company would like to know its equity beta if it altered its gearing to 40 per cent.</td></tr>
</table>

In this case we must use the full version of the model but replacing the weight of equity with one minus the weight of debt:

$$\beta_a = (1 - w_d)\beta_e + w_d\beta_d$$

The asset beta is then:

$$\beta_a = (1 - 0.45) \times 1.1 + 0.45 \times 0.05$$
$$\beta_a = 0.6275$$

Rearranging the formula to 'gear up' the beta to the level implied by 40 per cent debt:

$$\beta_a = (1 - w_d)\beta_e + w_d\beta_d$$
$$\beta_e = \frac{\beta_a - w_d\beta_d}{1 - w_d} = 1.0125$$

The correction for capital structure changes can be useful for a company that has or expects to make a significant change in its gearing. It can also be used for a non-listed company that cannot directly measure its equity beta and it is to that problem we turn next.

Introducing corporate tax into the estimation of asset beta

In most countries interest payments on debt are an allowable expense against corporation tax. We will examine this in more detail below but the key point for the moment is that the effective cost of debt capital will be reduced if the company can fully offset its interest payments for tax purposes. As far as the calculation of the asset beta is concerned the tax shield means that the effective exposure to financial risk, as measured by the market gearing ratio is reduced. The modified gearing ratio will be:

$$w_d = \frac{MV_d(1-T)}{MV_e - MV_d(1-T)}$$

where T is the corporation tax rate.

Unfortunately this means that we have to go back and recalculate the gearing ratio in full applying the impact of the tax shield to the market value of debt.

FINANCIAL REALITY

Friendly Grinders (2005) plc has two types of capital: debt where there are loans outstanding with an estimated market value of £48million and equity where there are 40 million 25p shares in issue with a market value of 210p each. The equity beta for the company is 1.27 and the average rate of corporation tax on its profits is 30 per cent.

The adjusted market gearing for Friendly Grinders is given as follows:

$$w_d = \frac{48(1-0.3)}{84 + 48(1-0.3)}$$
$$w_d = 0.2857$$

This compares with a market gearing ratio of 0.364 before tax. We can then use this ratio to calculate the asset beta as before:

$$\beta_a = \beta_e(1 - w_d)$$
$$\beta_a = 1.27 \times (1 - 0.2857)$$
$$\beta_a = 0.907$$

The sensitivity of beta to financial risk presents a significant problem in the historical measurement of beta. Whenever a firm's stock price rises its gearing falls and hence its equity beta will fall and vice versa when its stock price falls. This means that the observed beta will always be changing as the market gearing of the firm changes. As Ray Ball (2003) has pointed out this alone may be sufficient to explain many of the anomalies which have been observed in the empirical literature on the efficiency of markets including the mean reversion phenomenon, the size and other effects noted by Fama and French.

Default risk and the static trade off theory

An assumption within the Modigliani and Miller analysis is that no matter how high the firm gears itself it is not exposed to default. In practice this would mean that debt investors would not be able to put a firm that failed to pay interest or redeem its debt at the due time into receivership. This, as we discussed in Chapter 4 is not the case and the greater the gearing of a firm generally the higher its risk of failure and the lower its credit rating. In response to their critics on this point Modigliani and Miller attempted to argue that if increasing default risk results in a higher rate of return on debt then the firm's equity investors will require a lower rate. Exhibit 6.10 shows what Modigliani and Miller argue will happen.

The problem was that Modigliani and Miller could not offer a coherent explanation as to why the cost of equity might fall in this way. If one accepts the proposition that a firm's business risk is a fixed 'cake' (albeit a cake nobody wants) to be shared between the investor groups then it is possible to argue that if the debt holders demand a higher rate (implying they are accepting more risk) then the equity investors will be taking less.

Unfortunately, default risk is not quite like that – it is not just a 'rebundling' of business risk – it is a separate class of risk because of the contractual liability entered

EXHIBIT 6.10

The Modigliani and Miller version of what happens to the cost of capital as the threat of default at high levels of gearing increases

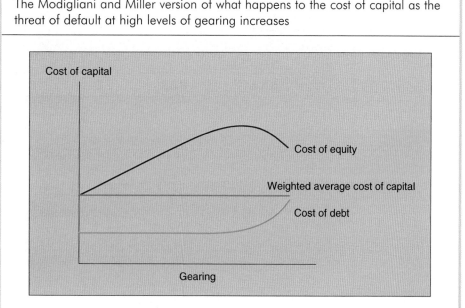

into by the firm with the debt investors. If the cost of debt capital does turn up as shown in Exhibit 6.10 with no commensurate reduction in the cost of equity then when taxes are added into the analysis the resulting weighted average cost of capital function is shown in Exhibit 6.11. Does this look familiar? It should do – it is exactly the relationship between cost of capital and gearing predicted by the traditional view and, as Ezra Solomons (1963) pointed out: 'Assuming that the straightforward logic of this argument is accepted, what we are left with is something very similar to the U-shaped curve envisaged by traditional theory'.

Stewart Myers put these insights together into what he referred to as the 'static–tradeoff' theory of capital structure:

> 'of course none of these developments disprove M&M's irrelevance theorem, which is just a "no magic in leverage" proof for a taxless, frictionless world. M&M's practical message is this: if there is an optimal capital structure, it should reflect taxes or some specifically identified market imperfections'.

Myers went on to argue that managers seek to trade off the tax savings on debt against the downside costs of issuing more debt capital. The threat of default would, Myers argued, be most severe for companies whose assets are largely intangible in nature and that as a result we would expect mature firms whose asset structure is mostly in the form of tangible assets to borrow more. One consequence of this is that high growth firms who are heavily invested in intangible assets are unlikely to pursue high levels of gearing even if this means that they forego valuable investment opportunities. Thus it is likely that such firms will face an 'underinvestment problem' at high levels of gearing, while mature firms that are heavily invested in real assets are likely and more prone to over-invest unless prevented from doing so.

EXHIBIT 6.11

The relationship between the weighted average cost of capital under the impact of tax and default risk

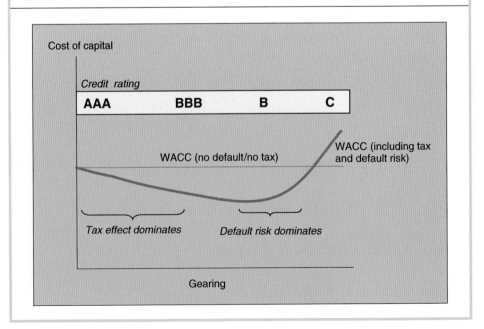

Adjusting the weighted average cost of capital under the static trade-off theory

An alteration in gearing when no taxes are present does not cause a significant problem as the weighted average cost of capital should remain unchanged. However when taxes are introduced and following the static trade-off theory we can identify three effects upon the weighted average cost of capital:

1 the cost of equity will change reflecting the alteration in gearing, and

2 there will be an alteration in the impact of tax,

3 there may also be an alteration in the default premium.

To analyze out the impact of these changes on the weighted average cost of capital and create an adjusted figure to discount the new investment opportunity we reintroduce a version of the *WACC* formula from Chapter 5. This version if you remember isolates the component return premiums within the model.

$$WACC = R_f + (1 - w_d)[\beta_i \, ERP] + w_d \delta_d$$

To correct that model for tax we return to the original weighted average cost of capital formula:

$$WACC = (1 - w_d)r_e + w_d \, r_d$$

which under tax this model becomes:

$$WACC = (1 - w_d)r_e + w_d \, r_d(1 - T)$$

However, as we noted in Chapter 5, the cost of debt capital consists of two parts: the T-Bill or risk free rate and a default premium δ. Thus the debt cost component of the weighted average cost of capital model is given by:

$$w_d \, r_d(1 - T) = w_d \, R_F(1 - T) + w_d\delta(1 - T)$$

Given that the cost of equity capital is given by:

$$r_e = R_F + \beta_e \times ERP$$

EXHIBIT 6.12

The meaning and corrections to the premium version of the weighted average cost of capital

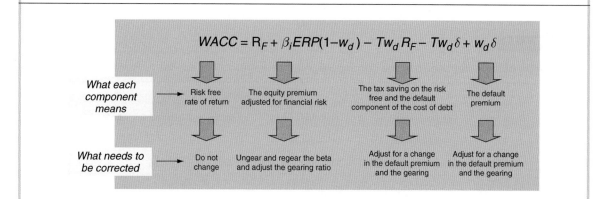

then by substitution the weighted average cost of capital becomes:

$$WACC = R_F + \beta_i\, ERP(1 - w_d) - Tw_d\, R_F - Tw_d\delta + w_d\delta$$

This premium version of the weighted average cost of capital isolates all the changes we need make to correct the weighted average cost of capital to reflect a change in the firm's gearing.

In Chapter 5 we calculated the weighted average cost of capital for Friendly Grinders as 7.355 per cent. Here is the exercise again but this time using the premium version of the weighted average cost of capital.

FINANCIAL REALITY

Friendly Grinders (2005) plc has two types of capital: debt where there are loans outstanding with an estimated market value of £48million and equity where there are 40 million 25p shares in issue with a market value of 210p each. The equity beta for the company is 1.27 and the average rate of corporation tax on its profits is 30 per cent. The company's existing cost of debt capital is 5.91 per cent. Jack Grinder is considering, at his bank manager's suggestion, taking out an extra loan to finance a project which has a capital outlay cost of 19.1 million. The loan would carry an arrangement fee of 2 per cent of the amount of the loan and the loan would carry interest at the current required rate of return of 6.30 per cent. Jack would like to analyze the impact of this alteration in gearing on the company's cost of capital.

The weighted average cost of capital using the data as shown before the introduction of new debt is as shown in Exhibit 6.13.

Now we can correct each component for the alteration in the firm's gearing if this project is accepted. To do this we go through the following steps:

1 Calculate the revised gearing ratio assuming that the new debt is acquired. The original gearing ratio for this company was 0.3636 (see Chapter 5) based upon debt of £48 million and equity of £84 million. With the acquisition of the new debt the gearing ratio will rise to:

$$w'_d = \frac{(48 + 19.482)}{(84 + (48 + 19.482))}$$

$$w'_d = 0.4454$$

EXHIBIT 6.13

Estimation of the components of the current weighted average cost of capital

	Risk free	Equity premium	tax saving on risk free rate	tax saving on default premium	default premium
WACC=	R_F	$+\beta_i ERP(1-w_d)$	$-Tw_d R_F$	$-Tw_d\delta$	$+w_d\delta$
	4.75%	$+1.27\times3.5\% \times (1-0.364)$	$-.3 \times 0.364 \times 4.75\%$	$-0.3 \times 0.364\times1.16$	$+.364 \times 1.16\%$
7.355%	4.750%	2.827%	-0.519%	-0.126%	0.424%

2 Calculate the revised cost of debt and hence the revised default premium. In practice we would have to decide whether the increase in the return required by the bank is because of the alteration in the credit status of the company that the increased gearing would entail or whether it is because of different terms attaching to the loan (remember debt of different terms to maturity will normally carry different rates of return). If it is the former then the appropriate rate to use for all of the firm's debt is the new rate required by the bank. If it is the latter then we need to calculate a weighted average cost of debt. We will choose the latter approach here to demonstrate the method: (note that the new borrowing of £19.1m has been increased by 2 per cent)

$$r_d' = \frac{48}{(48+19.482)} \times 5.91\% + \frac{19.482}{(48+19.482)} \times 6.30\%$$

$$r_d' = 6.0217\%$$

$$\delta' = 6.0217\% - 4.75\%$$

$$\delta' = 1.2717\%$$

3 Ungear and regear the company's beta. We know from earlier that the asset or pure equity beta for this company is 0.907. We proceed as follows to regear:

The tax adjusted gearing ratio for correcting the asset beta to the new level of gearing is given by:

$$w_d'' = \frac{(48+19.482)(1-0.3)}{(84+(48+19.482)(1-0.3))}$$

$$w_d'' = 0.3599$$

Using this net version of the gearing ratio we calculate the revised equity beta as follows:

$$\beta_e' = \frac{\beta_a}{1-w_d''}$$

$$\beta_e' = \frac{0.907}{1-0.3599}$$

$$\beta_e' = 1.417$$

Inserting these revised figures into the premium version of the weighted average cost of capital we obtain Exhibit 6.14.

EXHIBIT 6.14

Estimation of the components of the weighted average cost of capital taking into account the new loan

	Risk free	Equity premium	tax saving on risk free rate	tax saving on default premium	default premium
WACC=	R_F	$+\beta_i ERP(1-w_d)$	$-Tw_dR_F$	$-Tw_d\delta$	$+w_d\delta$
	4.750%	$+1.417 \times 3.5\% \times (1-0.4454)$	$-.3 \times 0.4454 \times 4.75\%$	$-0.3 \times 0.4454 \times 1.2733\%$	$+0.4454 \times 1.2717\%$
7.262%	4.750%	2.750%	−0.635%	−0.170%	0.567%

This suggests that the company is still not at its optimal position as far as the weighted average cost of capital is concerned. Analyzing the difference between the components of the weighted average cost of capital before and after the change in gearing suggests that the tax effect is still greater than the default premium.

Agency effects and capital structure

The idea that firms trade off the tax advantage of debt against the costs of distress leads to the idea that different firms with different mixes of intangible and real assets and at different stages in their growth are likely to migrate towards different capital structures. This issue was picked up by Michael Jensen whose work on agency theory was outlined in Chapter 1.

Jensen argued that large mature firms with high and stable cash flows which exceed their investable opportunities are prone to overinvestment as a result with management pursuing 'vanity projects' such as ill judged acquisitions or by excessive investment in perks and other managerial rewards. A firm in this situation that wishes to maximize shareholder value can return the free cash flow to its investors through higher distributions or alter its gearing in favour of debt. As we shall see later it can achieve this by repurchasing its equity using new debt. The leveraging of the equity of the firm through debt has the effect of concentrating the equity capital and as Jensen argued, reducing the agency costs of managers siphoning off the firm's value to their own advantage.

The combination leads to the conclusion that debt has a powerful effects in controlling managerial behaviour and in reducing wasteful investment in firms where that may be an issue given their maturity and asset mix. However, another piece of the argument about capital structure needs to be put into place.

The pecking order hypothesis

In general, the empirical evidence suggests that markets react more favourably to firms that increase rather than decrease gearing. The reason for this is not too hard to find. Because, debt requires a steady stream for future cash flows to service the necessary interest payments then the issue of debt signals to the market management's confidence that such cash flows will be available. Equity issues on the other hand appear as bad news to the markets and Clifford Smith (2003) has demonstrated that share value can fall by up to 3 per cent on news of an equity issue. This effect creates a bias in favour of debt finance and particularly in those situations where management believe that their firm is undervalued.

Management is also likely to be influenced by the relative costs of raising new external finance. These transaction costs include the costs of preparing for the issue, the publication of the prospectus and other regulatory documents, and the commission taken by any financial intermediaries or underwriters. If the capital is raised in an overseas market or on the Eurobond market then there may be exchange losses to bear as well.

This led Stewart Myers (1984) to propose what is known as the 'pecking order hypothesis'. Contracting costs and information signalling effects create a pecking order of attractiveness of different sources of finance: internal finance in the form of retained earnings are likely to be favoured over (in descending order of attractiveness) 'safe debt' such as bank loans, bond issues, and then onto hybrid finance such as convertibles and finally equity in the form of rights and new issues. Only in a situation where management believe that their firm is overvalued by the market are they likely to wish to issue equity (which by definition is what is overvalued) in preference to debt.

However, the situation is made more complex by transaction cost economics arguments. Although we do refer to the 'equity market' and the fact that firms raise equity finance from the primary market, firms are not in a position to freely transact equity. They can raise new equity finance but it is much more difficult to return that capital to the market although share buy-backs are now permitted in company law. As a result we refer to equity finance as 'internalized finance'. Debt finance can, on the other hand be rescheduled or redeemed as the firm gains a particular advantage in doing so. In an important sense debt is 'hired' from the market for a specific purpose and returned once that purpose is accomplished. As a result equity finance is more suited to the acquisition of assets which are intrinsic to the firm and highly specific in their function. As such they have little value in the debt market (because of their low marketability) as collateral security against a loan and therefore loan finance will not be the finance of choice for acquiring such assets. Where the purchase of 'real' assets is involved they are likely to be financed out of equity issues whereas 'intangible assets' are more likely to be financed out of earnings. Where real assets have more general use then their marketability is likely to be higher and they will be more attractive to lenders as security against a debenture issue or mortgage.

REVIEW ACTIVITY 6.3 Friendly Grinders plc is heavily invested in real assets and commands a powerful niche in its market sector. Many of its assets are highly specialized within the diamond grinding and polishing business. It does enjoy good levels of profitability and cash flow. What issues should it bear in mind if it should decide to expand its available capital through borrowing?

Dividend policy

As a company earns profits it can do one of two things with that surplus: it can pay it back to its investors by means of a dividend or it can retain it within the business as an addition to the shareholders' equity account in the balance sheet. It may of course decide to do a bit of both. In terms of the underlying cash generation of the firm earnings are strictly the free cash flow available for distribution to equity investors after all prior charges and taxes have been paid. The retained earnings of the firm are then an accumulation to its capital account and providing there is available cash on the asset side of the balance sheet then the firm can reinvest in new capital investment opportunities. If on the other hand the firm decides to redistribute it is passing that surplus back to the equity market giving investors the opportunity to either reinvest it themselves or to spend it. In its turn, if the firm that has distributed wishes to raise capital for reinvestment it can do so by returning to the capital markets and raising new equity or debt as it sees fit. That's the theory. However, it begs a lot of important questions: does it matter as far as the value of the firm is concerned whether the firm finances new investment internally through retentions or externally through the capital market? Does it matter to investors whether they get their money now in the form of a dividend or later through capital appreciation? To what extent can managers exploit their power to give or withhold dividends to their own advantage? It is obtaining answers to these questions that the dividend policy debate is all about.

EXHIBIT 6.15

The capital cycle of the firm showing the distribution of free cash flow between dividends and capital reinvestment

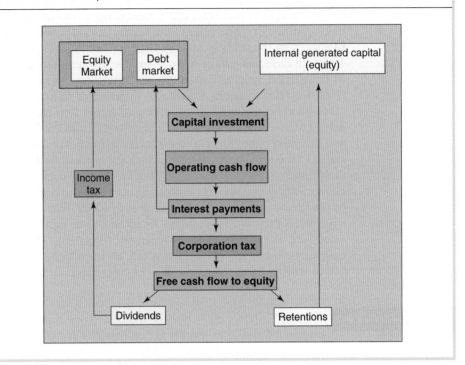

In a perfect capital market it is straightforward to see why dividend policy should be irrelevant in determining the value of the firm. This was an argument advanced by Modigliani and Miller in 1961. Again, like their capital structure argument, their dividend irrelevance hypothesis was part of their exploration of the problem of valuing the firm under conditions of uncertainty.

You may remember from our discussion of the Fisher Hirshliefer separation theorem that the means by which a project is financed is strictly independent of its value. Modigliani and Miller's capital structure argument was in terms of the substitutability of debt and equity, the dividend irrelevance argument is in terms of the substitutability of retentions and new equity in financing new investment.

Remember a perfect capital market is one where the firm has unlimited access to external funds free of transaction costs and taxes and where there is complete and free access to information on the part of both the firm and investors. The Modigliani and Miller argument can be constructed as follows:

1 If a firm has positive Net Present Value projects (when discounted at its weighted average cost of capital) then it should invest in those projects.

2 The means by which it finances those investment projects is strictly irrelevant: if the company has insufficient internally generated funds then it can raise the capital on the external market. Indeed, if it so chooses, it can pay its cash surpluses as dividends and refinance itself through the capital market to meet its investment needs. Indeed, given Modigliani

and Miller's cost of capital arguments it does not matter whether this external finance is obtained through the equity or the debt market – the cost of capital will remain the same.

3 The firm's investors are indifferent to whether the firm distributes or not providing what is retained is invested at a rate equal to or more than their required rate of return. If they require personal liquidity they can create 'home made dividends' by selling an appropriate portion of their shares which will have increased in value by the Net Present Values of the firm's new, positive Net Present Value investment.

What this dividend irrelevance hypothesis relies upon is the perfect substitutability in the investor's mind between current dividend and future dividend (where that future dividend is the product of the profitable exploitation of positive Net Present Value investment opportunities by the firm). When uncertainty is entered into the analysis it also assumes that the rate used by investors to discount near term dividends is that required to discount far term dividends and that this rate is the one used by the firm in evaluating its own investment opportunities.

However, the dividend irrelevance argument only works while the firm has a supply of positive Net Present Value investment opportunities. What should it do when (as surely will become the case at some stage) it has exhausted all the opportunities available? In that case it must return its earnings to its investors as dividends or by some other means. What this leads to is that Modigliani and Miller are in effect proposing a 'residual' dividend policy.

EXHIBIT 6.16

Comparative analysis of firms facing different investment conditions

NPV<0 IRR<WACC	NPV=0 IRR=WACC	NPV>0 IRR>WACC
Investment will reduce the value of the firm	Investment will leave the value of the firm unchanged	Investment will increase the value of the firm
Cash rich firm: weak investment opportunities with many products in their mature phase	Cash generative but surpluses in balance with return paid to investors through dividends or other means	Cash poor firm: high investment programmes consuming cash at a faster rate than its generation through ongoing activities
Company should return surplus cash to investors either as dividends or via share repurchase	Company should seek to resolve the investment as either value adding or destroying and then act accordingly	Firm should accept all positive Net Present Value investments either through retained earnings or new capital issue or both
Firm whose core business is contracting either through market or managerial failure	This state arises in highly competitive markets where NPVs are driven down to zero with little opportunity for product differentiation. Inefficient firms will move towards failure	Firm is expanding its business opportunities and investing heavily in both real and intangible assets

Problems with the dividend irrelevance argument

Although theoretically sound the irrelevance argument is based upon a number of critical assumptions which are all to a greater or lesser extent violated in practice:

Transaction costs There are transaction costs in real markets which will make it more costly for an investor to finance their short term liquidity requirements through the 'home made dividend' mechanism which the irrelevancy argument implies. It may also be very inconvenient for investors to have to sell shares to match a reduced dividend with the necessary portfolio rebalancing that this will entail. However, it may be cheaper for the equity investor to create a home-made dividend by selling some shares than for the firm to raise new capital on the equity market. In this case what will matter is the relative transaction costs between the firm selling (issuing) equity and the private investor selling equity to finance their respective liquidity requirements.

The impact of taxes The different tax treatment of capital gains and dividends means that investors will not be indifferent between financing new investment through retention or new equity issue. Presumably investors will prefer to take dividends if the tax system favours that alternative rather than those dividends being invested to finance future growth and hence increasing their exposure to capital gains tax liability. That capital gains liability may be postponed or may be incurred immediately depending on whether the investors resort to selling equity to replace dividends immediately or are willing to wait to take their capital accumulation at a later date.

Information asymmetries Because investors do not have the same access to information as management dividend payments are likely to be construed as an information signal about management's future intentions. It is not hard to see the logic: in the absence of any concrete evidence about future investment a cut in dividend could be regarded as a signal that the firm's future prospects are not as bright as the investors had been led to believe or that management has discovered a new investment opportunity. Likewise, an increase in dividend could be read the other way around as signalling optimism about future prospects or that management has run out of ideas about how to profitably invest the surplus generated by the firm.

The problem of uncertainty and the 'bird in the hand argument' In a vigorous rebuttal of the irrelevancy argument, Myron Gordon in 1963 argued that investors are always likely to prefer near term dividends rather than long term dividends because the latter are inherently more uncertain. However, the fallacy of this argument is that it is the uncertainty of the future earnings of the firms which drives the uncertainty attaching to dividends and investors, in valuing the firm, will base their assessment of risk (and hence the rate of return they require), on the uncertainty of the earnings flow.

The clientele effects The issues discussed above may create a clientele effect whereby investors who require a steady income flow, or where the tax regime favours dividends over capital gains, will be attracted to high dividend payout firms while those who are looking for growth will favour companies that offer future capital gain through a high retention policy. This idea that companies attract particular types of investor who can take advantage of their distribution policies does appear to be a common feature of the way the equity markets operate.

Dividend policy

In principle there are a range of dividend policies that a firm can pursue:

1 A constant or growing money payout related to the nominal value of the share. The advantage of this approach is it offers some consistency and predictability in the flow of dividend payments to investors. For a mature firm with high and stable free cash flows this may be attractive to investors first by promising a steady or growing dividend yield over time and second by reducing the potential of management to divert that surplus cash generation to non-profitable activities. The disadvantage is that if there is a downturn in earnings the firm may be forced to cut its dividend with all the negative signals that may give to the market.

2 A constant payout ratio may be used by firms who wish to maintain a stable link between their earnings, their rate or reinvestment and the dividend they pay out each year. The difficulty of course is that it does not signal management's intentions to the market nor does it offer any predictability for investors in terms of their dividend receipts from the company.

3 A zero dividend policy is a common option taken by firms during their growth phase as all available surpluses are reinvested within the business. In this case the market will be capitalizing on the potential growth opportunities and the increase in future earning power that they represent. Inevitably, however, the firm will exhaust its growth (i.e. positive NPV) opportunities and at that point it will begin to accumulate cash. This will be the stage at which the firm will be forced to contemplate returning cash to its investors either in the form of a dividend payment or by some other means.

4 A residual dividend policy is one where a dividend is only paid if there are no further current investment opportunities that can be exploited. This type of policy is likely to be pursued by firms that are in a growth phase and do not have ready access to external financing or where (remembering the pecking order hypothesis) it is disadvantageous seeking new debt or equity finance on transaction cost grounds. The difficulty with this type of dividend policy is that it does not offer any predictability to the investor in terms of the cash flow they receive and from management's point of view may be unsustainable. If the signalling hypothesis is true then any increase in dividends will be seen as favourable by the market but a cut will suggest that the firm does not have investment opportunities to exploit.

Estimating a firm's dividend capacity

Given that dividends are a direct cash withdrawal from the business the firm needs to be able to estimate the amount of cash that is surplus from its current operations but before any further capital investment is undertaken. The term 'free cash flow to equity' (FCFE) relates to the annual cash surplus generated by the firm which can be used, either for reinvestment or for distribution. Exhibit 6.17 shows the sequence of the calculations from the cash flow statement.

EXHIBIT 6.17

The potential dividend release from a firm's free cash flow

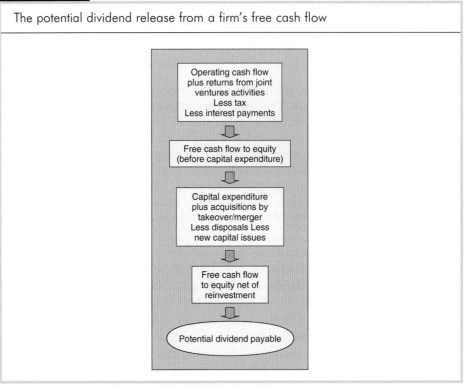

FINANCIAL CASE

Cobham's cash flow statement from its 2004 accounts is as shown in Exhibit 6.18. The company has 111 606 905 shares in issue and during the year it paid a combined dividend of 34.6p per share. What was the maximum dividend capacity of the business before and after capital expenditure and other financial investment?

The free cash flow to equity from the cash flow statement is as follows:

$$\text{FCFE} = \text{operating cash flow } (+\pounds163.1\text{m})$$

plus

dividends received from joint ventures (+£5m)

less

net interest paid (−£7.6m)

less

tax. (−£22.9m)

$$\text{FCFE} = \pounds137.6 \text{ million}$$

which on a per share basis:
potential dividend per share (assuming full distribution) = 123.29p per share.

EXHIBIT 6.18

Consolidated cash flow statement for Cobham plc

Consolidated Cash Flow Statement
for the year ended 31 December 2004

£m	NOTES	2004	2003
Net cash inflow from operating activities	22	163.1	147.8
Dividend received from joint venture		5.0	–
Returns on investments and servicing of finance	24a	(7.6)	(11.0)
Taxation		(22.9)	(20.3)
Capital expenditure and financial investment	24b	(39.7)	(39.2)
Acquisitions and disposals	24c	(73.8)	(115.0)
Equity dividends paid		(32.3)	(27.6)
Net cash outflow before use of liquid resources and financing		(8.2)	(65.3)
Management of liquid resources	24d	0.2	–
Financing	24e	7.2	105.1
(Decrease)/Increase in Cash	23	(0.8)	39.8

Now deducting net capital reinvestment we can determine the potential dividend payable:

$$\text{FCFE (net)} = \text{FCFE}$$
$$\text{less}$$
$$\text{(capital expenditure plus acquisitions less new capital issued)}$$
$$\text{FCFE (net)} = £137.6\text{m} - (39.7 + 73.8 - 7.2) = £137.6\text{m} - £76.3\text{m}$$
$$= £31.3 \text{ million}$$

The potential dividend per share after retention to finance net investment = 28.04p per share. This would suggest that the company in attempting to maintain a consistent dividend policy has over-distributed by £7.3 million or 6.56p per share.

Share repurchase

Since the 1981 Companies Act in the UK it has been possible for companies to redeem shares that they already have in issue. Up until that date the only shares which could be redeemed were redeemable preference shares. The idea behind a share purchase scheme is that the company can buy back a portion of its shares by either a direct offer to the current shareholders or by purchasing the required shares through the market. The company law requirements vary from country to country but the main requirements of a share repurchase scheme are as follows:

1 The power to redeem a company's shares must be stated in its articles of incorporation.

2 A buy-back must be approved by both the Board of Directors and by resolution of the shareholders. Under certain circumstances an application must also be made to the Courts for permission to reduce capital.

3 The buyback must be financed out of the firm's distributable reserves.

4 A transfer must be made from the distributable reserves to a 'capital redemption fund' of a sum equal to the nominal value of the shares to be redeemed.

5 That all shares redeemed must be cancelled (although there are proposals to permit up to 10 per cent of the purchased shares to be held by the firm on its own account).

The principle behind these legal requirements is to protect the rights of the remaining shareholders and to prevent a reduction of capital to the point that it is detrimental to the firm's creditors. There are broadly three ways in which a company can repurchase its shares:

1 A fixed price tender offer where the company offers a fixed price (invariably at a significant premium over the current market price) to all its current shareholders in order to induce them into selling whole or part of their holding. The fixed price premium may be up 40 per cent above the current market price.

2 Open tender offer where the company invites its shareholders to make a 'bid' (usually within a range of prices) for a price at which they are prepared to part with their shares. When the bids are received the firm's management will rank the bids along with the number of shares offered back to the company in reverse order in order to determine the group of shareholders who have offered the lowest price and whose shares will, in total, satisfy the firm's repurchase requirements. The highest price in the group accepted for repurchase then becomes the price used for the repurchased. Normally, the premium paid by the company at the bottom of a tender offer range is approximately 10–15 per cent above the open market price.

3 Open market repurchase where the company either directly or through an intermediary buys back their shares on the market.

Of these method 3 is the most common as it ensures that the price paid by the company for the repurchase is as close as possible to the current equity price although it is quite likely that the market will have adjusted the price in anticipation of the repurchase.

The consequences of a share repurchase

The most obvious consequence of a share repurchase is that it will entail a transfer of cash from the company to the shareholders and it is, therefore, a form of distribution. Unlike a dividend it will be treated as a capital transaction by the tax authorities and the investor will be required to pay 'capital gains tax' on any increase in the value of the shares since they were purchased. The rules for calculating capital gains vary from country to country and are complex but it is common for such gains to be taxed at a lower rate than income and for there to be a significant 'zero rate' band. Again many jurisdictions allow capital losses to be offset against gains in working out the overall tax payable. Dividends on the other hand are defined as 'investment' income and will attract a rate of tax either at, or in excess of, the investor's highest rate of tax.

For the company a share repurchase will have the effect of increasing the earnings per share as the number of shares in issue will be reduced. Other things being equal we would also expect to see an increase in the company's gearing where it is partly financed by debt. The net effect will be to increase the rates of return on equity and capital employed in the business on the assumption that the repurchase does not impair the earning capability of the firm.

However, the real consequences of share repurchase schemes operate at a much deeper level. There is strong evidence that markets regard the announcement of share repurchases as good news. There are a number of reasons for this. It may be that shareholders believe that the firm's management are signalling that the shares are undervalued in the market. It may also be viewed as potentially reducing the scope of managers to over-invest. You will remember from Chapter 1 that there can be a conflict between the interests of the shareholders and management creating agency loss as the latter use the information they have to the detriment of the former.

A share repurchase restricts the scope of this agency loss by distributing free cash flow back to the investors. Like the agency argument concerning capital structure above markets look favourably upon actions by the firm which limit the scope of management to exploit their position.

Share repurchase versus dividends

However, the more important issue is why should companies wish to repurchase their equity? There are a number of possible answers to this question although what we can say is that if a company's equity is fairly priced in the market and there is no difference in the tax treatment of capital gains and dividends then there should be no difference in principle between a repurchase and a dividend payment. However, there are a number of possible explanations:

1 A firm may wish to alter its capital structure in favour of higher gearing without issuing new debt capital. Over time, as a company accumulates profits in its owner's equity account gearing within its balance sheet will fall. If the directors believe that a certain level of gearing is optimal then a share repurchase may be able to re-establish the desired level.

2 Where a company has run out of new value adding investment opportunities it may find it to its advantage to cut back the size of the firm refocusing its attention on what is often referred to as its 'core business'. A share repurchase may be the only option for doing this if the company is ungeared or is unable to redeem its debt early.

3 Where dividends are taxed less than capital gains (as used to be the case with dividend receipts to pension funds prior to 1997 in the UK) then that would be an incentive for a firm to distribute via dividend rather than through repurchase. However, in the more usual situation capital gains are taxed more favourably than dividends and as a result share repurchase would be preferred. Surprisingly this has not always been the case and in the US dividends have dominated repurchases as the favoured mode of returning cash to the shareholders even though the dividends were more heavily taxed than capital gains.

4 As we noted above changes in dividend payout signal different things to the stock market. Repurchases are invariably seen as a positive sign by the markets and a signal that management believe that the company is undervalued in the market. Further flesh was put on the signalling argument by Guay and Harford (2000) who suggested that repurchases are more likely to occur when firms experience sudden but temporary improvements in their cash flow, while firms who have strong and consistent cash flows tend to distribute via dividends. Their empirical evidence lends some support to this hypothesis in that the reaction of prices to increasing dividends tends to be more favourable than the announcement of a repurchase.

There is still no clear consensus as to why firms do decide to opt for one method of distribution to shareholders over another. It is clear in the UK that the regulatory and other transactions costs incurred in a share repurchase are a substantial disincentive to management thinking of taking this route. Clearly the situation varies from country to country and in the US, repurchases have grown in popularity over the last 20 years. There are a number of readings at the end of this chapter which will allow you to explore this issue more fully.

SUMMARY

In the late 1950s Modigliani and Miller overturned the received wisdom in finance in two important ways. They argued that the logic of the Fisher Hirshliefer Separation Theorem applied in a world that admitted risk. Neither capital structure nor dividend policy had any impact on the value of the firm, only a firm's earnings and its exposure to business risk were important. Although the assumptions they invoked were very simplistic their theorems have stood the test of time and, as Stewart Myers has said, what matters is not whether Modigliani and Miller were right or wrong, they clearly were right given their assumptions, but how market imperfections disturb their analysis. There is still no definitive resolution of the irrelevancy debates however, we do now accept that agency effects, transactions costs, information signalling, taxation and the possibility of default all have a part to play in what is one of the most complex areas of decision making faced by the financial manager.

If there is an answer it is this: the value maximizing firm should adopt that capital structure and dividend policy which allows it to continue to expand value through investment in positive Net Present Value projects. The exact balance between different sources of finance will be shaped by imperfections in the financial markets and it should recognize that policy changes will bring transaction costs whether incurred through organizing a new tranche of debt, an equity issue or a repurchase scheme to buy back its own shares. The skilful financial manager needs to keep the financial policy of the firm in line with the company's needs and to ensure that when it needs cash it can get it and when it has too much that it is returned to its investors.

Further Reading

Ball, R., (2003) *The Theory of Stock Market Efficiency – Accomplishments and Limitations* in Stern, J.M., and Chew, D.H., (2003) *The Revolution in Corporate Finance* (4th Ed.), Blackwell, Oxford

Barclay, M.J. and Smith, C.W. (2003) The capital structure puzzle: another look at the evidence, in Stern, J.M. and Chew, D.H. (2003) *The Revolution in Corporate Finance* (4th Ed.), Oxford: Blackwell.

Barclay, M.J., Smith, C.W. and Watts, R.I. (1995) The determinants of corporate leverage and dividend policies, *Journal of Applied Corporate Finance* 7:4.

Dittmar, A.K. (2000) Why do firms repurchase stock?, *Journal of Business*, 73:355–384.

Gordon, M., (1963) *Optimal Investment and Financing Policy*, The Journal of Finance, XVIII, 2, 264–272

Grullon, G. and Michaely, R. (2002) Dividends, Share Repurchases, and the Substitution Hypothesis, *The Journal of Finance* 57:1649.

Grullon, G. and Ikenberry, D.L. (2003) What do we know about share repurchases? in Stern, J.M. and Chew, D.H. (2003) *The Revolution in Corporate Finance* (4th Ed.), Oxford: Blackwell.

Guay, W., and Harford, J., (2000) *The cash flow permanence and information content dividend increases vs. repurchases*, Journal of Financial Economics 57, 385–415.

Hamada, R.S. (1969) Portfolio Analysis, market equilibrium and corporate finance, *Journal of Finance*, 24:13–31.

Jagannathan, M., Stephens, C.P. and Weisbach, M.S. (2000) Financial Flexibility and the choice between dividends and stock repurchases, *Journal of Financial Economics*, 47:355–384.

Jensen, M. (1986) Agency costs of free cash flows, corporate finance and takeovers, *American Economic Review* 76:323–329.

Maxwell, W.F. and Stephens, C.P. (2003) The Wealth Effects of Repurchases on Bondholders, *The Journal of Finance* 58:2: 895–920.

Michaely, R., Thaler, R.H. and Kent, L. (1995) Price reactions to dividend initiations or omissions: overreaction or drift, *The Journal of Finance*, 50:573–608.

Miller, M.H. (1977) Debt and taxes, *Journal of Finance* 32.

Miller, M.H. (1986) Financial innovation – the last twenty years and the next, *Journal of Financial and Quantitative Analysis* 21.

Miller M.H. (1988) The Modigliani-Miller Propositions after thirty years, Reprinted in shortened form in Stern, J.M. and Chew, D.H. (2003) *The Revolution in Corporate Finance* (4th Ed.), Oxford: Blackwell.

Miller, M.H. Modigliani, F. (1961) Dividend policy, growth and the valuation of shares. *Journal of Finance* 17.

Miller, M.H. and Modigliani, F. (1966) Some estimates of the cost of capital to the electrical utility industry (1954–57), *American Economic Review* 56:3.

Modigliani, F. and Miller, M.H. (1958) The cost of capital, corporation finance and the theory of investment, *American Economic Review* 48.

Myers, S.C., (1984) *The Capital Structure Puzzle*, Journal of Finance, 39, 581–582.

Myers, S.C. (2003) Still searching for optimal capital structure, Reprinted in shortened form in Stern, J.M. and Chew, D.H. (2003) *The Revolution in Corporate Finance* (4th Ed.), Oxford: Blackwell.

Solomons, E., (1963) *Leverage and the Cost of Capital*, Journal of Finance, XVIII, 2, 273–79.

Smith, C., (2003) *Raising Capital – theory and evidence* in Stern, J.M., and Chew, D.H., (2003) *The Revolution in Corporate Finance* (4th Ed.), Blackwell, Oxford.

PROGRESS CHECK

1 What were the assumptions that underpinned the Modigliani and Miller capital structure and dividend irrelevance arguments?

2 What are the two principal irrelevancy arguments and how do they relate to the Fisher Hirshliefer Separation Theorem?

3 How does financial risk differ from business risk?

4 Under the traditional view of capital structure what happens to the firm's cost of capital as gearing is increased?

5 How does default risk arise and how does it differ from financial risk?

6 State the Modigliani and Miller propositions 1 and 2.

7 What is the impact upon the weighted average cost of capital if interest payments by companies (but not by individuals) are a tax deductible expense?

8 Define Modigliani and Miller's proposition 3.

9 List four possible challenges to the practical significance of the Modigliani and Miller propositions.

10 What do you understand by the term 'static tradeoff theory'?

11 How do agency factors influence the level of gearing that a firm might adopt.

12 What is the formula which links beta to a firm's level of gearing?

13 What are the two mechanisms by which a firm can return cash to its equity investors and under what cash flow circumstances might it choose either?

14 Outline the Modigliani and Miller dividend irrelevancy argument.

15 How would a firm assess its capacity to pay a dividend?

QUESTIONS (answers at end of book)

1 Two companies HI and LO plc are of identical business risk. The rate of return for a pure equity firm of that risk is 8 per cent. LO's earnings are £100 000 per annum and it is financed solely through equity. HI's distributable earnings are twice that figure and it has a gearing ratio (market value of debt to market value of equity) of 50 per cent. Hi's cost of debt finance is 6 per cent. What is the market value of HI's equity?

2 A company has a market gearing ratio (market value of debt to market value of equity) of 40 per cent. It pays corporation tax at 35 per cent and its debt interest payments are tax deductible. The rate of return on its debt capital is 4 per cent and its current cost of equity capital is 7 per cent. What is the implied rate of return on a pure equity firm of the same risk class?

3 A company has a beta value of 1.6. Its current gearing ratio is 45 per cent (market value of debt to total market capitalization). It is considering increasing its gearing to 60 per cent. What will its beta be after this alteration in its capital structure? Ignore tax.

QUESTIONS (answers on website)

4 Alphatron plc has 50million 25p shares in issue trading at 150p each. The firm's current cover ratio is three times dividends and the dividend it paid in the last financial year was 5p per share. Its current cost of equity capital is 8 per cent. It has one loan outstanding of £25 million upon which it pays 6 per cent fixed interest. The debt is due to be redeemed in three years and the company's lenders have told them that at current rates they could reschedule their debt and increase their loan to £30 million for a ten year term at an interest rate 25 basis points higher than the rate they would require on new loan finance if their existing loan was due for redemption immediately. The company pays corporation tax at 40 per cent.

You are required to:

(i) Calculate the current market value of the firm's equity.

(ii) Calculate the pure equity rate for a company of this risk class.

(iii) Calculate the cost of equity if the firm reschedules the debt as proposed.

(iv) Calculate the company's weighted average cost of capital both before and after this refinancing package.

(v) Comment upon any other issues the company may with to bear in mind when considering this proposal.

5 A company has a beta value of 1.6. Its current gearing ratio is 45 per cent (market value of debt to total market capitalization). The value of its debt in issue is £20 million and it pays tax at 40 per cent. It is considering increasing its gearing to 60 per cent. What will its beta be after this alteration in its capital structure?

6 Thomson Teazers plc is a stable company in the comic book publishing business. It has a mature market (in more ways than one) and earns a free cash flow after interest and tax of £150 million per annum. It currently operates with little debt but has found very few opportunities for expansion in its core business over the last five years. Last year it attempted a take over of Patsy (Stationary) Ltd for £25 million before it realized that it was the wrong sort of stationery and had to withdraw. The directors have currently refurbished the head office, installed a gymnasium and pool for senior staff in the basement and bought two new flag poles to carry the company's coat of arms and a flag bearing the symbol of the Queen's award for industry which they won two years previously. Walt Teazer the company's founder, chairman and honorary life president has currently had a new company car delivered – an Aston Martin Vanquish.

The company's shareholders include a number of significant institutional investors have become concerned at the low levels of dividends paid in recent years and the last AGM was a somewhat bad tempered event. The company share price had fallen by 8 per cent against the market trend in the last six months even though the company has significant cash reserves and the current year's earnings are on target.

Talking to a particularly aggressive fund manager at the reception that followed Walt was surprised to hear that the fund manager felt that a leveraged buy back of equity should be considered by the board. Walt nearly choked on his caviar canapés but after recovering his composure aided by another large glass of Bollinger (*gran cuvee*) did promise to consider the idea.

As the company's chief financial officer you are given the task of considering the options for improving the company's position with its shareholders. In your report you decide to expose a number of the issues which may be of concern to investors.

7   The summarized accounts and selected notes for Splash Computers plc are as below.

The company is run by two brothers who are the sole shareholders and company directors. They own 50 per cent of the equity each and have taken substantial dividends as well as paying themselves directors' emoluments of £600 000 each before arriving at operating profit for the year.

During the year they agreed and received an additional £400 000 of borrowing from the bank and also issued themselves, for cash, a further 150 000 shares each.

They have asked you for your opinion on how much further dividend this company could release. You note that the firm's accountants have not prepared a cash flow statement.

You are required:

(i)   To prepare a cash flow statement for the year to 31 December 2005.

(ii) To estimate the company's free cash flow to equity and its current dividend capacity in total and on balance for this year after the current dividend declared is paid.

EXHIBIT 6.19

Accounts for Splash Computers plc

Splash Computers plc
Summarized balance sheet

As at 31 December	2005	2004
Fixed assets	4 756 640	3 814 020
Current assets		
stocks and work in progress	695 600	511 500
debtors and prepayments	698 000	104 350
cash in hand	2 760 550	1 210 350
	4 154 150	1 826 200
Less current liabilities	2 770 138	1 470 010
	1 384 012	356 190
Total assets less current liabilities	6 140 652	4 170 210

Less long term debt	2 400 000	2 000 000
	3 740 652	2 170 210
Shares (£1 ordinary)	800 000	500 000
Profit and loss reserve	2 940 652	1 670 210
	3 740 652	2 170 210

Splash Computers plc
Extract from the profit and loss account

For the year ended	**2005**	**2004**
Operating profit for the year	3 789 000	1 909 000
Surplus on the disposal of fixed assets	125 680	305 050
	3 914 680	2 214 050
Interest paid and payable	114 000	95 000
	3 800 680	2 119 050
Tax at 35 per cent	1 330 238	741 668
Profit available for distribution	2 470 442	1 377 383
Less dividend proposed	1 200 000	1 000 000
Profit retained	1 270 442	377 383

Notes to the accounts

Debtors and prepayments		
Trade debtors	130 500	65 000
Prepayments and accrued income	18 000	
Balance due on sale of fixed assets	500 000	
Other debtors	49 500	39 350
	698 000	104 350
Current liabilities		
Trade creditors	230 400	367 090
Tax payable	1 330 238	95 000
Dividend payable	1 200 000	1 000 000
Interest payable	9 500	7 920
Outstanding liabilities at the year end	2 770 138	1 470 010
Fixed assets		
Opening value at cost	5 944 900	7 569 000
acquisitions	1 768 000	230 500
	7 712 900	7 799 500
Less disposals	540 900	1 854 600
	7 172 000	5 944 900
Depreciation		
opening balance	2 130 880	2 649 150
less depreciation released on disposals	432 720	1 112 760
	1 698 160	1 536 390
Depreciation charge for year	717 200	594 490
Accumulated depreciation	2 415 360	2 130 880

Producing a cash flow statement

This appendix presents a simple algorithm for producing a cash flow statement. The layout is as for FRS1 but the information provided by the algorithm can be rescheduled into IAS7 format. For our purposes the algorithm allows the easy calculation of the free cash flow to equity.

The logic of this method is based upon the balance sheet equation which describes the formal relationship between a firm's assets and the claims on those assets:

$$FA + St + Db + C = STL + LTL + OE$$

This means that the fixed assets, stocks, debtors and cash on the left hand side of the equation must necessarily equal on the right: the firm's short and long term liabilities and the owner's equity.

Between the beginning and end of the year the changes on each of these items must also balance. Using the delta (Δ) symbol to signify differences the changes in the balance sheet values over a year give the differential balance sheet equation as follows:

$$\Delta FA + \Delta St + \Delta Db + \Delta C = \Delta STL + \Delta LTL + \Delta OE$$

In order to explain the cash change over the period of account we rearrange this equation:

$$\Delta C = (\Delta OE + \Delta STL + \Delta LTL) + (\Delta FA + \Delta St + \Delta Db)$$

With the exception of cash, we have taken the changes in all assets values to the right hand side and shown them as a deduction from the changes in the values of the claims. Note how we have kept the changes in claims and assets separate and also, for convenience, how we have reordered the claims so that the change in owners' equity is shown first. The two groups of changes impact upon cash in different ways. Changes in claims represent what we term 'positive cash drivers' and changes in assets 'negative cash drivers'. What this means is that an increase in the value of a claim, if it impacts on cash will have a positive effect and vice versa for an increase in the value of an asset.

To illustrate the method we will use a simple set of accounts as shown in Exhibit 6.20.

Using the differential cash flow equation above we can show how the change in cash reconciles to the changes in the other balance sheet values as shown in Exhibit 6.21.

Our task now is to analyze each of the differences into the respective cash flow headings as shown in Exhibit 6.22.

Note: We have not, in this example, included a column for the management of liquid resources (i.e. the buying and selling of near money market instruments such as government and corporate bonds or increases or decreases on deposit accounts) between dividends paid and financing. In practice, the inclusion of this item rarely causes any problems. I prefer to split out the liquidity elements from the net cash flow at the end of the analysis. If you wish to include a separate column remember that liquid resources like other assets will appear in the negative cash driver part of the master schedule.

The first part of the analysis focuses on the three positive cash drivers: the change in the owner's equity account, the change in short term liabilities and the change in long term liabilities. Taking owner's equity first, the change of +37 in the balance sheet

EXHIBIT 6.20

Balance sheet, profit and loss, and notes to the accounts

Balance sheet			Profit and loss		
	2004	**2003**		**2004**	**2003**
Fixed assets	190	163	Sales turnover	100	70
Less accumulated depreciation	45	40	less operating costs	38	22
	145	123	Operating profit	62	48
Current assets			Interest paid	6	6
stocks	10	6	Profit before tax	56	42
debtors	18	12	Tax payable	12	10
cash	8	2	Distributable profit	44	32
	36	20	Dividends	11	10
less short term liabilities	24	23	Profit retained	33	22
Net current asset/(liabilities)	12	(3)			
	157	120			
less long term liabilities	90	90	Note: short term liabilities		
	67	30	trade creditors	6	9
			tax	12	10
Owners capital	12	8	dividends	6	4
Profit and loss reserve	55	22		24	23
	67	30			

EXHIBIT 6.21

The explanation of cash flow from the balance sheet

	C	=	(OE	+	STL	+	LTL)	–	(FA	+	St	+	Db)
2004	8	=	(67	+	24	+	90)	–	(145	+	10	+	18)
2003	2	=	(30	+	23	+	90)	–	(123	+	6	+	12)
Difference	6	=	(37	+	1	+	0)	–	(22	+	4	+	6)

EXHIBIT 6.22

Column headings for the master cash flow schedule

Δ	Operating cash flow	Interest paid/received	Taxation	CapEx Disposals	Dividends Paid	Financing

is derived from two sources: a +33 change in balance on profit and loss reserve and +4 arising from a new equity issue. To proceed, lay out the detail of the profit and loss account below the operating profit line until arriving at the figure for retained profit. Then extend each item to its respective FRS1 heading as shown below. Operating profit itself goes to operating cash flow, interest paid to the interest paid/received column and so on. Keep positive values positive and negatives, negative. Do not change sign and do not extend the totals. Likewise extend the new equity issue to the 'financing column'. Repeat for the changes in short and long term liabilities, rule off, cast each column and check that the sum of the analysis columns equals the sum of the cash differences for the positive cash drivers (38) as shown in Exhibit 6.21.

We learn from the balance sheet note that the change in the short term liabilities over the year (1) consists of a decrease in trade creditors (−3) which is posted to the operating cash flow column, an increase in tax payable (2) and an increase in dividends paid (2) posted to the tax and dividends paid columns respectively. These changes can be picked up from the notes to the balance sheet. Finally, we turn our attention to the negative cash drivers to complete the master schedule as shown in Exhibit 6.23.

With fixed assets the net change of 22 is explained by acquisitions (27) and an increase in accumulated depreciation of (5). The value of the acquisition represents a positive change in the fixed asset value in the balance sheet and the change in accumulated depreciation is a negative change. We post the former to the CAPEX column and the latter (because it passes through operating costs in the profit and loss) to the operating cash flow column. Note again how we keep the signs unchanged as we extend them across the schedule.

Finally, we total up the 'negative cash drivers', check the cross cast, and then deduct them from the corresponding changes in the 'positive cash drivers' totalled above to give the cash flow analyzed under the cash flow headings.

EXHIBIT 6.23

The master schedule

	Δ	Operating cash flow	Interest paid/ received	Taxation	CapEx Disposals	Dividends Paid	Financing
Positive cash drivers							
Operating profit	62	62					
Interest paid	(6)		(6)				
Profit before tax	56						
Tax payable	(12)			(12)			
Distributable profit	44						
Dividends	(11)					(11)	
Profit retained	33						
New equity issue	4						4
Change in owner's equity	37						
Short term liabilities							
Trade creditors	(3)	(3)					
Tax	2			2			
Dividends	2					2	
Change is STL	1						
Change in LTL	0						
Positive cash drivers	38	59	(6)	(10)	0	(9)	4

Negative cash drivers							
Fixed assets							
Acquisitions	27					27	
Accumulated depreciation	(5)	(5)					
Change in fixed assets	22						
Change in stocks	4	4					
Change in debtors	6	6					
Negative cash drivers	32	5	0	0	27	0	0
Cash flow analysis	6	54	(6)	(10)	(27)	(9)	4

All that remains is to layout the figures in vertical form and to reconcile operating profit with the cash flow from operations using the data in the operating cash flow column of the master schedule.

EXHIBIT 6.24

The final statement of cash flow and reconciliation

Statement of cash flow			Reconciliation of operating profit with cash flow from operations	
	2004			**2004**
Cash flow from operations	54		Operating profit	62
			add back depreciation	5
				67
Net interest paid	(6)			
Taxation	(10)		Increase in stocks	(4)
			Increase in debtors	(6)
Capital expenditures/disposals	(27)		Decrease in trade creditors	(3)
Dividends paid	(9)		**Cash flow from operations**	54
Financing	4			
Net cash flow for the year	6			

It really is as easy as that! You need only remember the balance sheet equation and the headings to use the technique. You do not need to add back depreciation, movements to reserves, or any of the other adjustments required by the conventional method of producing a cash flow statement. The technique eliminates all non-cash changes automatically. For example, a revaluation surplus posted to a revaluation reserve during the year would show up as a positive change in the owner's equity account and would be posted to the CAPEX column. The corresponding increase in the fixed asset account in the balance sheet would likewise be posted to the CAPEX account cancelling the earlier entry.

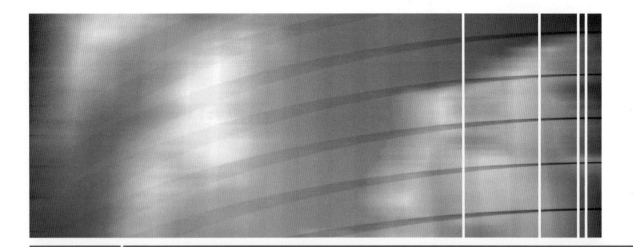

III Developments in Corporate Finance

Modelling inflation, tax and uncertainty

This chapter develops the use of the Net Present Value and other investment appraisal models under conditions of inflation, tax and uncertainty. The analysis of inflation covers the use of the Fisher formula and the techniques for converting real into nominal rates and vice versa. Given the problems of falling prices in certain markets deflation and its impact is also discussed. The elements of corporation tax systems are then described categorized into a small number of distinct groups presenting common features to the analyst. The UK system is described in some detail and its impact upon the value of investment is explored. We also describe the adjusted Net Present Value method for handling tax. Finally, using numerous practically based case exercises, various financial modelling techniques are demonstrated which when supplemented by sensitivity analysis and simulation can be used to inform managerial judgement in investment appraisal.

Learning outcomes

In this chapter you should achieve the following:

1 Understand the impact of price changes upon investment decisions and be able to undertake an investment appraisal in either real or nominal terms.

2 Identify when a short term capital rationing situation exists and deploy the profitability index in order to construct a capital investment plan.

3 Adjust future cash flows for the impact of corporation tax and calculate the Net Present Value of a project on that basis.

4 Calculate the adjusted Net Present Value in an analysis and explain the advantages and disadvantages of this technique.

5 Test the sensitivity of a project to changes in its key variables and to determine which variables are critical to the analysis.

6 Simulate a simple project and calculate the project Net Present Value at risk.

Investment appraisal and changing price levels

When considering the impact of changing price levels upon a project it is important to recognize that these price changes consists of two parts:

1 general price changes reflecting the average movement in price levels throughout the economy, and

2 abnormal price changes specific to the project where the prices obtained and the cost levels incurred by the firm differ from the general rate that prices are changing throughout the economy.

Inflation is the term used to describe the general increases in prices within the economy. There are a number of measures used to describe the phenomenon and different countries have different statistical methodologies for its measurement.

It is beyond the scope of this book to describe in detail the factors that influence the level of inflation in the economy. However, many scholars (and politicians) believe that it is purely a function of changes in the supply of money. If government increases the volume of money in circulation then the purchasing power of the currency will fall and prices will rise. Others take a broader view and look at the factors influencing both the supply and demand for money leading to a consideration of factors within the real economy. From our point of view we need not concern ourselves with how inflation comes about but just to recognize its importance.

What is a mistake, however, is to assume that although inflation as a general phenomenon may not have the importance currently as in previous decades that the problem of changing price levels has gone away altogether. Firms have different exposures to changing prices. Profit levels in the aviation industry, for example, are heavily influenced by the price of oil which while being an important factor across the general economy can be critical in the determining the performance of an airline.

In capital investment appraisal changes in future prices, whether they affect revenues or costs, are dealt with in one of two ways: by including the impact of all price changes in as far as they can be foreseen, or by excluding them from the analysis.

Real and nominal cash flows and rates of return

In dealing with inflation in investment appraisal two terms are important: 'real' cash flows or rates of return and 'nominal' cash flows or rates of return. A real cash flow projection is one which is expressed in current day price levels while a nominal projection uses the expected future price levels when estimating costs and revenues. A real rate of return is one which does not reward the investor for bearing inflation while a nominal rate does reward the investor for bearing the impact of future changes in price levels.

Obviously, if a cash flow has been projected in 'real' terms then the appropriate discount rate is the real rate of return required by investors. If the projection is in nominal terms then the appropriate rate to use is the nominal rate. So far so good, however, there is a trap for the unwary and that is to assume that when projecting cash flows in current day price levels then future price changes can be ignored. This is only true if the future price changes on all revenue and cost flows are expected to be at the level of general price inflation in the economy. In many businesses and especially the diamond grinding industry occupied by Friendly Grinders plc which imports much of its diamond paste from overseas suppliers this is certainly not the case as the next financial reality demonstrates.

Jack Grinder was reviewing a capital investment bid put forward by his product development team in the Diagrit business division. The capital investment for £3.5 million would be fully written off over the life of the project. The proposal included a cash flow projection which ignored price changes. Revenues, Jack knew, were based upon prices which tended to rise at 3 per cent more per annum than the general rate of price increases in the UK. Currently the Bank of England put the mid term inflation forecast at the government's target level of 2 per cent. Direct cost levels on the other hand had generally risen at a faster rate than revenues at about 6 per cent per annum while strict control of indirect costs kept their increases at or just below the rate of inflation in the UK. Friendly Grinders' cost of capital is currently estimated to be 8 per cent per annum (see Chapter 5).

The revenue and cost forecast relating to the new proposal DG05/01/14 provided by the division were as follows:

EXHIBIT 7.1

Summary cash flow projection for the DG05/01/14

DG05/01/14 Summary cash flow statement (sterling million)	1	2	3	4	5	6
Project revenues	2.100	2.250	2.290	2.310	2.400	1.960
less direct expenditures	−0.630	−0.675	−0.687	−0.693	−0.720	−0.588
indirect expenditures	−0.693	−0.743	−0.756	−0.762	−0.792	−0.647
Project operating cash flow	0.777	0.832	0.847	0.855	0.888	0.725

Jack gives a heartfelt sigh and decides to correct the projections himself.

What Jack is dealing with here is a projection which has ignored price changes completely. It is not expressed in current day price levels so to do that Jack first uplifts each line of the projection by its appropriate rate of price increases as shown in Exhibit 7.2

Note that for each line Jack has adjusted the original figures using the formula:

$$\text{Nominal value}_n = \text{unadjusted value}_n \times (1 + s)^n$$

where 's' is the specific rate of price increase and 'n' is the number of years until that cash flow arises.

The final summarized figure for each year is the 'nominal' project cash flow. Once the nominal cash flow projection is arrived at, we can then proceed to express that nominal flow in real terms by discounting using the rate of inflation. Jack's revision to real cash flow terms is as in Exhibit 7.3.

Note that in this case Jack has used the Bank of England quoted inflation figure to eliminate the impact of general inflation using the formula:

$$\text{Real cash flow}_n = \frac{\text{nominal cash flow}_n}{(I + h)^n}$$

where h is the rate of inflation.

EXHIBIT 7.2

Cash flow projection for the DG05/01/14 project after price level adjustments

DG05/01/14 Summary cash flow statement (sterling million)		1	2	3	4	5	6
Project revenues		2.100	2.250	2.290	2.310	2.400	1.960
price level adjustment	5% pa	x (1.05)^1	x (1.05)^2	x (1.05)^3	x (1.05)^4	x (1.05)^5	x (1.05)^6
Nominal project revenues		2.205	2.363	2.405	2.426	2.520	2.058
less direct costs		−0.630	−0.675	−0.687	−0.693	−0.720	−0.588
price level adjustment	6% pa	x (1.06)^1	x (1.06)^2	x (1.06)^3	x (1.06)^4	x (1.06)^5	x (1.06)^6
Nominal direct expenditures		−0.668	−0.716	−0.728	−0.735	−0.763	−0.623
less indirect expenditures		−0.693	−0.743	−0.756	−0.762	−0.792	−0.647
price level adjustment	2% pa	x (1.02)^1	x (1.02)^2	x (1.02)^3	x (1.02)^4	x (1.02)^5	x (1.02)^6
Nominal indirect expenditures		−0.707	−0.757	−0.771	−0.778	−0.808	−0.660
Nominal project operating cash flow		0.830	0.890	0.905	0.913	0.949	0.775

Jack now has two alternatives to consider: a nominal cash flow and a real cash flow. The first should be discounted using his company's cost of capital in the normal way (see Exhibit 7.4). Using the methods described in the previous chapters we have calculated the current cost of capital which reflects not only risk but also the reward investors require for bearing the potential loss caused by increasing price levels. The cost of capital is technically, therefore, a 'nominal rate of return' and is appropriate for discounting cash flows expressed in nominal terms.

EXHIBIT 7.3

Cash flow projection for the DG05/01/14 project adjusted to real terms

DG05/01/14 Summary cash flow statement (sterling million)		1	2	3	4	5	6
Project revenues		2.205	2.363	2.405	2.426	2.520	2.058
less direct costs		−0.668	−0.716	−0.728	−0.735	−0.763	−0.623
less indirect expenditures		−0.707	−0.757	−0.771	−0.778	−0.808	−0.660
Project nominal operating cash flow		0.830	0.890	0.906	0.913	0.949	0.775
price deflator	2% pa	/(1.02)^1	/(1.02)^2	/(1.02)^3	/(1.02)^4	/(1.02)^5	/(1.02)^6
Project real operating cash flow		0.814	0.855	0.853	0.844	0.860	0.688

EXHIBIT 7.4

Calculation of the Net Present Value for the DG05/01/14 project using the nominal rate of discount on the nominal cash flow projection

DG05/01/14 Summary cash flow statement (sterling million)	0	1	2	3	4	5	6
Nominal project operating cash flow		0.830	0.890	0.905	0.913	0.949	0.775
Capital investment	−3.500						
	−3.500	0.830	0.890	0.905	0.913	0.949	0.775
Discounted cash flow at 8 per cent	−3.500	0.769	0.763	0.719	0.671	0.646	0.488
Net Present Value	0.556						

The use of the Fisher formula

If Jack had decided to work on the real cash flows he would need to adjust the company's cost of capital to exclude the impact of inflation. The simplest adjustment would be to deduct the rate of inflation from the nominal rate but this neglects the fact that the component parts of the nominal rate (i): the return required for bearing general levels of price inflation (h), the difference in return required for bearing changes in specific as opposed to general price levels (r_s), the investors' liquidity premium (r_l) and the return required for risk (r_σ) are compounded together to give the return on one pound invested for one year. Thus:

$$(1 + i) = (1 + r_l)(1 + r_\sigma)(1 + r_s)(1 + h)$$

What we term the real rate is all the components of return except for the rate of inflation so the above formula can be simplified to:

$$(1 + i) = (1 + r)(1 + h)$$

This very important formula is named after the late early 20th Century economist Irvin Fisher and is known as the 'Fisher formula'.

Using the Fisher formula to convert a nominal rate of return of 8 per cent into a real rate given an inflation rate of 2 per cent we obtain:

$$(1 + i) = (1 + r)(1 + h)$$

$$(1+r) = \frac{(1+i)}{(1+h)}$$

$$(1+r) = \frac{1.08}{1.02} = 1.0588$$

$$r = 5.88\%$$

Using this rate to discount the real cash flows Jack arrives at an identical answer to his NPV calculation in Exhibit 7.5.

EXHIBIT 7.5

Net Present Value projection for the DG05/01/14 project using real cash flows
discounted using the real cost of capital

DG05/01/14 Summary cash flow statement (sterling million)	0	1	2	3	4	5	6
Project real operating cash flow		0.814	0.855	0.853	0.844	0.860	0.688
Capital investment	−3.500						
	−3.500	0.814	0.855	0.853	0.844	0.860	0.688
Discounted cash flow at 5.88 per cent	−3.500	0.769	0.763	0.719	0.671	0.646	0.488
Net Present Value	0.556						

Comparing the result of real and nominal analysis

So, in principle, there is no difference between a nominal analysis and a real
analysis – both give exactly the same answer. With a real analysis the intention is
that only the changes in the volume of activity are taken into account and that
changing price levels are ignored. In practice it is not possible to convert a nominal cash flow to a real cash flow for a given firm unless you know the specific rate
of price changes to which that firm is subject. Where a company has sector specific
price change which are significantly different from the general rate of inflation the
elimination of that inflation from its nominal cash flows will lead to a cash flow
projection that is neither fish nor fowl: the effect of price changes will have not
been properly accounted for and so what is left is neither a real cash flow nor a
nominal cash flow. The information derivable from a real terms analysis is therefore of questionable value.

Early studies revealed that many firms when undertaking discounted cash flow
techniques preferred to project in real terms but then failed to realize the importance of using the real as opposed to the nominal discount rate. It is also a
common mistake to assume that a real terms analysis can be based upon a cash
flow projection that ignores future price changes completely. That can only be
done if the firm could identify, and could isolate from the discount rate, the effect
of price changes that impact upon that project specifically. From a technical point
of view undertaking a real analysis is hardly worth the effort because to achieve
the desired result, future abnormal price changes must still be incorporated into
the analysis.

REVIEW ACTIVITY 7.1 Discount the project cash flows for the DG05/01/14 proposal on the
following bases:

1 Discount the original nominal cash flows as presented by the Diagrit
   division using the real rate of discount as calculated above and identify the
   degree of overvaluation of the project that this represents.
2 Discount the real cash flows using the nominal rate and identify the degree
   of undervaluation of the project that this represents.

Deflation

In recent years inflationary pressures within some western economies have been replaced by the reverse phenomenon of reducing as opposed to increasing price levels. In Japan, following the Plaza Accord of 1985 the Yen was realigned against the dollar. There has been a sustained period of deflationary pressure within the economy partly fuelled by the revaluation but also by the success of Japanese firms at producing large quantities of consumer goods at ever lower cost and with increasing quality. The problems caused by the realignment for Japanese export markets and the ability of firms to supply goods at ever lower prices led to supply outstripping demand and as a result a downward price spiral began to take hold.

Deflation, as it is termed, produces strong disincentive effects within the economy as consumers believe it is to their advantage to delay spending. As a result the inflation and the liquidity premium in the cost of capital turns negative. In principle, the method of dealing with deflation is exactly the same as with inflation. Projections are best constructed in nominal terms and a nominal discount rate applied to produce the Net Present Value. However, in those projections there will be considerable uncertainty because unlike inflation it is much more difficult stimulating demand than restraining it and it is relatively easy for a country to slip into what is termed a 'deflationary spiral'.

In most western economies with floating exchange rates and where the management of interest rates and the money supply is in the hands of the central banks the risk of deflation is minimized. Central banks who are less concerned with winning elections than politicians tend to take less risks with the economy. In the UK, the government when granting control of interest rates to the Monetary Policy Committee of the Bank of England established a 'symmetrical' inflation target of 2.5 per cent (now 2 per cent). The MPC is required to ensure that divergence of forecasted inflation below as well as above the target rate is quickly corrected. The Bank of England (at www.BankofEngland.co.uk) has a number of publications concerning its management of the monetary system.

The problem of capital rationing

Capital rationing can occur in the short run for any firm even though the firm's balance sheet shows substantial reserves and the company would not normally have any difficulties obtaining finance in the capital markets. As we noted in Chapters 2 and 3 although the capital markets are highly efficient raising substantial sums of new money through the fixed interest, equity or risk capital markets, it will take time and will involve at least some transaction costs. Technically a situation of capital rationing will arise where a firm, possessing value adding (positive NPV) investment projects, cannot raise sufficient finance at a cost of capital commensurate with the risk that it presents to the market, or without incurring transaction costs which would overwhelm the value added by the proposed investments. We will deal with transaction costs when we explore the adjusted present value technique later in this chapter.

We can summarize capital shortages therefore as follows:

1 *Capital market failure*: where finance of the type the firm needs is unavailable at any price. This is likely to be a temporary problem providing that the business prospects offered by the firm to the market are sound given the level of risk the company presents. Small firms or businesses new to market are more likely to face this problem than larger more established enterprises.

2 *Money market failure*: where the firm has significant positive value adding business already established and significant reserves but where its current liquidity is such that it needs to raise short term finance in the money market to supplement its treasury cycle. In this situation it may not be appropriate for the firm to raise new capital but instead it may attempt to raise short term debt finance through (usually) the banks or through trade finance. An inability to raise short term finance in this way would constitute a failure in the money market.

In both situations the problems are likely to be only short term but while exhausting for management to deal with do not present too many problems from a technical point of view. However, the Net Present Value rule does not provide sufficient information for the company to make the critical 'rank and yank' decisions concerning new project bids during the current year. The so called 'profitability index' can provide an indication of the ability of an investment to deliver positive value relative to its outlay.

FINANCIAL REALITY

Jack Grinder is back at his desk reviewing a long list of projects from the various divisions of the firm. The Board of Directors have decided that the capital markets would react badly if they were to announce a cut in dividends to help finance the current year's investment round. Jack had agreed strongly with that decision, but it did mean that the current levels of cash available at three months' notice was just £26 million.

EXHIBIT 7.6

The list of projects under review during the current investment round at Friendly Grinders plc

	0	1	2	3	4	5	6	7	8	NPV	IRR
OG05/06/01	–19.100	6.450	6.550	4.340	4.221	4.200	2.110			3.224	14.38%
OG05/09/02	–12.000	5.150	8.930	3.400						3.124	22.53%
DG04/01/03	–5.333	7.232	2.440	2.320	–3.000	–0.005				3.088	66.57%
DG05/03/11	–3.650	–3.000	2.400	2.200	1.866	1.750	1.500	1.000	–0.600	0.884	13.64%
DG05/01/14	–3.500	0.830	0.890	0.905	0.913	0.949	0.775			0.556	13.07%
DG05/02/11	–4.010	2.300	2.245	1.001	0.995	–1.540				0.522	18.02%
NM04/04/10	–4.000	–0.055	0.001	0.150	2.202	1.890	1.850			0.140	8.76%

Looking at this list seemed to suggest to Jack that the Optical Group were very likely to get finance, but that Nuclear Medicine at the other end of the list would lose out again. He had reviewed each proposal that had passed the Board's scrutinizing committee to see whether they had an option to defer and the list in front of him now represented only those projects where immediate commencement was necessary on commercial grounds. He knew that some of the smaller projects were reasonably scalable (down not up) but he was sure that this was not the case with the two highest NPV projects: OG05/06/01 and OG05/09/02. What to do now? Nothing for it – so Jack decided to do some thinking on the golf course.

EXHIBIT 7.7

A first attempt at ranking the current project submissions by Net Present Value

	0	1	2	3	4	5	6	7	8	NPV	IRR
OG05/06/01	−19.100	6.450	6.550	4.340	4.221	4.200	2.110			3.224	14.38%
OG05/09/02	−12.000	5.150	8.930	3.400						3.124	22.53%
DG04/01/03	−5.333	7.232	2.440	2.320	−3.000	−0.005				3.088	66.57%
DG05/03/11	−3.650	−3.000	2.400	2.200	1.866	1.750	1.500	1.000	−0.600	0.884	13.64%
DG05/03/11	−1.567	−1.288	1.030	0.944	0.801	0.751	0.644	0.429	−0.258	0.380	13.64%

Jack's problem here is that he is attempting to rank the project bids put to the board purely in terms of the Net Present Value each project promises to deliver. As things stand, he can opt for the projects as highlighted taking his total investment to £26 million but relying upon a scaling of DG05/03/11.

The highlighted investments in Exhibit 7.7 offer a Net Present Value of £6.692 million. However, these projects may not be as efficient at converting scarce capital into Net Present Value as others. For this reason Jack should rank all his positive Net Present Value projects using the following ratio:

$$\text{Profitability index} = \frac{\text{Net Present Value}}{\text{Capital invested}}$$

This index is useful for ranking projects where capital is unavailable for one year and it also gives us the short run opportunity cost of finance which the company can use in its negotiations in the money markets. Ranking each of the projects by their profitability index produces quite a different ordering to that suggested by NPV alone.

In Exhibit 7.8 we show the capital outlay, NPV, IRR and the profitability index. We have ranked the projects according to the profitability index and introduced a column showing the accumulated capital spend as we go down the ranked list of investments. Given that OG05/06/01 cannot be scaled back this suggests that this project should be eliminated from the list although before the plan is finalized it is worth checking whether

EXHIBIT 7.8

Ranking of projects by the profitability index

	Capital Outlay	Cum. Capital	NPV	IRR	PI
DG04/01/03	−5.333	−5.333	3.088	66.57%	0.5791
OG05/09/02	−12.000	−17.333	3.124	22.53%	0.2603
DG05/03/11	−3.650	−20.983	0.884	13.64%	0.2422
OG05/06/01	−19.100	−40.083	3.224	14.38%	0.1688
DG05/01/14	−3.500	−43.583	0.556	13.07%	0.1588
DG05/02/11	−4.010	−47.593	0.522	18.02%	0.1302
NM04/04/10	−4.000	−51.593	0.140	8.76%	0.0350

EXHIBIT 7.9

Analysis of the finalized capital expenditure plan with DG05/02/11 scaled and split

	Capital Outlay	Cum. Capital	NPV	IRR	PI
DG04/01/03	−5.333	−5.333	3.088	66.57%	0.5791
OG05/09/02	−12.000	−17.333	3.124	22.53%	0.2603
DG05/03/11	−3.650	−20.983	0.884	13.64%	0.2422
DG05/01/14	−3.500	−24.483	0.556	13.07%	0.1588
DG05/02/11	−1.517	−26.000	0.198	18.02%	0.1302
DG05/02/11	−2.493	−28.493	0.325	18.02%	0.1302
NM04/04/10	−4.000	−32.493	0.140	8.76%	0.0350
OG05/06/01	−19.100	−51.593	3.224	14.38%	0.1688
Capital Budget	**−26.000**		**7.850**	**22.55%**	**0.3019**

substituting this for the other large scale project OG05/09/02 delivers a superior Net Present Value. Dropping OG05/06/01 produces an investment plan, or capital budget, as shown in Exhibit 7.9. Four proposals are included in whole and one (DG05/02/11) in part generating a Net Present Value of £7.850 million which is £1.158 million better than Jack's original ranking.

There is still one question to be resolved and that is whether substituting OG05/06/01 for OG05/09/02 produces a better plan. In fact it produces the same outcome as the original ranking by Net Present Value and thus can be dismissed as an option.

If the least valuable project in the list of accepted projects is perfectly scalable then the profitability index for that project tells us the maximum additional rate which the firm should be prepared to pay for money market finance to overcome its short term capital shortage. Friendly Grinders could in principle pay this rate for a maximum £2.493 million of additional finance providing it repays that finance within one year. The maximum borrowing rate would therefore be:

Opportunity cost of finance   =   market rate with no market failure

+

profitability index (as a percentage)

Opportunity cost of finance   =   8% + 13.02% = 21.02%

The 8 per cent is used as the discount rate in calculating the Net Present Value on the marginal project. So if the company pays an additional 13.02 per cent for borrowing of £2.493 million for one year, the interest payment will be the remaining Net Present Value on this marginal project. Thus any additional rate of less than 13.02 per cent will generate a positive Net Present Value and is worthwhile. Clearly, for funds above the figure required to complete DG05/02/11 the additional rate which is worthwhile is just 3.5 per cent. Finally, if Jack were to seek the full finance required to complete the plan the maximum additional rate would be given by the weighted average of the profitability index on the partially complete project and the two remaining projects. The weights to use are given by the capital requirements for each project in Exhibit 7.10.

EXHIBIT 7.10

Calculating the weighted average of the profitability indexes for the rejected projects

Project	Capital required	weight by capital	PI	Weighted average
DG05/02/11	−2.493	0.097	13.02%	1.27%
NM04/04/10	−4.000	0.156	3.50%	0.55%
OG05/06/01	−19.100	0.746	16.88%	12.60%
	−25.593			14.41%

Rather unusually the weighted average rate is greater than that suggested for the marginal investment and that is because Jack has been forced to forego OG05/06/01 because of its lack of scalability and the size of the capital investment entailed.

REVIEW ACTIVITY 7.2 Jack is on his way for a round of golf with his bank manager. She is not a good golfer but she is willing to listen to a proposal (at least in the area of finance). He calls you on the mobile and says that he wants to know the maximum rates he should be prepared to negotiate for (a) an additional £2 million, (b) an additional £6 million and (c) an additional £19 million. You have five minutes or . . .

Where capital is in short supply for longer than one year then the firm will almost certainly need to raise additional finance in the capital market. The problem of deciding upon the optimal budgeting plan is somewhat more complex and may involve setting up a linear programming model where the Net Present Value can be optimized subject to  the capital constraints in the years in which they apply. Where, as in this case, the problem also involves 'integer' type solutions, i.e. where one or more projects must be accepted in their entirety or not at all, the mathematics becomes more formidable. Readings at the end of this chapter will guide you further, although it is worth noting that in practice such long term capital rationing is a signal that the firm should be looking to expand its capital base through a new issue to the markets. Short term financial problems can invariably be overcome through the money market as we discuss in Chapter 13 unless of course the company is deluding itself about the value of its project investment portfolio and that the range of positive Net Present Value projects presented to the Board of Directors for approval are not as financially valuable as their promoters claim.

The impact of taxation upon investment appraisal

There are a number of taxes which need to be taken into account when undertaking capital investment appraisal:

1 *Corporation tax*: this is a broadly based profits tax levied on companies. The profits of the firm will be adjusted eliminating any non-allowable expenditures (usually the cost of the enjoyable parts of running a business but also

including depreciation, amortization and other similar figments of the accountant's imagination). In the place of the company's depreciation charges it will be able to offset against its tax burden what are referred to as 'capital allowances'. Small firms pay a lower rate than larger firms and they may also find that there are a number of anti-avoidance provisions which are designed to prevent the owners taking advantage of the fact that corporation tax rates tend to be lower than income tax rates (which creates an incentive for them to retain their profits rather than distribute them).

2 *Value added tax*: this is a tax which accumulates along a supply chain and which is paid by the end customer for the product or services concerned. A company normally charges its customer VAT at the appropriate rate (usually the standard rate but other rates may apply for different types of supply) against which it offsets any VAT it has paid to its own suppliers. The difference between the former (the 'output tax') and the latter, its 'input tax', is normally paid or recovered within the quarter. VAT for a company is therefore normally self cancelling unless it makes supplies that are exempt from VAT. In that situation it will not have any output tax to offset its input tax and will have to include any VAT in the cost of its supplies. This can be significant for capital investment where, for example, a new building is constructed which will bear VAT on the construction costs, but where that tax cannot be offset against VAT charged on its outputs from the project.

3 *Local taxes*: apart from corporation and value added tax which are (in most European countries) nationally imposed taxes, companies may also have to bear regional taxes based on their property values or some other means of assessment. There may also be offsets available for companies that have a charitable purpose or are in specific industries such as agriculture. These taxes should also be taken into account is assessing the merits of a particular investment.

For a company operating in different countries the distinction between national as opposed to local taxes is important. With the former there are usually 'double tax agreements' whereby a liability for tax in one country can be offset in another. However, the offset may not be perfect in that the full amount of tax cannot be recovered and net liability results. The company operating across national borders may also face import duties that are non-recoverable. In summary, the diversity of taxes involved and the particular way in which they will impact upon a specific project can present a substantial problem in investment appraisal. This means that the relevant tax expert should always be present in the analysis of any significant new investment project.

However, leaving aside the impact of tax law, the financial modelling of a specific investment project raises a number of complexities:

1 Some taxes (notably corporation tax) allow that losses incurred on a specific project can be offset against profits made elsewhere, other taxes (such as a property tax on land) do not allow this. Where there are insufficient other profits in the year in question it may be possible to carry the losses forward until the point is arrived where they can be offset (or indeed be reclaimed against prior year liabilities already discharged). Because of this, there may be uncertainty about the impact of a given tax upon the future cash flows of the firm.

2 With most taxes there is a difference between the time at which the underlying profit or loss arises and when the tax has to be paid or can

be recovered. With corporation tax the liability is assessed on the profit for the year. Under some tax jurisdictions this means that the tax is paid in the year following (i.e. the tax is assessed on a prior year basis), in others a payment in advance of the eventual liability has to be paid during the year of assessment and any over- or under-payment collected in the following year. Because there are often heavy penalties for under-estimating the advance payment most companies err on the side of caution and overestimate. This induces 'fiscal drag' on company tax which can have a small but significant impact upon the firm's cash flows.

Corporate tax modelling

Modelling tax depends upon a careful understanding of its impact upon the company's overall tax burden, the timing of the resulting cash receipts or offsets and the adjustment of the discount rate to reflect the affect of any tax shield. In Chapter 5, we showed the procedure for adjusting the weighted average cost of capital to include the impact of taxation on the return a company must deliver to its debt investors. Our job here is to examine the effects of modelling the tax flows and their impact upon the underlying investment decision. We will take as our working example the DG05/01/14 case and extend the analysis taking into certain details concerning the tax system that Friendly Grinders plc operates under.

FINANCIAL REALITY

EXHIBIT 7.11

The nominal cash flow on project DG05/01/14 before tax

DG05/01/14 Summary cash flow statement (sterling million)	0	1	2	3	4	5	6
Nominal project operating cash flow		0.830	0.890	0.905	0.913	0.949	0.775
Capital investment	-3.500						
Nominal project cash flow	-3.500	0.830	0.890	0.905	0.913	0.949	0.775

The capital cost of the plant (−£3.5 million) is deemed to be a qualifying expenditure against which capital allowances can be claimed. Friendly Grinders has adequate profits elsewhere to offset the capital allowances.

The company can claim a first year allowance of 50 per cent of the qualifying expenditure and 40 per cent per annum on a reducing balance basis. Once the plant is written off, the unexpired capital allowances can be claimed in full. The company's marginal rate of corporation tax is 30 per cent and the tax on additional profits is payable 12 months after the liability arises. Friendly Grinders' cost of capital (post tax) is currently 7.355 per cent (see Chapter 5 for the detailed calculation of this figure for Friendly Grinders (2005) plc).

EXHIBIT 7.12

Analysis of the correction for corporate tax in Net Present Value analysis

DG05/01/14

Summary cash flow statement (sterling million)

		0	1	2	3	4	5	6	7
Nominal project operating cash flow			0.830	0.890	0.905	0.913	0.949	0.775	
Capital investment		-3.500							
Nominal project cash flow		-3.500	0.830	0.890	0.905	0.913	0.949	0.775	
Calculation of capital allowances									
Unexhausted capital allowance	50%	3.500	1.750	1.050	0.630	0.378	0.227	0.136	
First year allowance		-1.750							
Writing down allowances	40%		-0.700	-0.420	-0.252	-0.151	-0.091	-0.054	
Carried forward		1.750	1.050	0.630	0.378	0.227	0.136	0.082	
Capital allowance claimed		-1.75	-0.700	-0.420	-0.252	-0.151	-0.091	-0.054	
Tax saving in following year	30%		0.525	0.210	0.126	0.076	0.045	0.027	0.016
Tax on operating cash flow:									
Operating cash flow			0.830	0.890	0.905	0.913	0.949	0.775	
Increase in corporation tax liability	30%			-0.249	-0.267	-0.272	-0.274	-0.285	-0.232
Nominal project cash flow		-3.500	0.830	0.890	0.905	0.913	0.949	0.775	
Less tax on operating profits				-0.249	-0.267	-0.272	-0.274	-0.285	-0.232
Post tax cash flow before capital allowances		-3.500	0.830	0.641	0.639	0.642	0.675	0.490	-0.232
Tax benefit of capital allowances			0.525	0.210	0.126	0.076	0.045	0.027	0.016
Post tax project cash flow		-3.500	1.355	0.851	0.765	0.717	0.720	0.518	-0.216
Discount cash flow at 7.355 per cent	7.355%	-3.500	1.262	0.738	0.618	0.540	0.505	0.338	-0.132
Net Present Value		0.370							
Internal Rate of Return		11.52%							

Annotations:

(i) calculate the first year allowance as 50% of the initial capital outlay

(ii) calculate the writing down allowance as 40% of the reducing capital balance

(iii) work out the tax saving at 30 per cent and show it in the year in which the benefit will be received

(iv) work out the additional tax which will have to be paid as the operating cash flows increase the company's tax liability

(v) calculate the impact of the tax as a two stage process, first deduct the additional tax on the operating cash flows then add the benefit of the capital allowances

The analysis shown in Exhibit 7.12 proceeds through a number of stages:

1 The tax calculations are performed upon the nominal cash flows as these form the basis upon which future tax will be calculated.

2 Corporation tax is deducted from the project's operating cash flows on the assumption that these will form an incremental addition to the taxable profits of the firm. Tax is assessed on the project operating cash flows at the marginal rate for the firm. The effective rate should not be used as this is the average rate the firm pays whereas the project leads to an additional liability over and above the existing liability of the firm to tax. The cash effect of the additional tax will occur at the point the cash is paid to the Inland Revenue Service not at the point the liability arises. In tax jurisdictions where tax is paid 'on account' then the cash flow and the point the liability arises may well be the same. In jurisdictions where no advance payments are made then the cash flow is likely to be in the year following that when the liability arises.

3 The capital allowances are calculated using the rates specified in the ruling tax legislation for assets of the type concerned. Usually they are calculated on a reducing balance basis using the pooling method. What this means in practice is that all of the firm's assets form a 'pool' against which the writing down allowance (but not the first year allowance) can be applied. When a new asset is acquired, the first year allowance is taken and the balance of the asset's value (50 per cent in the example above) is taken to the fixed asset pool. Once in the pool it is charged annually with the prevailing writing down allowance until its is eventually disposed of.

4 The tax benefits associated with the capital allowances are kept as a separate line in the calculation. As with the additional tax on the operating flows from the project the cash benefit associated with the capital allowance will occur either in the year the liability arises if the firm is required to pay tax on account or in the year following.

5 The project is discounted at the company's post tax weighted average cost of capital reflecting the benefit of the tax shield on Friendly Grinder's cost of debt.

Using the tax model above we can determine how the NPV of the project responds to changes in the tax rate. Clearly, as the tax rate increases the NPV will fall. However, with this particular tax regime once the tax rate goes above 77 per cent (see Exhibit 7.13) the Net Present Value of the project goes negative. Note that in performing this analysis we have assumed for the sake of simplicity that the company's cost of capital remains unchanged. In practice of course that will not be the case.

This tax regime is therefore not neutral with respect to the value of the project and hence with respect to capital investment generally. A neutral tax regime is one where the reduction in the value of the project is in direct proportion to the tax rate. The conditions required for a corporation tax system to be neutral with respect to value of corporate investment are as follows:

1 Only a first year allowance (0%–100%) on the original capital investment should be given.

2 The incidence of the tax receipts and benefits should be at the point the liability to tax arises.

3 The cost of debt capital should not benefit from a tax shield.

EXHIBIT 7.13

The impact of corporation tax on the Net Present Value of a project

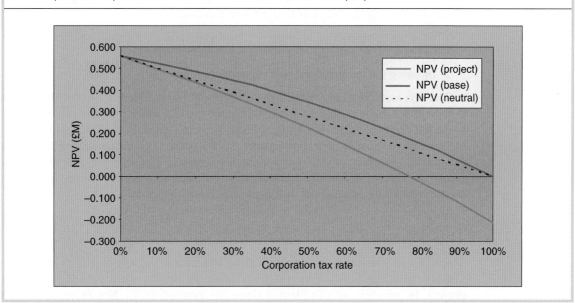

In Exhibit 7.13 we show the effect of the tax system as defined (NPV project) upon the value of the project and have included the effect of giving a 100 per cent first year allowance (and hence no writing down allowances) and setting the incidence of tax in the year in which the liability arises. This base case NPV returns a zero value if the tax rate is set at 100 per cent, however, it is not quite neutral because of the tax advantage of the tax shield on the cost of debt.

Evaluating the impact of structural changes in investment appraisal

The idea underpinning the use of the weighted average cost of capital in investment appraisal is that the risk profile of the firm will not be changed. In the majority of situations that is the case. However, a project may be of such significance that it does alter the business risk of the firm or at the very least while leaving the business risk unchanged causes a significant alteration in the equity investors' exposure to financial and default risk. In the worst case everything changes. We will defer a detailed examination of how we deal with structural change in business risk until Chapter 12 when we look at the problems of mergers and acquisitions. However, the method is straightforward in that the firm must establish the likely impact of the change in exposure by combining the beta of the firm and that of the new project/acquisition into an 'appraisal beta' which is used to revise the firm's cost of capital for evaluation purposes.

When a project entails a significant alteration in the firm's capital structure the use of the firm's existing weighted average cost of capital is inappropriate. There may also be significant tax benefits associated with a change in the gearing of the firm. There are broadly two ways of dealing with this issue:

1 by using the weighted average cost of capital adjusted for the alteration in gearing,

2 by using the 'adjusted present value' technique.

The first method is conceptually the most straightforward and accords with the idea that there is a single capital pool upon which the firm draws to invest. As we discovered in the last chapter, a significant alteration in the firm's gearing affects all of the parameters within the cost of capital: the equity premium, the tax benefits and any change in the default premium. A different approach recognizes that a project that necessarily entails an increase in the firm's gearing will also bring an associated tax benefit which can be considered as a distinct cash flow with its own exposure to risk.

The adjusted Net Present Value

The adjusted present value method allows the firm's decision maker to separately identify the components of the value added to the firm by the proposed investment project. In principle we can identify three components in the Net Present Value of a project:

1 The capital invested and the net of tax project cash flows.

2 The tax shield effect because of the use of debt finance to fund the project.

3 Any other exceptional issue costs caused by the project.

The technique can be expanded to also account for any special grants or other incentives attaching to the particular project.

Element 1 in the analysis should be discounted at the pure equity rate for a company of the specified risk class. This can either be achieved using Modigliani and Miller's proposition 2 (as modified for a company which can deduct its loan interest payments against tax) or by using the Capital Asset Pricing Model and ungearing the firm's beta. Element 2 should normally be discounted at the firm's cost of debt as the tax shield effect is unlikely to be affected by business risk, and Element 3 is an investment outlay and does not need to be discounted.

The logic of the method is that in the absence of a tax shield on debt interest the pure equity rate should be the same as the weighted average cost of capital at any level of gearing if the Modigliani Miller hypothesis is accepted. The only benefit of debt financing is that it offers a benefit to the project in the form of the tax shield.

FINANCIAL REALITY

Jack Grinder following his discussion with his bank manager has come away with an offer of a further £19.1 million of borrowing in order to finance project OG05/06/01. An upfront administration fee of 2 per cent of the loan would be payable. The new loan would run for the term of the project and would carry interest at 6 per cent being the rate of return required by the bank for a loan of this duration. This project will be eligible for a 100 per cent first year capital allowance. The company's corporation tax rate is 30 per cent and it has sufficient profits elsewhere to offset the tax effects. The project cash flows are as follows:

Project OG05/06/01							
	0	1	2	3	4	5	6
Nominal cash flows before tax	−19.10	6.45	6.55	4.34	4.22	4.20	2.11

The company's asset beta is 0.907 (see Chapter 6 for the calculation of this figure), the risk free rate of return is 4.75 per cent and the equity risk premium is 3.5 per cent.

To calculate the adjusted present value we proceed through the following steps:

1 Calculate the firm's pure equity cost of capital. We can use either Modigliani and Miller's proposition 2 or ungear the firm's equity beta. We will take the second approach which gives a pure equity cost of capital:

$$r'_e = R_F + \beta_A \times ERP$$
$$r'_e = 4.75\% + 0.907 \times 3.5\%$$
$$r'_e = 7.92\%$$

This is the rate we will apply to the firm's post tax operating cash flows on the basis that because the tax effects from the project bear the same risk as the project then this is the appropriate rate to use.

2 Discount the project's cash flows after accounting for the first year allowance and the tax on the subsequent operating cash flows. For this project this gives a Net Present Value of £2.631 million.

3 Calculate the interest that the firm will pay. In this case the project will entail a loan of £19.1 million plus issue costs of 2 per cent which equals 0.382 million. The interest payable on this debt at 6 per cent is £1.1689 million. The tax saving is then calculated at 30 per cent of the interest charge before being discounted at 6 per cent. The present value of the tax saving is £1.7244 million.

4 Calculate the present value of any issue costs. As these are incurred at outlay their present value is simply the amount paid of £0.382 million. If the issue costs were spread over more than one period then they should be discounted at the rate appropriate for the type of finance to which they are attached. In this case the rate of return required by the lender would be the appropriate rate.

The resulting adjusted Net Present Value is £3.703 million as shown in Exhibit 7.14. The advantage of this method is that it shows the sources of the present value of the project. In some situations a project may have a negative present value attaching to its project cash flows but a positive benefit from the tax shield. Such an outcome might give management pause for thought if the only reason for acceptance of the project is the tax shield then they might simply be better off revising the firm's gearing and foregoing the investment opportunity.

The adjusted Net Present Value approach exploits the Modigliani and Miller capital structure arguments to surmount the problem of valuing projects where a change

EXHIBIT 7.14

The estimation of the adjusted Net Present Value for project OG05/06/01

Project OG05/06/01	0	1	2	3	4	5	6	7
Operating cash flows before tax		6.450	6.550	4.340	4.221	4.200	2.110	
Tax on the operating cash flows (at 30%)			-1.935	-1.965	-1.302	-1.266	-1.260	-0.633
Operating cash flow less tax		6.450	4.615	2.375	2.919	2.934	0.850	-0.633
Project outlay	-19.100							
Tax impact of FYA		5.730						
Project cash flow	-19.100	12.180	4.615	2.375	2.919	2.934	0.850	-0.633
Discounted cash flow at 7.92 per cent	-19.100	11.286	3.962	1.890	2.152	2.004	0.538	-0.371
Net Present Value of project flows	**2.361**							
Interest paid on outstanding debt								
Loan value = 19.482 million								
Interest charge per annum		1.169	1.169	1.169	1.169	1.169	1.169	
Tax saving on debt interest paid		0.351	0.351	0.351	0.351	0.351	0.351	
Discounted value at company's cost of debt (at 6%)		0.331	0.312	0.294	0.278	0.262	0.247	
Present value of tax saving	**1.724**							
Present value of issue costs	**-0.382**							
Adjusted Net Present Value	**3.703**							

in capital structure is brought about by a change in the firm's gearing. Where it comes unstuck is where the new investment opportunity alters the firm's exposure to business and in particular to market risk. In this situation we are forced to undertake a revaluation of the firm using a revised weighted average cost of capital. We will return to this topic in Chapter 12 when we look at the problems of valuing other companies for the purposes of acquisition.

Modelling uncertainty

Generally there are two strategies for handling risk and uncertainty in investment appraisal. The first approach assumes that the cash flow projections are known for certain and then applies a discount rate which incorporates an element of return for the perceived risk of the project. This approach works well for the routine analysis of projects which do not entail significant disturbances to the value of the firm. This method also allows the 'spot' valuation of a project and as we shall see later can be modified to incorporate significant variations in the financing of the firm and in its taxable position. The second approach takes the project cash flows and the firm's target discount rate and explicitly models the uncertainty in the project either by a sensitivity analysis, simulation or stress testing. Each method focuses upon a different part of the examination of uncertainty and each has its own disadvantages.

Sensitivity analysis

The simplest approach to the analysis of uncertainty is by examining the marginal impact upon Net Present Value of changes in the underlying variables in the discounted cash flow analysis. In principle there are four sensitivities of concern to us:

1 the sensitivity of the project to changes in the capital investment outlay,

2 the sensitivity of the project to changes in the magnitude of any one of the project's future cash flows,

3 the sensitivity of the project to changes in the discount rate, and

4 the sensitivity of the project to changes in the average timing of the future cash flows.

Setting up a very simple mathematical description of a capital investment project:

$$NPV = -A_0 + \frac{A_1}{(1+i)^1} + \frac{A_2}{(1+i)^2} + \frac{A_3}{(1+i)^3}$$

where A_0, A_1, A_2 and A_3 are the project cash flows and i is the discount rate.

We can now explore the sensitivity of the project to changes in the variables involved using some simple mathematics:

1 *Capital sensitivity*: the marginal impact of changes in capital invested upon the project's Net Present Value is given by:

$$\frac{d(NPV)}{dA_0} = -1$$

This makes the obvious point that any change in the amount invested induces an exactly opposite change in the Net Present Value of the project. Thus a £1 increase in capital outlay will lead to a £1 decrease in Net Present Value and vice versa.

2 *Cash flow sensitivity*: the marginal impact of changes in any one of the cash flows is given by:

$$\frac{d(NPV)}{dA_n} = \frac{1}{(1+i)^n}$$

This again makes the intuitively obvious point that changing the magnitude of any of the future cash flows will have a direct bearing on the project's Net Present Value depending upon the magnitude of the discount factor used to discount that cash flow. The further away in time that a change in the value of cash flow occurs the lower the impact upon the value of the project.

3 *Discount rate sensitivity*: this sensitivity reintroduces a concept developed in Chapters 2 and 4 which is the duration of the project. Duration, you may recall, is the weighted average of the time when each cash flow arises where the weights are calculated with respect to the Net Present Value of the project. Here is the maths:

$$\frac{d(NPV)}{di} = -\frac{1}{(1+i)}\left[1\frac{A_1}{(1+i)^1} + 2\frac{A_2}{(1+i)^2} + 3\frac{A_3}{(1+i)^3}\right]$$

Multiplying the top and bottom of the right hand side of the above equation with the present value of the future cash flows gives:

$$\frac{d(NPV)}{di} = -\frac{1}{(1+i)}\left[\frac{1\frac{A_1}{(1+i)^1}+2\frac{A_2}{(1+i)^2}+3\frac{A_3}{(1+i)^3}}{PV}\right]PV$$

$$\frac{d(NPV)}{di} = -\frac{1}{(1+i)}\times D\times PV$$

where D is duration and PV is the present value of the future cash flows. Unfortunately the impact of changes in interest rate is not as intuitively obvious as was the case with changes in the cash flows analyzed previously. Because duration and the present value of a project's future cash flows are both a function of the discount rate we need to calculate all three terms on the right hand side of the expression. However, the maths does tell us one rather simple and obvious point that increasing the discount rate will surely reduce the Net Present Value. This should be well established in your thinking by now but it's nice to prove the point!

4 *Timing sensitivity*: because duration is our most comprehensive measure of the average time it takes a project to deliver its value to the firm it is this we target to measure the sensitivity of a project's values to either delay or, on the positive side, to more rapid realization of the project cash flows. Given that duration is defined as:

$$D = \left[\frac{1\frac{A_1}{(1+i)^1}+2\frac{A_2}{(1+i)^2}+3\frac{A_3}{(1+i)^3}}{PV}\right]$$

Then by rearrangement and letting K equal the numerator:

$$PV = \left[\frac{1\frac{A_1}{(1+i)^1}+2\frac{A_2}{(1+i)^2}+3\frac{A_3}{(1+i)^3}}{D}\right]$$

Deduct the capital outlay from each side and we have the Net Present Value of the project's cash flows on the left hand side of the equation:

$$NPV = -A_0 + \left[\frac{1\frac{A_1}{(1+i)^1}+2\frac{A_2}{(1+i)^2}+3\frac{A_3}{(1+i)^3}}{D}\right]$$

Substituting K on the right hand side we have the following expression:

$$NPV = -A_0 + \frac{K}{D}$$

Taking the first differential of NPV with respect to the duration we obtain:

$$\frac{d(NPV)}{d(D)} = -\frac{K}{D^2}$$

Multiplying top and bottom of the right hand side by the present value of the future cash flows:

$$\frac{d(NPV)}{d(D)} = -\frac{K}{PV}\frac{1}{D^2}PV$$

But given that the duration is $\dfrac{K}{PV}$ the differential resolves to:

$$\frac{d(NPV)}{d(D)} = -\frac{PV}{D}$$

Again, when stated this result is obvious that increasing duration will lead to a decrease in NPV but with lesser and lesser impact the larger the project's duration.

These four results do not capture all that can go wrong with a project. They do assume that only one variable changes at a time and that the change is very small – this is particularly important with interest rate and timing changes where the relationship between the variable and the Net Present Value of the project is non-linear. Sensitivity analysis does not reflect how variables interact no their contingent effects over time. However, our analysis does point to the usefulness of duration in determining the exposure of the project to uncertainty in its constituent elements.

FINANCIAL REALITY

Jack decided to have a closer look at the bids that had been put in front of the Board for consideration. In particular he was interested to see how they all compared with respect to interest rate risk and timing. This was the data that Jo-Jo his new Assistant Financial Controller had put together:

EXHIBIT 7.15

Analysis of the sensitivity of the project plan (refer back to Exhibit 7.6 for the individual project cash flows)

Project	CAPEX	PV	NPV	Profitability Index	duration	interest rate sensitivity	time sensitivity
DG04/01/03	−5.333	8.421	3.088	0.579	0.899	−7.007	−9.371
OG05/09/02	−12.000	15.124	3.124	0.260	1.863	−26.090	−8.117
DG05/03/11	−3.650	4.793	1.143	0.313	5.253	−23.316	−0.912
OG05/06/01	−19.100	22.324	3.224	0.169	2.787	−57.611	−8.010
DG05/01/14	−3.500	4.056	0.556	0.159	3.278	−12.311	−1.237
DG05/02/11	−4.010	4.532	0.522	0.130	1.334	−5.600	−3.396
NM04/04/10	−4.000	4.140	0.140	0.035	4.882	−18.712	−0.848

Jack was perfectly aware of the impact of changing capital spend: one extra pound spent on any of the projects would bring about a direct decrease of £1 in the value of the project. He also understood that any reduction in a subsequent cash flow would have an impact on the value of the project directly proportional to the discount rate for the year in question. What Jack could not understand is what these sensitivities meant.

The calculation of duration is straightforward and follows the procedure described in Chapter 2 using the present value of the project as the base for the weight measurement. Thus, for project DG04/01/03 the duration is calculated as follows:

$$D = \frac{1\dfrac{7.232}{1.08^1} + 2\dfrac{2.440}{1.08^2} + 3\dfrac{2.320}{1.08^3} + 4\dfrac{(-3.000)}{1.08^4} + 5\dfrac{(-0.005)}{1.08^5}}{8.421}$$

$$D = 0.899$$

Using the interest rate sensitivity formula we can calculate the impact upon the NPV of this project of a small change in interest rate of (say 1 per cent):

$$\frac{d(NPV)}{di} = -\frac{1}{(1+i)} \times D \times PV$$

$$d(NPV) = -\frac{1}{(1+i)} \times D \times PV \times di$$

$$d(NPV) = -\frac{1}{(1.08)} \times 0.899 \times 8.421 \times 1\%$$

$$d(NPV) = -£0.07007 \; million$$

EXHIBIT 7.16

The effect of interest rate changes upon Net Present Value (calculated directly versus using interest rate sensitivity)

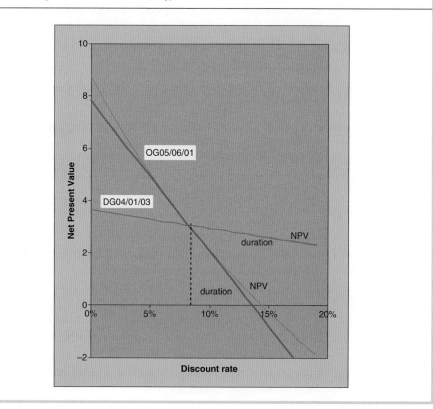

This sensitivity measure gives a comparative index of sensitivity of each project to tiny changes in the firm's cost of capital. However, with some projects the convexity effect (see Chapter 4) is noticeable as the change in interest rate used to measure the sensitivity of the project's Net Present Value is increased. Exhibit 7.16 shows a plot of the Net Present Values of two projects (which at the discount rate of 8 per cent have very similar NPVs) where one value is calculated in the normal way for the different discount rates and the other using the discount rate sensitivity measure based upon duration. As you can see from that exhibit the project from the Optical Group has a higher convexity which is itself associated with the rate of change of Net Present Value with interest rate.

Nevertheless, given that the cost of capital is designed to compensate the investors for the risk they are carrying then this sensitivity measure is a very useful measure of the relative exposure of different investment opportunities to interest rate risk. It is also worth making the point that when this sensitivity measure is low, errors in measuring the cost of capital are much less significant than when the sensitivity measure is high.

Time sensitivity is more difficult to interpret. This measure shows the sensitivity of a project to variation in the average time required to recover the cash flows from the project (i.e. its duration). This, like the previous measure is a useful index for evaluating an investment's sensitivity to overall variation in the project cash flows. The first three projects in the ranked list highlight the differences in that the two highest ranked projects are highly sensitivity to delays in the timing of the cash flows, while the third is far less sensitive to timing. From the point of view of value creation this index shows the relative importance that management should place in trying to bring forward the future benefits from different projects. The first two projects will reward that effort handsomely; the third will produce relatively little overall benefit.

EXHIBIT 7.17

The four principal sensitivity measures

Capital sensitivity	Cash flow sensitivity	Interest rate sensitivity	Timing sensitivity
$\dfrac{d(NPV)}{dA_0} = -1$	$\dfrac{d(NPV)}{dA_n} = \dfrac{1}{(1+i)^n}$	$\dfrac{d(NPV)}{di} = -\dfrac{1}{(1+i)} \times D \times PV$	$\dfrac{d(NPV)}{d(D)} = -\dfrac{PV}{D}$
Need to know:	**Need to know:**	**Need to know:**	**Need to know:**
• Capital investment	• Discount rate • Year cash flow arises	• Interest rate • Project duration • Present value of future project cash flows	• Present value of future cash flows • Project duration
Highly critical to the success of the project as variations in capital expenditure directly influence the value of the project	The impact of uncertainty of future cash flows diminish the further the cash flows are into the future	The impact of uncertainty in the cost of capital depends on the magnitude of this complex measure. Values greater than 100/i mean that this is the most critical measure of the four in determining a project's exposure to risk	This sensitivity measure focuses on the average time it take to recover the cash flow from a project. Improving the throughput of value generates a significant benefit in terms of value added to the firm

Simulation

Simulation starts from the proposition that managers and planners are able to define the parameters of the distributions of each of the variables in the model they are considering and the extent to which they interrelate. The method is simple to describe but rapidly grows in complexity with the number of variables in the model.

Jack had another proposal on his desk which was giving him more concern than the DG05/01/14. This project from the optics division was of a more short term nature and would entail a significant outlay of capital investment in order to capture the benefits of a short term government contracts. The cash flow projections looked strong in terms of the base case Net Present Value and Internal Rate of Return. However, OG05/09/02 had considerable uncertainties attached to the forward projections of cash flow. The basic proposal was as follows:

EXHIBIT 7.18

The project analysis for OG05/09/02

OG05/09/02	0	1	2	3
Sales revenue		10.500	15.900	8.000
Direct project costs		–3.150	–4.770	–2.400
Indirect project costs		–2.200	–2.200	–2.200
Operating cash flow		5.150	8.930	3.400
Capital cost	–12.000			
Net cash flow	–12.000	5.150	8.930	3.400
Discounted cash flow at 8%	–12.000	4.769	7.656	2.699
Net Present Value	3.124			
IRR	0.225			

Jack was concerned with the levels of uncertainty attached to the proposal.

The capital expenditure was imprecise where the development team had said under questioning that they could not be precise about the range of possible outcomes but believed that the build cost would at best be £11.5 million and at worst £12.5 million.

They had been more precise about the likely revenue outcomes and this is what gave Jack concern. They believed that the distribution of returns could be given an average value as shown but with a variation in outcome (as measured by the standard deviation) of 10 per cent in the first year growing in magnitude at 4 per cent per annum. Under questioning the team leader had conceded that the uncertainty was likely to be normally distributed with a small but definitely extreme level of downside risk.

The uncertainty attaching to the direct production costs had been defined in terms of an expected gross profit margin of 70 per cent, but with a 7 per cent predicted variability in the first year and 8 per cent thereafter. The fixed costs had, as Jack suspected, a much lower 2 per cent variability in each year. The company's cost of capital was set for the current year at 8 per cent with a standard error of 1 per cent. This was expected to hold over the next three years.

All distributions could be assumed to be normal except for the CAPEX which was assumed to be rectangular. The mean outcome was as stated in the relevant year except for the cost of capital where the mean for the current year was the outcome from the previous year.

Jack would dearly like to know the distribution of possible Net Present Values on this project and the magnitude of the potential financial loss that the company might incur within a 99 per cent confidence limit.

Although a very simple capital budgeting decision in its deterministic form, when we start to define each variable as a distribution the complexity of the problem soon become apparent. The definition of the problem we can summarize as a data table as shown in Exhibit 7.19.

Using Excel we can demonstrate the process but for more complex systems a specific program designed for simulation studies of this type is necessary. The concept of simulation is simple: from each distribution described we draw a randomly selected trial value for the variable concerned. So for the revenue in the first year, using the inbuilt random number generator (=RAND()) and the function for a normal distribution (or whichever distribution is specified) we take a trial value of revenue and then, using the same procedures trial values for each of the other values in the model. Exhibit 7.20 describes the sequence of activities necessary to obtain a trial value of the discounted cash flow in year one.

EXHIBIT 7.19

The preliminary estimates for input into the simulation

	0	1	2	3
Mean revenues (£million)		10.500	15.900	8.000
revenues sigma		10%	14%	18%
Gross margin		70%	70%	70%
variation (sigma) on gross margin		7%	8%	8%
Project indirect costs		2.200	2.200	2.200
Indirect cost sigma		2%	2%	2%
Capital cost (highest estimate)	−12.500			
Capital cost (lowest estimate)	−11.500			
Discount rate		0.080	PY	PY
Discount rate sigma		0.010	0.010	0.010

PY = prior year outcome

EXHIBIT 7.20

The sequence of activities for the first trial of a simulation

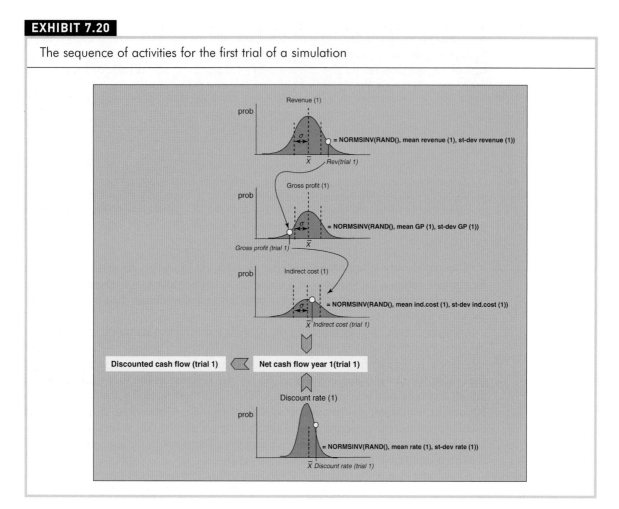

One sample from each of the variables in the model and the calculation of the Net Present Value (and Internal Rate of Return) is called a 'trial'. The larger the number of trials the more specimen results that can be drawn from the model and eventually a frequency distribution of Net Present Values and Internal Rates of Return for the project can be produced.

For Jack's project, a thousand trials on the spreadsheet produced the familiar bell shaped function as the distribution of Net Present Values as shown in Exhibit 7.22. If we repeat the exercise again and again we will get different results where the degree

EXHIBIT 7.21

The first four trials of the simulation

Trial	Rev1	Rev2	Rev3	GM1	GM2	GM3	FC1	FC2	FC3
1	11.491	16.510	7.131	9.274	12.575	4.814	2.217	2.183	2.238
2	9.702	15.020	8.373	6.410	10.193	5.851	2.158	2.267	2.118
3	10.379	10.925	7.900	6.561	7.148	5.834	2.160	2.177	2.203
4	9.175	13.974	6.457	6.002	10.242	4.366	2.151	2.175	2.176

of difference is governed, (a) by the number of trials we undertake, and (b) by the standard deviation of the underlying distributions. The accuracy of a simulation increases with the square root of the number of trials and that this is proportional to the standard deviation of the underlying distribution. So one thousand trials would reduce the standard deviation of the outcomes to 3.2 per cent $\left(\sqrt{1000} / 1000 \right)$ and 10 000 trials to 1 per cent of the standard deviation of the underlying distributions.

The means and standard deviations give us important information about our exposure to the risk that this project will turn out to have a Net Present Value of less than zero. Note that the averages for the Net Present Value and Internal Rate of Return (£3.146 million, 22.40 per cent) are very close to those determined from the base model (£3.124 million, 22.50 per cent). However, the standard deviations are large and we can work out, using standard normal tables the likelihood that the actual outcome for the Net Present Value of this project will be below zero.

Given a standard deviation of £1.949 million and a mean NPV of £3.146 million we calculate that zero is 1.614 standard deviations below the mean value. Using standard Z tables or the (=NORMSDIST(Z)) function in Excel we discover that 1.614 standard deviations below the mean encloses 94.9 per cent of the distribution above or 5.1 per cent of the distribution below zero. There is, therefore, just over a 5 per cent chance that this project will not return a positive Net Present Value. Whether this is acceptable or not depends upon the company's attitude towards risk. If Friendly Grinders is unwilling to accept any project which does not hold a better than 95 per cent likelihood of returning a positive Net Present Value then this project would just fail under that criterion. Using the standard normal tables it is possible to calculate the potential loss in value which might occur with the likelihood of it occurring.

At the 95 per cent level there are 1.6449 standard deviations below the mean and at the 99 per cent level there are 2.3263 standard deviations below the mean. Thus, at the 95 per cent level there is a 5 per cent chance of making a loss in excess of:

$$\text{Loss (prob} = 5\%) = Z(95\%) \times \sigma - \text{mean (NPV)}$$
$$\text{Loss (prob} = 5\%) = 1.6449 \times 1.949 - 3.146 = £0.0598 \text{ million}$$

And at the 99 per cent level there is a 1 per cent chance that there will be a loss in value in excess of:

$$\text{Loss (prob} = 1\%) = 2.3263 \times 1.949 - 3.146 = £1.3881 \text{ million}$$

With any normally distributed values there is always a chance that a loss may be incurred given that the distribution has (theoretically) infinite tails. However, in practice, companies that use this type of statistical analysis of the value at risk will set a cut of point (at the 95% or some other level) which effectively curtails the downside

Rate1	Rate2	Rate3	Capex	NCF1	NCF2	NCF3	NPV	IRR
0.062	0.075	0.070	−11.654	7.057	10.392	2.576	6.085	37%
0.090	0.099	0.074	−11.938	4.252	7.926	3.733	1.546	16%
0.089	0.085	0.080	−11.643	4.401	4.971	3.630	−0.499	6%
0.070	0.073	0.071	−11.904	3.851	8.067	2.190	0.481	10%

EXHIBIT 7.22

The distribution of the simulated outcomes from the project

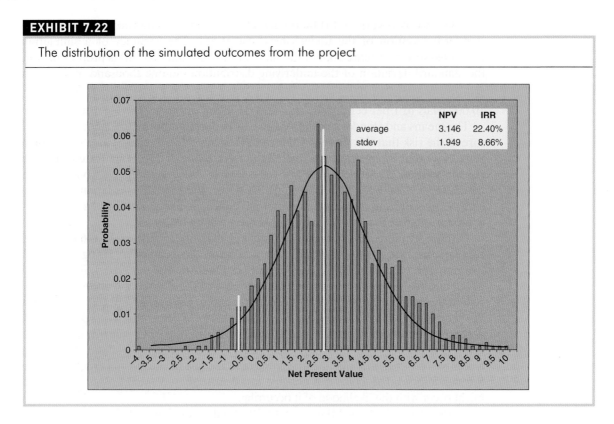

of the distribution. This topic is an extension of an important risk management measure called 'value at risk'. Further treatment of this topic is beyond this book but Jorion (2002) offers an excellent introduction to the topic.

The weakness of the simulation approach described above is that it makes some rather strong assumptions about the variables in the analysis and how they are related:

1 It is assumed that successive revenue and cost terms in the model are serially independent. It may be however that there is a degree of serial correlation in the variables concerned, such that if revenue is above average in year one, for example, then the revenue in year two is more likely than not to be above the average for that year. Likewise with costs. This problem in the modelling tends to reduce the likelihood of revenue sequences (+++) or (−−−) below what they would be if serial correlation were permitted and thus extreme outcomes tend to be damped down.

EXHIBIT 7.23

Potential loss associated with given levels of probability

Z	probability	Likelihood of loss	Loss
1.6142	0.947	5.3%	0.0000
1.6449	0.950	5.0%	0.0598
2.3263	0.990	1.0%	1.3881

2 Our simple simulation assumes that the variability of costs and revenues are also independent. Again there may be a degree of correlation between the two such that if revenues are exceptionally high, costs will tend to be higher than the gross margin ratio (in this case) would suggest. The simulation assumes that there is just as much chance that the costs will be below the level predicted by the gross margin as above. However, this effect tends to make the results more volatile than they should be if autocorrelation were permitted.

3 We have assumed that the time scale of the project is set at three years. It may be that time is a variable and that a distribution of outcomes over time is possible. This means that the terms in the model have both temporal as well as value variability.

4 The model assumes that management cannot act to curtail extreme sets of outcomes occurring. In practice this is unlikely to be the case especially if the project has what is known as 'real option' value. The concept of real options will be discussed in the next chapter.

These assumptions can all be surmounted using more sophisticated modelling packages than Excel. However, the statistical techniques involved become more and more complex as each refinement is added. The problem that Jack Grinder was aware of is that his Board of Directors who ultimately have to make their minds up, have enough trouble keeping tally of their golf score and think that 'par value' relate to the number of strokes on an average hole at the local club. Trying to explain anything to them which entails symbols, numbers and tables of data would produce immediate disbelief. The finer refinements of the techniques used can however be found in the readings at the end of this chapter.

Stress testing

Stress testing is a simple idea which has developed within the risk management literature. Essentially, it is designed to test the sensitivity of the project (or more strictly the project's value at risk) under the worst set of assumptions that can be reasonably expected to incur. Like simulation it relies upon a definition of the underlying distributions, however, it also requires a careful evaluation of the worst possible outcomes – possibly by considering the outcomes of similar projects undertaken in the past, or by looking at the response of the model to extreme external events. For example, in 1992 interest rates doubled in the UK as the government resisted the pressure on sterling caused by its relative overvaluation within the European Exchange Rate Mechanism. Stress testing considers what would happen to the value of the model if such events recurred. Again Jorion's (2002) book provides a very good introduction to this topic.

Testing the capital requirement for a project – the test framework

Of all the factors that determine a project's success the initial capital expenditure is the most critical. The magnitude, timing and management of new capital expenditure has a direct one to one bearing upon the value of the project and hence of the firm. The TEST framework is simple and designed to assist in critically evaluating the assumptions in forecasting capital expenditures.

T: technology The technological specification of the expenditure identifying those elements of the proposed technology which are well understood by the firm and those which are novel in design or in application. If a project concerns a product which is new into the market then it is likely that the technology of production will be new in concept and design. Where a company is a 'second entrant' then much of the technology will be well understood although the company may be seeking to capture a competitive edge through technological innovation that allows it to offer the same product at a better price.

E: expenditure The expenditure specification identifies not only the direct procurement costs of the new equipment, plant or other capital resources but also the costs of their integration into the asset fabric of the firm. In Chapter 11 we discuss in more detail the problems of capital integration and the hidden costs of embedding new technology within the company's existing asset (real and intangible) structures.

S: supply the supply specification relates to the conversion of the company's technological and expenditure requirements into a specification which can be used as the basis for an invitation to bid, or for the firm's negotiators when dealing with potential suppliers. In many situations the supplier contract may involve the transfer of technology or the creation of cooperative design teams working together on the design stage of the project. Supplier relationships are key to the successful implementation of any new project and when they fail it may be very difficult, if not impossible, to recover the situation.

T: timing all projects rely upon skilful project management using the best available planning techniques and risk management methods. Even small projects in terms of their capital expenditure can have a significant impact upon the operation of the firm. For significant projects a specialist project manager would be necessary to lead the development and implementation team and his or her first task would be to define the critical path to the stage that the project is implemented and is handed over to the ongoing operations management of the firm.

FINANCIAL REALITY

In 1997 the decision was taken to create a new Spa in the world heritage city of Bath. Bath was originally founded by the Romans to the enjoy the benefits of its hot water springs. In 2002 a grand opening was staged with a concert given by the three tenors. The only trouble was there was a leak and the paint kept peeling off the bath. Here is an edited extract from a newspaper article:

Bath's troubled spa now has too much water

By Richard Savill (Daily Telegraph, 13/01/2005)

The Bath Spa project, already more than three years behind schedule and £20 million over budget, has been hit by fresh problems including a water leak and the need for two boreholes to safeguard water supplies . . . the project, partly funded by the Millennium Commission, has been besieged by embarrassing and costly setbacks – including a wrangle about how to deal with flaking paint in the swimming pool area – and there is still no opening date.

It has also been blighted by arguments between Bath and North-East Somerset council, which owns the site, the main contractor, Mowlem, and the architect Nicholas Grimshaw. The cost of the additional repair work and the boreholes is estimated to be £4 million. The overall cost of the project has risen from £13.5 million in 1996 to a projected £33.3 million. A legal battle over who is to blame for the delays is likely to go to court.

The taxpayers' share of the cost could be £20 million, compared to an original figure of £4 million. However, the council said it hoped to recoup a "considerable amount" of this in the courts. Dan Norris, the Labour MP for Wansdyke, north-east Somerset, said the project had now cost every man, woman and child in the area £98. "That is more expensive than the Millennium Dome, which cost £17 a head," he said. "It is more expensive than the Scottish Parliament."

SUMMARY

In this chapter we have explored a number of practical issues in implementing capital investment appraisal techniques in practice. We have reviewed the two approaches for dealing with changing prices using both nominal and real analysis and introduced you to the very useful Fisher formula. We then turned our attention to the problem of handling capital rationing where, for the short term, a company has insufficient funds to finance its capital investment plans. The method of solution used involves the calculation of the 'profitability index' which under certain conditions can indicate the maximum additional return the firm might be willing to offer to the short term financial markets in order to raise the extra finance that it needs. Another problem area in corporate investment appraisal is taxation and, in particular, the impact of corporate taxes upon the viability of a given project. One concept we introduced here is the notion of a 'neutral tax system' being one which reduces the Net Present Value of a project directly in line with the tax rate but which does not 'confiscate value' at any rate below 100 per cent. Tax, and the incidence of capital transaction costs lead us to the 'adjusted present value' method where the benefits of the tax shield on debt interest and the impact of issues costs can be separately identified and accounted for. Finally, we looked at different ways of assessing the impact of uncertainty using sensitivity analysis and simulation. These techniques allow management to gauge the exposure of a given project proposal to different types of risk and therefore direct attention on those aspects of a project which need the most attention. In particular we focused attention on a critical part of the investment cycle and recommended the TEST procedure focusing upon the 'technological', 'expenditure', 'supply' and 'timing' aspects of the capital expenditure phase of the project.

Further Reading

Ashton, D. (1989) Textbook formulae and UK taxation: Modigliani and Miller revisited, *Accounting and Business Research*, Summer.

Benninga, S. (2000) *Financial Modelling* (2nd Ed.), Cambridge Mas: MIT Press.

Carsberg, B.V. *Analysis for Investment Decisions*, London: Haymarket Press.

Day, A. (2003) *Mastering Risk Modelling*, Harlow: FT Prentice Hall.

Fisher, I. (1930) *The theory of interest*, New York: Augustus M Kelly publishers. Reprinted 1965.

Hax, A.C. and Wigg, K.M. (1976) The use of decision analysis in capital investment problems, *Sloan Management Review* 17: 19–48.

Jorion, P. (2002) *Value at Risk* (2nd Ed.), Boston: McGraw Hill International Edition.

Myers, S.C. (1974) Interactions of Corporate Financing and Investment Decisions – implications for capital budgeting, *Journal of Finance*, 29: 1–25.

Weingartner, H.M. (1977) Capital rationing – n authors in search of a plot, *Journal of Finance* 32: 1403–1432.

PROGRESS CHECK

1 On what two bases can cash flows be projected and discount rates be quoted?

2 State the Fisher formula and define the terms it contains.

3 What ratio is appropriate for ranking projects under a situation of one-period capital rationing?

4 What is the significance of the marginal project in capital rationing?

5 What three taxes are likely to impact upon a firm?

6 What conditions are required for a tax system to be said to have a neutral impact upon an investment project?

7 The adjusted Net Present Value technique separately identifies three elements of a project investment appraisal. What are they?

8 Under what conditions could a project with a negative NPV attaching to its project cash flows still be regarded as acceptable?

9 What four sensitivity factors can be identified for a simple investment appraisal?

10 How is the sensitivity of a project to changes in its discount rate defined?

11 Outline the steps required to undertake a simulation of a capital investment project.

12 What is the meaning of the TEST acronym and how is it applied?

QUESTIONS (answers at end of book)

1 A company operates in an economic environment characterized by changing price and labour costs. Its current forecasts based upon both internal and governmental data is as follows:

	0	1	2	3	4	5
Labour rate		4%	4%	4%	4%	4%
Specific price changes (sales)		4%	4%	2%	2%	2%
Specific price changes (raw materials)		5%	5%	5%	3%	3%
General price inflation		2%	4%	4%	2%	2%
Real cost of capital		5%	5%	5%	5%	5%
Units sold		5%	5%	5%	5%	5%

It is considering an investment project that has a five year life.

Capital plant and equipment to be purchased immediately for $550 000. This plant and equipment is expected to lose value at a rate of 30 per cent per annum on its reducing balance. The plant would come on line immediately and would be scrapped for its written down value at the end of the fifth year of operation.

Sales of 10 000 units would be produced at a current price of $40 per unit. The first year's sales are expected to yield this price adjusted for the specific price change shown in the chart above.

Labour costs currently are $25 per labour hour and one labour hour produces two units of output. During the first two years the deployment of labour on this project must be found internally and the contribution foregone on other activities is expected to be approximately $76 000 and $56 000 in the first and second year respectively.

Material costs are $10 per unit at current prices.

Project specific overheads in current prices are $45 000 and these are expected to rise in line with general price inflation.

You are required:

(i) To project a statement of money (nominal) cash flows taking into account stated price changes for the five years of this project and to include capital expenditure and eventual sale proceeds of the plant and equipment for scrap.

(ii) To evaluate this project using the Net Present Value criterion *plus* one other investment appraisal technique of your choosing.

(iii) To advise management on the acceptability of this project outlining the theoretical and technical issues you have considered.

2 A company has the following investment project (expressed in £million):

	decision point	year 1	year 2	year 3	year 4	year 5
Outlay	−650					
Net cash flow from operations		210	240	240	150	
Scrap value of plant						25

The company's cost of capital for equity is 14 per cent and its cost of debt is 8 per cent. The company has a market gearing ratio of 0.7.

The projected cash flows have been produced in real terms including the projection of the scrap value on the capital equipment involved in year five. The company pays corporation tax at 40 per cent one year after the liability arises and is eligible for a 100 per cent first year capital allowance on its capital outlay. The proceeds from the disposal of capital equipment are taxed at the corporation tax rate. Interest on borrowing is tax deductible. The current rate of inflation is 4 per cent which is expected to continue into the foreseeable future. The company has adequate profits elsewhere to absorb any tax saving on this project.

You are required:

(i) To project the cash flows in money terms including the impact of corporation tax.

(ii) To calculate the Net Present Value of this investment at the cost of capital for the firm taking into account the impact of tax.

(iii) Use the adjusted present value technique to identify the relative benefits of the different sources of value in this project.

QUESTIONS (answers on website)

3   The real rate of return for a company is 4 per cent and the inflation rate is 3 per cent. What is the nominal rate?

4   A company has a portfolio of six capital investment projects (quoted in £million):

year	0	1	2	3	4
A	−1.50	1.00	1.00		
B	−3.90	−1.90	2.00	3.00	3.50
C	−0.50	0.70			
D	−8.00	−2.00	7.00	4.00	3.00
E	−2.00	1.00	1.80		
F	−0.10	0.05	0.08		

You may assume that none of the projects are mutually exclusive, that capital will be freely available within one year and that the projects are perfectly divisible. The company has a cost of capital of 10 per cent per annum.

You are required:

(i)   to advise the company which of these projects should be accepted if there is £8 million of investment funds available.

(ii) Identify the minimum rate of return required for any other project considered for immediate investment.

(iii) Outline any other assumptions required for the capital investment technique you have chosen to be valid.

(iv) Discuss the extent to which the assumptions, which underpin this model are likely to hold in practice.

5   A small equity financed company is considering a range of opportunities that would have a significant impact upon the value of the firm. It has filtered each of these projects according to their Net Present Value and Internal Rate of Return as shown below and is considering which project to accept given the availability of new equity of £300 000 at the company's current cost of capital of 8 per cent per annum. Funding above this limit would incur a significant increase in the rates of return required by investors. Generally, all projects can be scaled down but not up.

The projects are as follows:

	01-Jan	31-Dec-01	31-Dec-02	31-Dec-03	31-Dec-04	31-Dec-05	NPV	IRR
alpha	−130 000	0	0	0	0	220 000	£19 728.30	11%
beta	−9 000	3 000	3 000	3 000	3 000	3 000	£2 978.13	20%
gamma	−199 000	200 000	80 000	0	0	0	£54 772.29	31%
delta	−44 000	−22 000	70 000	10 000	12 000	0	£12 402.03	18%
epsilon	−97 000	20 000	38 000	50 000	25 000	10 000	£18 970.58	16%

The company has projected its accounting figures (before the investments proposed above) for the next five years as follows:

	01-Jan	31-Dec-01	31-Dec-02	31-Dec-03	31-Dec-04	31-Dec-05
Turnover		780 500	820 000	861 000	904 000	949 200
Gross profit		172 000	180 400	190 000	199 000	208 500
Capital employed	1 021 250	1 075 000	1 127 500	1 187 500	1 243 750	1 303 125

The company calculates depreciation on all new investments at 10 per cent of the acquisition value of any fixed capital investment incurred within the year concerned. The company's annual depreciation charge is 10 per cent of the original cost in each of the subsequent years of the asset's life.

You are required to:

(i) Advise the company as to which of the above projects the available capital should be allocated and the increase in the equity value of the firm which can be expected following that investment.

(ii) Given your advice above, advise management on the maximum rate of return it should be prepared to pay on the additional funds required to complete this portfolio of investments.

(iii) Calculate the increase in the expected gross annual rate of return on capital employed for this business if your project investment plan is accepted.

(iv) Comment upon the assumptions that you have made in formulating your advice to management.

6   Bernie Flower runs a garden landscaping service and is considering purchasing a Digemup Mini Digger. He currently hires a minidigger from the local building merchants at a daily hire rate of £75. During the previous year he hired a digger for 45 days although he could have used one for 60 days saving himself 30 days of labourer time at £50 per day. A new minidigger would cost £24 000 and would last ten years at which time he expects to be able to sell it on for £4000. He estimates that its running costs including diesel, servicing and insurance would be £480 per annum. Hire charges and costs are rising in his business at approximately 4 per cent per annum. Bernie is self-employed and pays tax at a marginal rate of 40 per cent and payments fall due one year after profit is earned. The new minidigger would attract a first year allowance of 50 per cent and 25 per cent per annum thereafter on a reducing balance. If Bernie bought the new machine he would need to invest in trailer and trailer bar for his flatbed truck which would cost an additional £6000 and which would be written off over the life of the minidigger. These additions to his truck would also attract capital allowances the same as the minidigger. Bernie has enough taxable income to absorb his capital allowances. Any unexhausted capital allowances at the end of the project can be claimed and offset against any tax liability on the sale proceeds of his mini digger at that time. Bernie has a cost of finance of 8 per cent per annum.

You are required to:

(i) Find the Net Present Value, Internal Rate of Return, payback and discounted payback for this project.

(ii) Test the sensitivity of this project to changes in capital spend and discount rate.

8 | Introduction to options and option pricing

I n this chapter we explore the nature and pricing of options. Options are one of three important types of derivative contract the other two being swaps and futures which we consider in Chapter 14. Options are particularly important because they allow us to value future choice. Supposing you particularly like a friend's car and he or she indicates that it might be up for sale in the spring. How much would it be worth to you to have first refusal on purchase of the car at a currently agreed price? Choices like this appear in a multitude of different situations and in this chapter we provide the background necessary for you to develop a sound understanding of how options (and the markets in options) for financial securities work and how options can be valued.

For what appears to be a simple type of agreement the mathematics required in their valuation is formidable. In this chapter we introduce the Black and Scholes option pricing model which apart from securing a Nobel Prize for its originators also released a wave of developments both within the markets and for investors in the field of financial engineering and risk management. We also demonstrate the binomial option pricing model which while being simpler to understand than Black and Scholes and more flexible in application is less deterministic in the results it delivers. Throughout this chapter we will restrict ourselves to options on equity shares. However, as we shall see in the next chapter particularly and in later chapters the option pricing framework can be used in widely different contexts ranging from currency dealing to capital investment appraisal.

Learning outcomes

In this chapter you will be able to achieve the following:

1 Gain familiarity with the different terms used to describe options and how they are traded and settled.

2 Draw a payoff diagram showing the profit and losses on simple option positions.

3 Identify the five principal drivers of option value and how they impact upon different types of option.

4   Gain a basic understanding of the Black and Scholes option pricing model and be able to build an Excel template to value either put or call options using the model.

5   Know how to extend the Black and Scholes model for the case where there is a dividend paid on the underlying security.

6   Be able to identify the significant sensitivities of the Black and Scholes model and calculate an option delta.

7   Understand the mechanics of delta hedging and how to form a delta neutral portfolio.

8   Be able to construct a binomial tree for both European and American put and call options and be able to derive the option value in each case.

9   Modify the binomial method for dividends paid in the underlying security.

The derivatives markets

In around 600 BC Thales of Miletus spotted an opportunity in the oil pressing business in ancient Greece. Thales was one of the earliest philosopher/mathematicians but like most academics he was usually short of cash. Here is how Aristotle three centuries later described Thales' technique for making money:

> *'There is the anecdote of Thales the Milesian and his financial device, which involves a principle of universal application . . . According to the story, he knew by his skill in the stars while it was yet winter that there would be a great harvest of olives in the coming year; so, having a little money, he gave deposits for the use of all the olive-presses in Chios and Miletus, which he hired at a low price because no one bid against him. When the harvest-time came, and many were wanted all at once and of a sudden, he let them out at any rate which he pleased, and made a quantity of money. Thus he showed the world that philosophers can easily be rich if they like, but that their ambition is of another sort.' ARISTOTLE POLITICS BOOK 1,*XI TRANSLATED BY BENJAMIN JOWETT http://classics.mit.edu/Aristotle/politics.1.one.html

What Thales purchased we would now describe as a 'call' option on the use of the oil presses – he didn't have to exercise his option if the harvest was poor and the actual rentals for their use at harvest had been less than the rental he had agreed to pay.

The option that Thales purchased was what we term an 'over the counter' transaction. Thales wanted the option for his own use but if he had lived two millennia later he might have discovered another way of making money. In 17th Century Osaka he might have been tempted to buy and sell rice futures on an exchange established for that purpose. Organized markets in commodity futures such as those for tin, lead, coffee beans and oil have been a feature of the more general commodity exchanges for many centuries. However the trading in financial futures and options is a relatively recent phenomenon with the first significant exchange established by the Chicago Board of Trade in the mid 1970s. Since that time trading in financial derivatives has become a key method for managing financial risk.

What is a derivative?

A derivative is a contract written on some underlying real asset (such as a commodity), a financial security, an economic event or a financial liability. Derivative contracts fall into three categories:

1 Where one party (the 'writer') grants a right to a counterparty (the 'holder') allowing them to purchase or sell the underlying asset or security at or before a specified time and at a specified price. This is an option contract.

2 Where one party agrees to buy or sell the underlying asset or security at a specified price and time. This type of derivative is a 'forward' contract where both parties commit to the delivery of the 'underlying' asset or security.

3 Where one party agrees to swap a commitment against an underlying asset or liability with another party. Such swap agreements may involve the swapping of interest rate liabilities, foreign currency loans or credit agreements.

Derivatives serve a number of purposes: they can be used as a way of making money by exploiting a potential market opportunity but more importantly they offer a way of managing risk. The farmer who is worried about a likely fall in the price of wheat may enter into a forward agreement with the miller to sell her harvest at an agreed price per tonne. The miller, who is worried about the prospect of a rise in the price of wheat would be quite happy with such a deal as it means that his supply is guaranteed at a fixed price. The farmer and the miller have both protected themselves against the downside risk of concern to them through the mechanism of the forward agreement.

The use of derivative contacts as a hedge against future uncertainty led to the development of a secondary market in derivatives and this in turn has led to an explosion in the range of financial products in the market as well as the growth of pseudo-derivative markets such as spread betting. The principal markets are in options and forward contracts that can be exchange traded and in the latter case they are known as 'future contracts'. A market in swaps is organized through the major banks and other financial houses.

However, options are an important form of derivative agreement. Options appear in many different guises: there are of course option contracts as traded between counterparties and in organized markets. But the concept of an option appears in many other contexts as well. An equity share in a geared firm and where there is limited liability is a form of option. Both the equity and the debt in issue by a firm can be valued using option pricing theory. The potential for management to alter or change direction in the future suggests that many investment projects have 'optionality' built in. Indeed when we start to look carefully options start appearing everywhere. For this reason we devote this chapter to option pricing. There is one warning however: the mathematics of option pricing is demanding and there are some particularly tricky parts that we must in this book glide over. There are ample references at the end of the text which will allow you to build your understanding of this vital area in modern finance.

An option contract

An option is a legally binding agreement between two parties: the 'writer' and the 'holder' which gives the holder the right to buy or to sell an underlying asset depending on whether it is a 'call' or a 'put' at or before a specified future date. The rather quaint expressions 'call' and 'put' give the flavour of the transaction quite nicely.

A call option gives the holder the right to 'call' which means to buy the underlying asset from the option writer at a specified time at a specified price. A 'put' gives the holder the option to put the asset concerned into the hands of the writer at a specified time and for a specified price.

When two individuals come together as counter-parties to an option contract then the deal is said to be 'over the counter' or OTC. With an OTC contract, the writer gives the option contract to the holder and receives in exchange a fee in compensation called the 'option premium'. If at the exercise date the price is favourable then the holder will exercise the option and the writer is bound to honour the deal and either sell or purchase the asset concerned at the agreed price.

However, with the formation of options exchanges in the United States, followed by the United Kingdom and then other countries around the world, option contracts have become 'securitized'. What this means is that the exchange permits the writing of options which are then freely traded, and at the exercise date the exchange settles the options that have been exercised and calls in the outstanding liabilities of the option writers. The exchange will in setting up an 'option' series will standardize the agreement.

In the UK, the principal derivatives market is the London International Financial Futures Exchange or 'LIFFE' (pronounced 'leafy'), LIFFE specifies that its standard

EXHIBIT 8.1

Equity options on Rolls Royce share

Equity Options on LIFFE Market Shares

ROLLS-ROYCE GROUP PLC

Mnemo: RR	**MEP:** LON
Exercise type: American	**Unit:** £

Underlying: ROLLS ROYCE GROUP	**ISIN:** GB0032836487	**MEP:** OTH
Unit: XXX	**Last:**-	**Last change:** 0
Volume:-	**Best bid:** 0	**Best ask:** 0

Unit of trading	One option normally equals rights over 1000 shares[1]
Expiry months	March Cycle (M): means the 3 nearest expiry months from Mar, Jun, Sep, Dec cycle[2]
Quotation	Pence per share
Minimum price movement (tick size and value)	0.5 pence per share/£5.00 0.25 pence per share/£2.50[3]
Exercise day	Exercise by 17:20 on any business day, extended to 18:00 for all series on a Last Trading Day
Last trading day	16:30 Third Friday in expiry month
Settlement day	Settlement Day is four business days following the day of exercise/Last Trading Day
Trading hours	08:00–16:30

Source: London International Financial Futures Exchange (LIFFE), 2005

The LIFFE trading floor in action before the introduction of computerised trading

contract is for 1000 shares, the price is quoted in pence per share and the minimum price movement is 0.1 per cent (this is known as a 'tick'). In Exhibit 8.1 we show the typical specification for an equity option such as that for shares in Rolls Royce plc. This standardization allows writers to enter the market, writing large numbers of common contracts which sare then traded on the exchange as securities in their own right. Invariably the exchange will ask the writer to submit an initial cash 'margin' which is then adjusted by subsequent variation 'margins' which reflect any potential losses the writer might face under the contract. The margin mechanism provides protection against default risk.

American, European and Asian options

You may have noted in Exhibit 8.1 that the options in Rolls Royce shares are referred to as 'American options'. This rather odd terminology relates to the conditions under which an option can be exercised rather than anything to do with where they are registered as a security. An 'American' option can be exercised at any point up to the exercise date, while a 'European' option can only be exercised on the exercise day itself. In both cases the value of the option at exercise is found by comparing the ruling price of the underlying security at the exercise date with the exercise price. With an 'Asian' option the average of the share price over a specified period before the exercise date is used to calculate the value of the option.

Charting the payoff on an option

The payoff, or 'intrinsic value' of an option is equal to the profit or loss on holding the option at maturity. For a call option if the share price is lower than the exercise price there will be no point in the holder exercising the option. The original writer of the option keeps the premium paid (i.e. that's the loss to the purchaser of the option). However, if the actual price of the share at the date of exercise is greater than the exercise price then the profit to the holder will be the difference between the two. By exercising the option the holder can either keep the shares or sell them to realize their profit immediately.

In Exhibit 8.2 we show a standard form of option payoff diagram. This is a vital tool in the option trader's kit bag. It shows the intrinsic value of a call option which will be zero if the option is 'out of the money' and positive if the option is 'in the money'. By deducting the premium (the price paid for the option) from the intrinsic value we get the overall pay off to the holder. There is one danger with this diagram which will become more obvious as we proceed. As the option moves from the day it was created to the point it expires it will also have time value. This diagram ignores that time value but with that in mind it is a useful tool for understanding the eventual payoffs if an option is held until it expires.

EXHIBIT 8.2

Payoff diagram for a call option

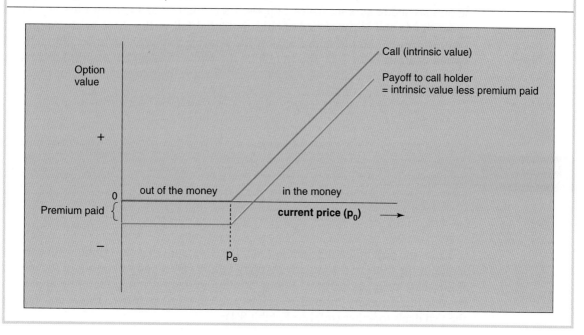

In the absence of transactions costs what the holder gains the option writer loses (an option contract is a zero sum between writer and holder).

With a put option the reverse logic applies. With a put the option holder has the right to sell the security concerned to the option writer. This will only be worthwhile if the actual price at the exercise date is less than the exercise price. If that is the case then the holder of the put option can purchase the shares in the market at the lower price and sell them to the writer at the exercise price. Again, the writer and the holder are in a zero sum situation (see Exhibit 8.3).

EXHIBIT 8.3

Payoff diagrams for the writer and holder of both call and put options

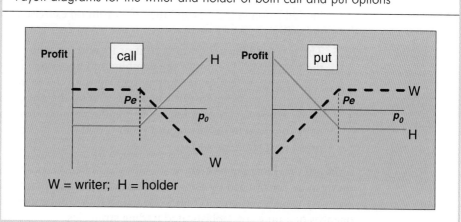

How to build a more complex option position

Payoff diagrams are very useful devices for envisaging the consequences of investing in options and related securities. Suppose for example that an investor has purchased some shares and is concerned about a potential fall in the share price. An option contract can be used to hedge against the possible rise in share price. Normally an option contract is for 1000 shares (100 in the United States) but we will have a look at the case of the purchase of a single share and how the payoff diagram for the security and the option combine.

FINANCIAL REALITY	Twelve month put options on Friendly Grinders plc shares are quoted at 12p with an exercise price of 240p. The current share price is 240p per share. How will a long hedge with these two securities combine?

From the put option diagram in Exhibit 8.3 we note that the option will be in the money if the value of the underlying share falls in value, and will be out of the money if the share price appreciates. A long position in the put would therefore appear to provide the necessary 'insurance' against a fall in the share price. This is how we put the two deals together (refer to Exhibit 8.4):

1 Construct a graph showing + and – value change (y axis) i.e. the profit or loss on either or the sum of the two transactions. The x axis is the price of the underlying.

2 Mark the current price of the share and the exercise price on the x-axis (they are both the same in this case).

3 Enter the profit or loss on the purchase of the share. This is a 45 degree line of positive slope passing through the current share price (240p). Obviously if the share price rises a profit will be made and if it falls a loss will be incurred.

4 Superimpose the payoff on the put option. If the share price is, at exercise, above 240p then the option will not be exercised and the loss is 12p irrespective of how far the share price may rise. Below 240p the option is worth exercising and so a 45 degree line of negative slope is drawn from point A showing first the reduction in the loss and then the profit on exercise of the put through to point B.

5 The two solid lines show the profit or loss on the long position in the share and the put option. Then draw the combination line which is the net of the other two – we show that as the dotted line. Up until the exercise price the combined position shows a net loss of 12p as the gain on the put offsets the loss on the share. However, from point A, the combination line first shows the loss overall being reduced to the breakeven point C and then proceeding into greater profit through to point D.

Payoff diagrams can be created for all sorts of hedged positions and combinations – they can be constructed by using an Excel table and the charting function but they are also very valuable when carefully sketched as they can be used to examine the consequences of a range of sophisticated trading strategies.

EXHIBIT 8.4

The payoff diagram for a long position in a security hedged by a long position in a put option

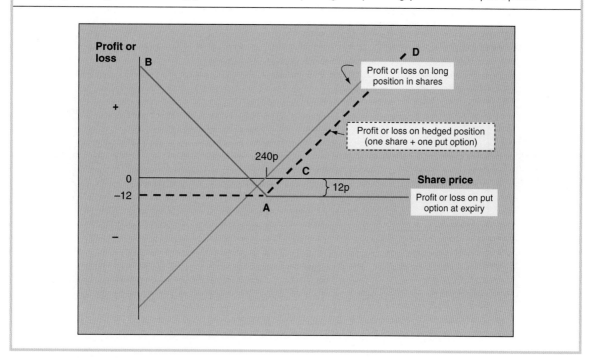

REVIEW ACTIVITY 8.1 Using a payoff diagram show the profit and loss of the resulting position:

1 Short in a share (current price = 240p), long in a call option (exercise = 240p, premium = 30p).
2 Long in a call option (exercise = 250p, premium = 20p), long in a put option (exercise = 225p, premium = 10p).

The basics of option valuation

At one extreme the value of a call option cannot be more valuable than the security against which it has been written. No rational investor would pay more for the right to buy a share in a company than its current market value. The current market value represents the upper boundary on the value of a call option.

At the exercise date an option will either be 'in the money', which means that for a call option the share price is greater than the exercise price or 'out of the money' which means that the exercise price is greater than the share price and the option is worthless.

We can represent the maximum value of a call option and its value at exercise using a profit graph as in Exhibit 8.5.

The problem is that the value of the call option will be somewhere between the upper and the lower boundary. The trick in option pricing is to find out exactly where between the lower and upper bound the option is placed at any point in time between when it is issued and when it is exercised.

EXHIBIT 8.5

The limits on the value of a call option

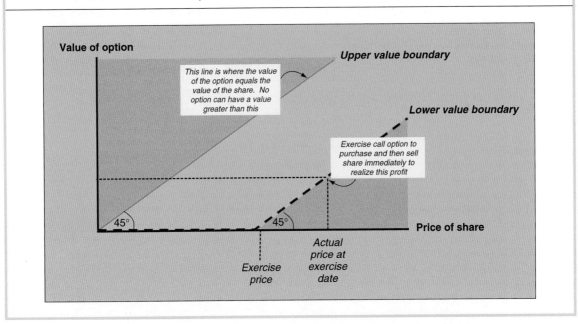

Although there may be many factors that actually drive an option's value, five are particularly important:

1   *The actual price of the shares concerned.* The higher the price of the shares when the option is exercised the more valuable a call option on the company's equity. The reason? The holder can purchase the shares at the exercise price from the option writer and immediately sell them for a higher price on the market. However, with a put option the reverse is the case. The lower the value of the shares the more valuable the option.

2   *The exercise price which is set at the commencement of the option contract.* The cheaper the price agreed by the option writer for eventual sale of the shares concerned the more valuable the option will be in the hands of the holder. Thus there is an inverse relationship between the exercise price and the value of the call option.

3   *When valuing a call option how much we have to pay, or the value we have to deliver, at the exercise date must be converted into a present value.* Therefore the greater the rate of interest used to discount the exercise price the less the present value of that eventual payment. Thus, the greater the discount rate the more valuable a call option will be. The reverse is the case with a put option where the holder receives the sale proceeds of the asset at expiry and hence the greater the discount rate the less valuable that future cash flow and therefore the option will be.

4   *The time to expiry of the option.* Generally, the longer an option has to run the more valuable it is – the most obvious reason being that an option with greater time to exercise has more time in which to move 'into the money'.

5 *The more volatile the underlying security against which the option is written the more valuable the option.* The reason is that an option allows us to curtail downside risk; we are left as the holder with upside volatility to give us the eventual payoff. The greater the volatility the greater the potential payoff.

These factors give what we term 'intrinsic value' and 'time value' as shown in Exhibit 8.6.

In our simple analysis of options we will assume that the underlying asset does not pay a dividend or interest. If it does then this will affect the option value – a topic we will return to after having dealt with the 'simple' stuff.

Intrinsic value and time value

Intrinsic value is the difference between the current price of the security and the exercise price:

$$\text{If} \quad P_0 - P_e > 0$$

then a call option is 'in the money', it has positive intrinsic value and if this condition holds at the exercise date then the holder will exercise the option. If it is a put option the option is 'out of the money' and the holder will not exercise the option.

$$\text{If} \quad P_0 - P_e < 0$$

then a call option is 'out of the money' and would not be exercised at the exercise date. If it is a put option then it will be exercised.

Time value is the value inherent in the option given its time to run until expiry. It will be influenced by three of the five factors above: the risk free rate of return, the

---

EXHIBIT 8.6

How option value is influenced by the five value drivers

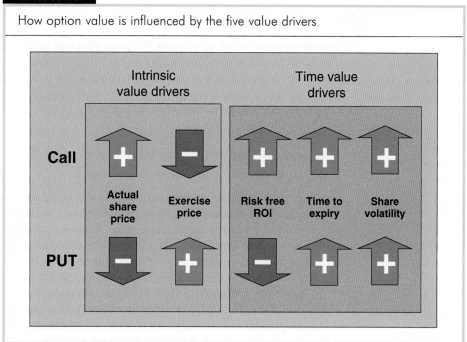

EXHIBIT 8.7

Quoted values of put and call options on Rolls Royce ordinary shares
(29 March 2005)

Option		. . . . Calls. . . .			. . . .Puts.		
		Jun	**Sep**	**Dec**	Jun	Sep	Dec
Rolls-Royce	240	**13.0**	**19.5**	**22.0**	5.0	10.5	13.5
(*243.5)	260	**4.0**	**9.0**	**13.0**	17.0	20.5	24.0

Note (*243.5) is the latest quoted share price and 240p and 260p the exercise prices.

---

time to expiry of the option, and the volatility of the underlying shares. Each of these terms will be defined as we develop the theory of option pricing which is really the theory of pricing time value. Time value diminishes to zero at the expiry date and at the last moment available for exercise the value of the option will be simply its intrinsic value.

REVIEW ACTIVITY 8.2   You purchase a call option on 1000 Rolls Royce shares. The share price goes down. What would you expect to happen to the value of the option?
    You are deciding to write a put option on 1000 Rolls Royce shares for a 240p series maturing in December. Is the value of the option likely to be less than or more than 13.5p?
    If the Rolls Royce options were due to expire today which of the option series would be in the money for a put and for a call?

Put-call parity

A natural question to ask is whether the price of a call option is related to that of a put. Indeed, there is a very close relationship which is ensured by arbitrage principle discussed in Chapter 1. If you proceeded through the following sequence of trades where there is a common exercise date (and assuming for the moment that Rolls Royce shares can only be exercised at the exercise date (i.e. a European style option).

1 Purchase 1000 Rolls Royce shares.
2 Write or sell a call option on 1000 Rolls Royce shares.
3 Buy a put option for 1000 Rolls Royce shares.

Now note what happens: at the exercise date if the call option is in the money you, as the writer, will be required to deliver the 1000 shares you hold and sell them to the holder of the call option at the exercise price. You will not exercise your put option, you will now have no shares but you will have the exercise price in cash.

If the put option is in the money, you will not receive a call from the holder of the call option but you will be able to sell your shares via the put option at the exercise price. So again you will hold no shares but you will have the exercise price in cash.

So the payoff on the deal is the difference between the purchase price of the shares now and the present value of the cash you receive at exercise. To make this potential gain in value on the underlying shares you have paid for a put option and received the premium on the sale of the call option. For the trade to yield zero profit (the zero arbitrage condition):

The gain on the underlying = the net cost of the options

$$P_0 - PV(P_e) = c - p$$

Where:

$PV(p_e)$ is the present value of the exercise price

P_0 is the cost of the shares

c is the cash received on the sale of the call

p is the cash paid for the put

This is the put-call parity relationship. Unfortunately it only works perfectly with European options rather than Americans where the option can be exercised at any time between issue and the final day of trading.

FINANCIAL REALITY

On the assumption that the Rolls Royce options are European style what should the put price be given the data shown in Exhibit 8.7? The risk free rate is 4.75 per cent and the time to exercise is 135 trading days. As we discuss later, using trading days (of which there are 250 in a year) give a more accurate result than using either a 365 or 360 day year count. For reasons we will explain later the risk free rate must be converted to a basis assuming continuous compounding. This gives a rate of 4.64064 per cent per annum.

Using the put-call parity relationship:

$$P_0 - PV(P_e) = c - p$$
$$p = c - P_0 + PV(P_e)$$
$$p = 19.5 - 243.5 + 240 \times e^{-.0464064*135/250}$$
$$p = 10.06$$

The quoted value is 10.5p. In principle the model should work for an American option if we knew the effective date of exercise but where that date is unknown we are unable to accurately determine the discounted value of the exercise price.

Valuing an option contract

Because an option grants the holder a valuable right to deal in an asset at a previously agreed price it would be rather desirable to discover the value of the option contract itself. Essentially two approaches have been developed with innumerable variations:

1 Three researchers Robert Merton, Fischer Black and Myron Scholes developed a 'closed formula' for pricing European style options. Their central insight was that a perfect hedge could be created from a long position in shares (i.e. purchasing shares with a view to sale at the exercise date on the option) and short position on a call option (effectively writing a call option). We show below how this 'hedging' procedure works but in principle a perfectly hedged

position in a security is riskless and thus should only offer the risk free rate of return to the investor. This insight combined with some assumptions about the nature of the return distribution and a heavy dose of stochastic calculus led to one of the most important models in finance. We will show the underlying insights behind this model and the method of derivation below.

2 Cox, Ross and Rubenstein (1979) building on an insight Cox and Rubenstein attributed to William Sharpe developed a binomial option pricing approach. The binomial model operates in discrete as opposed to continuous time and is conceptually easier to understand than the Black Scholes model. It is computationally more demanding than the continuous time model but does give the ability to price a wide variety of options which cannot be handled by the Black and Scholes Model.

In order to help highlight the logic behind these two approaches we will work with a simple example and develop the logic of the hedged position.

FINANCIAL REALITY

Friendly Grinders' current share price is 200p per share and Jack is looking at the price of 90 day call options on his company's shares. He is convinced that in 90 days, if things go well with the discussions concerning the acquisition of NASA technology for producing diamond beads the share price could be 250p. If it doesn't work out the share price is almost certain to lose its recent gains and return to the 150p per share where it has been stuck for the last six months. The risk free rate of return is currently 5 per cent and Jack is looking at share options with an exercise price of 210p. Ignoring issues of insider dealing and the impact a spell in prison might have on his golf handicap he decides to calculate the value of an option contract for 1000 shares. Jack decides to use a 360 day year count.

This is a very straightforward example because the share price at the date of exercise of the option can only have one of two values. A perfectly hedged position would be one, for example where the payoff from the holding of a given number of shares less the loss on the sale of a single call option is identical no matter whether the share price rises or it falls. The key number here is exactly how many shares we need to purchase which combined with the loss on writing one call option gives an identical payoff irrespective of whether the share price rises to 250p or falls to 150p.

If the share rises to 250p the option will be exercised by the holder of the call and the loss on the option contract to the writer will be (250p − 210p) 40p. If Δ shares were purchased the value of the shares will have risen and the combined position at exercise date would be:

$$\text{Value (up)} = 250p \times \Delta - 40p \cdots\cdots (i)$$

If the shares fall in value to 150p the value of the position would be (holding Δ constant):

$$\text{Value (down)} = 150p \times \Delta - 0 \cdots\cdots (ii)$$

because the option will be valueless and therefore not exercised by the holder.

For this to be a perfect hedge, all risk in the position must be eliminated which means that that the value of the position if the shares go up must be the same if they go down:

$$250 \times \Delta - 40 = 150\Delta - 0$$

therefore:

$$\Delta = \frac{40-0}{250-150} = 0.4$$

What this means is that the risk in holding 0.4 share is exactly offset by writing one option, or that of holding 400 shares is offset by writing an option contract on 1000 shares.

Substituting the value for Δ into either (i) or (ii) and discounting at the risk free rate gives the payoff on the position in present value terms. To obtain a Net Present Value of zero (which means that only the risk free rate of return has been earned overall) the discounted value of the payoff must equal the net cost of creating the position (share purchase less the premium received on writing the call).

$$NPV = PV(\text{payoff}) - \text{net cost of position} = 0$$

Therefore

$$PV(\text{payoff}) = \text{net cost of position}$$
$$(250 \times 0.4 - 40) \times e^{-0.05*90/360} = (0.4 \times 200 - C)$$
$$c = 0.4 \times 200 - (250 \times 0.4 - 40) \times e^{-0.05*90/360}$$
$$c = 20.74p$$

This means that if Jack were to purchase (say) 400 shares (at a cost of £1000) and sell a call option contract on 1000 shares for £207.40 his net gain would simply be the risk free rate of return on his net outlay over 90 days irrespective of whichever way the share price moves. Before generalizing this model it is worth noting some key points:

1 If the market price of the options happened to be greater than 20.74p Jack, in writing his call contracts, would make a rate of return on his position which is greater than the risk free rate. This would be an arbitrage profit and the rush of investors writing call contracts in an attempt to capture that excess gain would, as a consequence of the increased supply of contracts on the markets, push the option price down to its equilibrium value of 20.74p. The reverse logic would apply if the price happened to be less than 20.74p. The supply of contracts would fall as writers become scarce given the low return, as demand would exceed supply the price would rise until, again, the zero arbitrage price of 20.74p per option was obtained.

2 The value of the option is strictly independent of the probabilities of the share moving up, or moving down, but rather on the spread of the possible values which are obtained at the exercise date. Given that probabilities do not enter into the pricing formula, there is nothing in this approach to valuing options which is dependent upon the risk preferences of the investor. The zero arbitrage argument works whether the investor is an inveterate gambler at one extreme or would not be prepared to play a game of cards for matchsticks at the other. Because risk preferences are irrelevant in pricing options we will be able to see later how Black and Scholes were able to build a model assuming that all investors are risk neutral and thus would not demand any premium over and above the risk free rate as compensation for the volatility of the underlying shares.

3 The hedge ratio is the proportion of shares to options required to cancel the risk in the underlying position. To formalize this let u = factor to apply if the share price should rise (1.25 in the example above) and d = the factor to apply

if the share price goes down (0.75 in the example). The perfect hedge is created when:

$$u\Delta P_0 - c^+ = d\Delta P_0 - c^-$$

Where P_0 is the current price of the underlying share, c is the value of the call option and c^+ and c^- the two values of the call at exercise.

Rearranging:

$$\Delta = \frac{c^+ - c^-}{uP_0 - dP_0}$$

Thus the hedge ratio is the possible range in the value of the option at exercise divided by the possible range in the share price. This ratio underpins the technique of 'delta hedging' where options are used to eliminate the risk in an underlying position.

4 Combining the hedging ratio with the zero arbitrage position:

$$NPV = [(u\Delta P_0 - c^+)e^{-rt}] - [\Delta P_0 - c] = 0$$

Therefore:

$$c = \Delta P_0 - (\Delta u P_0 - c^+)e^{-rt}$$

We will need this formula again when we return to the binomial model later in this chapter.

THEORETICAL NOTE

The approach towards creating a riskless hedge described above is that adopted by Black and Scholes. There is an alternative approach where a replicating portfolio is established. It can be demonstrated that an option has the same payoffs as a combination of a loan (for an amount L) and share purchase. If Jack were (i) to purchase Δ shares at 200p and (ii) take out a loan which with interest at the risk free rate matures at the exercise date with a value of L, then the payoffs would be:

$$P_0 u\Delta - L = c^+$$

$$200 \times 1.25 \times \Delta - L = 50 \quad \ldots \ldots \ldots \text{(i)}$$

(if the price of the share rises to 250p) and

$$P_0 d\Delta - L = c^-$$

$$200 \times 0.75 \times \Delta - L = 0 \quad \ldots \ldots \ldots \text{(ii)}$$

(if the price falls to 150p and the call is worthless)
Rearrange (ii) in terms of L and substitute in (i) and we obtain:

$$P_0 u\Delta - P_0 d\Delta = c^+ - c^-$$

$$\Delta = \frac{c^+ - c^-}{uP_0 - dP_0} = \frac{40 - 0}{250 - 150} = 0.4$$

and,

$$L = uP_0(\Delta - 1) + P_e$$

$$L = 250 \times - 0.6 + 210$$

$$L = 60p$$

The value of the call is simply net cost of establishing the replicating portfolio being the cost of the shares purchased less the present value of the loan:

$$c = P_0\Delta - Le^{-rt}$$

$$c = 200 \times 0.4 - 60 \times e^{-0.05 \times 90/360}$$

$$c = 20.74p$$

which is exactly what we had before.

REVIEW ACTIVITY 8.3 What would be the value of the call option on Friendly Grinders if the share prices are expected to be either 10 per cent up or 10 per cent down at exercise? The exercise price remains at 210p.

What would be the value of the option on Friendly Grinders if the exercise price was 190p and the potential values were as originally stated?

What would be the value of the original option if the time to exercise was 180 days?

What would be the value of the option if the current share price was 190p?

What would be the value of the option if the risk free rate rose to 8 per cent?

The general option pricing model (Black and Scholes)

Because of the central importance of the Black and Scholes option pricing model in many different areas of finance it is worth outlining the maths involved in its derivation. The first thing to note is that the derivation assumes that the market for securities is weak form efficient. The second point to note is that it prices call options on a zero arbitrage argument. To explain how this model is derived we must first return to a topic first addressed in Chapter 3 about how share prices move through time. First, the market in shares is assumed to be weak form efficient and that share prices follow a version of a random walk called a 'geometric Brownian process'.

The assumed pricing process

In Chapter 3 we used the following formula to simulate share price movements.

$$\frac{\Delta P}{P} = \mu \Delta t + \xi \sigma \sqrt{\Delta t} \dots\dots\dots\dots (iii)$$

This is a discrete time model in that it assumes a time interval between price observations (Δt). This model assumes that the returns on a share generated over subsequent time periods are drawn from a normal distribution of returns of mean (μ) and standard deviation (σ). Put intuitively, this model implies that the future return over a given period Δt is the sum of two components: a deterministic component which is the average level of return (μ) appropriate for the time period (this is sometimes referred to as the 'drift factor' and a stochastic element which is controlled by the standard deviation. The ξ symbol is a random number generated from a standard normal distribution (mean 0 and standard deviation 1). If there is just one time period involved (say one year) and the standard deviation of returns is based upon annual returns then the model simply becomes:

$$\frac{\Delta P}{P} = \mu 1 + \xi \sigma \sqrt{1} = \mu + \xi \sigma$$

Now supposing we are interested in discovering the price change over two intervals $(t = 2)$. What we are in effect doing is summing two normal distributions. You may remember from our discussion of risk in Chapter 3 that when we combine the variances of independent distributions (i.e. where there is zero correlation between them) that they are simply additive. In a time series context, when we combine standard deviations the result is proportional to the square root of the time:

$$\sigma_{\Delta t=2} = \sqrt{1^2 \sigma^2 + 1^2 \sigma^2} = \sqrt{2\sigma^2} = \sigma \sqrt{2}$$

So instead of simply adding standard deviations through time we recognize that standard deviations increase (and decrease for that matter) by the square root of time.

The formula for the change in prices (iii) above is a finite difference equation. If we reduced the time gaps between price change measurements eventually we approach the situation where the gap in time is infinitely small giving a continuous time version of the model. So rearranging so that the model is expressed purely in terms of price change:

$$\Delta P = \mu P \Delta t + \sigma P \xi \sqrt{\Delta t}$$

the continuous version of the model becomes:

$$dP = \mu P dt + \sigma P dz$$

If we assume a very small but discrete change in time and that the random numbers from the standard normal distribution are strictly independent of one another then we can demonstrate that the 'risk term' (σdz) can be expressed as:

$$\sigma dz = \sigma \xi \sqrt{\Delta t}$$

in its discrete form (i.e., with small but measurable time intervals):

$$\Delta P = \mu P \Delta t + \sigma P dz \dots \dots \dots (iv)$$

or in its continuous form:

$$dP = \mu P dt + \sigma P dz \dots \dots \dots (v)$$

The log normal distribution

A log normal distribution occurs if the variable concerned (in this case share price) can be shown to be the mathematical product of a large number of independent, identically-distributed variables. A normal distribution follows if the variable is the sum of a large number of independent, identically-distributed variables. The log normal distribution therefore arises from a series of multiplicative effects whereas the normal distribution arises when those effects are additive.

The stochastic model of share price formation discussed in the last section forms the basis for the Black and Scholes model. If share price changes follow the continuous price change process described by equation (v) then we can demonstrate (as shown in the appendix) that the logarithm of share prices are normally distributed or, to put it another way, share prices are log normally distributed.

EXHIBIT 8.8

The general shape of the log normal distribution

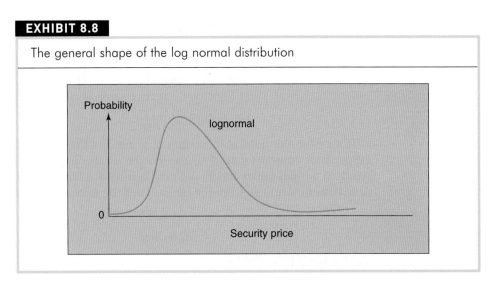

When compared with the normal distribution, the lognormal distribution has a strong downward 'skew' or bias and a limit to its downside value of zero as shown in Exhibit 8.8.

If P_T is the price of the share at time T and P_0 is the current price then the mean and the standard deviation of the distribution of share prices (assuming that the model above reflects the statistical properties of share price behaviour) is given by the following:

EXHIBIT 8.9

How the statistical function for the log-normal distribution is defined

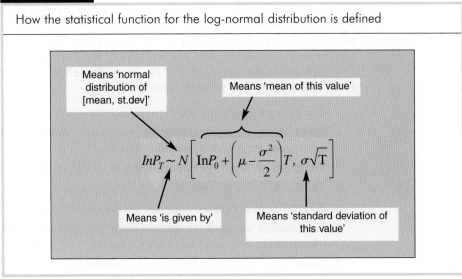

The share price of Friendly Grinders currently stands at 200p and its mean return over the last 12 months is 10 per cent and the standard deviation of the annual return on its shares has been 20 per cent. Jack would like to know the potential range of share value (within a 99 per cent level of confidence in 12 months).

FINANCIAL REALITY

Taking the formula above the mean and the standard deviation of the distribution is given by:

$$InP_1 \sim N\left[In200 + \left(0.1 - \frac{0.2^2}{2}\right)1,\ 0.2\sqrt{1}\right]$$

$$InP_1 \sim N[5.38,\ 0.2]$$

If we have the natural logarithm of a number then the antilog is given by the exponential constant raised to the power of the logarithm. In this case using standard normal tables the 99 per cent confidence level is given as 2.575 standard deviations up or down from the mean. Thus the upper price limit is:

$$P_1^+ = e^{(5.38 + 2.575 \times 0.2)}$$

$$P_1^+ = 363p$$

and the lower price limit is:

$$P_1^+ = e^{(5.38 - 2.575 \times 0.2)}$$

$$P_1^+ = 130p$$

In many respects given the slight upward drift in share prices over time, the impossibility of a negative price and the fact that share volatility does expand over time then the log normal distribution is likely to be a better approximation to the statistical properties of share prices than the normal distribution itself.

The derivation of the Black and Scholes model

Using our understanding of how the underlying share prices change over time we can now explore the way in which Black, Scholes and Merton sought to model a call option whose value, in part, depends upon the price of that share, the volatility of its returns and the time to exercise. The mathematics of the derivation is not easy and is more fully explored in the appendix. For the moment we will focus upon the assumptions Black and Scholes used for their analysis:

1 The options are Europeans.
2 Share prices are log-normally distributed and they follow a random walk in continuous time with a constant variance.
3 There are no arbitrage opportunities available in the market.
4 The markets are frictionless (i.e. no transaction costs or taxes).
5 No dividends are paid during the period of the option.
6 It is possible to adjust the investment in the underlying share continuously which means that short sales are permitted.
7 There is a risk free rate of interest available for borrowing or lending and that the term structure of interest rates is flat.

We will discuss the limitations these assumptions impose on the model after we have done the hard bit. The development of the model relies upon a mathematical theorem called Ito's Lemma after the Japanese mathematician Kiyosi Ito who in the early 1950s developed the principles of the stochastic calculus. The stochastic calculus is concerned with the mathematics of random processes through time. Using Ito's Lemma, Black, Scholes and Merton produced a differential equation which forms the basis of the model. The derivation of this differential equation is in the appendix.

The Black and Scholes model

At the end of the first and most important stage of the derivation of the model an equation emerges which links the value of a call option (c) to the share price (P), the risk free rate of return (r), time t and the volatility of the share price distribution σ:

$$\frac{\partial c}{\partial t} + \frac{1}{2}\sigma^2 P^2 \frac{\partial^2 c}{\partial P^2} + rP\frac{\partial c}{\partial P} = rc$$

This equation, from a mathematician's point of view, describes the value of a call option. The only problem is that it is not expressed in terms of the call option value itself but in terms of the rate of change of value of the option over time

$$\frac{\partial c}{\partial t}$$

the rate of change in the value of the option with respect to the underlying share price

$$\frac{\partial c}{\partial P}$$

and, to cap it all, the 'rate of the rate of' change of c with respect to the share price

$$\frac{\partial^2 c}{\partial P^2}$$

Reducing this back to an equation expressed purely in terms of c depends upon the definition of 'boundary conditions' which are the constraints upon the values that the chosen type of option can take. The partial differential equation above can be solved for all sorts of options, but our interest is in a call option which must have a value between zero, if it is not exercised and the difference between the share price and the exercise price if it is.

The Black and Scholes model that results is a closed form solution of the differential equation above and similar in structure to the two state model discussed earlier.

$$C = N(d_1)P_0 - N(d_2)P_e e^{-rt}$$

where:

$$d_1 = \frac{\ln(P_0/P_e) + (r + 0.5\sigma^2)t}{\sigma\sqrt{t}}$$

$$d_2 = d_1 - \sigma\sqrt{t}$$

where $N(d_1)$ and $N(d_2)$ are the areas under the normal distribution given by d_1 and d_2 respectively.

The replicating portfolio approach outlined earlier to creating a riskless hedge for the two state case gives an intuitive understanding of the model. Remember:

$$c = \Delta P_0 - Le^{-rt}$$

So by analogy $N(d_1)$ is the hedge ratio required to produce a riskless combination of shares and options, and $N(d_2)P_e$ is the value of a loan required to create the replicating portfolio. The value $N(d_2)$ also has another useful property in that it represents the probability, in a risk neutral world, that the call will be exercised.

Finding the inputs to the Black and Scholes model

The most significant problem in using the Black and Scholes equation is the calculation of these 'risk bearing' terms $N(d_1)$ and $N(d_2)$. The exercise price (P_e) and the current price (P_0) of the security concerned are easy to discover. The remaining three variables, the risk free rate (r), the time to expiry (t) and the volatility (σ) are more problematic:

The risk free rate of return

The discovery of the risk free rate of interest is straightforward although, unlike the case with the Capital Asset Pricing Model, a Treasury Bill rate of the same term as the option concerned is appropriate. However, the Treasury Bill rate normally quoted in the financial press is calculated using simple compounding to get the annual equivalent rate. However, in option pricing we are using continuous time discounting and the more accurate estimate of the continuously compounded rate of return is given by:

$$r = \text{In}(1 + R_f)$$

Where Rf is the annualized T-Bill rate using discrete compounding. Thus if the FT quoted rate is currently 4.75 per cent, the continuously compounded rate is

$$r = \text{In}(1.0475)$$
$$r = 0.0464 \equiv 4.641\%$$

The time to expiry

The time to expiry can be calculated using either calendar days or trading days. In practice, because of the relatively low variance of returns over non-trading days compared with trading days a trading days calendar of either 250 or 252 days is recommended (see Hull (2006) and Kolb (2003)). From now on we will use the trading day basis in valuing options

Volatility

The most difficult issue is the determination of the volatility of the underlying security. Because the Black and Scholes model works on the basis that share prices form a continuously generated time series therefore the returns that result are assumed to be continuously generated. More simply it is assumed that the return interval is infinitely short and the volatility is the standard deviation of those returns. We will return to the issue of volatility and its estimation once we have established the mechanics of operating the model itself.

Using the Black and Scholes model

Using an Excel spreadsheet operating the model is very straightforward:

1 Lay out a lookup table consisting of the five data elements required for the model: current price of the underlying, exercise price, risk free rate, time to exercise and the volatility (shown as a percentage variation).

2 Calculate d_1 and d_2 using the LN (natural logarithm) and SQRT (square root) functions. Exhibit 8.10 shows the necessary formula and a useful layout for this type of table.

3 Using the = normsdist() function calculate the total area under the normal curve given by the values of $d1$ and $d2$. Tables of the normal density function are available but usually these are only based upon half the area under the curve so 0.5 must be added to the result.

4 Calculate the call value using the Black and Scholes model using the EXP function to obtain the discounted value of the loan component of the model.

FINANCIAL REALITY

Using the data in Exhibit 8.7 determine (i) the price of September call options for Rolls Royce assuming that they are European type options and (ii), using put call parity determine the price of the equivalent put option. Assume that the volatility (annualized) is 20 per cent and that there are 135 trading days until exercise.

Exhibit 8.10 shows the data loaded into a simple Excel spreadsheet model and the resulting call value. The model generates a price for the call of 19.21p which is less than the quoted value of 19.5p. There are two possible reasons for this: (i) the quoted figure is for an American style option and/or (ii) the assumptions upon which the model is based are invalid, or (iii) the volatility is not correctly measuring the expected volatility but rather the historical position.

EXHIBIT 8.10

Excel template for the Black and Scholes option pricing formula applied to a call

A	B	C	D	E	F
1	**Black and Scholes Option Pricing Model**				
2					
3	Current price	243.50			
4	Exercise price	240.00			
5	Risk free rate	0.046406			
6	Time to exercise (days)	135			
7	Volatility	0.2000			
8					
9	d1	0.34250		= (LN(C3/C4) + (C5 + 0.5*C7^2) *C6/250)/(C7*SQRT(C6/250))	
10	d2	0.19553		= C9 – C7*SQRT(C6/250)	
11					
12	N(d1)	0.63401		= NORMSDIST(C9)	
13	N(d2)	0.57751		= NORMSDIST(C10)	
14					
15	call value	19.21		= C12*C3–C13*C4*EXP(–C5*C6/250)	
16					

EXHIBIT 8.11

The variation of call price with share price

Black and Scholes Option Pricing Model

Current price	0.00	40.00	80.00	120.00	160.00	200.00	240.00	280.00	320.00	360.00
Exercise price	240.00	240.00	240.00	240.00	240.00	240.00	240.00	240.00	240.00	240.00
Risk free rate	0.0464	0.0464	0.0464	0.0464	0.0464	0.0464	0.0464	0.0464	0.0464	0.0464
Time to exercise (days)	135	135	135	135	135	135	135	135	135	135
Volatility	0.200	0.200	0.200	0.200	0.200	0.200	0.200	0.200	0.200	0.200
d1	0.00	−11.95	−7.23	−4.47	−2.51	−1.00	0.24	1.29	2.20	3.00
d2	0.00	−12.09	−7.38	−4.62	−2.66	−1.14	0.10	1.15	2.05	2.86
	0.00									
N(d1)	0.00	0.00	0.00	0.00	0.01	0.16	0.60	0.90	0.99	1.00
N(d2)	0.00	0.00	0.00	0.00	0.00	0.13	0.54	0.87	0.98	1.00
call value	0.00	0.00	0.00	0.00	0.04	2.31	17.06	47.96	86.18	125.96
intrinsic value	0.00	0.00	0.00	0.00	0.00	0.00	0.00	40.00	80.00	120.00

Testing the model for different share prices and time to exercise

Using the formulas in the spreadsheet above we can create a data table of different call values for different values of the underlying shares. We have also introduced a further row into the analysis showing the intrinsic value of the option (which is the lower boundary of option value) at exercise.

When the values are plotted as a function the result lies close to the lower boundary of value see Exhibit 8.12. The curved functions are the values as generated by the Black and Scholes model and these curves answer the question posed at the beginning of the chapter as to where, between the upper and lower boundaries of option value, the price of the call would be located. Note how the curve progresses towards the intrinsic value of the option as the time to exercise decreases.

Valuing a put option using the Black and Scholes model

The value of a European put option can be found by either using put call parity theory or a modified version of the Black and Scholes model.

Using the put call parity relationship we can value a Rolls Royce put option quite simply as follows:

$$P_0 - PV(p_e) = c - p$$
$$p = c - P_0 + PV(p_e)$$
$$p = 19.21 - 243.5 + 240 \times e^{-.0464*135/250}$$
$$p = 9.77$$

Alternatively we can use a modified version of the Black and Scholes model for a European style put:

$$p = N(-d_2)P_e e^{-rt} - N(-d_1)P_0$$

where $d1$ and $d2$ are calculated as before.

EXHIBIT 8.12

The variation in the value of a call option with price (for different times to expiry)

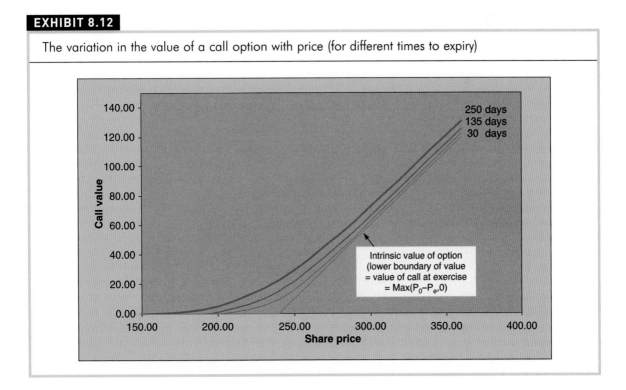

Implementing this version of the Black and Scholes model in Excel is straightforward. Using the call layout above (Exhibit 8.10) modify cell C12 and C13 to deliver $(N-d1)$ and $(N-d2)$ respectively. The put formula can then be inserted in cell C15 as follows:

$$= C13*C4*EXP(-C5*C6/250) - C12*C3$$

and you should obtain the result shown in Exhibit 8.13.

REVIEW ACTIVITY 8.4   Jack Grinder is keen to get a value on both put and call options of Friendly Grinders Plc. Friendly Grinders' current share price is 200p per share and Jack is looking at the price of 90 day options on his company's shares. The risk free rate of return is currently 5 per cent and the options have an exercise price of 210p. The volatility of the company's equity is 20 per cent.

Correcting for dividends

It is a relatively straightforward matter to adjust for dividends during the life of the option providing that the date the share price goes ex-div can be anticipated with a reasonable degree of accuracy and, of course, the value of the dividend can also be predicted with some accuracy. The technique is simply to reduce the current share price by the value of the dividend discounted at the risk free rate. The logic behind this is that the option is valued on the basis of the risky component of the share value whereas an impending dividend would be regarded as close to risk free. However, when the volatility of the share returns has been calculated using historical data it will reflect variability in the share price including any dividend effect. To be consistent, if we remove the dividend component from the share price we should also remove it from the volatility.

EXHIBIT 8.13

Excel template for the Black and Scholes option pricing model applied to a put

A	B	C	D
1	**Black and Scholes Option Pricing Model (Put)**		
2			
3	Current price	243.50	
4	Exercise price	240.00	
5	Risk free rate	0.046406	
6	Time to exercise (days)	135	
7	Volatility	0.2000	
8			
9	d1	0.34250	
10	d2	0.19553	
11			
12	N(-d1)	0.36599	
13	N(-d2)	0.42249	
14			
15	put value	9.77	
16			

The reason for this is that the presence of a (relatively) risk free component in the share price will dampen the variability of price changes. We need to obtain the volatility of the risky component of the share price. A relatively simple adjustment is to multiply the volatility estimate by the ratio of the current share price to the current share price with the discounted value of the dividend removed. This adjustment should only be used when volatility has been estimated on the basis of past data.

Therefore before entering data into the Black and Scholes model we make two adjustments to the input parameters:

$$P_0 = P_0' - d_{t(XD)}e^{-rt(XD)}$$

and

$$\sigma = \sigma' \times \frac{P_0'}{P_0' - d_{t(XD)}e^{-rt(XD)}}$$

FINANCIAL REALITY

The share price of Friendly Grinders plc is due to go ex div in six weeks' time with the payment of a 25p dividend. What is the revised value of both the call and the put option taking into account this dividend payment?

In this example the adjustment of the share price and the volatility for the effect of the dividend payment is as follows:

$$P_0 = 200 - 25e^{-0.05 \times \frac{30}{250}}$$

$$P_0 = 175.15$$

and

$$\sigma = \sigma' \times \frac{P_0'}{P_0' - d_{t(XD)}e^{-n(XD)}}$$

$$\sigma = 0.20 \times \frac{200}{175.15}$$

$$\sigma = 0.2284$$

(remember six weeks is 30 trading days).

Using the above inputs into the call and put models above we obtain

$$N(d1) = 0.13041$$

$$N(d2) = 0.10357$$

$$c = 1.48$$

and

$$N(-d1) = .86956$$

$$N(-d2) = 0.89641$$

$$p = 32.58$$

Where longer options are involved the dividend payments cannot always be predicted with accuracy. This is particularly important when we come to the topic of real options and the use of the option pricing model in valuing assets and liabilities over longer time scales. We will discuss the problem of handling longer dividends over longer time scales in the next chapter.

American calls and puts

The Black and Scholes model is based upon a set time of exercise. This creates difficulty when attempting to value an American call and in particular an American put option. Rolls Royce's quoted options are listed as Americans but in a situation where no dividend is due to be paid during the life of the option then a rational investor would normally seek to keep the option to its maturity. Where a dividend is due the situation changes in that it may be optimal to exercise just prior to the dividend date and thus capture the payment on the underlying stock. The decision whether to exercise early can be resolved by comparing the value of the option with early exercise (at the date the stock is due to go ex-div) against the value if it is kept until the expiry date but on the assumption that a dividend is paid (thus correcting the price of the share and the volatility as shown above)

With a put option the reverse is true. If a put option is deep in the money then it is worth exercising. The reason for this can be seen from the shape of the log normal distribution. Given the bias of the distribution the probability of further price decreases is lower than the probability of price increases – indeed when the share price gets to zero (as deep in the money as one can get with a put option) then the only way it can go is back up. So logic says that with a put option that is deep in the money it is worth exercising the option. If a put is near the option the motive of holding options as a hedge may suggest keeping it until it expires. Thus near the money American puts are likely to be closely approximated by the Black and Scholes model, whereas deep in the money Americans will invariably have a higher value than that predicted by the Black and Scholes model.

In the case of the Rolls Royce example (Exhibit 8.7) the quoted price for the September calls is 19.5p whereas the Black and Scholes model delivers 19.21p. Using the same input parameters the value of the equivalent put is 9.77p. This compares with a quoted price of 19.5p and 10.5p respectively for the call and the put. Given that the 240 series is close to the money we would expect the valuation as though they were European options to be close to the quoted figures – the situation is somewhat different as we move away from the money with the 260p series.

REVIEW ACTIVITY 8.5 Repeat the valuations for the September and December calls and puts for Rolls Royce on the 260p series and compare them with the quoted figures. How do you explain the difference?

Estimating volatility

The measure of the volatility of the underlying security is the annualized standard deviation of the continuously compounded rate of return. If the measurement interval is reasonably short (say daily returns are taken) then the volatility (σ) is given by the following formula:

$$\sigma = s\sqrt{t}$$

Where s is the standard deviation of the sample of individual daily returns, t is the number of time periods in one year. This, for daily data, is normally set as the number of trading days during a year (250 days).

The data table opposite gives us the information for both the estimation of the 'raw' volatility and for revising the volatility for influences that are closer to the end of the time sequence rather than further away.

We will now explain the steps required to generate this table:

1 Download daily price data for the selected time series (CLOSE column)
2 Calculate the price relative (current day price divided by previous day price) (PRREL column)
3 Calculate the logarithm of the price relative (use ln() function in Excel).
4 Use the standard deviation function to get the daily standard deviation.
5 Annualize the standard deviation by multiplying by the square root of 250.

The standard deviation of the sample of daily returns for Cobham is:

$$s = 0.00872$$

The estimate of the annualized value is given by:

$$\sigma = s\sqrt{t}$$
$$\sigma = 0.00872 \times \sqrt{250}$$
$$\sigma = 0.1378 \equiv 13.78\%$$

FINANCIAL CASE

Cobham plc wished to determine the volatility of its returns. A 20 day trading period was used and the following data produced:

EXHIBIT 8.14

Estimation of the volatility of a securities returns using the standard and the weighted method

n	Close	PRREL	ln(PRREL)	W	DEVSQ	W × DEVSQ
20	1410.50	1.00894	0.00890	0.09524	3.137E-05	2.988E-06
19	1398.00	1.00287	0.00287	0.09048	1.894E-07	1.713E-08
18	1394.00	0.99928	−0.00072	0.08571	1.614E-05	1.384E-06
17	1395.00	1.00647	0.00645	0.08095	9.925E-06	8.035E-07
16	1386.03	1.00124	0.00124	0.07619	4.238E-06	3.229E-07
15	1384.31	0.99878	−0.00122	0.07143	2.044E-05	1.460E-06
14	1386.00	1.00524	0.00522	0.06667	3.696E-06	2.464E-07
13	1378.78	1.02056	0.02035	0.06190	2.908E-04	1.800E-05
12	1351.00	1.00198	0.00198	0.05714	1.748E-06	9.990E-08
11	1348.33	1.00736	0.00733	0.05238	1.625E-05	8.514E-07
10	1338.48	1.00111	0.00111	0.04762	4.814E-06	2.292E-07
9	1337.00	0.99987	−0.00013	0.04286	1.180E-05	5.057E-07
8	1337.18	1.00088	0.00088	0.03810	5.845E-06	2.227E-07
7	1336.00	0.99553	−0.00448	0.03333	6.055E-05	2.018E-06
6	1342.00	1.00600	0.00598	0.02857	7.175E-06	2.050E-07
5	1334.00	0.99035	−0.00970	0.02381	1.690E-04	4.023E-06
4	1347.00	1.01370	0.01360	0.01905	1.062E-04	2.022E-06
3	1328.80	1.01668	0.01654	0.01429	1.753E-04	2.505E-06
2	1307.00	1.00849	0.00845	0.00952	2.654E-05	2.527E-07
1	1296.00	0.98152	−0.01865	0.00476	4.819E-04	2.295E-06
0	1320.40					
210	average		0.00330		sum =	0.00004
	st deviation		0.00872		stdev =	0.00636
	st dev × sqrt (250)		0.13784		st dev × sqrt (250)	0.10057

The problem of using this type of analysis is that we are trying to calculate the forward volatility from a series of historical return measurements. Unfortunately the volatility of a share is a stochastic variable. Using historical data therefore becomes more unreliable the further back in time we use as our sampling period. Similarly, the length of the time period over which the volatility is measured will have a significant impact as well. For most practical estimation purposes we should use daily returns and the past estimation period should be no longer than the duration of the security we are attempting to value. For this reason we would not collect a data series of more than 12 months of daily return measurements.

There are a number of procedures for 'updating' volatility measures. One straight-forward procedure is to weight the recent return measures more heavily than those collected earlier in the data series. To achieve this we multiply the squared deviation for each (Ln PRREL) value and then use the following formula (which when n is large is accurate enough for measuring the standard deviation of a sample of days):

$$s = \sqrt{\sum_1^n W_j (u_j - \bar{u})^2}$$

where u_j is the natural logarithm of the price in period (j) of the data series and u is the mean value. In Exhibit 8.14 we have calculated the weights based upon the first day having a weight of 1 and the last in the series as having a weight of 20. The sum of the weights is one and each weight is calculated as a fraction of the sum of the integers from 1 through to 20 which equals 210.
Thus:

$$w_1 = \frac{1}{210}$$

and

$$w_{20} = \frac{20}{210}$$

Multiplying these weights by the squared difference between the observed log return and the average log return gives the $W \times DEVSQ$ column. The sum of this column is the daily variance, the square root of which gives the daily standard deviation. When we scale this up to the annualized version we note that favouring the most recent observations reduces the volatility measure compared with the original approach.

REVIEW ACTIVITY 8.6 The directors of Cobham would be interested to know the value of an OTC call option on their company's shares. The volatility estimate is 13.80 per cent, the risk free rate is currently 4.75 per cent and the time to exercise is one year. The exercise price is to be set at the current share price of 1410.5p per share.

Using historically derived volatility for forecasting future volatility is particularly problematic but also particularly important for deriving forward price estimates of both call and put options. We have used a simple day weighted technique which places proportionately greater weight on the most recent return observations. Other weighting regimes using both geometrical and exponential weighting methods can also be used. A variety of procedures have been developed which are believed to offer superior forecasts to the standard or weighted approaches described above. The GARCH (which stands for 'generalized autoregressive conditional heteroscedasticity') method is one such approach which is now popular in practice. GARCH models the patterns in changing volatility over time and uses these to project forward volatility values. This method is not for the feint-hearted but further readings at the end of this chapter will give some insights into how this method works.

Implied volatility

One particularly popular approach at discovering the volatility variable is to use the Black and Scholes model to imply the volatility given that a particular option value is already known. One minor problem is that the Black and Scholes model cannot be rearranged in terms of volatility. However, resorting to Excel and the 'goal seek' function easily solves the problem. Using the Rolls Royce example given earlier we can enter the basic data into the spreadsheet entering a 'guess' value for the volatility as in Exhibit 8.10. The goal seek function can then be applied to the Excel table as follows:

set cell: C15

to value: 19.50

by changing cell: C7

This returns an answer in cell C7 of 0.2043 which is the implied volatility for Rolls Royce shares. The most significant problem here is that the validity of this volatility estimate relies upon the validity of the Black and Scholes model. Early studies (see Becker, 1981) demonstrated that implied volatility provides a better forecast of future volatility than the then available procedures for estimating volatility using historical data.

The sensitivity of option prices

If the Black and Scholes model is a fair reflection of the underlying pricing process then measurements of how the model responds to changing values of the underlying variables can be a powerful indicator of how the option itself might behave. This is critically important for the use of derivatives in the management of risk. In this section we will examine how option prices vary with share price (the option '*delta*'), and the related relationship between *delta* and the underlying share price (the option '*gamma*'). We will then review '*theta*' which measures how option value varies with time, '*vega*' which is how the option varies with volatility and finally '*rho*' which gives the sensitivity of option values with changes in the interest rate. These various sensitivity measures go under the name 'the Greeks' – although *vega* is the odd one out. *Vega* is named after the fifth brightest star in the sky and comes from Arabic meaning a 'falling vulture'. *Vega* is also known as *Kappa* which although not particularly memorable does have the advantage that it, like the others, is named after the letter K of the Greek alphabet.

The basic mechanics for discovering the Greeks (apart from *Gamma*) is to differentiate the Black and Scholes model by each variable in turn. *Gamma* is derived as the second differential of *delta* with respect to price. Although the resulting formulas look formidable they are relatively straightforward to program into Excel or another spreadsheet package. We have included all of the formulas for the sake of completion but will, in this section, be principally concerned with the first two: *delta* and *gamma*.

Delta and 'delta hedging'

When we first met the variable delta we considered a single time period model with just two future share price possibilities. However, in the Black and Scholes world share prices are changing continuously and hence the value of *delta* will change also. As a result a portfolio manager who wished to offset the possibility of an adverse movement in her portfolio by hedging would need to continuously adjust the balance of options and shares to maintain a risk neutral position. This process is known as 'dynamic delta hedging'.

EXHIBIT 8.15

Differentiating the Black and Scoles model by each variable in turn

Greek	Sensitivity	Formula (no dividends)
Delta (Δ)	Underlying share price	$\Delta(call) = N(d_1)$ $\Delta(put) = N(d_1) - 1$
Gamma (Γ)	Second derivative of delta with respect to price	$\Gamma = \dfrac{\left(\dfrac{e^{-\frac{1}{2}(d_1)^2}}{\sqrt{2\pi}}\right)}{P_0 \sigma \sqrt{T}}$
Theta (Θ)	Time to exercise	$\Theta(call) = -\dfrac{P_0\left(\dfrac{e^{-\frac{1}{2}(d_1)^2}}{\sqrt{2\pi}}\right)\sigma}{2\sqrt{T}} - rP_e e^{-rt}N(d_2)$ $\Theta(put) = -\dfrac{P_0\left(\dfrac{e^{-\frac{1}{2}(d_1)^2}}{\sqrt{2\pi}}\right)\sigma}{2\sqrt{T}} - rP_e e^{-rt}N(d_2)$
Vega	Volatility	$Vega = P_0 \sqrt{T}\left(\dfrac{e^{-\frac{1}{2}(d_1)^2}}{\sqrt{2\pi}}\right)$
Rho (P)	Interest rate	$P(call) = P_e Te^{-rT}N(d_2)$ $P(put) = -P_e Te^{-rT}N(-d_2)$

FINANCIAL REALITY

Friendly Grinders' current share price is 200p per share and Jack is looking at the price of one year options on his company's shares. The risk free rate of return is currently 5 per cent and the exercise price of 210p. The volatility is 20 per cent.

The Black and Scholes model gives a value of $N(d1) = 0.54$ and a call value of 16.04p. What this means is that for every 10p change in the underlying share price there will be a 5.4p increase in the price of the option. So, if Jack had purchased 1000 shares in Friendly Grinder plc he would need to sell short $1000/0.54 = 1852$ options to neutralize the risk of a fall in share price. If the share price did happen to move up by 5p per share, Jack would gain £50 on his shares but this would be offset by the loss of $0.54 \times 5p \times 1852 = £50$ on his options. If, on the other hand, the value of his shares fell he would make an equivalent gain on his short sale of options.

How does this hedging work in practice? The process is straightforward: the short seller writes a call option contract and the proceeds (the option premium paid by the holder) belong to the writer. If the option falls in value (i.e. it goes out of the money) then the option writer can either 'close' their position by buying back the calls at the lower price or wait until the exercise date when the call (if it is still out of the money) will have zero value. If the position is closed before the exercise date the difference in the two prices (the premium received on writing the call less the price paid to buy them back *i*) is the profit on the short sale. This profit should exactly match the loss in the value of the underlying shares if the hedge has been correctly set. If on the other hand the calls rise in value then closing the position creates a loss which will be offset by the rise in the underlying shares.

The problem with hedging when a share (or indeed any underlying security) is this close to the money is that delta is very sensitive to the price of the underlying. Indeed, even a small change of 5p in the share price revises the option value to 18.88p which is an increase of 2.84p. Jack's loss would be £52.60 (2.84p × 1852) indicating that he is over-hedged.

Delta will approach a constant value of 1.00 as the call goes deep into the money or zero as the call goes out of the money. The relationship between *delta* and share price is shown in Exhibit 8.16. The message of this for the portfolio or fund manager is that when an option contract is near the money the balance of shares and options required to keep a '*delta* neutral position' must be revised frequently. As the option moves deep into the money the revision can be less frequent.

EXHIBIT 8.16

Delta as the slope of the option curve at any point

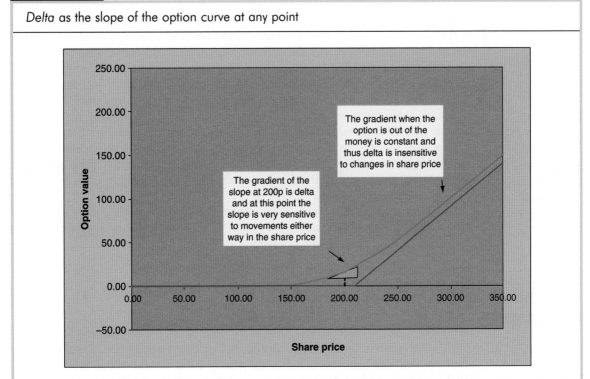

The gradient when the option is out of the money is constant and thus delta is insensitive to changes in share price

The gradient of the slope at 200p is delta and at this point the slope is very sensitive to movements either way in the share price

Option value

Share price

EXHIBIT 8.17

Gamma as the slope of the delta *curve*

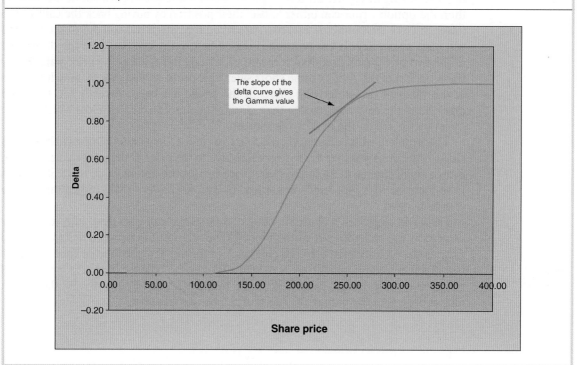

The slope of the *delta* curve as shown in Exhibit 8.17 gives the option *Gamma*. At the top of the curve (and at the bottom) the *Gamma* value reverts to zero – however at a position centred over the current share price the *Gamma* value is at a maximum. The definition of in the money, out of the money and near the money are all tied to this *Gamma* curve. From the curve we can see that the option is completely out of the money at 100p and completely in the money at 350p – indeed once these price thresholds have been reached the likelihood of the option moving to the other extreme is vanishingly small. The *Gamma* peak indicates the position where the *delta* value is most sensitive to changes in share price. Knowing the *Gamma* allows a portfolio manager to balance their portfolios such that they can minimize price risk (through *delta* hedging) and also minimize their exposure to hedging error by creating 'Gamma' neutral portfolios.

The other sensitivity measures: *theta, vega* and *rho* each have their uses in portfolio management and the references as the end of this chapter will allow you to build your knowledge of this important area of study.

The binomial model

The Black and Scholes model was a triumph in the mathematics of finance. It offered a comparatively simple formula for pricing traded options and for many other applications. However, it is only strictly valid for European style options. The binomial model uses a decision tree methodology to project a series of binary price movements through to the exercise date. We dealt with a simple one period binary approach when we examined Friendly Grinders in the early part of this chapter. In that case there were just two future prices permitted (up or down) at the exercise date. However, it is quite straightforward to project a price path with any number of intermediate time steps. We can restrict the price generation within the tree such that an 'up' movement from a lower price equals the 'down' movement from the higher price. Cox and Rubenstein who originated the technique suggested:

$$u = \frac{1}{d}$$

but there are other possibilities such as $u + d = 2$ which also works.

So, if for example the 'up' movement in the share price over the defined period happened to be 5 per cent, the u would be 1.05 and d would 0.9524. Let us trace a binary tree over six time steps. If the starting price is set at 100p Exhibit 8.18 shows where the price should be at the end of each branch of the tree. Note that a blank box has been created at each node against the price – this is for the option value at that point which we will calculate shortly.

REVIEW ACTIVITY 8.7 Construct a tree as shown in Exhibit 8.18 using a starting price of 100p and an up factor of 8 per cent. Highlight those boxes which would be out of the money for a put option with an exercise price of 90p.

The binomial model proceeds through a number of stages. We will first describe those stages and give the formula to be employed before working through the Rolls Royce example. The binomial method, like the Black and Scholes model, works on the basis that investors are risk neutral. This does not mean that up and down movements are of equal probability but that investors are unconcerned about the magnitude of the probabilities and are prepared to set the price according to the expected value of the shares.

Building the binomial model

1. Calculate the step length which is the time to expiry (in years, if the standard deviation of returns is quoted as an annual figure) divided by the number of steps you choose to undertake (N). If an option has T time to expiry (where T is expressed in fractions or multiples of a year) then:

$$\Delta t = \frac{T}{N}$$

2. For a given standard deviation of returns on the security concerned calculate the up/down changes which over the number of time steps of the tree will give the closest approximation to an overall return distribution that matches that volatility. If $u = 1/d$ is used then a simple set of equations tumble out which give the parameters we need to know in order to represent the volatility in these variables:

$$u = e^{\sigma \sqrt{\Delta t}}$$

$$d = e^{-\sigma \sqrt{\Delta t}}$$

EXHIBIT 8.18

Price propagation across a 6 time step binomial tree (100p = seed value being the current price of the share)

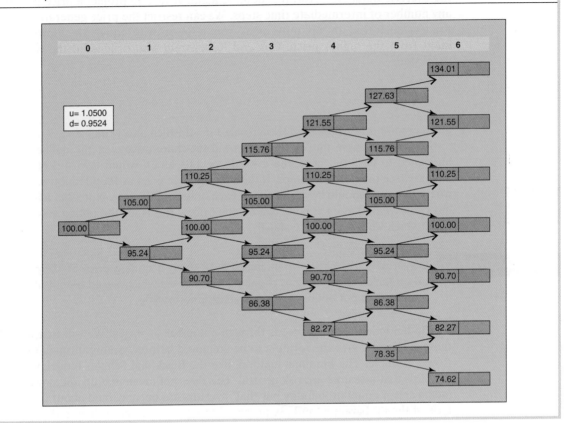

Although we do not derive these formulae in this book they make some intuitive sense in that 'u' is a continuous time compounding factor using the percentage standard deviation over the step length to uplift the share price over each period. The 'd' is the equivalent continuous time discounting factor for the 'downstep' in share prices.

3 Using the derived up/down factors (u and d) draw the tree (or use an analytical procedure as described in Hull (2006) or Cox and Rubenstein (1985).

4 Given that the underlying distribution of share prices at each step is assumed to be log normal then we can also assume that the likelihood of an upward movement in share price will not be the same as a downward movement. We therefore need to calculate the probabilities (p and $1-p$) of an up and a down movement at each node. Given that the expected future value of the price changes up and down must equal the starting price adjusted for the risk free return generated over the time step then given risk neutrality on the part of investors:

$$puP_0 + (1-p)dP_0 = e^{r\Delta t}P_0$$

Where r is the risk free rate of return and p is the probability of an upward movement in price. This formula on rearrangement gives:

$$p = \frac{e^{r\Delta t} - d}{u - d}$$

5 Given that subsequent share prices are separated by the time step of the tree we calculate the appropriate discount factor for each time step.

$$v = e^{-r\Delta t}$$

6 Once the tree is drawn out we can then work out given the final array of prices what the intrinsic value of the option is at the terminus of each branch. Using the discount rate from (5) and the probabilities from (4) we can then backward chain through the tree to get the option value at the start.

FINANCIAL REALITY

Use the binomial tree method to place a call value and a put value on the options in Rolls Royce. The data to be used is

$$P_0 = 243.5$$
$$P_e = 240.0$$
$$r = 0.0464$$
$$T = 135 \, days = 0.54 \, years \, (based \, on \, 250 \, day \, year)$$
$$\sigma = 20\%$$

we will assume six time steps.

Here are the steps in developing the binomial model as shown in Exhibit 8.19.

1 The step length is given by:

$$T = \frac{135}{250} = 0.54 \, years$$

$$\Delta t = \frac{T}{N} = \frac{0.54}{6} = 0.09 \, years$$

2 Using the formula for up and down in the price movement:

$$u = e^{\sigma\sqrt{\Delta t}} = 1.06184$$

$$d = e^{-\sigma\sqrt{\Delta t}} = 0.94176$$

3 Using these factors draw the price changes for each step:

$$P_1^+ = uP_0 = 243.50 \times 1.06184 = 258.56$$

and

$$P_1^- = dP_0 = 243.50 \times 0.94176 = 229.32$$

Then using these revised prices the calculation is repeated to obtain four new prices at time step 2 and so on.

EXHIBIT 8.19

Six time step binomial trees for call and put options (European) in Rolls Royce shares

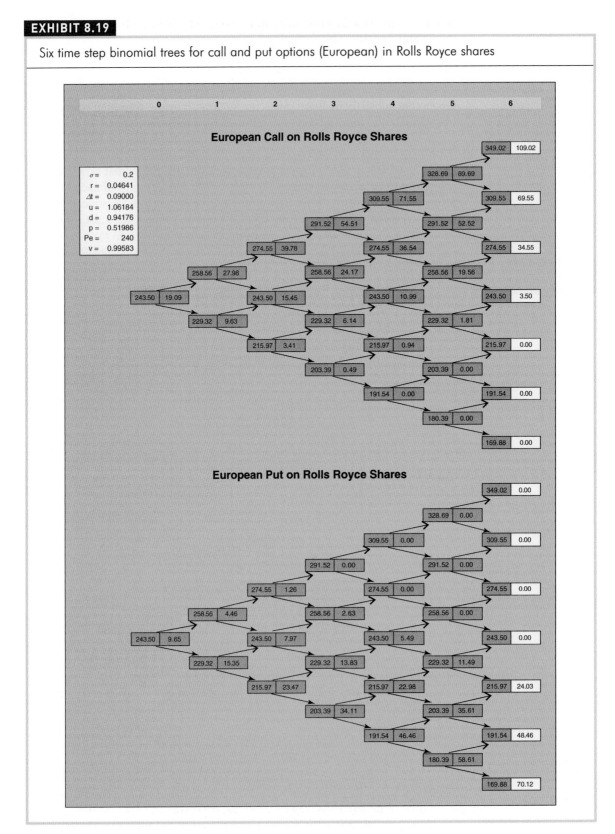

4 Calculate the probability of an up movement in price at each node:

$$p = \frac{e^{r\Delta t} - d}{u - d} =$$

$$p = \frac{e^{0.0464064 \times 0.09} - 0.94176}{1.06184 - 0.94176}$$

$$p = 0.51986$$

5 Calculate the discount rate for each time step:

$$v = e^{-0.0464064 \times 0.09}$$

$$v = 0.99583$$

6 Armed with this data we can now start to unravel the tree. With both the call and the put option calculate the intrinsic value of the option at that stage. Excel has a conditional IF function which simplifies the procedure. The Excel IF function is of the form:

$$= IF(Logical\_test, value\_if\_true, value\_if\_false)$$

Using this call insert the following formula alongside each of the final prices on the tree:

$$= IF(([P_6] - [P_e]) > 0, [P_6] - [P_e], 0)$$

Or for the put:

$$= IF(([P_e] - [P_6]) > 0, [P_e] - [P_6], 0)$$

Stepping back to time step 5 in this example we then calculate the expected value of the option at each preceding node. So for the call, when the share price is at its highest value at time step 5 (328.69) the option value is given by the discounted value of the two subsequent option prices weighted by the probabilities (p):

$$\text{Option value } (5, P = 328.69) = v[pc_6^+ + (1-p)c_6^-]$$
$$= 0.99583 \times [0.51986 \times 109.02$$
$$+ (1 - 0.51986) \times 69.55]$$
$$= 89.69$$

It is a straightforward task to copy this Excel function into each call value at each price point in the tree (excluding the final values at time step 6 of course). Eventually, the value of 19.09p emerges as the call value at the root of the tree and 9.65p is the put value. Even after six steps the binomial model has converged to a figure which is close to that predicted by the Black and Scholes (call = 19.21 and put = 9.77). For traded options a tree with more than 20 time steps will be required to bring the binomial model into close agreement with the Black and Scholes model (after 20 steps the model produces a value of 19.26p). For longer dated options (see Chapter 9) many more time steps may be required.

Using the binomial model to value American options

The Binomial model is reasonably straightforward to implement on a spreadsheet and although it is not as straightforward to use as the Black and Scholes model it is more flexible in its application. In particular, it provides a sure method for valuing American put options which are the nemesis of its more celebrated rival.

The downside of the binomial model is that a relatively large number of time steps are required to generate the accuracy of the Black and Scholes model.

Once a tree is set up then the process is straightforward: at each preceding price point before exercise check to see whether early exercise is justified. This is done by comparing the profit on exercise against the value of the option at each price point. If the option is more valuable (indicating that exercise is more worthwhile) leave the value in place, if not replace it with the profit on immediate exercise. Exhibit 8.20 shows the modified tree.

Taking the two lowest prices at the exercise date 191.54p and 169.88p we have an option value at the preceding node of 58.61p (see Exhibit 8.19). However, the profit on exercise would be (240.00 − 180.39) = 59.61p. Because, the value at exercise is greater than the value of the option early exercise is worthwhile at this node and hence the profit on exercise replaces the option value at that node. We then proceed backwards as before but testing and substituting at each node if early exercise is worthwhile at that point. When the tree is complete the model gives a value for the put option of 10.10p. This is closer to the true value (10.50p) than that produced by the Black and Scholes estimate based upon no early exercise. Again a standard tree can be built in Excel with perhaps 30 steps and a conditional statement which will put a node value to zero if the option is out of the money at maturity or to the higher of the profit on exercise or the option value if it is in the money.

EXHIBIT 8.20

Six time step binomial tree for an American put option in Rolls Royce shares

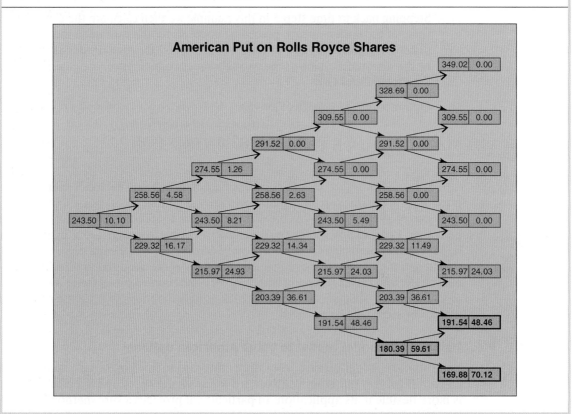

In the next chapter we demonstrate a simpler technique for laying out the binomial model in Excel or similar spreadsheet package.

How to correct the Binomial Model for dividends

Where an expected dividend yield (ratio of dividend to share price) and the payment date can be predicted then the correction of the tree is straightforward. First, identify the time step which covers the ex-dividend date (remember this is the date the dividend payment to the investor becomes irrevocable). Before the dividend payment the prices as calculated for each price path through the tree remain the same. However, all the prices after the ex-div date are reduced by the yield. Using the Rolls Royce example above, let us assume that a dividend of 20p was due to be paid in time step 4, going ex-div in time step 3. Note the importance of identifying accurately the time step in which the share is due to go ex-div as this is the date at which holders of the share become entitled to the dividend irrespective of whether or not they dispose of their shares subsequently. This is the date we would notice the drop in share price on the market reflecting the fact that it no longer carried the entitlement to the next dividend payment.

The yield promised by this payment is:

$$YLD = \frac{20}{243.5} \times 100 = 8.21\%$$

So, from time step 4 onwards the prices are reduced (both up and down) by 8.21 per cent (see Exhibit 8.21). Do note that only the time step 4 values need to be deflated by the dividend yield as time step 5 and 6 will carry forward this reduced value.

Notice now that the put value has now risen to 20.65p. This reflects the fact that the payment of a dividend reduces subsequent share prices by the yield percentage. A reduction in price pushes a put option further towards the money.

You may wonder why we have not simply reduced the value of the subsequent prices beyond the ex-div date by the value of the dividend. The obvious reason is that unless the volatility is altered to reflect the dividend payment the tree will not recombine (i.e. up prices will no longer equal down prices beyond the dividend date) and the tree will sprout extra branches. At time step 3 in Exhibit 8.20 four nodes will create eight nodes rather than five at time step 4. Although it is possible to handle such a tree it does make the process considerably more cumbersome.

REVIEW ACTIVITY 8.8 Friendly Grinders' current share price is 200p per share. The risk free rate of return is currently 5 per cent and Jack is looking at 90 day put options with an exercise price of 210p. The volatility of the shares is 20 per cent. Jack Grinder had a crafty idea: a large and surprise dividend payment which went ex-div in two months' time might yield a substantial profit – especially if he had 500 put contracts. He wonders whether the profit might be sufficient to purchase a new Aston Martin for £185 000 – that would certainly impress Gloria. The expected interim dividend yield would be 8 per cent. Value the put options using a 6 step binomial tree.

The answer is on the website but in a nice book like this we feel impelled to warn Jack that his new car may come at a heavy price. This would be deemed to be insider dealing.

EXHIBIT 8.21

Six step binomial tree for an American put option in Rolls Royce showing the impact of a dividend payment in time step 3

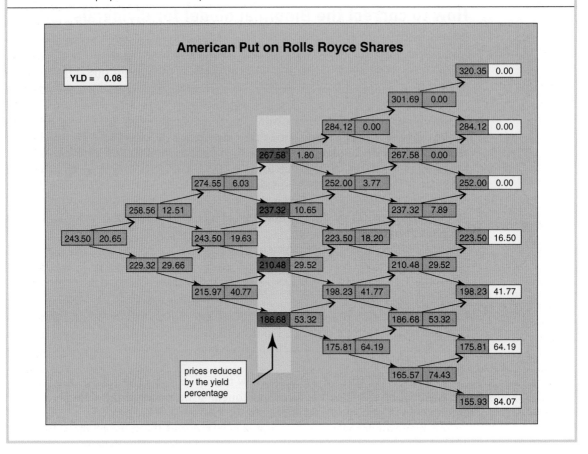

How to boost the accuracy of small tree in valuing American options

The greater the number of time steps in a binomial tree the closer will its results converge upon those predicted by the Black and Scholes model in those situations where the model is valid. We can use this to test the likely magnitude of error introduced through using a smaller tree.

Compared with the Black and Scholes model our 6 step tree produced a value for the Rolls Royce option (assuming no early exercise) of 9.65p rather than 9.77p using the model. This is an error of +1.23 per cent which indicates that the binomial values should be increased by this amount to bring them into convergence with the Black and Scholes model. Using this we can correct the American put value created by the binomial method to give $10.10 \times 1.23\% = 10.22$p.

SUMMARY

There is no doubt that mastering options is one of the more difficult aspects of learning finance. What looks to be a superficially straightforward idea soon becomes complex as we try to express the ideas in mathematical form. However, if you have followed the chapter to this point you will have gained some understanding of two important ways of valuing options of the major kinds: puts, calls, Europeans and Americans. The two models are not competitors for your affections but rather alternatives which have their relative strengths and weaknesses. The Black and Scholes model is perfect for a rapid estimation of an option's value and in the right situation where it is being used to value a European style option it can produce very precise results. It is a much more straightforward model for the manager to use when hedging risk exposure. The binomial model has much greater descriptive power and can be used in a wide range of complex modelling situations for which the Black and Scholes model is not applicable. In the next chapter we will take these two workhorses of finance and use them in valuing strategic alternatives in capital budgeting.

Further Reading

Aitchison, J. and Brown, J.A.C. (1957) *The Lognormal Distribution, with Special Reference to Its Use in Economics*, New York: Cambridge University Press.

Black, F. and Scholes, M. (1972) The Valuation of Option Contracts and a Test of Market Efficiency, *Journal of Finance*, 27:399–417.

Black, F. and Scholes, M. (1973) The Pricing of Options and Corporate Liabilities, *Journal of Political Economy*, 81:637–654. This is the paper that started it all – tough in places but very clear on the underlying logic of their model.

Black, F. and Scholes, M. (1974) The Effects of Dividend Yield and Dividend Policy on Common Stock Prices and Returns, *Journal of Financial Economics*, 1:1–22.

Black, F. (1989) How We Came Up with the Option Formula, *The Journal of Portfolio Management*, 15:4–8.

Cox, J.C. and Rubenstein, M. (1985) *Options Markets*, New Jersey: Englewood Cliffs. It is a shame that this book has not been updated. Cox and Rubenstein along with Stephen Ross developed the binomial model which has an important part to play in the strategic use of options.

Cox, J.C., Ross, S.A. and Rubenstein, M. (1979) Option Pricing – a simplified approach, *Journal of Financial Economics*, 7:229–64.

Daigler, R. (1993) *Advanced Option Trading*, New York: McGraw Hill. This book is a little dated now but it is clear and accessible.

Hull, J.C. (2006) *Options Futures and other Derivatives* (6th Ed.), New Jersey: Pearson Prentice Hall. This book is magnificent; buy it if you want to study options and other derivatives further from here.

Merton, R.C. (1973a) Theory of Rational Option Pricing, *Bell Journal of Economics and Management Science*, 4:637–654.

Merton, R.C. (1977) On the Pricing of Contingent Claims and the Modigliani-Miller Theorem, *Journal of Financial Economics*, 5:141–183.

PROGRESS CHECK

1 What is the difference between a European and an American put contract?

2 If you wished to hedge the risk of a share falling in value what type of option contract would be most suitable?

3 List the five drivers of the value of an option and which one is inversely related in its impact with the value of a call.

4 Define the put–call parity relationship and what general financial principle underpins its operation.

5 Explain the logic of the riskless hedge which forms the basis of the Black and Scholes model.

6 List the assumptions upon which the Black and Scholes model is based and which of these most constrains its practical use?

7 Write down the Black and Scholes model and outline how each variable within the model can be determined.

8 What change is made to the Black and Scholes model when dividends are paid on the underlying?

9 How do historical and implied volatility differ?

10 What do the five 'Greeks' refer to and what sensitivity does delta and gamma represent?

11 When is a position said to be delta neutral?

12 Describe the steps required to modify the binomial model to handle a put option.

QUESTIONS (answers at end of book)

1 The equity shares of TwoWay Plc are currently quoted at 90p which could rise by 10 per cent or fall by 10 per cent in 90 days' time. The current risk free rate is 5 per cent and an investor is seeking a call option contract for 1000 shares with an exercise price of 90p. Unfortunately she cannot find one either traded or OTC. How could she construct a replicating portfolio of investments which would generate an identical payoff to a call option on 1000 shares and what would be the net cost to her of that portfolio?

2 A traded 90 day call option on Parity Plc has a current price of 22p for the 200p series. The share price is currently 204.5p and the risk free rate of interest is 5 per cent.

You are required to:

(i) Calculate the price of the same dated put option in the same series.

(ii) Describe the arbitrage free mechanism by which put call parity comes about.

(iii) State the assumptions upon which put call parity is based.

QUESTIONS (answers on website)

3 The quoted prices for options in Rolls Royce shares are as follows:

Option		.... Calls			.... Puts		
		Jun	**Sep**	**Dec**	Jun	Sep	Dec
Rolls Royce	240	**13.0**	**19.5**	**22.0**	5.0	10.5	13.5
(*243.5)	260	**4.0**	**9.0**	**13.0**	17.0	20.5	24.0

You are required:

(i) To draw a profit diagram for a combination of a December call in the 260 series and a December put in the 240 series.

(ii) Under what circumstances would the above combination be in the money?

(iii) What is the cost to a speculator of establishing such a combination when one contract is purchased of each of the put and the call?

4 The price of shares in Black Plc are currently quoted at 214/220p being the difference between the bid and the ask price. The volatility of the shares is 30 per cent per annum and the current risk free rate is 5 per cent per annum. The cost of an OTC options contract for 100 000 shares for one year is being sought with an exercise price of 215p. What is the likely price that would be charged for such a contract for either a call or a put which can only be exercised on the date the contract expires? The dividend yield on these shares is expected to be 2.5 per cent.

5 Below is the specification for a European style option on the Financial Stock Exchange 100 index. The option is a cash contract in that settlement is in cash rather than securities. What do you think each term in the specification means?

FTSE 100 Index Options (European-Style Exercise)

Unit of trading	Contract valued at £10 per index point (e.g. value £65 000 at 6500.0).
Delivery months	Nearest eight of March, June, September, December plus such additional months that the nearest four calendar months are always available for trading.
Quotation	Index points (e.g. 6500.0).
Minimum price movement (tick size and value)	0.5 (£5.00)
Exercise day	Exercise by 18:00 on the Last Trading Day only.
Last trading day	10:30:30 Third Friday in delivery month.[1]
Settlement day	Settlement day is the first business day after the Last Trading Day.
Trading hours	08:00–16:30
Related documentation	Option Contract On FTSE 100 Index (No. 129E)
Last update	20/12/04

6 The price of a three month European call on Nuance Plc which has an exercise price of 80p is 24p. The current share price is 90p and the risk free rate of return is 5 per cent being the

quoted annualized rate on a 90 day Treasury Bill. There are 250 trading days in the year and there is estimated to be 124 days when the exchange will be open before the expiry of the option.

You are required to:

(i) Estimate as accurately as you can the implied volatility of the shares in Nuance Plc.

(ii) Given the data state the option delta at the current share price and the option gamma.

(iii) What would be the revised values for delta and for gamma if the shares (a) rose in value by 10 per cent, (b) fell in value by 10 per cent?

(iv) Explain the significance of the values you have calculated in (i) and (ii) above.

7 A company's current share price is 180p per share, its volatility is 35 per cent and the risk free rate is 5 per cent. Estimate using a 10 step binomial model the following:

(i) The value of a 90 day American put option with an exercise price of 210p.

(ii) The value of a 90 day American call option with an exercise price of 190p.

(iii) The value of both if a dividend of 10p per share is expected to go ex div in 30 days' time.

(iv) To compare and contrast the results of (i) and (ii) with those obtained for an equivalent European option.

The mathematics of the Black and Scholes Merton differential equation

Taking the process describing the share price:

$$dP = \mu P dt + \sigma P dz \ldots \ldots \ldots \ldots (i)$$

We can simplify this by substituting $a = \mu P$ and $b = \sigma P$:

$$dP = adt + bdz$$

If we assume that the price of a call option changes over time by a similar process then:

$$dc = pdt + qdz \ldots \ldots \ldots \ldots (ii)$$

Our job is to see how the two unknown (p) and (q) in this function relate to (a) and (b) in the price function. Ito's Lemma provides the solution in that the two functions p and q can be shown to be the following:

$$p = \frac{\partial c}{\partial P}a + \frac{\partial c}{\partial t} + \frac{1}{2}\frac{\partial^2 c}{\partial P^2}b^2$$

and

$$q = \frac{\partial c}{\partial P}b$$

Now plugging these functions back into (ii) above and replacing the values for a and b:

$$dc = \left[\frac{\partial c}{\partial P}\mu P + \frac{\partial c}{\partial t} + \frac{1}{2}\frac{\partial^2 c}{\partial P^2}\sigma^2 P^2\right]dt + \frac{\partial c}{\partial P}\sigma P dz$$

The discrete version of this equation is (assuming that the interval of time is small):

$$\Delta c = \left[\frac{\partial c}{\partial P}\mu P + \frac{\partial c}{\partial t} + \frac{1}{2}\frac{\partial^2 c}{\partial P^2}\sigma^2 P^2\right]\Delta t + \frac{\partial c}{\partial P}\sigma P \Delta z \ldots \ldots \ldots (iii)$$

Now remember that in the simple case described earlier we established a perfect hedge consisting of Δ shares at current price P and sold one call. Remember that the hedge ratio Δ is the change in the value of the option divided by the change in the value of the underlying security. In terms of the calculus:

$$\Delta = \frac{\partial c}{\partial P}$$

And so the value of the position (V) is given by:

$$V = \frac{\partial c}{\partial P}P - c \ldots \ldots \ldots (iv)$$

Over a small interval of time Δt:

$$\Delta V = \frac{\partial c}{\partial P}\Delta P - \Delta c$$

We also know that the change in value of this position over a set interval of time must be equal to the risk free rate of return for that time period $r\Delta t$ times the opening value of the position V. Therefore:

$$\Delta V = \frac{\partial c}{\partial P}\Delta P - \Delta c = rV\Delta t$$

Therefore using (*iv*) we obtain:

$$\frac{\partial c}{\partial P}\Delta P - \Delta c = r\left[\frac{\partial c}{\partial P}P - c\right]\Delta t$$

Substituting for Δc using (*iii*) above and for ΔP using (*i*) we obtain:

$$\frac{\partial c}{\partial P}\left[\mu P\Delta t + \sigma P\Delta z\right] - \left[\frac{\partial c}{\partial P}\mu P + \frac{\partial c}{\partial t} + \frac{1}{2}\frac{\partial^2 c}{\partial P^2}\sigma^2 P^2\right]\Delta t - \frac{\partial c}{\partial P}\sigma P\Delta z = r\left[\frac{\partial c}{\partial P}P - c\right]\Delta t$$

Untying and simplifying both sides of the above equation:

$$\frac{\partial c}{\partial P}\mu P\Delta t + \frac{\partial c}{\partial P}\sigma P\Delta z - \frac{\partial c}{\partial P}\mu P\Delta t \frac{\partial c}{\partial t}\Delta t - \frac{1}{2}\frac{\partial^2 c}{\partial P^2}\sigma^2 P^2\Delta t - \frac{\partial c}{\partial P}\sigma P\Delta z = r\left[\frac{\partial c}{\partial P}P - c\right]\Delta t$$

therefore

$$-\frac{\partial c}{\partial t}\Delta t - \frac{1}{2}\frac{\partial^2 c}{\partial P^2}\sigma^2 P^2\Delta t = \frac{\partial c}{\partial P}rP\Delta t - rc\Delta t$$

Divide through by Δt and rearrange to obtain the differential equation:

$$\frac{\partial c}{\partial t} + \frac{1}{2}\sigma^2 P^2\frac{\partial^2 c}{\partial P^2} + P\frac{\partial c}{\partial P} = rc$$

Options and the valuation of assets and liabilities

9

In the last chapter, we discussed the nature of an option contract. In this chapter we extend the idea of the option as a contingent claim upon some underlying asset. In so doing we show how the logic of the option and, to a certain extent the techniques of option pricing, can be applied in a wide range of different circumstances. We will commence our discussion of real options analysis by first exploring the weaknesses which are perceived within the conventional Net Present Value approach. In this chapter we extend the options approach to the situation where the underlying asset is the future cash flows arising as a product of capital investment. We will distinguish between four real option archetypes: the option to delay, to expand, to redeploy and to abandon a project. We then turn our attention to the valuation of intangibles such as patents, copyrights and brands. Finally, we consider how options can be used to assess the risk of default and hence the credit spread in valuing corporate bonds and calculating the cost of debt capital. As we proceed we will address the issue of 'technique stretch' or how far is it legitimate to translate the methods for valuing financial securities into the domain of asset pricing and investment appraisal.

Learning outcomes

By the end of this chapter you will be able to:

1 Understand the options embedded within capital investment projects.

2 Identify and measure the five drivers of real option value.

3 Solve simple real options using Black and Scholes and the binomial model.

4 Build an Excel binomial model incorporating 100 time steps.

5 Correct option value for dividend yield affects.

6 Correct the underlying Net Present Value of a project to take into account the presence of real options.

7 Use the option pricing methodology to determine the value of corporate debt and the potential yield spread.

Can we do better than Net Present Value?

In a recent study of America's largest companies, the Net Present Value technique was discovered to be the most popular capital budgeting tool followed by Internal Rate of Return and payback. In that survey over 85 per cent of companies said that they used Net Present Value always or often when making their capital investment decisions. This is a change on the situation up until the mid-1990s when the Internal Rate of Return was reported to be the most popular tool and indeed of the five major studies conducted over the last 20 years in various countries only Pike (1996) departed from the consensus view reporting that payback was more widely used than IRR.

A number of other tools apart from Net Present Value analysis are used by management to support their long term decision making. Of these sensitivity analysis and scenario analysis are the most popular as is shown in Exhibit 9.1. However, for academics no matter how successful or popular a method might be there are always improvements that can be made – and so it is with Net Present Value analysis.

In principle the Net Present Value technique should capture the impact of a project upon the cash flow of the business and, through the use of the market rate of return for a firm of a given risk class, deliver an assessment of the 'value added' to the shareholders of a given investment decision. That's the theory.

However, there is a perceived problem with Net Present Value analysis in practice in that although it incorporates a wide range of financial judgement it does not

EXHIBIT 9.1

The most popular investment appraisal techniques

First Line Techniques	%	Subordinate Techniques	%
Net Present Value	85.1	Sensitivity Analysis	20.5
Internal Rate of Return	76.7	Scenario Analysis	10.5
Payback	52.6	Inflation Adjusted Cash Flows	12
Discounted Payback	37.6	Economic Value Added	12
Profitability Index	21.4	Incremental Internal Rate of Return	8.5
Accounting Rate of Return	14.7	Simulation	3.1
Modified Internal Rate		Market Value Added	3.7
of Return	9.3	Pert/CPM	1.1
		Decision Tree	1.1
		Complex Mathematical Models	1.1
		Linear Programming	0
		Option Pricing Model	0
		Real Options	0.5

Percentage of respondents claiming that they used the named technique on greater than 75% of occasions where capital budgeting decisions were involved.
Sample surveyed 1000 CFOs from Fortune 1000 companies, 205 responses
Ryan and Ryan (2002)

Note: Highlighted items relate to topics discussed in this book.

include significant senior management judgement. If the NPV of a project is positive on the basis of the best estimates of future cash flows, and using the 'correct' discount rate, then the rule is: the firm should invest. Any positive Net Present Value project ignored is an opportunity missed to add value to the company. We have already discussed the assumptions which underpin the practical application of the Net Present Value approach in earlier chapters but it is worthwhile summarizing them again at this stage:

1   The model relates not to specific projects in isolation but rather to the impact of a given project upon the cash flows of the firm.

2   In its basic form the model assumes that future cash flows are deterministic (i.e. the future is known for certain) and that there is a perfect capital market where finance can be borrowed or lent at the prevailing market rate of interest in any amount free of transaction costs.

3   The presence of uncertainty is handled either by adjustments to the expected cash flows or by a risk adjustment to the discount rate. If the discount rate represents the opportunity cost of capital, fully adjusted for the risk of the firm, then the Net Present Value model should reveal the increase in the market capitalization of the business if a given project is undertaken.

4   The opportunity cost of capital should represent the rate of return, on average, of all classes of investors within the firm and that the capital structure of the business will remain undisturbed by the presence of a new project. If a new project is adopted which disturbs the risk of the firm as perceived by the market, then the discount rate should be revised.

Related to these we can identify three problems with standard Net Present Value analysis: first, the problem of achieving a consensus forecast about the impact of a project upon the cash flows of the firm (to give the project cash flows), second, identifying future contingencies where alternative courses of action are potentially open to the firm and where it can adapt its production or its assets to other uses thus mitigating its exposure to downside risk, and third, choosing an appropriate discount rate reflecting the impact of the project on the firm's exposure to risk. Many managers would add that the technique is too simplistic. New projects create assets which sit within the firm's existing network of assets. The firm also has a history and more importantly a future and it is the role of management to identify the strategic intentions of the firm and to create strategies and plans to realize the aims and goals it has set itself.

However, the strength of the technique is only as good as the financial estimates which support it and a number of writers have identified the problems associated with estimating the impact of contingent decisions upon the value of any given investment proposal. A project may offer the firm the ability to reconstruct different aspects of its business. An airline that invests in a new generation of quieter aircraft for its long haul business may open up the possibility of routes to different airports. The new aeroplane will make different demands on its ground crews and its maintenance staff. In addition they may all have a better second-hand price on the market and there may be favourable options available from the manufacturer on deliveries, engines and internal layout of seating for different classes of passenger. As the firm begins the process of deliberating upon the impact of its new capital purchases it will begin a process of which may affect the future viability of its operations and ultimately its survival.

The logic of the real options approach

So far we have discussed the technicalities of valuing options. However, the concept of an option has more fundamental roots. An option is the 'instantiation' of the opportunity cost concept as a claim (which in the case of a financial option takes the legal form of a contract binding the writer to the holder) but in other areas may be contractual or it may be embedded within the holder's property rights over some assets that they hold or are held by someone else. The key notion within the option is that it gives the right (or the opportunity if you like) to the holder to 'walk away' from a potential future claim and to pursue the next best alternative available to them. Thus the option premium is the opportunity cost of exercising the choice that the option represents.

To be more precise: you should now be thoroughly familiar with the idea that an equity option presents the opportunity to the holder to buy or to sell the shares concerned at some future date for a stated price. The intrinsic value of an equity option is the potential difference between the actual price and the exercise price when the option expires. The 'walk away' is, depending upon whether a call or a put is involved, the opportunity presented to the holder to hold their money or their shares and exploit the next best alternative open to them

However, and this point was first made by Black and Scholes (1973), the equity of a firm is also an option whose value is derived from the holder's claim over the value of the assets of the firm. The option value emerges when the equity investors have limited liability. If the asset value falls below the value of the external claims (the firm's short and long term liabilities) then the equity shareholders can simply walk away placing the firm in a member's voluntary liquidation. Indeed, we can use this intuition to place a value on the equity of the firm as we shall see in the next chapter.

Finally, the market value of any business asset is derived from the future cash flows it can generate for the firm over and above what it would have earned in the absence of that asset. From a business perspective assets do not have value in their own right but only in terms of the extent to which they can enhance the future cash flows of the firm overall. We all for example admired Concorde which was probably one of the most beautiful aeroplanes to grace the skies. However, the British and the French airlines that flew the supersonic airliner as a commercial business recognized that its value to them was the net cash flow it generated flying high value passengers at nearly twice the speed of sound across the Atlantic. Once it could no longer offer the prospect of earning that future cash flow, Concorde no longer had value and the remaining aeroplanes were given to museums.

It is a mistake that is often made about the Net Present Value approach to investment appraisal. The Net Present Value of a project represents, if the method is rigorously applied, the change in the value of the firm as a whole arising from the investment. Real options, a term first coined by Myers in 1974, arise when we recognize that investment in an asset creates an opportunity to create cash flows for the firm in many different ways which are not easy to capture within conventional investment appraisal.

FINANCIAL REALITY

Case studies now abound in the use of real options. Some of these directly use the financial modelling methods discussed in the last chapter, others use real options as mode of thinking strategically about investment projects. Here are some examples of where the methods have been used in practice:

Stealth Tier – an expansion option in the cable industry

In the late 1990s cable companies in the United States had expanded their cable capacity to 750 MHz (a measure of the capacity of a cable to carry digital signals) of which 14 per cent was unused in delivery services to the customers (Exhibit 9.2). Thus excess capacity was referred to as the 'stealth tier' because it presented an opportunity to the suppliers of on-line services to expand their offering into such areas as on-line shopping, video phones and so on. The cable companies therefore had a valuable asset on their hands which in conventional Net Present Value terms was valued at zero as no revenue stream was currently attributable to that capacity.

EXHIBIT 9.2

Analysis of the 750 MHz Cable Plant Usage

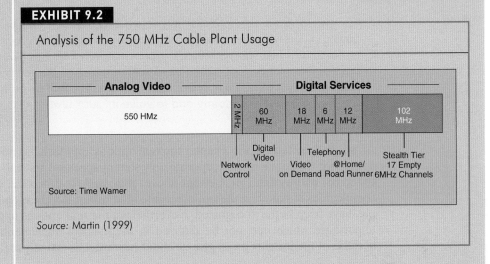

Source: Martin (1999)

In this case the analysts recognized the potential of real options to place a value on the unused capacity. Using conventional NPV analysis five potential scenarios were addressed for using each of 6 MHz channels within the stealth tier generating present value per household of between $15 and $150 per channel. Using this, the marginal capital spend per home, an estimated ten year project life and a standard volatility across the scenarios, a range of call option values was created ranging from $11.60 to $116.40. Given the availability of 17 channels this gave an option value of between $197 and $1979 per home which was 50 per cent of the current trading value per home.

Amazon.com – the option smorgasbord

In Chapter 10 we show how real options analysis has been used in a celebrated case study to value the company at a stage where it was still a long way from full profitability. However, Amazon has through its on-line trading systems developed a business model which gives it enormous flexibility in being able to enter, expand or withdraw from product markets. Its early success in creating an online book selling business allowed it to develop ordering, processing and delivery systems which could be rapidly expanded into the music, DVD, computer software and more recently consumer electronics and DIY equipment. Apart from the potential new product areas Amazon's systems development has been expanded in

▶

capacity in order to cope with significantly greater demand. The identification of potential within both its systems and its market for future expansion has created, analysts argue, a substantial real option component in the company's share valuation.

Merck – innovation in options analysis and simulation

The pharmaceutical business is characterized by huge investment in Research and Development and very long lead times for products to come to market. On average only one in every 30 000 newly synthesized chemicals has commercial potential and survives the many layers of testing and regulatory approval before coming to market. Merck, since the early 1980s has developed project valuation techniques using both options analysis and Monte Carlo simulation techniques:

' . . . when you make an initial investment in a research project, you are paying an entry fee for a right, but you are not obliged to continue that research at a later stage. Merck's experience with R&D has given us a data base of information that allows us to value the risk or the volatility of our research projects . . . I use option theory to analyse that investment, I have a tool to examine uncertainty and to value it.' JUDY LEWENT, CFO, MERCK (1994).

As we shall see later in this chapter the real options approach has not, as yet, become a standard technique in the corporate, investment appraisal arsenal. Indeed, some of the initial enthusiasm (see Lewent above) may well have become tempered as the complexities of handling the options embedded within R&D expenditure, for example, have been better recognized. Nevertheless, the real options approach has great importance which may not be realized in its practical implementation but rather because of the insights it can give us about how value is actually created in business.

The real options method

The practice of real options analysis is to use the vocabulary and techniques of the options pricing literature and apply it to the lower levels of analysis applied in firm valuation and investment appraisal. Given that the value of an asset resides in the present value of the net cash flows it generates over the period of its ownership then the present value is the direct analogue of the share price within option pricing. The means of capturing that present value is normally the capital investment outlay although in other types of real option it may be some future outlay incurred in altering the use of the asset or disposing of it in the case of the option to abandon. The outlay is therefore the analogue of the exercise price.

The time to exercise with a real option is rarely fixed at one point in time. Real options are therefore 'American' options. This limits the applicability of the Black and Scholes model and presents us with the opportunity (option) of using the binomial model which you have laboured over developing in the last chapter. Again we also use the risk free rate on the assumption that the principles of risk neutral valuation apply to management investors in real assets as much as they do to investor in equity options.

The final element in the translation of the option pricing framework concerns the issue of volatility. It is a truism to say of course that without risk there is no opportunity, and likewise options only arise when there is future uncertainty about the returns promised by an equity share, the value of the underlying assets and finally the cash flows of the business. Ultimately, it is the uncertainty reflected in the volatility of the firm's cash flows which deliver the volatility in the firm's equity. En route leverage effects may influence the volatility in the returns at each level and in principle, if the financial market is efficient at pricing the underlying value generation of firms, it should be possible to infer the volatility of a firm's cash flow from the observed volatility (historical or implied) of its equity and vice versa. Real options therefore use the concept of volatility in the same way as their financial counterparts. But it is this which provides the most significant insight from our study of real options.

Conventional methods of investment appraisal suggest that the lower the risk attaching to a project, the greater should be its value. Real options analysis would suggest quite the reverse. If a capital investment project is a call option on the future net cash flows that result then the greater the volatility of those cash flows, the more valuable the option. The reason for this apparent contradiction is quite straightforward: conventional methods assume that the firm is exposed to the full impact of the project's risk, however by exercising the inbuilt options within a project the firm may be able to avoid downside risk and only capture the benefits of the upside of the distribution of project performance. If this is successful then the 'average' outcome becomes the minimum level of performance and a project with high volatility gives greater upside opportunities compared with less risky alternatives. As a result, conventional Net Present Value with its emphasis on the expected project outcomes tends to lead to underinvestment. The addition of the real option premium to those projects which possess risk hedging characteristics corrects this tendency.

Technique stretch

One common criticism of the real options approach is that it is applying the techniques of analyzing the prices of securities actively traded in the capital markets to assets where there is no ready market. It is certainly true that the financial modelling

EXHIBIT 9.3

The translation of risk from cash flow to the securities market

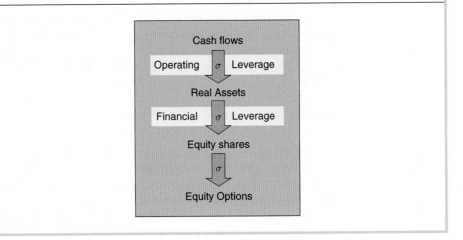

of options is mathematically sophisticated and the models are constrained by assumptions that are not perfectly valid in practice. However, the translation of financial markets methods to the analysis of investment opportunities has been done before and is now widely accepted. Compounding and discounting cash receipts and payments was a common feature of credit transactions in medieval Florence and Venice as the laws prohibiting the charging of interest on loans were relaxed. Irvin Fisher's 1930 work on the theory of capital and interest was concerned more with the theoretical principles of financial exchange than with corporate investment. Indeed, it was only in the 1950s that discounting methods entered the world of management accounting practice and began its slow process of acceptance within the business community. As we have observed before in this book, decision making models within firms are inherently less reliable than those used within the context of financial markets. What matters is do the models that are used capture some essential aspect of reality that would otherwise escape attention. Net Present Value methods focused attention on the problem of time and the cost of finance. Real options focus on future as well as current choice in investment selection and the potential value in flexibility.

The types of real option

In order to set the scene consider the next move in Friendly Grinders expansion from family business led by the irascible Fred Grinder to a dynamic public company under the control of his grandson, Jack. Friendly Grinders is considering significant expansion.

FINANCIAL REALITY

Friendly Grinders plc is considering the development of a new production facility in Grumbleton. It has achieved outline planning permission for a new grinding plant and has access to new capital for a £400 million building and development programme. A key feature of this programme will be the creation of Europe's first manufacturing plant to produce perfectly spherical diamonds.

There is a three-year period over which the capital investment could be delayed before the planning approval would lapse and a lengthy period of reapplication (with a strong possibility of refusal) to follow.

Although a minimum capital budget has been set aside if the market for the factory's principal product matures then the company would have the opportunity to expand its capacity quickly to take advantage of the situation.

If the market does not materialize there would be a substantial period over which the firm would have the opportunity to redeploy its assets to other uses. It would also have the option to rescale its level of diamond bead production.

It could also foresee a period where the firm would be able to abandon production and salvage its investment possibly releasing the land for a housing development.

Each of these future alternatives present options to management which allow them to manage the future risk inherent in the project. All are features of this capital project but none of them are easily captured within the conventional Net Present Value model. Real option pricing theory attempts to value the future alternatives that may be available and to give a means of distinguishing between competing projects which differ only to the extent that they offer differing real options.

EXHIBIT 9.4

The real option profile

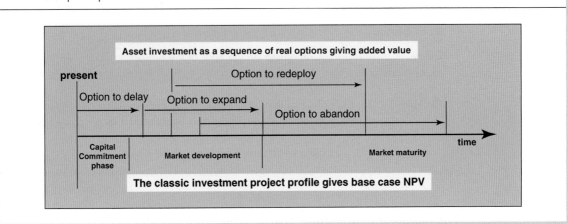

The development of the real option pricing literature allows us to identify a number of real option archetypes. Broadly these archetypes fall into two categories: simple and compound. A simple option is where one option exists to change the anticipated course of a project, while a compound real option is where there are a number of options which a firm can pursue some of which are contingent on others being exercised. Further reading on compound options are given at the end of the chapter.

Four of the most important simple option archetypes are as follows:

The delay option This option exists within a project when a particular alternative course of action allows the decision maker to defer the commitment of capital expenditure until some future date. It may be that the firm recognizes that there may be a change in its external circumstances, such as change in government regulations, or the future release of information by a competitor, which would make their given capital investment decision by the more or less worthwhile than expected given the current state of knowledge.

The expansion option Within the stealth tier case example we saw that a situation where excess cable capacity gives the company options over the future expansion of its business. The key idea here is that some capital projects have closed capacity that limits the investment opportunity. Other alternatives may achieve the same effect but give the firm the opportunity to expand capacity or indeed, as in the case of the system developments at Amazon, give it the opportunity to open up and exploit completely new market opportunities.

The redeployment option This, as the name suggests, is where a project offers the ability to redeploy the assets in use to some alternative activity thus capturing the economic value of that alternative rather than, perhaps, being forced to withdraw and scrap the resources concerned. The redeployment option (unlike the expansion option) allows the firm to hedge against the downside risk attaching to the distribution of project outcomes. The building in of utility services throughout an office block for rent would be the option premium paid if, in the course of time, office rentals collapsed and the firm decided to convert the building to living accommodation and rent it as flats.

EXHIBIT 9.5

Four generic real options

Real Option	Nature of the real option
Delay	Call option on the NPV of the project
Expand/contract	Call/put option on the cash flows resulting from changed capacity
Redeploy	Call option on the cash flows that would be generated in the alternative use (may also be extended to a choice between two or more valuable alternatives)
Abandon	Put option to sell (dispose) of the assets

The abandonment option It may be that even though a given capital investment decision looks highly profitable in terms of its Net Present Value that there is some uncertainty about future states of the world. In such a situation an alternative investment choice which offered the ability to abandon the project might be favoured over one where such a choice was not available. The capability of withdrawing at a time of the firm's own choosing may be an extremely valuable option especially when future uncertainty is high.

Within each of these options we can identify certain key features. First of all, there is a period of time over which the option can be exercised. For example, if a particular piece of machinery is purchased which is more general in its application than other alternatives, then redeployment may be a possibility for a substantial part of the economic life of the asset concerned. Thus an American option exists where the option to redeploy can be exercised at any time up until the date defined by the useful life of the asset. Second, a project at any stage of its life will have an economic value equal to the present value of its future cash flows assuming that once the capital investment is made the project is taken through to its ultimate completion. The economic value of the project is a direct analogy of the price of the underlying asset in the conventional options analysis. We also have the analogy of an exercise price which generally speaking is the cost of the capital investment concerned. In other situations, the exercise price of the real option may be different from this value – and these we consider further below.

The final characteristic which we can identify with each of the real options discussed above is their uncertainty. Obviously, the expected volatility is very difficult to determine with accuracy; however, in principle, the real option allows us to create a hedge against this uncertainty in the same way as with the conventional option. The greater the expected volatility of a project's cash flows, the greater the value of a real option which allows some hedging of the downside risk involved.

Estimating the volatility

There are broadly three ways in which the volatility of a project cash flows can be estimated:

1 By taking the variability of net cash flows on previous projects of a similar type and calculating their standard deviation. This entails the company keeping a database of the firm's cash flows analyzed by

project. The difficulty of course is where it is difficult to disentangle the cash flows from one activity against another and as a result any revenue (as well as cost) attributed to a given project is likely to suffer from allocation distortions.

2 At a first level of approximation it may be appropriate to take the volatility of the firm's equity or the volatility of traded companies whose business is focused in similar areas to that being currently contemplated. This can be a useful technique especially if the firm is entering into a novel business area where other firms already have an established position. However, using volatilities in this way the firm will need to 'ungear' the observed volatility in two stages: stage (i) to remove the increase in volatility attributable to financial gearing and, stage (ii) to remove the increase due to the firm's operating leverage. Operating leverage is the ratio of the firm's fixed costs to total costs and the conversion formula is as follows:

$$\sigma_{adj} = \frac{\sigma_{raw}}{(1+G_f)(1+G_o)}$$

where G_f and G_o are the financial and operating gearing ratios respectively.

Using its own volatility in this way does remove one of the potential benefits of real options analysis in that only scale and time effects will effectively be used to discriminate between competing projects.

3 By the use of simulation analysis. In Chapter 8 we described a simple version of Monte Carlo simulation for capital investment appraisal purposes. One of the outputs of the simulation model is the standard deviation of the cash flows based upon the parameter estimates entered into the model for revenues, expenditures, and the anticipated discount rate. Simulation analysis requires a specification of the expected distributions within the project cash flow model and in the most advanced modelling applications correlations between variables and across time can also be built in. Simulation, by its nature, is computationally demanding and time consuming although a number of simulation packages such as @RISK® and CrystalBall® are available that can simplify the process.

Adjusting the Net Present Value model

We can adjust the simple Net Present Value model to include the impact of a real option in the following way. If the Net Present Value of an investment is defined using the conventional weighted average cost of capital discussed in Chapter 5 then the Net Present Value of a project to which real options attach can be described as follows:

$$TPV = NPV_u + V_h$$

where NPV_u is the Net Present Value of the project assuming that the investment is unhedged by the presence of a real option and V_h is the option premium which is the additional benefit to the firm of adopting a project which is such an internal hedge.

Van Putten and McMillan (2004) argue that this formula should always include abandonment value as an explicit term. Following their argument about the significance of cost volatility, the ability to abandon allows managers to recover at least some of the project cost in the event that the investment does not survive for its expected economic life.

The valuation of real options

We now turn our attention to four simple real options which are present to a greater or lesser degree in most capital investment problems. With each we need to identify the following:

1 *The payoff if the option is exercised*: this will normally be the present value of the future cash benefits (or costs avoided) if the option is exercised.

2 *The exercise price*: this will usually be the capital expenditure required if the option is exercised.

3 *The uncertainty* which attaches to the future cash flows attributable to the current investment.

4 *The risk free rate* which should be determined from a risk free government bond of similar term structure to the real option.

5 *The time to exercise* and whether the option is either an American (most common) or a European.

Finally, if the option involves the sacrifice of some of the cash flows (e.g. the decision to delay exploiting a time constrained resource such as a fixed licence agreement) then there will also be the equivalent of a dividend payment as the value of the residual cash flow is reduced.

The delay option

The option to delay capital investment usually arises because of uncertainties about the future cash flow which will arise given certain specified, but unrealized future conditions. There may be some anticipated regulatory or legal change which given the right circumstances could give a project added value or it may be uncertainties about the future level of demand. The delay option allows the firm to realize the value of a capital investment once the crucial information is made known. Clearly, the delay option only has value if the firm has some exclusive right to the technology or product. If the investment is unprotected then any delay will mean that competitors may move into the market and take market share reducing the potential Net Present Value of the project.

The option to delay may also imply that the project cash flow will reduce progressively. This can be treated in a similar way to a dividend payment (in the form of a dividend) or by calculating the reducing profile of present values over the delay

FINANCIAL REALITY

Friendly Grinders plc has licensed technology for the production of nuclear grade carbon dust from NASA a condition of which is that it must begin manufacturing within 12 months. The Net Present Value of the project is −£5 million, and the present value of its future cash flows is £90 million. The expected volatility on the future cash flows is 35 per cent, and the risk free rate of return is 5 per cent. Jack Grinder would like to know what the Net Present Value of the project would be assuming that the company waits 12 months to see whether the level of demand predicted by NASA is realized.

period. We will defer considering this issue at this stage and revisit it when we review the option value attaching to exploiting intellectual property later in this chapter.

Using the procedure for solving the Black and Scholes model as shown in the last chapter and using the Friendly Grinders example above:

EXHIBIT 9.6

The Black and Scholes template for a real option

A	B		C	D
1	**Black and Scholes Option Pricing Model**			
2				
3	Current price		90.00	
4	Exercise price		95.00	
5	Risk free rate		0.05	
6	Time to exercise (days)		250	
7	Volatility		0.3500	
8				
9	d1		0.16338	
10	d2		−0.18662	
11				
12	N(d1)		0.56489	
13	N(d2)		0.42598	
14				
15	call value		12.35	
16				

Note that we have used 250 trading days for a year. It is possible to modify the model so that it accepts inputs in years rather than in days in which case the time shown in row 6 will not be expressed as a fraction or multiple of a year by dividing by 250 as has been done here.

As things stand Friendly Grinders plc is facing a project with a negative Net Present Value. Assuming that the project is commenced in one year's time then the rights to the licensed technology have a value of £12.35 million as opposed to a negative Net Present Value of £5 million if the project commenced immediately.

However, this analysis assumes that the delay option is a European Call upon the Net Present Value of the project. An obvious difficulty arises when the option to delay is present and can be exercised at any time. In which case we are dealing with an American style option where the 'right' to take up the option can be exercised at any time within a year as specified by the licence agreement. As we noted in the last chapter, where there is no dividend payable and where time value still exists it is still worthwhile to hold an American call option until expiry. However, in this situation it is highly unlikely that if the project did become favourable in terms of its Net Present Value during the year that the option to invest would not be taken up. The valuation of the option to delay as a European style call would therefore represent the lower limit on the value of this option.

The expansion option

The expansion option arises when a firm has the ability to expand its production or service capacity in the future. In many cases firms engage in new technology in a small way especially when there is considerable uncertainty about the future demand for the product concerned. However, engaging with a new technology gives the firm the option to expand its future level of output if the product does begin to take off in the market. Clearly, the value of the expansion option is greatest when the uncertainty attaching to future outcomes is highest. We would normally expect a high level of volatility to reduce the perceived value of the project to the firm and indeed, in the absence of the expansion option a company might well choose to adopt a very high rate of discount over and above its weighted average cost of capital in order to compensate for the level of perceived risk. The real options approach allows the firm to value the ability to capitalize on the development of the project at a time of its choosing.

FINANCIAL REALITY

Jack is considering a novel grinding process to produce spherical diamond beads which have applications in the photoelectric generation business. Because the government has announced that it is considering offering development grants in this area which will apply to certain types of technology there is the possibility that demand could take off very quickly following a favourable announcement. If Friendly Grinders were to undertake an immediate investment there would be the possibility of further expansion of the production facility on the back of the new technology that has been developed. The Net Present Value of the project as it currently stands is £5 million and the present value of the future cash flows from the project is estimated to the £70 million. The cost of expansion in three years would be £150 million pounds which is the timescale Jack expects the government to come to a decision. Taking into account the range of possible demand for spherical diamonds including the impact of a favourable outcome from the government's review, Jack believes that the standard deviation of the estimate of future cash flows is 35 per cent. The risk free rate of return is currently 5 per cent.

The real option that Jack is contemplating is one to expand capacity in the future when demand becomes clearer for spherical diamond enabled photoelectric cells. He has, through a current commitment to the novel technology, created a call option on an enhanced cash flow which he can exercise by the future investment of £150 million in three years' time. If in three years' time the present value of the future cash flows does not justify the expansion investment (i.e. the real option is out of the money) then he can ignore the opportunity and proceed with his current capacity. If the present value of the future cash flows is in excess of the value of the required investment then the difference is the Net Present Value of the project at that time (see Exhibit 9.7).

As Jack's problem presents a European style call option then its value can be found through the Black and Scholes option pricing model (see Exhibit 9.8).

REVIEW ACTIVITY 9.1 Using the spreadsheet template for calculating the value of a call option using the Black and Scholes option pricing model developed in the last chapter, calculate the value of the option to expand assuming the inputs to the Black and Scholes model as shown in Exhibit 9.8.

Answer $N(d1) = 0.23989$ $N(d2) = 0.09461$ call value = £4.58 million

EXHIBIT 9.7

The intrinsic value of a real call option on expansion of a project

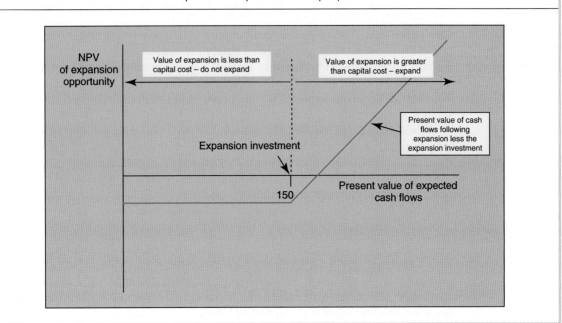

Jack's project has a call value of £4.58 million. This suggests, given that the Net Present Value of this project is £5 million that the overall value of the project to the firm is:

$$NPV = NPV_u + V_h$$
$$NPV = £5\,m + £4.58\,m$$
$$NPV = £9.58\,m$$

The option to expand production effectively doubles the Net Present Value of this particular project. Indeed in many situations, a project can have a Negative Net Present Value when calculated in the conventional way but has a positive Net Present Value when the effect of the real option is taken into account.

EXHIBIT 9.8

Using the Black and Scholes option pricing model to find the value of future cash flows

Variable	Value	
Current price of assets	£70 million	Present value of the investment project
Exercise price	£150 million	Capital investment required to exercise the option to expand
Time to exercise	3 years	Time at which the expansion should be undertaken
Volatility	35 per cent	Estimated volatility of project cash flows
Risk free rate	5 per cent	Continuously compounded rate of return on a risk free investment of three years to maturity

Modelling expansion as an American call option

Now let us reconsider this expansion option on the assumption that the decision to expand could occur at any time over the next three years. This situation invokes analogy with an American call option but with one key difference namely that as soon as the option value goes into the money then it will be exercised. This is different to the situation with an American equity call option. With the expansion option the natural assumption is that once the call is in the money (i.e. the present value is greater than the cost of exercise) then the firm will immediately expand its capacity. Working on these assumptions we then proceed to calculate the necessary precursors for a binomial tree.

We will assume for the sake of simplicity that the value propagation occurs over 12 time steps through the three year period and we will use a reduced form of spreadsheet model where the tree is collapsed into a matrix of future prices.

Using this approach with a few minutes extra work it is possible to expand the model to a hundred steps or more.

We will assume that the binomial 'ups and downs' u and d are related as follows:

$$u = \frac{1}{d}$$

where: $u = e^{\sigma\sqrt{\Delta t}}$ and $d = e^{-\sigma\sqrt{\Delta t}}$. Using the standard deviation (0.35) as given and a step length of 3 months the values of u and d are 1.1912 and 0.8395. From these values a 'probability' value is calculated as follows:

$$p = \frac{e^{r\Delta t} - d}{u - d}$$

$$p = \frac{e^{0.05 \times .25} - 0.8395}{1.1912 - 0.8395} = 0.4921$$

and finally the discount t factor (v) is given by:

$$v = e^{-r\Delta t}$$

$$v = e^{-0.05 \times 0.25} = 0.9876$$

REVIEW ACTIVITY 9.2 Using Excel or another equivalent spreadsheet build the model using the following steps as described. When you have successfully replicated the model as shown in Exhibit 9.9 extend your model to 100 time steps. This is more than sufficient for most applications in modelling options.

We proceed through the following steps to produce an easily extendable spreadsheet valuation model:

(i) Layout the data table as shown and then construct an nxn matrix. Below is shown a 12×12 matrix for 12 time steps. Put the present value of the project (£70 m) as the seed price in the matrix at location 0, 0 (this would be the current price of the share if you were using this model for calculating the value of an equity call option). Enter zero in all cells below the seed value (0, 1 to 0, 12).

(ii) Create an 'up' formula for generating prices along the first row only (this is very important).

$$p_1^+ = p_0 u = 70 \times 1.1912 = 83.39$$
$$p_2^+ = p_1^+ u = 83.39 \times 1.1912 = 99.33$$

and so on.

(iii) For all the other cells except the first row and the first column use the down formula but calculate the required value using the price in the cell above it and one to the left. So, the value in 1,1 is given by:

$$P_1^- (1,1) = P_0 d = 70 * 0.8395 = 58.76$$

Copy this formula into all the other cells of the matrix excluding the first row and the first column. You should end up with the price generation table as shown in Exhibit 9.9.

(iv) Construct an identical sized matrix immediately below as shown. This second matrix contains the derived option values. In the final column of the matrix build an Excel formula to deliver a value of 0 if the corresponding price in the matrix above is out of the money or $(P_{12} - P_e)$ if the option is in the money. Thus at cell 1,12 the value of the project is shown as 571.63, for a call option this is in the money with a value of $(571.63 - 150.00) = 421.63$. A suitable Excel formula would be:

$$= \text{IF}((P_{12} - \mathbf{P_{e^-}}) > 0, (P_{10} - \mathbf{P_e}), 0)$$

Note that the bold values should be entered using absolute ($) referencing.

(v) Now the tricky bit – every other cell in the analysis table should be filled in using a formula which achieves the following:

- IF the value of the option at a given cell is greater than zero
- AND IF the value of the option if exercised at any time step is greater than the call value at that point
- THEN (if true) enter the profit on exercise
- OR (if false)
- IF the option value is greater than zero enter the option value
- ELSE enter zero.

Here is an Excel formula to achieve the desired effect. Take cell (0,11):

$$= \text{IF}(\text{AND}((\mathbf{f_{0,12}}^* \mathbf{p} + (1 - \mathbf{p})^* \, \mathbf{f_{1,12}})^* \mathbf{v} > 0, P_{0,11} - \mathbf{P_e} > (\mathbf{f_{0,12}}^* \mathbf{p} + (1 - \mathbf{p})^* \, \mathbf{f_{1,12}})^* \mathbf{v}),$$
$$P_{0,11} - \mathbf{P_e}, \text{IF}((\mathbf{f_{0,12}}^* \mathbf{p} + (1 - \mathbf{p})^* \, \mathbf{f_{1,12}})^* \mathbf{v} > 0, (\mathbf{f_{0,12}}^* \mathbf{p} + (1 - \mathbf{p})^* \, \mathbf{f_{1,12}})^* \mathbf{v}, 0))$$

Again, the emboldened variables should have absolute cell referencing and all the others relative referencing.

Once you have successfully entered this formula simply copy it to every other cell in the matrix. You should achieve the result as shown in Exhibit 9.9. The value of the call option is in the 0,0 cell of the analysis matrix.

The binomial model shows that for this example there is close agreement with the Black and Scholes model indicating that early exercise will not occur (indeed given how far out of the money this option would be at commencement this is not surprising).

The redeployment option

During particular stages of a project's life a company may have the option to redeploy the assets involved into a new use. This option to redeploy entails an understanding of

EXHIBIT 9.9

A spreadsheet template for solving an American call option

σ =	0.3500
r =	0.0500
Δt =	0.2500
u =	1.1912
d =	0.8395
p =	0.4921
Pe	150.00
v =	0.9876

(i)

American Call Option – price/value generation table

	0	1	2	3	4	5	6	7	8	9	10	11	12
0	70.00	83.39	99.33	118.33	140.96	167.92	200.04	238.29	283.86	338.15	402.82	479.86	571.63
1	0.00	58.76	70.00	83.39	99.33	118.33	140.96	167.92	200.04	238.29	283.86	338.15	402.82
2	0.00	0.00	49.33	58.76	70.00	83.39	99.33	118.33	140.96	167.92	200.04	238.29	283.86
3	0.00	0.00	0.00	41.41	49.33	58.76	70.00	83.39	99.33	118.33	140.96	167.92	200.04
4	0.00	0.00	0.00	0.00	34.76	41.41	49.33	58.76	70.00	83.39	99.33	118.33	140.96
5	0.00	0.00	0.00	0.00	0.00	29.18	34.76	41.41	49.33	58.76	70.00	83.39	99.33
6	0.00	0.00	0.00	0.00	0.00	0.00	24.50	29.18	34.76	41.41	49.33	58.76	70.00
7	0.00	0.00	0.00	0.00	0.00	0.00	0.00	20.56	24.50	29.18	34.76	41.41	49.33
8	0.00	0.00	0.00	0.00	0.00	0.00	0.00	0.00	17.26	20.56	24.50	29.18	34.76
9	0.00	0.00	0.00	0.00	0.00	0.00	0.00	0.00	0.00	14.49	17.26	20.56	24.50
10	0.00	0.00	0.00	0.00	0.00	0.00	0.00	0.00	0.00	0.00	12.16	14.49	17.26
11	0.00	0.00	0.00	0.00	0.00	0.00	0.00	0.00	0.00	0.00	0.00	10.21	12.16
12	0.00	0.00	0.00	0.00	0.00	0.00	0.00	0.00	0.00	0.00	0.00	0.00	8.57

(ii) (iii) (iv)

American Call Option – tree analysis

	0	1	2	3	4	5	6	7	8	9	10	11	12
0	4.35	7.22	11.80	18.94	29.82	45.90	68.86	100.38	141.75	193.67	256.53	331.72	421.63
1	0.94	1.68	2.96	5.17	8.87	14.98	24.79	40.03	62.77	94.95	137.57	190.02	252.82
2	0.13	0.25	0.48	0.91	1.70	3.17	5.85	10.63	18.99	33.15	56.01	90.15	133.86
3	0.01	0.02	0.04	0.08	0.16	0.32	0.66	1.36	2.79	5.74	11.82	24.32	50.04
4	0.00	0.00	0.00	0.00	0.00	0.00	0.00	0.00	0.00	0.00	0.00	0.00	0.00
5	0.00	0.00	0.00	0.00	0.00	0.00	0.00	0.00	0.00	0.00	0.00	0.00	0.00
6	0.00	0.00	0.00	0.00	0.00	0.00	0.00	0.00	0.00	0.00	0.00	0.00	0.00
7	0.00	0.00	0.00	0.00	0.00	0.00	0.00	0.00	0.00	0.00	0.00	0.00	0.00
8	0.00	0.00	0.00	0.00	0.00	0.00	0.00	0.00	0.00	0.00	0.00	0.00	0.00
9	0.00	0.00	0.00	0.00	0.00	0.00	0.00	0.00	0.00	0.00	0.00	0.00	0.00
10	0.00	0.00	0.00	0.00	0.00	0.00	0.00	0.00	0.00	0.00	0.00	0.00	0.00
11	0.00	0.00	0.00	0.00	0.00	0.00	0.00	0.00	0.00	0.00	0.00	0.00	0.00
12	0.00	0.00	0.00	0.00	0.00	0.00	0.00	0.00	0.00	0.00	0.00	0.00	0.00

(v)

the present value of any alternative use over the time period in which the redeployment option could be exercised. Where a number of alternative uses are available, the normal opportunity cost principles apply in that the present value of the next best alternative should represent the price at which the redeployment option could be exercised. Given the extended periods over which the redeployment option may exist there are problems in finding an exact solution. One way of tackling this is to calculate the abandonment values at different points in time assuming that the option to exercise is effectively a European call. There are suitable readings at the end of this chapter which will allow you to extend your knowledge of the techniques for handling the redeployment option. However one variant of the redeployment option is particularly important and that is where the company is in a position to abandon the project at any time during its life. It is to this type of real option that we now turn our attention.

The abandonment option

As a project draws towards the end of its life, the abandonment decision will depend upon the relationship of the present value of the existing cash flows to the value which could be realized if the assets involved were scrapped or salvaged. In other situations, it may be that the firm has a business opportunity or product which could be sold off to another party at any time over its life. For example, a pharmaceutical company may have the licence to produce a drug over the remainder of the period for which it holds the patent rights but at any time during that period it could sell its rights to a third-party rather than continue production itself.

The option to abandon has the characteristics of an American style put option. The binomial option pricing approach offers the most straightforward way of valuing this type of option although the Black and Scholes model would provide the most conservative estimate of its value.

FINANCIAL REALITY	The conditions have turned favourable for the production of nuclear grade carbon dust under the NASA agreement. The Board of Directors of Friendly Grinders plc has decided on the immediate commencement of the project. Its latest estimate of the Net Present Value of this project is £10 million against the capital build of £90 million. The licence agreement with NASA is indefinite but the life of the current project is ten years. Friendly Grinders would have the option to sell the technology on for an estimated £40 million. The expected volatility on the future cash flows is 45 per cent, and the risk free rate of return is 5 per cent.

The nature of the put option available to Friendly Grinders in this case is very straightforward. If at any time the expected present value of the future cash flows falls below £40 million, it would make sense for the company to immediately wind up production and transfer its agreement with NASA to the third party. Clearly there are issues in making reliable estimates of future abandonment values and in particular the problems of putting a value on a put option of this type. The first step is to calculate the minimum value which would hold if the abandonment was delayed until the end of the project. For this we use the Black and Scholes model as modified for a put option.

This suggests that the Net Present Value of this project is somewhat more than the £10 million identified through conventional Net Present Value analysis but is now £15.03 million reflecting the value of the abandonment option. Given that the option

---

EXHIBIT 9.10

The Black and Scholes template for a put option

A	B		C	D
1	**Black and Scholes Option Pricing Model (Put)**			
2				
3	Current price		100.00	
4	Exercise price		40.00	
5	Risk free rate		0.05	
6	Time to exercise (days)		2500	
7	Volatility		0.4500	
8				
9	d1		1.70678	
10	d2		0.28376	
11				
12	N(d1)		0.04393	
13	N(d2)		0.38830	
14				
15	put value		5.03	
16				

---

to abandon is available at any time during the life of the project then we would expect the option premium to be more than the £5.03 million calculated for a European style option.

With real options of this type where the opportunity to redeploy or withdraw extends over a substantial period of time then the Black and Scholes model is less applicable. We now examine the value of the put option using the binomial tree approach. In this example we will use a ten step model for illustration purposes (which gives a step length of one year) and assume that the abandonment option could be exercised at any time up to the ten year point.

The model inputs and the results are shown in Exhibit 9.11. The two critical Excel formulas to handle the logic within the tree analysis are as follows:

$$= IF((P_e - P_{10}) > 0,(P_e - P_{10}),0)$$

For the terminal option values and

$$= IF(AND((f_{0,\,10}{}^*p + (1 - p){}^* f_{1,\,10}){}^*v > 0, P_e - P_{0,\,9} > (f_{0,\,10}{}^*p + (1 - p){}^* f_{1,\,10}){}^*v),$$
$$P_e - P_{0,\,9}, IF((f_{0,\,10}{}^*p + (1 - p){}^* f_{1,\,10}){}^*v > 0,(f_{0,\,10}{}^*p + (1 - p){}^* f_{1,\,10}){}^*v, 0))$$

for the interior option cell values.

This analysis suggests that the value of this withdrawal option is £5.86 million. Using 100 time steps a more accurate answer of £6.16 million is obtained.

Real options and the discount rate

The presence of real options in capital investment appraisal is an important indicator of the degree of flexibility that management possesses in the reduction of risk. In certain types of industry, with very short lead times to new markets and highly

EXHIBIT 9.11

The value of an American Put option on abandonment

σ=	0.4500
r=	0.0500
Δt=	1.0000
u=	1.5683
d=	0.6376
p=	0.4445
Pe=	40.00
v=	0.9512

American Put Option – price/value generation table

	0	1	2	3	4	5	6	7	8	9	10
0	100.00	156.83	245.96	385.74	604.96	948.77	1487.97	2333.61	3659.82	5739.75	9001.71
1	0.00	63.76	100.00	156.83	245.96	385.74	604.96	948.77	1487.97	2333.61	3659.82
2	0.00	0.00	40.66	63.76	100.00	156.83	245.96	385.74	604.96	948.77	1487.97
3	0.00	0.00	0.00	25.92	40.66	63.76	100.00	156.83	245.96	385.74	604.96
4	0.00	0.00	0.00	0.00	16.53	25.92	40.66	63.76	100.00	156.83	245.96
5	0.00	0.00	0.00	0.00	0.00	10.54	16.53	25.92	40.66	63.76	100.00
6	0.00	0.00	0.00	0.00	0.00	0.00	6.72	10.54	16.53	25.92	40.66
7	0.00	0.00	0.00	0.00	0.00	0.00	0.00	4.29	6.72	10.54	16.53
8	0.00	0.00	0.00	0.00	0.00	0.00	0.00	0.00	2.73	4.29	6.72
9	0.00	0.00	0.00	0.00	0.00	0.00	0.00	0.00	0.00	1.74	2.73
10	0.00	0.00	0.00	0.00	0.00	0.00	0.00	0.00	0.00	0.00	1.11

American Put Option – tree analysis

	0	1	2	3	4	5	6	7	8	9	10
0	5.86	3.14	1.29	0.31	0.00	0.00	0.00	0.00	0.00	0.00	0.00
1	40.00	8.57	4.92	2.19	0.58	0.00	0.00	0.00	0.00	0.00	0.00
2	40.00	40.00	12.28	7.55	3.69	1.10	0.00	0.00	0.00	0.00	0.00
3	40.00	40.00	40.00	17.20	11.34	6.10	2.08	0.00	0.00	0.00	0.00
4	40.00	40.00	40.00	40.00	23.47	16.58	9.88	3.93	0.00	0.00	0.00
5	40.00	40.00	40.00	40.00	40.00	29.46	23.47	15.55	7.44	0.00	0.00
6	40.00	40.00	40.00	40.00	40.00	40.00	33.28	29.46	23.47	14.08	0.00
7	40.00	40.00	40.00	40.00	40.00	40.00	40.00	35.71	33.28	29.46	23.47
8	40.00	40.00	40.00	40.00	40.00	40.00	40.00	40.00	37.27	33.28	33.28
9	40.00	40.00	40.00	40.00	40.00	40.00	40.00	40.00	40.00	38.26	37.27
10	40.00	40.00	40.00	40.00	40.00	40.00	40.00	40.00	40.00	40.00	38.89

specific assets then the level of adaptability which management has in delaying projects, expanding or contracting production, or redeploying to new uses, will be very limited. In this case, the firm has limited scope to hedge project risk and thus investors will be fully exposed to, and will expect to be rewarded for carrying this level of risk. Where significant adaptation is available, management has the opportunity to 'hedge' the volatility of project returns and this we would expect to see reflected in a reduction in the discount rate which investors impose upon the firm.

Arguably, therefore, the discount rate used by the firm should reflect the lower risk imputed to the firm's earnings because of the presence of real options within its capital budgeting plans. The only time in which a real option would become valuable to investors is if it promises flexibility over and above that which would normally be anticipated by the market for a firm of that type. From this perspective, adding an option premium to the Net Present Value of the expected cash flows discounted by the appropriate rate of return is double counting the benefit of adaptation unless the option was not one which would be anticipated by the market.

More correctly, if the securities markets are correctly pricing firms given their inherent adaptation and managers are making efficient project selection decisions then the base case NPV includes within it the relevant option premium. What this means is that the formula discussed above:

$$NPV = NPV_u + V_h$$

describes the base case NPV, which is the Net Present Value of the expected cash flows discounted at the current opportunity cost of capital, in terms of two components: the Net Present Value of the expected cash flows if discounted at a higher rate assuming that no managerial adaptation is available to the firm plus an adaptation premium created by the availability of real options. The key point here is that in an efficient market, the option premium is imputed by the market and managers do not themselves need to undertake the exercise. All they need to do is to discount the expected cash flows from projects at the appropriate market rate – the market in setting that rate will already have discounted the adaptability inherent in the business. Of course, if markets are not efficient then neither the Net Present Value model nor the option pricing model are likely to be effective at valuing projects in the hands of their investors.

The real options approach, therefore, implicitly assumes that investors do not perfectly price the firm's ability to adapt and mitigate its exposure to project risk. So far, little evidence has been discovered to support this view. What value then does real options analysis have in assessing the value added by any particular project? The most convincing case that can be made for real options analysis is that it allows management to think about 'project hedging' and the factors which are likely to influence their ability to adapt to changing circumstances. Arguably, markets understand perfectly well those business situations where such adaptation is a possibility and will price that into shares. Across the portfolio of holdings, managers will have differing abilities to capitalize upon the inherent flexibility within the investment opportunities available to their firms. However these differing abilities are simply a component of the unsystematic risk which within the classical analysis described in Chapter 3 we assume would be diversified away by rational investors.

The real options process

Some writers would argue that real options analysis should not be regarded as a 'bolt on' technique to the Net Present Value model. Rather, it is part of a portfolio of methods designed to assess the impact of a project upon the firm in both the short and the long term. In Chapter 11 we discuss this topic in more detail when we look at managerial models of investment appraisal in more detail. However, Munn (2002) has suggested the following steps in undertaking a real options analysis of new investment proposals:

1   *Qualitative management screening* – this is a 'coarse filter' where management decide whether a given project is likely to fit within the firm's overall business strategy. This may be simple where a proposal to replace an existing asset is made or it may be more complex where the proposal is to engage in a completely new line of business.

2   *Base case Net Present Value analysis* – if the project survives the coarse filter the 'financial ruler' is passed over the project. On the basis of the best guess forecasts the project's Net Present Value is calculated using an appropriate risk adjusted hurdle rate.

3   *Monte Carlo simulation* – given the problems of relying upon single point estimates of future cash flows the first step is to conduct a sensitivity analysis to identify the most influential variables upon the project's Net Present Value analysis. These variables and the correlations between them will then be projected forward using Monte Carlo simulation techniques. The simulation will deliver to the investigator important information about the volatilities of each variable and of the project overall.

4   *Real options project framing* – drawing on knowledge of the strategic possibilities from 1 as modified by the rigours of 2 and 3 a range of 'optionalities' are identified for the project. Real options analysis tends to focus attention upon adaptation within the project whereas what is just as important is how a project increases the firm's overall ability to adapt. The typology of real option types discussed earlier provides the framework of delay, expansion, redeployment and abandonment.

5   *Real options modelling and analysis* – using the inputs from the base case Net Present Value analysis and the simulation studies the analyst can then develop 'prices' for the options embedded within the project. This allows the modification of the base case Net Present Value required to estimate the overall project value to the firm.

6   *Portfolio and resource optimization* – in a step that Munn describes as 'optional' the firm can assess the significance of the project upon the firm's overall portfolio of investment opportunities. In Chapter 6 we discussed the use of the profitability index as a means of ranking projects under single period capital rationing. That would form part of this stage of the analysis although what Munn suggests is more radical. Munn suggests that the correlations between projects (and indeed the real options on projects) should form the basis of a selection procedure along the lines of the Markowitz portfolio analysis discussed in Chapter 3.

7   *Reporting* – Munn makes the important point that management must understand the underlying rationale supporting project proposals. They will never, he argues, accept the results from a 'black box' if they do not understand the assumptions upon which the analytical models are based. For this reason the reporting process where not only recommendations are made but also the rationale for those recommendations are given.

8   *Update analysis* – underlying real options analysis is the fact that the future is uncertain. Once a project is accepted and implemented it is then important to update the analysis on a regular basis as options mature and new opportunities become available.

The evidence for the use of real options and the underinvestment problem

There is no doubt that real options analysis captured the imagination of both corporate managers and academics alike. In the 1970s and 1980s a number of scholars suggested that the standard Net Present Value techniques systematically undervalued investment opportunities within firms. This it was assumed was the fault with the method rather than with the use of an inappropriately high discount rate. Myers in 1974, and writers subsequently, identified the problem of relative adaptation as being the cause of this underinvestment and that the classical investment appraisal techniques failed to recognize the flexibility open to management when valuing projects. Options analysis appeared to offer the tool necessary to overcome the perceived deficiency in the Net Present Value approach. A number of firms have experimented with the use of real options analysis although recent studies of US practice suggest that the technique is not gaining acceptance and indeed has declined in use as many firms have abandoned it as impractical.

> *The survey shows that tool usage is high across all industries and in all countries, with the average respondent using 13 of the top 25 tools. Yet 77% of executives report that tools promise more than they deliver, and even highly rated tools vary widely in their ability to improve financial results, customer quality, and competitive advantage . . . Some tools seem to exasperate those who try them . . . The survey found that 46% of North American firms that experimented with real options analysis gave up, perhaps because it is too rarefied a concept . . . Indeed, management tools are not silver bullets that will instantly eradicate the problem. They are more like chain saws potentially powerful when applied to the right problems, but extraordinarily dangerous in the wrong hands.* EXTRACTED COMMENT FROM: *FAD OR FAILURE OF THE MONTH: MANAGERS MUST DECIDE BUSINESS DAY (SOUTH AFRICA)* 10/18/2000 BY CRAWFORD GILLIES

In a recent study, Ryan and Ryan (2002) reported that the use of options generally and real options in particular were currently ranked as the least used of a set of supplementary capital budgeting tools put to CFOs within the Fortune 1000. In the most recent survey conducted by Bain and Co., of management tools used by US top companies real options analysis had dropped out of the list!

This evidence does not necessarily disprove the value of real options analysis to companies, and indeed some very large companies such as British Petroleum, Merck and Hewlett-Packard have used real options analysis. What it may simply point to is a first mover phenomenon. Highly innovative and technically adept companies may have been early adopters of the real options technique and some of those may have abandoned it as an approach for a variety of reasons. If real options analysis follows the trajectory of development of the Net Present Value technique then it will only gradually become accepted when it forms part of the professional development of accountants both when training and in practice.

The valuation of intangible assets using real options

Some of the classic cases in the use of real options (as with the case of Merck cited earlier) have involved estimating the future benefits available from patents and other forms of intellectual property. Given that many company acquisitions and joint ventures are driven by the desire to capture intellectual property rights it is important to estimate their value to the firm. A patent (which provides legal protection against others exploiting an invention for 17 years in the first instance) is effectively a call option on the exploitation of the product or service concerned. The only problem here is that as the patent proceeds through its life we would expect the present value of the future cash flows to decline. Once a patent expires we can assume that competitors will enter the market and rapidly drive the Net Present Value of the investment opportunity to zero. Circumstances differ of course, and it may be that an application to the court to extend the patent, or the possession of certain proprietary technology that would make it difficult for new entrants to gain access to the business, could extend the useful life of the project.

FINANCIAL REALITY

Jack Grinder has diverted some of his firm's R&D effort to the development of a project close to his heart. The Friendly Grinders' scientists have discovered a process for making microscopic diamond dust particles which have the reflective properties of larger flawless diamonds. This when added to specially formulated paint pigment results in the paint molecule encircling the diamond (the paint is technically called a 'clathrate' after the latin for 'cage'). When this pigment is used in the outer layer of a golf ball (the 'dimple) the ball shines in flight and is much easier to locate. What is more it adds an extra 5 per cent of flight compared with a conventional four piece ball. The G3B (Grinders Glowing Golf Ball) as Jack has dubbed his new creation is now covered with a 17-year international patent. The present value of the project if an exclusive licence to make and sell the balls is granted to a prominent sports goods manufacturer is £8.5million. The cost to Friendly Grinders of manufacturing the dust in the required quantities is £3.8 million. A simulation study suggests that the project cash flows will have a standard deviation of annual returns of 25 per cent reflecting the expected variability in the royalties received from the manufacturer. The risk free rate is 5 per cent.

In this case Jack has a call option on the exploitation of the new patent. However, the time value element (as this is a call) will tend to make delay worthwhile, while the loss in the value of the project will tend to make early exercise more desirable. The delay factor can be regarded as a 'dividend' which effectively reduces the value of the project as it proceeds through its life in the same way that a share paying a dividend will have a lower value than it would have had if the dividend had not been paid.

Adjusting for a known dividend yield

The simple method of correcting for the reduction in project value (the analogue of a known dividend yield and assuming that it does not impact upon the project's volatility) is to reduce the present value by the dividend yield. Given that the patent has 17 years to run then the simplest approach is to assume a dividend yield of 0.0588 (i.e. 1/17) which implies a smooth decrement in the value of the project through time. The Black and Scholes model then becomes:

$$c = N(d_1)P_0e^{-yt} - N(d_2)P_ee^{-rt}$$

where:

$$d_1 = \frac{\ln(P_0/P_e) + (r - y + 0.5\sigma^2)t}{\sigma\sqrt{t}}$$

$$d_2 = d_1 - \sigma\sqrt{t}$$

and y is the dividend yield. The revised Black and Scholes template becomes:

EXHIBIT 9.12

The valuation of a call option with imputed dividend

A	B	C	D	E	F
1	**Black and Scholes Option Pricing Model**				
2					
3	Current price	8.50			
4	Exercise price	3.80			
5	Risk free rate	0.05			
6	Time to exercise (days)	4250			
7	Volatility	0.2500			
8	Dividend	0.0588			
9	d1	1.15089		= (LN(C3/C4) + (C5 – C8 + 0.5*C7^2) *C6/250)/(C7*SQRT(C6/250))	
10	d2	0.12012		= C9 – C7*SQRT(C6/250)	
11					
12	N(d1)	0.87511		= NORMSDIST(C9)	
13	N(d2)	0.54781		= NORMSDIST(C10)	
14					
15	call value	1.85		= C12*C3*EXP(–C8*C6/250) – C13*C4*EXP(–C5*C6/250)	
16					

This suggests that this project has a total project value of £6.55 million of which £4.7 million is base case NPV and £1.85 million being the value of a call option on the value of the project. The same correction can be applied when using the binomial tree technique except that the risk neutral probability is adjusted to reflect the reduction in the risk free return by the dividend yield:

$$p = \frac{e^{(r-y)\Delta t} - d}{u - d}$$

The input parameters into a 100 step binomial tree would be as follows:

$$\Delta t = 17/100 = 0.17$$
$$u = e^{\sigma\sqrt{\Delta t}} = e^{.25\sqrt{.17}} = 1.1086$$

$$d = e^{-\sigma\sqrt{\Delta t}} = e^{-.25\sqrt{.17}} = 0.9021$$

$$p = \frac{e^{(r-y)\Delta t} - d}{u - d} = \frac{e^{(.05-0.0588)\times0.17} - 0.9021}{1.1086 - 0.9021} = 0.4670$$

$$v = e^{-r\Delta t} = e^{-0.05*0.17} = 0.9915$$

These values generate a call value of £3.83 million suggesting that in these circumstances early exercise carries a substantial benefit over that implied by the Black and Scholes model.

Option pricing and valuation of corporate liabilities

In their 1973 article, Black and Scholes commented on the fact that equity can be regarded as a call option on the value of the firm's underlying assets. This point was developed by Merton (1974) who generated the first closed form model for estimating default spreads and the probability of default.

As we have noted before in this chapter, the key requirement for optionality to occur in equity is limited liability. Let us presume for a moment that the firm has outstanding liabilities 'L' and total assets 'A', then at the point of maturity of those assets the shareholders can exercise the option granted through their limited liability. If the value of the firm's assets is in excess of the value of the outstanding liabilities they can pay off the liabilities and their gain is what is left. If not, they can exercise their limited liability and 'walk away'. Their option is therefore a European Call whose intrinsic value is given by:

$$E = \max[(A_e - L), 0]$$

where 'A_e' is the value of the assets at exercise, L is the value of the liabilities (being the exercise price of the option) and E is the value of the equity being a call option on the firm's underlying assets.

In practice, the value of L is normally taken to be only those short and long term liabilities (bank loans, long term loans, finance leases etc.) which contribute to the firm's exposure to financial risk. Accounts payable (creditors) are not included and so 'A' is regarded as assets less short term liabilities.

In the last chapter we examined the Black and Scholes equation. Merton derived an identical model for the equity value of a firm partly financed by a discount bond (a bond with no coupon payments which is issued below its nominal value) repayable at time t and where the firm has a current asset value (A_0) of volatility (σ_A).

Black and Scholes	Merton's (1974) model
$c = N(d_1)P_0 - N(d_2)P_e e^{-rt}$ where:	$E = N(d_1)A_0 - N(d_2)Le^{-rt}$ . . . .(i) where:
$d_1 = \dfrac{\ln(P_0/P_e) + (r + 0.5\sigma^2)t}{\sigma\sqrt{t}}$	$d_1 = \dfrac{\ln(A_0/L) + (r + 0.5\sigma_A^2)t}{\sigma_A\sqrt{t}}$
$d_2 = d_1 - \sigma\sqrt{t}$	$d_2 = d_1 - \sigma_A\sqrt{t}$

Given (from Modigliani and Miller's Theorem) the value of a firm's equity plus the market value of the firm's debts must be equal to the market value of the firm as a whole and given that the value of equity is the value of the call option then:

$$D = A_0 - E$$

Once we have that debt value it is easy to calculate the yield (y) on a discount bond. Using continuous time discounting:

$$e^{yt} = \frac{D}{L}$$

$$y = \frac{1}{t} \ln\left(\frac{D}{L}\right)$$

and the spread is the difference between the yield and the risk free rate (r) :

$$spread = y - r$$

$$spread = \frac{1}{t} \ln\left(\frac{D}{L}\right) - r$$

Before we implement the model there are some important insights to be obtained about the nature of debt and the bond holders' exposure to default risk:

1 The greater the asset value of the firm to the value of the outstanding debt (i.e. the smaller its gearing ratio) the lower the likelihood of default. This is an obvious result (although it's nice to have it confirmed from option pricing theory).

2 The greater the volatility of the firm's asset value (σ_A) the greater the likelihood of default and hence the greater the value of the equity (as a call option) against the asset value of the firm compared with the situation where the investors had unlimited liability. Remember that a call option can be used as a hedge against potential downside losses in the underlying asset (the asset value of the firm in this case). The greater the volatility, the more valuable the call option as an insurance against default.

3 The greater the time to maturity of the bond (t) the greater the chance of default. If the value of the firm is following a stochastic process then the longer the time the process runs the greater the chance it will drop below the value of the debt (L) and hence the greater chance the firm will default.

Implementing the Merton model

The Merton model requires as inputs: the value of the firm's assets (A), the volatility of those assets (σ_A), the par value of the firm's debt (L), the time to maturity (t) and a risk free rate of return (r). The problem is that we cannot observe (σ_A) nor the current value of the firm's assets directly. What we can observe is the value of the firm's equity (σ_e) and the value of its total equity capitalization (assuming that it is traded). The equity value of the firm will therefore be the market's view of the value of the call option on the firm's underlying assets (E).

Because we assume that the stochastic process used to generate share prices is the same as that used to generate the changing asset value of the firm we can use Ito's

Lemma (we do not prove it here) to connect the volatility and the value of the firm's equity to the volatility of its assets and its asset value:

$$\sigma_e E = \frac{dE}{dA}\sigma_A A_0$$

where E (the firm's equity value) is the value of the call in the Merton model and A_0 (the firm's asset value) is the value of underlying and so $\frac{dE}{dA_0}$ is the hedge ratio or $N(d1)$. We therefore obtain:

$$\sigma_e E = N(d_1)\sigma_A A_0$$

therefore

$$E = \frac{N(d_1)\sigma_A A_0}{\sigma_e} \dotsc\dotsc\dotsc\dotsc\dotsc\dotsc\dotsc .(ii)$$

We calculate E by taking the share price and multiplying by the number of shares in issue. Therefore equation (ii) and the original Merton equation (i) now contain just two unknown values (A_0) and (σ_A). Two equations and two unknowns must in principle be solvable – but not, unfortunately, by simple algebra. There are a number of proprietary software packages that will do the job but the easiest method is to use the 'solver' tool in Excel. The technique is straightforward. We rearrange (i) and (ii) as follows:

$$E - N(d_1)A_0 - N(d_2)Le^{-rt} = 0$$

$$E - \frac{N(d_1)\sigma_A A_0}{\sigma_e} = 0$$

and ask the solver to minimize the sum of the squares of these two equations by varying the asset value and the asset volatility.

To demonstrate the method and to answer a question first raised in Chapter 5 about how we estimate the cost of debt capital we return to the case of Cobham plc.

FINANCIAL CASE

The financial debt outstanding for Cobham plc in the notes to the accounts is shown in Exhibit 9.13:

EXHIBIT 9.13

Cobham's short and long term borrowing

Designation in notes to the accounts	Nominal value ($m)	Nominal value (£m)	Term to maturity	Interest rate	weight	Weight × term	weight × rate
Senior notes – totalling £125.0m	55.00	30.6	7	5.14%	0.1145	0.8014	0.0059
	170.00	94.4	10	5.58%	0.3538	3.5385	0.0197
	10.00	6.2	7	6.28%	0.0232	0.1627	0.0015
Bank loans – totalling £15.5m	15.00	9.3	10	6.42%	0.0349	0.3486	0.0022
Loan notes		10.3	2	4.25%	0.0386	0.0772	0.0016
Short term borrowing		116.1	0.5	6.06%	0.4350	0.2175	0.0264
		266.9			1.0000	5.1458	0.0573

The current share price is 1375p and 111 606 905 shares in issue (see Chapter 5). The volatility of the company's equity is estimated at 13.78 per cent (see Chapter 8). The risk free rate of return of the firm's debt which is raised in the US market (separately identified in Exhibit 9.13) is shown in Exhibit 5.13 as 4.2 per cent and the risk free rate for the UK is 4.75 per cent.

The Merton model assumes that a single, zero coupon bond, is in issue. That is clearly not the case with Cobham. One way of tackling this is to calculate the sum the cash flows on an equivalent single bond with a repayment of £266.9 million and average coupon rate derived from Exhibit 9.13 and to assume that this is repaid not at maturity but at the nominal duration date. Exhibit 9.13 shows the average term to maturity (5.1458 years) and an average coupon rate of 5.73 per cent. This coupon rate when applied to the nominal value of the debt gives a cash flow to the investors each year of £15.3 million. This value can be taken straight from the face of the accounts as the interest payable.

The nominal duration of the debt is given by weighting the payment in each year by the year value (see Exhibit 9.13). This (to a reasonable approximation) reveals that firm has to repay a loan with interest which equates to a single repayment value of £343.41 million in 4.55 years.

	1	2	3	4	5	Total
Cash flow to the investor	15.301	15.301	15.301	15.301	282.21	343.41
Cash flow/total cash flow × year number	0.045	0.089	0.134	0.178	4.11	4.55

The final input into the model is to collect the risk free rates of return. Of the nominal debt of £266.9 million £140.5 million was US$ debt and the balance, £126.4 million UK denominated. The average maturity of the US$ component of the Cobham debt is 9.2 years (Exhibit 9.14).

EXHIBIT 9.14

Calculation of the average term to maturity of the US$ debt in Cobham's long term debt

Designation in notes to the accounts	Nominal value ($m)	Nominal value (£m)	Term to maturity	Interest rate	weight	Weight × term
Senior notes – totalling £125.0 m	55.00	30.6	7	5.14%	0.2175	1.5222
	170.00	94.4	10	5.58%	0.6722	6.7216
Bank loans – totalling £15.5 m	10.00	6.2	7	6.28%	0.0442	0.3091
	15.00	9.3	10	6.42%	0.0662	0.6623
		140.5			1.0000	9.2152

From Exhibit 5.14 we discover that the US risk free rate for debt with a maturity of 9.2 years is 4.2 per cent, so weighting this by value with the UK denominated debt we obtain an average risk free rate as follows:

$$r_f = W_{us}r_{f(US)} + W_{UK}r_{f(UK)}$$

$$r_f = \frac{140.5}{266.9} \times 4.2\% + \frac{126.4}{266.9} \times 4.75\%$$

$$r_f = 4.46\%$$

The equivalent continuously compounded rate is given by:

$$r_f = \ln(1.0446)$$

$$r_f = 4.364\%$$

EXHIBIT 9.15

The Merton structural debt model (before solution using the solver routine)

A	B	C	D	E
1	**Merton (1974) Structural Debt Model – call value**			
2				
3	**Current asset value**	**1000.00**	guess	
4	**Asset Volatility**	**0.1000**	guess	
5				
6	Value of outstanding debt	343.41		
7	Risk free rate	0.04364		
8	Time to exercise (days)	1137.5		
9	Value of equity	1534.6		
10	Volatility of equity	0.1378		
11				
12	d1	6.04828		
13	d2	5.83497		
14				
15	N(d1)	1.00000		
16	N(d2)	1.00000		
17				
18	Value of the equity call on the firm's assets	718.44		
19				
20	Actual equity – call	816.16	= C9–C18	
21	Equity less Ito estimate of equity value	808.91	= C9–(C15*C4*C3/C10)	
22	**Squared total**	**1320445.11**	= E20^2 + E21^2	
23				
24	**Value of debt**	281.56		
25	**Spread**	1.9826E-11	= (1/(C8/250))*LN(C6/C24)–C7	

In Exhibit 9.15 we show the call model before using the Solver routine. We have reordered the data table from that used for the basic Black and Scholes model into a convenient layout for Solver. The current asset value (which is the analogue of the current share price in the Black and Scholes model) is set at a guess value and a new line introduced for the asset volatility which again takes a guess value. The value of equity and the volatility of equity are then picked up in two new lines (rows 9 and 10) The calculation of all the other parameters is as with Black and Scholes model coming down to the value of the equity call (remembering to pick up the asset volatility and not the volatility of equity in the calculations).

To use the solver routine you will need to select 'solver' from the tools menu in Excel. Within the input dialogue window:

$$\text{Set target cell} = C22$$
$$\text{Equal to} = \text{'min'}$$
$$\text{By changing cells} = \$C\$3{:}\$C\$4$$

and Exhibit 9.16 results.

EXHIBIT 9.16

The Merton structural debt model (after using the solver routine)

A	B	C	D	E
1	**Merton (1974) Structural Debt Model – call value**			
2				
3	**Current asset value**	**1816.16**	guess	
4	**Asset Volatility**	**0.1164**	guess	
5				
6	Value of outstanding debt	343.41		
7	Risk free rate	0.04364		
8	Time to exercise (days)	1137.5		
9	Value of equity	1534.6		
10	Volatility of equity	0.1378		
11				
12	d1	7.62966		
13	d2	7.38130		
14				
15	N(d1)	1.00000		
16	N(d2)	1.00000		
17				
18	Value of the equity call on the firm's assets	1534.60		
19				
20	Actual equity – call	0.00	=C9–C18	
21	Equity less Ito estimate	0.00	=C9–(C15*C4*C3/C10)	
22	**Squared total**	**0.00**	=E20^2 + E21^2	
23				
24	**Value of debt**	281.56		
25	**Spread**	5.3429E-16	=(1/(C8/250))*LN(C6/C24)–C7	

The model gives a value of £281.56 million being the current value of the debt outstanding discounted at the yield. The risk neutral default probability (given by $(1 - N(d_2))$) is zero and as a result there is zero spread over the risk free rate (5.3429^{-10} is effectively zero). This agrees with our view in Chapter 5 that Cobham is essentially default free.

If we use the above modelling procedure we can calculate the cost of its debt for a range of different gearing ratios and asset volatilities. However, before doing that let us have a look at Friendly Grinders plc.

FINANCIAL REALITY

Jack Grinder has been exploring with Gloria the maximum debt capacity that his company could carry. Currently the total equity value of the firm is £440 million and the current level of borrowing is £240 million which with total interest payable over the term to maturity is £320 million. The nominal duration of the debt is six years. The volatility of the firm's equity is 35 per cent.

The outputs of the model using the solver routine reveal that the current value of the firm's assets is £674.19 million, its asset volatility is 0.2324 and its likelihood of default is 6.04 per cent. The value of its debt is £234.19 million implying a yield of 5.203 per cent. The spread is therefore just 20 basis points. This represents a very low likelihood of failure and a very low credit risk premium. If we calculate the present value of the outstanding debt and compare that with the market value of the debt as generated by the model we have the potential loss to the lender on holding the debt:

$$Loss = Le^{-rt} - D$$
$$Loss = 237.06 - 234.19 = £2.87 \ million$$

As a percentage of the present value of the debt this gives a loss in percentage terms of 1.21 per cent. The actual probability of default is 6.04 per cent, thus we can easily calculate the potential recovery that a lender would achieve. The model reveals that there is £6.04 per £100 at risk of which £1.21 is likely to be loss and the balance recovered. Therefore the recovery is:

$$Recovery = \frac{0.0604 - 0.0121}{0.0604} = 79.9\%$$

If we vary the level of debt held by Friendly Grinders assuming different volatilities the result is as shown in Exhibit 9.17.

This shows Jack his room for manoeuvre when negotiating new levels of debt.

REVIEW ACTIVITY 9.3

Jack still doesn't have an answer to his question: what would happen if he raised the value of his debt outstanding by £180 million repayable over the same term as his existing debt? He assumes that the total asset value of the firm would remain the same.

The Merton model is the prototype for a wide range of models which use option pricing to evaluate the credit risk of companies and the credit spread. The shortcomings of the model are obvious: it makes the same range of assumptions as the Black and Scholes model and it assumes that asset values follow the same stochastic process as the share price. It also assumes that the underlying assets are freely divisible and are traded in open markets. In practice we would expect there to be a non-traded

EXHIBIT 9.17

Variation in spread with different levels of debt and different volatilities

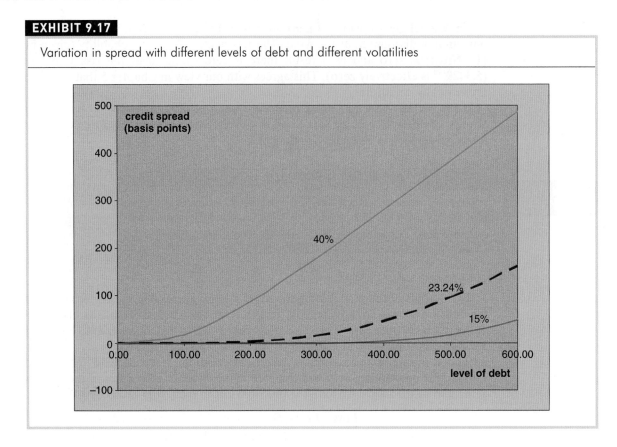

premium for companies such as Cobham and Friendly Grinders which will increase the value of any calculated spread.

Finally, and most problematic of all, it assumes that the firm's debt financing is a single discount bond. However, the evidence is that while the model does not accurately predict observed spreads it does produce results which are highly consistent with them. The model also appears to predict default probabilities with accuracy and this can be used with published data to produce a more accurate estimate of the required spread.

SUMMARY

In this chapter we have extended the role of option pricing to cover the valuation of investment opportunities in real assets. This has produced the rather surprising conclusion that where future options exist the volatility of a project's future cash flows may actually increase its value. We have explored the application of the Black and Scholes and binomial model in pricing four important types of real option: the option to delay, the

option to expand, the option to redeploy and finally the option to abandon a project. Real option pricing does focus attention upon of the value that is added to a project through management's discretion to alter the terms of its continuation at a later stage. However, there is some doubt whether in a perfectly efficient market we can simply add together the Net Present Value of a project with the value generated via the real option.

We then turned our attention to the use of real options in valuing intangible assets where there is some predictability about the future cash flows which can be earned through their exploitation. Finally, we have returned to the problem of estimating the cost of capital and in particular the calculation of the yield spread on a company's debt. Although option pricing methods are not particularly accurate in determining spreads in practice, they do provide a very consistent ranking of default probability and the relative magnitudes of spreads when compared with published data.

However, the story of option pricing is not yet over and in the next chapter we will review the use of these important derivatives, and their valuation methodology, in estimating the value of firms as a whole.

Further Reading

Black, F. and Scholes, M. (1973) The Pricing of Options and Corporate Liabilities, *Journal of Political Economy*, 81, 637–654.

Cooper, N., Hillman, R. and Lynch, D. (2000) Interpreting Movements in High Yield Corporate Bond Market Spreads, Bank of England publication, www.BankofEngland.co.uk

Damodaran, A. (2003) The Promise of Real Options, published in Stern, J.M., and Chew, D.H. (2003) *The Revolution in Corporate Finance* (4th Ed.), Oxford: Blackwell publishing. This provides a brief overview of the different types of real option, however the discussion does not go as far as solving American put and call options using the binomial method.

Finger, C.C. (2002) Credit Grades TM, technical document, www.riskmetrics.com. This is an excellent overview of the use of option pricing in the assessment of corporate liabilities.

Howell, S. (2001) *Real options: Evaluating Corporate Investment Opportunities in a Dynamic World* Harlow: Financial Times Prentice Hall. This is an excellent and thought-provoking book with numerous case examples. Some of the appendices on option pricing using both the Black and Scholes and the binomial model are very useful indeed.

Lewent, J. (1994) Scientific Management at Merck: an Interview with the CFO Judy Lewent, *Harvard Business Review*, January–February 1994: 89–99. This is an early and interesting example of the application of option pricing in a commercial setting.

Martin, L.A. (1999) Portfolio Managers Series: New Valuations for Cable Plant, Credit Suisse First Boston *Equity Research*, April 30 1999.

Merton, R.C. (1974) on the pricing of corporate debt: the risk structure of interest rates, *The Journal of Finance*, 29:23. This was the seminal article on the use of option pricing in valuing corporate debt. Although complex in parts the article is beautifully written and it is relatively easy to gain an understanding of what the author intends.

Mouboussin, M.J. (1999) Get real: using real options in the security analysis, Credit Suisse First Boston.

Munn, J. (2002) *Real Options Analysis: Tools and Techniques for Valuing Strategic Investments and Decisions*, New Jersey: Wiley Finance. This is a useful book for developing your study of real options from this point forward. It focuses on the practical implementation of the techniques and uses Crystal Ball simulation software for many of the applications.

Myers, S.C. (1974) 'Interactions of Corporate Financing and Investment Decisions: Implications for Capital Budgeting', *Journal of Finance*, 29: 1:1–25, March 1974.

Myers, S.C. (1977) 'Determinants of Corporate Borrowing', *Journal of Financial Economics*, 5:147–175, November 1977.

Pike, R. (1996) A Longitudinal Survey on Capital Budgeting Practices, *Journal of Business, Finance and Accounting*, 23, 79–92.

Ryan, P.A. and Ryan, G.P. (2002) Capital Budgeting Practices of the Fortune 1000: how things have changed? *Journal of Business and Management*, 8:4, Winter. An excellent and up-to-date article on the current state of play in the use of capital budgeting techniques.

Trigeorgis, L. (1996) *Real Options: Managerial Flexibility and Strategy in Resource Allocation*, Massachusetts: The MIT Press. Cambridge. An early edition of what has become a classic within the real options literature.

Van Putten, A.B. and MacMillan, I.C. (2004) Making Real Options Really Work, *Harvard Business Review*, December 2004:134–141.

PROGRESS CHECK

1 Identify three problems with standard Net Present Value analysis and state which of these can be influenced by real options analysis.

2 What ultimately determines the volatility of an equity option?

3 Identify four types of simple real option and note how they differ from one another.

4 Name and briefly describe three approaches to estimating the volatility of a firm's cash flows.

5 List the five principal drivers of real option value.

6 What limits the usefulness of the Black and Scholes option pricing model in pricing real options?

7 How is the intrinsic value of an option to expand determined?

8 Give an example of an abandonment option.

9 What evidence is there concerning the use of real options in practice?

10 What type of real option would be used to value a pharmaceutical company's rights to exploit a patent for a new drug?

11 What critical condition must exist for an equity investment in the shares of a company to have option value?

12 In what respect does Merton's (1974) model differ from the original Black and Scholes option pricing model?

QUESTIONS (answers at end of book)

1 A company is considering an investment project requiring the outlay of £12 million. A constant cash flow return of £1.5 million is likely for each of the next ten years in real terms. The current discount rate that the firm uses in evaluating its investment projects is 8 per cent (nominal) and the current rate of inflation is 2.5 per cent. The company has the option to delay capital investment for three years without sacrificing any loss of value from the project. The company estimates that the volatility of the cash flows from this project is 30 per cent per annum, and the risk free rate is 5 per cent.

You are required to:

(i) Estimate the Net Present Value of this project in nominal terms.

(ii) Calculate a minimum estimate of the value of delay for three years.

(iii) Calculate value of the option to delay on the basis that the company can exercise its option at any point over the next three years.

(iv) Discuss the extent to which the value of the delay option such as this can be added to the Net Present Value of the project in order to capture its full value added to the firm.

2 A company has a listed share capital with a market capitalization of £250 million with 100 million shares in issue. The volatility of the company's equity is 60 per cent per annum and the risk free rate is 5 per cent. The company has outstanding zero coupon debt of £150 million which is repayable at par in five years. You are required to:

(i) Estimate the volatility of the firm's assets and their current value.

(ii) Calculate the value of the firm's debt and the implied yield.

(iii) Calculate the probability of default, the potential loss to the lender and the percentage recovery.

3 A company is assessing the likely value added of a capital investment project. The Net Present Value of the project is –£2 million but an assessment of its real option value is £6 million. The company's discount rate is 10 per cent which has been developed as the firm's best estimate of the average rate of return required by its investors. To what extent is it legitimate to regard the value added of this project as £8 million?

4 The UK Olympic Association has commissioned a new stadium for the 2012 games to be held in London. The expected total cost of construction in present value terms is £150 million over three years and the Net Present Value of the project is £10 million. The expected volatility of the construction cost is 20 per cent per annum. The risk free rate of return is 5 per cent per annum.

The City of London Insurance Company has offered to indemnify the Association if the expected final build cost should at any point exceed £200 million. In that eventuality the Association could sell the stadium to a consortium established by the insurance company for the value of the construction costs to date. Once the development rights are sold the consortium would complete the project and take over the stadium and its facilities following the games.

You are required to:

(i) Describe the nature of the option being offered to the Olympic Association.

(ii) Sketch a diagram showing the intrinsic value of the indemnity agreement to the Association.

(iii) Using three month time steps construct a binomial tree showing the paths of expected construction cost.

5 Friendly Grinders is considering the production of a diamond-like dust made from Boron Nitride. Although difficult to manufacture the final product has excellent conductive properties and can be constructed in a crystalline structure which is second only to diamond in its hardness. The patented process has reduced construction costs and Jack Grinder expects the plant to be up and running within 12 months at a cost of £16 million. The future cash flows from the project are estimated to have a present value of £20 million. After five years of initial exploitation the rights to manufacture under the patent could be sold for £10 million diminishing at £1 million per annum for the next ten years. The volatility of the expected future cash flows is 30 per cent and the risk free rate of return is 5 per cent. The company's cost of capital is 8 per cent.

You are required:

(i) To define the type of real option which Friendly Grinders possesses with the disposal of the patent rights.

(ii) To calculate the option value on the assumption that the firm commits itself to production for only five years.

(iii) To describe how this option could be modelled using the binomial option pricing approach where the company could exercise its rights at any time between five and 15 years.

(iv) To calculate the necessary inputs into modelling this using the binomial approach and assuming quarterly time steps.

6 A large pharmaceutical company has successfully trialled a new drug and won approval for its use as a prescription only treatment for old age. ELIXO as the drug is called has ten years before its initial patent expires and there is reasonable assurance that a further five years would be granted. The commercial exploitation will start with a £50 million capital investment which promises a £10 million Net Present Value. The anticipated volatility is 50 per cent per annum and further expansion would be possible from one year forward at a cost of a further £40 million. The risk free rate of return is 4 per cent.

Assuming that the patent will be extended and that the present value of exploitation diminishes at a constant rate you are required to:

(i) Estimate the value which the option to expand offers to the company.

(ii) Estimate the value added to the business by this project.

(iii) Determine when it is most likely that the company will exercise its option to expand.

IV | Valuation

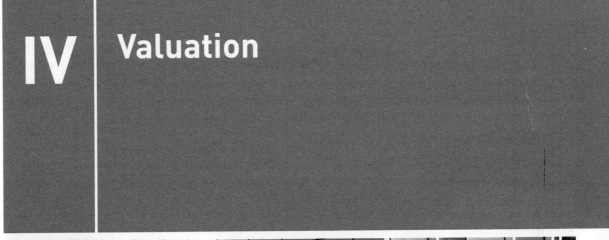

10 | Valuing the firm

I
n this chapter we review the theory and methods involved in valuing a company. Our first topic is a brief discussion of the accounting processes that underpin valuation focusing upon the distinction between two principal accounting flows: the flow of earnings and the firm's cash flow. We then discuss in outline the methods of detecting the application of 'creative accounting' procedures. Once we have confidence in the underlying reported information we can then move on to the application of a range of financial methods designed to identify the current value of the business. In this chapter we consider four basic methods of valuation: the asset based approach, relative valuation methods, flow methods and contingent methods of valuation. Of these, flow valuation has the greatest application in practice. In this chapter we focus on the valuation of dividends and in Chapter 12 extend our analysis to consider the valuation of future cash flows of the firm as a whole. This chapter also includes a discussion of Economic Value Added (EVA®) and how it relates to other valuation methods.

Valuation is an inexact science at best, and all of the methods discussed in this chapter include different degrees of subjectivity. However, different methods have different advantages in different situations and some capture important aspects in valuing a business which are not recognized by others.

Learning outcomes

By the end of this chapter you will be able to achieve the following:

1 Recognize potential biases and misstatements in financial reports and calculate valuation relevant figures from the accounts.

2 Distinguish between the earnings and cash flows of the business and understand their usefulness in different valuation procedures.

3 Undertake an asset based valuation of a company making suitable adjustments for the imputed value of goodwill and other intangible assets.

4 Estimate the value of a company using relative valuation techniques and understand the significance of Tobin's Q.

5   Value a company using a variety of flow techniques including the dividend discount model, its free cash flow to equity equivalent, shareholder value analysis and economic value analysis.

6   Understand the contingent methods of valuation and be able to describe and follow through a valuation using simulation and option based techniques.

Introduction to valuation

In an efficient capital market, the best estimate the value of the firm is given by the current share price multiplied by the number of shares in issue. There is only one element of value which is missing from this calculation and that is the difference between the firm as it is currently operated, and the value of the firm as it could be operated adopting the best management practices available, minimizing the firm's cost structure, and maximizing its available product opportunities. This difference in value between how the firm is currently, and what it potentially could be, we term the control premium. The problems of determining the control premium will be discussed in Chapter 12.

Given the high level of efficiency of the equity markets an obvious question is why would we wish to value a firm by any other means than simply taking its share price and multiplying by the number of shares in issue. The first and most obvious point, of course, is that not all firms we may wish to value are traded in equity markets. It may be that the management of a firm are considering the acquisition of another company and need to value their target in order to decide upon an appropriate bid price. Also, if we can build a generally valid model of firm valuation (in that it enables us to consistently predict share values) then we may also gain an understanding of the principal 'drivers of firm value' in the market and gain a deeper understanding of how the market itself operates. Finally, we may, as investors, simply think we might strike lucky and find a firm which is systematically undervalued or as managers believe that imperfections in the way that information is transmitted have led to a situation where the market has simply got it wrong. Our concern in this chapter is to develop a range of valuation methods for firms and to define the situations under which each method is likely to be most useful.

In principle, there are four approaches to valuing the firm:

1   *Asset valuation*: where a summary of the assets less the liabilities of the firm are valued on some agreed basis.

2   *Relative valuation*: this involves valuing some measurable attribute of the firm, such as its current level of earnings, dividends, or book value, in terms of the price that the market is prepared to pay per pound or dollar of these attributes.

3   *Flow valuation*: this entails identifying a value flow (usually earnings, dividends or cash flow) and converting them to a present value.

4   *Contingent valuation*: where the firm is valued in terms of the present value of the expected cash flows plus some premium for any future growth options.

EXHIBIT 10.1

The four principal methods of valuing a firm and the underpinning theory of valuation

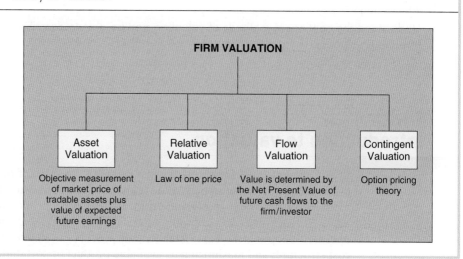

Each of these approaches has different strengths, weaknesses and range of application. Within each method a particular theory of value dominates (see Exhibit 10.1) and with each there is a different trade-off between the objective and subjective elements of the valuation process. However, before we get into all of that a little basic accounting is in order.

The two financial flows

The first step in understanding the basics of valuation is recognizing the financial flows within the firm. Any business is dominated by two financial flows: the first and most important is its cash flow. The cash generation and expenditure of the firm determine the short term success and the long term survival of the business. The second flow is where revenues are recognized as chargeable to the year in question and accounting costs are matched to the process of earning that revenue and then allocated to different categories of account. These two flows, in as far as they impact upon the financial reports of the business are shown in Exhibit 10.2.

These two flows have broad similarities but also some crucial differences and it is easy to become confused between the two. The cash flow of the firm is reasonably straightforward: as operations generate surplus cash (the operating cash flow) interest and tax payments will be made and the remainder is Free Cash flow to Equity (FCFE) before reinvestment. From that FCFE dividends are paid to investors and the balance retained for further reinvestment. From the analytical point of view greater reliability can be placed upon the cash flow statement than the profit and loss account. It is much more difficult to manipulate the reporting of cash flow figures although it is possible for operating expenditures to be reported as capital expenditure and vice versa. This form of mismatching will have an impact on the estimation of the free cash flow to equity which is an important number in determining the firm's dividend capacity (see Chapter 6).

EXHIBIT 10.2

The two financial flows through the firm

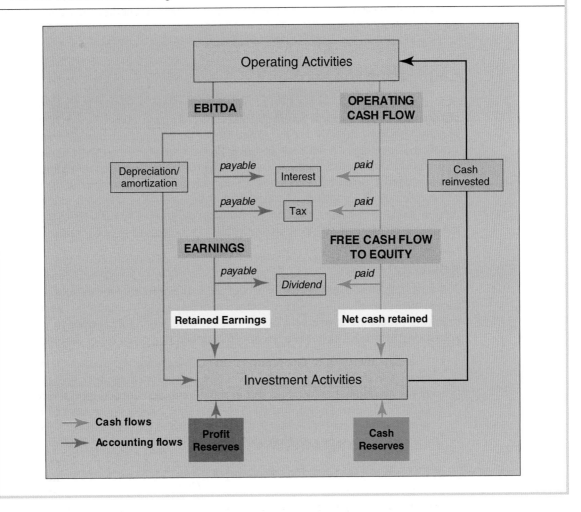

The 'accounting' flow represents the creation of shareholder surplus over time which is accumulated in the owner's equity account. The closest analogue to operating cash flow within the profit and loss account is 'EBITDA' or earnings before interest tax, depreciation and amortization. The accountant will have used various recognition rules for revenues and costs before arriving at EBITDA but there should, at steady state, be approximate parity between EBITDA and operating cash flow. From EBITDA a substantial charge will be made for depreciation and amortization representing the matching to the period in question of the value represented by both real and purchased intangible assets (such as goodwill on acquisition, patents and licences). Further charges will then be made for interest and tax but note the key distinction here is that what is charged is what is deemed to be payable and not necessarily what has been paid. This leads to an earnings figure which is a measure of smoothed income available for distribution to investors and out of which the directors may decide to declare (make payable) a dividend. What are then left are retained earnings which go to increase the capital account of the investors.

The accounting flow is a very limited interpretation of the extent to which shareholder value has been earned via the business transactions undertaken during a period of account. The cash flow model shows the increase in the consumption power of the investor over the period of account irrespective of whether the cash is distributed directly or reinvested.

Laundering the accounts

Before proceeding with any method of valuation the analyst will need to check the financial accounts of the business concerned and correct for any anomalies. The first stage of the checking exercise is to test the extent to which the company has been engaged in 'creative accounting'. Creative accounting is the art of manipulating the reported figures to produce either more favourable earnings figures (aggressive accounting) or reduced earnings figures (defensive accounting) to suit perceived circumstances. In the very long run accounting distortions must cancel out to the neutral position but along the way there is scope to enhance or deflate the value of earnings. The first step is to measure the degree of 'aggressiveness' or 'defensiveness' in the reporting of earnings.

Reliability testing

Although this book is not primarily concerned with accounting techniques it is useful for the analyst to check a company's stance with respect to its financial reporting. The following procedure is one very useful test for determining the extent to which the accounting principles have been 'creatively' applied in a given set of accounts.

1 Calculate the Cash to Operating Profit (COP) Ratio. Where there is no expansion or contraction of the level of sales the opening and closing accruals in the accounts should cancel out in their combined impact upon the reported earnings figures. Therefore EBITDA should be closely approximated by the reported operating cash flow (OCF). The ratio of EBITDA to OCF we term the cash to operating profit (COP) ratio:

$$COP(actual) = \frac{EBITDA}{OCF}$$

and at steady state should be equal to one.

2 Given an identified percentage level of revenue change ($\Delta(Rev)\%$) in the profit and loss account we can predict using the prior year figures the maximum or minimum value the COP ratio should be. We would normally expect *EBITDA* to grow at the rate of $\Delta(Rev)\%/(1-G)$ where G is the prior year's cost gearing ratio. So the *COP* ratio should be, assuming no corresponding change in the firm's underlying cash flows:

$$COP(predicted) = 1 + \frac{\Delta(Rev)\%}{1-G}$$

The cost gearing ratio is calculated using the fixed operating costs (less depreciation and amortization) over total operating costs (less depreciation and amortization).

3 Calculate the COP bias, that is the ratio of COP actual to COP predicted. A figure of greater than one suggests that aggressive accounting is being used and the extent of the distortion from neutrality, a figure of less than one indicates the reverse.

The summarized operating profit statement for Cobham plc is shown in Exhibit 10.3 (the full accounts can be obtained from *www.cobham.com*):

EXHIBIT 10.3

Summarized statement of operating profit for Cobham plc (2004)

	2004	**2003**
Turnover	983.0	832.6
Cost of Sales	714.6	585.3
	268.4	247.3
Selling and Distribution Costs	−55.5	−48.2
Administrative Expenses	−83.3	−73.2
Operating Profit	129.6	125.9

For 2004 the charges for depreciation and amortization were £42.5 million and £21.6 million respectively and the operating cash flow was £163.1 million. The 2003 charge for depreciation was £33.7 million (charged to cost of sales) and for amortization was £16.3 million (£0.8 million charged to cost of sales).

From 2003 to 2004 the growth in Cobham's turnover was 18.06 per cent and the cost gearing ratio in 2003 was:

$$G = \frac{48.2 + 73.2 - 15.5}{585.3 + 48.2 + 73.2 - 33.7 - 16.3}$$

$$G = 0.1613$$

Our prediction of the COP Ratio is therefore:

$$COP(predicted) = 1 + \frac{0.1806}{(1 - 0.1613)}$$

$$COP(predicted) = 1.2153$$

The actual COP ratio for Cobham is:

$$COP(actual) = \frac{\text{operating profit} + \text{depreciation} + \text{amortization}}{\text{operating cash flow}}$$

$$COP(actual) = \frac{129.6 + 42.5 + 21.6}{163.1}$$

$$COP(actual) = 1.1876$$

The COP bias measures the degree to which the firm is being aggressive or defensive in the use of its accounting policies:

$$COP(bias) = \frac{COP(actual)}{COP(predicted)}$$

$$COP(bias) = \frac{1.1876}{1.2153}$$

$$COP(bias) = 0.9772$$

This suggests that Cobham is tending (either by accident or design) to understate its performance compared with its cash generation by approximately 2.28 per cent. From a practical point of view this difference is very small but is a point we should bear in mind when using earnings based valuation measures for this company.

> *The flow of cash in and out of Enron told a less spectacular story than its soaring revenue, In 1998, Enron actually had a negative cash flow of $59 million . . . . In 1999, Enron had a positive cash flows of $177 million – but that came from a rise in short term borrowing, while the net cash generated by operating activities fell by 25 per cent from 1998 levels . . . . Investors might have started to wonder if they had paid closer attention to these subtler measures of efficiency and profitability rather than to earnings, or to 'operating earnings'.* LOREN FOX, *ENRON – THE RISE AND FALL,* PP 175–176.

The one important type of accounting misclassification that is not highlighted by the COP ratio is the claiming of capital receipts as income or, more problematically, the inappropriate capitalization of costs. The problem with this type of misclassification error is that it impacts just as much upon the cash flow statement as upon the reported accounts. Although the financial statements are often opaque when it comes to this type of misclassification there are some steps which can be taken to help identify the extent of the problem:

1 Check to see if there have been any changes in the accounting policies particularly with respect to the recognition of revenues and expenditures and the rules for charging depreciation and amortization.

2 Identify all acquisitions and disposals of fixed assets and intangible assets in the notes to the accounts. Details of such movements should be noted and reference to the capital expenditure can be checked with the various statements that precede the financial reports. If the case is sufficiently important or there is doubt concerning the reliability of the reported figures details of acquired companies and the cost of acquisition can be obtained from the central registration authority for the acquired company (see Chapter 12).

3 Because the tax authorities are very clear as to what it is legitimate to capitalize and what is not, the revised tax liability should agree with the tax paid and any differences clearly justified in the notes to the accounts. Because of timing lags in the payment of corporation tax a margin for the increase or decrease in turnover may not be significant. However, inexplicable adjustments for deferred tax which cannot be reconciled to the notes relating to the acquisitions and disposals of fixed assets may indicate a problem with what is being charged and what is not.

Readings are given at the end of the chapter which give further information on reliability testing. The appendix to this chapter contains a summarized procedure for the pre-valuation correction of accounting data.

REVIEW ACTIVITY 10.1 Cobham plc shows the movements on its fixed assets as shown in Exhibit 10.4 along with a statement from the Chairman's Report.

Referring to Cobham's accounts identify any other indications of the reasons for the movements and determine the extent to which you can place reliance upon the company's reporting of its capital expenditures.

EXHIBIT 10.4

Isolating the significant additions to fixed assets and tracing their justification within the annual reports

CORPORATE DEVELOPMENT

During the year the Group successfully pursued its strategy of sustained development through organic growth and acquisition. Six acquisitions were completed for a total consideration of £61m. In addition, in December, agreement was reached to acquire H Koch and Sons (Koch) for a cash consideration of US$63m and Remec Defense & Space Inc. (Remec) for a cash consideration US$260m. Both of these acquisitions are expected to complete in the second quarter of 2005, subject to certain approvals. Remec, in particular, positions the Group well in the network enabling capability market. Three further small acquisitions for the Chelton group were announced in February of 2005. Chairman's Report. Cobham Financial Report 2004

10 INTANGIBLE FIXED ASSETS

Group: £m	GOODWILL	OTHERS	TOTAL
Cost			
At 1 January 2004	391.2	5.6	396.8
Foreign exchange adjustments	–	(0.1)	(0.1)
Addtions	(49.3)	0.2	50.1
Adjustments to contingent consideration in respect of prior year acquisitions (note 18)	(0.5)	–	(0.5)
At 31 December 2004	**440.6**	**5.7**	**446.3**

11 TANGIBLE FIXED ASSETS

Group: £m	INVESTMENT PROPERTIES	LAND AND BUILDINGS FREEHOLD	LONG LEASES	SHORT LEASES	PLANT AND MACHINERY (INCLUDING AIRCRAFT & VEHICLES)	FIXTURES FITTINGS TOOLS AND EQUIPMENT	PAYMENTS ON ACCOUNT AND ASSETS UNDER CONSTRUCTION	TOTAL
Cost or valuation								
At 1 January 2004 – cost	–	80.4	16.9	4.3	312.3	55.3	10.2	479.4
At 1 January 2004 – valuation	4.1	–	–	–	–	–	–	4.1
Foreign exchange adjustments	–	(1.4)	(0.2)	(0.5)	(4.0)	(0.9)	(0.3)	(7.3)
Additions	–	(5.4)	0.3	4.5	(38.0)	4.7	4.9	57.9
Undertakings acquired	–	0.1	–	–	5.7	0.9	–	6.7
Disposals	–	–	–	(0.2)	(3.7)	(2.1)	(0.4)	(6.4)
Reclassifications	–	2.8	(1.9)	1.6	7.3	0.4	(10.2)	–
At 31 December 2004	**4.1**	**87.3**	**15.1**	**9.8**	**355.6**	**58.3**	**4.2**	**534.4**

Asset valuation

The traditional approach to valuation is to add together the value of all the firm's tradable assets less any outstanding liabilities. For an ongoing business the appropriate basis for the valuation of its assets is their replacement cost. Providing all of the firm's assets are captured within the valuation process, then presumably if the investors were by some mischance deprived of the firm then they could reinstate it in its original condition by repurchasing all of the assets involved. There are some obvious problems with this in that many assets are not tradable and, indeed, are accumulated over long periods of time. Some assets may be of an intangible nature and are not directly replaceable in the market. More problematically, assets exhibit differing degrees of 'entanglement' (see Chapter 11) with one another. So the idea that the value of a firm is equal to its replacement cost is only true at the level of the business as a whole and is not the same as saying that it is equal to the sum of the replacement costs of its parts.

However, this approach has been widely used particularly for the valuation of small businesses. There are a variety of valuation rules which are used depending upon the age, business type and existing profitability of the business. Two common rules are:

$$\text{Entity value} = \text{sum of all real assets at book or replacement cost} + m \times \text{annual profits}$$

$$\text{Entity value} = \text{sum of all real assets at book or replacement cost} + m \times \text{annual turnover}$$

The factor (m) is agreed by negotiation and is designed to compensate the seller for the value of the business goodwill. Although the method appears simplistic there is an underlying logic to the multiple of profits approach. In terms of the real assets of the business, no purchaser should be willing to pay more than their replacement cost as this represents the open market, buying in price of the assets concerned. On the assumption that annual profits are the result of operating the business successfully then m can be regarded as the inverse of the capitalization rate for converting a perpetual stream of future profits at the current rate to a present value. The smaller the value of m which is chosen the higher the capitalization rate reflecting the riskiness of the profits generated by the business and hence the volatility attributable to the valuation of the firm's goodwill.

FINANCIAL REALITY

Before he left, Fred, the irascible owner of Friendly Grinders Ltd had a long talk with his grandson Jack, who at that time was a rather junior director with little experience of business. Fred told him that when he died the business was his. Six weeks later Fred died a happy man and Jack took over the reins of Friendly Grinders Ltd. When the business was valued for estate duty the value of its stock and equipment was valued at £210 000, the lease on the factory and head office was valued at £150 000 and the annual profits at £110 000. Tickitt, Hoppitt and Co., a local firm of accountants handled the negotiations with the Inland Revenue's valuation office. The Inland Revenue argued that the appropriate basis was assets plus 80 per cent of annual turnover which stood at £820 000. The argument finally boiled down to a question of the type of industry and the company's profit history. Mr Tickitt had pointed to the variability in profits in the recent past under Fred's erratic style of leadership. Finally a figure of £550 000 was agreed for the goodwill being five years of annual profits.

The obvious attraction of this approach to valuation is its simplicity. It also provides an auditable basis for the core component of the valuation and where small firms are involved whose principal assets are stock and the leases of the property that they occupy then little more may be required to come to an agreed valuation between vendor and purchaser. In larger firms where the bulk of the value is resident in the intangible assets of the business then this approach becomes less viable.

FINANCIAL CASE

Given the figures shown in Exhibit 10.20 (in the appendix) what would be the value of Cobham per share on the basis of (a) a five years' and (b) a ten years' multiple of earnings? The goodwill included in the firm's net assets is £347.2 million. On sale all of the provisions and contingent liabilities would be realized. There are 111,606,950 shares in issue.

In the case of Cobham plc, Exhibit 10.20 (in the appendix) shows equity capital which is equal to total assets less all outstanding liabilities of £657.33 million. Deducting the value of goodwill and the addition of £72.50 million this implies that the company would have net assets of £241.40 million as shown in Exhibit 10.5. The estimated share prices of 746p per share and 1280p under the two bases of calculation are both significantly lower than the current share price of 1440p.

This method of valuation is widely used in practice by professional company brokers attempting to place a value upon a small business. Exhibit 10.6 shows a selection of the rules of thumb used for valuing small businesses. Note that the valuation covers the business element and not the transfer of land, buildings or other fixed assets.

For larger firms with dominant corporate or product brands an indication of the premium attaching to the firm through its brand value can be achieved through the use of specialist valuation firms such as Interbrand Ltd in the UK or Financial World in the US (who use the Interbrand methodology). There is some evidence (Barth *et al.* (2003))

EXHIBIT 10.5

Calculation of the value of Cobham's equity on the basis of asset value plus earnings multiples

	£million
Capital invested less outstanding debt	657.33
Less goodwill in the acounts	−347.20
Less goodwill adjustment	−72.50
Net assets	237.63
Add 5 years of earnings (5 × £119.04million)	595.20
Estimated value of Cobham	832.82
Estimated share price (5 years earnings basis)	746 p
Net assets	237.63
Add 10 years of earnings (10 × £119.04million)	1190.40
Estimated value of Cobham	1428.03
Estimated share price (10 years earnings basis)	1280 p

EXHIBIT 10.6

Valuing a small business

Type of Business	'Rule of Thumb' valuation
Accounting Firms	100%–125% of annual revenues
Auto Dealers	2–3 years net income + tangible assets
Book Stores	15% of annual sales + inventory
Engineering Practices	40% of annual revenues
Food/Gourmet Shops	20% of annual sales + inventory
Grocery Stores	11%–18% of annual sales + inventory
Insurance Agencies	100%–125% of annual commissions
Janitorial & Landscape Contractors	40%–50% of annual sales
Legal Firms	40%–100% of annual fees
Off Licences	25% of annual sales + inventory
Restaurants (non-franchised)	30%–45% of annual sales
Sporting Goods stores	30% of annual sales + inventory
Public Houses and Bars	55% of annual sales
Veterinary Practices	60%–125% of annual revenues

Source: The Business Reference Guide, 2003

that the results produced by these two organizations are positively associated with equity values. The Interbrand methodology works by the following formula:

$$\text{Brand value} = \text{net brand related profit} \times \text{brand strength multiplier}$$

For products the net brand related profit is calculated as the difference between the brand net operating profit after tax (NOPAT) and the level of profit that would be earned by a generic product returning a 5 per cent return on capital employed. For a company brand the difference in net operating profit after tax less a suitable charge for the opportunity cost of the capital employed (we will consider this later in this chapter when we examine the concept of Economic Value Added).

The brand strength multiplier is calculated using an indexation system where points are awarded to a brand's leadership, stability, market presence, international recognition, trend, support (in terms of the firm's ongoing investment in the brand) and protection (such as patents, registered marks etc.). The points are weighted to create an index on a 0 to 100 scale and this is then translated into an income multiplier which normally has a range of between 5× and 20× income. In an illustration of the method, Barth *et al.* (2003) cite Gillette for example as having a brand multiplier of 17.9× to give a brand value of $10.3 million dollars.

In summary, the asset valuation approach covers a wide range of possibilities. The essential argument is the extent to which the value of a firm can be regarded as the sum of its parts. For a small firm with low brand value and restricted capability the intangible value of the business is likely to be transient and highly volatile. For this reason, 'under new management' may not be a guarantee that any of the old goodwill of the business will survive a change of ownership. Therefore the process of valuing the business as the sum of its replaceable assets plus a highly discounted premium for its earning power may be entirely appropriate. With larger firms and especially those with very large brand power such as those listed in Exhibit 10.7

EXHIBIT 10.7

Top 10 brands (2003)

		Country	Brand value $B
1	COCA-COLA	US	70.45
2	MICROSOFT	US	65.17
3	IBM	US	51.77
4	GE	US	42.34
5	INTEL	US	31.11
6	NOKIA	Finland	29.44
7	DISNEY	US	28.04
8	MCDONALD'S	US	24.70
9	MARLBORO	US	22.18
10	MERCEDES	Germany	21.37

Source: Business Week 4 August 2003

the problem of valuing the firm is dominated by the problem of valuing the brand. Our problem is that the large majority of traded companies do not have 'valuable brands' but they do have very large intangible resources. For these the asset valuation method is quite inappropriate. We will explore the problem of the valuation of intangibles in greater depth in the next chapter.

Relative valuation models

When a firm has moved to a size that the 'rule of thumb' approaches are no longer acceptable then some form of market based pricing mechanism must be used. The principle here is to find some common variable within companies which appear to be consistently priced by the capital market. Obviously, there are a large number of such variables including annual earnings, sales turnover, book value, fixed asset value, and net worth. The three most common in practice are:

- Price Earnings (P/E) multiples.
- Market to net worth (Tobin's Q).
- Market to book (M/B) value ratios.

Of these the P/E and M/B ratios rely upon some benchmark valuation of earnings or book value from either the market as a whole or for a reference firm or industry. Tobin's Q is assumed, for theoretical reasons we discuss later, to have a value of one. Of these there are subvariants such as the price earnings per unit of growth (PEG) ratio.

Price earnings multiples

The price earnings ratio is calculated as the ratio of the price per share divided by the underlying earnings per share. Normally a company publishes its earning per share under a number of different bases: basic earnings per share which is simply the published earnings divided by the numbers of shares in issue. If the company has a number of share options in issue to its employees and directors then it will also produce a 'diluted' earnings per share calculated on the basis that all options are taken up. Finally, underlying earnings per share is presented which is the basic earnings per share with the goodwill amortization added back.

Most financial newspapers carry the PE ratio and in Exhibit 10.8 we show the price earnings ratios for all the firms in the aerospace and defence industry in the UK excluding Cobham plc. In order to value Cobham we can use the average price–earnings ratio for its industrial sector as a first approximation of the value that the market places upon one pound of earnings in this industry.

The weighted average of the price–earnings ratios within the industrial sector to which Cobham belongs is 19.98 with a standard deviation of 3.96. In 2004 Cobham declared underlying earnings per share of 94.8p. This equates to a value of 1894p per share. Cobham's actual PE ratio is 15.2 which places it close to the bottom of the range of ratio values for companies in this sector.

Different variants of the PE ratio are used by different analysts. Some prefer to use a historical PE using the average of quoted figures over the last 12 months. This historical or 'trailing' PE ratio is claimed to remove price 'noise' (the random fluctuation) from the share price. Other analysts prefer a 'leading' PE ratio being the estimate from forecasts of the next 12 months' earnings figures. Figure 10.9 shows a summary of analysts' forecasts for Cobham's earnings per share for the next four years.

As we shall see after we have discussed flow valuation methods there is some rationale in the use of PE ratios. The magnitude of the PE ratio indicates the degree of volatility attaching to the firm's earnings stream. A low ratio suggests a low value is being placed on the earnings stream and hence (other things being equal) the higher its volatility and vice versa.

The problems with the PE method are numerous: first it is reliant upon an accounting estimate of earnings. As we outlined earlier, the accounting model makes a number of assumptions about the temporal matching of cash flows to time periods which even though firms may be acting quite consistently in their application of the Generally Accepted Accounting Principles (GAAP) can result in quite different outcomes across

---

EXHIBIT 10.8

Weighted price earnings ratios for firms in the aerospace industry

	Mkt Cap	weight	P/E	weight × PE
Rolls Royce	4.4400	0.2173	21.6	4.69
Smiths	4.8900	0.2393	20.7	4.95
BAe	8.5900	0.4204	18.6	7.82
Chemring	0.1429	0.0070	15.0	0.10
Hampson	0.0607	0.0030	88.1	0.26
Meggitt	1.1300	0.0553	20.0	1.11
UMECO	0.1383	0.0068	18.8	0.13
Ultra Elec.	0.4988	0.0244	18.6	0.45
VT	0.5410	0.0265	17.2	0.46
Total Market Cap.=	20.4317	1.0000	26.5	19.98

EXHIBIT 10.9

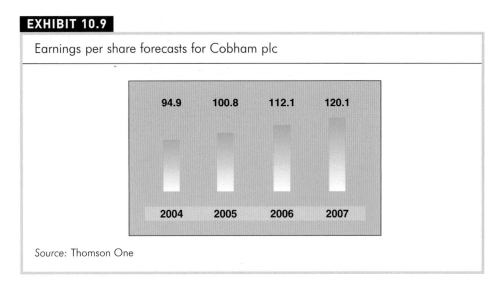

Earnings per share forecasts for Cobham plc

| 94.9 | 100.8 | 112.1 | 120.1 |

| 2004 | 2005 | 2006 | 2007 |

Source: Thomson One

and between industries. The second problem is that the model avoids the valuation issue in that it is transferring the problem of valuation to the market in assuming that a benchmark PE, however constructed, represents an appropriate price for earnings either across the market or across the industry. Finally, it assumes that the market does in fact value earnings rather than some other aspect of the companies financial output such as dividends, or growth in earnings or indeed risk.

Tobin's Q

This particular ratio has an impeccable academic pedigree. It was first proposed by the Nobel Prize winning economist James Tobin in 1969 and since that time has developed a small but influential following. Its principal advantage as a metric is that it would appear to allow us to determine whether a market is over or undervalued although its use at the individual stock level is more questionable.

Tobin defined Q as the ratio of total capital value (equity plus debt) to the replacement (or reproduction cost) of all capital market assets. The long run equilibrium for this ratio is one. Taking this ratio to the firm level:

$$Q = \frac{\text{market capitalization of the firm}}{\text{replacement cost of the firm's assets}}$$

Following Modigliani and Miller's proposition 1 that total market capitalization is the sum of the value of equity and the value of debt then an 'equity version of Q' can be defined as:

$$Q = \frac{\text{market capitalization of the firm} - \text{market value of debt}}{\text{replacement cost of the firm's assets} - \text{total debt}}$$

$$Q = \frac{\text{market value of equity}}{\text{net worth of the firm}}$$

When viewed this way all that Tobin's Q is saying is that the rate of return the firm generates on the replacement cost of its net assets is equal to the rate of return required by equity investors. To see this let us assume that the market value of the firm's equity is the capitalized value of the economic earnings of the business (E):

$$MV = \frac{E}{r_e}$$

However, the economic profit of the business is the replacement cost of the firm's net assets (C_R) multiplied by the rate of return on that invested capital (r_{RC}):

$$MV = \frac{r_{RC}C_R}{r_e}$$

as a result Q becomes:

$$Q = \frac{MV}{C_R} = \frac{r_{RC}C_R}{r_e C_R} = \frac{r_{RC}}{r_e}$$

If $Q = 1$, then this ratio simply asserts that at long run equilibrium the rate of return on invested capital must equal the firm's cost of capital (i.e. the required rate of return on equity) or, to put it another way, the rate of return on new capital invested in firms (the Internal Rate of Return on the capital invested) is equal to the rate of return on existing capital traded in the market (the required rate of return on equity). We have met this concept already in that in the long run the Net Present Value of internal investment is driven down to zero, i.e. the point at which the Internal Rate of Return on the firm's investments equals the firm's cost of capital. This is an important (if rather unsurprising result) for reasons we return to when we discuss the problems of estimating the growth rate of the firm.

To what extent can Tobin's Q and the implied relationship between equity value and a firm's net worth be used for prediction purposes? Smithers and Wright (2000) have conducted studies into the properties of their equity version of Q. They demonstrate that over time, and at the level of the market Q exhibits strong mean reversion. This is what we would expect if at the market level the Internal Rate of Return on invested capital was markedly different from the prevailing market required rates of return. Firms that earned greater than the market rate would attract investors and hence their equity prices would rise and firms earning a lower than market rate would find their share price falling.

There is some evidence that Q is also a superior leading indicator for share price changes than either the P/E ratio (where earnings is the fundamental lead indicator) or dividend yield (where dividends are the fundamental lead indicators). In causality tests Smithers and Wright report that net worth (the fundamental in the Q ratio) has only a 1.4 per cent probability of no predictive power, while dividends and earnings have 43.8 per cent and 88.6 per cent probability respectively. They also found that net worth only really works as a predictor when used as a ratio with equity value rather than on its own.

The historical evidence (see Exhibit 10.10) is that Q has been considerably less than one for the market as a whole for long periods and only greater than one for relatively short periods. However, the evidence on Q is not persuasive: measurement problems and the approximation of book value to the replacement cost all serve to distort the picture. The variations in Q in Exhibit 10.10 suggests long periods when the stock market significantly undervalued corporate assets – the principal downturns being around the period of the Wall Street crash in the 1920, the recession of the 1930s and the sustained bear market of the 1970s following the turmoil in the

EXHIBIT 10.10

Tobin's Q 1900–2000

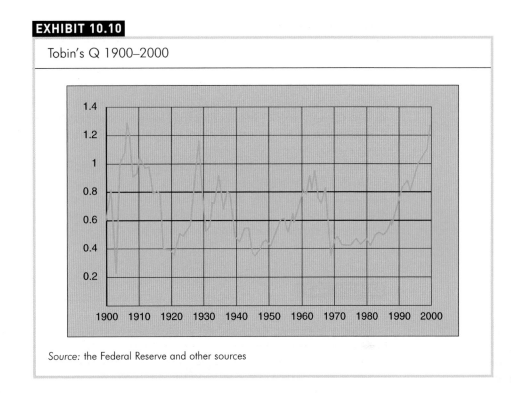

Source: the Federal Reserve and other sources

Middle East and the oil price shocks that followed. Nevertheless, from our perspective the problems in valuing Q reduce its value considerably:

1 As we shall see in Chapter 11, assets in firms acquire value not because they are held in isolation but because they are held within a network of other assets. So when we talk about the replacement cost of the firm's assets what we actually mean is the replacement cost of the firm as a whole and that is not directly observable from the accounts.

2 Many assets do not trade in what we technically call 'complete markets'. A firm, for example, is unlikely to be able to purchase its part finished goods on the open market. Similarly, it is difficult to purchase an asset which is a direct replacement for a fixed asset in use. It may be easy to purchase a completely new asset but not one of the exact age and condition as that currently held.

Although there is some theoretical support for Q, and at the aggregate market level it does have a strong mean reversion bias, this unfortunately does not mean that we can record the sum of the replacement costs of a firm's assets and these would equal the total market value of the firm. But how would we expect it to do as a relative measure? The answer is just as badly. Only if two firms were shown to have comparable yields on their internal investment would we expect to be able to translate the rate of return on equity from one to the other and hence obtain a valuation of that firm's equity.

In practice, the application of Tobin's Q invariably relies upon the use of accounting information as a proxy for replacement cost. This leads to the more measurable market to book ratio.

Market to book ratio

The market to book ratio is a pragmatic interpretation of Tobin's Q. This ratio assumes that there is a consistent relationship between market value and the net book value of the firm, or to put it another way that the market prices one pound (dollar) of book value in one firm, the same as in another. In Exhibit 10.11 we put that to the test with Cobham. This time we show the price to book values of all the companies in its FT industrial classification and calculated the average of the ratio using market value as the weight.

Exhibit 10.11 shows the average market to book ratio for the sector to be 2.974. Given that Cobham has a book value of assets less all outstanding liabilities of £509.7 million this would imply that its market value should be £1515.85 million which is 1358p per share on the basis of 111 606 905 shares in issue. This result is reasonably close to the current market value of 1 440p per share.

EXHIBIT 10.11

The calculation of the weighted average price to book ratio for the aerospace industry (excluding Cobham plc) – values shown in £billion

	Mkt Cap	Price to book	weighted average
Rolls Royce	4.4400	2.570	0.558
Smiths	4.8900	4.330	1.036
BAe	8.5900	2.21	0.929
Chemring	0.1429	2.31	0.016
Hampson	0.0607	1.83	0.005
Meggitt	1.1300	2.88	0.159
UMECO	0.1383	2.03	0.014
Ultra Elec.	0.4988	6.22	0.152
VT	0.5410	3.92	0.104
Total Market	20.4317	Average = 2.974	

An aero engine plant

Exhibit 10.12 shows the table of market capitalizations for the aerospace sector in the UK excluding Rolls Royce. The book value of Rolls Royce plc is £2307 million and there are 1704.77 million shares in issue. What is the predicted value of the price per share of Rolls Royce?

EXHIBIT 10.12

The calculation of the weighted average price to book ratio for the aerospace industry (excluding Rolls Royce plc)

	Mkt Cap	Price to book	weighted average
Cobham	4.4400	2.98	0.648
Smiths	4.8900	4.33	1.036
BAe	8.5900	2.21	0.929
Chemring	0.1429	2.31	0.016
Hampson	0.0607	1.83	0.005
Meggitt	1.1300	2.88	0.159
UMECO	0.1383	2.03	0.014
Ultra Elec.	0.4988	6.22	0.152
VT	0.5410	3.92	0.104
Total Market	20.4317		Average = 3.063

The price to book ratio would appear to be useful in the relative valuation of companies. However, as we shall see later in this chapter the price to book ratio has a relationship to the fundamentals of the firm and in particular the linkage to the return spread.

Relative valuation methods are popular with market analysts. Computationally they are straightforward but the problem comes in identifying an appropriate benchmark for a specific company. Underpinning these methods is the idea that similar companies of similar business and with similar exposure to financial and other risk should carry the same value scaled by the size of their earnings, book value or net worth. This is a straightforward arbitrage argument but one that because of the problems of making appropriate comparisons does not lead to methods that have the reliability necessary for practical application.

However, the relative valuation measures arguably have value in their time series. As companies or indeed the markets move through their cycles these ratios can help indicate exactly where on the cycle they are. This is not the same as saying that the companies or the market are overvalued when the ratios are higher than average or the long run trend or vice versa when the ratios are lower than average or the trend. There may be very good reasons why firms and markets are more or less valuable than the average at different points in time or indeed why one firm is more or less valuable than its business neighbour. It is towards providing answers to these issues that we now turn out attention.

Flow valuation methods

Flow valuation is based upon the ideas we have already discussed about the valuation of individual investment projects using the Net Present Value technique. When valuing the equity of the firm, the most obvious flow candidate is the cash flow received by the investors. In terms of what is paid to the investors by the firm (and ignoring any share repurchase scheme) all they receive is a flow of variable dividend payments. Therefore the investor can be regarded as holding a variable interest rate bond of indefinite term. However, many firms do not pay dividends and for these some alternative flow measure is necessary. One approach is to use projections of the annual free cash flow to the equity investors which is retained within the firm. Another method is to use some measure of residual value from the company's accounts again projected over the lifetime of the firm. The problem with these methods is that they rely upon (a) a calculation of an appropriate discount rate and (b) the forecasting and projection of the future flow measures.

The dividend valuation model

In Chapter 5 we derived an equity valuation model for the firm from the standard definition of return which states that return is the total monetary gain or loss to the investor, both from capital gain and dividends, over a specified holding period. So over the next holding period (however long that may be) the return is the difference between the current price and end of period price plus any dividend paid.

$$r_1 = \frac{p_1 - p_0 + d_1}{p_0} \quad \dots\dots\dots\dots\dots(i)$$

or by rearrangement:

$$p_0 = \frac{p_1 + d_1}{(1 + r_1)}$$

Because this model refers to a future time period it is described as an *ex-ante* model and the return (r_1), the price at the end of the period (p_1) and the dividend receivable (d_1) are all expected values.

Given that the return formula (i) is purely definitional the question then arises as to what is the simplest set of assumptions necessary to create an equity valuation model which is not dependent upon some future estimate of the value of the equity concerned. Three assumptions dramatically simplify the model:

1 The firm is a going concern which implies there is no foreseeable prospect of its failure.

2 The rate of return in future periods is expected to be constant which implies that there is a flat term structure on equity returns.

3 There is an expectation of a constant rate of change in the dividends paid over the indefinite life of the firm.

Invoking these assumptions we can demonstrate that the current price of the firm's equity is simply the present value of the future dividend stream (which 'grows' at a constant rate 'g') accruing to the investor. In fact the rate of growth can be assumed to be a zero or indeed a negative value without doing violence to the underlying integrity of the model.

The resulting model is as derived in Chapter 5:

$$p_0 = \frac{D_0(1+g)}{(1+r_e)} + \frac{D_0(1+g)^2}{(1+r_e)^2} + \frac{D_0(1+g)^3}{(1+r_e)^3} + \dots\dots\dots\infty$$

Which resolves to the dividend growth model first derived by John Burr Williams in 1938:

'A stock is worth the present value of its future dividends, with future dividends dependent on future earnings. Value thus depends on the distribution rate for earnings, which rate is itself determined by the reinvestment needs of the business'. WILLIAMS, J. B. (1938) *THE THEORY OF INVESTMENT VALUE*

This insight was developed by Myron Gordon in 1962 into what is now known as Gordon's Growth Model:

$$p_0 = \frac{D_0(1+g)}{(r_e - g)}$$

Thus the current share price is a function of just three variables: the dividend paid during the last 12 months (D_0), the rate of return required by equity investors when discounting the dividend flow receivable by them (r_e) and the expected growth rate attaching to those dividends over the lifetime of the firm (g).

The three assumptions upon which the dividend growth model is based 1 to 3 are an example of the rigorous application of Ockham's Razor to the problem of how expectations are built in the equity market. Each assumption is designed to reduce the model to a progressively simpler form while retaining the key features of the valuation process.

One common objection to the dividend growth model is that it violates Modigliani and Miller's dividend irrelevance hypothesis (see Chapter 6). This is a misconception partly brought about by focusing on the 'dividend' in the model's name and forgetting that the model values both dividends and dividend growth and partly because of a misclassification error. Dividend growth is generated by, among other things, the firm's ability to retain earnings for future investment so in reality the model is valuing dividends and reinvestment capacity which are both created by earnings. That is exactly Modigliani and Miller's position with respect to valuation.

The dividend growth model can be classified, depending on how you view growth as either an accounting flow model where earnings are either distributed or retained for growth or as a cash flow model where the shareholders value the cash flows they receive as dividends and as capital gain. Given the importance of the model and its analogues we will review the assumptions upon which it is based in some detail.

The perpetuity assumption

The dividend growth model represents the limiting value of a firm's equity in the hands of its shareholders. In principle, the value of the shares is assumed to be the present value of an infinite stream of constantly growing dividend payments discounted at the investors' required rate of return. Any finite stream of discounted dividend payments assuming the same rates of growth and return will necessarily have a present value less than the value generated by this model.

Normally, a limited company is assumed to have an indefinite life. This is embedded in the accountant's 'going concern' concept. However, this is a fairly restricted concept in that it requires that management should prepare their accounts on a 'going concern basis' unless they 'intend to liquidate the entity, cease trading, or have no realistic alternative to do so' (IAS1). In a market based setting we mean something more than this in that shareholders do not have any expectation that the company will cease trading and will therefore continue indefinitely.

Where there is a significant difference between the expected rate of growth of the firm and the rate of return required by the equity investors then the cumulative present value of the dividends paid to investors rapidly approaches the present value of a stream of dividends extending into perpetuity. However, where the difference is narrow the model does not resolve towards its limiting value quickly and even assuming a 60-year life there may be a considerable difference between the value generated by the model and an equivalent dividend pattern but assuming a finite life of 60 years (i.e. $p_{61} = 0$).

We demonstrate this effect in Exhibit 10.13 where we show the value of a firm of different lifetimes (from 1 to 250 years) assuming a 10p initial dividend growing at the rates

EXHIBIT 10.13

How the value of the firm changes with different assumed time horizons to failure

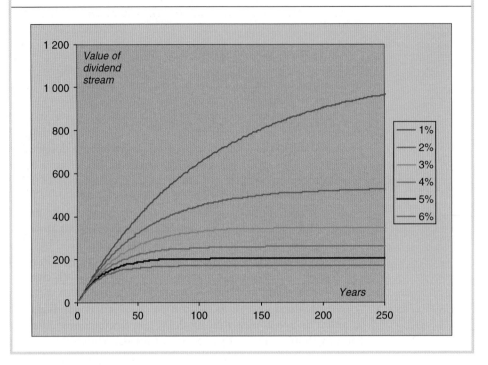

as shown and with a required rate of return on equity of 8 per cent. Note how a high growth rate brings the model into agreement with the perpetuity (i.e. the point where the curve become horizontal) much more quickly than when lower growth rates are applied.

One way of dealing with this problem is to use a time restricted version of the growth model:

$$P_0 = \frac{D_0 \left[1 - \dfrac{(1+g)^n}{(1+r_e)^n} \right](1+g)}{(r_e - g)}$$

REVIEW ACTIVITY 10.3 Calculate the value of a share currently paying a dividend of 20p per share with an expected growth rate on dividends of 5 per cent and a rate of return on equity of 8 per cent assuming (i) a 20 year life (ii) 50 year life (iii) 100 year life. What fraction of the perpetuity value is achieved in each case?

This suggests that the dividend growth model is only likely to be a fair representation of corporate value where the growth return spread is greater than 4 per cent. In periods of high nominal returns this may be reasonable, in periods where both real and nominal returns on equity are very low this severely limits the validity of the model.

The constant return assumption

The rate of return which we assume investors use to discount the dividend flow from a company should be the rate that they would use to discount an earnings stream of that risk in the market. Given that dividends (and the growth on dividends) are an equity flow we should assume that the rate to use is the minimum required rate of return for an investment of that risk.

In Chapters 3 and 5 we explored the use of the Capital Asset Pricing Model as a predictor of the equity investors' required rate of return. In principle the Capital Asset Pricing Model is a one period model in that it measures the expected return over a single holding period. The extent that it is legitimate to extend the rate of return predicted by the Capital Asset Pricing Model over a long series of holding periods is open to question. Bansal, Dittmar and Kiku (2005) were concerned with this issue. Using a process called stochastic cointegration these researchers investigated the relationship between asset beta and consumption beta over long time horizons. The Bansal *et al.* study demonstrated that in the short run, variations in returns are principally explained by transitory price shocks but over the long run it is dividend shocks that are the major source of return volatility. However, although dividends appear to be the strongest predictor of consumption betas over the longer time horizon, and the consumption betas are closely related to the asset betas, there is little to suggest the consistency in the term structure that the valuation model requires. This throws a question mark over the use of the model if long run returns are not valued by investors in the same way as short run returns. One answer to this problem is that over the very long run errors in the discount rate will have a receding impact upon current valuations. However, near term errors are likely to be much more significant.

The constant dividend growth assumption

What this implies is that future dividends grow at a constant, predictable rate. At first sight this appears to be very unlikely but the important question when building a valuation model is not what we think might happen but what the market as a whole expects to happen. Given our earlier discussion about the pricing process in markets variability and inconsistency in growth assumptions are likely to be cancelled out and a single dominant expectation of future growth emerge. Our simplest assumption is that future growth is a constant percentage (predicting changing rates adds a layer of complexity which we can incorporate at a later stage if the circumstances suggest that is appropriate). The model also requires what we will term the long run equilibrium growth rate, that is a growth rate which assumes that the firm's opportunities for earning a rate of return in excess of the cost of its capital have been exhausted (which we assume will be the case over the long run).

The use of the dividend growth model

The relationship between the underlying earnings per share (94.8p) and the dividends per ordinary share (31.00p) in 2004 imply that currently Cobham is reinvesting the following proportion of its earnings:

$$b = \frac{EPS - DPS}{EPS}$$

$$b = \frac{94.8 - 31.0}{94.8}$$

$$b = 0.6730$$

Cobham's financial record over the last five years is as follows:

EXHIBIT 10.14

Cobham's financial records 2000–2004

Pence	2000	RESTATED 2001	RESTATED 2002	2003	2004
Dividend per ordinary share	20.20	23.23	25.60	28.16	31.00
Earnings per ordinary share – underlying	64.2	75.4	86.4	93.5	94.8
Earnings per ordinary share – basic	63.0	59.4	70.7	17.2	76.0
Earnings per ordinary share – fully diluted	62.3	58.8	70.2	17.1	75.5
Net assets per ordinary share	273	311	294	412	457

The rate of return required by its equity investors (see Chapter 5) is 7.2 per cent.

This, as a proportion of the required rate of return on equity gives the long run growth rate if these payout and retention ratios remain constant:

$$g = br_e$$
$$g = 0.6730 \times 0.072$$
$$g = 4.846\%$$

The dividend growth model therefore predicts a share price for Cobham:

$$p_0 = \frac{D_0(1+g)}{(r_e - g)}$$
$$p_0 = \frac{31.0 \times (1.04846)}{0.072 - 0.04846}$$
$$p_0 = 1380\,p$$

The same result can be obtained by simplifying the dividend growth model. Given that dividends are simply earnings less retentions and if growth is retention ratio times the required rate of return then the following replaces (i):

$$p_0 = \frac{E_0(1-b)(1+br_e)}{(r_e - br_e)}$$
$$p_0 = \frac{E_0(1-b)(1+br_e)}{r_e(1-b)}$$
$$p_0 = \frac{E_0(1+br_e)}{r_e} \quad \dots\dots\dots\dots\dots (ii)$$
$$p_0 = \frac{E_0}{r_e} + E_0 b$$

Substituting the figures for Cobham gives exactly the same answer as before:

$$p_0 = \frac{E_0}{r_e} + E_0 b$$

$$p_0 = \frac{94.8}{0.072} + 94.8 * 0.6730$$

$$p_0 = 1380 \, p$$

This calculation reveals the true nature of the dividend growth model. It is the capitalized value of next year's expected earnings (equation (ii)) as:

$$p_0 = \frac{E_0(1+br_e)}{r_e} = \frac{E_1}{r_e}$$

So, if we assume that the firm is able to achieve the shareholders' required rate of return on new equity invested (in this case retained earnings) then the dividend valuation model is simply the capitalized value of the forward earnings figure. Indeed, if we use the analyst's prediction of next year's earnings for Cobham of 100.8p per share then the share price is:

$$p_0 = \frac{E_1}{r_e}$$

$$p_0 = \frac{100.8}{0.072}$$

$$p_0 = 1400 \, p$$

It might be objected that the appropriate rate of return to use for the reinvestment of earnings should be the Accounting Rate of Return on owner's equity employed. After all what is being reinvested is 'accounting earnings' and this surely means that the accounting and not the shareholder rate should be used to estimate the firm's rate of growth. In Cobham's case that would be a rate of 18 per cent using our adjusted figures or 19.25 per cent (as shown in the appendix) on the basis of the company's accounts. Although many sources use this rate it is clearly incorrect. Retained earnings are new equity investment and it will be investment partly in real assets but mostly in intangible assets. The rate of return on equity employed (ROE) is the rate of return on the book value of accumulated capital. We also know that the balance of reserves is incomplete because it fails to take into account investment in 'non-purchased' intangibles. However, the rate we are after is the firm's Internal Rate of Return on its current invested capital which is not directly observable.

If we use the required rate of return on equity to determine the rate of growth the model represents a long run equilibrium valuation of the firm and, if we assume that the assumptions of the model hold then three outcomes can occur:

1 The model gets the share price right (as in the Cobham case). This suggests that the market believes that the company's potential for earning excess returns over its cost of capital is currently exhausted and that there is no residual growth left within the firm's current portfolio of assets that can be exploited to improve market value. The market also does not recognize further options for the company's expansion. We will return to this point again at the end of the chapter.

2 The model under predicts the actual share price. This suggests that the market does anticipate further exceptional growth feeding through from its current investment and/or further options for expansion which could be exploited in the future.

3 The model over-predicts the actual share price. This suggests that the true rate of return the company is earning on its reinvestment is less than the market expects.

However, these three interpretations of the results from the model must be viewed with extreme caution. In each of the three cases the model may simply be misspecified in one way or other or in the first case in ways that are self-cancelling.

REVIEW ACTIVITY 10.4 Below are the analysts' expectations for Cobham shown in Exhibit 10.15 as a buy/sell/hold and for earnings. To what extent do the valuation procedures support this consensus among analysts?

EXHIBIT 10.15

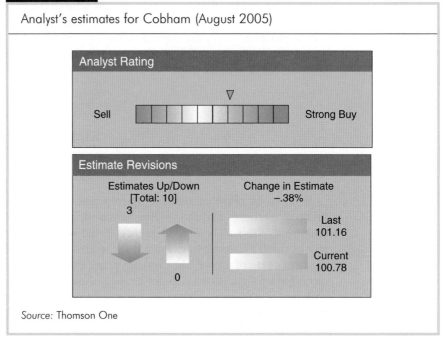

Analyst's estimates for Cobham (August 2005)

Source: Thomson One

How value varies with growth

The dividend discount model has some important implications. First it places a limit on the long run rate of growth (*g*) which cannot exceed the investors' required rate of return when discounting dividends. This is often taken as a fatal flaw with the model but a moment's thought reveals that it is not the model that is at fault. If a firm's limit on growth is constrained by its ability to create new investment through retention then in the very long run the rate of return on new investment must converge on the investors' required rate of return (to assume otherwise implies that the firm can keep finding positive Net Present Value projects indefinitely). If the firm reinvests all of its surpluses then the maximum rate of return it will earn is the rate of return required by its equity investors and that will be the rate of growth of its capital account. If it only reinvests 50 per cent of its earnings (say) then the maximum growth rate will be 50 per cent of the shareholders' required rate, and so on. What it cannot do is consistently reinvest more than 100 per cent of what it earns.

The second implication concerns the volatility of value and its relationship to growth. Where growth is low relative to the shareholders' required rate of return then the volatility of the share price will also be low, where growth is high volatility will be high. If growth relative to return is very high then even minor changes in investor sentiment towards future growth rates can have sudden and dramatic effects upon market values (see Exhibit 10.16). Much has been talked about bubbles and crashes in the equity markets with the most recent and spectacular occurring in the years 1999–2000. However, what the model suggests is that these are not due to 'irrational exuberance' in the pricing of shares (Robert Schiller, 2001) nor necessarily to the domination of the market by speculators.

The model suggests that prices will always rise steeply when beliefs about future growth rates converge on the required rates of return on equity. Any irrational exuberance arose because the markets believed in the year 2000 that the new technologies promised higher than historical levels of corporate earnings growth and that these levels of growth were a permanent feature of the new economy. However, when the mood bursts, even fractionally, the collapse in share prices will be dramatic. At the other end of the growth scale, when expectations of corporate growth are very low, then the markets exhibit very low levels of volatility induced by shocks impacting upon the growth rate. This is the stage (usually associated with the flat bottom of a bear market) where the market appears resistant to nearly all external stimulus.

The Gordon Growth Model does, therefore, give us some very interesting insights into the way real markets may work. However, concerns about the veracity of earnings numbers, or indeed, when faced with a company that does not pay dividends, may lead us to an alternative flow valuation method.

The free cash flow to equity model

This modelling procedure is based upon the concept behind the dividend valuation model except that instead of dividends we employ the Free Cash Flow to Equity (FCFE) after reinvestment in their place. The intuition behind the model is slightly different in that instead of working from the definition of return we work from the idea that the

EXHIBIT 10.16

The variation in share price with growth rate using the Gordon Growth Model

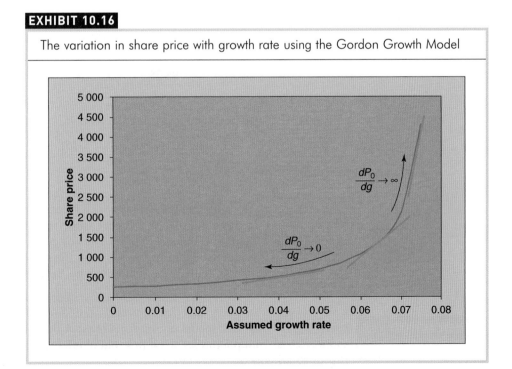

value of the firm to its investors is the discounted value of the future net cash flow available either for payment as dividend or for reinvestment. Working on the basis of the net free cash flow to equity per share then the price of the share is given by:

$$p_0 = \frac{FCFE_0(net)(1+g)}{(1+r_e)} + \frac{FCFE_0(net)(1+g)^2}{(1+r_e)^2} + \frac{FCFE_0(net)(1+g)^3}{(1+r_e)^3} + \cdots \cdots \infty$$

Therefore:

$$p_0 = \frac{FCFE_0(net)(1+g)}{(r_e - g)}$$

Following the same intuition as before the growth rate will be the rate of cash reinvestment (b_c) times the rate of return on reinvestment.

This model is a 'pure cash flow' model and as such there is no ambiguity about the reinvestment rate – it should be the firm's current Internal Rate of Return on future investment. However, given that we are again trying to impute a long term rate of growth we can make the case again that the simplest assumption is, that over the longer run, the firm's Internal Rate of Return will be driven down to its cost of capital and so the formula above becomes:

$$p_0 = \frac{FCFE_0(net)(1+b_c r_e)}{r_e(1-b_c)}$$

Cobham's Free Cash Flow to Equity before net reinvestment was 123.29p per share (see Chapter 6). Of that it retained 95.25p per share for capital reinvestment. Its cost of equity capital is 7.2 per cent.

The rate of reinvestment for Cobham is:

$$b = \frac{\text{Net reinvestment}}{FCFE}$$

$$b = \frac{95.25}{123.29} = 0.7726$$

the FCFE (net) is 28.04p per share and using the model:

$$p_0 = \frac{28.04 \times (1+0.072 \times 0.7726)}{0.072 \times (1-0.7726)}$$

$$p_0 = 1808\, p$$

The current share price for Cobham is 1440 which means that the free cash flow to equity model has, in this case, placed a higher value on the firm's equity than the market. On the assumption that the market has not got it wrong this suggests that the market does not believe that in the long run the company will be able to earn the rate of growth on reinvestment implied by the firm's current cost of capital.

REVIEW ACTIVITY 10.5 Assuming that the FCFE model above is not misspecified what does the current share price of 1440p imply for the firm's rate of return on reinvestment or its cost of equity capital?

Economic value added

Economic value added (EVA®) offers a means of valuing firms which bridges the two flow concepts discussed earlier. The EVA® method was developed by Stern and Stewart and combines the intuition behind the Net Present Value model with the accounting numbers that the firm produces in the form of its annual profit and the total of its invested capital.

The EVA® model is related to the concept of Shareholder Value Added first developed by Alfred Rappaport, (SVA is simply the discounted value of the future expected cash flows earned by the firm discounted at the firm's weighted average cost of capital). The SVA concept requires a specific time horizon and a means of establishing the terminal value of the firm at the end of the discounting period. The EVA® model uses a similar approach but connects the discounted cash flow model with the financial reporting system of the firm.

The EVA® model is defined as a firm's invested capital (C) times its return spread. The invested capital is not simply the market capitalization of the firm but the sum of its asset values in the balance sheet less non-financial liabilities. The argument for this approach is that the market tends to value both future growth opportunities and assets currently held while EVA® is concerned only with the return on the latter. The return spread is the difference between the Accounting Rate of Return on that investment (r_a) and the firm's weighted average cost of capital $(WACC)$ which for the sake of brevity we label simply as 'r':

$$Spread\% = r_a - r$$

In value terms, EVA® is derived as follows:

$$EVA = spread\% \times C$$
$$EVA = r_a C - rC$$

However given that the Accounting Rate of Return can be defined as net operating profit after tax $(NOPAT)$ divided by capital invested then the firm's Economic Value Added is given by:

$$EVA = \frac{NOPAT}{C} \times C - rC$$
$$EVA = NOPAT - rC$$

Turning to the Net Present Value of the firm we can define it in terms of EVA® in the following way:

$$NPV = -C + \frac{NOPAT_1}{(1+r)} + \frac{NOPAT_2}{(1+r)^2} + \frac{NOPAT_3}{(1+r)^3} + \cdots\cdots$$

However, the capital invested in the business can be represented by a perpetual stream of outflows as follows:

$$-C = -\frac{rC}{(1+r)} - \frac{rC}{(1+r)^2} - \frac{rC}{(1+r)^3}\cdots\cdots$$

substituting for $-C$ in the equation for the Net Present Value of the firm gives:

$$NPV = \left[\frac{NOPAT_1}{(1+r)} - \frac{rC}{(1+r)}\right] + \left[\frac{NOPAT_2}{(1+r)^2} - \frac{rC}{(1+r)^2}\right] + \left[\frac{NOPAT_3}{(1+r)^3} - \frac{rC}{(1+r)^3}\right] + \cdots\cdots$$

$$NPV = \frac{EVA_1}{(1+r)} + \frac{EVA_2}{(1+r)^1} + \frac{EVA_3}{(1+r)^2} + \cdots\cdots\cdots$$

Thus, by this simple piece of logical manipulation, the developers of EVA® as a management tool have constructed a valuation model for the firm. As the present value of the business is formally the value of the capital invested plus the Net Present Value of that investment then:

$$PV = C + \sum_N \frac{EVA_n}{(1+r)^n}$$

For a value maximizing firm the EVA® approach implies that a firm should seek to maximize the difference between the net operating profit of the business after tax and a capital charge which is based upon the return required by the investors and the value of the invested capital. One interesting aspect of the mathematics of the model is that it works irrespective of the basis upon which the invested capital is valued. If C is stated in replacement cost terms rather than historical (book) value then the magnitude of the annual EVA®s will be reduced but the overall present value of the business will remain unchanged. The EVA® method therefore incorporates whatever asset valuation system the company may choose to use in preparing its financial reports.

As a managerial tool EVA® has enjoyed great success, at one level it is easy to understand its simple message that value is created when the company makes a greater rate of return than the market requires given the fixed capital invested in the business.

The problem with implementing the EVA® approach is that it does require a large number of accounting adjustments to remove any distortions caused by the application of the Generally Accepted Accounting Principles. The purpose of these adjustments is to bring the NOPAT figure into close alignment with the operating cash flow of the firm and to exclude asset write offs such as goodwill and capitalized R&D expenditure which are likely to generate positive cash flows in the future. In the appendix we discuss the principal adjustments necessary for the conversion of the published accounting figures to NOPAT in a form suitable for application within the EVA® model.

There are a number of ways that the EVA® measure can be converted into a valuation tool. If we assume that with consistent reinvestment at the current rate the firm can achieve the above EVA® consistently then the value of the firm is the sum of the capital invested plus the EVA® capitalized using the cost of capital:

$$PV = C + \frac{EVA}{r}$$

The revised invested capital for Cobham is £1000.39 million (see appendix) and therefore, using the firm's existing weighted average cost of capital (6.81 per cent – see Chapter 5), we have an Economic Value Added for Cobham of:

$$EVA = NOPAT - rC$$
$$EVA = 183.69 \times (1 - 0.3) - 0.0681 \times 1000.39$$
$$EVA = £60.46\ million$$

In practice, some 100 different adjustments can be made to a set of accounts in order to bring them into closer alignment with what is perceived to be the underlying operating profitability and level of capital invested. However, the adjustments shown in the appendix are the most common and the ones which are likely to be the most significant in terms of their impact upon the assessment of NOPAT.

Using the EVA® calculated above the value of Cobham (assuming a perpetuity) becomes:

$$PV = C + \frac{EVA}{r}$$

$$PV = 1004.39 + \frac{60.46}{0.0681}$$

$$PV = £1888.20 \; million$$

However, this is a whole firm value. The equity value is then the present value of the firm less the value of outstanding debt. The total debt (short and long term) within Cobham is £267.40 million. There is also the capitalized value of the leases and hire agreements of £75.66 million. The residual equity claim is given by:

$$Equity = PV(firm) - debt \; outstanding$$

$$Equity \; (£m) = 1888.20 - (267.40 + 75.66)$$

$$Equity = £1545.14 \; million$$

with 111 606 905 shares outstanding this gives an equity value per share of 1384p compared with a current quoted figure of 1440p.

In summary, flow techniques capture some important elements within the valuation problem. They incorporate growth, risk (via the discount rate) as well as the fundamental value driver in the form of earnings, EVA® or cash flow. However, of the methods examined the dividend valuation model came closest to the actual valuation of Cobham. This could be for two reasons: luck or, more likely, this is the model that best expresses the actual valuation process within the market.

Step valuation procedures

A limitation of the flow valuation models as we have developed them is that they assume that growth in dividends will be constant from the next year forward. This may not be a reasonable assumption especially if there is evidence of unexpired growth in recent investment which is being priced by the market. The analyst's job is to estimate how long that period of unexpired growth will run for and what the magnitude of the growth will be.

We have (see Chapter 7) noted that Cobham's current growth in dividends appears to have stabilized at 10 per cent per annum. Analyst's forecasts (see Exhibit 10.9 show an average expected compound growth rate over the next three years of 8.2 per cent.

REVIEW ACTIVITY 10.6 Using the data in Exhibit 10.9 calculate both the average and the geometric average growth rate in expected earnings. What would be implied if the earnings grew at the rate analysts predict and the rate the company appears to be currently maintaining on the growth of its dividends?

The procedure is very straightforward. First we project the current dividend payment of 31p per share for the next three years at 8.2 per cent being the analysts' expectation of future earnings and hence dividend growth (assuming a constant payout

EXHIBIT 10.17

Step valuation for Cobham plc

	0	1	2	3	
Projected dividends growing at 8.2 per cent per annum		33.54	36.29	39.27	
Discounted value of first three years' dividends ($r_e = 0.072$)		31.29	31.58	31.88	$P_3 = \dfrac{D_3(1+g)}{(r_e - g)}$
Present value of first three years' dividends	94.75				
Year 3 dividend				39.27	$P_3 = \dfrac{39.27 \times (1.04846)}{0.071 - 0.04846}$
Value of perpetuity at the end of year 3				$1749.07 \leftarrow$	$P_3 = 1749.07\,p$
Discounted value to year zero	1423.77 $\leftarrow$				
Value of equity	**1518.51**				

and retention ratio). Second, using the dividend at the end of year 3 (39.27p) we calculate the value of the firm at that date, as before, using the dividend growth model. Finally, we discount that future firm value using the company's cost of equity capital. The sum of the discounted dividends for the next three years plus the terminal value at year 3 gives the revised value of the firm (see Exhibit 10.17).

Using this technique any range of future growth patterns can be modelled. It may be that we can predict a high rate of growth for an initial period followed by a deceleration of growth through the middle term leading to a stable long term growth rate to perpetuity. Although there is no limit to the modelling imagination there comes a stage where incorporating future assumptions about growth add to the complexity of the analysis without adding significantly to the value of the output. Once we reach that point we stop and try our hand at something different.

Using flow models to explain the investor ratios

If we believe that the dividend growth model (or its FCFE equivalent) reasonably reflects the real pricing process in the equity markets then we can settle the argument about what *P/E* and *M/B* ratios actually measure. The *P/E* ratio is easily derived from the dividend valuation model. We will assume that the long term rate of return on reinvestment is equal to the minimum rate of return required by equity investors. If that is the case then the following sequence of steps takes us to an estimate of the long run equilibrium *P/E* ratio:

$$P_0 = \frac{D_0(1+g)}{(r_e - g)}$$

$$P_0 = \frac{E_0(1-b)(1+br_e)}{(r_e - br_e)}$$

$$\frac{P_0}{E_0} = \frac{(1+br_e)}{r_e}$$

$$\frac{P}{E} = \frac{1}{r_e} + b$$

So the long run P/E ratio is simply the reciprocal of the firm's cost of equity plus the reinvestment rate (b). Given that Cobham's required rate of return on equity is 7.2 per cent and the current rate of retention is 0.6730 we can predict its P/E ratio:

$$\frac{P}{E} = \frac{1}{r_e} + b$$

$$\frac{P}{E} = \frac{1}{0.071} + 0.6730$$

$$\frac{P}{E} = 14.76$$

Cobham's actual P/E ratio is 15.2 suggesting that the company is (a) either marginally undervalued in the market, or (b) the actual rate of return on reinvestment is expected, over the long run, to be marginally higher than the current rate of return on equity. We can use the model to find what that internal rate of reinvestment might be:

$$P_0 = \frac{D_0(1+g)}{(r_e - g)}$$

$$P_0 = \frac{E_0(1-b)(1+br_c)}{(r_e - br_c)}$$

$$\frac{P}{E} = \frac{(1-b)(1+br_c)}{(r_e - br_c)}$$

$$15.2 = \frac{(1-0.6730)(1+0.6730 \times r_c)}{(0.072 - 0.6730 \times r_c)}$$

Rearranging and solving implies an internal reinvestment rate (r_c) of 7.34 per cent. In practice, the current internal rate of reinvestment may be somewhat higher than this value if it is expected that the rate will converge on the market rate of return over the short run.

Can we, in fact infer much from this analysis? The answer is that we cannot infer any more than our previous observation that the Gordon Growth model correctly predicts the current share price. Nevertheless, for investors who like to observe the movements of P/E ratios and worry about what drives them the answer is straightforward: the market rate of return for the firm's given level of risk, the firm's Internal Rate of Return on new investment and the retention ratio.

Contingent methods of valuation

The option pricing approach discussed in the last two chapters offers a clue as to how the equity in the firm may be valued. If we recognize that an equity investor in a geared firm with limited liability has a call option on the underlying assets of the firm then we have, potentially, a method for valuing the business. Although conceptually a powerful approach, the use of option pricing methodology does present difficulties in estimating the necessary input parameters into the model. Using the real options methodology, one approach is to simulate the future cash flows of a firm given realistic current conditions and estimates of the volatility of key input variables. With this we can generate an overall estimate of the future volatility of the business and then using a specified set of assumptions about the terminal value of the business generate an option value for the business. This modelling approach has many refinements but essentially provides both methods and insights into the valuation of all firms that are financed partly by debt and, in particular highly leveraged, fast growing start-up companies.

The limits on value

Traditionally, the value of the firm in the hands of its investors will have a lower limit equal to the break up value of the firm less all external claims on the business (the sum of its short and long term liabilities). Generally it was argued that once the present value of the firm's future cash flows (when discounted at the equity investors rate of return) fell bellow this value then it would be rational for the investors to cut their losses, liquidate the firm and salvage what value they could. However, this rather simple analysis is tempered in the light of options theory. From an options perspective the equity investors in a geared firm have a call option on the value of the firm's assets over and above the value of the debt. If the value of the assets should fall below the value of the debt then given limited liability the equity investors could put the firm into members' voluntary liquidation and walk away leaving the debt holders to bear the loss. Thus in a geared firm the equity value of the business is the value of a call option on the firm's net assets. In an ungeared firm the option value does not exist and thus the value of the firm to the equity investors is simply the present value of the net cash flows anticipated over the lifetime of the business.

This analysis suggests that valuing a firm depends upon the existence of gearing and that the value of the firm is not simply the present value of its assets in use less the value of its outstanding debt. If the firm is ungeared the critical numbers are:

1 the realizable value of its assets, and

2 the present value of the firm's assets in continued use.

The greater of these is its equity value. In the presence of gearing the important numbers are:

1 the present value of the firm's assets, and

2 the value of the firm's outstanding debt.

The value of the firm in this case will be the value of the option to continue in business.

This perspective on the value of a firm suggests that the following variables are critical:

1 The present value of the firm's assets in use. Generally the greater this value the greater will be the value of a call on those assets at exercise.

2 The value of the outstanding debt (the exercise value of the firm) – generally the lower this value the more valuable the call becomes until at the limit of zero gearing the call value equals the present value of the firm's assets in use.

3 The term to maturity of the debt – the longer the term the greater the value of the equity call.

4 The risk free rate of return used to discount the exercise value multiplied by the probability of exercise. Given the inverse relationship between exercise value and firm value this would suggest that the greater this rate the greater the call value. However, this is not likely to be the case overall given that the

EXHIBIT 10.18

The boundaries of firm value

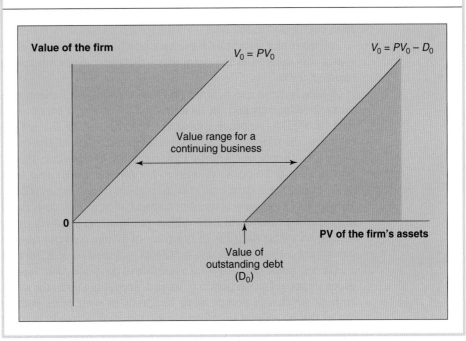

present value of the firm's assets will be determined in part by the discount rate and that this in its turn is partly influenced by the risk free rate.

5 The expected volatility of the present value of the firm's assets. This leads to the rather paradoxical result that the higher the uncertainty about future cash flows the more valuable is the call option on those cash flows.

Valuing the firm as an option

In the last chapter we explored Merton's approach to the valuation of debt and by implication the valuation of equity. However, in that model we presumed that the firm was traded on the equity market and that, as a result, the asset value and the volatility of future cash flows could be imputed from the observed volatility of the security's returns. In the more general valuation context, the firm's equity may not be traded or we may have reason to believe that the true valuation is considerably different from that revealed by the share price.

Schwartz and Moon (2000) developed a procedure for the contingent valuation of equities using option pricing and simulation methods. They used as their case study Amazon.com which at that time had been in business for just over three years. The company was still not profitable in the conventional sense but was growing its market and its revenues at a rapid rate. In March 1996 the quarterly sales of Amazon.com was \$0.875 million. By September 1999 its sales had risen to \$355.8 million. Here, in outline, is the procedure Schwartz and Moon followed:

A stochastic model was created of the firm's revenue generating process and its cost structure. This model contained a drift term which reflects the expected rate of growth in its revenues and a stochastic term reflecting the degree of uncertainty about that growth rate. The expenditure model reflected not only the company's fixed and variable cost structure but also the impact of taxation upon the company's profits. Refinements of this stochastic model included a mean reverting process to the estimated long run rate of revenue growth as well as a procedure for carrying forward losses for tax purposes from one period to the next.

A bankruptcy condition was imposed where given a starting amount of cash bankruptcy was defined as the point when the amount of cash and other monetary assets reached zero.

A time horizon was defined for the simulation of the firm's future cash flows and a terminal value invoked. In their study Schwartz and Moon set the final value as ten times EBITDA. Another approach would be to take the net cash flow figure and to capitalize the following year's projected earnings at risk free rate of return less the terminal growth rate of earnings. However, the time horizon should be such that by that time the equity holder's option is so far into the money that there is zero default risk.

A simulation is then undertaken to generate a large number of cash flow paths. In Exhibit 10.19 we show a simulated series of quarterly cash flows for Amazon assuming a starting revenue of £356 million per quarter, a growth rate of 11 per cent a quarter and an initial volatility of revenues of 10 per cent per quarter. The firm's starting balance of cash resources available was assumed to be £200 million.

The key point to note is that a number of the price paths have been generated one of which shows default in period 5. Indeed, depending upon the software used a model can be built which will permit many hundreds of such price paths to be generated. The model can be refined to reflect a wide range of different circumstances: different patterns of growth and the decline in growth as the firm matures, different cost structures, correlation between variables, differing tax regimes and different initial conditions. From the simulation the volatility of the cash flow projection can then be determined and the likely default in each period determined. This volatility, expressed as the

EXHIBIT 10.19

Simulated cash flow paths for Amazon.com over 12 quarters

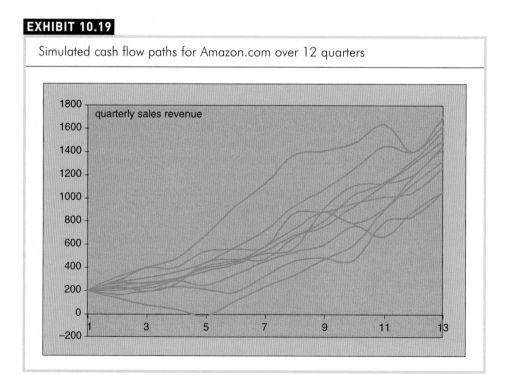

standard deviation of the company's future cash flows can then be adjusted to a continuous time basis as described in Chapter 8 and a valuation of the option component of the company's valuation determined.

The problem with this approach to firm valuation lies in estimating the initial volatilities of the future revenue growth and, in later variants of the model, the volatilities of future costs. Nevertheless, the technique does offer a potential route for valuing companies that are in their early stages of growth and which rely upon substantial investment in intangible assets.

SUMMARY

In this chapter we have surveyed a range of different valuation techniques looking for the model which best explains (and therefore help us efficiently predict) share price. Using Cobham plc as our case example we demonstrated that the methods often used in the context of small firm valuation do not help us when it comes to large quoted companies. We then reviewed a range of relative valuation techniques which gave different results depending upon which fundamental was assumed to be driving the value of the firm. We noted that while simple to apply these methods did not capture the elements which we believed important in equity valuation: the firm's future growth rate, the rate of return required by investors and, most important of all, the firm's risk. To overcome these difficulties we then explored flow valuation methods that rely upon the discounting of the future financial flows which we assume drive value. Of these, in Cobham's case, the dividend valuation model got the right answer. However, that could have been largely a matter of good fortune and although the empirical evidence suggests that the dividend model explains greater than 70 per cent of share value there is still room for error.

Finally, we turned our attention to contingent valuation methods which use the real options approach to determine share value. This approach, while challenging, does hold out the prospect of valuing firms that are very difficult to value by other means either because of their stage of growth or, as in the case of Amazon.com, because of the extraordinary range of real options the firm has created through its innovative business model.

Further Reading

Barth, M.E., Clement, M.B., Foster, G. and Kasznik, R. (2003) Brand Values and Capital Market Valuation, in Hand, J. and Lev, B. (2003) *Intangible Assets – values measures and risks*, New York: Oxford University Press.

Barker, R. (2001) *Determining Value – valuation models and financial statements*, Harlow: FT Prentice Hall.

Bansal, R., Dittmar R., and Kiku, D., (2005) Long Run Risks and Equity Returns, Unpublished Manuscript, Duke University.

Damodaran, A. (2001) *The Dark Side of Valuation – valuing old tech, new tech and new economy companies*, New Jersey: FT/Prentice Hall.

Fox, L. (2003) *Enron – the rise and fall*, New Jersey: Wiley.

Gordon, M. (1962) *The Investment, Financing and Valuation of the Corporation*, IL., Irwin: Homewood.

Grant, J.L. (2003) *Foundations of Economic Value Added*, New Jersey: Wiley Finance.

Mulford, C.W. and Comiskey, E.E. (2002) *The Financial Numbers Game – detecting creative accounting practices*, New York: Wiley.

Schiller, R.J., (2001) Irrational Exuberance, Broadway Books, New York.

Schwartz, E.S. and Moon, M. (2000) Rational Pricing of Internet Companies, *Financial Analysts Journal* 56:3:62–75.

Schwartz, E.S. and Moon, M. (2001) Rational Pricing of Internet Companies Revisited, *Financial Review*, 36:7–26.

Smithers, A. and Wright, S. (2000) *Valuing Wall Street – protecting wealth in turbulent markets*, New York: McGraw Hill.

Tobin, J. (1969) A general Equilibrium Approach to Monetary Theory, *Journal of Money Credit and Banking*, Feb. 1969, 1(1):15–29.

PROGRESS CHECK

1 Identify two reasons why valuing the company might be a useful exercise to undertake.

2 List the four methods of firm valuation and state of the underpinning theory of valuation which applies in each case.

3 Operating cash flow reflects the cash flow from day-to-day operations. What is the nearest analogue in the accounting flow?

4 What does a COP(bias) value of less than one represent?

5 What are the two principal components of the asset valuation of a company?

6 Brand value, as determined by the Interbrand methodology, consists of two components. What are they?

7 Identify three problems with the use of price-earnings ratios in relative valuation.

8 Define Tobin Q and state what value this ratio should take at equilibrium.

9 Describe two problems in the use of Tobin's Q.

10 List the three assumptions which underpin the dividend valuation model.

11 How is growth in dividends related to the current rate of reinvestment?

12 What would you expect to be the impact upon the firm value as expected growth rates converge on the rate of return required by equity investors in the firm concerned?

13 Define Economic Value Added and write down the formula for its calculation in terms of NOPAT.

14 Define the price earnings ratio in terms of the required rate of return on equity and the reinvestment rate.

15 What are the boundaries of firm value as far as equity investors are concerned when the company is partly financed through debt capital?

QUESTIONS (answers at end of book)

1 APE (Training) Ltd provides a range of training programmes for large multinational companies in the computer, telecommunications and financial services industry. These training courses range from short intensive programmes updating software engineers in the latest systems programmes to 'sheep dip' courses in Excel, Word and other office products. The company also employs a team of in house experts developing new training materials for use by tutors and clients. Some tutors are on full time contracts, others are university professors or consultants who work for APE on a part time basis.

The company was established in 1989 by two brothers and since that time has developed into a multi-million pound turnover business. The brothers own the majority of the equity capital and are considering either a flotation or a sale of the company outright. Ape currently has 10 million, 50p shares in issue. There are few competitors although Beaser (training) plc does have a listing on the Alternative Investment Market. Ape has become more diversified than Beaser in recent years with a considerable portfolio of work in the financial services sector contributing one third of its total revenue. Beaser's beta as estimated by the Imperial Risk Management Service is 1.6, there are 50 million shares in issue with a market price of 670p. As a whole the financial services sector carries forty per cent more market risk than the average but is very lowly geared with a sector debt to equity ratio of 0.05. Other summary statistics for both companies for the year ended 31 December 2004 are as follows:

	Ape	Beaser
Net assets at book value (£million)	12	35
EPS (p)	95	40
DPS (p)	40	25
Gearing (debt to equity)	5%	12%
Five year historic earnings growth	12%	8%

Analysts forecast revenue growth in computers and telecommunications to be 6 per cent per annum, but the financial services sector is expected to grow at just 4 per cent.

Background information:

The equity risk premium in the UK is 3.5 per cent and the rate of return on short dated government stock is 4.5 per cent.

Both companies can raise debt at 3 per cent above risk free.

Corporation tax is 40 per cent

You are required to:

(i) Calculate the equity and weighted average cost of capital for Ape (Training) and explain in which circumstances either rate would be used.

(ii) Advise the principal shareholders in APE (Training) of the likely range of issue price for the company.

(iii) Describe the limitations of the valuation procedure that you have used and the assumptions that you have made.

2 Fullopep plc is a newly formed biotechnology company which is growing rapidly but is still not at full profitability. Its current net cash flow is £85 million which is expected to grow at a rate of 12 per cent per year for the next ten years. The standard deviation of its cash flows is 22 per cent per annum. Its current debt is £380 million and the company has £90 million of cash reserves. The firm's current cost of capital is 8 per cent per annum and the risk free rate is 5 per cent. At the end of ten years the terminal value of the business can be assumed to be the present value of a perpetuity of the final year earnings discounted at the firm's cost of capital.

You are required to

(i) Estimate the current market capitalization of the firm on the basis that there is no uncertainty concerning the firm's future rate of growth.

(ii) Estimate the minimum value of a call option in the hands of the equity investors on the firm's assets to be held for the next ten years.

(iii) On the basis of (ii) and the terminal value of the business calculate the equity value of the firm.

QUESTIONS (answers on website)

3 Although world equity markets have lost between 40 and 60 per cent of their value since the peak in Spring 2000 many firms are still trading at many multiples of their book value. Discuss the reasons why this is the case and the extent to which the inclusion of brand values, unrealized holding gains and internally generated goodwill would bridge the gap.

4 Roboflop plc is a mature company in the private security business. Its free cash flow to equity is £450 million and its rate of return on equity is 8 per cent. The company has 400 million 25p ordinary shares in issue. In the current year its net capital expenditure is expected to be £280 million financed by £20 million of new borrowing and the balance from its own resources.

You are required to:

(i) Estimate the current share price using the free cash flow to equity model.

(ii) Compare and contrast the free cash flow to equity growth model with the dividend growth model.

5 Below is a statement of the current and expected balance sheet and profit and loss account for a limited company. The company accounts are expressed in £'000. The company has 1 million £1 ordinary shares in issue at a current share price of £8.40 per share. The company's management expects the firm to grow at 5 per cent into the indefinite future. The rate of return required by its equity investors is 8 per cent.

Balance Sheet		year + 1	Profit and Loss			year + 1
Fixed assets	2 500	2 944	Revenue		2 500	2 750
Accum Depreciation	1 000	1 294	cost of good sold		1 250	1 375
	1 500	1 650	Gross profit		1 250	1 375
Stocks	104	115				
Debtors	208	301	Administrative expenses	400		440
Cash	0	−32	Depreciation	250		294
	312	384			650	734
Creditors	52	57	Earnings before interest and tax		600	641
	260	327	interest paid		88	99
	1 760	1 977			512	542
Long term borrowing	880	989	Tax at 50%		256	271
	880	988	Net profit for distribution		256	271
Owners capital	100	100	Dividends		154	163
Profit reserves	780	888	Profit retained		102	108
	880	988			256	271

You are required to:

(i) Calculate the firm's current EPS, its actual P/E ratio and the P/E ratio expected at long run equilibrium.

(ii) Provide two alternative valuations of the firm's equity using the growth figures suggested by the company's management and its own retention policies.

6 Appended are the profit and loss account, balance sheet and cash flow statements with supporting note 18 for Virgin Atlantic Ltd an unquoted company in the airline

business. The statement below contains data relating to British Airways plc (courtesy of Thomson One).

Key Fundamentals

Forward P/E*	11.01	Dividend Yld	0.00
Price to Book	1.25	1 Yr Tot Return(%)**	25.07
Price To CF	2.96	Beta**	2.01
1 Yr Sales Growth	−1.66	1 Yr EPS Growth	80.60
Current Market Cap** (£ million)	3,026.71		

Source: Worldscope, *FirstCall, **Datastream

You also note the following:

The current risk free rate is 4.5 per cent, LIBOR is 4.5 per cent and the equity risk premium (rate of return on the market less the risk free rate) is estimated at 3.5 per cent for the UK equity market.

The ratio of total debt to total capital (debt plus equity) for British Airways is 60.11 per cent and of total debt to equity is 186.7 per cent. The yield spread for British Airways debt over risk free is 50 basis points.

The current share price for British Airways is 288p per share and its current PE ratio is 10. The corporation tax rate for both companies is 30 per cent.

On the basis that Virgin Atlantic's asset beta is likely to be the same as that of British Airways you are required to:

(i) Estimate the equity cost of capital and the weighted average cost of capital for Virgin Atlantic on the assumption that its yield spread on the cost of debt is the same as that borne by British Airways plc.

(ii) Calculate the Economic Value Added for the year of account for Virgin Atlantic noting those further accounting adjustments you would consider in order to refine your estimate.

(iii) Estimate the value of Virgin Atlantic using EVA and any two other methods that you consider appropriate.

Virgin Atlantic Limited and subsidiary companies
Directors' report and consolidated financial statements
28 February 2005

Consolidated profit and loss account
for the year ended 28 February 2005

	Note	**Year ended 28 February 2005**	10 months ended 29 February 2004
		£million	£million
Turnover: Group and share of joint venture		**1,640.1**	1.287.3
Less: share of joint venture's turnover		**(9.9)**	(15.3)
Group turnover	2	**1,630.2**	1,272.0
Cost of sales before exceptional item		**(1,330.6)**	(1,042.8)
Exceptional item	6	**30.9**	–
Gross profit		**330.5**	229.2
Administrative expenses		**(269.6)**	(216.1)
Group operating profit	2	**60.9**	13.1
Share of operating profit in *joint venture*		**0.6**	0.1

	Note	£million	£million
Profit on disposal of fixed assets		**1.0**	–
Profit on disposal of joint venture		**16.0**	–
Other interest receivable and similar income	4	**9.0**	14.8
Interest payable and similar charges	5	**(19.5)**	(7.1)
Profit on ordinary activities before taxation	6	**68.0**	20.9
Tax on profit on ordinary activities	8	**(20.8)**	(11.1)
Profit for the financial year		**47.2**	9.8
Preference dividends paid and accrued	9	**(7.2)**	(5.1)
Retained profit for the financial year	19	**40.0**	4.7

The profit for the year arises from continuing operations. The difference between reported and historical cost profits and losses is not material.

Consolidated balance sheet
at 28 February 2005

	Note	28 February 2005			29 February 2004		
		£million	£million	£million	£million	£million	£million
Fixed assets							
Intangible assets	10			**38.9**			32.2
Tangible assets	11			**448.2**			421.3
Investment in joint venture:	12						
Share of gross assets			**–**			7.3	
Share of gross liabilities			**–**			(3.8)	
			–			3.5	
Other investments	12		**8.7**			9.6	
				8.7			13.1
				495.8			466.6
Current assets							
Stocks	13		**26.1**			20.4	
Debtors due within one year	14	**146.6**			179.5		
Debtors due after one year	14	**66.7**			41.3		
			213.3			220.8	
Cash at bank and in hand			**265.5**			209.1	
			504.9			450.3	
Creditors: amounts falling due within one year	15		**(568.6)**			(516.2)	
Net current liabilities				**(63.7)**			(65.9)
Total assets less current liabilities				**432.1**			400.7
Creditors: amounts falling due after more than one year	16			**(154.7)**			(193.8)
Provisions for liabilities and charges	17			**(196.2)**			(165.6)
Net assets				**81.2**			41.3
Capital and reserves							
Called up share capital	18			**0.3**			0.3
Share premium account	19			**140.0**			140.0
Other reserves	19			**(228.7)**			(228.7)
Profit and loss account	19			**169.6**			129.7
Shareholders' funds / (deficit)							
Equity			**(18.8)**			(58.7)	
Non-equity			**100.0**			100.0	
				81.2			41.3
Shareholders' funds	20			**81.2**			41.3

Consolidated cash flow statement
for the year ended 28 February 2005

	Note	**Year ended 28 February 2005**		10 months ended 29 February 2004	
		£million	**£million**	£million	£million
Net cash inflow from operating activities	23		**191.2**		92.3
Dividends from joint ventures and associates			–		0.1
Returns on investments and servicing of finance					
Interest received		**9.0**		4.6	
Interest paid		**(3.2)**		(2.7)	
Interest element of finance lease rental payments		**(7.9)**		(4.0)	
Preference dividends paid		–		(6.1)	
			(2.1)		(8.2)
Taxation					
Overseas taxation paid			**(0.6)**		(0.2)
Capital expenditure					
Purchase of tangible fixed assets		**(109.4)**		(76.6)	
Purchase of intangible fixed assets		**(8.3)**		(11.6)	
Sale proceeds on disposal of tangible fixed assets		**2.8**		2.1	
Sale proceeds on disposal of other investments		**1.2**		–	
Return of aircraft progress payments		–		11.7	
			(113.7)		(74.4)
Acquisitions and disposals					
Proceeds from sale of interest in joint venture			**20.0**		–
Cash inflow before management of liquid resources and financing			**94.8**		9.6
Management of liquid resources					
Decrease / (increase) in short term deposits			**40.2**		(20.8)
Financing					
Repayment of secured loans		**(17.9)**		(26.0)	
Capital element of finance lease and hire purchase contract payments		**(20.8)**		(10.0)	
			(38.7)		(36.0)
Increase/(decrease) in cash in year	24		**96.3**		(47.2)

18 Share capital

	28 February 2005	29 February 2004
	£	£
Authorised		
3,000,000 ordinary shares of 10p each (equity)	**300,000**	300,000
150,000 cumulative redeemable preference shares of 1p each, linked to LIBOR plus 2.5% (non-equity)	**1,500**	1,500
	301,500	301,500
Allotted, called up and fully paid		
2,797,297 ordinary shares of 10p each (equity)	**279,730**	279,730
100,000 cumulative redeemable preference shares of 1p each, linked to LIBOR plus 2.5% (non-equity)	**1,000**	1,000
	280,730	280,730

7   An internet based company started up two years ago. It is 80 per cent geared and the firm's cash flows are highly volatile. The business is growing rapidly in spite of difficult trading conditions. Interest rates have fallen back 75 basis points since the firm was founded and the owners are confident of their continuing success. Describe the steps you would take to value this firm using real option pricing methodology and explain the reason why such methods are particularly useful for this type of company.

The pre-valuation corrections of accounts

Our concern is to ensure that the reported earnings are a fair indication of the actual earnings of the business during the year in question and any distortions are corrected. The procedure we describe below is designed to produce earnings numbers which can be used in a wide range of valuation procedures.

The COP ratio gives an indication of the direction of any bias in the presentation of the operating profit of the business. If the COP bias is neutral then nothing more need be done above the operating profit line apart from ensuring that there has been no change in depreciation and amortization policy. However, here is a checklist of points which may need to be considered and corrected for before using the accounts for valuation purposes:

1 Has the depreciation/amortization policy been changed or additional impairments been made which are likely to distort the reported performance in the current year, if so these should be reversed and the bottom line earnings figure been corrected.

2 Consider whether the amortization of intangibles is appropriate given their longevity and whether the amortization charge should be corrected. The traditional position was that purchased goodwill and other intangibles should be written off as quickly as possible. It is now recognized under FRS10 and IAS 38 that goodwill may have an indefinite life and that amortization of its value might not be appropriate.

3 Check to see if any increase in the bad debt provision has been included and remove.

4 Consider whether any R&D expenditures should be capitalized. R&D is expenditure designed to produce cash flows in the future which is not reflected in the GAAP requirement to write it off in the year it is incurred. This expenditure should be capitalized over its useful life which depends on the expected life cycle of the business. A useful guide is the length of time which the company uses to depreciate its fixed plant. To capitalize R&D expenditure for the last n years growing at a constant rate (g) use the following formula:

$$R \& D(cap) = R \& D_0 \left[\frac{1 - (1+g)^n}{g} \right]$$

The make a charge to the profit and loss account take the capitalized value and write off over the capitalization period (n).

5 Check for operating leases and hire purchase agreements. Consider capitalizing the annual payments at the company's current cost of debt capital (before tax) over the expected life of the asset (again the company's current depreciation policy for similar owned plant and equipment can be used to estimate the expected life). Then charge an implied interest charge to the profit and loss account on the capitalized sum at the firm's cost of debt capital (gross).

6 Check for any exceptional items and remove (including any profits on the sale of fixed assets or other disposals). Similarly remove any exceptional

restructuring charges and pension fund deficits or surpluses debited or credited to the profit and loss account.

7 Check for any exceptional severance payments to directors or other employees not included in restructuring.

Now, with a well scrubbed profit and loss account, you are in a position to calculate the revised earnings per share and the level of retained earnings for the current year. Finally, having added any revised capitalized values to the balance sheet, the firm's return on equity capital employed can be recalculated (note that the capitalized values of any leases will be added to the debt balance and not to the owner's equity account. The accounts should also easily reveal the Net Operating Profit after Tax (NOPAT) which forms the basis of the Economic Value Added method discussed earlier in this chapter.

FINANCIAL CASE

The 2004 net operating profit for Cobham plc prior to amortization of goodwill is £135.9 million. Goodwill is amortized by the company over its useful life of 20 years. In the current year £20.50 million was written off and the accounts reveal that £72.5 million is the accumulated amortization to date. The firm is of the view that this level of amortization of goodwill reflects the economic life of the assets acquired.

Research and Development expenditure is written off in the year it is incurred and in 2004 £48.7 million was written off. The company believes that the benefits of its current R&D expenditure are realized over five years. The prior year charges for R&D (in £million) were 40.4 (2003), 31.6 (2002) 28.2 (2001) and 21.6 (2000). Further charges of £21.1 million were also made under long term hire purchase agreements and operating leases with an average life of nine years. The company's marginal rate of corporation tax is 30 per cent and during the year it paid interest of £12.8 million.

The balance sheet showed net assets of £509.7 million and long and short term borrowing of £151.3 million and £116.1 million respectively.

Cobham's weighted average cost of capital is 6.81 per cent and its cost of debt capital is 4.8 per cent.

When reviewing the accounts of Cobham the COP ratio suggests that there has been little distortion in arriving at operating profit compared with the operating cash flow. However, a range of adjustments suggest themselves.

First, we add back to the operating profit the amortization charged, the R&D expenditure written off and the hire and lease charges. Of these, the goodwill figure will be corrected to the assumption that the intangible assets have an indefinite life. The accumulated depreciation in the balance sheet for intangible assets is £72.50 million and this is added back to the net assets of the business. Likewise the annual charge for goodwill is £20.50 million and this is added back to the operating profit.

The Research and Development expenditure has a useful life of five years and assuming straight line depreciation we can calculate an appropriate amortization charge based upon one fifth of the R&D expenditure in each of the previous five years. The total amortization to date will be 50 per cent of the previous five years' charges to the profit and loss account (assuming straight line depreciation). This means that of the total charge of £170.5 million over five years, £89.02 million should be added to the value of the capital invested. Amortization of the R&D expenditure is then calculated as one fifth of the total charge.

REVIEW ACTIVITY 10.7 Calculate the value of the previous five years' R&D expenditure and assuming straight line depreciation calculate the net book value of the unexpired charge to the profit and loss.

The hire and lease charges are costs incurred in financing long term assets and these charges are capitalized at the cost of debt capital. We use an annuity calculation to obtain the necessary multiple of the annual charge:

$$\bar{A}|_5^{0.048} = \frac{1 - \dfrac{1}{1.048^9}}{0.048}$$

$$\bar{A}|_5^{0.048} = 7.17$$

When multiplied by the annual charge of £21.10 million this gives a capitalized value of £151.32 million as the debt capital represented by this method of financing assets. The current book value of these assets, assuming a consistent retirement and replacement policy over a nine-year life would therefore be 50 per cent of the capitalized value (£75.66 million) and the settlement value of the leases would be approximately 50 per cent of the capitalized value. The straight line depreciation is one ninth of the capitalized value of the assets.

Finally, we adjust the value of the tax charge at the standard rate of 30 per cent of taxable profit.

The revised earnings per share for Cobham on the basis of 111 606 950 shares in issue is 101.39p per share and the revised return on equity capital (earnings/equity capital employed) is 19.25 per cent.

EXHIBIT 10.20

The final adjusted accounts for Cobham plc

Cobham – summary profit and loss account (revised)

	£m	£m
Operating profit (excluding discontinued operations)		135.90
Add back Goodwill amortization		20.50
R&D expenditure written off		48.70
Hire and lease charges		21.10
		226.20
Less amortization of R&D	34.10	
depreciation of leased and hired assets	8.41	
		42.51
Revised operating profit		183.69
Less: net interest payable as per the accounts	10.00	
imputed interest on leases and hire agreements	3.63	13.63
Adjusted profit before tax		170.06
Less Adjusted tax payable		
Tax rate at 30 per cent of adjusted profit		51.02
Revised earnings		119.04

Cobham – summarized balance sheet 2004 (revised)

	£m
Net assets as per the accounts (excluding long and short term financial liabilities)	777.10
add accumulated amortization of goodwill	72.50
add R&D not written off	85.25
add capitalized value of leases and hire agreements	75.66
	1010.51
Less increase in tax payable	10.12
Invested capital	1000.39
Financed by:	
Short and long term debt	267.40
Capitalized value of leases	75.66
Total debt	343.06
Equity capital	657.32
	1000.39

The valuation of intangibles

I n this chapter, we develop our understanding of the nature and valuation of intangible assets. In the first part of the chapter we briefly explore the relationship between the management of intangibles and the value they represent, and the underlying economics of the firm. We then review two methods that have been proposed for the financial estimation of the value of intangibles in general before moving on to explore both an empirical and the normative model of the structure of the intangible assets of the firm. We then turn to the problem of capital investment in assets which gain their value through their strategic value or through their instrumental value or indeed both. The resulting managerial model of corporate investment appraisal highlights the different aspects of the managerial task in making capital budgeting decisions. The models explored in this chapter, to a greater or lesser extent rely upon the input of more formal financial techniques. We will focus on two such techniques that are progressively becoming established in practice: scenario planning and the Financial Appraisal Profile model.

Learning outcomes

By the end of this chapter you will have gained a greater understanding of the nature of intangibles and their role in creating firm value. More specifically, you will also be able to:

1 Define the key attributes of value based management and in particular how it relates to the underlying economics of the firm.

2 Measure the financial value of a firm's intangible assets using both 'calculated intangible value' and Lev's valuation procedure.

3 Recognize the different intangible drivers of value within the CBI's Value Creation Index.

4 Define the concepts of prepotency, entanglement, sufficiency and emergence in as far as they relate to the asset structure of the firm.

5 Undertake an audit of a firm's asset structure testing it for sufficiency within each asset category and prioritizing investment to maximize the firm's value advantage.

6 Develop a managerial process for any given capital investment decision using the Financial Appraisal Profile model.

The problem of intangibility

For traditional accountants, Microsoft is, as Winston Churchill said famously in his 1939 radio broadcast about Russia, 'a riddle wrapped in a mystery inside an enigma'. The software giant in 1998 had total revenues of $14.4 billion and total assets worth $22 billion, but its market capitalization – based on a stock price of $90 a share on September 28 – now exceeds $466 billion. This represents a huge chasm between the company's value as measured by conventional accounting norms and its market value. MEASURES THAT MATTER: ALIGNING PERFORMANCE MEASURES WITH CORPORATE STRATEGY (KNOWLEDGE AT WHARTON, SEPT 2004).

A recurrent feature of our study of corporate finance and valuation to this stage has been the importance of a firm's intangible assets in creating value. However, the regulators of accounting practice have been reluctant to countenance the capitalization of expenditures on the development of intangible assets. There are a number of reasons for this: the problems of measurement, the consequential difficulty of creating a trail of evidence to support the asset concerned, uncertainty about the future benefits the asset will bring and so on. Intangible assets are rarely traded in complete markets and many such assets are deeply entangled with one another within the 'asset network' of the firm.

These are the pragmatic reasons for the profession's reluctance to allow the inclusion of non-purchased intangibles into the framework of financial reporting. However accounting is also constrained in its approach to the problem of valuation by a tradition which regards it as axiomatic that the value of the firm is the value of the sum of its parts. This naïve reductionism is enshrined in company law, and was articulated by the eminent 19th Century accounting scholar F.W. Cronhelm:

'It is the primary axiom of the exact sciences, that the whole is equal to the sum of its parts: on this foundation rests the whole superstructure of bookkeeping.'
DOUBLE ENTRY BY SINGLE, 1818:4

Nevertheless, accountants, over the last half century have been forced through a 'paradigm shift'. The old belief was that intangible assets, and particularly those we might refer to as 'knowledge based', exist to leverage value out of real assets. Now the perception has reversed. The modern view is that real assets have a purely instrumental role in leveraging value out of the knowledge and skills of a firm's people and its systems. This reversal in thinking has also created problems for a profession which attaches great importance to the objectivity it brings to financial measurement and hence to the reliance that can be placed upon its financial judgement and integrity.

Formally, accountants distinguish between intangible assets that are purchased and those that are not. But, as we have already seen purchased goodwill will only form a small part of the hidden value of the ongoing valuation of firms. Goodwill cannot be added to, it need not be amortized (in recognition of its longevity) but where it is not written down a regular impairment review is required to ensure that its carrying value in the balance sheet is not greater than its economic value to the firm. Even in those situations where a firm has grown entirely through acquisition rather than organically, the balance sheet value of goodwill will not have much relevance in determining the current value of the firm.

In general, all assets represent claims on future cash flows. Real assets are those assets which have a real and physical presence, and intangible assets are those that do not. Sometimes, intangible assets may have legal rights attached to them in the form of patents, copyrights, service agreements, or guarantees.

However, in many firms the bulk of intangible assets subsist in the knowledge base that they have created over time, the network of relationships upon which they depend and the trust which is vested in their name and in the products and services they sell.

<table>
<tr>
<td>**REVIEW ACTIVITY 11.1**</td>
<td>Select four firms from the following industries: pharmaceuticals, software and computer services, food producers and processors, and aerospace and defence. For each firm chosen determine, using the resources available on Thomson One or from the company's investor website directly, the proportion of their stated asset value which is in the form of goodwill and the proportion of their annual expenditure which is incurred in the creation of intangible asset value. Here you should include research and development expenditure, elements of the firm's advertising and marketing expenditure, training and staff development and any other separately classified items which would, in your opinion, enhance the underlying value of the firm rather than just being incurred as part of the process of earning revenue during the year in question.</td>
</tr>
</table>

Intangibles and strategy

A key 'intangible' for any firm is the strategy that the firm has in place for exploiting its asset capabilities in order to gain 'value advantage' in its market place. The subject of corporate strategy and strategic planning are based upon the assumption that the formation of a coherent business mission, clear business objectives and the strategies for achieving them is a vitally important part of delivering firm value. To discuss this connection between strategy and intangible value, it is useful to make a rather nuanced distinction between competitive and value advantage.

Competitive advantage relates to a firm's ability to open up new product markets, develop existing markets and capture market share. It is a concept borne out of what Williamson (1991) refers to as the 'strategizing' approach to corporate strategy – an approach which he argues is all about the power of the firm to shape its markets and to control its competitive position. The antithesis of this approach to corporate strategy is what Williamson refers to as the 'economizing approach'. The economizing approach gives equal, if not more importance to finding the least costly way of creating the firm's outputs while delivering improved value into the hands of the customer rather than to the search for market influence which is the hallmark of the Harvard School strategists.

Economizing has its roots in transaction cost theory which we introduced in Chapter 1. Transaction Cost Economics relies upon Coase's theorem (see Chapter 1) that firms can only exist and prosper if they can achieve a given set of economic outputs at lower transaction costs than can be achieved by leaving them to open market transacting. However, more than that, Williamson argues that economizing is about finding the most efficient governance structures for the firm – this he refers to as 'alignment', i.e. finding the most appropriate ways of configuring the organization to match the requirements of the markets in which its is operating.

> '. . . between economising and strategising, economising is much the more fundamental. That is because strategising is relevant principally to firms that possess market power – which are a small fraction of the total (ephemeral market advantages ignored). More importantly, I maintain that a strategising effort will rarely prevail if a program (ed: business enterprise) is burdened by significant cost excesses in production, distribution, or organisation. All the clever ploys and positioning, aye, all the king's horses and all the king's men, will rarely save a project that is seriously flawed in first order economising respects.' WILLIAMSON (1991): 75.

Seeking value advantage underpins the principles of value management which we can characterize by the following key attributes:

1 *Resource optimization*: which means developing the 'stock' of financial, real and intangible assets which the firm has at its disposal and where its ultimate value resides.

2 *Resource alignment*: this is the ability of the firm to align its management, its organization, and its structures in order to best fit the contingencies of its business environment.

3 *Adaptation*: which is the ability of the firm to reorganize and reconfigure the resources at its disposal in order to capture the maximum value from opportunities as they present themselves.

4 *Cost minimization*: this is the firm's willingness to seek minimum cost solutions to its production problems. This broadly encompasses not only the issues of alignment and adaptation but also the elimination of waste.

FINANCIAL REALITY

The Disney approach to project planning

The Walt Disney Corporation of America produces family entertainment for a global market. Its films, theme parks and merchandizing have been highly successful and its 'Dream, Believe, Dare, Do' philosophy is designed to emphasize flair and invention in the planning process. Walt Disney himself was highly cost conscious and believed that idea generation should be built into the corporate processes. He instituted a nine step planning process (summarized in Capadagli and Jackson's 'The Disney Way', McGraw Hill, 1998):

Blue sky:	ideas are encouraged and 'story building' and fantasy are given full reign.
Concept development:	from the many ideas generated one is identified as having the most potential for development.
Feasibility:	the chosen alternative is tested for feasibility; this may include building and market testing a prototype.
Schematic:	finalize the master plan outlining the business processes required to bring the product to market.
Design objectives:	specify the design details; develop an implementation and budget strategy.
Contracting:	establish sources of key inputs of materials and services.
Production:	commission the build programme, start production.
Install:	bring the product to its market, 'install the show'.
Close out:	summarize the project, monitor performance and celebrate a successful launch.

> You can see from this process that the Disney management practices attempt to marry the process of project development with an environment conducive to the creation of new ideas and problem solving. One such project was the construction of the castle that forms the centrepiece of Disney World, Florida and whose design has been copied at the other Disney theme parks in France, Hong Kong, Tokyo and elsewhere.

We have already seen how the real options method, if successfully applied by management, can help maximize the opportunities for enhancing the value of the firm through adaptation. However, all of these four attributes rely upon the skills and ability of management as a source of value advantage. As a result, we observe the interesting paradox that the managerial process of investment appraisal, for example, can be a significant source of value for a new project and that the present value of the future cash flows is as much a return on the appraisal effort as on the capital investment itself. For this reason the strategic appraisal of projects in terms of the value of the investment to the firm as a whole is an important part of any appraisal process.

The financial measurement of intangibles

A number of attempts have been made to develop valuation models for intangibles at both the firm and the project level. We will discuss two methods here: the measurement of 'Calculated Intangible Value' (CIV) and Lev's Knowledge Earnings.

Calculated intangible value (CIV)

The CIV is based upon the difference between a company's observed return on assets employed and what would be expected for either (i) another company in the same industry of similar size and structure or (ii) an average drawn from its industry. The CIV is derived as the present value of the firm's return on asset spread where the spread is measured as the difference between the firm's rate of return and that of an average competitor. In this respect CIV has a commonality of approach with EVA® discussed in the last chapter. The most significant difference being that CIV focuses on the intangible element of asset value and uses an accounting spread rather than the spread between a firm's accounting return and its cost of capital:

$$\Delta r_A\ (\%) = r_{A,F}A - r_{A,I}A$$
$$\Delta r_A\ (\text{£}) = net\ profit - r_{A,I}A$$

where $r_{A,F}$ is the return on assets and A is the asset value invested in the firm concerned, $r_{A,I}$ is the return on assets in the competitor or in the industry.

The calculations above are on a pre-tax basis and so the CIV measure is taken as the discounted value of the post tax returns using the firm's weighted average cost of capital.

In the financial year 2004, Rolls Royce plc had made an operating profit of £320 million on assets employed in the business of £1626 million. However, Cobham Plc had made an operating profit of £129.6 million on an asset base of £241.0 million. Cobham's retained earnings are £50.1 million. Cobham's monetary assets are £101.3 million and its weighted average cost of capital is 6.81 per cent. The expected rate of return of the highly knowledge based biotechnology, pharmaceutical and software industries is 6 per cent higher than risk free. The expected return on tangible assets is 2.75 per cent above risk free. The corporation tax rate is 30 per cent.

Rolls Royce and Cobham plc both manufacture planes like these

The return on assets is based upon operating profit and tangible assets only and thus excludes any costs of financing, extraordinary items and tax. Currently the rate of return earned by Rolls Royce is:

$$ROA_{RR} = \frac{320}{1626} = 19.68\%$$

The value spread for Cobham is therefore:

$$\Delta r_A \ (\pounds) = net\ profit - r_{A,I} A$$
$$\Delta r_A \ (\pounds) = 129.60 - 19.68\% \times 241$$
$$\Delta r_A \ (\pounds) = \pounds 82.17\ million$$

There are a number of approaches to capitalizing the earnings derived from the intangible assets of the firm. One approach is to capitalize the year forward estimate of earnings using, as derived in the last chapter, the current rate of reinvestment times the firm's required rate of return (which we assume to be the firm's weighted average cost of capital). However, because we are using the weighted average cost of capital we should employ Cobham's Net Operating Profit after Tax (NOPAT) rather than its earnings after interest charges (see appendix to Chapter 10).

$$g = \frac{retained\ earnings}{NOPAT} \times WACC$$
$$NOPAT = \pounds 129.60\ million \times (1 - 0.3)$$
$$g = \frac{50.1}{90.72} \times 0.0681$$
$$g = 3.761\%$$

Note that this is a lower rate than the rate of growth of dividends which benefits from the gearing effect.

$$CIV = \frac{\Delta r_A (1 - t)(1 + g)}{WACC}$$

$$CIV = \frac{82.17(1-30\%)(1.03761)}{0.0687}$$

$$CIV = £889 \; million$$

REVIEW ACTIVITY 11.2 Taking Cobham's CIV measure test its sensitivity to changes in (i) the rate of the expected growth in earnings and, (ii) the firm's weighted average cost of capital. Of these, which do you think is likely to be most critical in determining the value of CIV?

If we combine this value into the Cobham Balance Sheet we arrive at an estimate of net assets employed of £1130 million giving an equity valuation of 1010p per share.

The problems with the CIV method are numerous. Most of the issues in using the relative methods of valuation discussed in the last chapter resurface with CIV. Not only should the average competitor be in the same industry with a similar asset portfolio but it should also have similar cost gearing. However, most problematic of all the CIV is a difficult measure to interpret. Presumably the comparator firm will also have some intangible assets and so any CIV is a measure of the surplus intangible value over and above the base company employed.

Lev's knowledge earnings method

An alternative approach to the valuation of a firm's intangibles has been developed by Baruch Lev (2001). His method, like CIV is based upon the capitalization of excess earnings but rather than benchmarking against a competitor or an industry average, Lev calculates a net earnings figure after deducting two charges:

1 a charge for the use of the firm's monetary assets (taken as the risk free rate × the monetary assets employed), and

2 a charge for the use of the firm's tangible assets (average return on tangible assets across the economy of companies predominantly driven by their investment in tangible assets).

Once the knowledge earnings have been estimated, he proposes a three step discounting procedure (see: Mintz (2000)):

- Five years at the company's current rate of growth.
- Six to ten years at a declining growth rate towards the long term predicted rate.
- Eleven years forward being the present value of all subsequent earnings growing at the long term predicted rate.

Lev argues that the rate of return for discounting intangible returns should be greater than that for either tangible or monetary assets. The rationale for this is the greater uncertainty that attaches to intangible asset returns. The average expected return premium of high knowledge intensive industries (such as pharmaceuticals, software and biotechnology firms) is estimated at 6 per cent above risk free (Stewart, 2001).

In Exhibit 11.1 we have proceeded through the following steps in order to calculate the value of the intangible assets in Cobham:

1 Using the current year's earnings we have deducted a charge for the monetary assets employed (£101.3 million) at 4.75 per cent and for the tangible assets employed (£241 million) at 7.25 per cent.

EXHIBIT 11.1

Calculation of intangible value using the Lev Knowledge Earnings method

	0	1	2	3	4	5	6	7	8	9	10	11
Forecast earnings (Exhibit 10.9)	94.9	100.8	112.1	120.1								
Charge for monetary assets employed	−4.8											
Charge for real assets employed	−17.5											
Knowledge earnings	72.6											
Growth rate expected (years 1–5)	8.17%											
Long term growth rate	3.76%											
Decay rate (years 6–10)	87.86%											
Projected growth		8.17%	8.17%	8.17%	8.17%	8.17%	7.18%	6.31%	5.54%	4.87%	4.28%	3.76%
Projected knowledge earnings (years 1–11)		78.5	85.0	91.9	99.4	107.5	115.2	122.5	129.3	135.6	141.4	146.7
Discounted earnings (years 1–11)	1131	70.9	76.7	83.0	89.8	97.1	104.1	110.6	116.7	122.4	127.7	132.5
PV of terminal intangible asset value	461											1416
Value of intangible assets	1592											

2 Using analysts' estimate for the growth in forecast earnings we can estimate near term growth at 8.17 per cent and long term growth at 3.76 per cent as above. The intervening growth figures between years five and 11 we calculate as the decay rate required to bring the growth of 8.17 per cent to 3.79 per cent in six years (year 11 is the first year at which the lower growth rate applies). The decay percentage is calculated as follows:

$$Decay\,rate = \sqrt[6]{\frac{3.76\%}{8.17\%}} = 87.86\%$$

This percentage is applied to the prior year growth in earnings to obtain the projected figure for knowledge earnings in each of the years 6–11 inclusive.

3 The projected knowledge earnings are then discounted at a rate of 10.75 per cent reflecting the risk premium over the risk free rate. The terminal value is estimated using the modified version of the earnings growth formula:

$$\text{Terminal value} = \frac{KE_{11}(1+g_{10})}{r_k}$$

$$\text{Terminal value} = \frac{146.7 \times (1.0379)}{0.1075}$$

$$\text{Terminal value} = £1416\,million$$

this value is discounted over 11 years at 10.75 per cent to give a present value.

There is some evidence that Lev's approach generates intangible asset values which are well correlated with total investment returns. Stewart (2001) claims that the correlation between Lev's measure of knowledge earnings and returns is 0.53 compared with a coefficient of 0.29 between earnings and returns. In terms of explanatory power this equates with an R^2 of 28.1 per cent and 8.41 per cent respectively. However, Lev's method contains numerous approximations and there is little clarity in the literature on the appropriate mechanism for measuring earnings. Lev appears to favour an approach based upon an average of three years' past and three years' forecast earnings with a double weighting given to the latter. We have used the current year's earnings figures to avoid double counting the near term growth estimate.

Much about the Lev method is 'suck it and see if it works'. Undoubtedly, the higher volatility of intangible assets would lead to a higher rate of investment in those assets if, conceptually, they can be disentangled from the underlying real assets of the firm. If one accepts that they can, there are still problems in using the rate of what he refers to as highly knowledge based industries. The pharmaceutical and biotechnology industries are typically very rich in highly specific real assets as well as the intellectual resources driven by their research and development programmes. The same is true to a lesser extent with software firms. As a result we still have an entanglement problem in extracting a pure 'knowledge rate'.

In Exhibit 11.2 we summarize the balance sheet breakdown of net assets invested in Cobham plc and recast them using the intangible asset values derived from the two models above. The Lev model does produce an overall asset value that approximates to the value of the firm as revealed by its share price. In forming your view about the usefulness of these models you may wish to reflect upon the relative success of the various flow models discussed in the last chapter. Arguably, neither model has given us noticeably superior results to that obtained using conventional valuation procedures.

EXHIBIT 11.2

Comparative statements of net assets for Cobham plc using both the CIV and Lev models

Statement of Net Assets

	Accounts	CIV	LEV
Fixed Assets			
Intangible assets at value	374	889	1592
Tangible assets	241	241	241
Investment in joint venture	16	16	16
Investment in associates	1	1	1
Net Current Assets	125	125	125
Total assets employed	757	1272	1975
less long term liabilities and provisions	248	248	248
	510	1024	1727
Per share (p)	457	915	1544

Prioritizing investment in intangibles

Neither the CIV method nor Lev's approach to the valuation of knowledge-based assets provide the fineness of detail required for management to prioritize investment in intangibles. Indeed both methods take us little further than justifying the difference between the book value of assets in the balance sheet and the company's market value. So far, the only definitive tool at our disposal for measuring such investment is the real options approach discussed in Chapter 9.

We now discuss two methods, one empirical and the other normative, for helping management prioritize investment. The first method developed by Cap Gemini, the consulting division of Ernst & Young, was based upon a survey of analysts' opinion identifying the key intangible value drivers in different industries and a series of statistical tests designed to validate the model which resulted. The second method is derived from the resource based approach in corporate strategy and focuses upon the natural ordering of capital assets within the structure of any firm.

The value creation index

The value creation index (VCI) arose from work done by the Cap Gemini Centre for Business Innovation who published an influential study in 1997 called Measures That Matter. On the basis of an extensive research study polling analysts as well as academic opinion the CBI team came up with nine categories of non-financial performance that appeared to determine corporate value creation:

1 innovation
2 quality
3 customer relations
4 management capabilities
5 alliances

6 technology

7 brand value

8 employee relations

9 environmental and community issues.

Under each of these headings, the team then developed a number of measurement metrics designed to capture the crucial features of each category. Using a range of statistical techniques, these metrics were tested for explanatory power across the S&P500 companies. Once the process of selecting candidate metrics was completed and ensuring, as far as possible that each measure was as independent as possible from one other, a model was then designed which explained the market value of the companies tested.

The nine categories of the VCI described above were discovered to have different levels of importance in different industries. Low (2000) reporting on the creation of the VCI claims that over 50 per cent of traditional corporate value is based upon the nine factors, rising to over 90 per cent for e-commerce companies. In the development of the index, noticeable differences arose between the relative importance of the various factors identified as important by analysts and the weightings delivered by the subsequent statistical analysis. Across the industries analyzed, 'connectedness' in the form of alliances such as joint ventures partnerships and other co-operative arrangements, was revealed to be much more significant than believed by analysts and other respondents. Rather interestingly, technology and customer satisfaction did not reveal themselves as important value drivers in the statistical study whereas they had been given much greater significance by respondents. There are a number of explanations for this the most likely being that these are now taken for granted and are no longer influential in the price setting process.

In Exhibit 11.3 we show the most important value drivers for the various industries analyzed by the CBI study. We have categorized the value drivers according to their power in explaining share price.

EXHIBIT 11.3

The most important value drivers in the VCI

The Most Important Value Drivers

Airlines	Financial Services	Manufacturing (non-durables)	Manufacturing (durables)	E-commerce
Human capital	Alliances	Innovation	Innovation	Alliances
Efficiency	Human capital	Management	Employee	Innovation
Safety	Management	Employee	Management	Number of users
Alliances	Brand	Quality	Alliances	Brand
Fare index	Innovation	Brand	Brand	Minutes per page
Cabin service	Technology	Technology	Technology	Change in usage
	Customer	Customer	Customer	Market share

High

Medium

Low

There are a number of conclusions we can draw from this study:

- The broad accounting categories of intangibles into: 'goodwill', 'brand', and 'R&D expenditure' does not capture the fineness of classification required to explain company value.
- Within different industries different types of intangible asset have different importance in driving firm value.
- Network effects are very important, in most industries, in explaining company value and these effects manifest themselves not only through formal and informal alliances but also through measures of customer satisfaction.

A significant problem with the Cap Gemini study is that it does not distinguish between those intangibles which have a primary impact upon the company's ability to deliver value and those whose effect is largely instrumental. As a result, the impact of a given intangible may appear to be only weakly associated with share price but its presence within the asset structure of the firm is critical for another level of intangible to operate effectively. It is this issue which we explore in more detail with our second model.

REVIEW ACTIVITY 11.3   Taking any of the companies that you analyzed in the previous review activity identify, in as far as it is possible, the level of expenditure which the firm incurred in the last year of account on any of the value drivers in the VCI. What inaccuracies might be present in determining the value invested in asset formation as a proportion of the total expenditure you have identified?

The MAKENT© model – an emergent model of firm value

The MAKENT© model is a development of the resource based perspective within business strategy. Following the work of Birger Weirnerfelt (1984), Barney (1991) and more recently Venugopal (1999) the perspective of business strategists has moved away from the preoccupation with the firm's external environment characterized by the Harvard School of Business Strategy to one which is more concerned with the internal resources of the business and the capabilities they create. The resource based view seeks to build sustainable value advantage by procuring and configuring the available resources so as to gain the maximum resource yield being the difference between the returns generated by those resources and their opportunity cost.

Resource based strategists have come up with a number of different ways of categorizing resources. Hall (1992) for example clusters assets in the following way: organizational attributes, intangible assets that confer legal protection, information assets, personal and inter-organizational networks and financial assets. Others come up with slightly different subclassifications. The problem with these asset constructions is that there is no particular rationale for the way they are. The MAKENT© model addresses this problem. Underpinning this model are some basic ideas about the nature of different assets types: these can be summarized as 'prepotency', 'entanglement', 'sufficiency', and 'emergence'.

Prepotency

Prepotency is familiar enough to those who have studied elementary motivation theory. It is the idea that certain needs (in motivation theory) and assets (in our example) have to be in place before other needs can be satisfied or in our case other assets can either be procured or put to the job of creating value. If a need of higher prepotency is thwarted then we immediately seek to resolve that need before returning to seeking to fulfil their higher aims in life – and so it is with assets.

The first, and most prepotent of all assets are monetary assets (M) followed by the real assets of the firm (A). The real assets such as land, building, physical plant and inventories have a fineness of categorization which we will not go into in detail here. The possession of real assets of themselves requires the application of general knowledge and skills which are transferable and in the public domain. The pilot of the airliner possesses publicly available knowledge in the form of his or her knowledge of how to fly. This publicly available (K) knowledge is the 'ticket to the value game' in the sense that the intelligent ordering and utilization of the firm's real assets is dependent upon the existence of, and the firm's continuing investment in, knowledge of this type. There is something of a chicken and an egg problem when we talk about real assets and the knowledge of how to use them. However, because the knowledge of how to use many real assets lies within the pool of labour a firm has at its disposal that knowledge is more easily replaced than the asset itself. This is a topic we will return to in Chapter 12 when we discuss the problems of information assets and synergy in the context of the acquisition decision.

The next level of ordering of assets takes us to the firms 'E' value, E is the private enterprise knowledge of assets in use that a firm accumulates as it learns to configure the subordinate monetary, real and 'K' assets in more intelligent ways than its competitors. A firm's E knowledge can subsist at many levels within the firm. It partly resides in superior strategies and structures which enable the firm to compete and create value more easily than its neighbours. It also takes the form of systems and databases as well as the knowledge that management and other employees possess about their firm's products and processes. This private knowledge can be regarded as the glue which cements the firm's internal asset 'net' and which is vital for winning and sustaining competitive advantage and superior value in the market.

At this point we conceptually make a transition from the internal asset network of the firm to the external network of relationships with suppliers, distributors, customers, competitors and all the other external stakeholders of the firm. The value of this network (N) is the penultimate piece in our value jigsaw. The final piece arises as the firm begins to successfully transact with its suppliers, customers and external stakeholders. As it does so it will begin to create 'T' value, which is the value attaching to the trust placed in the firm and its products by external stakeholders and in particular by customers. Customer 'T' we generally call 'brand' value although the term brand with its association with corporate or product name is a weak signal of the social capital that a firm accumulates to its products or directly or by proxy to itself. In total this 'T' value can be partitioned into three components in ascending order of prepotency: product 'T' being the reputation vested by the firm's potential and actual customers in the products sold; corporate 'T' being the reputation vested by customers in the corporate name and, finally, social 'T' which is the wider value in 'good citizenry' that a firm accumulates over time.

Entanglement

The concept of prepotency in value is related to the idea of entanglement. Entanglement expresses the idea that many assets derive their value from their interconnectedness with other assets in very specific ways. High prepotency assets, such as cash and near cash have very low entanglement. These assets can be freely exchanged and the market for their replacement is relatively complete. An aeroplane is of relatively low entanglement with the other assets of the airline because its deprival can be easily repaired by its replacement. However, even at this level an aeroplane, for example, will become weakly entangled with its maintenance systems and as a result its deprival value will be in excess of its buying in price because knowledge of any new plane in use has to be acquired over time and effective maintenance protocols developed before full efficiency in that aspect of the asset's management can be captured. However, the degree of entanglement represented by an enterprise resource planning system or at another level by the relationships established by the firm with its customers and suppliers can be a significant source of company value. At this level any disturbance with one relationship is likely to cause disruption to the whole network and ultimately the ability of the firm to create value.

FINANCIAL REALITY

At the peak of the 2005 holiday season British Airways found itself embroiled in an industrial dispute with its catering supplier, GateGourmet. Here is how The Times described the situation:

> At lunchtime on Wednesday, Dave Siegel was alone in a meeting room at Heathrow's Hilton hotel with Tony Woodley. Six days of talks between Siegel's company, GateGourmet, and Woodley's Transport and General Workers' Union had made slow progress, and now the two men were trying to work out a deal without distractions.
>
> The stakes were high. Exactly a week earlier, the company had sacked 650 workers when a festering industrial-relations problem erupted into the open. Sympathy strikes by British Airways workers grounded the airline, stranding more than 100,000 passengers. Little-known GateGourmet, the world's second-largest provider of airline meals, had overnight become a household name.
>
> With the resumption of BA flights last week, the public thought the crisis was over. But it was only a hiatus. In reality, GateGourmet's UK operations were spiralling towards collapse, with potentially nasty consequences for BA.
> THE TIMES BUSINESS FOCUS: DOG'S DINNER AUGUST 21 2005

What BA had not appreciated when it outsourced its in-flight catering activity to GateGourmet was that many of the sacked workers were husbands, wives or partners of the baggage handlers, check-in and other staff who worked for BA.

British Airways had thought outsourcing was a smart move but they had not anticipated the network effect and how disastrously it would work against them. They had seen outsourcing as an opportunity to slash over £70 million from its expenditures over the term of its five year contract with GateGourmet, the cost of this dispute in terms of lost business and trust in the 'world's favourite airline' could easily trump that sum many times over. The most obvious lesson here is that BA had not appreciated quite how deeply its assets (in house and outsourced) were entangled with one another, nor did they recognize the risk to which they were exposing themselves across their whole asset network by relying upon one outsourcing contract.

As a rule high prepotency assets are generally weakly entangled and are easy to value. The value of such assets will either equal or closely approximate their market price. Low prepotency assets are generally highly entangled and are likely to have a value in use which is many orders higher than the replacement cost the original assets concerned, if indeed they can be replaced at all.

Sufficiency

At each level of the asset hierarchy there needs to be sufficient availability of the underlying assets to permit the growth in value at the higher level. A firm must have sufficient cash (but no more) to release growth at the higher levels. As cash is generated in excess of that which is sufficient for its value generation purposes it should be returned to its investors. If an airline finds itself with more aeroplanes than it needs then they should be sold releasing resource for other use. At any of the value levels within the firm we can express sufficiency in different ways:

1 Insufficiency for survival which is where an asset level has been damaged, undermined or lost to the point that the firm has insufficient at that level to allow the higher levels of asset value to be created or to emerge.

2 Sufficiency for zero growth which is where an asset is just sufficient to maintain the value of the super-ordinate assets of the firm but insufficient to allow their development.

3 Sufficiency for the firm's current rate of growth. This is where the firm has just sufficient assets at a given level to maintain the current level of value growth within the firm but no more.

4 Sufficiency for the planned rate of growth: this is where there is sufficiency of the asset concerned to support the rate of growth set by the firm in its current business plans and budgets.

5 Sufficiency for extraordinary levels of growth: this is where the available capacity of the assets held offers future expansion options and opportunities for the exploitation of new markets.

The trick of course is that, following the prepotency idea and the ordering that results, the overall growth of the firm is constrained by the lowest level of sufficiency in the asset resources the firm holds.

Emergence

The final property of asset growth that the MAKENT© model points to is the concept of 'emergence'. The idea here is based upon the Hayek, Coase and Williamson notion of adaptation briefly outlined earlier in this chapter and which underpins the 'economizing' approach and indeed much of our discussion of real options. Because of the relative lack of market power, which characterizes all but the largest firms in a particular industry, management can never predict the full nature of all future investment opportunities and the magnitude of their Net Present Values. As a result management must make their Net Present Value 'luck' by having in position the resources and the adaptability to respond to profitable opportunities as they arise. What matters is not so much the firm's purpose but its 'fitness for purpose'. It achieves this state of asset readiness by minimizing its costs of transacting at all levels and in particular minimizing those costs relating to the changing the fixed means of production (change costs), changing the location of operating resources (logistic costs) and control costs (Ryan, 2001).

From the point of view of asset creation the economizing approach sees the creation of value as much an emergent phenomenon as a deliberate process of planning and strategic selection. The message of the MAKENT© model becomes even more blunt at the higher asset orders: management cannot deliberately create trust in its products without ensuring appropriate investment at lower levels – indeed direct investment in, for example, brand enhancement without ensuring that the capacity to deliver what is promised is almost certainly counterproductive and value destroying.

Asset growth – good and bad

Growth is only valuable if it leads to an increase in the Net Present Value of the firm overall. The promise of an increase in the reported earnings of the firm or indeed an improvement in the return on equity (or total capital) employed does not necessarily mean that the underlying asset growth is value adding. Indeed, asset growth can be value destroying if the rate of return delivered is lower than the firm's opportunity cost of capital. The problem that the MAKENT© model highlights is that value creation at the level of the firm can only be achieved by the appropriate development of the firm's asset base throughout its entire ordering. This leads to a useful categorization of investment.

Value enhancing Where new investment supported by a sufficiency of assets of the correct type and mix elsewhere leads to the creation of new positive Net Present Value business.

Value enabling Where new investment releases potential for growth in higher order assets previously constrained by insufficiency at a lower level.

Value sustaining Where new investment is required within the total structure of assets required to maintain the value generation of the whole.

Using the MAKENT© model

The MAKENT© model can be employed as a strategic reasoning tool helping management to think about the positioning of their asset investment and the priorities

EXHIBIT 11.4

The MAKENT© model

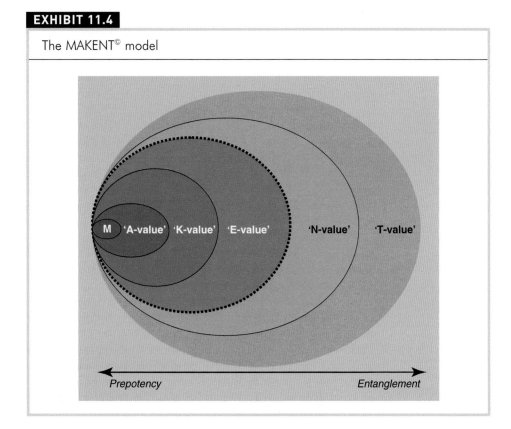

they should pursue to maximize the value advantage from their investment portfolio. Here is one approach to the development of a metrication system for the model which is based upon an analysis of the potency of the different asset classes in driving firm value within a given industrial grouping and a sufficiency analysis which investigates the extent to which a given firm's current levels of asset investment are sufficient to sustain growth.

Potency analysis

The first step is to identify within each of the MAKENT© levels a small number of useful subclassifications. Under monetary assets for example it would make sense to split the category into capital and monetary resources, the real assets into operational and structural and so forth. The fineness of detail can be adjusted as the model is developed in a particular application.

Then, using external sources (supply and demand side as well as analysts and other industry experts) the 'potency' of each asset class and subclass is assessed in terms of its ability to drive value. This opinion can be quantified in a number of ways – one approach is by obtaining a preference vote from those consulted where each is invited to distribute (say) 1000 points across the various alternatives. This can be achieved by a simple importance scale (1–10) which is converted to a potency score for each asset classification as follows:

$$Potency\ score = \frac{score\ (1-10)\ under\ each\ heading}{total\ score\ for\ all\ headings} \times 1000$$

FINANCIAL REALITY

Jack Grinder was aware that his company was taking a big step forward with its expansion plans and he had high hopes of its success and in particular the new developments at Grumbleton. However, he had become concerned over the last 12 months that the high rates of growth in his early years as CEO had not been sustained. Years of investment in new product development and production had been successful but never quite achieving the results that he had hoped for. Gloria had been a great help and it was through her that he had learned about the MAKENT© model. He had asked John Towser a recent appointment from one of the UK's best business schools to undertake an investigation. John, or Bozzo to his friends, had proved himself already, he was a first class facilitator and decision maker and, critically, he was very adept at synthesizing the views of others into a consensus agreement.

The first task Bozzo set himself as he started work on this new project was to obtain a consensus on the subclassifications of the MAKENT© model that most readily captured the value drivers of the business. At the end of his analysis he had achieved a scoring of the potency of the MAKENT© asset classifications at delivering value in the type of business in which Friendly Grinders was engaged.

In this exercise a uniform rating scale was used in order to calculate the scores. It is possible to 'stretch' the extremities of the scale by using a non-linear weighting system for transferring the suggested level into the distribution of the thousand points.

Jack and his board reviewed this stage of the analysis and while surprised at some of the results accepted the logic of the various judgements. They also noted that the results were in broad agreement with the 'Measures that Matter' study that had been undertaken by Ernst & Young's Centre for Business Innovation in 1997.

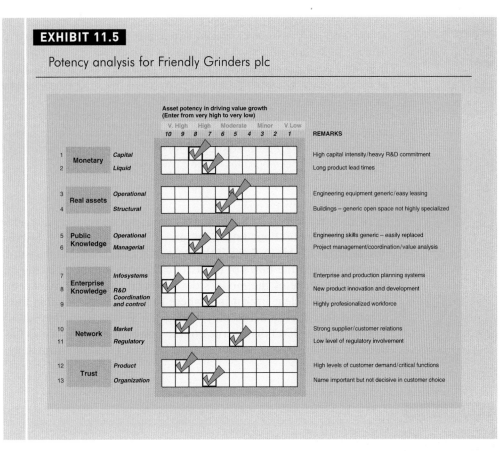

EXHIBIT 11.5

Potency analysis for Friendly Grinders plc

The value of this stage of the exercise is that it brings into the decision/judgement process external opinion on the importance of the various components of the firm's asset resource in driving value. Empirical evidence on the importance of different asset classes in driving firm value is very scarce and the original CBI studies suggest a wide variation in practice between one industry and another. The CBI (1997) report suggests that R&D, for example (an E asset component within the MAKENT© framework) is critical for driving value in the pharmaceutical business but is of much lower significance in the computer, food industry and oil and gas sectors.

Sufficiency analysis

The objective of this stage of the analysis is to undertake an asset audit at each level of the MAKENT© structure distinguishing between asset capability within the scale ranging from 'sufficient for failure' through to 'sufficient for extraordinary levels of growth'. In the metrication method chosen at Friendly Grinders a 10 point scale was used for assessing sufficiency under each heading and the audit focused upon the capability, constraints, contingency and costs of the pool of assets concerned. At this stage of the MAKENT© audit there is no *a-priori* consideration concerning the relative importance of each asset category or subclass.

Finally, once the sufficiency and potency audit is complete an index scaled from −1 to +1 can be created:

$$\text{Sufficiency index} = \text{potency score} \times \text{sufficiency score}$$

At the end of the analysis Bozzo produced a summary analysis as shown in Exhibit 11.6 advising that the asset priorities were that the firm's liquidity problems were now a binding constraint upon its development and indeed were at a level which would threaten the survival of the business in the short term. In addition the liquidity constraints were such that any further asset development would be very difficult to sustain and this was supported by the low levels of capital availability. The two other binding constraints on the company's development were the adequacy of its management team and the low level of investment and development of the firm's information systems.

In many respects this type of analysis does not reveal the value added by any given investment proposal but rather the priorities for investment. Subsequent stages of development of this tool entail the refinement of metrics to measure the firm's performance across the range of the asset categories identified by the model. However, even at this stage of the model's development the senior management of Friendly Grinders had a clear insight into where the problems lay within the firm. It may be objected that the model is only telling the Board what they should have known already – at one level that is true but the power of models such as this is that it helps decision making by reconstructing their knowledge of their firm in more useful ways.

EXHIBIT 11.6

Sufficiency analysis for Friendly Grinders plc

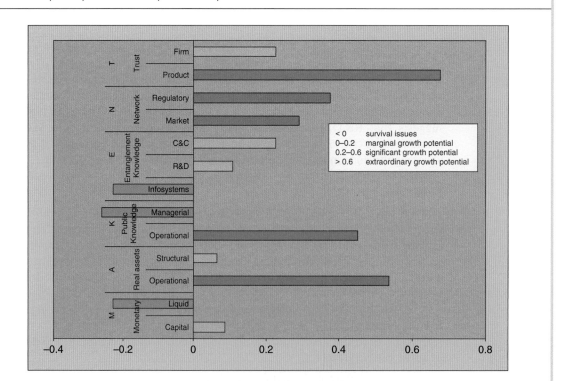

Managerial models of investment appraisal

If we accept that management effort in decision making is in itself a value adding activity we need to make sure that the managerial processes we prescribe:

1 Recognize the strategic importance of the intangible aspects of the investment decision and the options for hedging strategic risk (strategic impact assessment).

2 Capture the firm wide financial implications of the alternatives under scrutiny (financial impact assessment).

3 Recognize the uncertainty which attaches to those alternatives (the risk assessment profile).

4 Identify the options open to management and the opportunities for hedging both operational risks.

Two techniques can help in establishing the managerial processes described in Exhibit 11.7 scenario planning and the Financial Appraisal Profile (FAP) Model.

Scenario planning

Scenario planning is a general methodology which allows managers to speculate upon, analyze and prepare for a range of alternative futures. In capital investment appraisal it forms a context in which particular investment decisions can be undertaken. It does not replace the formal techniques already discussed within this book but is a useful

EXHIBIT 11.7

Summary of the four components in the managerial process model of capital budgeting

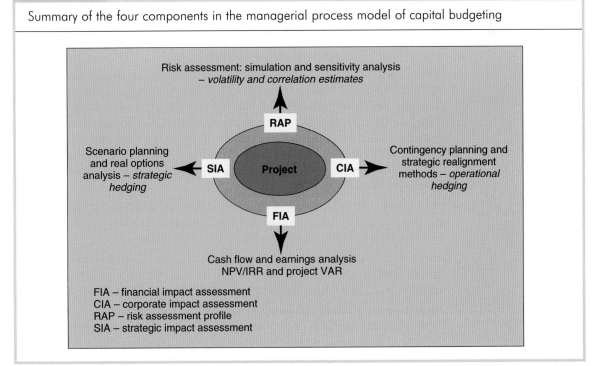

FIA – financial impact assessment
CIA – corporate impact assessment
RAP – risk assessment profile
SIA – strategic impact assessment

precursor to any definition of the real options available to the firm or, indeed, the definition of the strategic and risk components of the FAP model.

Scenario planning commences from the basis of the firm's current position and puts the question what possible future states of the world can be derived from the existing business model? A scenario is coherent narrative defining a business environment in which the firm could find itself. A scenario may or may not appear unlikely but it must be both plausible and logically derivable from present circumstances. A scenario is neither a prediction nor a forecast although when alternative scenarios are investigated they may be underpinned by more detailed forecasts using a wide variety of techniques. Advocates of scenario planning also suggest that scenarios should challenge the existing mindset within the firm and present an opportunity for the firm to both engage with, and learn about the future.

In essence, scenario planning is a brainstorming technique which follows a loose prescriptive methodology in its application:

1 A team of managers is brought together led by a facilitator with a brief to seek out a range of plausible scenarios as they can. Nothing is ruled in or ruled out although the only condition is that each scenario must follow logically from the current situation.

2 The group, in exploring scenarios will work through their common assumptions and ensure that they have a clear understanding of the firm's current position and the constraints upon it. At this stage it is important to capture the 'scenario in use'. This scenario is the narrative which integrates the common set of assumptions about the future held by management; it may be embedded within the current business plan or articulated within other strategic planning exercises undertaken by the firm.

3 As future scenarios are articulated they are analyzed for:
 (i) logical coherence,
 (ii) plausibility,
 (iii) strategic fit with the organization's aspirations and goals,
 (iv) potential for future options for change.

4 Within each scenario, as it is developed, certain common structures will emerge, there will be what Hodgson (2003) describes as 'predetermined elements' such as population statistics, 'driving forces' such as increasing globalization of financial markets and 'current trends'. Current trends are the more proximate movements, for example, in exchange rates and interest rates. As these structures emerge the team should seek to establish turning points where alterative scenarios could emerge and identify the signals that such turning points are imminent.

5 At this stage the groups should seek to integrate their defined scenarios creating a series of future timelines which articulate, usually, no more than four or five possible scenario timelines should be developed.

6 Along each scenario timeline the management team will seek to define the various options which present themselves, the likely impact of intervening variables as each scenario unfolds, and the future outcomes for the firm.

7 Subgroups are given timeframes to explore. The timeframes will be dictated by the planning horizons of the firm which to a certain extent depend upon the type of business in which the firm is engaged. However, the normal split

between near, middle, and distant future is sufficient for most purposes. Each group will seek to build the narrative within their time frame of each of the candidate scenarios.

8 The subgroups will reconvene to integrate their work building a narrative for each scenario describing:

(i) key elements of each scenario as it unfolds,

(ii) the likely impact upon the firm,

(iii) the options available,

(iv) the turning points in each scenario, and

(v) the signals of change.

9 The group will then seek to develop a core strategy which is designed to work across all scenarios and contingent scenario specific strategies which would only be successful if a particular scenario were to emerge.

Although a general methodology, the scenario planning exercise can lead to the definition of different layers of capital expenditure:

- Core investment which is designed to support all future scenarios: investment in knowledge systems and information processing is a clear example of this type of investment. Such investment is likely to be on creating assets which enhance the organization's ability to adapt and to capture new business opportunities. This investment is likely to be of low relative risk.

- Scenario specific investment which is designed to capture value within the boundaries of specific business scenarios as they emerge.

- Contingent specific investment which is designed to capture value by engineering turning points or the firm's ability to exploit those turning points as they arise.

The wide popularity of scenario planning methods reflects partly the ease with which they can be applied, the marketing power of the consultancies that 'sell' them and in the longer run their usefulness to firms who sell them as products to time strapped management. Scenario planning can be particularly useful in established firms (and not for profit organizations) whose senior team have become locked into their current ways of thinking and who are prone to what Janis and Mann (1977) referred to as 'groupthink'. Indeed, it is this problem which scenario planning, the MAKENT© model and our next and final managerial model are (in part at least) designed to overcome.

The financial appraisal profile model

The financial appraisal profile model (FAP) is a systematic attempt to bring together the strategic, financial and risk implications within investment appraisal: into a single modelling framework. Unlike conventional investment, FAP appraisal techniques focus as much on optimizing the managerial processes involved in corporate investment decision making as on refining investment appraisal techniques. A key insight within FAP is that value is gained through the rigour of the processes of forecasting and testing data and assumptions as it is through designing greater abstraction into the modelling process.

The FAP model requires management to work upon three parallel streams of activity:

1 A financial appraisal which leads to the Net Present Value profile. The NPV profile is simply an array of the Net Present Value, discounted payback, the discounted payback index and the marginal growth rate of the project (see Chapter 2 for the mechanics of producing each of these project statistics). These statistics, the authors of the FAP model claim, give a rounded view of the value added and the 'liquidity' of the project. High project liquidity is required to enable the expansion and redeployment, real options and indices such as the discounted payback and the discounted payback index are simple indicators of the flexibility offered by a given project.

2 *A strategic review which leads to a strategic index.* The implementation of the model requires the firm to define its strategic priorities by creating a corporate ranking (CR) of the strategic benefits it expects to get from any given project on a 1–10 scale. Once the scale values have been produced weights are then produced (the total of which add to one) showing the relative importance of each strategic benefit. The strategic index is then created for a given project as follows: first, using a team based approach, a 'project strategic score value' (PSSV) is created by identifying the extent to which the project offers 'strategic benefits' to the firm (again a score against each perceived benefit is awarded on a 1–10 scale). Second, agreement is achieved on the PSSV score across the project team by an iterative process using a 'quasi-delphi' technique which is designed to eliminate (as far as possible) undesirable aspects of group decision making such as 'group-think'. Once the PSSV is established then combining the corporate ranking with the result will give the strategic index on a range from 1–10.

3 *The project risk profile.* This aspect of FAP requires the determination of the following modelling components: a risk impact value and probability, a corporate risk threshold (CRT), a disutility impact value (DIV) and a department risk value (RV). These are combined to give an overall risk area index (RAI). The logic of the four components of the analysis is straightforward: the assessment of the impact of the risk is multiplied by its probability of occurrence to obtain a risk impact by area. These risk values are modified by the disutility factor and combined to produce a risk value for the project as a whole. The disutility factor represents the degree of aversion to risk by both departments affected by the project within the firm and for the firm as a whole.

Exhibit 11.8 shows how each of the three different elements of the FAP model integrate with one another.

Case study: applying the FAP model

Jack Grinder has been talking to his bank about his firm's capital funding requirements and Gloria, his lending manager, is proving yet again to be very helpful. His primary interest is in securing a deal for £19.1 million of finance to support project OG05/06/01. This project is for a new computer controlled precision laser for cutting mirrors for scientific instruments. The market for high specification mirrors in telescopes and other applications is growing rapidly.

EXHIBIT 11.8

The FAP model

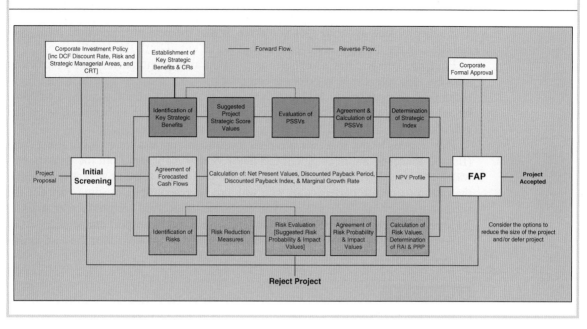

Gloria had attended a seminar in Manchester given by one of the authors of the FAP and had been very impressed. Exhibit 11.9 shows the current NPV analysis as undertaken by the firm's finance office and as corrected by Jack.

The installation of the new laser grinder will have a profound impact upon the productivity of the production department. It will mean far lower set up costs and shorter production times for each new job and allow the company to be much more flexible in its approach to meeting its customer requirements in building complex, multicomponent mirror arrays for the new generation of orbital telescopes. In addition, the new laser grinding facility will substantially reduce the environmental dust and the usage of large quantities of water-based lubricants associated with the old processes.

EXHIBIT 11.9

The financial appraisal for project OG05/06/01

Project OG05/06/01	0	1	2	3	4	5	6	7
Operating cash flows before tax		6.450	6.550	4.340	4.221	4.200	2.110	
Tax on the operating cash flows			−1.935	−1.965	−1.302	−1.266	−1.260	−0.633
Operating cash flow less tax		6.450	4.615	2.375	2.919	2.934	0.850	−0.633
Project outlay	−19.100							
FYA		5.730						
Project cash flow	−19.100	12.180	4.615	2.375	2.919	2.934	0.850	−0.633
Discounted cash flow at 7.92 per cent	−19.100	11.286	3.962	1.890	2.152	2.004	0.538	−0.371
Net Present Value of project flows	**2.361**							

The new process will be much cleaner from an environmental perspective and will lead to more comfortable working conditions for the staff involved. Since Gloria had been working on Jack's 'feminine side' he had come to appreciate the importance of maintaining a healthy working environment for his staff as well as for the directors. The only problem, as far as Jack could see, is that the new process would mean special training for the staff involved and that would entail both time and money.

Friendly Grinders has a very strong position as a 'niche player' in its particular markets although there is growing competition from the new South Indian high-technology companies. Jack is sure, however, that their technological lead will only be enhanced by the acquisition of the laser grinder although in business, as on the golf course, a substantial lead is always difficult to maintain.

Jack decides to put together a capital investment appraisal team again using John (Bozzo) Towser as an independent facilitator. Senior managers from the departments within the optical group affected will also form part of the team as well as representatives from corporate departments who will also be responsible, in some part, for the success or otherwise of the project. The departments involved are production, marketing, environmental, public relations, human resources and transport and logistics.

Seven key strategic benefits have been established by the board for the assessment of capital projects. They are:

EXHIBIT 11.10

The seven key strategic benefits

Strategic benefit	CR
1 Production flexibility and responsiveness	9
2 Market leadership in terms of product quality and design	10
3 Logistical efficiency	9
4 Developmental potential	10
5 Organizational efficiency	7
6 Growth potential	10
7 Environmental impact and sustainability	6

The board when drawing up their list of strategic benefits applied a corporate ranking on a scale of one to ten indicating how important they felt each benefit would be to the future development of the firm. The board then turned its attention to its assessment of the specific risk attaching to projects and identified the following risk management areas: operations, marketing, environment, human resources, and logistics. It also determined a corporate risk threshold (CRT) of 7.5 to reflect (out of 10) the maximum level of risk it was prepared to accept across all areas. The board struggled with the concept of a disutility factor but accepted the need that extreme values should be given greater importance in the assessment than values within each midrange.

In the end, the board accepted Jack's proposal for a simple formula to take into account the DIV factor. The board also agreed that 7.92 per cent was an appropriate cost of capital given Jack's extensive analysis and the current situation in the capital markets.

The FAP protocol

A few days after the board meeting, a file containing the project proposal documents was sent to Bozzo and to the other members of the capital investment appraisal team.

The enclosed PRP and SI forms required each team member to identify the specific risks relating to their own area of responsibility and the specific strategic benefits that they could identify within the current project in as far as they impacted upon them.

Four weeks later the completed FAP documents were returned. Each member of the investment appraisal team had done a reasonable job of identifying the relevant risk areas, had provided some justification for each, and provided estimates of the likely probability of the risk occurring and the anticipated impact that each risk element would have on the project as a whole. In line with the FAP protocol each of the team members worked on their documentation independently and were required not to discuss their judgement with other team members. This approach is what is often referred to as a quasi-Delphi technique in decision making and forecasting. Strictly, within the Delphi technique, participants in the process should not be known to one another.

In two further iterations, Bozzo collated the information on the returned forms making comments on the risks and strategic benefits identified, noting and clarifying issues that were either unclear or ambiguous. At each stage, team members were asked to enter probability and impact values for the risk areas identified by other members.

Once the quasi-Delphi stage of the FAP protocol was completed Bozzo called a team meeting for one week later. At this meeting all the extreme values were debated and in some case modified and a wide-ranging discussion followed leading to some modification in the estimates provided by team members of their PRP and SI values.

One further meeting was conducted a week later for team members to resolve outstanding issues and at that point Bozzo and Jack were able to complete the FAP documentation.

Calculation of the Net Present Value profile

The Net Present Value profile consists of five estimated values: the project's Net Present Value, its discounted payback the discounted payback index, the marginal growth rate and an estimate of the average annual discounted value of the abandonment values for the first two years (see Exhibit 11.11). The board had decided that abandonment was only likely within the first two years if on technological grounds the

---

EXHIBIT 11.11

The NPV profile – basic calculations

Project OG05/06/01

	0	1	2	3	4	5	6	7
Project cash flow	−19.1000	12.1800	4.6150	2.3750	2.9190	2.9337	0.8500	−0.6330
Discounted cash flow at 7.92 per cent	−19.1000	11.2861	3.9625	1.8895	2.1519	2.0040	0.5380	−0.3713
Cumulative discounted cash flows	−19.1000	−7.8139	−3.8514	−1.9618	0.1901	2.1941	2.7322	2.3609
Net Present Value of project flows	**2.3609**							
Discounted payback				**3.9117**				
Discounted payback index	**1.1236**							
Marginal growth rate	**1.6789**							

Abandonment values		14.6000	9.0000					
Average discounted abandonment values	10.6280							
Proportion of capital cost	55.64%							

equipment proved unable to achieve the high specifications demanded of it. The abandonment value did not include any estimates for market failure because the board was convinced, on the basis of its existing order book that it was very unlikely that abandonment would be brought about because of lack of potential sales.

The project risk profile

The various team meetings resulted in a statement showing the calculation of the agreed risk probabilities and impact values for each of eight key risk elements identified by the team. Each management area was asked to assign a probability and an impact value to each of the risk elements. These probabilities are independent assessments of the perceived likelihood of the particular peril occurring. In order to cope with the impact of extreme values upon the firm a simple disutility function was defined:

$$DIV = I \times (1 + d) + (I \times d)^2$$

where d is a percentage reflecting the degree of disutility for larger rather than smaller impact values (I).

The board agreed that 10 per cent would represent an appropriate rate. The effect of this function on impact values is shown in Exhibit 11.12.

The table of agreed values to go into the risk profiling component within FAP model are shown in Exhibit 11.13. The probabilities and impact values provided by the responsible area concerned are highlighted. In calculating average values some additional weight may be given to reflect the greater expertise and indeed responsibility for the risk element concerned. In implementing the FAP procedure the board weighed up the pros and cons of a special weighting for specific areas of responsibility but decided against it. This decision was motivated by what they thought was the considerable likelihood that individual areas would overstate the impact of area specific risk on the project except of

EXHIBIT 11.12

Effect of the disutility factor upon impact values

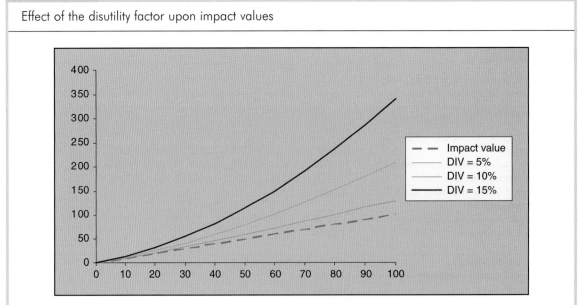

EXHIBIT 11.13

The risk profile

Calculation of the agreed risk probability and impact values for the key risk elements

	Management areas of responsibility – suggested values					Average Values	Coefficient of variation
	Operations	Marketing	Environment	Human Resources	Logistics		
Risk area (operations) (1) — Technological complexity							
Probability	0.25	0.18	0.2	0.35	0.5	**0.296**	**39.78%**
Impact	14	15	8	12	12	**12.2**	**19.67%**
DIV	17.36	18.75	9.44	14.64	14.64	**14.966**	**21.30%**
Risk area (operations) (2) — System maintenance							
Probability	0.4	0.35	0.45	0.5	0.5	**0.44**	**13.25%**
Impact	5	8	6	5	5	**5.8**	**20.11%**
DIV	5.75	9.44	6.96	5.75	5.75	**6.73**	**21.30%**
Risk area (marketing) (3) — Sales volume							
Probability	0.05	0.2	0.09	0.08	0.1	**0.104**	**48.88%**
Impact	30	45	24	25	35	**31.8**	**24.15%**
DIV	42	69.75	32.16	33.75	50.75	**45.682**	**30.07%**
Risk area (marketing) (4) — Delivery times							
Probability	0.05	0.05	0.02	0.08	0.06	**0.052**	**37.29%**
Impact	12	25	18	10	15	**16**	**32.83%**
DIV	14.64	33.75	23.04	12	18.75	**20.436**	**37.37%**
Risk area (Environment) (5) — Laser hazards							
Probability	0.05	0.01	0.1	0.04	0.04	**0.048**	**60.95%**
Impact	8	12	15	8	10	**10.6**	**25.03%**
DIV	9.44	14.64	18.75	9.44	12	**12.854**	**27.39%**
Risk area (Human Resources) (6) — Altered working practices							
Probability	0.1	0.15	0.1	0.1	0.16	**0.122**	**22.24%**
Impact	5	8	8	15	10	**9.2**	**35.98%**
DIV	5.75	9.44	9.44	18.75	12	**11.076**	**39.03%**
Risk area (Human Resources) (7) — Training							
Probability	0.03	0.05	0.05	0.05	0.02	**0.04**	**31.62%**
Impact	3	6	5	10	2	**5.2**	**53.57%**
DIV	3.39	6.96	5.75	12	2.24	**6.068**	**56.09%**
Risk area (Logistics) (8) — Technological complexity							
Probability	0.16	0.1	0.2	0.2	0.09	**0.15**	**31.55%**
Impact	5	3	8	6	6	**5.6**	**29.01%**
DIV	5.75	3.39	9.44	6.96	6.96	**6.5**	**30.23%**

Agreed $DIV = Impact(1 + 10\%) + (Impact \times 10\%)^2$

course, in those situations, where the area concerned was promoting the project being assessed. The board took the view that it was impossible to 'double guess' departmental motivations and biases and that no fixed rule could be applied.

Each risk element is summarized by an average value for the probabilities and impact values and the coefficient of variation calculated in each case (taken as the standard deviation of each probability or impact value divided by the respective mean). From the summarized results it was clear that a major area of concern appeared to be the ability of the new capital equipment to deliver the sales volume required to meet demand.

The next stage of the exercise was the calculation of the departmental risk values (RV) for each department. By multiplying the probability of the risk occurrence by the disutility value in each case an importance rating and risk value was calculated for each department and a total importance rating derived. Given that there are eight risk areas (n) identified in the analysis the risk value for each area is calculated as follows:

$$RV = \frac{rating}{n} \times -10$$

EXHIBIT 11.14

The departmental risk values

Departmental Risk Values (RV)

Details of Risk Element	Probability of occurrence	DIV	Importance Rating/RV
Operations			
Risk element 1	0.30	14.97	4.43
Risk element 2	0.44	6.73	2.96
Total importance rating			7.39
Operations risk area (RV)			**−9.24**
Marketing			
Risk element 3	0.10	45.68	4.75
Risk element 4	0.05	20.44	1.06
Total importance rating			5.81
Marketing risk area (RV)			**−7.27**
Environment			
Risk element 5	0.05	12.85	0.62
Total importance rating			0.62
Environment risk area (RV)			**−0.77**
Human Resources			
Risk element 6	0.12	11.08	1.35
Risk element 7	0.04	6.07	0.24
Total importance rating			1.59
Human Resources risk area (RV)			**−1.99**
Logistics			
Risk element 8	0.15	6.50	0.98
Total importance rating			0.98
Logistics risk area (RV)			**−1.22**

Bozzo Towser highlighted the departmental risk values as follows: first the area which presented the highest value overall (to give the risk area index (RAI)), second the risk element which presented the highest impact value upon the firm (and the degree of disagreement among team members about that value) and third, the risk element where there was the highest disagreement among the team members. These values are entered into the overall financial appraisal profile summary document (Exhibit 11.16).

The strategic index

The calculation of the project strategic score values was relatively straightforward compared with the problem of calculating the project's risk profile. Because the board had already identified seven strategic benefits and applied a corporate ranking to them all, what was left was for each departmental team to assess the project from their point of view under each of those seven headings. In this case it was decided to give more weight to the department for whom the strategic benefit concerned was most relevant. Double weight for example was given to the operations department in assessing the strategic score attaching to 'production flexibility and responsiveness'.

In Exhibit 11.15 the shaded values are those where strategic benefit is identified with a particular department. Each department was allowed to score each benefit on a scale one to ten, and then all the scores for the particular benefit were totalled doubling the value for the highlighted department. The project strategic score value was calculated as a simple average using the number of departments plus 1 in the case where just one department was team responsible for the benefit concerned and plus 2 in the case where two departments were involved.

Using the corporate rankings to form a weighted average of the PSSVs a strategic index of 8.31 (out of 10) was derived for this project.

The FAP summary

The FAP summary presents relevant facts and opinions concerning this project in a straightforward form for assessment by management. For this particular project it is clear that it offers a positive Net Present Value and a reasonably short discounted payback period. The rather low discounted payback index reflects the relatively low present value of future cash flows compared with the capital cost of the project and this, coupled with the very low marginal growth rate suggests that this project is only marginal financially. However the relatively high abandonment value may give the Board of Directors some comfort that if the project does not work out as planned that a substantial proportion of the initial outlay could be quickly recovered.

The highest risk area index at −9.24 suggests a significant level of risk within the operations department although the highest area risk impact is in marketing where achieving appropriate sales volume will be critical for the success of the project. The high probability attaching to system maintenance problems within the operations department is an area of concern and one where the company's management would seek to mitigate the risk in some way or other.

Finally, the project has a very high strategic index value of 8.31 which suggests that although the project may not yield highly in terms of its financial performance and does carry significant risk exposure that it would present an important strategic opportunity for the firm.

EXHIBIT 11.15

Calculation of the project strategic score values

Calculation of the project strategic score values	CR	operations	marketing
1 Production flexibility and responsiveness	9	10	9
2 market leadership in terms of product quality and design	10	9	9
3 logistical efficiency	9	9	7
4 developmental potential	10	8	9
5 organizational efficiency	7	9	8
6 growth potential	10	10	9
7 environmental impact and sustainability	6	9	8

Concluding comments on the FAP model

In a series of studies the FAP model was shown to have very high acceptability among professional managers (see Ryan and Lefley, 2005). It was perceived that the model captured the essential elements of corporate investment decision making and allowed management to focus on the most significant risk areas and the strategic benefits that the project would offer the firm. However, this type of modelling approach is based upon the assumption that subjective judgements can be reliably converted into numerical scores or index values. Intuitively, this would appear to be plausible, although there are question marks about the additivity of subjective estimates and the process of averaging which the model requires.

It is worth noting that the FAP model uses only very simple capital budgeting techniques and relies upon an absence of agency effects between team members working

EXHIBIT 11.16

The financial appraisal profile

The Financial Appraisal Profile
Project OG05/06/01 Computer Controlled Laser Grinder

Basic Data	Capital cost of the project	£19 100 000
	Cost of Capital	7.92%
	Estimated Life of Project	7 years
Financial	Net Present Value	£2 360 890
NPV Profile	Discounted Payback	3.912 years
	Discounted Payback Index	1.124
	Marginal Growth Rate	1.68%
	AV's classification	High
Project Specific Risk	Risk Area Index (operations)	−9.24
Project Risk Profile	Extreme Risk Impact: marketing (sales volume)	45.68
	Variance: risk element 5, environment	0.61
Strategic Benefits: strategic index		8.31

environmental	human resources	logistics	PSSV	weight of CR	Strategic index
8	7	7	8.50	0.15	1.25
9	8	7	8.50	0.16	1.39
8	7	8	7.83	0.15	1.16
8	9	8	8.43	0.16	1.38
8	7	8	7.83	0.11	0.90
7	7	8	8.57	0.16	1.41
9	7	8	8.33	0.10	0.82
			Strategic index=		**8.31**

the model and more senior management who are ultimately responsible for the decision. The case which is made for this type of procedure is that it enhances the quality of decision-making by, first of all, being more rigorous in the collection and presentation of opinions, but also by being more inclusive in its approach. The empirical studies on the acceptability of the technique suggest that it may have important side benefits apart from the decision-making process:

- It will enable management to make a more considered and persuasive case for funding for a given project. FAP sits naturally with the business planning process and could be a useful adjunct as the firm attempts to put together a case for acquiring further capital resources.
- With its supporting documentation it provides an important history of the decision-making process and allows more considered post project evaluations to be conducted. Given that relevant evidence is available concerning the judgements of individual areas within the firm this should lead to greater accountability as the project unfolds.

SUMMARY

In this chapter we have explored the problems of valuing the intangible assets of the firm. In so doing, we have attempted to obtain some financial precision in the analysis by using two techniques for valuing the hidden component of a firm's value. Although these techniques promise much we are still a very long way from being able to put financial values on the most relevant components of a firm's intangible asset structure. We then stepped aside from the rigours of financial analysis and considered two approaches to understanding the intangible structure of firms and their relative importance in driving firm value. Finally, we explored two process based techniques of capital investment appraisal. The first scenario planning allows the firm to understand, in a systematic way the alternative possibilities and future options available to it. The second technique attempts to harness the various dimensions of investment appraisal which we believe to be important to managers within a single profiling technique.

Further Reading

Barney, J.B. (1991) Firm resources and sustained competitive advantages. *Journal of Management*, 17:99–120.

CBI (1997) Measures that Matter. Since the closure of the Center for Business Innovation in 2003 this article is now hard to find. One source that requires registration is www.zdnet.co.uk.

Grant, R.M. (1991) The Resource-based Theory of Competitive Advantage: Implications for Strategy Formulation, *California Management Review*, 33:3

Grant, R.M. (2002) *Contemporary Strategy Analysis – Concepts, Techniques, Applications* New York: Blackwell Publishing.

Hall, R. (1992) The Strategic Analysis of Intangible Resources *Strategic Management Journal*, 13:135–144.

Hodgson, T. (2003) Strategic Thinking with Scenarios, www.Metabridge.com

Janis, I. and Mann, L. (1977) *Decision Making: A Psychological Analysis of Conflict, Choice and Commitment* New York: Free Press.

Low, J. (2000) The Value Creation Index, *The Journal of Intellectual Capital*, 1: 3:252–262.

Hand, J. and Lev, B. (eds) (2003) *Intangible Assets – values measures and risks*, Oxford: Oxford University Press.

Lev, B. (2001) *Intangibles, Management, Measurement and Reporting*, Washington DC: The Brookings Institute.

Mintz, S.L. (2000) The Second Annual Knowledge Capital Scorecard: a knowing glance, *CFO magazine*, February at www.CFO.com.

Ringland, G. (1998) *Scenario Planning: Managing for the Future*, New York: John Wiley & Sons.

Ryan, R.J. (2001) *Strategic Accounting for Management*, London: Thomson.

Ryan, R.J. and Lefley, F. (2005) *The Financial Appraisal Profile Model*, Basingstoke: Palgrave Macmillan.

Schoemaker, P.J.H. (1995) Scenario Planning: A Tool for Strategic Thinking. *Sloan Management Review*, Winter 1995:25–40.

Stewart, T.A. (2001) *The Wealth of Knowledge*, London: Nicholas Brealey.

van der Heijden, K., Bradfield, R., Burt, G., Cairns, G. and Wright, G. (2002) *The Sixth Sense: Accelerating Organizational Learning with Scenarios*, New York: John Wiley & Sons.

Venugopal, R. (1999) *Contemporary Strategic Management*, Delhi: Vikas Publishing House Pvt Ltd.

Wack, P. (1985) Scenarios: Shooting the Rapids, *Harvard Business Review*, November/December: 139–150.

Wernerfelt, B. (1984) A Resource-based View of the Firm, *Strategic Management Journal*, 5:171–180.

Williamson, O.E. (1991) Strategising, Economising and Economic Organisation, *Strategic Management Journal*, Winter 12:75–94.

PROGRESS CHECK

1 Give two reasons why the accounting profession might be reluctant to incorporate non-purchased intangibles in the annual financial reports of a firm.

2 Value advantage and a competitive advantage are closely related concepts. However what disagreement between corporate strategists does this conceptual distinction reflect?

3 What are the four key attributes of value base management?

4 How is Calculated Intangible Value measured and what other important financial metric does it closely resemble?

5 How are the three subcomponents of earnings decomposed by Lev's Knowledge Earnings method capitalized?

6 List the nine categories of non-financial performance identified within the Value Creation Index.

7 What four asset attributes underpin the MAKENT© model?

8 How are the concepts of prepotency and entanglement related in the hierarchy of asset value defined by the MAKENT© model?

9 What are the six asset categories within the MAKENT© model?

10 Outline the steps involved in a scenario planning exercise.

11 What in outline are the three component parts of the Financial Appraisal Profile model?

12 List possible advantages of the Financial Appraisal Profile model compared with conventional investment appraisal techniques.

QUESTIONS (answers at end of book)

1 The earnings before interest and tax of a company in the food retail sector are £41 million per annum and the tax rate on company profits is 30 per cent. The average return on real assets employed in the sector is 15 per cent and the assets employed in the company concerned are carried in the balance sheet at £100 million. The expected growth rate in its earnings is 4 per cent per annum and the company's cost of capital is 8 per cent.

You are required to:

(i) Estimate the Calculated Intangible Value for this business.

(ii) Suggest the principal components of the intangible value of a company of this type.

(iii) Discuss the advantages and disadvantages of the CIV measure for calculating intangible value.

QUESTIONS (answers on website)

2 Nucleon plc, is a little known company producing high pressure valves in the energy supply industries. The rate of technological change in the industry is fast moving and the company invests 10 per cent of turnover each year in research and development of new products. Currently the forward earnings of the business are £70 million and its current weighted average cost of capital is 7.5 per cent. The firm currently holds £5 million of net monetary assets and £180 million of real assets. Short term growth is expected to be of the order of 12 per cent per annum for four years declining to the long run, underlying rate of growth of 5 per cent within ten years. The current risk free rate of return is 5 per cent, and using Lev's estimates of the rate of return on real assets of 7 per cent and on intangible assets of 10 per cent:

(i) Calculate the value of the firm's investment in intangible assets.

(ii) Compare and contrast the assumptions within the Lev model with other models that claim to measure the value of intangible investment within the firm.

(iii) What are the advantages of using the LEV approach to the capitalization of intangibles rather than simply deducting from the capitalized value of earnings a charge for the employment of monetary and real assets respectively?

3 A large established company which is a household name for the provision of a wide range of domestic cleaning goods is considering employing a firm of consultants who undertake brand valuation using the Interbrand methodology. They have been advised that alternative approaches are available for putting a value on the intangible assets of the firm. In what way is the Interbrand approach different from other methods of intangible valuation and what would be the benefit to a company of obtaining a brand valuation by these means?

4   A company has completed the following potency analysis for the subdivisions of its asset structure suggested by the MAKENT© model.

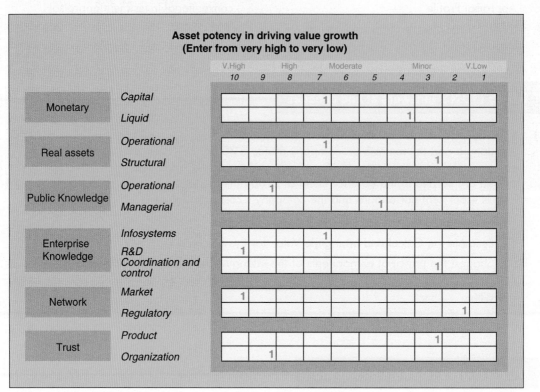

Asset potency in driving value growth
(Enter from very high to very low)

		V.High		High	Moderate			Minor			V.Low
		10	9	8	7	6	5	4	3	2	1
Monetary	Capital				1						
	Liquid							1			
Real assets	Operational				1						
	Structural								1		
Public Knowledge	Operational		1								
	Managerial						1				
Enterprise Knowledge	Infosystems				1						
	R&D	1									
	Coordination and control								1		
Network	Market	1									
	Regulatory									1	
Trust	Product								1		
	Organization		1								

An audit of the firm's resources reveals that its monetary assets, operational and managerial assets are sufficient for planned levels of growth while trust in the firm's products is on the cusp between sufficiency for zero growth and sufficiency for current growth. There is a perceived deficiency in the firm's operational knowledge base and its information systems. Research and development is revealed to be just sufficient to maintain the current level of growth but no more. All the other asset levels appear to be sufficient for superior levels of growth over the longer run.

You are required:

(i) Using the above data to propose a plan of action for boosting the firm's overall level of growth prioritizing those areas where the maximum early gains in performance could be achieved.

(ii) Discuss the advantages and disadvantages of techniques such as the MAKENT© model in setting an agenda for management investment decision making.

5   The FAP model attempts to integrate various aspects of the investment decision making process within a simple profile. To what extent does this approach absolve the company from the problem of measuring directly the impact of project specific risk upon the value of an investment?

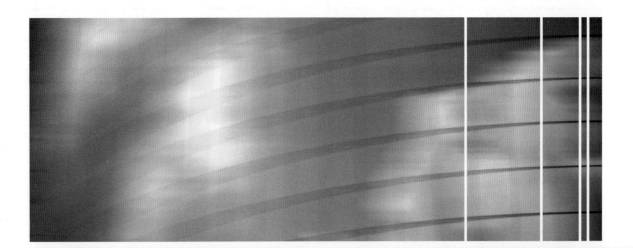

V | Corporate Financial Control

12 | Mergers and acquisitions

Mergers and acquisitions are possibly the most significant investment decision that any company will be required to make. An important lesson from the literature of this subject is that most acquisitions do not enhance shareholder value for the acquiring firm and indeed, in a significant proportion of cases, actually destroy value. In this chapter we explore some of the motivations for merger and acquisition activity by companies, the mechanisms for their accounting and most importantly, their implications for the value of the firm. What is not often appreciated is that significant acquisitions lead to a change in the value of the acquiring firm's pre-existing business. We will investigate this problem in some detail and come to the conclusion that the problem of valuation for the purposes of acquisition is not one of valuing the target firm, but rather one of revaluing the acquiring firm on the presumption that the acquisition proceeds.

Learning outcomes

By the end of this chapter you will be able to achieve the following:

1. Distinguish between friendly and hostile takeover bids and the way in which firms seek to defend themselves against the latter.
2. Describe the reasons why firms acquire other businesses.
3. Understand the broad regulatory principles which govern mergers and acquisitions.
4. Identify the most likely sources of finance for acquisitions of different size.
5. Create a simple consolidated balance sheet for two companies following acquisition.
6. Propose reasons why merger and acquisition activity tends to occur in waves.
7. Know the difference between the value added upon acquisition (VAA) and the control premium.
8. Explain the differences between the three broad classes of acquisition in terms of their impact upon the underlying risk of the firm.
9. Value a type III acquisition using the iteration function within Excel.
10. Determine the negotiation parameters for a bid to acquire another firm.

Introduction to mergers and acquisitions

Mergers and acquisitions occur when two firms decide to combine their businesses either by both businesses combining to create a new entity (merger) or by one purchasing a controlling stake in another business (acquisition). The opposite can also occur when a part of a business is 'spun off' or 'demerged'. The terms merger and acquisition from a technical point of view represent two different modes of business combination although in much of the research literature the term 'merger' is used to cover both.

Acquisitions are the more common form of business combination and it is with this type of activity that we will be most concerned in this chapter. An acquisition occurs when a company acquires more than 50 per cent of the shares of the target company. Once a company has more than 75 per cent it is able, under UK company law, to undertake the sorts of activities (e.g. change its name, change the purpose of its business) which require a special resolution of the shareholders. At that point the target company will also lose its listing under Stock Exchange rules. Once the company has more than 90 per cent of the equity it can enforce the purchase of the remaining shares from the minority investors.

Hostile bids and takeover defence

The large majority of takeovers are negotiated between the directors of the two firms involved and receive the support of the target firm's directors. Some, however, are resisted by the directors who believe:

1 That the acquisition is against the interest of their shareholders in that the offer price is too low given the value of the firm. In this respect they may believe that they can deliver higher value to investors in the longer run or they may believe that a return of capital to investors is possible via a share repurchase scheme. The implication of this line of reasoning is that the market has not efficiently priced the firm's shares and that by changing strategy the managers can improve the firm's market performance. For this argument to be sustainable, investors need to have confidence in their Board's ability to deliver improved shareholder value. In some cases this may be achieved by changes in the firm's senior management.

FINANCIAL REALITY

In May 2004, the entrepreneur Phillip Green started a battle to acquire control of Marks & Spencer, once the doyen of the high street but whose value had fallen over the previous three years. Green's initial offer valued at 370p was insufficient to convince the Board of M&S and their new Chief Executive Stuart Rose of the merits of the takeover. Rose had been appointed after heavy City pressure to remove Geoffrey Holmes the previous Chief Executive. Rose's appointment was well received by investors and put the M&S Board in a strong position to resist Green's advances. The third and final approach by Green amounted to a 400p offer in the form of 335p in cash and the balance in equity participation. The M&S Board's defence was that the offer under-valued the company even though the share price prior to the bid had been trading in the 260p–280p range. Investors took the view that Rose, who had been influential in turning around the fortunes of Green's Arcadia Group, would be able to extract more value from the ailing high street giant. They were no doubt influenced by Rose's promise to return £1 billion in cash

▶

to investors through a share repurchase scheme and to return the share price to more than 400p share. Less than 18 months later the company was trading at more than 425p per share in difficult retail conditions for the UK economy.

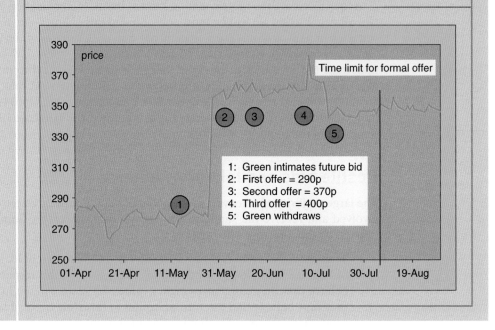

EXHIBIT 12.1

The price of Marks & Spencer plc ordinary shares over the time period of the offer for the company made by Phillip Green (May–June 2004)

1: Green intimates future bid
2: First offer = 290p
3: Second offer = 370p
4: Third offer = 400p
5: Green withdraws

2 That the acquisition is against the interests of management. Clearly many if not all of the managers in a firm subject to a hostile bid are likely to lose their jobs and the command over the perks that they enjoy. Given their vulnerability it is not surprising that managers attempt to resist the interests of the corporate raiders. Here are some of the resistance strategies that have been tried at some time or other (Exhibit 12.2).

EXHIBIT 12.2

Resistance strategies put forward by managers against hostile bids

Asset revaluation	Revalue the firm's assets – this assumes that the market has not efficiently priced the assets involved and is only limited to assets carried on the balance sheet.
Buyout	Launch a management buyout using debt; the 'leveraged buyout' (LBO).
Counter-bid (pacman defence)	Make a reverse bid for the predator – this is only viable where the predator is a public company with a diverse shareholding. Where the predator is largely owned by a single individual then this is unlikely to work.

Crown jewel defence	Where management sell off the firm's most valuable assets (or engage in sale and lease back as appropriate) thus reducing the attractiveness of the firm to potential predators.
Defensive bid	Where the company makes a bid designed to enlarge the company or diversify its interests such that it is less attractive to the predator company.
Dividends and share repurchases	By returning cash to shareholders the aim is to improve shareholder perceptions of the value in the company. The City Code (see below) does not permit repurchase schemes once an informal offer has been made.
Golden parachutes	Contractually committing to generous severance packages for management which would make the target less attractive in the eyes of the bidder.
Inflate profit forecasts	This tactic has to survive the credibility test unless the market is convinced that it is supported by a viable plan for improving revenue growth and/or cutting costs.
Poison pills	Issuing new types of finance (convertibles, mezzanine debt and other forms of intermediate finance) which would be expensive for a successful bidder to honour.
Regulatory defence	Invite investigation by the regulatory authorities on the basis that the acquisition would be uncompetitive and against the public interest.
White knights	Invite a counter bidder who is less likely to be hostile to the interests of management.

Many of these were developed during the wave of hostile bids in the US during the 1980s as nearly one third of all listed companies were subjected to a takeover attempt at some stage. In the UK, the City Code (see below) has largely prevented what are known as 'shark repellants' which include: 'poison pills', parachutes, the crown jewel defence and others which are in the naked interest of management and against the interests of the shareholders. Since the 1980s it has become more and more difficult to mount a hostile bid without the consent of the board of directors. Indeed, as we shall see later in this chapter, much of the current regulation is designed to regulate hostile bids and to circumscribe the tactics that can be used by either side in the battle.

Why acquire?

Why do firms acquire other businesses? In an efficient capital market it would seem highly likely that it will always be cheaper from the investors' point of view to gain the benefit of investment in two companies by combining them in a portfolio rather than for management to attempt to achieve the same result through

EXHIBIT 12.3

Diversification and integration strategies

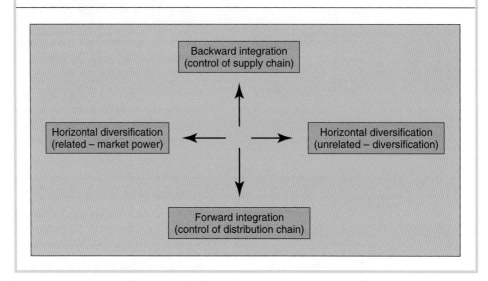

acquisition. It is also true that many acquisitions are likely to increase a firm's exposure to market risk rather than reduce it. If we accept the basic idea that investors are particularly concerned about this type of risk then this is likely to bring about a reduction in the equity value of the acquiring firm.

Here are some of the arguments that have been advanced for and against acquisitions.

Backward/forward integration Acquisition of companies up and down the supply chain allows a company to gain a greater slice of the industry value added. This can be achieved through economies in transacting, the capture of related technology, the reduction of risk in the supply chain or distribution network, and so on. However, the problem with integration strategies is that they are particularly likely to expose the firm to enhanced risk as the returns generated by suppliers and distributors are likely to be highly correlated with those of the acquiring company. From the perspective of market risk the beta of the company post acquisition (ignoring changes in gearing effects) will be a linear combination of the betas of the pre-acquisition company and its target. As a consequence investor perceptions of the risk of the acquiring company will change and with it their perception of its value.

However, this linear combination of risk assumes that prices and hence returns are solely influenced by market risk and that industry or firm specific factors are irrelevant. We know for our discussion of the capital asset pricing literature in Chapter 3 that this may be an optimistic assumption. The more proximate problem is that an increase in overall risk exposure may lead to a fall in the acquirer's credit rating with a commensurate increase in its cost of debt capital. This, combined with an increase in gearing in order to finance the acquisition may lead to a significant reduction in the capitalized value of the firm.

In its 2004 accounts Cobham plc had made further acquisitions continuing its strategy of growth, in its principal markets, by backward integration. The company has pursued a policy of acquiring key technology and know-how by the cash purchase of target companies many of whom it has developed ongoing business relationships over a number of years. None of these bids are hostile and are achieved by negotiation with the companies concerned.

EXHIBIT 12.4

Acquisitions undertaken by Cobham plc (financial year end 31 March 2005)

Name	Business Description	Consideration	Date Acquired	Country	Group Division
Precision Antennas Ltd	Design and manufacture of antenna systems for airborne, land based, satellite, vehicular, wireless and telecommunications.	£3.1m	January 2004	England	Chelton
Trade and Assets of Pentar Communications	Applications for use in the cabin and on the flightdeck of commercial aircraft including internet and email, in-flight entertainment, security, maintenance and system control.	C$3.2m C$0.6m deferred	March 2004	Canada	Chelton
NEC Aero SA	Design and manufacture of control panel face plates, lighting and signage for aircraft and vehicles.	€4.5m	April 2004	France	Chelton
DTC Communications Inc.	Design and manufacture of wireless communication equipment used in LENS.	US$48.0m US$0.2m deferred	April 2004	USA	Chelton
Spectronic Denmark A/S	Design and manufacture of wired and wireless audio communication products, as well as system level monitoring solutions, to government agencies and a select group of OEM manufacturers worldwide for LENS.	DKr225m	October 2004	Denmark	Chelton
Temex SA (Division)	Design and manufacture of ferrite and cavity components and the development and production of diodes principally for switching, alternator and multiplier applications, for use in military, space and telecom markets.	€7.7m	December 2004	France	Chelton

Horizontal integration From the investor's perspective horizontal integration will only be worthwhile from a portfolio point of view if one or more of the following conditions hold:

- The net effect is to reduce the firm's exposure to market risk. This implies that the weighted sum of the firm's betas will be less than the beta of the acquirer before acquisition.

- The integration of the two firms takes the combination to a size which is more efficient from a transaction cost perspective. What this means in practice is that the firm can gain advantage through managerial efficiencies of scale. If a firm is of efficient size from a transaction cost perspective and over-expands then managerial inefficiencies will reduce shareholder value and there will be considerable internal pressure within the firm to disaggregate.

- The integration of the two firms allows the acquirer to capture constrained resources which are blocking its growth more quickly than it could achieve by organic expansion. A firm which has an intensive research and development commitment and a portfolio of relatively young products may find it attractive to acquire a competitor which has a portfolio of products which are more mature in their life cycle and are more cash generative.

- Where a firm manages through acquisition to acquire a greater degree of monopoly power through market concentration. Although the Competition Commission of the European Union or the Member State is likely to examine any acquisition which threatens to reduce competition (see later) an acquirer may be able to argue the case for an acquisition on the grounds of the market power held by other firms in the industry.

FINANCIAL REALITY

Telefónica in £17.7bn deal with the UK's O2

Telefónica, Spain's biggest telecoms group, on Monday emerged with an agreed £17.7 bn ($31.4 bn) offer for the second largest UK mobile operator.

The all-cash deal is priced at £2 a share, a 22 per cent premium over Friday's closing price. It follows recent interest in O2 from KPN of the Netherlands and Deutsche Telekom of Germany. If completed, the deal will make Telefónica the world's second largest listed international telecoms group by market capitalisation, behind the UK's Vodafone. Analysts said on Monday that it might spark further consolidation in Europe. The move was partly motivated by the failure of an ambitious €5 bn share buyback programme to lift Telefónica's share price this year. On Monday the shares fell more than 2 per cent to €13.3, off a 12-month high of €14.5. O2 rose 25.3 per cent to 205¾p, up 41½p giving it a market capitalisation of £18.03 bn, above the Telefónica bid.

France Télécom's aggressive Orange brand is expected to intensify competition in Spain, where Telefónica has seen its market share halved since liberalisation. The Spanish operator has been eyeing O2 for at least a year, although it has never admitted to formal takeover talks. There were also high-level approaches to KPN. O2 will add 24.6 m clients in the UK and Germany to Telefónica's 90m-strong subscriber base, which is mainly in Latin America and Spain.

O2 was targeted for a takeover. Shareholders in O2 may well be excused for wondering what to do next. After Monday's 200p a share bid by Telefónica the question is whether another bidder is likely to emerge.

If the Telefónica bid is successful, Peter Erskine, O2's chief executive, could earn up to £7.5 m, assuming the company's remuneration committee allows him to exercise all his options. David Finch, chief financial officer, could receive up to £4 m.

The acquisition is expected to be completed in January. It will be financed via a bridging loan arranged by Goldman Sachs and Citigroup. Telefónica bonds weakened and, in the credit derivatives market, the cost of buying protection against the company defaulting rose about 13 per cent, or 6 basis points, to 50bp. O2 widened 2bp to 47bp. Standard & Poor's on Monday cut Telefónica's rating one notch to A– and warned it would cut it a further notch to BBB+ if the deal went through. FINANCIAL TIMES: OCTOBER 31 2005 EDITED EXTRACT

Synergistic effects The concept of 'synergy' was first introduced by Igor Ansoff (1962) who argued that firms, when they combine, should seek to create a whole which is greater than the sum of its parts. He used the memorable bit of maths: '2 + 2 = 5' which although doing some violence to the laws of arithmetic suggests that there is a possibility of gain in combination for firms which is not available if they act alone. What this suggests is that there are possibilities in aggregating firms which are not available to the individual investor who independently creates a portfolio of the two companies. When synergistic effects are being claimed as a benefit of integration the case needs to be made out on two grounds: first is it likely that the combined business will earn greater revenue than before? It may be, for example, that the two firms have complementary technologies that create future options for growth not available to either firm acting in isolation. It may be that the combined firm would have the power to access markets which are close to them as independent entities. However, revenue gains are often the easiest to overestimate and the hardest to realize. Second, is it likely that the combined business will be able to operate more cost efficiently than the two firms separately? As we will discuss later, increased size often brings about greater internal coordination costs and any potential cost savings through combined operation must be sufficient to defeat these 'deadweight' extra costs. Finally, it may also be the case that there are financial synergies in that the combined firm will be able to gain access to the capital market more readily than either firm on its own. Some of these synergies are straightforward, some are subtle – these we deal with later.

Tax and debt benefits On occasions an acquisition may be desirable for purely financial reasons. If a target company has tax losses from previous years, or capital allowances that cannot be fully absorbed by taxable profits, then an acquirer may be able to utilize those potential tax benefits to offset its own tax liabilities. Where a company has a loss making overseas subsidiary or unexpired capital allowances it may be beneficial to acquire a profitable company within that tax jurisdiction to offset those losses or capital allowances before consolidation. Much will depend upon the differences between the tax regime in the acquirer's base country compared with those of the target.

Where an acquirer and a target have complementary cash flows such that a negative correlation exists between them then a portfolio effect will arise giving an overall cash flow of lower volatility than the originals. The lower volatility attaching to the cash flow may improve the credit status of the combined company and thus reduce the company's overall cost of capital.

Window dressing If a company acquires a smaller firm with a lower P/E ratio than itself then, assuming that the market does not downgrade the value of its earnings, the increase in earnings on consolidation should generate a greater than proportionate increase in its share price. Likewise the acquisition of a firm which has a lower return on capital employed will tend to improve the reported returns for the acquirer on consolidation. However, from a financial perspective these effects can be considerably outweighed by other effects on its share value and its returns as we shall see later in this chapter.

REVIEW ACTIVITY 12.1 How would you classify the following acquisitions (backward or forward integration, related or unrelated diversification) and what might be the rationale?

1 Volkswagen acquire Skoda.
2 British Airways acquire British Airports Authority.
3 Telefónica acquire O2.
4 Diageo acquire Hilton.
5 Volkswagen acquire EuroDisney.

Note: some of these have happened, others have not. This should not be taken as any encouragement to any of the Boards of Directors of the companies named.

The transactions cost dimension to the acquisition decision

Enlarging a firm through either organic growth or more rapidly by acquisition may bring some economies of scale in management. However, these economies will only exist up to a certain point where further expansion will create more cost than benefit. This comes about for two broad reasons:

1 The relative advantage that a hierarchy has over open market transacting in terms of the number of implied contracts in the case of the former compared with number of actual contracts in the case of the latter required to coordinate production.

2 The transaction cost advantage of coordinating work within a hierarchy (implied contracting) compared with the transaction cost of setting up a sequence of coordinated market transactions (actual contracting).

Ronald Coase (1937) argued that creating or increasing the size of a firm is justified, as we have shown, where the frequency of a given transaction is high. However, firm based production has economic advantages where the assets employed are highly specific to the given job or the outcomes are uncertain and thus less straightforward to incorporate into a formal open market contract. So for certain types of economic transactions the cost advantage would tend to lie with firms owning the means of production rather than leaving the free market to do the job. For simple, infrequent low complexity business, open market transacting is likely to be more cost efficient. As we have discussed before, as the complexity, frequency or uncertainty rise the marginal cost of market transacting rise as well. Coase argued that a point can come where the additional benefit of coordinating the economic resources gained through enlarging the firm is exactly equal to the additional cost of contracting those resources through the open market. This extension of the marginality rule in economics determines the point of optimum size for the firm.

> '... *as a firm gets larger, there may be decreasing returns to the entrepreneur function, that is the costs of organising additional transactions within the firm may rise. Naturally a point must be reached where the costs of organising an extra transaction through the firm are equal to the costs involved in carrying out the transaction in the open market ... The firm will tend to expand until the costs of organising an extra transaction within the firm become equal to the costs of carrying out the same transaction by means of an exchange on the open market ...' COASE (1937) THE NATURE OF THE FIRM*

From a transaction cost perspective it does not matter, in the longer run, whether the firm achieves its optimum size through organic growth or acquisition. Indeed, acquisition may be a straightforward means of optimizing the use of its management resource to best effect. However, transaction cost economics tend to suggest that mergers and acquisitions by large firms can lead to overexpansion and the creation of a conglomerate where the competitive benefit of the firm over the market is lost. The corollary of course is that small firm acquisitions are more likely to be successful where the efficiencies of scale in management have not yet been achieved.

The market for corporate control

One argument for the prevalence of mergers and acquisitions is the idea that there is an active market for corporate control. This idea, first proposed by Henry Manne in 1965, has strongly influenced the thinking of both academics, practitioners and regulators. However, the concept of a market for corporate control has its roots in the problem of the separation of management and control first described by Berle and Means (1932). Berle and Means posed the question as to why rational investors would continue to invest in companies run by people motivated by 'prestige, power or the gratification of personal zeal'. Michael Jensen (1986, 1988) among others, sought an answer through agency theory. Acquisitions are a means by which a competitive market, in this case the market for the control of corporations, purge weak or over opportunistic management.

From our discussion of the problem of agency in Chapter 1 and in Chapter 6 you may remember that the separation of shareholders (the principals) from the management (their agents) presents managers with the opportunity to over-consume perks and other side benefits to the disadvantage of the investors. Managers have a number of advantages in the relationship with shareholders – they have better access to relevant information and they can distort the type of business that they undertake to their own rather than the shareholders' interest. Agency theorists assume that managers will seek to maximize their own value and will act opportunistically to achieve that. Given the circumstances and the resources available, agency theorists argue that unless there are effective controls in place managers may well indulge in 'vanity' projects, i.e. investments which do not increase shareholder value but simply make the management 'look good'.

There are a number of signals that a corporate raider, suspecting management over-indulgence might look for: relative underinvestment, over-diversification, weak profitability, the accumulation of cash resources, low dividends and no other attempts to return surplus cash to shareholders. Such corporate raiders or 'asset strippers' as they are sometimes known engage in hostile takeover bids targeting weakly managed firms. There is a strong argument that such activity enhances economic efficiency, it removes weak management, it releases unused or underemployed assets back into the economy and it returns cash to the investors for them to invest elsewhere.

There has been considerable research into the existence of the market for corporate control, its strength and the mechanisms through which it operates. The evidence is not clear cut although there is some evidence that relatively low profitability firms and firms that pay high dividends are more susceptible to takeover. However, there is no evidence to support the view that firms that are particularly cash rich make an attractive target. The explanation for this could be that firms with strong cash reserves are more able to defend themselves than those that are not in such a strong position. We will return to the problem of management attitudes later when we consider the 'eat or be eaten' explanation for merger waves.

Merger waves

There is evidence that merger activity comes in waves. The idea of a wave in this context can mean one of two things: that there are peaks and troughs in merger activity in terms of the numbers of bids made, or that there are peaks and troughs and that they are of predictable frequency. What is evident from the past UK data is that there are minor wave patterns. However an examination of the quarterly data does not reveal a predictable frequency. When we look at the annual data, the data series since 1969 shows two significant peaks in the early 1970s and the mid 1980s. There is good evidence of high correlation between stock market booms and high levels of merger activity. A number of different explanations have been put forward to account for this. Mitchell and Mulherin (1996) suggest that sudden technological or industrial changes can cause shocks within certain industries and where a cluster of industries are affected in this way a wave of merger activity will appear. The problem with this explanation is that it does not explain why the waves appear to be highly correlated with market booms.

Two explanations of wave behaviour have, however, received considerable attention in the literature: the managerial hubris hypothesis and more recently the 'eat or be eaten' hypothesis.

The managerial hubris hypothesis

The idea that merger wave activity is triggered by management's belief that companies are systematically misvalued has been around for some time.

Astute managers, spotting the potential advantage, seek to make acquisitions in order to capture the misvaluation. This, Roll (1986) and others argue is likely to lead to a loss of shareholder value because of managerial overconfidence either in terms of their ability to value the companies concerned or indeed simply to manage them.

EXHIBIT 12.5

Number of UK acquisitions and mergers

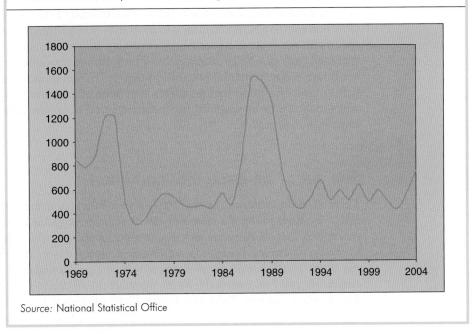

Source: National Statistical Office

This is a theme taken up by Ferris and Pecherot Petitt (2002) who referred to this hubris phenomenon as 'the winner's curse'. They suggest that there are possibly five principal explanations for the degree of loss of shareholder value to the acquirer:

1 Overestimation of the target firm's growth.

2 Overestimation of the expected cost and/or revenue synergies. In the last chapter we discussed the emergent and entangled nature of a firm's asset structure. Bringing together two disparate organizations and rebuilding both the internal and external networks of the organization is both costly and time consuming and may well overwhelm any synergistic benefits that may be available.

3 Overbidding for the firm concerned.

4 Failure to appreciate the magnitude of the risks to which the target firm is exposed and the additional risk which may arise post consolidation. A common source of the latter is where the large firm because of its increased size attracts the attention of regulators leading to anti-trust investigations of various sorts.

5 Failure to successfully integrate the acquired firm following acquisition.

To these we could add the following:

6 The economics of the aggregation are against the increase in the size of the expanded firm and managerial failure occurs (the transaction cost economics argument).

7 Mistakes in valuation where the acquirer's management do not appreciate that changes in the risk of their business may lead to an increase in their cost of capital and a reduction in the market value of their underlying business.

The managerial hubris hypothesis for merger waves relies upon the existence of systematic misvaluation of companies within the capital markets, or at least the belief by managers that equity values are generally too low. This of course relies upon the assumption that markets do not efficiently price shares and that the efficient markets hypothesis does not hold. It may well be that managers do believe that their firms are over or undervalued at any specific point in time, and it may also be that managers can make similar sort of judgements about other firms in whom they are interested as potential acquisition targets. However, it is a big jump to go from that to the assumption that managers systematically believe that firms are undervalued which is what is required for the managerial hubris hypothesis to satisfactorily explain merger waves.

The eat or be eaten phenomenon

There is some evidence, Louis (2004) that a firm can defend itself from predatory attack by itself making a takeover bid. Louis investigated a number of banks and noted that targets for acquisition who subsequently made a successful acquisition themselves were less likely to find themselves under attack. However, such banks that did undertake defensive acquisitions of this type paid a higher premium for the companies acquired and earned a lower cumulative abnormal return than other banks. This is what Gorton, Kahl and Rosen (2005) referred to as the 'eat or be eaten' scenario. They further argue that such defensive acquisitions may explain the observed fact that mergers tend to go in waves. For example, if one company has the opportunity to make a purely rational takeover on the basis of some technological or regulatory shift in the market, or for some other reason which is likely to add value to their shareholders then it is quite likely that potential victims will themselves engage in defensive takeovers in order to protect their position.

Now the question is why should firms engage in defensive behaviour of this type? One answer could be in terms of the managerial incentives involved. If, for example, managerial compensation functions are such that they are likely to favour the maximization of shareholder value then we would presume that they would be less concerned about remaining independent and may welcome a bid. However, in a situation where managers are concerned about their own employment, and especially in situations where their firms might be seen to be failing, then they are likely to strongly resist an attempted acquisition. Gorton and his co-workers argue that this type of defensive acquisition is self-reinforcing in that as soon as managers recognize that the environment is becoming conducive for a takeover bid they themselves attempt defensive acquisitions inducing others within the industry to do exactly the same. So, if this theory is correct, one potentially value adding takeover attempt, or even the threat of it, can lead to a wave of related defensive acquisitions. Analytically, this account of merger activity is plausible. Using techniques of economic analysis, Gorton and his co-workers suggest the following:

1 Industries populated by similar sized firms will be characterized by defensive merger waves where the acquisitions are characterized by negative Net Present Values. The reverse is true of more heterogenous industries.

2 Large companies tend to overpay with a consequent loss of shareholder value while the reverse is true for small firms.

3 Small acquisitions are more likely to be value generating than large acquisitions.

The phenomenon of mergers, why they occur and the existence of merger waves is a continuing area of research. There are further readings at the end of the chapter which will help you develop this topic.

1 The economics of the aggregation are against the increase in the size of the expanded firm and managerial failure occurs (the transaction cost economics argument).

2 Synergistic benefits that were expected to occur do not materialize. In the last chapter we discussed the emergent and entangled nature of a firm's asset structure. Bringing together two disparate organizations and rebuilding both the internal and external networks of the organization is both costly and time consuming and may well overwhelm any synergistic benefits that may be available.

3 The managerial hubris phenomenon (i.e. managerial overconfidence) may lead to overbidding for control. As noted above when management become convinced that their company is being systematically misvalued.

4 Mistakes in valuation where the acquirer's management do not appreciate that changes in the risk of their business may lead to an increase in their cost of capital and a reduction in the market value of their underlying business.

5 Failure to appreciate the magnitude of the risks to which the target firm is exposed and the additional risk which may arise post consolidation. A common source of the latter is where the large firm because of its increased size attracts the attention of regulators leading to anti-trust investigations of various sorts.

The regulation of takeovers

The agency perspective, and the problems of the separation of ownership and control were magnified by the 1980s merger boom and a succession of corporate scandals. The movement to improve corporate governance and to ensure that firms complied with the principles of good management and corporate direction led to a spate of reports culminating in the Combined Code of Good Governance with which all firms listed on the London Stock Exchange are expected to comply. The City Code for Takeovers is designed to ensure, as far as possible, that takeover bids and acquisitions are conducted with the interests of shareholders foremost in the minds of the management concerned.

City Code for Takeovers

Mergers and acquisitions are controlled in the United Kingdom by the 1985 Companies Act. However, the City Code for Takeovers is designed to create equitable treatment between the shareholders of the target company and to prevent covert action on the part of their directors to frustrate a bid. On the other side, the code sets clear rules for the process of what is called 'stake building' where an individual or other firm attempts to acquire control by stealth by the piecemeal purchase of shares in the target company either by private treaty with individual shareholders or by purchases in the open market.

The City Code has no legal force but the parties to an acquisition who do not follow it may find that the London market withdraws their ability to trade in shares on the exchange or imposes other sanctions against them. The application of the City Code is administered by a takeover panel which is an independent body whose purpose it is to ensure that takeovers and mergers are conducted in a way which does not prejudice the interests of shareholders. The panel, which is appointed by the Bank of England, can ask the Financial Services Authority, which in the UK is the principal regulatory agency controlling the activities of the financial markets, to investigate the conduct of the parties to an acquisition. The FSA can, in its turn, impose substantial sanctions and fines on any party that it believes has acted against either the letter or the spirit of the Code.

Stake building

A common approach to acquiring a controlling interest in another company is for a potential predator to accumulate sufficient shares to the point where they take effective control by stealth. The City Code has a number of rules which regulate the substantial acquisition of shares (SARs). Unlike other aspects of the City Code, the rules on SARs only apply to UK companies:

- If the potential predator acquires shares in the target company in the three months prior to the formal announcement of a bid then the offer, when it is made, must be of the same or greater value than the earlier acquisition of shares.

- If the company acquires more than 10 per cent of the voting rights of another company then any subsequent offer within the following 12 months must be for a cash amount equal to the highest price paid for any of those shares acquired at any time. Exhibit 12.6 shows the various stages a bid must proceed through and the latest event dates to be in compliance with the Code.

EXHIBIT 12.6

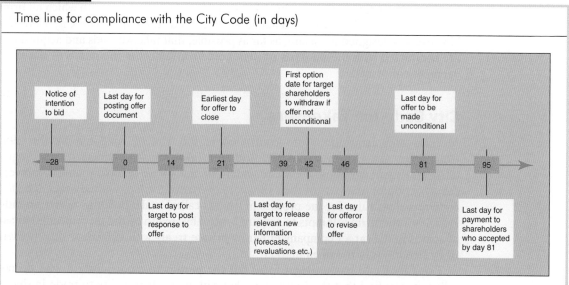

Time line for compliance with the City Code (in days)

The ten principles of the City Code:

1 All the investors in the target company should be treated similarly.

2 No party in an offer (actual or potential) should disclose information to one or more shareholders in the target company and not to others.

3 An offer should only be made by individuals or firms who have every reason to believe that they will be able to implement the offer in full.

4 The shareholders in the target company should be given sufficient information and advice to make a properly informed decision and should be given adequate time to do so.

5 All documentation, whether produced by the offeror or by the directors of the target company should be produced to the highest standards of accuracy.

6 All parties must do everything they can to ensure that a false market is not created in the securities of the acquiring or in the target company. A false market occurs when false information is given or information is withheld in such a way as to inhibit the free negotiation of prices. In other words it is a deliberate attempt by either party in the acquisition to undermine the efficiency of the market in the two companies' shares.

7 The Board of Directors of the target company must not take any action that might thwart an actual or a potential bid or deny the shareholders the opportunity to decide upon the merits of the bid proposal without the approval of the shareholders in an Annual General Meeting.

8 The rights of control exercised by either the offeror, or by the directors of the target company must be exercised in good faith and must not be oppressive to existing minority shareholders.

9 Directors on both sides of an acquisition must act in their company's interest and not have any regard for their own shareholding or that of their family or of any special interest group.

10 Where control is gained (i.e. more than 50 per cent of the shares of the target company are acquired) then a general offer should be made to all of the other shareholders of the acquired company.

The role of the Competition Commission

For many years, governments and regulators have sought, in the public interest, to prohibit or lay conditions upon mergers or acquisitions that might lead to a substantial lessening of competition within the economy or the industry concerned. There is a general belief that increased competition leads to lower prices of goods and services, higher quality, and more choice for consumers.

Some mergers or acquisitions present a threat to competition within a particular industry. This can occur when two companies combine to create an entity that by virtue of its size has substantial power either over the market as a whole or over a particular part of the supply chain. Indeed, even where firms grow organically they can find themselves subject to an investigation with the potential risk of action being taken to reduce their market power through divestment or some other means. However, powerful interests are at stake in many such investigations.

Pressure builds for Tesco power probe

*John Fingleton, the new chief executive of the OFT (Office of Fair Trading), will
make a submission in person to the All Party Small Shops Group's ongoing probe
into retail trends. . . . The group has been critical of the 'creeping centralisation'
on Britain's high street and is expected to use its findings to call for the power of
Tesco, Asda, J Sainsbury and Wm Morrison to be curtailed. . . . News that the
OFT will contribute to the All Party's report is the latest sign that the status quo,
which has allowed Tesco to grow its market share to 30 per cent, could be
reviewed. Last month, the OFT overturned its August ruling that it would not refer
the grocery market to the Competition Commission, the competition watchdog. . . .
Gerry Sutcliffe, the competition minister, told the inquiry that he believed there was
'something wrong' with the grocery market, and that 'something needed to be
done' to address it. TELEGRAPH, JAMES HALL (FILED: 06/11/2005)*

As the inset from the *Telegraph* makes clear the Office of Fair Trading which has
the power to refer issues to the Competition Commission has been reluctant to
engage the power of the large supermarkets and only after sustained lobbying
decided to refer a matter where one supermarket controlled in excess of 30 per cent
of UK food retailing. However, once the OFT makes a decision to refer the
Competition Commission will enter into the process shown in Exhibit 12.7.

The role of the UK Competition Commission is to ensure as far as possible that
merger activity does not lead to a substantial lessening of competition (the SLC test). A
number of tests are applied before the Competition Commission can become involved:

- *The turnover test*: an investigation will only be conducted if the target company
  has a turnover in excess of £70 million per annum.
- *The share of supply test*: the commission will only become involved if following
  the merger the combined company either supplies, or is supplied with more
  than 25 per cent of all the goods or services of a specified description. In
  determining whether the 25 per cent limit has been breached, the commission
  itself can decide whether to make its estimate on the basis of value, cost,
  price, quantity or even the number of employees involved.
- *The substantial lessening of competition test*: if the turnover or share of supply
  test has been applied and the competition commission decides that a merger
  should be investigated then it must satisfy itself that it is likely that a
  'substantial lessening of competition' will occur. In applying the SLC test, the
  commission will review the competitive constraints upon firms, any expected
  changes in the structure of the market, and the likely impact of the merger
  upon the rivalry which exists between firms.

Within the European Union, the European commission has exclusive jurisdiction
for mergers resulting in a worldwide turnover of more than €5 billion per annum and
a turnover within the European economic area of more than €250 million per
annum. Thus where a merger or an acquisition involves two countries within the
union there is a single 'one-stop arrangement' where either approval for the intended
acquisition or merger can be obtained. The European Union will seek to block a
merger if, in its view, it creates a dominant position for the companies involved
leading either to higher prices, a lessening of consumer choice or is proved to be
detrimental to innovation. The commission also now seeks to determine whether a

EXHIBIT 12.7

The steps taken by the UK's Office of Fair Trading and then the Competition Commission in assessing whether a proposed combination is against the public interest

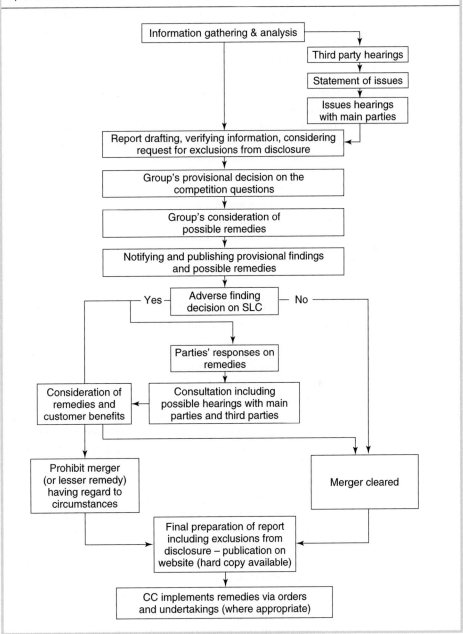

Note: SLC = substantial lessening of competition test, CC = the Competition Commission.

merger would 'significantly impede effective competition' and this may occur not by virtue of the merger itself but because of the position that the merged firm would be able to command in either a duopoly or oligopoly.

'The test contained in the EU Merger Regulation is that mergers which ". . . create or strengthen a dominant position as a result of which effective competition would be significantly impeded . . ." are to be declared incompatible with the Common Market. This dominance test sets a high threshold for intervention . . . the concept of dominance inherent in our merger control test has most frequently been applied to situations where a proposed merger would create a single market leader. These are situations where so-called "unilateral effects" are the predominant competition concern . . . But as well as single firm dominance . . . regulation can also be applied to situations of collective or oligopolistic dominance . . . (where) the Commission will examine the structure of markets to identify whether the merger would tend to lead to a higher degree of tacit co-ordination in the market. Normally, this analysis will entail an examination of: the role of any smaller players (the "competitive fringe"); market characteristics such as the degree of transparency, product homogeneity, market growth, innovation, barriers to entry, incentives to compete, the possibilities for retaliation, and so on . . . Last September this type of analysis lead to the prohibition of a proposed deal between two UK travel companies, Airtours and First Choice. This was the first case in which the Commission prohibited a merger, which would have resulted in a market with four players becoming a market with three. Or put another way, the decision was for the first time based on a finding of oligopolistic dominance.' EDITED EXTRACT FROM A SPEECH GIVEN BY MARIO MONTI, COMMISSIONER FOR COMPETITION POLICY, WASHINGTON, 26 JUNE 2000

The convergence of takeover regulation – the international perspective

Since the 1990s there has been an increasing awareness of the importance of good corporate governance and this is particularly important in the area of mergers and acquisitions. The UK model described above (found also in the United States and other countries who have developed their legal and regulatory systems from either the UK or the US) is based upon a particular 'market based' model of corporate ownership rather than what Goergen, Martynova and Renneboog (2005) describe as the 'block holder' or stakeholder perspective which predominates in Europe. What this means is that takeover regulation has been seen in the UK as a means of protecting the rights of a widely distributed shareholder base, whereas within the European model the emphasis has been on the protection of different stakeholder groups such as creditors, employees and indeed the wider national interest.

There is a debate as to which of these two systems (the Anglo-American or the European) is the most economically efficient and this has led to discussion about the way that corporate law and takeover regulation in particular should develop. There are three possibilities:

1 Convergence of the European model to the Anglo-European system. To a certain extent, this has already occurred with the agreement by the European countries of the 'equal treatment' principle as a basic tenet of company law as well as the introduction of the requirements concerning stakebuilding and the mandatory bid which are important features of the City Code.

2 The two systems could form the basis of a new regulatory model combining the best practice of both. Although there is a broadly held view that the Anglo-American model has many economic advantages others argue that the European system is better at handling the agency effects brought about by the

separation of ownership and control and in mitigating abuse of managerial power. This could be taken to suggest that European companies should be given the freedom to select the regulatory model which best satisfies their needs.

3 Countries should be encouraged to develop their own regulatory systems eliminating weaknesses wherever possible and borrowing good practice where appropriate.

Currently, the drift of European policy has been towards 1 partly because of the power of the US (and to the lesser extent the UK) capital markets to dictate corporate regulation and partly because of the recent economic success of the US and UK economies compared with those within the eurozone. However, in the shifting global market place nothing can be taken for granted and what is one year's consensus becomes last year's bad idea. Goergen, Martynova and Renneboog (2005) provide a very interesting overview of development in takeover regulation and corporate governance across thirty European countries based upon evidence from 150 corporate governance lawyers.

Financing and accounting for acquisitions

There is a broad range of financing options open to an acquirer. Much depends upon the size of the proposed acquisition in relation to the financial resources of the bidding firm. For a relatively small acquisition the cheapest source of finance is invariably the acquirers own retained earnings and in this respect the acquisition may be of little more significance than the acquisition of any fixed asset. As we have noted before, the availability of retained earnings in the balance sheet is only part of the story. In addition the firm must also have sufficient liquidity to finance the deal either from its own cash reserves or from the sale, or sale and leaseback of existing assets. A firm may also be able to finance a deal through a back to back sale of an existing subsidiary or an investment in an associated company. Where an acquisition is beyond the existing resources of the firm it has generally two routes to follow:

1 An offer for cash financed by debt issue. Where a large company acquisition is involved financing may be achieved by way of a new debt issue where the acquirer has access to the bond market. The problem with this approach is that it will signal to the market that a likely acquisition is imminent and cause a 'price rush' amongst the stocks of the likely targets. For this reason acquisitions for cash will usually entail the extension of a line of credit from a financial institution (a bridging loan) until the offer is accepted and the bond issue can proceed.

FINANCIAL REALITY

In its 2004 accounts Cobham plc reported acquisitions as follows:

During the year the company completed six acquisitions for a total cash consideration of £60.4m and deferred consideration of £0.4m. In December agreement was reached to acquire two further businesses for a cash consideration of US$323m. These transactions are likely to be completed in the first half of 2005. Three further acquisitions were completed in February 2005 for a total cash consideration of £10m and £3m of contingent consideration.

Its financing requirements for the year were achieved as follows:

- The March 1996 private placement of Cobham guaranteed senior notes which raised US$50m. These notes carry a fixed interest rate of 6.28 per cent for the seven year notes and 6.42 per cent for the ten year notes. Principal repayments to date amount to US$25m.
- The October 2002 private placement of Cobham guaranteed senior notes which raised US$225m. The facility comprises two series of notes repayable in seven and ten years. As a result of an interest swap the interest expense varies with LIBOR.
- The £200m club multi-currency credit agreement which was entered into in December 2002. The borrowings carry a variable rate of interest. At the end of 2004 £78.4m had been drawn under this agreement. The facility reduced to £150m after the first year of operation and is repayable in full in January 2008.
- In January 2005 the Group entered into a 12 month US$200m facility to provide short-term finance for the purchase of Remec and Koch.

Because Cobham has healthy cash generation its financing arrangements are achieved through cash payment with debt used to 'smooth' the short term consumption of cash.

2 Where a company does not have access to the bond market it will need to seek intermediated finance either through its own bank or some other financial institution. A number of factors will come into play with this type of finance: the lender's perception of the credit risk of the acquirer both before and after acquisition, the terms of the loan, the potential for equity participation, the amount of finance required and the security offered. Mezzanine finance is one particularly attractive source of debt. Although this type of debt is subordinated (see Chapter 4) it does offer a high rate of interest and usually the attraction of an equity stake in the form of warrants.

3 One disadvantage of a cash payment to investors is that their equity claim once liquidated is liable, where it is applied, to capital gains tax. An equity swap where shares in the acquirer company are exchanged with those of the target in a ratio appropriate to the value transferred is an attractive possibility in those situations where the acquirer is highly regarded by the market. Such a swap will not normally be regarded as taxable in the hands of the investors. As the transaction will be achieved by the creation of new shares there will be an immediate impact upon the gearing of the firm. However, as the acquisition is backed by the assets and earnings of the acquired firm there should be little or no dilution effect. The problem with a purchase through shares is that it does depend upon the perceived value of those shares by the target firm shareholders. The problems are less where the acquirer's shares are actively traded, but where a private company seeks to acquire another then it is highly unlikely that the shareholders in the target company will be easy to convince of the financial benefits of this method of financing.

Accounting for acquisitions

By understanding the accounting mechanics we can gain some insight into how the acquisition process operates. Unlike much of accounting the process is remarkably easy to follow. As we have noted there are two modes of financing an acquisition:

1 By a cash payment to the target shareholders.

2 By an issue of shares (sometimes combined with cash) to the target company shareholders at an agreed valuation of those shares.

The first move is to open the balance sheet into a useable format for analysis purposes. This we call the balance sheet equation:

$$FA + St + Db + C = STL + LTL + OC + SPA + PLR$$

where FA means fixed assets, St, Db and C are stock, debtors and cash, STL and LTL are the short and long term liabilities. The three emboldened headings are the owners capital introduced (OC), the share premium account (SPA) and PLR is the profit and loss reserve.

1 Lay out the accounting equation as shown above.

2 Using the parent company balance sheet proceed as follows:

(a) Open an 'Investment in Subsidiary' column (Inv) alongside fixed assets in the accounting equation.

$$FA + Inv + St + Db + C = STL + LTL + OC + SPA + PLR$$

(b) Enter the existing balance sheet values from the parent company in the accounting equation.

(c) Record the financing transaction showing the purchase of the investment in the subsidiary for cash or for a corresponding issue of shares.

3 Create a new accounting equation for the consolidated balance sheet renaming the 'Investment in Subsidiaries' column as Goodwill on Acquisition (GW) and introducing (if the acquisition is for less than 100 per cent of the equity) a minority interest column as an addition to the owner's equity columns at the right hand side.

$$FA + GW + St + Db + C = STL + LTL + OC + SPA + PLR + MI$$

4 Enter the values from the parent company balance sheet in the new accounting equation (put the 'investment in subsidiary' value in the goodwill column).

5 Enter the values from the subsidiary balance sheet.

6 Transfer the balances in the owner's equity account of the subsidiary to (a) the goodwill column (GW) and (b) the minority interest (MI) column in the proportions acquired by the parent company and retained by the minority.

Friendly Grinders plc decided to buy out RufDiamond Ltd at the date of the acquisition the two company balance sheets were as shown in Exhibit 12.8.

EXHIBIT 12.8

Balance sheets for Friendly Grinders and RufDiamond plc prior to acquisition

Friendly Grinders PLC Balance Sheet at date of acquisition (£million)			RufDiamond plc Balance Sheet at date of acquisition (£million)		
Fixed assets		640	Fixed assets		90
Current assets:			Current assets:		
Stocks	33		Stocks	12	
Debtors	12		Debtors	30	
Cash	35		Cash	8	
	80			50	
Less short term liabilities	24		Less short term liabilities	25	
		56			25
		696			115
Less long term liabilities		90	Loan		10
		606			105
Owner's Equity			Owner's Equity		
Share capital		20	Share capital		40
Share premium account		45	Share premium account		40
Profit and loss reserve		541	Profit and loss reserve		25
		606			105

The Board had decided to review the accounting implications of a purchase of 80 per cent of the equity of RufDiamond for:
(a) a cash payment of £140 million financed by a loan of £140 million, or
(b) an issue of 13 million 25p ordinary shares with a current market value of 1100p each.

Step 1 Lay out (Exhibit 12.9) the Friendly Grinders balance sheet on a table headed by the balance sheet equation including an INV column representing the investment to be made in a subsidiary company.

Step 2 Show the financing step. In this case we enter a transaction showing the creation of the new loan and the removal of £140 million from the cash account (Credit) and entering it into the INV account (Debit). This creates a new parent company balance sheet (transcribe the column totals to the balance sheet as shown in Exhibit 12.11.

Step 3 Lay out the new parent company balance sheet on the balance sheet equation which has the INV column renamed to GW representing 'goodwill' on

EXHIBIT 12.9

Friendly Grinders' Balance Sheet and the financing steps

	FA	Inv	St	Db	C	=	STL	LTL	OC	SPA	PLR
Friendly Grinders Balance											
Sheet pre acquisition	640		33	12	35		24	90	20	45	541
New Loan finance					140			140			
Purchase of											
RufDiamond plc		140			−140						
Friendly Grinders Balance											
Sheet post acquisition	640	140	33	12	35		24	230	20	45	541

acquisition and an additional column named MI representing the interest of the RufDiamond minority shareholders in the assets (less the liabilities of the group).

Steps 4, 5 and 6 are shown in Exhibit 12.10. Note in that exhibit how the assets and liabilities of the two companies are combined in total and the equity accounts of the new subsidiary company split between the investment in the subsidiary account (now shown as the 'goodwill' column) and the minority interest column.

The final consolidated balance sheet is straightforward as shown in Exhibit 12.12.

If the company were to arrange the transaction through a share issue the outcome would be the same except in the financing step a new share issue would be created part of the proceeds of which would be counted as capital introduced and part as share premium.

You can now proceed with the consolidation to produce a group account as before.

EXHIBIT 12.10

Consolidation within the balance sheet equation

	FA	GW	St	Db	C	=	STL	LTL	OC	SPA	PLR	MI
Friendly Grinders (parent)												
balance sheet	640	140	33	12	35		24	230	20	45	541	
RufDiamond balance												
sheet	90		12	30	8		25	10	40	40	25	
Transfer RufDiamond's												
equity												
80% to goodwill		−32								−32		
20% to minority interest										−8		8
Transfer RufDiamond's												
share premium account												
80% to goodwill		−32								−32		
20% to minority interest										−8		8
Transfer RufDiamond's												
profit and loss reserve												
80% to goodwill		−20									−20	
20% to minority interest											−5	5
Consolidated												
balance sheet	730	56	45	42	43		49	240	20	45	541	21

EXHIBIT 12.11

Balance sheet for Friendly Grinders (Parent Company) Ltd post acquisition

Friendly Grinders (parent company) Ltd
Balance Sheet at date of acquisition (£million)

Fixed assets		640
Investment in subsidiary		140
Current assets:		
Stocks	33	
Debtors	12	
Cash	35	
	80	
Less short term liabilities	24	
		56
		836
Less long term liabilities		230
		606
Owner's equity		
Share capital		20
Share premium account		45
Profit and loss reserve		541
		606

EXHIBIT 12.12

Balance sheet for Friendly Grinders (Group) plc post acquisition

Friendly Grinders (group) plc
Balance Sheet at date of acquisition (£million)

Fixed assets		730.0
Goodwill on acquisition		56.0
		786.0
Current assets:		
Stocks	45.0	
Debtors	42.0	
Cash	43.0	
	130.0	
Less short term liabilities	49.0	
		81.0
		867.0
Less long term liabilities		240.0
		627.0
Owner's equity		
Share capital		20.0
Share premium account		45.0
Profit and loss reserve		541.0
		606.0
Minority interest		21.0
		627.0

EXHIBIT 12.13

Balance sheet equation of financing step when an acquisition is financed by shares

	FA	Inv	St	Db	C	=	STL	LTL	OC	SPA	PLR
Friendly Grinders Balance Sheet pre acquisition	640		33	12	35		24	90	20	45	541
Purchase of RufDiamond plc issue of 13 million ordinary shares for 1100p											
13 million at 25p to issued share capital		3.3							3.3		
13 million at 1075p to the share premium account		139.8								139.8	
Friendly Grinders Balance Sheet post acquisition	640	143.1	33	12	35		24	90	23.3	184.8	541

REVIEW ACTIVITY 12.2 Produce a consolidated balance sheet at the date of acquisition for Friendly Grinders assuming:

1 acquisition of 90 per cent of the equity for £150 million, or
2 acquisition of 80 per cent of the equity for a payment of £80 million in cash and the balance by an exchange of 6.5 million 25p ordinary shares valued at 1100p each.

In both cases the cash component of the bid is to be financed by a loan of the same amount.

The creation of the group balance sheet entails the consolidation of the assets and liabilities of all the companies involved. However the subsidiary companies do not lose their identity unless they are wholly owned by the parent company and in that case they can still be maintained as an independent subsidiary company within the group. This means that the subsidiaries have their own board of directors, their own legal status and the important requirement in company law that the directors must work in the interests of the company and not necessarily the interests of the parent company. In practice of course, the parent company can replace the Board of Directors and can enforce their will if necessary if there is any divergence of view about how the enterprise should be run. In the situation where there are minority shareholders involved the situation become more difficult and the parent company must make sure that it does not operate in a way that is disadvantageous to them.

Valuing a target company

Many of the problems of company valuation have been discussed in earlier chapters. The problem we now confront is how to apply the general principles of valuation discussed earlier to situations where a controlling claim is being acquired in another firm and where the acquisition is likely to fundamentally alter the underlying nature of the acquirer's business. In many respects the problem faced is similar to that discussed in Chapter 7 where significant capital investment decisions alter the financial structure of the firm.

The general principle in valuing an acquisition is that what is important is not the value of the target company *per se*, but the value of the acquiring firm after the acquisition has taken place. Even when management intend to operate the acquired firm as a separate trading entity the new business will have an impact upon the consolidated cash flows and earnings of the acquiring business and on its investors' perception of risk. The problem of setting a bid price for an acquisition is determined by the alteration that will result, if the bid is successful, in the value of the acquirer.

The control premium and the value added on acquisition

The control premium is the difference between the pre-acquisition equity value of the target firm and the actual total price paid to obtain a controlling interest. The value added on acquisition is the difference between the acquiring firm's shareholders' part of the increase in the value of the firm overall and the amount they paid for the acquisition. With a 100 per cent stake all of the value gain goes to the acquiring company shareholders. With a less than 100 per cent stake the minority shareholders retain part of the increase in the value of the acquiring firm bought about by the takeover of their company.

FINANCIAL REALITY	The directors of Friendly Grinders have been getting cold feet over the acquisition of RufDiamond plc. They have asked Gloria, the new company CFO to go away and 'pass a ruler' over the figures justifying a revised offer of £1 per ordinary share in RufDiamond for 100 per cent of its equity. RufDiamond has 160 million 25p ordinary shares in issue. The original terms had been for an 80 per cent stake for a cash payment of £140 million. The share price of RufDiamond before the announcement had been trading at around 78p. Gloria's estimate of the combined value of the firm's cash flows of the firm post acquisition is £1110 million being £230 million more than the present market capitalization of the firm. Gloria decides to work out whether the 100 per cent acquisition is better value for the current investors in Friendly Grinders than the original bid.

Gloria works out the increase in Friendly Grinders plc's overall cash flows as a result of the acquisition (£230 million) before calculating the portion attributable to the Friendly Grinders' shareholders. She then deducts the cost of the acquisition to get the value added on acquisition (VAA) in both cases (Exhibit 12.14).

EXHIBIT 12.14

Calculation of the value added on acquisition based upon no change in the market value of the underlying business of the acquirer

Percentage stake in RufDiamond plc	80% £million	100% £million
Value of the combined firm	1110.00	1110.00
Pre-acquisition value of Friendly Grinders	880.00	880.00
Increase in PV of firm's cash flows	230.00	230.00
Share due to Friendly Grinders' investors	184.00	230.00
Cost of acquisition	140.00	160.00
Value added on acquisition to parent company investors (VAA)	**44.00**	**70.00**

She then moves on to the next step which is to calculate the control premium by deducting the open market value of the shares in RufDiamond acquired from the cost of the acquisition to Friendly Grinders.

EXHIBIT 12.15

Calculation of the Control Premium based upon no change in the market value of the underlying business of the acquirer

Percentage stake in RufDiamond plc		80% £million	100% £million
Premium paid on acquisition			
Cost of acquisition		140.00	160.00
Open market value of equity in RufDiamond		124.80	124.80
Open market value of shares acquired		99.84	124.80
Control premium		**40.16**	**35.20**

REVIEW ACTIVITY 12.3 Assuming that the underlying value of Friendly Grinders does not change and Gloria is correct in her estimation of the value of RufDiamond: what is the maximum offer that should be made on the basis of a 100 per cent and on the basis of an 80 per cent acquisition?

The problem for Gloria is that although she is happy with the current share prices of the two companies she is less than happy that the post acquisition value will simply be the sum of the current market value of Friendly Grinders plus the discounted value of the additional cash flows generated by the acquisition. She has every right to be concerned so before returning to the problem of valuing this type of bid we need to review the potential impact that acquisitions can have upon the underlying value of the acquirer. In our analysis we will focus on cash offers although the same principles apply to those made by an exchange of shares.

The three acquisition types

With all acquisitions the maximum price the acquirer should pay is the increase in its own total market value following the acquisition. The crunch is this: only in the very simplest of cases can we just add the value of the acquirer and the value of the target to get the value of the combination. Indeed, we can go as far as this: the stand alone valuation of the target firm is nearly always irrelevant in determining the price that should be paid for its acquisition. What matters, from the acquiring shareholders' point of view is whether the acquisition adds value to them. From a valuation perspective we can categorize acquisitions into three types.

Type I Acquisitions that neither disturb the business risk nor require additional external financing which is likely to change the firm's current weighted average cost of capital. Acquisitions such as those pursued by Cobham and described earlier in this chapter fall into this category. Usually such acquisitions will, compared with the size of the acquirer, be relatively small, require no expansion in the acquirer's capital and present no threat to its underlying business risk. Such acquisitions can be assessed as we would any other project. The value of the acquired company, and hence the maximum that should be paid for it, is the Net Present Value of the future cash flows of the target firm discounted at the acquirer's weighted average cost of capital.

Type II Acquisitions that do not disturb the business risk but do disturb the financing of the firm either through altering the firm's debt or its exposure to default risk. With this type of acquisition the discount rate can be calculated by regearing the weighted average cost of capital of the acquiring firm. However, because the weighted average cost of capital has changed, the total market value of the acquirer will also change and this needs to be assessed as part of the valuation exercise. The problem is that we immediately fall into a circularity in that we need to know gearing of the combined firm post acquisition (in order to calculate the revised cost of capital).

Type III Acquisitions that alter the firm's exposure to business risk and possibly its exposure to financial and default risk. In order to estimate the cost of capital we need to know the cost of equity of the combined business. However, the cost of equity of the combination is dependent upon the price that is paid for the target's equity – but again we do not know the price to be paid until we know the value of the target. Type III acquisitions, therefore, present all of the problems of Type I and Type II but with the added problem of the change in business risk.

Given that Type I acquisitions should represent little challenge to us given the methods for handling capital investment projects discussed in earlier chapters we will move on to Type II and Type III acquisitions where the underlying value of the firm will be disturbed.

Valuing acquisitions that alter the firm's exposure to risk

Both Type II and Type III acquisitions raise complexities in valuation because of the disturbance to the underlying risk of the acquirer. As a consequence of the change in risk the post acquisition value of the firm is not the sum of its pre-acquisition value plus the value of the firm acquired. In this situation the value of the combined firm is not a linear addition of pre-existing values. The combined firm is a new valuation entity with its own cost of capital based upon the business risk of the new asset and capital structure of the business.

To estimate the value of the combined firm we introduce a variation on the stepped valuation model discussed in Chapter 10. With this variant of the model we will value the free cash flows to all classes of investor to obtain a total firm value following the consolidation of the new acquisition. The value added to the equity investors by the acquisition (the VAA) is then given by the total firm value less the value of debt and loan finance outstanding.

The valuation model invokes a planning horizon over which the firm believes it can achieve a set level of growth and a terminal value is then calculated at the end of that period representing the residual value of the firm on the assumption that it survives in perpetuity. The method we show here is designed to estimate the increase in shareholder value caused by the acquisition concerned. Our approach has some similarities to the Adjusted Present Value approach discussed in

Chapter 6 except that we avoid the multiple discount rate problem which undermines the validity of that technique.

The first step in the analysis is to separate out the post-acquisition cash flows into risk streams representing the degree of business risk (as measured by their asset beta). Normally we would anticipate the following cash flow streams:

Stream 1 the projected Free Cash Flow for the acquiring firm at its planned rate of growth. This stream will have a value V_1 and an asset beta β_1.

Stream 2 the projected Free Cash Flow for the target firm at the rate of growth that the acquiring firm believes that it can achieve. This stream will have a value V_2 and an asset beta β_2.

Stream 3 any increase or decrease in the acquiring firm's cash flow caused by either synergistic effects or exceptional gains or losses on integration. This stream will have a value V_3 and an asset beta β_c.

The business risk attaching to stream 1 is that of the acquiring firm, stream 2 is that of the target firm and stream 3 is that of the post-acquisition or combined firm. The asset beta of the combined firm (β_c) will be given by the following:

$$\beta_c = \frac{V_1}{TMV_e} \times \beta_1 + \frac{V_2}{TMV_e} \times \beta_2 + \frac{V_3}{TMV_e} \times \beta_c$$

$$\beta_c = \frac{\dfrac{V_1}{TMV_e} \times \beta_1 + \dfrac{V_2}{TMV_e} \times \beta_2}{1 - \dfrac{V_3}{TMV_e}}$$

We can simplify this by multiplying the right hand side of the equation (top and bottom) by the total market value of equity to give:

$$\beta_c = \frac{V_1}{TMV_e} \times \beta_1 + \frac{V_2}{TMV_e} \times \beta_2 + \frac{V_3}{TMV_e} \times \beta_c$$

$$\beta_c = \frac{TMV_e \left[\dfrac{V_1}{TMV_e} \times \beta_1 + \dfrac{V_2}{TMV_e} \times \beta_2 \right]}{TMV_e \left[1 - \dfrac{V_3}{TMV_e} \right]}$$

$$\beta_c = \frac{V_1 \beta_1 + V_2 \beta_2}{TMV_e - V_3}$$

Unfortunately a combined asset beta is needed to determine the weighted average cost of capital of the post acquisition firm which in its turn is required to calculate the values of the individual streams V_1, V_2, V_3. Therefore we have a circularity problem which can only be resolved by a process of iteration. The procedure, in outline, is as follows: we set the valuation and cost of capital algorithms up within Excel and enter 'seed' values using the current market capitalization of the equity for the acquirer and the target and with zero for the value of the stream 3 cash flow. The model will iterate to a solution such that the values of each stream input into the cost of capital calculation give a WACC which delivers those input values.

The only way to see this piece of magic in action is to return to Friendly Grinders and see how Gloria is getting on sorting out the implications of the higher bid price for RufDiamond plc.

Gloria was back at her desk again. She had just two ambitions: the first to be CFO at Friendly Grinders. She had achieved that. The second concerned Jack Grinder but her plans there had not been fulfilled. With a sigh she returned to the job in hand. Gloria had realized that with all the firm's other capital commitments they would have to finance the acquisition of RufDiamond plc with new borrowing. However, she had concerns in that RufDiamond's equity beta was considerably higher than Friendly Grinders at 2.2. This was putting complexity into the case that she had not yet worked through. Her original valuation had suggested that if the acquisition went ahead the added value to Friendly Grinders' shareholders would be approximately £230 million (using a cost of capital based upon the combined values of the two firms' equity and £160 million of additional borrowing to finance the deal at an offer price of £1 per ordinary share). This would give a net increase in shareholder value of £70 million after deducting the cost of the acquisition.

The current level of debt in Friendly Grinders was £90 million (which Gloria believed to be close to its imputed market value), and there were 80 million, 25p equity shares in issue with a market price of 1100p each. The firm's equity beta now stood at 1.19, the current risk free rate was 4.5 per cent and the equity risk premium was 3.5 per cent. The firm currently paid 110 basis points over risk free on its borrowing and the corporation tax rate was 30 per cent. Gloria was concerned that a significant increase in the gearing of the firm to the level implied by the RufDiamond acquisition would reduce the firm's credit rating from BB+ to B and potentially raise the firm's existing cost of debt by a further 120 basis points. Not only would the company have to finance the full acquisition cost by borrowing but they would also be taking over a further £10 million of outstanding debt held by RufDiamond.

A lengthy analysis of RufDiamond's recent performance suggested that the business would generate £16.11 million of operating cash flow in the next 12 months and under Friendly Grinders' management business growth could be sustained at 6 per cent nominal for the next ten years (this was the planning assumption that Friendly Grinders had built into their own investment plans). What was important was that it would be also able to generate additional business through synergies between the operations of the two firms. This additional business would boost overall cash flow by £5 million in year 1 (net of reinvestment) and that this business would also be able to grow at a compound rate of 6 per cent. In the recent past Friendly Grinders had been generating a rate of return on Free Cash Flow of 15 per cent on its capital investment portfolio.

A number of additional factors also formed part of her analysis:

- The possibility of miscellaneous land sale in RufDiamond's portfolio of property assets worth an estimated £6 million and realizable immediately.
- The immediate disposal of a joint venture held by RufDiamond worth £7 million.
- Exceptional integration costs of £2 million in year 1 and £1.5 million and £1.0 million in years 2 and 3 incurred through the limited redundancies and other costs that would follow the acquisition.
- The ongoing level of capital investment required in RufDiamond to sustain a rate of growth of 6 per cent per annum.
- The net impact upon Friendly Grinders' own business (net of increased management charges) of the acquisition.
- The company's corporation tax burden which is assessed at 30 per cent and is paid in the year it arises. Capital expenditure attracts a 100 per cent capital allowance in the year in question.

In reviewing the impact upon the firm of this acquisition Gloria also had in front of her the firm's ten year planning assumptions. In the last 12 months the firm had earned free cash flow after capital refinancing but before tax of £65.01 million. The assumed rate of growth for the next ten years is expected to be 6 per cent.

Gloria decided to use a stepped valuation method valuing the ten year, cash flow projection, and then taking the terminal cash flow and assuming that would grow in perpetuity at 2.2 per cent per annum.

The acquisition of RufDiamond plc is clearly a Type III acquisition. The alteration in Friendly Grinders' debt position will alter the firm's cost of capital by altering the exposure of the equity investors to both business and financial risk and by altering the default premium.

Step 1 Establish the planned rate of growth for the planning horizon and project the Free Cash Flow to the firm.

Step 2 Estimate the capital reinvestment required to sustain the desired rate of growth. There are a number of approaches to this: we can project forward the capital spending from previous years or if sufficient back data is available we can test the relationship between capital spending and operating cash flow using regression techniques. Alternatively, using the rate of return on equity (r) quoted for Friendly Grinders of 15 per cent and a 6 per cent growth rate we can imply a retention ratio (b) using Gordon's approximation:

$$g = r \times b$$
$$0.06 = 0.15 \times b$$
$$b = 40\%$$

The case tells us that streams 1 and 3 are net of reinvestment. Our only concern is stream 2 which is the projected cash flows from the acquired business. The retention ratio should be applied to the cash flows after tax.

The resulting cash flows for each of the three streams are shown in Exhibit 12.16.

Step 3 We now proceed to set up the cost of capital model. The first step is to calculate the asset beta for stream 1 (Friendly Grinders' underlying business risk), stream 2 (RufDiamond's underlying business risk) and for the combined firm.

The asset beta for streams 1 and 2 is calculated as shown below:

Friendly Grinders plc	RufDiamond
$\beta_A = \beta_e \times \dfrac{TMV_e}{TMV_e + TMV_d(1-T)}$	$\beta_A = \beta_e \times \dfrac{TMV_e}{TMV_e + TMV_d(1-T)}$
$\beta_A = 1.19 \times \dfrac{880}{880 + 90(0.7)}$	$\beta_A = 2.2 \times \dfrac{124.80}{124.80 + 10(0.7)}$
$\beta_A = 1.11$	$\beta_A = 2.083$

EXHIBIT 12.16

The three cash flow streams arising upon acquisition

	DOA	1	2	3	4	5	6	7	8	9	10
Stream 1 – current projected cash flows for Friendly Grinders plc											
Free cash flow before tax (after reinvestment)		68.91	73.04	77.43	82.07	87.00	92.22	97.75	103.62	109.83	116.42
Tax on free cash flow at 30%		−20.67	−21.91	−23.23	−24.62	−26.10	−27.67	−29.33	−31.08	−32.95	−34.93
Planned cash flow (post tax)		48.24	51.13	54.20	57.45	60.90	64.55	68.43	72.53	76.88	81.50
Stream 2 – current projected cash flows for acquired business											
Operating cash flows		16.11	17.07	18.10	19.18	20.33	21.56	22.85	24.22	25.67	27.21
Tax on the operating cash flows		−4.83	−5.12	−5.43	−5.76	−6.10	−6.47	−6.85	−7.27	−7.70	−8.16
		11.28	11.95	12.67	13.43	14.23	15.09	15.99	16.95	17.97	19.05
Capital investment to maintain operating capacity (40%)		−4.51	−4.78	−5.07	−5.37	−5.69	−6.04	−6.40	−6.78	−7.19	−7.62
Tax benefit of capital allowances at 100%		1.35	1.43	1.52	1.61	1.71	1.81	1.92	2.03	2.16	2.29
		8.12	8.61	9.12	9.67	10.25	10.86	11.52	12.21	12.94	13.72
Stream 3 – additional cash flows contingent on acquisition											
Realizable assets											
land sale	6.00										
disposal of interest in joint venture	7.00										
Exceptional integration costs		−2.00	−1.50	−1.00							
Increase in Friendly Grinder's business	13.00	5.00	5.30	5.62	5.96	6.31	6.69	7.09	7.52	7.97	8.45
Tax on synergies and other contingent cash flows	−3.90	−0.90	−1.14	−1.39	−1.79	−1.89	−2.01	−2.13	−2.26	−2.39	−2.53
Increase in post tax cash flow	9.10	2.10	2.66	3.23	4.17	4.42	4.68	4.96	5.26	5.58	5.91

DOA = date of acquisition

Note: for simplicity we have assumed that the value of the outstanding debt is the same as its book value. This may be a reasonable assumption to make where there is an expectation that debt will be rescheduled at maturity and where current yields are reasonably well approximated by the coupon rate. Where that is not the case, the market value of the debt should be implied from the expected yield, the actual coupon rate and the term to maturity as described in Chapter 4.

The asset beta for the combined firm is also reasonably straightforward:

$$\beta_c = \frac{V_1\beta_1 + V_2\beta_2}{TMV_e - V_3}$$

$$\beta_c = \frac{880 \times 1.11 + 124.8 * 2.083}{1004.8 - 0}$$

$$\beta_c = 1.231$$

Now using this beta we can 'regear' to Friendly Grinders' position post acquisition:

$$1.231 = \beta_e \times \frac{1004.8}{1004.8 + 260(0.7)}$$

$$\beta_e = 1.454$$

Note that in this calculation we have summed the two original equity values (£880m + £124.80m to give £1004.8m) and the total of outstanding debt which is £160m (if £1 per share is offered) plus the £90m and £10m of debt held by the two firms before the acquisition.

Using the revised equity beta we obtain a cost of equity capital using the Capital Asset Pricing Model as follows:

$$E(r_e) = R_f + \beta_e \times ERP$$
$$E(r_e) = 4.5\% + 1.454 \times 3.5\%$$
$$E(r_e) = 9.59\%$$

The final step in the calculation of the weighted average cost of capital is as follows:

$$WAAC = \frac{TMV_e}{TMV_e + TMV_d}E(r_e) + \frac{TMV_d}{TMV_e + TMV_d}r_d(1 - T)$$

$$WACC = \frac{1004.8}{1004.8 + 260} \times 9.59\% + \frac{260}{1004.8 + 260} \times 6.80\% \times 0.7$$

$$WACC = 8.60\%$$

The Excel analysis table is shown in Exhibit 12.17.

Step 4 We can now value the three streams of cash using the weighted average cost of capital of 8.6 per cent.

Note that we have discounted each cash flow at the weighted average cost of capital and calculated a residual value as follows (using stream 1 as the example):

$$V_{10} = \frac{FCF_{10} \times (1 + g)}{WACC - g}$$

$$V_{10} = \frac{81.50 \times (1.022)}{0.086 - 0.022}$$

$$V_{10} = £1301.94 \text{ } million$$

EXHIBIT 12.17

Excel model for the weighted average cost of capital for Friendly Grinders

Cash flow stream	1	2	3
Value of the equity	880.00	124.80	0.00
Value of the debt	90	10	
Beta	1.190	2.200	
Asset beta	1.110	2.083	
Asset beta of combined firm	1.231		
Market value of combined firm equity	1004.80		
Total debt	260		
Revised equity beta	1.454		
Cost of equity	9.59%		
Cost of debt	6.80%		
Weighted average cost of capital	8.60%		

This value when discounted to a present value can be added to the present value of the ten years of projected free cash flows to give a total firm value of £970 million or £880 million in the hands of the equity investors given the £90 million of debt finance.

Step 5 We now have three values for the three streams:

Stream 1: £880 million, Stream 2: £153.24 million and Stream 3: £76.76 million.

The sum of the stream 2 and stream 3 values give the £230 million that Gloria believed RufDiamond was worth. The problem is that the valuations of the three streams put into the cost of capital calculation and the three derived values here do not agree. To solve this activate the iteration feature in Excel (shown in Tools > Options > Calculation) and set the values in the cost of capital calculation equal to the cells showing the stream 1–3 values in Exhibit 12.17. Without the iteration feature checked Excel will produce a circular referencing error.

The result is that we have three stream values as shown in Exhibit 12.19. Note that we have put in Gloria's figures (using the uncorrected cost of capital) and the revised figures.

There is a substantial difference in the value of this acquisition compared with Gloria's original estimate. The valuation of the stream 2 and stream 3 cash flows is £226.30 million compared with £230 million but more critically the value of Friendly Grinders' cash stream 1 has now been devalued to £864.63 because of the alteration in the business risk to which the firm is exposed, the change in the financial risk because of the gearing effect and the increased default risk. Overall the increase in shareholder value is £50.93 million compared with the anticipated £70 million.

It might be objected that the decline in the value of the stream 1 income is mainly due to the higher imputed business risk whereas it is a low risk stream and should be valued as such. Valuing the streams by their component costs of capital might appear to make some sense but a moment's thought will show that if we do the net outcome will be the same as the value of the target stream will be reduced and the value of the acquirer's stream will be increased by compensating amounts.

EXHIBIT 12.18

First iteration of the valuation of Friendly Grinders (post acquisition)

Valuation of Stream 1 (Friendly Grinders – original)	DOA	1	2	3	4	5	6	7	8	9	10
Planned cash flow (post tax)		48.24	51.13	54.20	57.45	60.90	64.55	68.43	72.53	76.88	81.50
Discounted cash flow		44.42	43.36	42.32	41.31	40.32	39.35	38.41	37.49	36.60	35.72
Present value	399.30										
Terminal cash flow											81.50
Terminal value											1301.94
Discounted value	570.70										
Original value of the firm	970.00										
less Friendly Grinders' outstanding debt	90.00										
Friendly Grinders original equity value	880.00										

Valuation of stream 2 (acquired Free Cash Flow)	DOA	1	2	3	4	5	6	7	8	9	10
Increase in post tax cash flow		8.12	8.61	9.12	9.67	10.25	10.86	11.52	12.21	12.94	13.72
Discounted cash flow		7.48	7.30	7.12	6.95	6.79	6.62	6.46	6.31	6.16	6.01
Present value	67.20										
Terminal cash flow											13.72
Terminal value											219.11
Discounted value	96.04										
Projected increase in the value of the firm	163.24										
less RufDiamond's outstanding debt	10.00										
Addition to the equity value of Friendly Grinders	153.24										

Valuation of stream 3	DOA	1	2	3	4	5	6	7	8	9	10
Valuation of the additional cash flow on acquisition											
Increase in post tax cash flow	9.10	2.10	2.66	3.23	4.17	4.42	4.68	4.96	5.26	5.58	5.91
Discounted cash flow	9.10	1.93	2.26	2.52	3.00	2.93	2.86	2.79	2.72	2.66	2.59
Present value	35.35										
Terminal cash flow											5.91
Terminal value											94.47
Discounted value	41.41										
Value of additional cash flows	76.76										

EXHIBIT 12.19

The corrected valuation for Friendly Grinders where the output values agree with the weights in the WACC calculation

	£ million (uncorrected)	£ million (corrected)
Stream 1 Valuation of Friendly Grinders' cash flow	880.00	864.63
Stream 2 Valuation of RufDiamond's cash flow	153.24	150.66
Stream 3 Valuation of the synergistic and combination cash flows	76.76	75.64
Combined value of cash flows	1110.00	1090.93
Additional borrowing to finance bid	160.00	160.00
Equity value of the firm post bid	950.00	930.93
Original equity value of the firm	880.00	880.00
Increase in the value of the firm	70.00	50.93

Negotiating the bid

To maintain shareholder value, the acquirer must be confident that the bid lies between two constraints:

1 The open market value of the target's shares as no shareholder is likely to give up their shares for less than this figure.

2 The net increase in the value of the acquirer as a result of the bid.

In Exhibit 12.20 we have reworked the valuation model for Friendly Grinders and established a range of acceptable bid prices.

At the current bid price of £160 million, 22p per share (100p – 78p) is being offered as the control premium which is £35.2 million and £50.93 million is the

EXHIBIT 12.20

The bid range for Friendly Grinders giving the maximum increase in shareholder value (78p per share) and zero (135.77p per share)

Bid Price (£million)	124.80	160.00	200.00	217.23
Bid Price (per share)	78.00	100.00	125.00	135.77
Stream 1 valuation	861.29	864.63	868.22	869.71
Stream 2 valuation	150.10	150.66	151.26	151.51
Stream 3 valuation	75.40	75.64	75.90	76.01
Combined value of cash flows	1086.79	1090.93	1095.38	1097.23
Proposed Bid	124.80	160.00	200.00	217.23
Equity value of the firm post bid	961.99	930.93	895.38	880.00
Original equity value of the firm	880.00	880.00	880.00	880.00
Increase in the value of the firm	81.99	50.93	15.38	0.00

value added on acquisition. In any bidding process the negotiation with the target's directors (who may have a substantial equity interest in their firm) or in the case of a hostile bid with the shareholders directly should be determined by the minimum amount which the acquirer believes is necessary to gain control. One common approach is to set a bid that splits the spoils between the two groups of shareholders in proportion to their equity capitalization. So in Friendly Grinders' case the available VAA is £92.43 million being the difference between the lowest acceptable bid to RufDiamond's investors and the maximum acceptable bid to the shareholders in Friendly Grinders.

Friendly Grinders' Share of VAA	RufDiamond's Share of VAA
$VAA_{FG} = \dfrac{880}{1004.80} \times 92.43$	$VAA_{RD} = \dfrac{124.80}{1004.80} \times 92.43$
$VAA_{FG} = £80.95\ million$	$VAA_{RD} = £11.48\ million$

This would suggest a bid price of (£124.80 m + £11.48 m) £136.28 million or 85p per share (160 million shares).

In general, getting the control premium right and making sure that there is an equitable distribution of the value generated by the acquisition will entail consideration of many factors:

1 The value that could be realized from the sale of disposable assets which do not influence the future earnings of the acquired business and which have no economic value to the acquirer.

2 Evaluation of the extent to which the earnings distribution of the target company can be managed to eliminate or reduce the current downside risk thus increasing the expected average future earnings from the assets acquired and possibly increasing their quality by reducing their volatility.

This control premium will be further enhanced by synergistic effects:

3 The extent to which synergies in operations and the utilization of human and capital assets will enhance the earning capacity of the combined business. It is important in this context to determine whether it is the target or the acquirer driving the synergistic benefit. If synergy could be achieved by acquiring a number of like firms then a synergy premium should not be applied to the target firm under consideration. If the synergy is only achievable with the specific target then a premium should be applied.

4 Assessment of the impact of the business upon the financial reports of the acquirer.

5 Assessment of the impact of the acquisition upon the intangible value of the acquirer and the target if it is planned that it should remain as a separate operating company within the group.

Acquiring another firm is probably the quickest way for any firm to grow and, if it is done correctly, increase shareholder value. However, in efficient and competitive markets the gains that can be made through acquisition are likely to be small and often illusory. Acquisitions, nevertheless, form part of the corporate landscape and, from time to time, give rise to waves of merger activity. In this chapter, we have outlined the nature of mergers and acquisitions and the ways in which they are regulated.

A critical problem for any firm considering an acquisition is how to value a given target firm. Only in the most insignificant of cases will an acquisition add value to a firm in a direct way.

Approximately half of all acquisitions appear to destroy shareholder value and only a relatively small proportion enhance it. We have therefore devoted substantial space in this chapter to the analysis of the impact of an acquisition upon the value of the acquirer. The mechanisms by which value is added or destroyed are complex but one important route through which it occurs is by disturbing the firm's exposure to various types of risk and hence by disturbing its cost of capital. In this chapter we have shown a method for estimating the impact upon the firm's value from acquisition and in so doing draw together many of the issues discussed in this book concerning capital valuation and the cost of capital.

Further Reading

Agrawal, A., Jaffe, J.F. and Mandelker, G.N. (1992) The Post-merger Performance of Acquiring Firms: A Re-examination of an Anomaly, *Journal of Finance*, September, 47:1605–1621.

Andrade, G. and Stafford, E. (2004) Investigating the Economic Role of Mergers, *Journal of Corporate Finance*, 10: 1–36 *Journal of Economics and Business*, January, 36:29–42.

Ansoff, I. (1957) Strategies for diversification, *Harvard Business Review*, Boston, 35:5:57 Sep/Oct

Ansoff, I. (1962) *Corporate Strategy*, New York: McGraw Hill.

Berle, A.A., and Means, G.C. (1932) The Modern Corporation and Private Property, New York; The MacMillan Company (Reprint, 1991, Transaction Publishers, N.J.)

Coase, R.H. (1937) The Nature of the Firm, in Williamson, O.E. and Winter, S.G. (eds) (1993) *The Nature of the Firm: origins, evolution and development*, New York: Oxford University Press.

Dong, M., Hirschleifer, D., Richardson, S. and Teoh, S.H. (2003), Does Investor Misvaluation Drive the Takeover Market?, Working Paper, *Economist*, (1993), Something in the Waves, 6:89–90.

Erard, B. and Schaller, H. (2002), Acquisitions and Investment, *Economica*, 69:391–414.

Ferris, K.R. and Pecherot Petitt, B.S. (2002) *Valuation: avoiding the winner's curse*, London: FT Prentice Hall.

Franks, J. and Mayer, C. (1996) Hostile takeovers and the correction of managerial failure, *Journal of Financial Economics*, Elsevier, 40(1): 163–181.

Goergen, M., Martynova, M. and Renneboog, L. (2005) Corporate governance convergence: evidence from takeover regulation reforms in Europe, *Oxford Review of Economic Policy*, 21:243–268.

Geroski, P.A. (1984) On the Relationship Between Aggregate Merger Activity and the Stock Market, *European Economic Review*, 25:223–233.

Golbe, D.L. and White, L.J. (1993) Catch a Wave: The Time Series Behaviour of Mergers, *The Review of Economics and Statistics*, 75:493–499.

Gort, M. (1969) An Economic Disturbance Theory of Mergers, *The Quarterly Journal of Economics*, MIT Press, 83(4):624–642.

Gorton, G., Kahl, M. and Rosen, R. (2005) Eat or be Eaten: a theory of merger and merger waves, Working paper.

Hay, D.A. and Liu, G.S. (1998) When do Firms go in for Growth by Acquisitions?, *Oxford Bulletin of Economics and Statistics*, 60(2):143–164.

Jensen, M.C. (1986) Agency Costs of Free Cash Flow, Corporate Finance and Takeovers, *American Economic Review*, May, 76:323–329.

Jensen, M.C. (1986) Agency Costs of Free Cash Flow, Corporate Finance, and Takeovers, *American Economic Review*, American Economic Association, 76(2): 323–329.

Jensen, M.C. (1988) Takeovers: Their Causes and Consequences, *Journal of Economic Perspectives*, American Economic Association, 2(1):21–48.

Jensen, M.C. and Ruback, R.S. (1983) The Market for Corporate Control: The Scientific Evidence, *Journal of Financial Economics*, 11:5–50.

Jovanovic B. and Rousseau P.L. (2002) The Q-Theory of Mergers, *American Economic Review Papers and Proceedings*, May, 198–204.

Linn, S.C. and Zhu, Z. (1997) Aggregate Merger Activity: New Evidence on the Wave Hypothesis, *Southern Economic Journal*, July, 64:130–146.

Loderer, C. and Martin, K. (1992) Post acquisition Performance of Acquiring Firms, *Financial Management*, Autumn, 21:69–91.

Louis, H., (2004) The cost of using Bank Mergers as Defensive Mechanisms against takeover threats, *The Journal of Business*, 77(2):295–310.

Machlin, J.C., Hyuk C. and Miles, J.A (1993) The Effects of Golden Parachutes on Takeover Activity, *Journal of Law & Economics*, University of Chicago Press, 36(2):861–876.

Mitchell, M.L. and Mulherin, J.H. (1996) The Impact of Industry Shocks on Takeover and Restructuring Activity, *Journal of Financial Economics*, 41(2): 193–229.

Moeller, S.B., Schlingemann, F.P. and Stulz, R.M. (2005) Wealth destruction on a massive scale? A study of acquiring firm returns in the recent merger wave, *Journal of Finance*, 60:757–782.

Mueller, D.C. (1969) A Theory of Conglomerate Mergers, *The Quarterly Journal of Economics*, MIT Press, 83(4):643–659.

Mueller, D.C. (2003) *The Corporation: Investment, Mergers, and Growth*, London: Routledge.

Myers, S.C. and Majluf, N. (1984) Corporate Financing and Investment Decisions When Firms Have Information that Investors do not Have, *Journal of Financial Economics*, 13(1):187–221:38.

Resende, M. (1999) Wave Behaviour of Mergers and Acquisitions in the UK: A Sectoral Study, *Oxford Bulletin of Economics and Statistics*, 61(1):85–94.

Roll, R. (1986) The Hubris Hypothesis of Corporate Takeovers, *Journal of Business*, University of Chicago Press, 59(2):197–216.

Scherer, F.M. (1988) Corporate Takeovers: The Efficiency Arguments, *Journal of Economic Perspectives*, American Economic Association, 2(1):69–82.

Schnitzer, M. (1996) Hostile versus Friendly Takeovers, *Economica*, London School of Economics and Political Science, 63(249):37–55.

Schwartz, S. (1982) Factors Affecting the Probability of Being Acquired: Evidence for the United States, *Economic Journal*, Royal Economic Society, 92(366):391–398.

Shleifer, A. and Vishny, R.W. (1988) Value Maximization and the Acquisition Process, *Journal of Economic Perspectives*, American Economic Association, 2(1):7–20.

Shleifer, A. and Vishny, R.W. (2003) Stock Market Driven Acquisitions, *Journal of Financial Economics*, 70:295–311.

Yakov, A. and Lev, B. (1981) Risk Reduction as a Managerial Motive for Conglomerate Mergers, *Bell Journal of Economics*, The RAND Corporation, 12(2):605–617.

PROGRESS CHECK

1 What is the formal distinction between a merger and an acquisition?

2 Name six resistance strategies that the board of directors might employ.

3 What is the difference between a diversification and an integration strategy in corporate acquisition?

4 Give four reasons that might justify horizontal integration.

5 What do you understand by the term 'synergy'?

6 What is the market for corporate control, and how is it believed to operate?

7 Many acquisitions lead to a loss of shareholder value. What are the five principal explanations of this provided by Ferris and Petitt (2002)?

8 How many days are allowed between the notice of intention to bid for a firm and the last day for posting the offer document under the City Code?

9 Outline the ten principles which inform the City Code.

10 In the UK, what three tests are applied before the Competition Commission can become involved in determining the outcome of a proposal for two firms to combine?

11 Why would the Competition Commission of the European Union seek to block a merger?

12 What are the two most important mechanisms for financing an acquisition?

13 How does a minority interest arise upon consolidation?

14 What is the difference between the 'Control Premium' and the 'Value Added on Acquisition'?

15 What are the characteristics of the three financial types of acquisition?

16 How is the asset beta of the combination of firms derived?

17 What limits the bid price that the firm might set for an acquisition?

QUESTIONS (answers at end of book)

1 FlyMe Ltd is an unquoted company in the airline business. It has, since it was founded in 1988, developed a strong transatlantic business as well as a substantial position in the long and medium haul holiday market. In the year to 31 December 2005 its reported turnover was in £1.7 billion and its profit for the financial year was £50 million. The company's net assets are £120 million and its carries £150 million of long term loans in its balance sheet. It has recently expanded its fleet of wide bodied jets suitable for its expanding holiday business and has orders placed for the new Airbus 380 super-Jumbo to supplement its long haul fleet. FlyMe Ltd has route licences to New York, and six other major US cities.

There is no other airline of comparable size and business mix although analysts regard British Airways as a useful comparator. The statement below contains data relating to British Airways PLC (courtesy of Thomson One).

Key Fundamentals			
Forward P/E*	11.01	Dividend Yld	0.00
Price to Book	1.25	1 Yr Tot Return(%)**	25.07
Price To Cash Flow	2.96	Beta**	2.01
1 Yr Sales Growth	−1.66	1 Yr EPS Growth	80.60
Current Market Cap**			
(£ million)	3,026.71		
Source: Worldscope, *FirstCall, **Datastream			

You also note the following:

The current risk free rate is 4.5 per cent and the equity risk premium (rate of return on the market less the risk free rate) is estimated at 3.5 per cent for the UK equity market. The current share price for British Airways is 288p per share and its current PE ratio is 10. The corporation tax rate for both companies is 30 per cent.

The ratio of total debt to total capital (debt plus equity) for British Airways is 65.12 per cent and of total debt to equity is 186.7 per cent.

You may assume:

(i) FlyMe Ltd has the same exposure to business risk as British Airways.

(ii) FlyMe Ltd has undertaken a consistent programme of reinvestment.

(iii) The debt in both companies is not expected to be sensitive to market risk.

There has been considerable consolidation in the airline industry and you are advising a large UK airline on the value of FlyMe Ltd as a potential target for acquisition. It is anticipated that over the longer run the domestic airline industry will settle down to a rate of growth in line with GDP growth in the UK economy which according to the latest Bank of England inflation report stands at 4 per cent (nominal). However, the current rates of growth for this company are likely to be sustained for the next five years before reverting to the GDP growth rate from the seventh year forward.

The acquiring company's principal market base is in the UK and Europe with routes to the Middle East. Its principal hub is at Stanstead where FlyMe also has its centre of operations. It has a small holiday business through its partnership with a number of independent tour operators. It has a good reputation as a business carrier within its European market earned through very high standards of punctuality and service. Currently, it has cash reserves of £860 million.

You are required to:

(i) Estimate the current cost of equity capital for FlyMe Ltd using the Capital Asset Pricing Model making notes on any assumptions that you have made.

(ii) Estimate the expected growth rate of this company using Gordon's approximation and the current rate of retention of Free Cash Flow for each of the next seven years. Make notes on any assumptions you have made.

(iii) Value this company on the basis of its expected Free Cash Flow to Equity explaining the limitations of the methods you have used.

(iv) Write a brief discussion paper outlining the considerations a likely acquirer might bear in mind when contemplating this acquisition including a discussion of any real options that may be available to the acquirer.

	Year ended 31 December 2005	Year ended 31 December 2004
Net cash inflow from operating activities	210.0	95.0
Return on investment and servicing of finance		
Interest received	12.0	6.0
Interest paid	(4.0)	(3.0)
Interest element on finance leases	(6.5)	(4.0)
	1.5	(1.0)
Taxation	(4.1)	(0.2)
Capital Expenditure	(120.2)	(75.0)
Acquisitions and disposals		
Proceeds from the sale of interest in joint ventures	10.0	15.0
Cash inflow before management of liquid resources and financing	97.2	33.8
Management of liquid resources		
Decrease/(increase) in short term deposits	35.5	(32.2)
Financing		
Repayment of secured loans	(31.0)	(25.0)
Increase/decrease in cash for the year	**101.7**	**(23.4)**

QUESTIONS (answers on website)

2 Ruskin plc and Alf plc decide to merge their business operations. Ruskin has a market capitalization of £6bn and Alf a market capitalization of £4bn. Ruskin's market gearing ratio is 40 per cent and Alf's market gearing ratio is 10 per cent. The beta for Ruskin is 1.8 and the effective tax rate for both firms is 30 per cent. Both firms have identical business risk.

You are required to:

(i)   Calculate the asset beta for both firms and Alf's equity beta.

(ii) Calculate the combined asset beta and the combined equity beta for both firms.

(iii) Give reasons why the combined asset beta might not be as you have calculated.

3

Aqualot plc Abstracted Balance Sheet	£ million	£ million	Permalot plc Abstracted Balance Sheet	£ million	£ million
Fixed Assets		1980	Fixed Assets		764
Current Assets			Current Assets		
stocks	205		stocks	20	
debtors	90		debtors	120	
cash	40		cash	5	
	335			145	
Short term liabilities	322		Short term liabilities	140	
		13			5
		1993			769
Long term Liabilities		260	Long term Liabilities		10
Net Assets		1733	Net Assets		759
Owners' capital, 25p ordinary shares		100	Owners' capital, 25p ordinary shares		30
Share premium account		450	Share premium account		90
Profit and loss reserve		1183	Profit and loss reserve		639
		1733			759

Abstracted Profit and Loss	£ million	£ million	Abstracted Profit and Loss	£ million	£ million
Turnover		2800	Turnover		380
Operating profit		440	Operating profit		120
Interest paid		13	Interest paid		0.5
Distributable profits		306	Distributable profits		84
Dividend per share		15p	Dividend per share		20p

Abstracted Cash Flow	£ million	£ million	Abstracted Cash Flow	£ million	£ million
Operating cash flow		640	Operating cash flow		240
Net reinvestment		−150	Net reinvestment		−10
Corporation tax paid		−112	Corporation tax paid		−50
Interest paid		−4.5	Interest paid		−0.5
Beta		1.5	Beta		2.4
P/E ratio		15	P/E ratio		10
Historic earnings growth		5.50%	Historic earnings growth		3%
Risk free rate		4.50%	Risk free rate		4.50%
Equity risk premium		3.50%	Equity risk premium		3.50%
Debt in the form of a bond issue 5 per cent 5 year senior note		£108%			

Aqualot is considering a bid for Permalot and is planning to finance the acquisition by an offer of equity and cash. New shares would be offered at Aqualot's current share price equal to 50 per cent of the Permalot equity value. Any control premium plus 50 per cent of the equity value of Permalot would be offered in cash. The balance would be raised by new borrowing although Permalot realizes that its cost of debt would be raised by 80 basis points given the increase in gearing that this acquisition would entail.

In addition to the consolidated cash flows Aqualot believes that it would be able to generate a further £14 million in the first year net of reinvestment and that this would grow at the company's target growth rate of 5 per cent. It also believes that it can sustain this growth rate on its existing and the newly acquired business indefinitely. There would be exceptional integration costs of £12 million in year 1 and £5 million in year 2.

You may assume that Aqualot would maintain its current rate of net reinvestment.

(i) You are required to establish the negotiating range for a takeover attempt by Aqualot stating the minimum price and the maximum price to be paid.

(ii) Assuming that an offer is accepted which represents a division of the value of the acquisition between the two groups of shareholders in proportion to their total equity investment (pre-acquisition) in the two companies, calculate the value of Aqualot post acquisition.

(iii) Describe the steps which Aqualot should take if the bid is treated as hostile by the directors of Permalot.

4 In 2003, US sports tycoon Malcolm Glazer took control of the icon of British Football, Manchester United. Below are two reports compiled by the BBC (reproduced by permission) and you are required to do the following:

© Len Grant Photography/Alamy

(i) In as far as the information allows, determine the motives that may have led Malcom Glazier to make this bid.

(ii) Discuss the economic purpose served by an acquisition of this type.

(iii) Describe the steps that he took and the constraints imposed upon him by UK and European Law and regulation.

(iv) Outline the steps that he should have taken to determine the bid price for a football club such as this.

(v) Outline the problems that Malcolm Glazer may face in the acquisition and in particular describe the likely areas of risk that he faces in realizing surplus value from the transaction.

Article 1: Monday, 16 May, 2005, 08:05 GMT 09:05 UK

He may be pursuing one of Britain's best-known institutions, but Malcolm Glazer remains, above all, a shining example of the American dream.

His pursuit of Manchester United has made him a household name in UK financial circles and a figure of suspicion for many ordinary fans. However, Malcolm Glazer's background couldn't be any further removed from the glamour and drama of the 'Theatre of Dreams'.

From a Lithuanian family which emigrated to the United States, he was born in 1928, just as the Wall Street Crash was about to propel America into a decade-long depression. The budding tycoon grew up in Rochester, New York State, what was then a provincial town an hour from the Canadian border and 300 miles north of New York City. His father ran a store selling watch parts and it was in this humble setting, that he first cut his teeth in business after his father's death in 1943.

Over the next thirty years, the aspiring businessman steadily transformed his small inheritance into a growing business empire, thanks to a series of shrewd investments. Yet, it was not until well into his mid fifties that Mr Glazer was to become embroiled in his first takeover battle.

In 1984, he launched an unsuccessful $7.6bn (£4bn) bid to buy the bankrupt freight rail company, Conrail, reputedly backed up by just £100m of his own money. The bid may have come off the rails but Mr Glazer avoided being shunted into the sidings. He successfully invested in a range of business spanning television, restaurants and property. He became famous for stalking icons of American life such as kitchen designer Formica and motorcycle manufacturer Harley-Davidson. Neither of these deals ultimately came off but his willingness to take a gamble and put himself in the firing line was clear.

This hard edge was not merely confined to his public life. In 1980, Glazer took his five sisters to court in a dispute over their mother's will. However, it was in the bearpit of American football that he was really to make his business reputation and cement his fortune. In 1995, he paid $192m for the underperforming NFL football team, the Tampa Bay Buccaneers. Quickly proving that he wouldn't just sit on the touchline, he sacked the team's coach at the end of his first season.

Several unremarkable seasons followed and the new owner incurred the wrath of the team's fans by threatening to move the team out of the city. In 2003, he spent $8m on luring one of the sport's most successful coaches, Jon Gruden, from rival team, the Oakland Raiders. The gamble paid off and that same year, the Buccaneers went on to win the Superbowl. His investment in the club was said to have quadrupled in value. However, he wasn't content to sit on his laurels. He soon tried and failed to buy the Los Angeles Dodgers baseball team.

More significantly, it was in March 2003 – the year that Manchester United last won the Premiership title – that Mr Glazer first paid £9m to buy into Britain's biggest football club. Any suggestions that he was merely in it for the prawn sandwiches were quickly dispelled as the tycoon's stake steadily rose, hitting 28% last October. The talk was of a bidding war between *him and two other legendary gamblers, financiers JP McManus and John Magnier who had also built up a significant holding in the club.*

After the club rebuffed an informal takeover approach last November, Mr Glazer showed his ruthless streak, effectively forcing three United directors off the board. This escalation of hostilities was seen as a mistake by some and Mr Glazer's main financial backer, JP Morgan, promptly withdrew. However, the American proved undaunted and returned with more detailed takeover proposals and fresh backers in February. The fans may not have liked it but Mr Glazer was proving, not for the first time, that he wouldn't take no for an answer.

Article 2 *Thursday, 12 May, 2005, 23:07 GMT 00:07 UK*

US sports tycoon Malcolm Glazer has won control of Manchester United through a £790m ($1.47bn) takeover bid acquiring the 28.7 per cent stake owned by the Irish racing tycoons JP McManus and John Magnier, and now has more than 70% of the Premiership club. Red Football Ltd, acting on behalf of Mr Glazer, said the Irishmen had sold their stakes for 300p a share.

Club fans have vehemently opposed Mr Glazer's ambition all along and fear that ticket prices will soar. The bid comes five days ahead of the 17 May deadline when Mr Glazer had to make known whether he planned to bid.

Timeline of a Takeover

- **March 2003** – *Glazer buys 2.9% stake in club*
- **March 2004** – *Glazer says he has "no current intention" of making a bid*
- **June 2004** – *Glazer's stake in club nears 20%*
- **October 2004** – *United confirms bid approach from Glazer, as his stake nears 30%*
- **November 2004** – *Glazer ousts three directors from United's board*
- **December 2004** – *Glazer makes revised bid*
- **February 2005** – *Glazer makes new bid approach, valuing United at £800m, the club later opens its books to the tycoon*
- **14 April 2005** – *Glazer moots £800m bid for club*
- **28 April 2005** – *Takeover Panel sets 17 May deadline for Glazer to announce whether he intends to buy United*
- **12 May 2005** – *Glazer launches formal takeover bid for United after upping his stake in the club to almost 57%*

Mr Glazer now wants to buy the rest of the club's shares. If he gets 75% plus one share, United could be delisted from the stock exchange and Mr Glazer could transfer his debt onto the club. If he can get 90% plus one share, he can make a compulsory purchase and scoop up the other 10% of the club's shares. With heavy trading in Manchester United shares taking place after the announcement, it is already looking increasingly likely that Mr Glazer will quickly reach the 90.01% stake he needs to force out any remaining shareholders. United's third-biggest shareholder Scottish mining millionaire Harry Dobson is already reported to have sold his 6.45% stake after the Irishmen sold theirs. Shares in Manchester United closed up 34.25 pence, or 12.92%, at 299.25p on Thursday.

Constitutional Affairs Minister Harriet Harman said the government had urged Mr Glazer to have talks with fans, the Football Association and the club in order to ensure there was "constructive involvement". She told BBC One's Question Time: "Manchester United is very important to English football and the government is keeping a very close eye on the situation. "The fans are very worried and obviously there is concern that ticket prices will go up and that there won't be investment in the players."

Mr Glazer first showed an interest in buying the club last autumn and tabled a formal proposal in October, which was rejected by the board. The owner of the Tampa Bay Buccaneers is thought to be keen to exploit the strength of the Manchester United brand in the US. Two weeks ago, the club board said it could not recommend Mr Glazer's second takeover proposal to shareholders because his business plan appeared to be too "aggressive". His offers were rejected on the grounds that his plans relied too heavily on borrowed money. The club's chief executive David Gill said Mr Glazer's business plan was "potentially damaging" to the club amid fears that the American could saddle it with up to £300m worth of debt. However, members of the board did agree that some shareholders might think the offer was a good one.

Manchester United fans are angry at the latest news. Last year, they formed a shareholders' association to buy club shares and try to protect it from Mr Glazer's clutches. A spokesman for Shareholders United, which represents 17% of the club's shareholders, told the BBC that Mr Glazer was "no Roman Abramovich" (the Russian Billionaire who purchased Chelsea Football Club).

"He's not turning up with a suitcase full of his own cash and he is, in effect, asking Manchester United fans to pay for his takeover, to pay for increased ticket prices and increased merchandising," said spokesman Oliver Houston. "We feel completely betrayed by John Magnier and JP McManus."

The Irishmen are estimated to have made a £70m profit from their stake. A spokesman for the duo said: "They saw it as an investment. They got a very good deal."

"I'm giving up my season ticket," said Shareholders United president Nick Towle. "I'm not putting a penny of my money into this guy's pocket." Mr Towle said Shareholders United still hoped to stop the tycoon getting a 75% stake. "If we can get to that 25% of the remaining shareholders, that would be great," Mr Towle added. "But it's looking like an uphill battle for us."

Analysts are convinced that the 76-year-old is unstoppable. "I think it's pretty much game over now as the key to all this was always going to surround what the Irish duo would do with their stake," said Richard Hunter of stockbrokers Hargreaves Lansdown.

5   Below is the summarized data for Marks and Spencer plc extracted from the ThomsonOne database. Phillip Green, who last attempted to acquire the company in 2003, is returning to the problem and would like to get answers to the following questions:

   (i)   What is the range of potential growth rate which is implied by the data and the equity price that is implied assuming that the risk free rate of return is currently 4.6 per cent and the equity risk premium is 3.5 per cent.

   (ii) If Green believes that he could generate a further 2 per cent growth (compound) from this business over the next ten years what would this imply for the increase in shareholder value that could be generated from this business?

   (iii) If Green was revisiting the question of whether to bid for Marks and Spencer plc what other issues should he consider in making up his mind about the appropriate bid price?

Analyst Rating

Sell ▮▮▮▮▮▮▮▮▮ Strong Buy

EPS Estimate Forecasts

20.58	29.09	32.50	34.84
2005*	2006	2007	2008	*actual

Estimate Revisions

Estimates Up/Down
(Total 19)

7

9

Change in Estimate
1.07%

Last
28.786

Current
29.093

MARKS AND SPENCER GROUP PLC

http://www.marksandspencer.com

		Price*– **11/21/2005**	**Shrs Out (th)***	**Mkt Cap (th)***
Exchange:	L	445.75	1 660 415	7 401 290
Country:	G			
	B			
	R			
DJ Sector:	Consumer, Cyclical	**PE Ratio**	**Tot Ret 1Yr***	**Beta***
DJ Industry:	Retailers, Broadline	12.18	0.34	0.51
Company Status:	Active			*Source:Datastream

Scaling Factor: Millions GBP   Currency: GBP

5 YR ANNUAL BALANCE SHEET	**3/31/2005**	**3/31/2004**	**3/31/2003**	**3/31/2002**	**3/31/2001**
Cash & Equivalents	279.60	720.60	471.90	816.10	414.40
Other Current Assets	551.70	1 369.60	1 269.70	1 277.40	1 389.70
Total Current Assets	831.30	2 090.20	1 741.60	2 093.50	1 804.10
Property, Plant & Equipment – Net	3 316.10	3 497.60	3 435.10	3 381.20	4 118.90
Other Assets	137.60	1 789.30	1 577.20	1 716.10	1 763.10
Total Assets	**4 285.00**	**7 377.10**	**6 753.90**	**7 190.80**	**7 686.10**

Long term debt	1 901.90	2 337.50	1 675.00	2 045.40	598.30
Other liabilities	1 861.70	2 585.60	2 042.30	2 065.50	2 434.10
Total Liabilities	**3 763.60**	**4 923.10**	**3 717.30**	**4110.90**	**3 032.40**
Shareholders' Equity					
Minority Interest	0.00	0.00	0.00	0.40	15.60
Preferred Stock	65.70	84.90	118.20	276.00	0.00
Common Equity	455.70	2 369.10	2 918.40	2 803.50	4 638.10
Total Shareholder's Equity	**521.40**	**2 454.00**	**3 036.60**	**3 079.90**	**4 653.70**
Total Liabilities & Shareholders' Equity	**4 285.00**	**7 377.10**	**6 753.90**	**7 190.80**	**7 686.10**
Equity Shares Outstanding	1 658.10	2 265.14	2 270.02	2 306.95	2 867.38
5 YR ANNUAL INCOME STATEMENT					
Sales	7 710.30	7 971.50	8 077.20	7 619.40	8 075.70
Operating Income	677.10	809.40	761.80	629.10	467.00
Interest Expense on Debt	119.00	59.10	51.30	19.60	0.00
Pretax Income	745.30	781.60	679.00	687.90	145.50
Income Taxes	158.30	229.30	197.40	195.10	142.70
Net Income Available To Equity	587.0	552.3	507.3	153.0	(5.5)
Dividends	(203.3)	(263.2)	(246.0)	(238.9)	(258.3)
Profit/(loss) for the period	383.7	289.1	261.3	(85.9)	(263.8)
PER SHARE DATA					
EPS	0.29	0.24	0.21	0.17	0.00
Fully Diluted EPS	0.29	0.24	0.20	0.17	0.00
5 YEAR ANNUAL CASH FLOW STATEMENT					
Net Cash Flow From Operating Activities	1 309.90	399.30	920.40	951.10	524.90
Net Cash Flow From Investing Activities	−250.20	242.60	334.00	−437.60	252.30
Financing Activities					
Net Proceeds From Sales/Issue of equity and preference stock	0.00	0.00	0.00	−9.30	0.00
Equity and preference stock	2 334.10	87.80	299.70	1 769.90	20.30
Purchased, Retired, Converted, Redeemed Long Term Borrowings	0.00	441.70	0.00	1 296.90	0.00
Inc(Dec) In ST Borrowings	855.60	−27.50	−110.40	−265.60	39.40
Reduction In Long Term Debt	98.00	2.50	310.70	0.00	310.80
Cash Dividends Paid – Total	239.70	250.10	232.20	256.70	258.60
Other Source/(Use) – Financing	0.60	3.60	0.00	0.00	0.50
Net Cash Flow From Financing Activities	−1 747.20	95.00	−933.40	−987.30	−550.00

Short term finance and the management of interest rate risk

13

U p until this stage we have been primarily concerned with the operation of the capital market, the appraisal of long-term investments and the estimation of the cost of capital. However, firms also need access to short-term finance to support their operating activities and occasionally bridge problems caused by short-term capital market failure. We will spend some time examining the nature of the money market and how it operates before turning our attention to the different mechanisms available for financing a firm's operating activities. The problem most firms confront in dealing with the money markets is managing their exposure to short-term interest rate risk. In Chapter 8, we introduced the idea of derivatives and explored options in some detail. Other types of derivative are also available that are specifically suited to the management of interest-rate risk. In this chapter we explore the application of two broad classes of money market derivative: the forward rate and the swap agreement.

Learning outcomes

By the end of this chapter you will be able to achieve the following:

1 Describe in outline the different types of money market instrument and explain their use in commercial transactions.

2 Locate prices and interpret their significance for purchasing and selling money market securities.

3 Have a sound knowledge of the principal drivers of interest rates and the role of the Central Bank in setting rates.

4 Describe the principal sources of short term finance and calculate the relative advantages of commercial paper issues and repo transactions compared with bank borrowing.

5 Decide on the most appropriate class of money market derivative for the management of interest rate risk.

6 Establish and price a hedging strategy for the management of short term interest rate risk using a Forward Rate Agreement and an interest rate future.

7 Determine the SWAP premium for a vanilla interest rate swap and describe the mechanism by which swaps are priced and traded on the money markets.

The money markets

Like the capital markets the money markets are where financial securities of different sorts are traded. Again like the capital market there is a primary money market where companies can raise new money to finance their operations, a secondary market where monetary securities are bought and sold and also a derivatives markets which trade in contracts whose value is based, in some way upon those securities. The only significant difference between the capital and the money market is in terms of the maturity of securities involved. In the money markets the securities when issued have a maturity of (normally) less than one year – very occasionally banks may issue money market securities of up to two years' maturity.

We do not delve too deeply into the wide variety of money market instruments that are traded. In Exhibit 13.1 we show a selection of the different types of money market security that are traded. They can be subdivided into three categories:

- *Coupons bearing securities*. These are fixed maturity securities which carry a specified rate of interest usually payable at maturity. Coupon bearing securities have much of the characteristic of the government and corporate bonds discussed in Chapter 4.

- *Discount securities*. These securities are issued at a lower price than their face value (say £100) which will be repaid at maturity. The gain to the holder is purely in terms of the capital gain over the holding period. The measurement of the discount yield is discussed later.

- *Derivatives*: these are contracts written on an underlying money market security and they are normally cash settled. This means that the security is not handed over at settlement but rather the profit and loss on the transaction is settled by a cash payment.

EXHIBIT 13.1

The principal money market instruments

Security	Issuer	Characteristics
Coupon bearing being securities which pay a set rate of interest on their face value:		
Certificates of Deposit (CD)	Banks, building societies, other financial houses	In exchange for a deposit of funds the issuer writes a receipt offering a one-off interest payment plus repayment of the face value of the deposit at maturity. The CDs are negotiable and can be traded.
Repo agreements (repurchase agreements) and reverse repos	Central banks, commercial banks and finance houses and corporates	When a bank/company agrees to sell a security at a given price it enters into a simultaneous agreement with the purchaser to buy the security back at a given future date and price. A reverse repo is simply an agreement to purchase a security with a simultaneous agreement to resell.

Security	Issuer	Characteristics
Discount instruments which are issued at a discount relative to their redemption value		
Treasury Bills	UK Treasury	These bills or government 'IOUs' are usually of one or three months maturity. They are highly liquid investments and easily traded.
Commercial paper	Corporates	Companies issue 'IOUs' against borrowed funds. They are issued at a discount and repaid at their face value and no extra interest is paid. CP are the short term equivalent of corporate bonds and can be asset backed or may be 'credit backed' where the issuing firm has a weak credit rating but can obtain credit support from another company. CP is not normally traded but is usually held until maturity once issued.
Bills of Exchange/Banker's Acceptance	Corporates	Bills of Exchange are issued by companies promising to repay borrowing from a bank. Once the bank accepts the bill of exchange it is called a 'banker's acceptance' and as such can be traded as a discount instrument on the money market.
Money market derivatives:		
Forward Rate Agreements (FRAs)	Banks and other financial houses	An agreement by the bank to enter into a notional loan or accept a deposit with a customer for a specified period of time and to settle with the customer the difference between the rate of interest agreed when the agreement is made and the rate prevailing when the notional loan/deposit is deemed to start.
Options on Forward Rate Agreements (Caps and Floors)	Banks and other financial houses	The bank as writer of the option agrees to cap the interest rate charged on a loan over a set period of time such that if the interest rate rises above the cap the difference in the rate is paid to the holder. If the interest rate does not reach the cap the holder does not have to reimburse the bank (as with the FRA). A floor is exactly the opposite where a minimum interest rate is set on a deposit.

Security	Issuer	Characteristics
Interest Rate Futures	Exchange Traded	These are notional securities traded on the futures markets whose prices depend upon prevailing interest rates. Thus the greater the interest rates the lower the value of the future and vice versa.
Options on Interest Rate Futures	Exchange Traded	As the name suggests there are options available for the purchase or sale of IRFs at a specified future date.
Interest Rate Swaps	Two counterparties: banks or corporates	Where two parties agree to swap their liabilities for interest rate payments on a given capital sum. This is usually, but not necessarily, a fixed for variable interest rate swap.
Options on swaps (swaptions)	Banks and corporates	Where two counterparties enter into an option agreement to enter into an interest rate swap at some future date.

Trading in the money markets

Much of our study of corporate finance has focused upon the problems of obtaining long term finance by companies. However, firms and other institutions also have short term financing requirements. Broadly we can categorize firms into two types depending upon the dynamics of their business and the stage their products have received in their life cycles.

1 *Cash generators*: being companies whose products and services are well established in the market and/or where the firm's treasury cycle is very short between the time a sale is made and the customer pays. Retail businesses tend to be cash generative particularly if much of their sales are on a cash basis. Some companies, even within a normally cash restrictive industry such as pharmaceuticals, may have a highly successful product line with strong patent protection. Warner Lambert, the US pharmaceutical company, discovered and brought to market 'Lipitor' the first of a new generation of anti-statins. Following the market launch in 1997 the company became progressively more cash generative until in the year 2000 it was taken over by Pfizer for $90 billion. Highly cash generative businesses will usually seek to lay off cash in the short term market while establishing the most profitable use for its resources or deciding whether to return cash to investors by way of a share repurchase or dividend payment.

2 *Cash consumers*: being companies who, by nature of the adverse terms of trade they face, or because of high levels of investment in research and development or new capital programmes are chronically short of cash. Many heavy manufacturing firms find themselves in this position because of the long lead times in production and the extended times they may face before customer accounts are settled. Such companies are likely to find themselves active in the money markets as short term borrowers. Young fast growing companies also tend to fall into this category.

Quoting price of money in the money markets

There are three types of short term interest rates quoted in the money market.

1. *Rates for buying and selling money market securities.* The rates are normally quoted two ways and so the one month Treasury Bill rate is (at 30 September 2005): $4_{21/32} - 4_{19/32}$. The higher rate is the discount rate on selling the bill (the higher the discount rate the lower the value of the bond) and the lower rate is the rate at which the bills can be purchased in the market. The first rate is thus the 'offer rate' or 'offer price' and the second the 'bid rate' or 'bid price'.

2. *The rate quoted for borrowing and lending.* In the money markets again two rates are quoted, the first is the lending rate and the second the deposit rate. So, for example, the sterling interbank rate is currently quoted at $4_{5/8} - 4_{1/2}$. The interbank market is a market for borrowing and lending between banks and the first rate is the rate a bank will quote to lend funds and the second is the rate the bank will pay on deposits. Again the higher rate is the offer rate and the lower the bid rate.

3. *Reference rates*: in many situations securities are valued using a benchmark rate. The most important is the London Interbank Offer Rate (LIBOR) which is collated on a daily basis by the British Bankers' Association from the offer rates quoted by the major banks for fixed maturity lending. The LIBOR is fixed every day at 11.00am. A corresponding bid rate (LIBID) is also collated and published at the same time. The LIBOR is quoted on the basis of interbank transactions on the London markets in sterling, dollars and a range of other currencies. The system has been copied elsewhere although LIBOR is the most often quoted rate internationally.

Changes in interest rates are usually quoted in 'basis points'. This is a term we met first when discussing the fixed interest market in Chapter 4. But to refresh your memory a basis point is 0.01 of a per cent. Thus a quarter percentage change would be quoted as 25 basis points and a half percentage change would be 50 basis points.

REVIEW ACTIVITY 13.1 The rate of discount on a Treasury Bill is quoted as $4_{12/16} - 4_{10/16}$. What rate would be appropriate for the purchase of a 90 day bill and what would be the subscription value of a bill with a face value of £50 000?

Finally, when deciding which rate is which it is always worth remembering the principle 'the customer always loses'. This simply reflects the fact that banks and other market makers in the money markets exist to make a profit out of the transactions concerned.

The drivers of interest rates

Short term interest rate movements are primarily signalled by changes in the base rate declared by the central bank. On a monthly basis the Monetary Policy Committee of the Bank of England, under the chair of the Governor of the Bank, reset the central bank's interest rate which is the overnight (i.e. very short term) repo rate at which it undertakes financial transactions with the major banks. In the major western economies, where the central bank is independent of political control, the primary aim in setting interest rates is the maintenance of stable prices. In the United Kingdom the Bank of England is set a target rate for inflation of 2.0 per cent and is required to set interest rates that are

The Bank of England

Image Source/Alamy

consistent with the maintenance of that target. Prior to 1997 the inflation target represented a maximum rate. Since that time it has been set as a 'symmetric' target in that variances in either direction should be regarded as equally undesirable. This reflects concerns that deflation is as significant a threat to the stability of the economy as excessive inflation.

If price levels are expected to move above 2.0 per cent the Bank will increase the base rate to slow credit formation and hence cut the demand for goods and services in the economy. If the rate falls below this figure the bank will move to cut rates and hence expand credit formation and thus demand.

There are a number of other factors that the Bank will bear in mind when managing interest rates:

- The supply and demand for money in the economy including the level of government borrowing.
- The level of confidence in particular areas of the economy such as housing, manufacturing and the retail sector.
- The level of the exchange rate (a high exchange rate for the domestic currency will elevate import prices and dampen export competitiveness – and vice versa).
- Market expectations as revealed by forward rates on the money market and other factors.
- Price changes in particular sectors and in different aspects of the supply chain. Increases in energy costs or high levels of wage settlements could presage inflationary pressure.

Altering interest rates is one instrument under the central bank's control. It also has the power to influence rates through its open market operations. If the central bank increases its net lending to the banking sector it will increase the supply of money in the economy which will tend to reduce interest rates. Conversely, if the central bank borrows money it tends to reduce the level of liquidity in the banking sector and hence short term interest rates will rise.

FINANCIAL REALITY

Following Hurricane Katrina in the US in August 2005 immense pressure was put on international oil prices following damage and closure of refineries in the Gulf of Mexico which provide over a quarter of the US supply of oil. Here is the edited conclusion of the team of economists and other experts who under the chair of Mervyn King, Governor of the Bank of England, decided on the level of UK interest rates for the month of September:

While there remained uncertainty about the likely effects of Hurricane Katrina on US GDP growth, past experience suggested that those effects might be relatively small and short-lived. However, higher oil prices continued to pose a downside risk to world demand and an upside risk to world export prices.

> *On the domestic front, the slight upward revision to Q2 GDP left growth slightly below trend for the fourth quarter in a row. Consumption growth had been weaker than expected, but this may have reflected mismeasurement issues relating to the net tourism figures. Acting in the opposite direction, export growth might have been overstated. Data releases and survey indicators relating to July and August suggested that GDP growth in Q3 was likely to be broadly similar to that in Q2.*
>
> *UK consumption and business investment and euro-area domestic demand had continued weak. If sustained, these developments were likely to push down on UK GDP growth and deliver a lower inflation outturn . . . Sterling's appreciation would also push down on inflation. However, equity prices had continued to increase, money growth was strong, and activity developments over the previous month could be viewed as having been broadly consistent with the August Inflation Report.*
>
> *There remained a risk that oil prices would rise further. This posed an upside risk to the inflation projection. But, there were few signs of any second-round effects arising yet from the increase in oil prices.*
>
> *Given these considerations, the Committee agreed (unanimously) that it was appropriate to leave interest rates unchanged at 4.5%.*
>
> Note the range of issues that have influenced the Monetary Policy Committee. A number of potential inflationary risks were identified in both the international economy and the domestic money markets. The Committee would also have had at its disposal the market's expectations of interest rate through both the long and the short term.

In setting interest rates the Central Bank will bear in mind the short term structure of interest rates projected in ways similar to that described in Chapter 4 and as shown in Exhibit 13.2. This curve is the short term version of the term structure (or yield curve) described in Chapter 4. The nominal spot curve reflects the interest rate on securities maturing within five years and the nominal forward rate curve reflects the forward rates implied by the nominal spot curve (we demonstrate the calculation of implied forward rates later in this chapter when we consider the valuation of swaps). From these curves we can note that the expectation of future interest rates is down by some 50 basis points compared with the current levels. This would suggest that the market expects inflationary pressure to ease in the near term and as a result the cost of short term money (in nominal terms) to reduce.

Money market finance

Companies have a number of sources of short term borrowing. For small firms, or young firms without a strong credit rating the simplest form of short term finance is bank borrowing. This borrowing may be for a fixed term and rate but will normally be against an overdraft on a variable rate. As with personal borrowing the rates of interest will vary depending upon the perceived credit risk. Where a company has made sales to low credit risk companies it may also be able to factor its receivables. With factoring a percentage of the value of the debt (usually about 80 per cent) is

EXHIBIT 13.2

The short term structure of interest rates

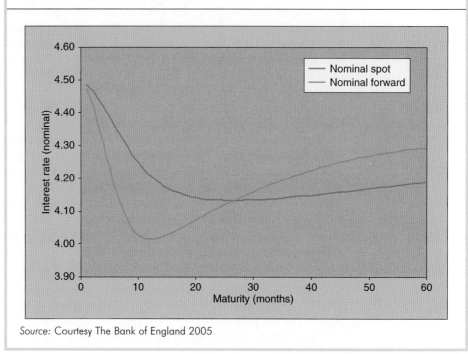

Source: Courtesy The Bank of England 2005

paid upon presentation of the invoice. The balance less commission and charges will be paid once the debt is collected from the customer. Some factors offer debt management and collection services.

Companies with stronger credit ratings may also resort to the issue of 'commercial paper'. This is the corporate equivalent of a Treasury Bill which is a discount security used to raise finance for the government's short term operational money needs. Commercial paper is issued at a discount and is almost always issued with a maturity of less than 270 days.

The primary market for CP is handled by banks and other financial institutions specializing in this type of market. The issue is invariably made within the context of a CP programme. Thus, a limit will be specified for the maximum amount of short term debt that can be issued by the company at any one time and a period of time over which the issues will be made is also specified. There are two principal commercial paper markets: the US dollar market which is worth over $1.5 trillion (2005) and the European commercial paper market where issues are made principally in sterling or euro(s) but also in Swiss francs and other smaller national currencies. The European market is estimated to be worth in excess of £500 billion.

FINANCIAL REALITY

As a large public limited corporation Friendly Grinders plc has a good credit rating and has decided to raise short term finance through the CP market. Friendly Grinders decides to limit itself to a five year programme of no more than £200 million in issue at any one time. The commercial arm of its bank arranges the issue of an initial tranche of £50 million for 90 days at a discount of 4.8 per cent.

In order to calculate the issue price for this commercial paper we need to apply the following formula:

$$PV_0 = \frac{FV}{(1 + r_d \times \dfrac{D}{365})}$$

In the United States and some other jurisdictions a 360 day count is used. However, as Friendly Grinders is issuing this first tranche in the UK money market the price quoted will be:

$$PV_0 = \frac{£50 \ million}{(1 + 0.048 \times \dfrac{90}{365})}$$

$$PV_0 = £49\ 415\ 141$$

Usually CP of this type is passed into the hands of financial institutions, investment funds and companies looking for a short term deposit of known maturity and yield. It is however negotiable and can be traded on the CP market. Obviously as interest rates in the short term money market fluctuate so will the prices at which the corporate paper will trade.

Normally commercial paper is unsecured and thus the investor must rely upon the credit worthiness of the issuer. However, there is a market for 'asset backed' commercial paper where the value of the issue is secured against certain specified assets of easily realizable commercial value (such as land, property and other generally tradable assets). In recent years lower credit rated companies have also entered this market where their commercial paper is backed by a higher credit rated institution such as a bank or merchant bank. In the equivalent way to granting a letter of credit for a commercial transaction, the money market guarantee given by the bank allows the company concerned to issue 'credit backed' paper.

The attractiveness of this type of market for an issuer is that it may be able to secure a more competitive rate for borrowing short term from the money market than it can obtain borrowing under normal commercial terms from a bank. However, against this the costs of issue are significant and can only be contemplated for large value issues.

Repo (repurchase) agreements

A bank, financial institution or indeed a company can enter into a repurchase agreement which is a simultaneous buy/sell arrangement where either:

1   The company sells a financial security for a stated price agreeing to repurchase that security at that price (plus interest) at a particular date, or

2   The company buys a financial security with a concurrent agreement to sell it back (a reverse repo).

The point of the repo agreement is it offers borrowing and lending secured against a financial security such as a Treasury Bond. As a result the effective rate of interest on the repo should be more favourable than unsecured borrowing or lending because of the collateral given by the repo'd security. When the repo market first opened in the UK in 1996 most of the activity was for overnight transactions between banks using gilt edged securities (Treasury Bonds). However, repo agreements are now struck with terms of up to six months and other types of business apart from banks have entered the market.

FINANCIAL REALITY

Friendly Grinders decide to use a repo agreement to achieve a more favourable rate on short term borrowing. Gloria enters into a repo agreement through the NatWest Repo desk whereby she sells £2 million (nominal) of long dated Treasury stock for £1 970 800 with a buy back in 30 days at £1 977 000. LIBOR is currently 4.2 per cent.

The effective interest rate that Friendly Grinders pays on the repo'd loan is:

$$r = \frac{1\ 977\ 000 - 1\ 970\ 800}{1\ 970\ 800} \times \frac{365}{30}$$

$$r = 3.83\ per\ cent$$

which is 37 basis points lower than LIBOR.

Currently the gilt repo market is standing in excess of £200 billion representing more than 25 per cent of the UK money market.

Using the money markets to finance trade

Apart from the tendency of a given firm to be cash rich or cash dry companies may also have a short term requirement to finance a particular trade deal. One of the most popular ways of doing this is through what is known as a 'Banker's Acceptance'. This entails the creation by the bank of a 'letter of credit' (traditionally also known as a 'Bill of Exchange').

FINANCIAL REALITY

Friendly Grinders has made a purchase of industrial grade diamonds worth £6 000 000 from a South African Company based in Johannesburg. Its bank is NatWest plc based in London and its suppliers, Dirand (SA) Ltd's bank is the SA Bank based in Johannesburg. The two companies agree that payment will be made 30 days after delivery and that acceptance financing will be used to avoid the credit risk that Dirand is exposed to. Friendly Grinders obtains the financing agreement for the transaction from the NatWest who issue a 'letter of credit' (LOC) stating that it will pay £6 000 000 in 30 days. This letter of credit is sent to SA Bank who in its turn notifies Dirand of its receipt. Dirand now ships the goods and passes the shipping documents plus a time draft requesting payment to the SA Bank. The letter of credit will contain the agreed conditions and the required documentation (invoice, bill of lading and insurance documents) that need to be attached. The SA Bank will then check that the documentation is in order and returns the letter of credit and the documentation to the NatWest in London.

Assuming that all the paperwork is in order the NatWest stamps the LOC as 'accepted' and at that point a 'Bankers Acceptance' is created. At this point the NatWest accepts responsibility for payment. NatWest pass the shipping documents to Friendly Grinders who are now happy in the knowledge that the goods ordered are underway and also returns the Bankers Acceptance to the SA Bank.

The SA Bank can request immediate payment of the discounted value from the NatWest or hold it until it expires in 30 days and claim the full £6 000 000. If the first course is chosen NatWest, in its turn, can hold the Banker's Acceptance which it can either retain until Friendly Grinders pays or it may sell it on to the market.

Whoever holds the acceptance when it matures can redeem it with the NatWest Bank for £6 000 000. Likewise, the SA Bank can hold the Banker's Acceptance rather than redeeming it early for its discounted value or it can sell it into the market. At the end of 30 days, Friendly Grinders pays the £6 000 000 to the bank and the bank redeems the Banker's Acceptance to whoever holds it at that time.

The sequence of steps involved in this financial transaction (see Exhibit 13.3) achieves a number of ends: first the credit risk to the two counterparties is minimized. Dirand (SA) is sure of getting its money and the NatWest in London will not accept the LOC until it has verified that the goods have been shipped in accordance with the specification agreed between the two counterparties.

Second, both parties achieve their desired terms of trade in that Friendly Grinders is granted 30 days to pay and Dirand (SA) can either take payment in full at 30 days or the discounted value of the transaction immediately. Finally, the Banker's Acceptance can be sold on in the money market or can be redeemed at the holder's discretion.

From the point of view of the two companies a significant amount of risk has been withdrawn from the transaction but there is a catch. Friendly Grinders will pay a substantial charge for the service as, in effect, it is purchasing the bank's creditworthiness. Problems may also materialize if, when the letter of credit is referred to the seller, they either cannot produce the required documentation or disagree with the terms of

EXHIBIT 13.3

The sequence of steps in the creation and discharge of a Banker's Acceptance

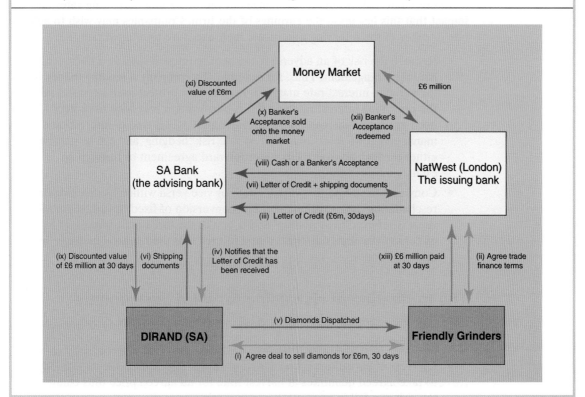

payment. The latter may occur if the goods in this case are priced in the importer's currency (as in this case) and there is a sudden and adverse change in the rate of exchange. However, financing trade through a letter of credit and Banker's Acceptance is a particularly common way of settling international transactions especially where the counterparties are not well known to one another.

A bank may collect a large number of Banker's Acceptances and where these have maturities of less than three months (in the UK) and are supported by a commercial transaction which will be completed within the specified timescale then the central bank may accept them as collateral for a loan. Not all Banker's Acceptances are eligible to be used in this way and many more find their way into the hands of fund managers as 'discount paper' to be redeemed on the due date for their face value.

The management of interest rate risk using money market derivatives

There are a number of ways in which a company can attempt to mitigate its exposure to interest rate risk. Where a company has its operations distributed across a number of different countries it may decide to borrow short term finance in different markets and hence diversify its exposure to interest rate risk. Likewise in the UK it may 'revolve' a number of different sources of short term finance balancing its fixed and variable rate borrowing. There are a number of internal measures that a company can take to smooth the variability of its interest payments. However, there may come a point where 'internal hedging' is insufficient and the company will need to have resort to money market derivatives to hedge its exposure.

Interest rate risk results from changes in the prevailing borrowing rates and the impact that this has upon the earnings of the firm. Companies may wish to achieve one or other of the following to mitigate their exposure to interest rate risk:

- Remove the risk of an adverse movement in interest rates in a borrowing or lending arrangement. Thus, for example, if a company is lending money in the variable interest rate market it may wish to protect itself against a fall in the prevailing interest rate and if it is borrowing it may wish to protect itself against an increase in the prevailing rate. This type of interest rate management we refer to as interest rate risk 'hedging' and can be achieved either through an over the counter forward agreement or through an exchange traded future agreement.

- Convert a fixed rate to a variable rate or vice versa without redeeming or rescheduling their existing debt. The conversion of fixed to variable or vice versa is referred to as a 'swap' and is one of the three most important types of derivatives alongside options and futures that the financial manager has at their disposal.

The mitigation of risk using forward agreements

Originally forward agreements were entered into to minimize the risk in buying and selling commodities:

- Growers of agricultural products would enter into arrangements with buyers to take agreed quantities at harvest time for an agreed price thus eliminating the risk of a fall in price on the open market from the point of view of the grower, or the risk of a rise in price from the point of view of the buyer.

- Shippers of commodities would agree a price for future delivery of a consignment of tea, coffee, sugar, spice or other goods. The shipper was thus protected against a fall in market prices and the receiving wholesaler from an increase.

Now virtually any commodity or security can be bought and sold 'forward' as an 'over the counter' agreement and a number of forward contracts have been standardized into a form where the resulting 'future' contract can be traded on one or more of a number of exchanges around the world. Future contracts provide a means of mitigating adverse price risk at low cost although given their nature it is not always possible to perfectly hedge the underlying risk. Our particular application is where forward and future agreements are used to manage adverse movements in the price of money.

The difference between the forward agreements and future contracts

Where the counter parties agree to undertake a future transaction at a given price or rate of interest then they are said to be entering into 'a forward agreement'. The forward agreements are 'over-the-counter' or OTC arrangements and can be arranged between individuals, companies and/or their financial institutions. Forward agreements of necessity means that each party to the arrangement accepts the risk that the other side may default. However, the benefit is that such an agreement can be tailored to meet the requirements of both parties exactly. This may be important if one or both parties require the forward agreement to perfectly hedge some underlying transaction.

Many forward agreements have been standardized and 'securitized' such that they can be traded between buyers and sellers on an exchange. Exchange traded forward agreements are known as 'futures contracts'. The advantage of the futures contract is that it avoids default risk by the mechanism of the margin payments which the exchange will require both parties to deposit as the contract proceeds to maturity. Normally, an initial margin will be required in the form of a cash payment into the exchange and this will be followed by 'variation' or 'maintenance' margin calls as one or other party begins to take a loss. Inevitably, both forward agreements and future contracts represent a zero sum between the two sides, as one party makes a profit, the other makes a loss.

Neither forward agreements nor future contracts can be settled prematurely if one or other of the two parties wishes to avoid further losses. So, if one party wants to avoid further losses they must 'close their position' by entering into another contract on the other side. So if an agreement has been made by one party to purchase goods at a future date at a contracted price then to 'close their position' they will need to enter into a similar agreement to sell those goods at a currently agreed future price and at the same date as the original agreement. One of the benefits of a futures contract is that it can be closed quickly and indeed if a margin call is not paid can lead to the very rapid closure of the position by the exchange. A forward contract can be closed by agreement if the other party is willing or by the purchase of an equivalent but opposite contract to buy or sell the security concerned. This will normally be a more costly and difficult process than dealing through the exchange.

Hedging interest rate risk using forward agreements

Two methods are available to hedge interest rate risk. The first uses a forward type agreement where the company nullifies the impact of an adverse interest rate movement by entering into an arrangement to notionally borrow or lend an equivalent sum such that the interest paid or received is sufficient to balance any loss that may result.

This type of interest rate hedging can be achieved either through an 'over the counter' arrangement called a 'Forward Rate Agreement' or through the use of interest rate futures. Interest rate futures are exchange traded forward agreements which can be entered into and 'closed out' at a later stage. The second approach is to use an interest rate option to hedge the exposure.

Forward Rate Agreements (FRA)

Forward Rate Agreements are the most common way in which companies hedge their interest rate risk. The idea is simple: if a company knows that it has a future liability to pay interest (say) on a loan at a variable rate it can take out a notional loan with an FRA market maker which we will call the 'bank' – although it may not be the company's bank but another financial institution specializing in this type of business – of the same amount of money for the period. The bank agrees that, in its turn, it will pay to the company the difference between the contracted rate of interest and the rate of interest ruling at the time if the difference is positive, or recover from the company the shortfall if it is negative. So, to get that absolutely clear:

- *Buying an FRA*: if a company is concerned about a rise in interest rates it buys an FRA from the market maker. This is a notional loan at a fixed

EXHIBIT 13.4

The time line for a Forward Rate Agreement

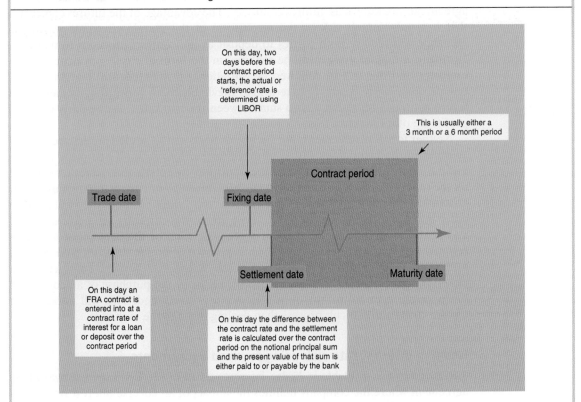

contracted rate where market maker (the seller) of the FRA agrees to compensate the buyer for a subsequent rise in interest rates above the fixed FRA rate.

- *Selling an FRA*: if a company is concerned about a fall in rates it will sell an FRA to the market maker which is equivalent to a notional deposit of the contracted sum such that if interest rates fall below the contracted deposit rate the company (the seller) will be reimbursed.

Therefore, in a situation where a corporate treasurer finds herself exposed to future interest-rate changes on borrowing in the money market she can use a Forward Rate Agreement to lock in a fixed rate of interest. Therefore, if interest rates move against the company such that the rates it has to pay on the actual borrowing are higher than they are currently then the FRA will yield the difference. If interest rates move in its favour then it will save interest on the underlying loan but will have to pay the difference over to the bank. The reverse is true if the company knows that it will be depositing a fixed sum at a variable rate of interest over a set period of time. A Forward Rate Agreement is therefore a notional loan or deposit with a bank over a set period (the contract period) which is set to start a specified date in the future.

In principle an FRA is converting an exposure to a variable rate to a fixed rate of interest or vice versa. Where there is considerable uncertainty in the money market (perhaps an imminent decision on interest rates from the Monetary Policy Committee) hedging through a Forward Rate Agreement may be an appropriate method for locking in current rates until the situation is clarified.

REVIEW ACTIVITY 13.2 You expect to take out a loan in three months to cover your second quarter's operational requirements. Given that the current interbank rate is 4.5 per cent would you buy or sell an FRA given the short term yield curve is (a) or (b) as shown in Exhibit 13.5.

EXHIBIT 13.5

Alternative short term yield curves in the money market

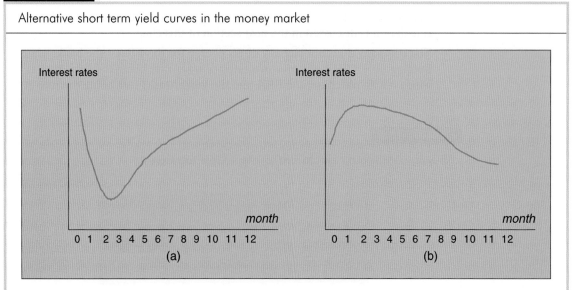

(a) (b)

When a company is rescheduling its debt (see Chapter 5) it may believe that rates on the roll-over are temporarily out of line with future expectations. This may be signalled by an inverted yield curve and it may be appropriate to use an FRA to lock in the lower expected future rate.

A company may also enter into a Forward Rate Agreement if it is a fixed rate payer and expects interest rates to fall. In this case it would be advantageous to sell an FRA to the market maker. If interest rates fall the market maker will pay the difference between the contracted rate and LIBOR at the settlement date to the company. If interest rates rise the company will pay the difference to the market maker.

FINANCIAL REALITY

Friendly Grinders has a short term borrowing requirement of £6 million commencing on 1 March, three months from now. The loan is required for six months. Gloria, who has now been appointed the company's CFO, decides to hedge the interest rate risk by purchasing an FRA (3v9) from the bank for a notional sum of £6 million. The contract rate is agreed at 4.5 per cent. Gloria believes that she could get a loan currently at 50 basis points above the short term money market rate. At the fixing date, two days before the settlement date, LIBOR has risen to 5.5 per cent. Gloria takes out the loan at 6.0 per cent on the 1 March.

Here we have the essentials of a Forward Rate Agreement. Here are some points to note:

- The Forward Rate Agreement in this case is quoted 3v9. The term of the contract is nine months, however, the notional loan or deposit starts after three months. A 3v6 would be one where the loan/deposit was for three months commencing in three months. A wide variety of forward agreements are available within a three month (1v4 to 6v9) and six month series (1v7 to 6v12). Also, FRAs are available for periods longer than 12 months.

- The fixing rate will be established with reference to LIBOR. The rates of interest on the underlying loan taken by Friendly Grinders will have a premium on top of this commensurate with their credit rating.

- The contract rate is set according to the forward rate for the loan and its calculation is discussed in the next section of this chapter.

- The company does not pay any direct charge for the FRA – the bank, when quoting for an FRA will give two rates: a lower rate being the (bid) rate at which it will 'purchase' the FRA and the higher (ask) rate being the rate at

---

EXHIBIT 13.6

Buying or selling an FRA to hedge interest rate exposure

Rate Exposure:	Money market exposure as:	
	Borrower	**Lender**
Fixed	Sell	Buy
Variable	Buy	Sell

which it will 'sell' an FRA to the company. The logic of this we will explain more fully when we look at the valuation of an FRA later in this chapter.

Conceptually it is all very straightforward – the problems come in figuring out the practice.

In the case above, at the settlement date, interest rates have indeed risen and the Bank will reimburse Friendly Grinders for the differential in interest rate between contract and fixing. The cash payment is received on settlement, which is at the beginning of the contract period, when the interest payment is discounted using the reference rate determined at the fixing date:

$$Settlement = \frac{(r_f - r_c) \times \dfrac{C}{365} \times Loan}{(1 + r_f \times \dfrac{C}{365})}$$

So in this case if the loan is for (C) 182 days (six months) and the reference rate r_f is 5.5 per cent and the original contract rate r_c was 4.5 per cent. The difference is 1 per cent which is calculated on a six month basis:

$$Settlement = \frac{(.055 - .045) \times \dfrac{182}{365} \times 6\,000\,00(}{(1 + .055 \times \dfrac{182}{365})}$$

$$Settlement = £29\,119$$

Once this settlement is received from the bank Friendly Grinders can do one of two things:

1 They can reduce the loan they take out by £29 119.

2 They can invest the £29 119 at the money market rate and offset the resulting amount at the end of the six month loan period against the interest on the loan.

Given the bank has given them a 1 per cent differential on the contracted amount through the Forward Rate Agreement this will offset the additional 1 per cent that Friendly Grinders has to pay on the loan.

Valuing Forward Rate Agreements

The ability to lock an interest rate into a Forward Rate Agreement will depend, among other things upon:

1 The current money market rates (the spot rate) for borrowing/lending of different maturities.

2 Expectations of the forward money market rates for loans commencing at the start of the contract period.

3 The contract periods involved.

In principle, three rates are involved in valuing an FRA:

1 The spot rate for a loan maturing at the settlement date (r_1).

2 The spot rate for a loan maturing at the end of the FRA contract period (r_2).

3 The forward rate of interest for a loan commencing at the settlement date and terminating at the end of the contract period (r_{fra}).

If we denote our day count in the same way then the spot rate for loan maturing at the end of the contract (r_2) should be related to the other two rates as follows (assuming a 365 day count):

$$(1 + r_2 \times \frac{t_2}{365}) = (1 + r_1 \times \frac{t_1}{365})(1 + r_{fra} \times \frac{t_{fra}}{365})$$

This can be rearranged in terms of the FRA contract rate:

$$r_{fra} = \frac{r_2 t_t - r_1 t_1}{t_{fra}(1 + r_1 \frac{t_1}{365})}$$

So, if the current spot rate for one month (30 day) is 4.5 per cent and for 90 days is 4.82 per cent then the contract for a (1v3) FRA would be 5.0 per cent. Because both the spot rates and the forward rates are in practice quoted as a spread, the market maker will not quote a single figure but a spread. The higher rate will be made to customers who wish to purchase an FRA (i.e. notionally deposit funds) and the lower rate to customers who wish to sell an FRA (i.e. notionally borrow funds).

$$r_{fra} = \frac{90 \times 0.0482 - 30 \times 0.045}{60 \times (1 + 0.045 \times \frac{30}{365})}$$

$$r_{fra} = 5.0\%$$

To see how this works to the bank's favour assume that the bank responds to the FRA enquiry with 4.9–5.1. What this means is that for a 1v3 FRA they will contract at 5.1 per cent where they sell the FRA and at 4.9 per cent when they buy. Exhibit 13.7 shows how this allows the bank to make its profit on the agreement.

Where the banks sells the FRA it sets a contract rate of 5.1 per cent and if LIBOR were to rise giving a fixing rate of 6 per cent it pays 0.9 per cent to its customer. Other

EXHIBIT 13.7

Who pays and the quote spread on an FRA

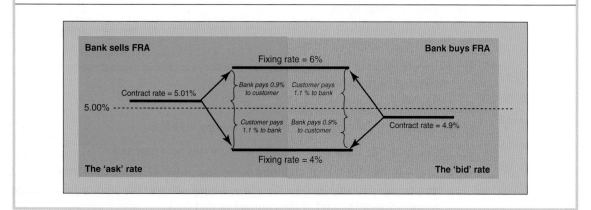

customers who had 'sold' FRAs to the bank would have been quoted 4.9 per cent and thus on a balanced book the bank makes 0.2 per cent. Because banks are in the business of making money exactly the same happens but the other way around if the fixing rate were to fall to 4 per cent.

If the customer decides that they wish to cancel a Forward Rate Agreement they have two ways of proceeding:

1 They can close their position if they have purchased an FRA by selling an equivalent FRA back to the bank. Likewise, if they have sold an FRA they can purchase an equivalent agreement.

2 They can request an immediate settlement of the position. The settlement amount will be calculated as the difference between the value of the agreement if settled immediately and its value if it proceeded through to completion.

The risks of a Forward Rate Agreement

With a Forward Rate Agreement both parties accept the default risk of the other. Apart from this, if a company is using a Forward Rate Agreement to hedge its interest rate risk on an underlying loan or deposit there is a possibility that LIBOR may move away from the rate of interest that the company actually has to pay. This unwanted difference between the actual interest rate paid and LIBOR is called 'basis risk'.

Forward Rate Agreement strips

If the company has a requirement to protect itself from adverse interest rate movement for a lengthy period of time it can proceed in one of two ways:

1 it can purchase an FRA agreement for the whole period of its exposure, or

2 it can purchase two or more FRA agreements where the contract periods run back-to-back over the period of its exposure.

So, if for example a corporate treasurer needed to hedge a nine-month loan commencing in three months' time he or she could purchase a 3v12 FRA or a sequence of FRAs such as: 3v6, 6v9 and 9v12. The advantage of this type of arrangement, which is called an FRA strip, is that first, a more favourable overall contract rate might be achieved and second, the Treasurer would have the ability to reverse the hedge at any of the intermediate points depending upon how interest rates have moved in the interim period. Further readings are available at the end of the chapter which will allow you to estimate the effective contract rate on an FRA strip.

Interest rate futures

An interest rate future is a securitized forward interest rate agreement. The standard specification for three month sterling IRFs are show in Exhibit 13.8. Note the key features: unlike an FRA (where the end of the contract period is agreed between the parties) there is a set maturity date (the delivery months) and a standard contract amount of £500 000. The price at which a given future is traded is calculated as 100 minus LIBOR. So if LIBOR was currently 4.5 per cent the IRF would be trading at a spread around 95.5.

EXHIBIT 13.8

The standard specification for a three month sterling IRF (LIFFE)

Three Month Sterling (Short Sterling) Interest Rate Futures

Unit of trading	£500 000
Delivery months	March, June, September, December
Quotation	100.00 minus rate of interest
Minimum price movement (tick size and value)	0.01 (£12.50)
Last trading day	11:00 – Third Wednesday of the delivery month
Delivery day	First business day after the Last Trading Day
Trading hours	07:30–18:00
Last update	18/08/04

Trading Platform:

- LIFFE CONNECT® Trading Host for Futures and Options
- Algorithm: Central order book applies a pro-rata algorithm, but with priority given to the first order at the best price subject to a minimum order volume and limited to a maximum volume cap
- Wholesale Services: Asset Allocation, Block Trading, Basis Trading

Based on the British Bankers' Association London Interbank Offered Rate (BBA LIBOR) for three month sterling deposits at 11:00 on the Last Trading Day. The settlement price will be 100.00 minus the BBA LIBOR rounded to three decimal places.

Contract Standard:

Cash settlement based on the Exchange Delivery Settlement Price.

In effect the standard three month sterling future contract is an agreement, on the part of the 'seller' to issue notional three month sterling discount bills with a face value of £500 000 where the discount yield is fixed at the 'delivery date' for three months' forward. The 'buyer' is the counterparty who agrees to purchase the bills at the current price. So, if current interest rates are 5 per cent, the seller of an IRF at the delivery date notionally issues bills to the buyer at a price of £95 per £100 nominal value. If interest rates had risen in between times, at the settlement date the issuer could purchase back bills at the fixing rate of (say) 6 per cent which gives a price of £94 per £100 nominal. Obviously if interest rates fall the seller of the IRF at 95 would lose as the issue price would be less than the notional buy-back price on delivery.

A key point about IRFs is that they are cash settled. The seller is not really forced to issue bills nor the buyer to subscribe to them. What is settled at delivery is the notional gain or loss on the future contract. Because each contract is 'closed out' at settlement one counterparty is said to be going 'long' (the purchaser of the notional bill) and the other is said to be going 'short' (the notional issuer or seller of the bill).

The operation of the financial futures exchange

There are a number of exchanges for the trading of derivatives in both commodities and financial securities around the world. There are two aspects of each exchange (although there are variations in how they work): the trading floor or system and the clearing house. Very few exchanges continue with a trading floor system but where they do this is where registered trading members of the exchange come to buy and sell securities on behalf of their clients (see Exhibit 13.9). The large majority of exchanges now manage their trading electronically.

A derivative is initially established between two counterparties but once it is accepted by the exchange for trading purposes the clearing house becomes the nominal counterparty to two transactions: it will take a short position with respect to the 'purchaser' of the IRFs and a long position with respect to a seller. The clearing house is the administrative unit where deals are registered and settled. With most of the global exchanges the clearing house is a unit within the exchange with the notable exception of the London exchange (LIFFE): and the Chicago Board Options Exchange (CBOT) where a separate clearing house manages the transactions.

Margins

In order to reduce default risk the clearing house will require that brokers on the exchange pay an initial margin of between 5 and 10 per cent of the value of new contracts bought or sold. The purpose of this initial margin is to protect the clearing house from gains or losses on the first day. As the contract proceeds through to settlement it is 'marked to market' on a daily basis and any gain or loss credited or debited to the broker's account. If profits are being made on a position, then the

EXHIBIT 13.9

The dealing sequence on a pit traded exchange

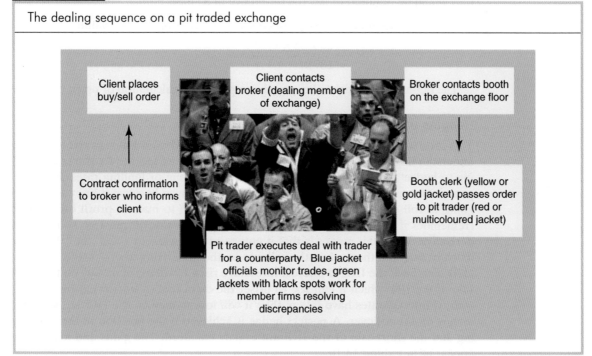

broker can withdraw margin against their account. However, if losses are made then the broker is required to submit to 'margin calls' and pay the variation margin into their account with the clearing house in the form of cash or securities of agreed value. On settlement, therefore, if the margin account is up-to-date the sum of the variation margins paid in will cover any outstanding liability to which the broker is exposed.

Ticks and settlement

In order to simplify the calculation of profit and loss on cash settled derivatives the value of the smallest unit of price movement is defined as a tick. With an interest rate future a tick is the value of a movement of one basis point (.01 per cent) for the proportion of a year over which the contract is deemed to run.

$$\text{Tick} = \text{unit of trading} \times \text{basis points (decimal)} \times \text{fraction of a year}$$

As a basis point is 0.01 per cent this as a decimal is 0.0001 and so the tick size for the sterling three month future is:

$$\text{Tick} = £500\,000 \times 0.0001 \times 1/4 = £12.50$$

So, if at settlement of the sterling three month futures LIBOR stood at 4.25 per cent then a trader who had agreed to purchase (say) ten contracts at 95.5 would face a settlement price of $100 - 4.25 = 95.75$ which is 25 basis points in their favour. The resulting cash payment they would receive would be:

$$\text{Settlement} = \text{number of contracts} \times \text{basis points} \times \text{tick value}$$
$$= 10 \times 25 \times £12.50$$
$$= £3125$$

On the other hand, an agreement to sell 20 contracts at (say) 95.4 is a notional issuer of bills at an implied rate of 4.6 per cent and given that LIBOR is 4.25 per cent they would be required to pay the difference of 35 basis points:

$$\text{Settlement} = \text{number of contracts} \times \text{basis points} \times \text{tick value}$$
$$= 20 \times 35 \times £12.50$$
$$= £8750$$

The definition of a tick value greatly simplifies the calculation of profit or loss.

Hedging using interest rate futures

This inverse relationship between the price of an IRF and interest rates is key to understanding how they work to the advantage of the corporate treasurer attempting to hedge against adverse movements in borrowing or lending rates. If a company is concerned about a rise in interest rates (maybe because it knows that it is going to roll over a loan at some future date) then to make a profit on the IRF (remember if interest rates rise the IRF will fall in value) it must go short in the derivative. What this means is that it enters into a contract to 'sell' the IRF at the delivery date and then, when the rollover on the underlying has occurred, immediately buys back the IRF. If interest rates have risen it will make money on the short sale of the IRF which it can use to offset the extra cost of borrowing on the rollover. If interest rates have fallen, then it will lose money on the IRF but will save money on the rollover. A perfect hedge is achieved if the position in the underlying and the short sale of the IRF are exactly balanced. The gains and losses thus appear as in Exhibit 13.10.

EXHIBIT 13.10

Payoff diagram for IRF versus the underlying (borrowing plus short in the IRF)

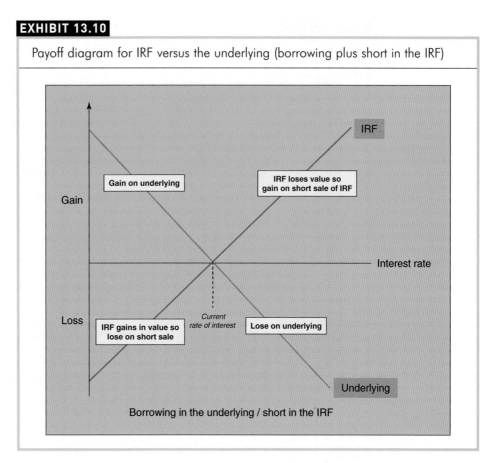

Conversely, if the company needs to deposit funds it will be concerned about a fall in rates. To hedge this potential loss it can 'buy' an IRF (i.e. agree to purchase at the stated price at settlement) and then, once the period to hedge has passed, contract to sell the derivative. This long position in the IRF will generate a gain if the level of interest rates fall and hence will compensate for the loss in the return on the funds deposited.

FINANCIAL REALITY

Gloria has a short term borrowing requirement for £6 000 000 for 30 days commencing in three weeks' time on 1 November. She is worried about an adverse interest rate move by the Bank of England. Current LIBOR is 4.5 per cent and she would like to fix that rate. In order to achieve this she contracts to sell 4 December IRFs at 95.4 immediately. She turns out to be correct and is forced to borrow at 25 basis points more than she planned with LIBOR at 4.75 per cent. As soon as the borrowing is agreed she closes her position by buying 4 IRF contracts at the quoted price of 95.15.

Gloria has calculated that she requires four contracts by dividing the amount to be hedged by the standard contract value and dividing again by the contract period (three months) over the exposure period (one month).

EXHIBIT 13.11

Payoff diagram for IRF versus the underlying (lending plus long in the IRF)

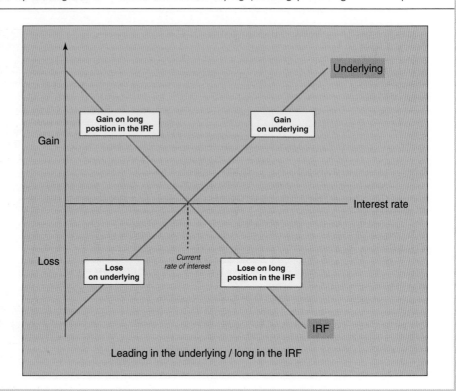

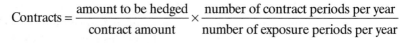

$$\text{Contracts} = \frac{\text{amount to be hedged}}{\text{contract amount}} \times \frac{\text{number of contract periods per year}}{\text{number of exposure periods per year}}$$

$$\text{Contracts} = \frac{£6\,000\,000}{£500\,000} \times \frac{4}{12} = 4$$

She is not concerned about the actual interest rate she pays (which will depend on the company's credit rating) but rather that an increase of base rate by the Bank of England would add the same rate increase to her own cost of borrowing.

On the underlying transaction in the money market her interest rate loss is 25 basis points for one month:

$$\text{Loss} = 0.0025 \times £6\,000\,000 \times 1/12 = £1250$$

On the short sale she sold four December contracts for 95.4 and bought them back for 95.15 this is 25 ticks in her favour which at £12.50 gives a gain as follows:

$$\text{Gain} = 4 \times 25 \times £12.50 = £1250$$

There are a number of problems with using interest rate futures as a hedging instrument compared with Forward Rate Agreements. Because the latter is an OTC contract it can be tailored to meet the company's needs exactly. Any amount of notional principal can be built into the forward rate contract whereas with an IRF the principal must be in multiples of the standard contract amount. It is often assumed, also, that exchange traded derivatives are free of default risk. This is not necessarily the case as the individual purchaser or seller of futures contracts will trade through a registered broker who is in their turn required to pay margins into the exchange in order to cover any potential losses on their book. However, brokers may permit their clients in certain cases to contract on a margin account which means, in essence, that the broker extends credit for the amount of the contract concerned. In some cases, where substantial losses have been incurred by a client, the broker has been forced to default. In those situations where a client is not allowed to trade on credit, the use of IRFs for hedging purposes will mean that both initial and variation margins are required as the contract proceeds through to settlement. With Forward Rate Agreements, such margin payments are not required and final payment is made or received at the settlement date. Like Forward Rate Agreements, IRFs are also subject to basis rate risk where the actual rate of interest that the company requires in order to undertake its own cash market transactions are different to the fixing rate used by the exchange.

In summary, although IRFs are cheaper and quicker to establish than Forward Rate Agreements they are not as flexible as a hedging tool nor do they entirely remove the possibility of default risk.

Swaps

A swap is an arrangement where two counterparties agree to swap their liabilities for interest payments. A swap is a more formalized and often more complex version of the Forward Rate Agreement discussed earlier in this chapter. With a Forward Rate Agreement, the client is exchanging exposure to a variable rate of interest for a guaranteed fixed rate, or a fixed rate for a variable rate, where the fixed rate is established at the point the contract is entered into with the bank.

A swap, on the other hand, can be entered into by any two parties and the terms and nature of the agreement can be varied to achieve almost any desired outcome. Interest rate swapping arrangements can be set up purely in the domestic market where one party wishes to swap a commitment to pay fixed interest for a variable rate and the other party wishes to do it the other way around. Swaps can also be arranged between different currency zones and these 'currency swaps' will be discussed in more detail in Chapter 14.

As with Forward Rate Agreement, the motivations for interest rate swaps are numerous: it may be that the holder of a fixed interest loan believes that interest rates may be about to fall and that moving to a variable rate could take advantage of the situation. Another party may have a variable loan and wish to convert the interest payments to a fixed basis to eliminate some of the interest rate risk that they face.

FINANCIAL REALITY

Many years ago Jack Grinder and his rather impecunious brother Roger had 25 year mortgages on their property, and both those mortgages were for £250 000.

Jack was, of course, in permanent employment and paid a fixed interest rate of 5 per cent on his £250 000 mortgage. He was sure at the time that interest rates were going to go down and his mortgage company told him that he would have to pay the Bank Base Rate plus 0.75 per cent in order to convert to a variable rate loan. He was not totally convinced he wanted to remortgage because of the legal costs of rearranging the loan and he felt that in 12 months' time he might regret the changeover.

▶

Roger was a portfolio worker and did not have a regular supply of income. He paid a variable rate given his credit rating of Base Rate plus 2 per cent but he wanted to move to a fixed rate on his £250 000 mortgage. His mortgage company told him that he would have to pay 7 per cent. Jack had spotted a way of saving some money by swapping their interest rate liabilities.

As Jack recounted this arrangement to Gloria some years later he was rather surprised that she was not as impressed with his financial acumen as he was. What solution did they come up with and what was wrong with it?

A common mistake made by those new to swap arrangements is that they assume that one party must be able to secure either fixed or variable rate finance at a cheaper rate than the other. As we will discover with this example this is not necessarily the case. In both the variable rate and the fixed rate markets Roger paid a higher rate of interest on his borrowing than Jack. What matters is that there must be some relative advantage. To explain let us see how Jack and Roger got on.

Jack paid 5 per cent to his mortgage company so Roger made a fixed interest payment to him (at a small premium over the 5 per cent Jack was paying) in exchange for a variable payment from Jack. The variable payment Jack made, of course, was less than what his brother paid, but when Roger compared his total interest bill compared with the amount he would have paid if he remortgaged he was better off.

Let us see how that will work in practice. Jack agreed to pay Roger the base rate plus 0.75 per cent and Roger in his turn agreed to pay Jack 5.5 per cent. Exhibit 13.12 shows the relevant interest flows. The receipt from Roger more than offsets Jack's fixed interest payment giving him a surplus of 50 basis points. Given that he is transferring a variable payment to Roger of base plus 0.75 per cent the net cost to him will be base plus 0.25 per cent. So Jack is now paying a variable rate on his mortgage but at a lower rate than if he had remortgaged with his own mortgage company.

EXHIBIT 13.12

An interest rate swap between two counterparties

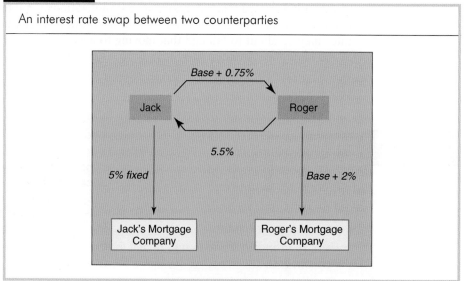

Roger in his turn receives base plus 0.75 per cent which he offsets against the variable payments he currently makes of base plus 2 per cent. His net overall payment is the residue of the fixed element of his variable payment (1.25 per cent) plus the 5.5 per cent he paid to Jack. His net interest cost is therefore 6.75 per cent which is lower than his own mortgage company required for a fixed interest mortgage (7 per cent). So Roger is happy too!

In Exhibit 13.13, Jack's column shows the interest payments he made under the swap less the interest he received. He paid 5 per cent to the mortgage company but Roger offered to give him 5.5 per cent in exchange for a payment of the base rate plus 0.75 per cent interest. Roger currently pays base plus 2 per cent but he can offset the rate he gets from his brother less the 5.5 per cent he pays Jack as his side of the swap arrangement.

When we net off each brother's interest receipts and payments Jack is 0.5 better off than the quoted remortgage rate and Roger is 0.25 per cent giving a cash saving of £1250 and £625 compared with remortgaging.

Exploiting the comparative advantage principle in swaps

This simple example also shows something else: when we look at the whole picture the exchange between the two brothers cancel out and in determining the overall benefit of the swap we look at the sum of the two rates required to remortgage, deduct the current rates paid by each party and we have the swap premium:

$$\text{Swap premium} = 7\% + (\text{Base} + 0.75\%) - (5\% - (\text{Base} + 2\%)) = 0.75\%$$

Or putting it another way:

$$\text{Swap premium} = 7\% - 5\% + (\text{Base} + 0.75\%) - (\text{Base} + 2\%) = 0.75\%$$

The 7 per cent minus the 5 per cent is the advantage Jack has over Roger in the fixed interest market and the difference in the variable rates is the advantage he has in the variable market. If we net off these two relative advantages that tells us instantly if the swap is worthwhile. This is what is known as the principle of competitive advantage in swaps.

Before we move on to consider how this works in the corporate world it is worthwhile reflecting on what is the dynamic which makes the swap work. It looks almost too good to be true in that both parties appear to be better off. Following the no pain

EXHIBIT 13.13

The financial arithmetic of the swap agreement

	Jack	Roger
Interest rate to mortgage company	−5.00%	−(base + 2%)
Interest received from brother	5.50%	base + 0.75%
Interest payment to brother	−(base + 0.75%)	−5.50%
Net interest paid	−(base + 0.25%)	−6.75%
Rate required to remortgage	−(base + 0.75%)	−7.00%
Interest saving on swap	0.50%	0.25%
Cash saving	1250	625

no gain maxim we note that Jack and Roger are not just swapping interest payments, they are also swapping risk. Jack is a low risk client of his mortgage company and that is reflected in the relatively low rates he has to pay. Roger is much higher risk and when Jack accepts the promise of fixed interest receipts he is also accepting some default risk. Roger, in his turn, when he accepts the variable payment, is accepting along with it some of Jack's creditworthiness.

Now, if Jack's mortgage company could see that he is accepting a risky income flow (from Roger) in exchange for his much more secure payments to his brother they might well insist on a higher variable interest rate for remortgaging. Roger's mortgage company would go the other way if it recognized that he has a much more secure source of income from his brother in exchange for interest payments to Jack which carry the added risk of his less reliable personal income. As a result they may be willing to drop the fixed rate they are asking for Roger to remortgage. The net effect is that if the system was transparent and efficient the benefit of the swap would be obliterated.

REVIEW ACTIVITY 13.3   On the basis of the facts above, devise a swap agreement that would allow the two brothers to share the swap premium equally.

The swap market

The type of arrangement between Jack and Roger is termed a 'vanilla' swap. With swap arrangements organized through money market intermediaries, the bank or other finance house involved sits as the counterparty between the individuals or firms engaged in the swapping arrangement. The institution organizing the swap quotes two interest rates: a rate at which they are prepared to receive a fixed interest cash flow stream (the ask rate) and the second the rate of fixed interest that they are prepared to pay (the bid rate).

FINANCIAL REALITY

Friendly Grinders plc currently has a short-term borrowing at a variable rate of LIBOR plus 60 basis points on a £15 million loan due to mature in 12 months. Gloria thinks that future interest rates are set to rise and decides to enter into a swap arrangement to convert to fixed interest. The treasurer of Cobham Plc has taken the opposite view and would like to swap an equivalent amount of the same maturity to a variable rate. Cobham currently pays 4.95 per cent fixed interest. A 12 month swap rate of 4.61 (bid) and 4.62 (ask) is quoted by the bank. Cobham's current quote for a variable interest loan is LIBOR plus 75. Friendly Grinders would be able to raise a £15 million fixed loan for 5.5 per cent.

In Exhibit 13.14 we show the structural arrangement for an interest rate swap organized through a bank. The key point to note here is that neither party deals with one another directly but only through the mediation of the bank, and that no principal is exchanged in the swap. The bank quotes two rates for swapping LIBOR and sterling interest rates quotes are given against six month LIBOR on an actual/365 basis.

Cobham would receive fixed interest of 4.61 per cent on the swap which would offset its own fixed interest payments of 5.05 per cent leaving 44 basis points difference. This when added to the LIBOR it pays to the swap bank gives an effective variable rate of LIBOR + 44 giving a net saving of 31 basis points over LIBOR + 75.

EXHIBIT 13.14

Swap agreement through an intermediary

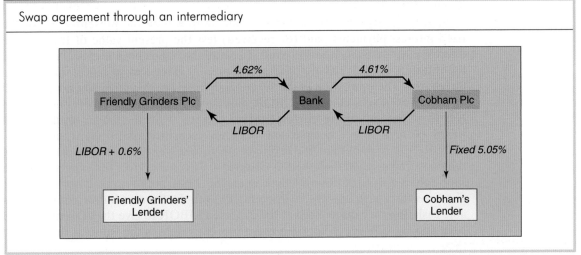

Friendly Grinders receives LIBOR from the bank, pays LIBOR + 60 on its own borrowing giving a difference of 60 basis points. It pays 4.62 per cent to the bank giving it an effective fixed rate 5.22 per cent – a saving of 28 basis points.

The combined saving is 59 basis points. We can check this. The difference between the current variable rate paid by Friendly Grinders and the variable rate that Cobham would have to pay is 0.15 per cent or 15 basis points. The difference between the respective fixed rates is 0.45 per cent or 45 basis points. This, combined gives a saving of 60 basis points from which the bank takes 1 basis point on the spread to give a net saving of 59 basis points. This gives a saving of £88 500 overall which goes £42 000 to Friendly Grinders and £46 500 to Cobham.

Valuing a swap

A vanilla interest rate swap is equivalent to the issue of a fixed interest rate bond of set maturity combined with the purchase of a variable rate bond of the same maturity by one party and the issue of a variable rate bond and the purchase of the corresponding fixed rate bond by the other. Formally, the issuer of the fixed rate

EXHIBIT 13.15

The financial arithmetic for a swap via an intermediary

	Friendly Grinders	**Cobham**
Current interest liability	−(LIBOR + 60)	−5.05%
Receipt from bank	LIBOR	4.61%
Paid to bank	4.62%	LIBOR
Interest flow after swap	5.22%	LIBOR + 44
Open market cost	5.50%	LIBOR + 75
Saving	**0.28**%	**0.31**%

bond (i.e. the payer of the fixed rate) is the 'seller' of the swap and the other party is termed the 'buyer'.

In either party's hands the value of the swap will be the present value of the fixed interest payments paid (or received) less the present value of the variable interest payments received (or paid). Because the bonds have identical maturities the transfers of principal are of identical present value and so cancel out and can be ignored. The estimation of the future cash flows on the variable bond are based upon a LIBOR spot curve. A LIBOR spot curve is one which assumes no interest is paid on the underlying instrument (see Chapter 4 for the longer term version) which permits direct comparison between securities of different maturities. LIBOR is only published for terms of up to one year but can be extended by the bootstrap method discussed in Chapter 4. This curve gives the expected future spot values for LIBOR and these plus the basis points agreed for the swap give the future cash flows to be discounted. Both the fixed cash flows and the variable cash flows are discounted at the expected LIBOR to give the present value of each and the difference between these present values is the value of the swap to the party concerned.

When a market maker such as a bank opens a swap book they will normally set the fixed rate offered such that the present value of the interest payments on the fixed and the variable flows net out to zero less a small profit margin. The profit margin will depend upon the bank's assessment of the counterparty's credit risk and will normally be 2 basis points for a swap with another bank or financial institution but can be much larger with non-banking clients. Because the fixed swap rate assumes that the variable receipt is at LIBOR then the variable cash flows (if discounted at LIBOR will always give a present value equal to the assumed par value of the swap).

FINANCIAL REALITY	The *Financial Times* (25 November 2005) quoted LIBOR spot, six months and one year at 4.42150, 4.62125 and 4.64 respectively. What would be the fixed rate that the bank would pay for a LIBOR receipt and give a 2 basis point profit on a one year swap?

Using the LIBOR rates available to us we can generate a table of cash flows as follows:

1 Project the variable cash flows using either a spot curve or the rates quoted in the FT. We need to calculate the rate of interest on this variable leg which will be generated using the LIBOR rate appropriate for the first six months and the LIBOR rate appropriate for the second six months. The first six months' rate is given (4.62125 per cent) but we do not have the rate of return for the second six months (the forward interest rate starting in six months and lasting until the end of the year. We get around this by calculating the implied forward rate.

The implied forward rate is the rate of return on a security commencing at the chosen forward date and terminating at the required maturity or end date. We can derive the implied forward rate by remembering that the annual spot rate is equivalent to two six monthly rates compounded together – the first six monthly rate as given and the second six monthly rate being the implied forward rate for the second six months:

$$(1 + LIBOR_{12}(spot)) = (1 + LIBOR_6(spot))^{\frac{1}{2}}(1 + LIBOR_{12,\,6}(fwd))^{\frac{1}{2}}$$

$$(1 + LIBOR_{12,\,6}(fwd)) = \left[\frac{(1 + LIBOR_{12,}(spot))}{(1 + LIBOR_6(spot))^{\frac{1}{2}}} \right]^2$$

$$\text{Implied forward rate} = \frac{(1 + LIBOR_{12})}{(1 + LIBOR_6)^{\frac{1}{2}}}$$

$$\text{Implied forward rate} = \frac{1.0464000}{(1.0462125)^{\frac{1}{2}}}$$

Implied forward rate = 1.0230286 (6 monthly)

or

$$\text{Implied forward rate} = 1.0230286^2$$
$$= 1.0465875 \text{ (annual equivalent)}$$

2 Calculate the present value of the variable flow using the LIBOR spot rate. In Exhibit 13.16 we show the LIBOR rate as a discount rate:

$$LIBOR_6 = \frac{1}{1.046213^{\frac{1}{2}}} = 0.977665$$

$$LIBOR_{12} = \frac{1}{1.046400} = 0.955657$$

3 Project the fixed payments (which at this stage are the unknown) using a 'guessed' value for the coupon payment. In this example we set the coupon payments at 2.5 per cent.

4 Discount the fixed payments using LIBOR spot as in 2.

5 Equalize the sum of the present value of the variable flow and the swap margin with the present value of the fixed flow by varying the assumed coupon rate. In Exhibit 13.16 we have used the goal seek routine in Excel.

The key point about valuation from the point of view of the counterparties involved is that when the swap is established its net value to each is zero (apart from the spread taken by the bank). However, if LIBOR subsequently increases the value of the swap will increase to the seller (i.e. the party who issues fixed and receives variable) and its value will decrease in the hands of the 'buyer' (the party who has issued variable and receives fixed). Both parties will need to revalue their position in the swap (mark the swap to market) from time to time.

We can use the valuation method shown above to calculate the value of the swap in the hands of either party.

REVIEW ACTIVITY 13.4 If LIBOR has risen after six months to 4.75 spot and 4.85 at six months, who is the gainer and who the loser in the Cobham, Friendly Grinders swap and what is the potential loss or gain to either party over the final six months of the loan?

EXHIBIT 13.16

A goal seeking routine for a vanilla interest rate swap

£100 nominal vanilla interest rate swap (one year)

	spot	6 months	12 months
LIBOR (quoted)	**4.42150**	**4.62125**	**4.64000**
LIBOR rate	0.044215	0.046213	0.046400
Discount rate		0.977665	0.955657
Forward rate (six monthly)		0.022845	0.023029
Variable receipt		**2.284530**	**102.302861**
Discounted variable receipts		2.233505	97.766495
Present value (variable receipts)	**100.00**		
Fixed payment		**2.283246**	**102.283246**
Discounted fixed receipts		2.232250	97.747750
Present value (fixed payments)	**99.98**		
Profit margin	0.02		
Fixed rate	**4.62**		

Set this 2.5 initially and the 12 month figure to 100 plus this value

Take the difference in the present values and set them equal to the required profit margin using the goal seek function in Excel

In the next chapter we will return to another type of swap where two parties exchange liabilities in foreign currencies.

SUMMARY

Even though governments, companies and other organizations may be able to gain access to the capital markets for their long term finance they still need short term finance to support operations and to bridge between capital transactions. It may also be the case that from time to time the organization concerned has surplus cash which it needs to invest for the short term while it decides what it wants to do with it. The money market is the market for short term finance and a wide range of money market securities and intermediaries have come into existence to service this need. The growth of different types of money market instruments has been enormous over the last 50 years and 'treasury managers' have emerged as a separate financial specialism devoted to exploiting this market.

Borrowing or lending on the money market gives rise to a particular short term exposure in the form of interest rate risk. To cope with this, and to give flexibility to traders in the market, money market derivatives have emerged: Forward Rate Agreements, interest rate futures and swaps being the three most important and dealt with in this chapter. We do not have the space to deal with the other types of derivative that are available and their specialist uses. However, the readings at the end of this chapter should slake your thirst for knowledge of these interesting, sometimes useful and invariably complex securities.

Further Reading

Choudry, M. (2005) *The Money Markets Handbook – a practitioner's guide*, New York: Wiley.

Ludwig, M.S. (1993) *Understanding Interest Rate Swaps*, McGraw-Hill Education.

Reuters (1999) *An Introduction to Foreign Exchange and Money Markets*, The Reuters Financial Training Series, New York: Wiley.

Stigum, M. (1995) *The Money Market* (4th Ed.) Homewood, Illinois: Irwin.

Stigum, M.L. and Robinson, F.L. (1996) *Fixed Income Calculations: Money Market Paper and Bonds* (Vol 1), Homewood, Illinois: Irwin Professional (USA).

Teasdale, A. (2004) The Process of Securitisation, *Journal of Bond Trading and Management*, 2:1, October.

Tuckman, B. (1996) *Fixed Income Securities*, New York: Wiley.

PROGRESS CHECK

1 What distinguishes securities traded in the money market compared with those traded in the capital market?

2 What are the three principal types of short-term interest rate quoted in the money market?

3 List five factors that the central bank will consider when managing short-term interest rates.

4 Identify the three sources of short-term finance that are available through the money market.

5 With a Banker's Acceptance, which party in the transaction guarantees the value of the transaction?

6 What is the essential difference between a Forward Rate Agreement and an interest rate future?

7 What does the term '3v6' mean with respect to a Forward Rate Agreement?

8 If a company has entered into an agreement to lend money to another party at a fixed rate of interest should it buy or sell a Forward Rate Agreement to hedge its interest rate risk?

9 Is the bid price the price at which a market maker is willing to purchase a Forward Rate Agreement or the price at which they are willing to sell?

10 How is a tick on a three-month sterling interest rate future calculated given that the unit of trading is £500 000 and the minimum price movement is 0.01 per cent?

11 Should a corporate treasurer buy or sell interest-rate futures if they believe that interest rates on variable rate borrowing are set to rise?

12 What do you understand by the term 'basis risk'?

13 What condition has to hold for a vanilla interest rate swap to be worthwhile?

14 If a bank organizes a swap agreement between two counterparties how does it make its money?

QUESTIONS (answers at end of book)

1 A company is likely to have £160 million of finance released through the sale of a subsidiary undertaking with completion in six months on 30 September. This money is to be used for a share repurchase scheme which will commence on 1 January. The current short term deposit

rate is 3.5 per cent. The group treasurer is looking at options to lock in this rate for the three month period. LIBOR is currently 4.5 per cent. He negotiates the sale of a Forward Rate Agreement at a contract rate of 4.4 per cent. On 28 September the rate is fixed at LIBOR which has fallen to 3.9 per cent. The firm's short term deposit rate has also fallen by 50 basis points. You are required to calculate the benefits and costs of this Forward Rate Agreement to the company.

2   Alfie Ltd and Ruskin Ltd are negotiating a £5 million swap agreement. Alfie currently pays LIBOR plus 150 but would like to move to a fixed rate basis. Alfie could reschedule to fixed at a rate of 6.8 per cent. Ruskin on the other hand currently pays fixed of 7.2 per cent but believes interest rates may fall to its advantage if it can convert its borrowing to a variable rate basis. Ruskin has been offered by its bank LIBOR plus 200. Both companies are in a similar line of business and have a good credit rating.

You are required to calculate swap terms which would balance any premium equally between the two companies.

QUESTIONS (answers on website)

3   Both the Bank of England and the British Bankers Association are sources of short term money market rates. However, they determine the rates by a different mechanism and for a different purpose. Outline the mechanism and the purpose by which each comes to the rates which are released to the money market.

4   Friendly Grinders plc has received an order from Matsui Engineering for diamond tipped drills. The order value is for £76 000 for delivery in two weeks. Neither company has dealt with one another. Matsui Engineering's Bank is the Matsui Finance and Banking Corporation (MFBC) who is prepared to provide acceptance financing for the transaction. The agreed terms are payment in yen at 30 days. Friendly Grinders bank is the Royal RatNest Bank plc (RRB). Describe the trade financing process through all its stages outlining the various options to each party as the transaction proceeds.

5   A company is likely to have £160 million of finance released through the sale of a subsidiary undertaking with completion in six months on 30 September. This money is to be used for a share repurchase scheme which will commence on 1 January. The current short term deposit rate is 3.5 per cent. The group treasurer is looking at options to lock in this rate for the three month period. LIBOR is currently 4.5 per cent. Describe the relative costs and benefits of hedging the interest rate risk to which the company is exposed through Forward Rate Agreements or interest rate futures.

6   The Medical Trust has a short term finance requirement for £20 million for one month commencing in one month time. The group treasurer has arranged finance at base plus 2 per cent but is concerned that the Bank of England may raise interest rates by between .25 and .50 per cent in three weeks time at the next meeting of the Monetary Policy Committee. The treasurer decides to lock in the current rates using interest rate futures. A three month sterling future is available that would cover the full exposure period. Current LIBOR is 4.6 per cent. The standard contract size is £500 000 and the tick size is 0.01.

The Bank of England increases the base rate at the next meeting by a quarter point and then again the following month by a further quarter point. After hedging the original exposure and just prior to obtaining the loan, the company finds that it can cut its borrowing requirement by £5 million. At this point LIBOR is 4.84 per cent. When the company repays the loan LIBOR is at 5.1 per cent. Calculate the net cost of the financing to the company and explain why the hedge is less than perfect.

7 The Royal RatNest Bank plc is quoting 4.72/5.75 for an interest rate swap. The day's LIBOR quote is given below:

	overnight	day	Change week	month	One month	Two months	Six months	One year
£ Libor	4.51625	+0.104	−0.144	+0.066	4.58500	4.61563	4.61563	4.62750

You are required to:

(i) Draw the 12 month LIBOR curve and comment on the reasons why it has the shape it does.

(ii) Calculate the value of £10 million swap in the bank's book.

(iii) Outline the advantages and disadvantages of swap finance in managing a company's exposure to interest rate risk.

14 | International financial markets

n this final chapter we explore the role and workings of the foreign exchange markets and their impact upon companies who undertake their trade across international frontiers. Foreign currency transactions expose firms to a type of risk which is not present in their domestic activities. In addition to the volatility of prices, which the firm faces as part of its day to day operations, it also has to cope with volatility in the value of the currencies it employs in its dealings with other parties. This chapter commences with an analysis of the different types of risk exposure that companies face when engaged in international trade. This is followed by a review of the FOREX markets and a formal treatment of exchange rates. The five arbitrage conditions are then examined as part of a wider discussion of the factors that influence exchange rates. We then demonstrate the methods for adapting conventional investment appraisal methods where foreign currency and remittances are involved. We then conclude this chapter by drawing together concepts developed in Chapter 8 with those of this chapter and offer a simple treatment of FOREX hedging methods.

Royalty-Free/Corbis

Learning outcomes

By the end of this chapter you will be able to achieve the following:

1 Make currency conversions using both direct and indirect rates of exchange and be able to calculate cross rates between any two currency pairs.

2 Estimate both future spot and forward rates using the five arbitrage conditions.

3 Project foreign exchange cash flows and calculate the Net Present Value of those flows in terms of the domestic currency.

4 Distinguish internal and external hedging techniques and be able to calculate the minimum exchange requirements for a complex series of inter and intrafirm indebtedness.

5 Establish and calculate the benefits of a forward exchange hedging arrangement.

6 Determine the appropriate use of a currency future in hedging exchange rate risk and set up such a hedge so as to minimize basis risk.

7 Estimate the net advantage to a firm in engaging in a fixed for fixed, or fixed for variable, currency swap agreement.

8 Estimate the value of the currency option and identify the circumstances where such an option could be used in hedging exchange rate risk.

Introduction to exchange rates

The first obstacle when learning about foreign currency transactions for the first time is what the different quoted rates mean. In the foreign exchange markets both direct and indirect quotes for foreign currencies may be given. The direct quote is the actual price of the foreign currency in terms of the domestic or 'base' currency. This is the direct analogy of asking for the price of say an orange at a market stall: the trader may say 'one orange costs 25p' – which is the direct price – or she may say 'four for a pound' – which is what we term the indirect price.

A quote of 0.67 as the exchange rate for dollars against sterling means that one dollar will cost the purchaser 67p. This is a direct sterling dollar exchange rate. If, on the other hand, the dollar exchange rate quoted is 1.4925 this represents the number of dollars that can be purchased for one pound. This is the indirect sterling dollar exchange rate. Notice that whichever way we give it, the base currency is always quoted first. Note also this obvious point: the sterling/dollar exchange rate is the inverse of the dollar/sterling rate and so for a given base currency the indirect rate is the inverse of the direct rate.

There are two simple conversion ratios that show how to convert a counter currency into a base currency and vice versa. Using the sterling/dollar rate we can work out the value in dollars of (say) £1 million relatively straightforwardly in Exhibit 14.1.

EXHIBIT 14.1

Currency conversion using both direct and indirect rates of exchange

Direct Rate of Exchange	**Indirect Rate of Exchange**
$\text{Direct rate} = \dfrac{\text{base currency}}{\text{counter currency}}$	$\text{Indirect rate} = \dfrac{\text{counter currency}}{\text{base currency}}$
Direct rate (£/$) = 0.5806	Indirect rate (£/$) = 1.7224
$\text{Counter currency} = \dfrac{£1\,000\,000}{0.5806}$	Counter currency = £1 000 000 × 1.7224
Counter currency = $1 722 356	Counter currency = $1 722 400

Two currencies are said to be at parity if the exchange rate is one. With respect to a base currency a high denomination currency is one where the direct exchange rate is greater than one and a low denomination currency is one where the exchange rate is less than one. This gives a useful way of telling whether a quote is direct or indirect with respect to a given base currency:

1 With high denomination currencies the direct rate is greater than the indirect rate.

2 With low denomination currencies the indirect rate is greater than the direct rate.

So if the foreign or counter currency is more highly denominated than the base currency, the higher quote is the direct quote and the lower the indirect quote. Taking the yen as an example, Exhibit 14.2 shows the dollar/yen exchange rate as 118.3 and .008453. Because 2 is the case for the yen, 0.008453 is the direct rate in that 1 yen costs $0.008453 and 118.3 is the indirect rate because $1 buys 118.3 yen.

For the Canadian dollar/sterling exchange rate sterling is the relatively high denomination currency and so of the two quotes: 0.4951 and 2.0198 the latter is the direct quote in that it costs 2.0198 dollars to purchase one pound sterling or conversely you get 0.4951 pounds per dollar. Note that in this case the Canadian dollar is the base currency.

To summarize: when dealing with foreign currencies make sure that you understand the basis upon which the quote is given and whether you are dealing with a direct quote or an indirect quote. In most situations it will be the latter (although not always!). The direct quote represents the cost of purchasing one unit of the counter currency using the domestic or base currency concerned, the indirect quote represents the amount of the counter currency which can be purchased using one unit of base currency.

EXHIBIT 14.2

Major currency cross rates

Major Currency Cross Rates

Currency Last Trade		U.S. $ N/A	Yen 9:55am ET	Euro 9:55am ET	Can $ 9:55am ET	U.K. £ 9:55am ET	AU $ 9:55am ET	Swiss Franc 9:55am ET
1 U.S. $	=	1	118.3000	0.8471	1.1726	0.5806	1.3546	1.3130
1 Yen	=	0.008453	1	0.007161	0.009913	0.004908	0.011450	0.011098
1 Euro	=	1.1805	139.6531	1	1.3843	0.6854	1.5991	1.5499
1 Can $	=	0.8528	100.8826	0.7224	1	0.4951	1.1551	1.1196
1 U.K. £	=	1.7224	203.7597	1.4590	2.0198	1	2.3331	2.2614
1 AU $	=	0.7382	87.3350	0.6254	0.8657	0.4286	1	0.9693
1 Swiss Franc	=	0.7616	90.1024	0.6452	0.8931	0.4422	1.0317	1

Source: Yahoo-finance 23 November 2005

EXHIBIT 14.3

The bid ask spreads with direct and indirect quotations for foreign currency

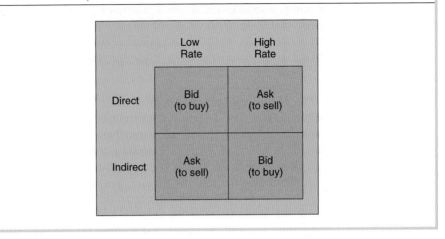

The bid offer spread

Whether a direct or an indirect quote is given the complicating factor is that you will confront two prices: the price at which the bank or other currency trader is prepared to sell, and the price at which he or she is prepared to buy the currency concerned. In the case of a direct quote the lower of the two is the buying price and the higher the selling price. So, for example, if you see dollars quoted as follows:

$$0.5800 - 0.5810$$

This means that you can sell the currency to the trader at the lower price or purchase it at the higher. The difference, or 'spread', is the margin that the trader makes upon the deal. An indirect quote is slightly more complicated. For example, if you see:

$$1.7220 - 1.7226$$

the higher figure will be used when the bank purchases currency from you, and the lower figure is the rate you will face when buying dollars.

To make things even more complicated direct quotes are invariably given in the US financial markets for domestic transactions and indirect quotes are used when trading overseas. In the United Kingdom and other European markets quotations are usually indirect.

Pips and big figures

The foreign exchange (FOREX) markets have a language of their own when giving quotes.

Gloria rings Mike (Ringo) Starky her old friend at the NatWest corporate currency desk for a quote on purchase US$ 4 million. After some friendly banter about the Diamond Grinders Christmas Ball they get down to business: 'Ringo, give me a cable in four dollars'. 'No problem' he replies 'buying or selling'. ▶

She laughs: 'don't push it – just give me the quote'. 'Ok, 22/26, what are you doing?' 'I'm buying $4 million at 23'. 'Gloria, I said 22'. 'Come on' she replies, 'give me a break, the dollar's dropping as we speak'. 'Alright 23, but never again' says Ringo resigning himself to the inevitable 'I'm contracting $4 million at 1.7223 spot' he concludes. Gloria, satisfied with her deal tells him he's the worst currency dealer she has ever met and with a chuckle they finish the call.

The phrase 'cable in four dollars' means a sterling dollar quote (a cable) for four million dollars. The origins of the term cable arose from the early cross Atlantic telegraph cable linking the London and New York currency markets. Two prices are quoted. In this case, because indirect quotes are being used the lower figure gives the price at which the trader is prepared to sell dollars in exchange for sterling and the higher being the rate the trader is prepared to buy dollars for sterling. Exchange rates are usually quoted to four decimal places. When the dealer quoted he knew that Gloria was aware that the 'big number' was 1.72 and all she needed to know was how many 'pips' (22 and 26) above that number for the ask and the bid price.

Spot and forward rates

The spot rate of exchange is quoted for immediate settlement where immediate normally means within two working days. The forward rate is the current rate applied to a foreign exchange transaction which will be completed at some time in the future. If the forward rate is higher than the spot rate (when using a direct quote) then the counter currency concerned is said to be trading at a premium. Conversely, if the forward rate is lower than the spot rate then the currency is trading at a discount. The inverse is the case when indirect quotes are given. So, for example, if the dollar sterling exchange rate (spot) is 1.65 and the forward rate is 1.67 then the dollar is trading at a forward discount relative to sterling and the percentage discount is calculated as follows:

$$Discount = \frac{f_0 - s_0}{s_0} = \frac{1.67 - 1.65}{1.65} = 0.0424 \equiv 4.25\,per\,cent$$

Note that the forward rate is not the rate at which the currency will be actually traded in the future; it is the rate at which the currency is traded currently for settlement at a specified future date.

Forward quotes are normally given relative to the current spot rate in terms of basis points (or 'pips'). So if a current spot sterling dollar rate of 1.7238 and a 12 month forward discount is given as '30' this means that the 12 month forward rate that will be quoted is 1.7268.

Cross rates

One obvious way to make money out of the foreign exchange markets would be to exploit differences in exchange rates between different pairs of currencies. Given the prominence of the dollar however most quotes are given in dollars so if a (say) Swiss franc/Canadian $ rate is required the two US$ rates are taken and a 'cross rate' calculated. As a result when quotes are created in this way 'triangular arbitrage' is not possible. However, a significant market developed in the 1980s for cross trading with the

German mark and now, following monetary union in Europe, with the euro. As a result it is possible to obtain derived cross rates where no arbitrage is possible and a traded cross rate where mispricing can occur such that a profit can be made. However, in competitive markets it is very difficult to find any profit from triangular arbitrage in this way.

For example, using the indirect dollar/yen, the direct euro/yen and the direct dollar/euro we can see whether a profit can be made using the mid market prices from Exhibit 14.2. The result is shown in Exhibit 14.4 and it is not particularly encouraging. The modest gain that is made on the investment of $1million dollars would be obliterated by the spreads and other dealing costs.

To obtain the cross rate for a given currency against another nominate the 'cross base' currency you wish to use and find:

1 The direct rate for the base currency of the pair of currencies you are targeting against the cross base.

2 The indirect rate for the counter currency of the pair of currencies you are targeting in your calculation against the 'cross base'.

To avoid problems with the bid ask spread at this stage we use the mid-market quote (i.e. the mid point value quoted between the two rates given).

$$\text{Cross rate (currency (base)/currency (counter))} = \frac{currency(base)}{\text{cross base}} \times \left[\frac{currency(counter)}{\text{cross base}} \right]^{-1}$$

Taking the dollar, as is usual, as the cross base we can calculate the sterling/euro rate as follows:

- Identify the base currency in the rate to be determined (sterling in this case) and find the direct rate of exchange using the dollar as the cross base. In this case:

$$\text{dollar/sterling (direct rate)} = 1.7224$$

- Identify the counter currency in the rate to be determined (the euro) and find the indirect rate of exchange using the dollar as the cross base. In this case:

$$[\text{dollar/euro (indirect rate)} = 0.8471]$$

The cross rate for sterling/euro = $1.7224 \times 0.8471 = 1.4905$ (indirect rate)

EXHIBIT 14.4

Triangular arbitrage

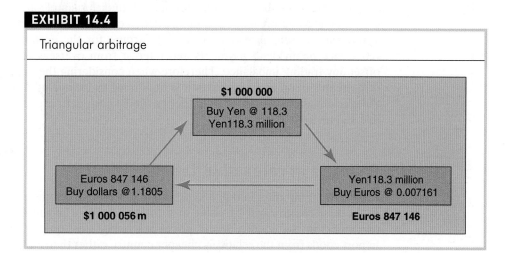

REVIEW ACTIVITY 14.1 Calculate the yen/sterling cross rate using the dollar as the cross base.
Calculate the SwFr/Can$ cross rate using the yen as the cross base.
Calculate the SwFr/dollar exchange rate using sterling as the cross base.

The determinants of exchange rates

As with any commodity the prices of foreign currencies on the international markets are determined by the laws of supply and demand. For any given currency an excess of supply over demand with respect to any other currency will lead to a decrease in its direct exchange rate against that currency. The converse is true if there is an excess of demand over supply. The problem, as with all truisms, is deciding what is likely to lead to an increase in relative supply and what to an increase in demand. A number of theories have been proposed which all, to a greater or lesser extent, help predict exchange rate movements.

The balance of payments

When a country purchases more goods by value from a foreign currency area than it sells to that area then this will create a deficit on that country's trading account. In order to pay for those purchases, buyers in the country concerned will need to acquire the relevant foreign currency in order to make settlement of their indebtedness. As a result, the increase in demand for that currency will lead to its appreciation with respect to the domestic currency concerned on the foreign exchange market. Normally, we would expect any country that runs a persistent trade deficit to suffer devaluation in its currency's exchange rate. Over the longer run we would expect to see an increase in demand for that country's goods as its price levels, denominated in other currencies, fall in line with the devaluation. On the other side of the equation, the cost of that country's imports should rise as its exchange rate declines making foreign goods relatively less attractive and hence reducing domestic demand for them. So in summary, a country which persistently exports more goods by value than it imports should see its domestic currency strengthen against those of its trading partners, while the reverse will be true from countries running a persistent deficit.

There are a number of factors which confound this simple analysis. For example, even though a country may be running a deficit on its balance of trade it may also have significant overseas investments earning income for the economy concerned. The remittance of dividend payments and interest from overseas holdings will tend to offset any trading imbalance. Therefore when considering the impact of the balance of payments upon exchange rates it is important to include all transactions between the economies concerned whether they be on the current or capital account, or for visible and invisible goods.

Changes in rates of inflation

If the rate of inflation in one country is greater than in another, the prices of goods in the first country will be rising at a faster rate than in the second. As a result, consumers in the country where prices are rising most quickly will be tempted to import goods from the relatively cheaper country rather than purchasing those goods on their own domestic market. This will have the effect of increasing the value of that other country's currency and we would expect this trading behaviour to continue to the point that the other country's currency has been revalued to a level which cancels out the differences in prices.

For example, if goods in the UK cost £100 and in the eurozone they cost €150 we would expect a direct exchange rate of sterling into euro(s) of 0.666 or an indirect rate of 1.5. Let us assume that prices are steady in the eurozone but rising at 5 per cent in the United Kingdom. At the end of the year, a consumer in the UK is wondering whether to purchase their goods at their local store for £105, or whether to purchase them in France for €150. If the exchange rate has not changed then it would clearly make sense (ignoring the cost of the ferry of course) to convert £100 into euro(s) and go for a shopping expedition in Calais. It is unlikely, however, that our intrepid consumer will be so lucky. What is likely to have happened in the meantime is that £100 will buy 5 per cent less euro(s) than it did before leading to an exchange rate of 1.35. Purchasing power parity or PPP is assumed to hold between currencies in that exchange rates will adapt to keep relative purchasing power between economies constant.

There is a simple formula for predicting the future spot rate given expected changes in rates of inflation between two currency zones. The spot rate in one year's time (s_1) is related to the current spot rate (s_0) and the respective rates of inflation (h_c and h_b) for the counter and base currencies as follows:

$$s_1 = s_0 \times \frac{(1 + h_c)}{(1 + h_b)}$$

For example: in the United States inflation is currently 3 per cent per annum, in the United Kingdom it is 1.8 per cent. These rates are expected to hold over the next 12 months. The current sterling/dollar exchange rate (indirect) is 1.8683. In this case the predicted 12 month spot rate is given by:

$$s_1 = 1.8683 \times \frac{1.03}{1.018}$$

$$s_1 = 1.8903$$

Note that in 12 months' time we expect to be able to purchase more dollars with our pound reflecting the relative weakening of the dollar against sterling in line with the higher inflation rate in the United States.

To summarize, countries with relatively high expected inflation rates should see their currency depreciate as consumers attempt to secure cheaper prices by buying from abroad. High inflation tends to lead to weak currencies, and low inflation to strong currencies. In practice, there are a number of factors which may militate against purchasing power parity operating in the way we have described.

Generally, if two countries have very dissimilar trading portfolios then changing inflation rates will impact upon the balance of imports and exports differently in each country. Purchasing power parity also assumes that there are no barriers to trade between countries such as tariffs and indeed transactions costs associated with buying and selling the goods or foreign currencies. The empirical evidence is that in the short run there are considerable divergences between economies and that PPP does not hold particularly well. In the longer run, there is some evidence that economies converge on a mean exchange rate predicted by purchasing power theory. There are readings at the end of this chapter which will enable you to explore the relationship between exchange rates and inflation in more detail.

Interest rates and interest rate parity

We would normally expect a country which offers higher interest rates in general compared with its competitors to enjoy a short run increase in the value of its currency as overseas investors attempt to purchase interest-bearing securities in the country concerned. However, once their holdings of financial securities mature then we would expect them to sell their investments and repatriate the proceeds into their own domestic currency. As a consequence, we would predict that the forward exchange rate in a high interest-rate economy will tend to be at the discount relative to the current spot rate.

Indeed, a canny investor in a low interest-rate economy may seize the opportunity to borrow funds in order to purchase interest-bearing investments in a relatively high interest-rate economy and immediately engage in a forward transaction to sell the expected proceeds of the investment thus realizing an arbitrage gain. This is how it works.

The sterling dollar spot and one year forward rates are both currently quoted at 1.8683. Interest rates in the United States are currently 6.5 per cent and in the UK 5 per cent. Given that the forward and spot rates are the same the difference in interest rates suggests that money can be made. Here is how it is done:

1 Borrow (say) one million sterling on the UK money market at the rate of 5 per cent.

2 Purchase $1.8683 million on the international Forex market and invest in the United States at 6.5 per cent and promising $1.9897 million in 12 months.

3 Sell $1.9897 million at 12 months forward at the current forward rate yielding £1.0650 million for delivery in 12 months.

4 Repay the loan in 12 months using the proceeds of the forward transaction collecting £15 000 profit (£1.065 million − £1.05 million).

Clearly to prevent this type of arbitrage opportunity prospering the sterling dollar forward indirect 12 month rate will rise, in a competitive market, to offset the arbitrage gain. We can calculate this new indirect rate by working out the maths of the relationship as follows.

Step (i) Borrow principal sum (P) at the interest rate (i_b) in the base economy.

Step (ii) Convert the proceeds of borrowing at the current spot rate and calculate principal plus interest in the overseas economy:

$$\text{Return on overseas investment} = P \times s_0 \times (1 + i_c)$$

Step (iii) Sell the future proceeds of the foreign investment on the forward market yielding on settlement in 12 months:

$$\text{Yield on forward contract} = \frac{P \times s_0 \times (1 + i_c)}{f_0}$$

Step (iv) Repay the original loan:

$$\text{Repayment} = P \times (1 + i_b)$$

For the no arbitrage condition to hold true the profit, being the difference on the yield from the forward contract, less the cost of the loan repayment should be zero i.e.:

$$\frac{P \times s_0 \times (1 + i_c)}{f_0} = P \times (1 + i_b)$$

On rearrangement the forward rate that gives zero profit on this set of transactions is:

$$f_0 = s_0 \times \frac{(1+i_c)}{(1+i_b)}$$

$$f_{£/\$} = s_{£/\$} \times \frac{(1+i_\$)}{(1+i_£)}$$

$$f_{£/\$} = 1.8683 \times \frac{1.065}{1.05}$$

$$f_{£/\$} = 1.8950$$

Let's see what happens to the arbitrage deal if this were the forward rate:

1 Borrow one million sterling on the UK money market at the rate of 5 per cent.

2 Purchase $1.8683 million on the international FOREX market and invest in the United States at 6.5 per cent and promising $1.9897 million in 12 months.

3 Sell $1.9897 million at 12 months forward at the current forward rate of 1.895 yielding 1.05 million sterling.

4 Repay the loan in 12 months using the proceeds of the forward transaction leaving no profit or loss.

This process of attempting to lock in the potential gain on investment in fixed interest overseas bonds through the use of the forward market is termed 'covered interest arbitrage'.

The Fisher Effect

Reviewing the two explanations of exchange rates above you may have noted that the forward rate is connected to the current spot rate through the relative interest rates in the two economies concerned, and the future spot rate is connected to the current rate through the relative rates of inflation. You may also remember from our discussion of the Fisher formula in Chapter 7 that nominal interest rates are connected to inflation rates as follows:

$$(1+i) = (1+r)(1+h)$$

where i, r and h are the nominal and real interest rates concerned, and h is the rate of inflation.

We can substitute this into the interest rate parity formula to get a rather extended version as follows:

$$f_0 = s_0 \times \frac{(1+r_c)(1+h_c)}{(1+r_b)(1+h_b)}$$

Now Fisher and others have argued that we would expect the real rate of interest to be the same across different economies. If this is the case $r_c = r_b$ in the above formula and the real interest rates cancel to leave:

$$f_0 = s_0 \times \frac{(1+h_c)}{(1+h_b)}$$

Or putting it another way:

$$\frac{(1+h_c)}{(1+h_b)} = \frac{(1+i_c)}{(1+i_b)}$$

So, if you know the interest rates prevailing in the domestic and overseas economy it is possible to predict the rate of inflation in one providing you know the rate of inflation in the other. This formula can also be organized another way by algebraic manipulation to give:

$$\frac{(h_c - h_b)}{(1+h_b)} = \frac{(i_c - i_b)}{(1+i_b)}$$

Or more succinctly:

$$\frac{\Delta i}{(1+i_b)} = \frac{\Delta h}{(1+h_b)}$$

What this formula tells us is that the differences in inflation between (say) the eurozone and the UK are directly related to the current difference in prevailing interest rates between the two. This predicted relationship between inflation and interest rate differentials is known as the Fisher Effect.

The International Fisher Effect

The International Fisher Effect concerns the relationship between current and future spot rates and changes in interest rates. Remember that the Purchasing Power Parity formula links current and future spot rates and the Fisher Effect formula links relative interest rates and inflation rates. Simple substitution of the latter in the former creates the formula for the International Fisher Effect.

The Purchasing Power Parity formula is:

$$s_1 = s_0 \times \frac{(1+h_c)}{(1+h_b)}$$

Substituting the Fisher formula:

$$\frac{(1+h_c)}{(1+h_b)} = \frac{(1+i_c)}{(1+i_b)}$$

We get:

$$s_1 = s_0 \frac{(1+i_c)}{(1+i_b)}$$

This formula says that the differences in interest rates drive differences in spot rates which is found by rearrangement:

$$\frac{s_1 - s_0}{s_0} = \frac{(i_c - i_b)}{(1+i_b)}$$

FINANCIAL REALITY

Current interest rates in the eurozone economies are 2.124 per cent and in the United Kingdom 4.516 per cent. The current sterling/euro rate is 1.4590. What is the expected spot rate in 12 months?

EXHIBIT 14.5

The five arbitrage conditions driving exchange rates

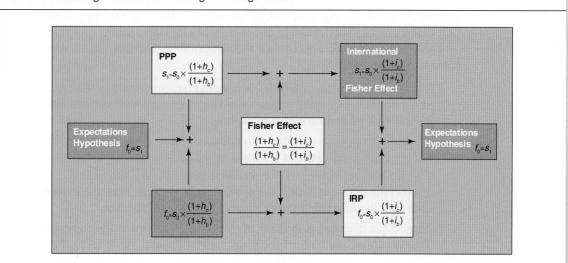

The expected spot rate in 12 months is:

$$s_1 = 1.4590 \times \frac{(1.02124)}{(1.04516)} = 1.4256$$

This is a sterling/euro rate of 0.7014 (direct).

The expectations hypothesis

There is one final drop of juice to be squeezed from these relationships. Putting the International Fisher Effect formula together with the Interest Rate Parity formula leads to the final and we hope obvious conclusion that the current forward rate should equal our expectation of the future spot rate. Indeed, this ought to be the case because if it was possible to take delivery of currency in say three months at the agreed forward rate and sell it at a different spot rate then there would be money to be made. So, if at the present day the expectations of future spot rates are different to forward rates this would lead to traders buying or selling in the forward market in an attempt to take advantage of the potential gain. This buying or selling pressure would achieve the effect of bringing the forward rate into line with the expected future spot rate.

Exhibit 14.5 shows the relationships between the various formulas and how they are derived. To get to all of them you need to be familiar with the three core relationships: Purchasing Power Parity, Interest Rate Parity and the Fisher Effect and do remember that the exchange rate used in these formulas is always the indirect rate.

International capital budgeting

An important application of this understanding of the drivers of exchange rates is in the area of capital budgeting. Foreign investment does raise a number of financial problems many of which are unique to the country concerned: access to local capital markets, taxation systems, regulations on the remittance of profits being just a few of the more important concerns. However, one problem that is relatively easily over-come is how to forecast future cash flows and apply the standard investment appraisal techniques when dealing with foreign currencies. The standard approach uses the purchasing power parity theorem as a means of estimating future spot rates.

There are four basic approaches to the appraisal problem, all of which should come to the same answer:

1 Project the overseas cash flows in nominal terms; convert to the company's domestic currency using estimates of future spot rates before discounting at the company's domestic cost of capital.

2 Project the overseas cash flows in nominal terms, discount at the company's cost of capital adjusted for the local rate of inflation and convert the resulting Net Present Value to domestic currency terms using the spot rate.

3 Project the overseas cash flows in real terms, convert using the current spot rate and discount using the company's real rate of discount.

4 Project the overseas cash flows in real terms, discount at the company's real cost of capital and convert the resulting Net Present Value using the spot rate.

<table>
<tr><td>FINANCIAL
CASE</td><td colspan="6">Friendly Grinders plc has a small investment opportunity in Germany which would entail the investment of €2.5million for five years generating future cash flows as follows:</td></tr>
</table>

	0	1	2	3	4
Nominal cash flows	−2.50	0.50	0.75	2.50	2.50

The rate of inflation in the euro economies is 1.5 per cent and in the UK it is 2.5 per cent. The current sterling/euro exchange rate is 0.7. The company's nominal cost of capital is 8 per cent per annum.

The first step is to set the analysis up by calculating the expected future spot rates using the Purchasing Power Formula (noting that we have been quoted a direct rate which needs to be converted to the equivalent indirect rate).

$$\text{Direct rate} = 0.7000$$
$$\text{Indirect rate} = 1/0.7 = 1.4286$$

Expected spot rate in years 1 and 2:

$$s_1 = s_0 \frac{(1+h_c)}{(1+h_b)}$$

therefore:

$$s_1 = 1.4286 \times \frac{1.015}{1.025} = 1.4146$$

$$s_2 = 1.4286 \times \frac{1.015^2}{1.025^2} = 1.4008$$

EXHIBIT 14.6

Four methods of calculating the Net Present Value of a project where the cash flows arise in a foreign country

	0	1	2	3	4
Direct exchange rate	0.7				
Indirect rate	1.4286				
Expected rates		1.4146	1.4008	1.3872	1.3736
1 + UK discount rate	1	1.0800	1.1664	1.2597	1.3605
1 + UK real rate	1	1.0537	1.1102	1.1698	1.2325
1 + euro base discount rate	1	1.0695	1.1438	1.2232	1.3082

Method 1 – nominal cash flow using expected spot rates and domestic nominal discount rate

	0	1	2	3	4
Nominal cash flows	−2.5000	0.5000	0.7500	2.5000	2.5000
Conversion to UK nominal	−1.7500	0.3534	0.5354	1.8022	1.8200
DCF (at 8 per cent)	−1.7500	0.3273	0.4590	1.4307	1.3377
NPV (UK) =	**1.8047**				

Method 2 – nominal cash flow using local nominal discount rate and current spot rate

	0	1	2	3	4
Nominal cash flows	−2.5000	0.5000	0.7500	2.5000	2.5000
DCF (Germany)	−2.5000	0.4675	0.6557	2.0438	1.9111
NPV (Germany)	2.5781				
NPV (UK) =	**1.8047**				

Method 3 – real cash flow using current spot rate and domestic real discount rate

	0	1	2	3	4
Nominal cash flows	−2.5000	0.5000	0.7500	2.5000	2.5000
Real cash flows	−2.5000	0.4926	0.7280	2.3908	2.3555
Convert at current spot	−1.7500	0.3448	0.5096	1.6736	1.6488
Discount at real discount rate	−1.7500	0.3273	0.4590	1.4307	1.3377
NPV (UK) =	**1.8047**				

Method 4 – real cash flow, discount at the real rate and convert using the current spot

	0	1	2	3	4
Nominal cash flows	−2.5000	0.5000	0.7500	2.5000	2.5000
Real cash flows	−2.5000	0.4926	0.7280	2.3908	2.3555
Discount at real discount rate	−2.5000	0.4675	0.6557	2.0438	1.9111
NPV (Germany)	2.5781				
NPV (UK) =	**1.8047**				

Our next step is to calculate the appropriate discount rates. We are told that the UK rate is 8 per cent which using the Fisher formula and the UK rate of inflation of 2.5 per cent gives a real rate of 5.367 per cent (note that we use the compound version of the formula to get the rates for subsequent years). We can use this UK real rate to calculate the German nominal rate by again using the Fisher formula but this time using the local inflation rate of 1.5 per cent.

We then proceed through each method as shown in Exhibit 14.6 yielding a Net Present Value in each case of £1.8047 million.

REVIEW ACTIVITY 14.2 Using the same cash flows as in the example above recalculate the Net Present Value in each method using current rates of inflation, interest rates and exchange rates. The *Financial Times* provides all of the relevant data.

Managing currency risk

When dealing in or holding foreign currencies businesses are subject to a variety of different risks. These risks are conventionally defined as follows.

Economic risk This is the long run risk of trading in a given country. This type of risk is an important driver of business risk although with the latter we are directly concerned with the volatility of the firm's operating cash flows which will also be influenced by its internal decisions on cost structure, technology and so forth. Economic risk is therefore the context in which the firm establishes its exposure to business risk by the production and operating decisions it makes.

Where a company trades solely in its domestic markets it is, more or less, tied to the economic risk of its home economy. We say more or less because even though the firm itself may not trade abroad its customers and suppliers may do so. As a result the domestically based firm may find itself exposed to the economic risk of other countries by proxy.

Economic risk in any country arises from a number of sources within the economy: there can be the risk of political change or upheaval (political risk), changes in the regulation under which companies are required to operate (regulatory risk), changes in the expectations and demands of the local population (social risk), changes in the local tax regime (fiscal risk) and, finally, changes in monetary conditions through interest rates changes or alterations in the money supply (monetary risk). The problem of any meaningful analysis of any of these different aspects of economic risk is their interdependence.

Another useful way of thinking about economic risk exposure is to classify the source of the risk in terms of structure; shocks; markets and noise. Structural changes in economies come through large scale political change or action. The collapse of the Soviet Union or the slower but no less dramatic economic liberalization in China are two examples of structural disturbance and sources of substantial risk. 'Shocks' are the shorter term events such as the South East Asia Tsunami or Hurricane Katrina in 2005 which while dramatic and devastating do not necessarily lead to longer term structural change. Market borne risk we have already met but this refers to the ebb and flow of demand within the economy for goods and services as tastes and incomes rise and fall. Finally, 'noise' is the term we give to the short term stochastic fluctuations in supply and demand which is a continuing feature of all economic systems.

The management of economic risk and its potential impact upon the long term cash flows of the firm can be achieved by diversifying operations across as many different countries as possible. The key to the successful management of economic risk is through the principles of diversification discussed in Chapter 3 and not simply restricting activity to those countries which appear safe from political or economic change. Choosing to balance international trade in different countries according to how the expected returns from the markets concerned covary with one another can lead to high average returns but with minimum overall risk exposure. Indeed, paradoxically, it can be easier to apply the principles of Markowitz diversification in international trade than it is in balancing investments within the domestic economy where all firms are under broadly similar market conditions and pressures.

Exchange rate or transactions risk This is the risk to which the firm is exposed because of variations in the exchange rate at which it is required to transfer cash flows across international borders. In the previous section we discussed some of the factors that influence exchange rates: the balance of payments, inflation and interest rates. Obviously, these influences are driven by the respective macro economies and thus exchange rate risk is influenced by structural changes and shocks, as well as market and noise effects. In the very short run exchange rate risk can have a significant impact upon the operating performance of the firm. How it deals with this risk depends to a certain extent upon its ability to naturally minimize its exposure by diversifying its operations across different economies. The more a business spreads its operations the more it can rely upon the natural negative covariance effects which exist between currencies. For the smaller firm, or for the firm that is heavily exposed to a small number of other currencies, the better strategy may be to attempt to hedge the exposure perhaps through the use of derivatives. We will return to this strategy for managing exchange rate risk in the next section.

Translation risk Where a company has assets and liabilities in another country it will be required to consolidate their value into the group balance sheet. Clearly, if these assets or liabilities are in countries where the exchange rate has fallen against sterling during the previous accounting period then a loss on translation will occur. From an accounting perspective such losses impact upon the carrying value of assets and liabilities in the balance sheet and should be disclosed in the accounts. Translation risk has no economic significance for the firm except in as far as it reflects upon the market's perceptions of its performance. In an efficient capital market we would expect translation risk to be ignored in the pricing process and in practice few companies seek to actively manage this type of exposure.

FINANCIAL REALITY

This is how Cobham plc manages the risk in its international operations (Financial Report, 2005).

Foreign currency risk is the most significant aspect for the Group in the area of financial instruments. It is exposed to a lesser extent to other risks such as interest rate risk and liquidity risk. The Board reviews and agrees policies for managing each of these risks and they are summarised below. The policies have remained unchanged throughout the year.

Foreign currency risk
The Group, which is based in the UK and reports in sterling, has significant investment in overseas operations in the USA, with further investments in other EU countries, Australia, Canada, South Africa and Asia. As a result, the Group's balance sheet can be affected by movements in these countries' exchange rates. The Group's policy is to reduce, or eliminate where practicable, both structural and transactional foreign exchange risk. Where significant, currency denominated net assets are partially hedged by currency borrowings. Currency exposures are reviewed regularly and all significant foreign exchange transactions are approved by the parent company.
The pound/US dollar exchange rate is the most important as far as Cobham is concerned, particularly given the level of US dollars which the subsidiaries expect to receive from their normal business activities. In addition to the longer term borrowing structure, a number of financial instruments are used to manage the foreign exchange position, such as forward contracts. As at

▶

> 31 December 2004, US$221m of forward contracts were in place and stretching out to 2014. These contracts are at an average exchange rate of $1.68: £1. It is the Group's current belief that the net dollar receipts from its subsidiaries will exceed the level of the outstanding commitment.
>
> The Group has transactional currency exposures. Such exposures arise from sales and purchases by operating units in currencies other than the unit's functional currency.
>
> The Group's policy is to minimise trading in subsidiaries' non operating currencies. However, where this is impractical the Group will seek to reduce its exposure through the use of forward contracts.
>
> The Group does not hedge balance sheet and profit and loss translation exposures. Generally, borrowings are arranged in local currencies to provide a natural hedge against overseas assets.

There are a variety of ways that companies can seek to mitigate their exposure to foreign exchange risk. These we broadly characterize as either internal or external hedging. Internal hedging is where the company chooses to establish its operations in such a way that its exposure to risk in minimized. External hedging is where derivatives are bought or sold in order to eliminate specified risks. The basic ideas of hedging have been discussed before in relation to options and interest rate derivatives but it is always worth coming back to the point that hedging is the process of eliminating the impact of exposure in the price movements of one asset by taking a position in another asset where we know or can reasonably anticipate that the price movements between the two assets will be perfectly negatively correlated. With OTC derivatives the pricing relationship is perfectly matched so that a long position in one security is covered by a corresponding short position in the other security and the negative price correlation is assured. With exchange traded derivatives the relationship between movements in the price of the derivative are not perfectly matched with those of the underlying security. This gives rise to a particular form of residual risk in hedging operations called 'basis risk'. Basis risk is the risk left over when a position in a security has been imperfectly hedged. It is the lurking enemy that stalks the treasury manager. We will return to this aspect of risk after reviewing the basic methods of hedging foreign currency positions.

REVIEW ACTIVITY 14.3 Distinguish between (i) country risk and economic risk and (ii) business risk and market risk.

Internal hedging

There are a number of simple techniques that a company can use to minimize its foreign exchange exposure. Wherever possible, these procedures should, on cost grounds, take precedence over external hedging techniques. For example: if a company wishes to invest in an overseas capital building programme it may make sense to raise the necessary capital in the country concerned. A natural hedge is then formed if the overseas borrowing is used to finance the overseas capital expenditure. Likewise a company may find it useful to establish an overseas banking facility to minimize the transactions costs and exchange losses of conversion. At the operational level 'leading and lagging' can be used where particular currency movements are anticipated by: making payments in advance if it is believed that the foreign currency concerned will strengthen or delaying payment if it is believed that the foreign currency will weaken.

Matching and netting

Of the internal hedging techniques matching and netting are very simple ways of managing foreign currency risk. A matching agreement is one entered into by two or more companies who have a trading association and mutual indebtedness between them. A netting arrangement, on the other hand, is one which is conducted between companies or operating entities within a single group. In practice matching and netting are very similar although with the former formal agreements between the parties are required and there may be taxation and other implications if the matching agreement is viewed by the authorities as a way of profit shifting.

We can, from an analytical point of view, treat both methods in the same way. The simplest way to set up a netting arrangement is to show the mutual indebtedness between parties as a network arrangement.

FINANCIAL REALITY

At the year end Friendly Grinders had subsidiaries and associates in France, the United States and Switzerland.

Friendly Grinders owed AmiGlace, a French associate €54 million while in its turn AmiGlace had a loan to repay Friendly Grinders of £10 million. It also owed, Friendly Grinders (US) $38million.

Friendly Grinders was owed £24 million by its US subsidiary who also owed the Swiss Diamond Importers (SDI) SFr 102 million. The SDI owed Friendly Grinders £32 million, on a separate account to Friendly Grinders (US) $6 million and AmiGlace €5 million.

Gloria embarked on a round of telephone calls to see if she could arrange a match and net for the year end to ensure, if possible, a single settlement. The relevant quotes for the netting arrangement were sterling/dollar = 1.7238, sterling/euro = 1.4624 and sterling/SFr = 2.2670.

EXHIBIT 14.7

Step (i): conversion to base

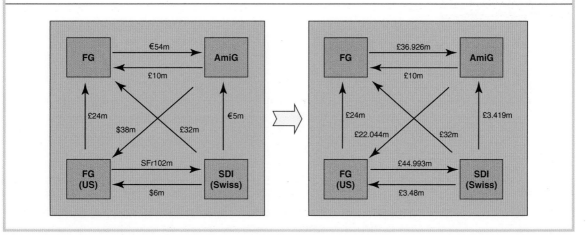

The success of a netting arrangement such as this is to ensure that all cash in transit is accounted for and all parties agree on the rate of exchange to be used. In the case of a parent company/subsidiary netting arrangement it is fairly straightforward. When other companies are involved agreements may be required in order to renominate indebtedness between the parties involved.

In this example we have used mid-market rates to establish the indebtedness between the parties. In practice the appropriate bid-ask rates would be used. In Exhibit 14.7 we show the network of financial commitments.

The netting then proceeds in a series of steps:

(i) *Convert to base using current spot rates of exchange.* With this step we convert all of the foreign currency flows to sterling using, the direct or indirect rates of exchange as convenient.

(ii) *Clear bilaterals.* Where two parties have a mutual indebtedness this can be netted off and the net position taken as shown in Exhibit 14.8.

(iii) *Clear circuits by deducting cross indebtedness from all legs.* A circuit is a triangular sequence of indebtedness (the direction of the arrows show a loop of commitments) and in Exhibit 14.8 we have highlighted two candidates to eliminate the debt of £22.044 million owed by AmiGlace to Friendly Grinders (US). Either could be chosen – for convenience we have taken the one which leaves the least negative values to contend with. So, in this case we have chosen the outstanding between AmiGlace and Friendly Grinders (US) and reduced this to zero; we have deducted their indebtedness from what Friendly Grinders (US) owes its UK parent company and, in turn from what Friendly Grinders (UK) owes to AmiGlace.

This leaves the position as shown in Exhibit 14.8.

(iv) Clear cross indebtedness. In this case SDI (Swiss) owes £32 million to Friendly Grinders UK. However, Friendly Grinders UK is owed £1.956 million from its US subsidiary to which it can add the £32 million

EXHIBIT 14.8

Steps (ii) and (iii): clearing bilaterals and identifying circuits

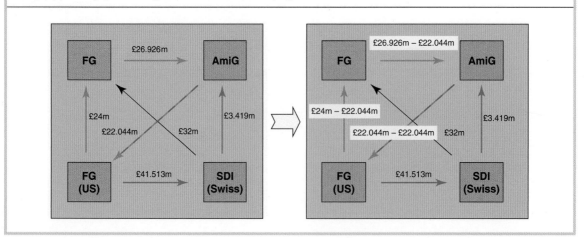

EXHIBIT 14.9

Step (iv): clear cross indebtedness

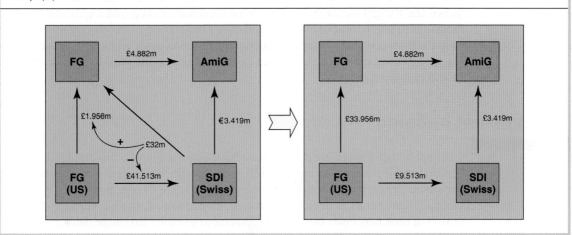

owed to Friendly Grinders by SDI (Swiss) reducing the payment due from the US subsidiary to SDI (Swiss) by the same amount.

(v)   Reduce the indebtedness between the parties by taking the smallest amount in the circuit and either adding or deducting the amount concerned from all connections in the loop depending by the direction of the liability. In this case we have taken the £3.419 million owing to AmiGlace from SDI(Swiss) and deducting it or adding it to the indebtedness on each of the other legs of the circuit.

So, by a sequence of netting arrangements Gloria has succeeded in reducing eight outstanding cross border accounts (valued at £176.862 million in transfer) down to three (with an outstanding value of £52.31 million) and eliminated one currency

EXHIBIT 14.10

Step (v): finalize the net

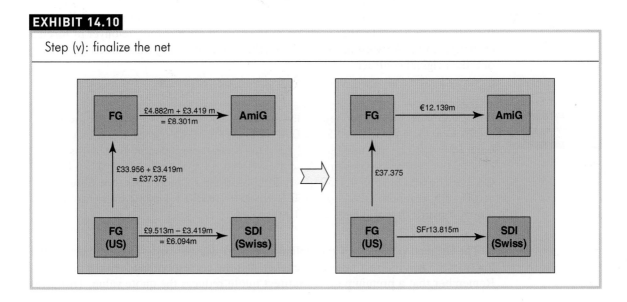

entirely from the settlement process. This simple technique of restructuring the network of indebtedness considerably simplifies settlement and in some cases can remove the need to deal in a specific currency. In 1998 the Malaysian Government pulled the Ringgit out of the international currency markets and imposed draconian measures to prevent capital flows in and out of the country. The strategy was bold but only partly successful as companies trading into Malaysia employed, among other things, extensive matching operations in order to defeat the need to move currencies in and out of the country.

External hedging

External hedging is achieved in ways we have already discussed in this book. First, a forward or future contract can be used such that the movement in the value of the derivative position offsets the movement in the value of the underlying. Second a company that needs to acquire the use of, or dispose of, foreign currency for a set period of time may enter into a swap agreement to either exchange the currency (FX swap) or to exchange the currency and interest payments associated with the underlying capital market transaction.

Forward contracts

Forward contracts on currencies offer one of the simplest ways of eliminating the downside on exchange risk. A forward currency agreement sets a 'price' (the rate of exchange) for delivery of a specified amount of the currency concerned on a specific date. Forward currency agreements, like other forward contracts are over the counter. This means that the contracts can be tailored to their exact purpose creating a perfect hedge against the underlying currency risk exposure. A company when purchasing or selling currency on the forward market may pay a commission to the bank although much of the cost is reflected in the quoted spread. Normally, large transactions between banks and corporate customers carry a small spread, lower value transactions a greater spread.

A forward contract commits both parties to deliver which means that both parties take the gain or loss (see Exhibit 14.11) determined by the actual price at delivery. If the rate moves against either party or, in the case of say a corporate buyer of foreign exchange on the forward market, then further losses can only be avoided by 'closing out' the original contract.

FINANCIAL REALITY

Friendly Grinders has arranged for the supply of some diamond grit in six months on 30 June for a payment of $240 000. Friendly Grinders agrees to buy from the bank $240 000 on 30 June but on 1 April the procurement department learns that only 75 per cent of the consignment can be delivered and agree to pay $175 000. On 1 January £/$ (spot) = 1.5010 – 1.5520 and the six month forward is quoted at 90 – 85 premium. On 1 April £/$ (spot) = 1.4950 – 1.5450 and the three month forward at that date is 20 – 10 discount.

The original purchase of the dollars required will be made on 1 January at the lower of the two indirect rates of exchange less the corresponding forward premium. Remember that a premium on an indirect quote reduces the quote value. This gives

EXHIBIT 14.11

Gains and losses on forward currency agreements

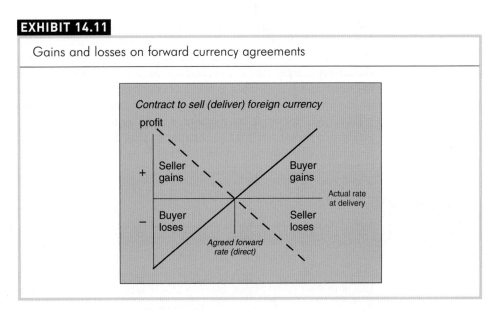

the rate of exchange that will be paid at delivery on 1 June and is not paid until that date. Given that the company needs a partial close out on 1 April we need the rate at that date at which it can place $650 00 back onto the market. In this case because the forward rate is at a discount we add it to the indirect rate and take the highest of the pair (the bank will buy back at the most favourable rate from its point of view).

1 January	Forward rate agreed = 1.5010 − 0.0090 = 1.4920
1 April	Forward rate agreed = 1.5450 + 0.0010 = 1.5460
1 June	Sterling cost on delivery of $240 000 = $240 000/1.4920 = £160 858
1 June	Sterling recovery on close out on $60 000 = $60 000/1.5460 = £38 810

The net cost of the transaction is £122 048 giving an effective rate of exchange on the transaction of 1.4748.

Forward contracts of this type are very straightforward. Friendly Grinders knows its exact foreign exchange commitment at the time of purchase of the goods concerned and can negotiate any anticipated transactions costs into the contract at the beginning. The downside of course is that it will suffer an opportunity loss if the currency moves against it. However, from the corporate trader's point of view that the future sterling flows are guaranteed (ignoring the default risk on the bank's part) and given that Friendly Grinders' business is in the diamond trade and not in taking risks on the foreign exchange markets then this type of hedge might be regarded as the most appropriate way of handling this type of transaction.

Money market hedge

An alternative to an open forward transaction is the creation of a synthetic forward position or 'money market hedge' in the foreign currency concerned. This relies upon the 'purchaser' of the foreign currency being able to borrow the required finance for the duration of the exposure. The technique is straightforward. The purchases of the foreign currency takes out a loan at the domestic money market rate and converts the principal to the overseas currency required which is then placed upon deposit at the money market rate in the country concerned. At the end of the required term the overseas currency holding is taken off deposit, the UK loan is settled and the transaction for which the currency was originally required is also settled . It sounds complicated but is simple in practice. Gloria is up to her tricks again and trying to establish whether it would be cheaper to raise $4.6 million dollars in six months via a forward transaction or a money market hedge.

FINANCIAL REALITY

Gloria is looking at a potential settlement of $4.6 million in six months' time on a capital construction project at Friendly Grinders (US) subsidiary. She has decided to raise the finance from the firm's UK reserves rather than attempt to raise further finance in the US at the current time. She can borrow at a fixed rate of 60 points above sterling LIBOR in the UK and achieve a deposit rate 60 points above dollar LIBOR in the United States. Sterling LIBOR is quoted at 4.42 per cent and US LIBOR at 4.04 per cent. The current sterling dollar spot rate is 1.7238 and the six month forward is 1.7250.

Gloria's first task is to borrow $4.6 million equivalent in sterling which at the US rate of interest (i_{us}) and over six months and using the 360 day count is calculated as follows:

$$\text{Current dollar equivalent (CDE)} = \frac{\text{future dollars required}}{(1+i_{US} \times \frac{days}{360})}$$

$$CDE = \frac{\$4.6m}{(1+0.0464 \times \frac{180}{360})}$$

$$CDE = \frac{\$4.6m}{(1.0232)} = \$4.4957m$$

At the current spot rate this converts to £2.608 million which is the present sum she needs to borrow. Using this borrowing she could purchase $4.4957 m dollars and deposit them in the United States with the prospect of realizing £4.6 million in six months.

If Gloria borrows this her repayment to the bank will be given as follows:

$$\text{Repayment} = £2.608\,m \times (1+i_{UK} \times \frac{days}{360})$$

$$\text{Repayment} = £2.608\,m \times (1+0.0502 \times \frac{180}{360})$$

$$\text{Repayment} = £2.6735\,m$$

The implied forward rate on this transaction is simply the dollars realized in six months ($4.6 million) divided by the sterling repayment of £2.6735 million. This gives a rate of 1.7206. She notes that this is more expensive than the forward rate and so would not proceed to raise her dollars through this route.

If the money market hedge had been worthwhile (i.e. gave an implied forward rate greater than the quoted forward rate) an arbitrage opportunity would be available. In practice a money market hedge will only be worthwhile if it offers lower transactions costs overall than purchasing on the forward market. Finally, it is worth recollecting that a money market hedge will only be profitable if there is an arbitrage opportunity using the interest rate parity principle. In practice the forward quoted rates rarely give that opportunity. Where a money market hedge can be valuable is if the fixed rate deposit and loan can be settled at call (i.e. immediately). This in effect allows the position to be closed at zero cost.

Currency futures

A currency future is a securitized forward contract which can be exchange traded. The future contract specifies a set amount of currency with set delivery days and are normally cash settled. What this means is that the position is invariably closed out prior to delivery and margins will be required to establish and maintain the position.

A variety of different currency contracts can be purchased on the international derivatives exchanges with the greatest variety established and traded on the New York Board of Trade (NYBOT) options and futures exchange. A more limited range is available on the London and other markets. Exhibit 14.12 shows the array of contracts available on the NYBOT exchange. Each has a settlement date on the third Wednesday of the settlement month of March, June, September and December. For each currency pair a contract size is specified (in the case of the sterling/dollar contract it is set at £125 000 or for a 'small' sterling dollar quote the minimum contract size is set at £62 500).

As with most exchange traded products the smallest price movement is defined as a 'tick' and with currency futures the tick will be .0001 of the counter currency per contract of the base currency. So the tick size of a small sterling dollar contract would be specified as $.0001 times 62 500 or $6.25. Although convoluted this method of measuring tick size greatly enables the calculation of gains or losses on the transaction.

The mechanics of creating a currency hedge using futures proceeds through a number of steps:

1 Calculate the currency requirement in base currency units. With an intended purchase of dollars for example we calculate, using the current spot rate, the equivalent sterling value.

2 The sterling equivalent is divided by the contract size and the nearest number of contracts is taken. In practice it is rare to get an exact match and so a less than perfect hedging arrangement will be created.

3 The contracts are purchased or sold depending upon whether an underlying purchase or sale of the underlying currency is to be made. The current open value is used and any initial margin is paid via the broker into the exchange clearing house.

4 Immediately the period of exposure is over the position is closed by making a reverse sale or purchase of the contracts held.

5 The difference between the rate for the purchase/sale is deducted from the rate required to close the position and the number of ticks calculated.

6 Using the number of ticks the profit or loss on the position is calculated and deducted from the dollar requirement if a gain or added to it if a loss. This net dollar requirement is purchased at the ruling spot rate.

EXHIBIT 14.12

Contract terms for a range of currency pairs

Contract	Contract Symbol	Contract Size	Price Quotation	Minimum Price Movement
Aus. Dollar – U.S. Dollar	AU	200 000 A. dollars	U.S. dollars per A. dollar to 4 decimal places	.0001 or 20 U.S. dollars per contract
U.S. Dollar – Swed. Krona	KU	200 000 U.S. dollars	krona per U.S. dollar to 4 decimal places	.0001 or 20 krona per contract
U.S. Dollar – Norw. Krone	NS	200 000 U.S. dollars	krone per U.S. dollar to 4 decimal places	.0001 or 20 krone per contract
U.S. Dollar – Swiss Franc	YF	200 000 U.S. dollars	S. francs per U.S. dollar to 4 decimal places	.0001 or 20 S. francs per contract
U.S. Dollar – British Pound	YP	125 000 B. pounds	U.S. dollars per pound to 4 decimal places	.0001 or 12.50 U.S. dollars per contract
U.S. Dollar – Japanese Yen	YY	200 000 U.S. dollars	yen per U.S. dollar to 2 decimal places	.01 or 2000 yen per contract
U.S. Dollar – S.African Rand	ZR	100 000 U.S. dollars	rands per U.S. dollar to 4 decimal places	.0005 or 50 rands per contract
U.S. Dollar – New Z Dollar	ZX	200 000 N.Z. dollars	U.S. dollars per N.Z. dollar to 4 decimal places	.0001 or 20 U.S. dollars per contract
Euro – U.S. Dollar Large	EU	200 000 euro	U.S. dollars per euro to 4 decimal places	.0001 or 20 U.S. dollars per contract
U.S. Dollar – Canadian Dollar	YD	200 000 U.S. dollars	C. dollars per U.S. dollar to 4 decimal places	.0001 or 10 C. dollars per contract
Euro – U.S. Dollar Regular	EO	100 000 euro	U.S. dollars per euro to 4 decimal places	.0001 or 10 U.S. dollars per contract
U.S. Dollar – Hungarian forint	UF	200 000 U.S. dollars	forint per dollar to 2 decimal places	.01 or 2000 forint per contract
U.S. Dollar – Czech Koruna	UZ	200 000 U.S. dollars	koruna per dollar to 3 decimal places	.001 or 200 koruna per contract
Small U.S. Dollar – Japanese Yen	SN	100 000 U.S. dollars	yen per US dollar to 2 decimal places	.01 or 2000 yen per contract
Small U.S. Dollar – Canadian Dollar	SV	100 000 US$	.0001 or 10 pound per contract	.0001 or 10 C. dollars per contract
Small U.S. Dollar – Swiss Franc	MF	100 000 US$	S. francs per U.S. dollar to 4 decimal places	.0001 or 10 S. francs per contract
Small British Pd. – U.S. Dollar	MP	62 500 pounds	U.S. dollars per pound to 4 decimal places	.0001 or 6.25 U.S. dollars per contract

Contract Months
March, June, Sept. & December.

Contract Settlement
Physical Delivery on the third Wednesday of the expiring month

Trading Hours
7:00 p.m. to 10:00p.m.
3:00 a.m. to 8:05 a.m.
8:05 a.m. to 3:00 p.m. (closing period commences at 2:59 pm)

Ticks
1/2 ticks on spread trades are permitted

Last Trading Day
Two business days prior to the third Wednesday of the expiring month, except for the U.S.$/Canadian $, which is one business day prior to the 3rd Wed. of the expiring month and the U.S./Hungarian forint, which is 3 business days prior to the 3rd Wed. of the expiring month

Source: NYBOT *www.nybot.com* standard contract specification list

The sterling cost of the net position (i.e. original dollar requirement plus or minus the profit on the futures) should, if a perfect hedge has been created give an effective sterling cost equal to the original sterling equivalent calculated in 1.

FINANCIAL REALITY

Friendly Grinders needs to purchase $11 million on 24 November. Gloria has decided to hedge the risk of an appreciation in the value of the dollar using small sterling dollar currency futures. The spot rate at 20 October is quoted as 1.7600 and the open price for a December contract is 1.7643. She opens her position on 20 October and closes her position on 24 November using the proceeds of the futures transaction to offset the amount of currency required. On 20 November spot has moved to 1.7184 and the future has moved to a settlement price of 1.7227.

Step (i) Calculate the exposure in sterling at the current spot rate:

$$\text{Exposure}(sterling) = \frac{\$11m}{1.7600} = £6.25 \text{ million}$$

Step (ii) Calculate the number of contracts required to hedge the exposure.

$$\text{Contracts} = \frac{\text{exposure (sterling equivalent)}}{\text{contract size}}$$

$$\text{Contracts} = \frac{£6.25 \text{million}}{£62\,500} = 100 \text{ contracts}$$

Step (iii) Purchase 100 contracts at the open price of 1.7643 on 20 October.

Step (iv) Sell 100 contracts at the settlement rate on 20 November at 1.7227.

Step (v) Calculate the difference between the opening rate and the rate used to close the positions (1.7227 − 1.7643) and calculate the number of ticks (416) and the tick value at $6.25 per tick ($2600).

Step (vi) As 100 contracts were purchased this represents a profit of $260 000 which is deducted from the dollar requirement to give a net purchase of $10.74 million. Using the 20 November spot rate of 1.7184 this gives a sterling cost of £6.25 million which is exactly the same as the cost at 20 October using the spot rate at that date (see Exhibit 14.13).

In practice using futures contracts to hedge FOREX transactions of this type rarely comes out exactly as shown. There are two reasons why the hedge might be less than perfect: the currency requirement may not yield an exact number of contracts and the futures rates may not move in line with changes in the spot rate. This latter problem is what we term we have already referred to as basis risk.

Basis risk

Basis is the name given to the difference at any point in time between the prices of two related financial securities. Variability in the value of basis in a hedged position

EXHIBIT 14.13

Hedging using currency futures

20-Oct Dollar purchase requirement	$11 000 000
20-Oct spot	1.7600
20-Oct Sterling equivalent	£6 250 000
standard contract size	£62 500
number of contracts to purchase	100
20-Nov sell 100 contracts at rate =	1.7227
20-Oct original cost at rate =	1.7643
profit on net position	–0.0416
ticks	–416
Tick value ($6.25)	–$2 600
Dollar requirement	$11 000 000
dollar gain on futures contract	–$260 000
20-Nov Net purchase (dollars)	$10 740 000
20-Nov spot	1.7184
Sterling cost	£6 250 000
Original cost	£6 250 000
Net gain or loss	$0

gives rise to basis risk. Basis risk is a problem which affects all derivative securities that are used to hedge price movements in some underlying assets. With interest rate futures discussed in the last chapter basis risk will arise if the change in the quoted price of the security does not match the corresponding change in the underlying interest rates that are being hedged. With currency futures the hedge will only work perfectly if a proportionate change in the underlying is reflected in an equivalent change in the value of the derivative. If the movements in the exchange rate in the spot market are not perfectly reflected in the futures market then there will be a gain or loss on the hedged position.

If basis is the difference between the spot and the future price at any time as shown in Exhibit 14.14 then we could create a perfect hedge if we knew the magnitude of b_c the basis at the point the position is closed. Unfortunately this is the uncertain element and it is the variability of b_c which is the basis risk in the hedged position. Clearly, as we approach settlement the variability of b_c will diminish as b_c drops to zero. This leads to the obvious conclusion that the way to minimize basis risk is to hedge with a future contract which is due to mature as soon as possible after the exposure in the underlying is cleared. Indeed, if the exposure in the underlying is cleared at exactly the same time as the future matures then the basis risk will necessarily be zero. So the rule for hedging currency risk is: look for a currency future maturing after, but as close as possible to, the currency purchase or sale which clears the exposure to changes in rate of the underlying. It is also critical to clear the position in the future or delivery will be enforced. With currency dealings, failing to close means that the currency will either be delivered or called and the loss will be the spread and commission in organizing a currency transaction at spot. If the underlying is in potatoes, or coffee beans then delivery could present you with an embarrassing problem.

EXHIBIT 14.14

Basis and basis risk over time

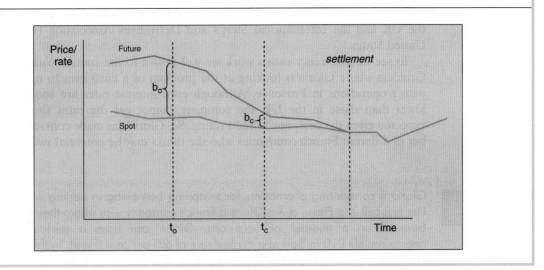

Currency swaps

In the last chapter we described a simple interest rate swap. Currency swaps work on the same principle in that they allow two parties to exchange interest rate commitments on borrowing in different currencies. However, unlike an interest rate swap, currency swaps entail an exchange of principal. When the swap is agreed, the two parties raise debt in their own currency and an exchange is made at an agreed rate of exchange (the original spot rate).

The value of a currency swap is that it allows a company, for example, to acquire finance in other than its base currency area at either a fixed or a variable rate to suit its circumstances. It would be possible to borrow in its base currency, convert its borrowing to the counter currency required and transfer the sum involved to an account denominated in that currency. The problem with this approach is that it may be able to borrow at a slightly better rate in its domestic market but it would bear substantial transaction costs. The other factor that is important in determining the value of a swap is the term structure of interest rates (see Chapter 4) for the two currencies concerned and the term structure of the exchange rate. If, for example, the term structure is upward sloping in one economy and downward sloping in another then a swap agreement can be configured which gives both parties the ability to benefit from the differences in the forward rates and the expected future spot rates.

During the tenure of a swap interest is exchanged at specified dates:

- With a fixed for fixed swap, interest is exchanged at a fixed rate agreed in the swap contract.
- With a fixed for variable swap, the parties swap variable interest at LIBOR plus an agreed number of basis points and the fixed rate of interest as originally agreed.

At the end of the agreed swap period the principal is re-exchanged at the original spot rate irrespective of how the exchange rate has changed over the intervening period. There are nuances in swap agreements about the timing of interest payments. In some the interest is paid in arrears, in others it is paid in advance. Whichever way is agreed the arrangement between the parties is formalized in a 'swap confirmation'. This legal form has been standardized by the British Bankers Association (BBA) in the UK and the International Swaps and Derivatives Association (ISDA) in the United States.

To see how currency swaps work we will return to the frantic world of Friendly Grinders where Gloria is looking at the problem of a euro loan to open the company's operations in Provence. Although euro interest rates are some 2 per cent lower than those in the UK the company cannot get the rates she would have expected given the company's credit rating. So, Gloria has made contact with a number of different French companies who she thinks may be potential swap partners.

FINANCIAL REALITY

Gloria is considering alternatives for swapping borrowing in sterling with euro(s). Her first call is to Pierre at AmiGlace a French company with whom they have done business on a number of occasions. Gloria can raise a sterling loan of approximately £10 million at a current rate of 6.0 per cent (fixed). In the eurozone she can raise an equivalent euro loan at 5.2 per cent, fixed. Gloria needs approximately €15 million for one year. AmiGlace can get a better rate of 4.8 per cent but can only get 6.4 per cent in the UK loan market. Pierre is looking to reschedule a one year UK loan of exactly £10 million. The proposal is for a fixed for fixed currency swap at today's sterling/euro spot rate of 1.4590. Interest will be settled between the two parties at six monthly intervals.

The mechanics of a fixed for fixed swap are straightforward. Both parties raise the required loan in their own currency at the best fixed rate which is also agreed between each party as the basis for the swap. In this case, if she went ahead, Gloria would notify Pierre that she was able to raise a £10 million, one year loan at 6.00 per cent. He in his turn raises an equivalent loan whose value is calculated, using the agreed spot rate, at €14 590 000. The principal is transferred between the parties at the date the loan is taken out and each party pays the other the interest due at the prevailing spot rate. At the end of the loan the principal is re-exchanged at the original and not the current spot rate. This is to ensure that both parties are able to repay the debt at its original value.

In this example (see Exhibit 14.15) Gloria and Pierre are contemplating a direct interest rate swap. There is no comparative advantage between the two parties in either market. In the UK market, Friendly Grinders can get 6.0 per cent and AmiGlace can get 6.4 per cent (a difference of 40 basis points). The same difference exists between the rate Friendly Grinders can get in the euro market (5.2 per cent) and the rate available to AmiGlace (4.8 per cent) – again 40 basis points.

A fixed currency swap of this type is valuable if both parties have an interest rate advantage in their own market compared with the other. This may arise even where companies have identical credit ratings for the simple reason that lenders recognize that a borrower raising debt in a foreign currency is bearing exchange risk. Because exchange rates are volatile the borrower therefore takes on some risk in their interest payments even though the rates are fixed.

A fixed for fixed swap is also valuable even if one party carries a higher credit risk and thus a higher cost of debt finance in both markets. In that case the idea of comparative advantage discussed in the last chapter tells us the maximum gain on the swap.

EXHIBIT 14.15

Fixed for fixed currency swap with no comparative advantage

	Friendly Grinders UK	AmiGlace Eurozone
month 0 Loan taken out	–£10 000 000	–€14 590 000
Principal received	€14 590 000	£10 000 000
Total interest paid	€700 320	£600 000
month 12 Principal re-exchanged	–€14 590 000	–£10 000 000
Principal received	£10 000 000	€14 590 000
Net cost	–€700 320	–£600 000
Cost if self-financed	–€758 680	–£640 000
Potential saving	€58 360	£40 000
Saving in domestic currency	£40 000	€58 360
Assuming a constant spot rate (£/euro) =	1.459	

FINANCIAL REALITY

Gloria's second alternative is a swap arrangement with a small French company she knows through her banking connections. Frere Franglais is a French owned cross channel general trading firm that is looking for £10 million to build a UK distribution facility in Kent. Frere Franglais could raise a euro loan at 8.2 per cent and a UK loan at 10.8 per cent.

To see whether a swap is worthwhile we compare the fixed rate differential between the two parties for borrowing in the UK market and compare it with the differential in the euro market:

$$\boxed{\text{Swap premium}} = \begin{array}{c}\text{Interest rate}\\\text{differential in the}\\\text{UK market}\end{array} - \begin{array}{c}\text{Interest rate}\\\text{differential in the}\\\text{euro market}\end{array}$$

Swap premium = (10.8% – 6%) – (8.2% – 5.2%) = 1.8%

If we look at the capital and interest flows on this swap (as shown in Exhibit 14.16) we see that Friendly Grinders could save annual interest of (5.2 per cent – 4.3 per cent) 0.90 per cent on its euro loan which is €131 310 (equivalent to £90 000 per annum at the current spot rate). Frere Franglais would save (10.8 per cent – 9.9 per cent) 0.9 per cent on its loan which is £90 000 per annum (equivalent to €131 310) as shown in Exhibit 14.16.

The question is: is this gain illusory? With the pure vanilla swap the comparative advantage in the two markets was down to a transfer of credit risk. Jack Grinder had not appreciated that he was swapping his own high quality income flow for a low quality flow

EXHIBIT 14.16

Fixed for fixed currency swap with comparative advantage

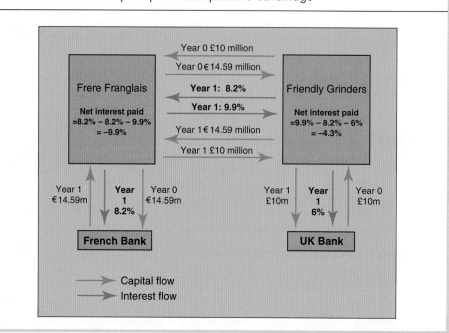

from his impecunious brother. In such a situation we would expect the lenders to adjust their rates to rectify the alteration in Jack and Roger's relative riskiness. With a currency swap it can be different if the comparative advantage has been brought about by differences in the tax treatment of interest payable in the two countries concerned. Nevertheless, any differential in rates caused by differences in credit rating (whether specific to the firm or caused by differences in exchange rate risk) should be eliminated if the credit market is perfectly efficient.

From the description of a fixed for fixed swap it is a straightforward step to a fixed for variable currency swap. Again, in this situation the gain that can be made relies upon there being some comparative advantage between the two parties that can be exploited.

FINANCIAL REALITY

Gloria's third alternative entailed a swap with another Anglo-French company Belltrane who was looking for a variable interest UK loan. Belltrane could secure a fixed loan at 5.6 per cent in the eurozone or LIBOR + 2.5 per cent in the UK. Gloria can secure a variable rate loan in the UK at LIBOR + 0.6 per cent or fixed at 5.2 per cent in the eurozone. In this case Gloria would be prepared to pay 5.0 per cent fixed in exchange for LIBOR + 120.

The comparative advantage suggests a swap premium as in Exhibit 14.17.

EXHIBIT 14.17

Suggested swap premium with comparative advantage

	Sterling (Variable) LIBOR+	Euro (Fixed)	Premium
Belltrane	250	560	
Friendly Grinders	60	520	
Interest rate differential	190	40	150

This indicates that there are 150 basis points to be shared between the two parties. To see how the distribution of interest rates works out we will use the diagram as in Exhibit 14.16 but this time in Exhibit 14.18 we do not, for the sake of clarity, include the principal transfers.

Friendly Grinders would have been able to secure a fixed interest loan in euro(s) for 5.2 per cent and as a result of the swap pays a net of 4.4 per cent giving a saving of 80 basis points. Belltrane would have been able to secure a UK loan at LIBOR + 250 but given the swap pays a net of LIBOR + 180 giving a saving of 70 basis points. The total saving between the two parties is 150 points as expected.

The mechanism for a fixed for variable swap is exactly as before with a fixed for fixed agreement:

1 Each party takes out a loan for an agreed term at an agreed interest rate and at the current spot rate. The principal is transferred between the two parties.

2 Using the prevailing spot rate the interest to be paid over by each party is calculated in the counter currency concerned at each agreed payment interval (six monthly in the Friendly Grinders case).

3 At the end of the contract the original amount is repaid. In this case Friendly Grinders would repay €14.59 m and Belltrane would repay £10 m.

EXHIBIT 14.18

Fixed for variable currency swap

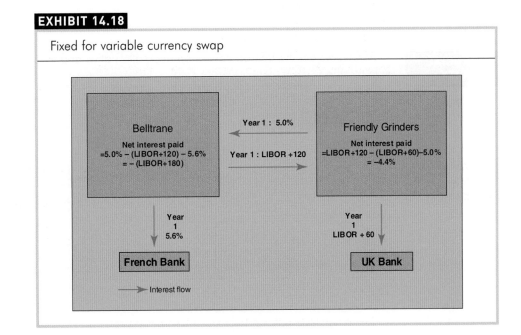

Valuing currency swaps

It may happen as in the above examples that two parties with identical borrowing requirements can enter into an OTC agreement. However, it can be quite difficult to find a counterparty whose requirements exactly meet one anothers needs. As with interest rate swaps a company can arrange a currency swap via a market maker – normally a bank or other financial institution that specializes in the swap business.

You may remember that a swap agreement can be replicated by the sale and purchase of two bonds maturing at the same time:

1 The swap 'seller' (Friendly Grinders in this case) issues a fixed interest rate bond of set term and receives from the buyer a variable rate bond of exactly the same maturity.

2 The swap buyer issues the variable rate bond and receives the fixed rate bond.

With a vanilla interest rate swap the market maker quotes a pair of fixed rates 'for LIBOR'. What this means is that in exchange for LIBOR received from one counter party it will pay fixed at the lower of the two rates quoted, and it will charge the higher rate to the counterparty to whom it pays LIBOR. The market maker sets the fixed rates such that the present value of the fixed interest payments received under the swap agreement equals the present value of the variable interest payments (in practice a slightly lower rate is set to give a profit margin). A zero coupon yield curve or 'spot' curve is used to generate the expected rates for LIBOR.

With a currency swap the same principle applies as with an interest rate swap but in this case:

$$V\ (swap) = V\ (base\_bond) - s_0 V\ (counter\_bond)$$

where $V(swap)$ is the value of the swap, $V(base\_bond)$ and $V(counter\_bond)$ are the values of the fixed or the variable rate bond issued in the base currency and in the counter currency respectively. s_0 is the spot rate (direct) used to convert the value of the bond issued in the counter currency into the base currency.

We can use these ideas to value the cost of finance to either counterparty through the swap mechanism.

FINANCIAL REALITY

Gloria works out the interest saving on each alternative and lays them out side by side.

EXHIBIT 14.19

Comparison of three currency swap alternatives

Option:		AmiGlace (fixed/fixed)		FrereFranglais (fixed/fixed)		Belltrane (fixed/variable)
Cost of self financing						
euro loan	5.20%	758 680	5.20%	758 680	5.20%	758 680
Cost of loan via swap	4.80%	700 320	4.30%	627 370	4.40%	641 960
Saving		58 360		131 310		116 720
Convert to sterling at						
spot (1.4590)		40 000		90 000		80 000

Gloria decides to value the Belltrane alternative if she went ahead with that deal. She would like to know the value of the swap agreement to Friendly Grinders, the gain and the fixed rate which would give her a zero Net Present Value on the swap There is, she believes some comparative advantage in the swap (unlike AmiGlace) as Belltrane has a very similar credit rating to Friendly Grinders. She notes that current LIBOR rates and exchange rates are as follows:

EXHIBIT 14.20

Current LIBOR rates and exchange rates

	spot	6 month	12 month
£ LIBOR	4.42125	4.62125	4.64000
euro Libor	2.17750	2.57425	2.73238
sterling/euro	0.6838	0.6900	0.6961

Gloria's calculation suggests that the net interest cost is likely to be 4.4 per cent yielding a saving in the cost of financing the loan of 80 basis points or £80 000. As with the vanilla interest rate swap discussed in the last chapter we value the two legs of the agreement:

1 The valuation of a purchase of a nominal sterling bond at LIBOR + 120. The future interest payments and redemption at par are calculated using LIBOR + 120 implied forward rates and then discounted using the appropriate sterling LIBOR spot rate.

2 The valuation of an issued Eurobond at 5 per cent fixed. This is discounted using the euro LIBOR rate.

In Exhibit 14.21 we show the valuation of the swap given that the current terms are agreed and the gain in value to Friendly Grinders compared with the company raising the euro loan at 5.2 per cent.

The first step in the analysis is to calculate the six monthly discount factors for both sterling and euro LIBOR. This currency swap like most that are transacted in the market is with interest payable six monthly. The discount factor for sterling LIBOR, for example, is:

$$LIBOR_6 = 4.6215\%(annual)$$

$$LIBOR_6 = 1.046215^{\frac{1}{2}} - 1$$

$$LIBOR_6 = 0.0228465(biannual)$$

$$LIBOR_6(discount\ rate) = \frac{1}{1.0228465} = 0.977665$$

and

$$LIBOR_{12} = 0.046400$$

$$LIBOR_{12}(discount\ rate) = \frac{1}{1.046400} = 0.955657$$

The second step is to calculate the variable receipts on the variable leg of the swap. In Exhibit 14.21 we work on a nominal sterling swap of £100. Because the receipts will be in sterling we use the sterling LIBOR + 120 implied forward rates to calculate the expected future cash flow. The forward rate for the first six months is, of course, the expected spot rate on a six month maturity. The forward rate for the second six months is as follows

$$£LIBOR_6 + 120 = 0.058213 \equiv 0.028695 (semi\text{-}annual)$$
$$£LIBOR_{12} + 120 = 0.058400$$
$$£LIBOR + 120(fwd) = \frac{1.058400}{1.028695} - 1 = 0.028877$$

These receipts we discount using the sterling LIBOR spot rate as quoted to give a present value of the variable leg of the swap of £101.13.

The third step is to calculate the present value of the fixed payments. These have been agreed at 5 per cent or two biannual instalments of 2.5 per cent on the principal. Because these are euro payments then we discount them at the euro LIBOR rate to give a present value (€149.17). This figure we then convert at the spot sterling/euro exchange rate of 0.6854 to give a present value on the fixed leg of £102.24. The difference in the present value of the two legs is the value of the swap which is –1.11. So, if Friendly Grinders were required to 'mark to market' this swap would be shown as a net liability of £111 000. Normally, if a swap is negotiated through a bank the fixed rate would be set against LIBOR to give a zero Net Present Value. In this case if Gloria wished to achieve a zero Net Present Value on the swap she would need to agree a rate of 3.87 per cent (this rate can be discovered from the model using goal seek and setting the value of the swap to 0 by changing the fixed rate payable).

However, what matters to Gloria is that she can access a euro loan at a net cost of 4.4 per cent. The gain on the swap is £0.76/£100 or 76 basis points over the year or £76 000 – which is not bad for half an hour's work on the telephone. This gain is the discounted value of the saving Gloria estimated at 80 basis points (which assumes that the saving is immediate).

Once the valuation model is established it is then possible to calculate the breakeven rates of interest in negotiation.

REVIEW ACTIVITY 14.4 After setting up the model and keeping all variables as agreed:

1 What is the minimum variable rate that can be accepted?

2 What is the minimum fixed rate that can be accepted?

There are other approaches to swap valuation based upon the idea that a swap can be construed as a sequence of Forward Rate Agreements or forward contracts. The readings at the end of this chapter outline the mechanics of the different methods. However, the comforting point to note is that they all come out to the same answer!

FX swaps

The currency swaps we have described above are a combined interest rate swap and foreign exchange swap. One obvious question is whether it is possible to simply swap foreign currencies without any payment of interest. Indeed it is. Foreign exchange swaps are purely concerned with exchanging currencies and for both counterparties

EXHIBIT 14.21

Valuation of a fixed for variable OTC swap

	spot	6 months	12 months
LIBOR STERLING (quoted)	4.42125	4.62125	4.64000
LIBOR EURO (quoted)	2.17750	2.57425	2.73238
£LIBOR	0.044213	0.046213	0.046400
£LIBOR discount factor		0.977665	0.955657
£LIBOR	0.021775	0.025743	0.027324
£LIBOR discount factor		0.987372	0.973403
Sterling bond value (LIBOR + 120)	**100.00**		
£LIBOR + 120	0.056213	0.058213	0.058400
£LIBOR + 120 (forward rates)		0.028695	0.028877
Variable receipt		**2.869456**	**102.887683**
Discounted variable receipts		2.805367	98.325385
Present value (Sterling) – variable receipts	**101.13**		
Eurobond value (FIXED 5%)	**145.90**		
Fixed Rate (%)		2.5	2.5
Fixed payment		**−3.647505**	**−149.547709**
Discounted fixed receipts		−3.601445	−145.570179
Present value (fixed payments)	−149.17		
Convert at spot	**−102.24**		
Value of the swap	**−1.11**		
Sterling bond value (LIBOR + 60)	**100.00**		
LIBOR + basis points		0.052213	0.052400
LIBOR + 60 forward rates		0.025774	0.025957
Variable payment		**−2.577410**	**−102.595689**
Discounted variable payments		−2.519843	−98.046339
Present value (variable payments)	**−100.57**		
Present Value of swap cash flows	**−101.68**		
Effective interest cost of euro loan (5.2%)	**145.90**		
Fixed Rate (%)		2.6	2.6
Fixed payment		**−3.793405**	**−149.693610**
Discounted fixed receipts		−3.745502	−145.712199
Present value (fixed payments)	−149.46		
Convert at spot	**−102.44**		
GAIN ON SWAP (£/£100)	**0.76**		

two transactions are involved in a simple 'spot against forward': a simultaneous spot sale of currency A and purchase of currency B is made by one side of the agreement. The other party purchases from the other party currency A, and sells back B. This is termed the first leg. Simultaneously with these spot transactions a set of reversing forward agreements are made to sell and buy back the two currencies at an agreed date (the second leg). It is also possible to enter into permutations of this type of swap. A forward against forward starts with a forward (rather than a spot contract) to exchange two currencies at the earlier of two future dates and at the second of the two dates the deal is reversed. Foreign exchange swaps are a useful mechanism for companies to exchange currencies for agreed periods of time and thus avoid the heavy transactions costs of buying and selling currencies on the open markets.

Currency options

Currency options have many of the features of equity options discussed in Chapter 8. 'Cash' options are written on the delivery of foreign exchange at a specified rate and at, or before, a specified future time. Such options can be written as calls where the writer agrees to deliver if 'called' the nominated amount of foreign currency at the specified exchange rate for exercise. Likewise they can also be written as puts where the writer agrees to purchase the nominated amount at the agreed rate. Cash currency options can be written OTC and are also available exchange traded.

A second type of exchange traded option is also available and these are written on futures contracts. So a call option on sterling dollar futures is one where the writer agrees to sell the future to the holder if 'called' at an agreed future rate. A put option does the reverse. The only significant difference in the trading terms of this type of option is that they are referred to by the maturity date of future contract and not the exercise date of the option.

Currency options are particularly useful where a company is in a tender bid situation and if successful will receive payment in an overseas currency. If the tender is successful the option can be exercised if it is in the money and the underlying currency transaction can be effectively hedged. If the tender is unsuccessful the option can be exercised and the profit taken.

FINANCIAL REALITY

Jack Grinder is bursting with news. 'Gloria', he exclaims 'I have just tendered for a huge order for diamond dust for the new CERN project in Switzerland – it's a €25 million order for delivery in six months!'

'Is that an agreed price?' enquires Gloria mildly. Jack pauses 'is that a problem?' he asks looking worried. Gloria explains the financial facts of life to Jack carefully: 'we need to ensure that the exchange rate ruling for euro(s) today is the one we get in six months. That's tricky to hedge in the normal way. If we don't get the contract we do not want to take delivery of the sterling if the forward rate is against us.'

'What are you saying?' said Jack. 'We could take a hit if the euro moves the wrong way and there is nothing we can do about it.'

'No, I'm not saying that' replies Gloria '– we could hedge the currency with a euro sterling option in the cash market but it will cost us. We will have to pay a premium to cover the position'.

'How would that work exactly?' asks Jack.

'Well what we can do is see if the bank will write us an option to buy the sterling equivalent of €25 million exercisable in six months. At today's spot of 1.4707 that's . . .' she tapped her calculator . . .'£17 million. So if we set that as the exercise price and the spot rate goes higher, say to 1.5, we will be in the money and take delivery of £17 million from the bank in exchange for the €25 million we receive from CERN. If the rate goes down below the agreed rate, we bin the option and convert our euro(s) on the spot market.'

'That's fine, if we get the contract, but what happens if we don't?' queried Jack who thought for one fleeting moment that he had caught her out. 'No problem' she replies. 'If we are in the money we buy the euro(s) at spot which will, using the rate before, be 1.5 and call the option at 1.4707 for a nice profit. If the rate falls below that we just bin the option.' 'And all we've lost is the premium – great, work it out with the bank and how about dinner tonight? 'There is something I have been meaning to ask you for a long time . . .'

The OTC options such as those contemplated by Gloria take the largest share of this specialized form of options trading. There are some exchange traded currency options available in the US but they are not widely available elsewhere. The London International Financial Futures Exchange offer dollar euro contracts as European style options. The readings at the end of this chapter will allow you to expand your knowledge of this particular market.

SUMMARY

In this chapter we have taken some initial steps into the world of the foreign currency markets at such a level as required for the corporate financial manager to keep their head above water. We have explored the nature of exchange rates and the factors that drive them. We described the so-called five arbitrage conditions which link the two monetary phenomena, inflation and interest rates, to spot and forward rates. However, trading in overseas markets bring specific risks some of which can be eliminated through the mechanics of hedging. Some hedging techniques are simply a matter of getting the pattern of operations right and to make sure that inter and intra company indebtedness is minimized. Some risks may require more sophisticated methods using one of the many derivative instruments available in the market. Derivatives impose costs and if they are not handled correctly can lead to substantial losses in their own right. The derivatives discussed in this chapter are reasonably straightforward but there are many more sophisticated variants which can

have unforeseen consequences if things go wrong. However, some would argue that financially engineered products such as these can be a great opportunity for the firm. So before we sign off with our final financial reality here is a quote from the famous 1990 Nobel Prize winning economist Robert Merton:

'Thanks to the inventiveness of the modern financial markets, managers can, in principle, engineer a company's capital structure so that virtually the only risks its shareholders, debt holders, trade creditors, pensioners, and other liability holders must bear are what I call value adding risks. Those are the risks associated with positive Net Present Value activities in which the company has a comparative advantage. All other risks can be hedged or insured against through the financial markets.

In most large companies, equity capital is used to cushion against a great many risks that the firm is no better at bearing than anyone else. If it can strip out the non-value-adding, or passive, risk, the company will be able to use its existing equity capital to finance a lot more value adding assets and activities than competitors, and its shares will be worth far more. So the potential for creating shareholder value through financial engineering is enormous.

This is not just a theoretical possibility: one innovation – the interest rate swap, introduced about 20 years ago – has already enabled a major industry, banking, to dramatically increase its capacity for adding value to each dollar of invested equity capital. With the range of derivative instruments growing, there is no reason other companies cannot do likewise, potentially creating tens of billions of dollars in shareholder value. The possibilities are especially important for private companies that have no access to public equity markets and therefore cannot easily increase their equity capital by issuing more shares.

In other words, smart financial engineering frees up equity capital for strategic investments, allowing a company to finance more value adding growth for the same amount of equity. And there is no increase in the level of risk a company bears, just a change in the risks nature. Better yet, as we shall see, managers can create all this value adding growth without changing the way their companies currently go about their business.' HARVARD BUSINESS REVIEW, November 2005

Finally, there is a one element of our story which we do need to bring to a conclusion. Given the highly technical nature of the subject you might be forgiven for thinking that that is what finance is all about. Nevertheless, there is a human dimension to all aspects of business. We often forget that markets, financial or otherwise, are human inventions and our tour of corporate finance and valuation through the last 14 chapters has been an examination of the implications of markets and our response to them. That response is intimately tied up with our attitude towards risk and how far we are prepared to go to exploit it, and what efforts we make to minimize it.

That's it – except to say that in a small restaurant in the depths of the Kentish countryside the financial future of Friendly Grinders hangs in the balance . . .

FINANCIAL REALITY

Jack Grinder passed a small box across the table to Gloria containing within it the product of many years' research by the company's R&D laboratory. He knew his grandfather who had founded the firm would have been very proud of their achievement. Gloria, her hand shaking with excitement flipped open the lid and there, flashing on a circle of gold, was a ten caret diamond of unimaginable purity and brilliance. 'We have a new business venture and . . .' Jack hesitated a moment, his eyes twinkling over an upraised glass of Bollinger. ' . . . what about a consolidation?' he leaned across the table 'Would you be willing to become Gloria Grinder?'

Further Reading

Backus, D., Gregory, A. and Telmer, C. (1993) Accounting for Forward Rates in Markets for Foreign Currency, *Journal of Finance*, 5:1887–1908.

Buckley, A. (2004) Multinational Finance (5th Ed.) Harlow England: FT Prentice Hall. A particularly scholarly text with a good discussion of the principles and evidence supporting the five arbitrage theorems.

Cumby, R.E. and Obstfeld, M. (1984) International Interest-Rate and Price-Level Linkages Under Flexible Exchange Rates: A Review of Recent Evidence, in Bilson, J.F.O. and Marston R. (ed.), *Exchange Rates: Theory and Practice*, Chicago: University of Chicago Press.

Cuthbertson, K. (1996) *Quantitative Financial Economics – stock bonds and foreign exchange,*

Series in Financial Economics and Quantitative Analysis, New York: Wiley.

Fama, E. (1984) Forward and Spot Exchange Rates, *Journal of Monetary Economics*, 14:319–338.

Hodrick, R.J. (1987) *The Empirical Evidence of the Efficiency of the Forward and Futures Foreign Exchange Markets*, Chur, Switzerland: Hardwood Academic Publishers.

Hodrick, R. J. (1989) Risk, Uncertainty and Exchange Rates, *Journal of Monetary Economics*, 23:433–459.

Hull, J.C. (2005) Options, Futures and Other Derivatives (6th Ed.) New Jersey: Pearson Prentice Hall. The best book on derivatives on the market.

Jorion, P. and Abuaf, N. (1990) Purchasing Power Parity in the Long Run, *Journal of Finance* 45:1.

Lucas, R.E., Jr. (1982) Interest Rates and Currency Prices in a Two-Country World, *Journal of Monetary Economics*, 10:335–360.

Mark, N. (1988) Time Varying Betas and Risk Premia in the Pricing of Forward Exchange Contracts, *Journal of Financial Economics*, 22:335–354.

Merton, R. (2005) You Have More Capital than You Think, *Harvard Business Review*, November 2005

Miller, M. (1997) *Merton Miller on Derivatives*, New York: Wiley.

Retz, R.W. (2005) *Currency Futures and Options*, New York Board of Trade available from www.nybot.com.

Reuters (1999) *Foreign Exchange and Money Markets*, The Reuters Financial Training Series, Singapore: Wiley.

Valdez, S. and Wood, J. (2003) *An Introduction to Global Financial Markets* (4th Ed.) Basingstoke, Hants: Palgrave.

PROGRESS CHECK

1 If you are given an indirect rate of exchange, which would be the highest: the bid rate or the ask rate?

2 Define a forward rate of exchange.

3 How is a cross rate calculated and what two types of cross rate are quoted?

4 What three principal economic influences drive interest rates?

5 Write down the formula for calculating a future spot rate given the rates of inflation in the domestic and overseas economy.

6 Describe the steps required to exploit a covered interest arbitrage opportunity.

7 Outline the four different approaches that can be employed in calculating the Net Present Value of a project when the cash flows arise in a foreign currency.

8 How do economic risk, exchange rate risk and translation risk differ from one another?

9 What is the difference between a matching and a netting arrangement?

10 What are the advantages and disadvantages of a money market hedge over a forward currency agreement?

11 With respect to currency futures how is a tick defined?

12 At what rate is the principal converted in the re-exchange at the end of a currency swap?

13 What is the principal difference between an FX swap and a currency swap?

14 In what way does a quotation for a currency option on a futures contract differ from that provided on other types of traded option?

QUESTIONS (answers at end of book)

1 The spot rate for the dollar/Japanese yen is 119.230. US LIBOR is 4.05250 per cent and Yen LIBOR is 0.04000 per cent. What is the implied forward rate at three months, six months and 12 months?

2 A Canadian subsidiary has submitted the following project for approval to its UK parent company:

Capital investment Can$6.6 million and five years real terms cash flow of Can$ 2.0 million. A 100 per cent first year capital allowance is available and Canadian corporation tax is charged at 20 per cent. Canadian tax is levied in the year following assessment. Under a double tax agreement Canadian Tax can be offset against UK tax which is levied at 30 per cent. Under the UK system a 100 per cent first year allowance is available for this class of expenditure. The group cost of capital is 8 per cent and the following statistics are available:

	UK	Canada
Spot rate of exchange		2.0079
Interest rates	4.6 per cent	2.99 per cent
Inflation	2 per cent	2.6 per cent

The company requires bids to be submitted at UK nominal and discounted using the group's cost of capital.

You are required to:

(i) Project the Canadian and the UK post tax cash flows for this project in nominal terms.

(ii) Calculate the Net Present Value of this investment.

3 The UK group treasurer is expecting the receipt of $12 million dollars in three months. She anticipates that she will need to hold this dollar balance before reinvesting it in France in six months time. The current sterling/dollar rate is 1.7201 and the three month and six month forward rates are 1.7195 and 1.7214 respectively. The current sterling/euro rate is 1.4585 and the three month and six month forward rates are 1.4510 and 1.4421 respectively. Calculate the total sterling exchange gain or loss on this set of transactions.

QUESTIONS (answers on website)

4 The following indirect rates with respect to the US$: $/Swiss franc 1.313, $/euro 0.8471.

(i) What is the implied euro/Swiss franc cross rate in both direct and indirect terms?

(ii) Is there an arbitrage opportunity between these two currency pairs?

5 A US company needs to purchase euro 20 million in four weeks on 12 December. The $/euro spot rate is 1.1793 and December dollar/euro currency futures are trading at 1.1721. The group treasurer is concerned about a potential appreciation of the euro and would like

to lock in the current rate. The dollar euro currency futures have a contract size of €200 000 and a tick is $20 per contract. At the date the loan is taken out the spot rate has moved to 1.1830. What close out rate would lead to a perfect hedge?

6   Define the different types of risk that can influence currency price movements and the ways that they can be mitigated.

7   Lucas Ltd a US company owes its Canadian subsidiary Can$14m which in its turn owes ¥2m to the Japanese subsidiary and €8 million to the European subsidiary. Lucas owes ¥16m to its Japanese subsidiary which on another account owes it $5m. The European subsidiary owes Lucas Ltd $15m but on another account it is owed by Lucas €5m. The direct rates are $/euro = 1.18, $/yen = 0.00839, $/Can$ = 0.8566. Work out the most efficient settlement at the current exchange rates between the group companies.

8   BP has approached Royal Dutch Shell to negotiate a £400m fixed for variable swap for six months. BP has fixed rate borrowing in the UK market but would wish to move to a floating rate over the next six months. Royal Dutch Shell is looking for fixed rate sterling of an equivalent amount and is willing to negotiate terms. The current sterling/euro spot is 1.4585 and the following data may be relevant:

Market rates (annualized)	overnight	3 months	6 months
Euro LIBOR	2.12375	2.46263	2.58475
Sterling LIBOR	4.51625	4.61563	4.61563

BP Rates	UK	Euro
Fixed (%)	4.55	2.80
Variable Basis Points over LIBOR (£)	60	65

RDS Rates	UK	Euro
Fixed (%)	4.75	2.30
Variable Basis Points over LIBOR (Euro)	75	75

Both companies have identical credit ratings. Interest will be settled three monthly in arrears.

You are required:

(i)   To determine the premium available on a fixed for fixed and a fixed for variable swap.
(ii) To establish terms for a fixed for variable swap which equalizes the value between each party.

9   Below is a section from the financial report of Cobham plc describing its risk management policies. On the basis of this and any other evidence you can discover describe the risk management policies of the business and in particular its approach to hedging through the use of derivative instruments. Are there any alternative approaches the group might take and what would be their advantages and disadvantages?

Foreign currency risk is the most significant aspect for the Group in the area of financial instruments. It is exposed to a lesser extent to other risks such as interest rate risk and liquidity risk. The Board reviews and agrees policies for managing each of these risks and they are summarised below. The policies have remained unchanged throughout the year.

Foreign currency risk

The Group, which is based in the UK and reports in sterling, has significant investment in overseas operations in the USA, with further investments in other EU countries, Australia, Canada, South Africa and Asia. As a result, the Group's balance sheet can be affected by movements in these countries' exchange rates. The Group's policy is to reduce, or eliminate where practicable, both structural and transactional foreign exchange risk. Where significant, currency denominated net assets are partially hedged by currency borrowings. Currency exposures are reviewed regularly and all significant foreign exchange transactions are approved by the parent company. The pound/US dollar exchange rate is the most important as far as Cobham is concerned, particularly given the level of US dollars which the subsidiaries expect to receive from their normal business activities. In addition to the longer term borrowing structure, a number of financial instruments are used to manage the foreign exchange position, such as forward contracts. As at 31 December 2004, US$221m of forward contracts were in place and stretching out to 2014. These contracts are at an average exchange rate of $1.68: £1. It is the Group's current belief that the net dollar receipts from its subsidiaries will exceed the level of the outstanding commitment. The Group has transactional currency exposures. Such exposures arise from sales and purchases by operating units in currencies other than the unit's functional currency. The Group's policy is to minimise trading in subsidiaries' non operating currencies. However, where this is impractical the Group will seek to reduce its exposure through the use of forward contracts. The Group does not hedge balance sheet and profit and loss translation exposures. Generally, borrowings are arranged in local currencies to provide a natural hedge against overseas assets.

Interest rate risk

The Group has various long and short term borrowings principally in sterling and US dollars at fixed and floating rates of interest. The Group is continually monitoring its exposure to movements in interest rates in order to bring greater stability and certainty with respect to borrowing costs. Group policy is to assess borrowings with regard to fixed or variable rates of interest depending on prevailing market conditions, including instances where interest rate swaps are used. Surplus funds are placed on short term deposit. These deposits have floating rates of interest, and thus there is some modest exposure to interest rates.

Liquidity risk

The Group has a strong cash flow and where practicable the funds generated by operating companies are managed on a regional basis. For short term working capital purposes in the UK, most operating companies utilise local bank facilities within an overall Group arrangement. In the USA a central treasury function is maintained which all US subsidiaries use. These practices allow a balance to be maintained between continuity of funding, security and flexibility. As regards liquidity, the Group's policy has throughout the year been to maintain a mix of short, medium and long term borrowings with their lenders. The private placement of Cobham guaranteed senior notes which raised US$225m in October 2002 enabled the Group to reduce short term and increase long term borrowings. Short-term flexibility is achieved by overdraft facilities. Details of the year end position, which is in accordance with this policy, are given in note 29. It is, in addition, the Group's policy to maintain undrawn committed borrowing facilities in order to provide flexibility in the management of the Group's liquidity; details are also given in note 29.

Accounting Rate of Return: the ratio of the average operating profit generated by a project (net operating cash flow less depreciation) to the average capital employed.

Accrued interest: this is the interest due to the seller when a bond is sold between two coupon payment dates. Accrued interest is reflected in the market price of the bond and gives the difference between the 'clean' price (i.e. the value of the bond discounted at its current yield) and the actual price (sometimes called the 'dirty' price).

Agency Theory: a theory of contractual relationships within the neoclassical tradition. The theory explains the phenomenon of 'agency loss' where one party to a contract of employment, the agent, has a differential advantage in terms of the information they hold and can use that information to gain personal advantage over and above that which would lead to an optimum relationship from the point of view of the principal. Information asymmetry generates 'moral hazard' and 'adverse selection'.

Alternative Investment Market: a UK market with close analogues in other countries which exist for the issue and trading in equity of small and intermediate size companies. The AIM has lower admission costs and regulatory requirements than the full market.

American option: an option that can be exercised at any time up until the exercise date.

Arbitrage Pricing Theory (APT): a multifactor asset pricing model which specifies security returns in terms of a range of linear factors under the assumption of zero arbitrage. The outcome is a series of risk premia associated with any number of factors. A single factor version of the APT reduces to the CAPM.

Arbitrage: the process of seeking risk free profit opportunities by the simultaneous buying and selling of the same security in different markets in contravention of the Law of One Price.

Arithmetic average: the simple average obtained by adding the value of n observations of a given variable and dividing by n.

Asset beta: measures the sensitivity of the underlying business to market risk. It is the beta we would expect to observe empirically if the firm was financed solely by equity.

Basis point: 0.01 of a per cent.

Basis risk: the variability in the prices of two related securities in the hedging arrangement. For example, if changes in the price of a currency future do not perfectly match the change in the price of the underlying security then a profit or loss may occur on the hedged position. This potential variability in the outcome of a hedge is basis risk.

Beta: a statistic which measures the sensitivity of security returns to factors influencing changes in the returns of the Efficient Market Portfolio. Beta is normally measured using proxies for the returns of the Efficient Market Portfolio. Such proxies are stock indices of sufficient breadth to capture market wide effects.

Bills: money market securities issued by government and others. They are normally offered to the market at a discount and do not carry interest but are repaid at par.

Bills of exchange/Banker's Acceptance: bills of exchange are issued by companies promising to repay borrowing from a bank. Once the bank accepts the bill of exchange it is called a 'banker's acceptance' and as such can be traded as a discount instrument on the money market.

Binomial option pricing model: a binary tree algorithm for determining the value of any type of option. The binomial model assumes that the pricing process in the underlying progresses in discrete rather than continuous time as is the case with the Black and Scholes option pricing model.

Black and Scholes option pricing model: a model expressing the relationship between the price of a European style option and five variables that drive option value: the value of the underlying asset, the exercise price, the time until the option matures, the risk free rate of return and the volatility of the continuously generated returns of the underlying security. The model also makes a number of assumptions about the nature of the underlying distribution of returns, the ability of traders to continuously update their position in the underlying security, and the absence of dividends.

Bond: a capital market security representing a liability upon the part of a borrower to repay a specified capital sum (its redemption or par value) at a specified future date. The bond will normally carry a rate of interest (the coupon rate).

Bootstrapping: a technique where the investor's required rate of return on a bond is calculated from a series of bonds with known maturities incrementing in six month intervals.

Business risk: the variability in a firm's earnings caused by the uncertainties within its business environment.

Calculated Intangible Value: the difference between a company's observed return on assets employed and what would be expected for either another company in the same industry of similar size and structure or, an average drawn from the industry concerned.

Call option: an option to purchase the underlying asset at a stated price on or before a given date from another party, the option 'writer'.

Capital Asset Pricing Model (CAPM): this is the first in a sequence of financial models which seek to explain expected returns in terms of risk. A CAPM is a single factor model where the systematic explanation of return is market risk as measured by the sensitivity of a given security's returns to changes in the efficient market portfolio. Within CAPM only market or 'systematic' risk is priced. All other sources of variation in return are unsystematic and are diversified away in the pricing process.

Capital market: the market for the purchase and sale of securities which have longer than one year to maturity.

Central Limit Theorem: the classical version of the theorem states that if X is a random, independent variable of mean μ finite variance σ^2 that the sampling distribution of the mean approximates a normal distribution as N (the sample size) increases. Informally, the distribution of sample means will approach normality as N increases irrespective of the shape of the underlying distribution of X from which the samples are drawn.

Certificates of Deposit (CD):   in exchange for a deposit of funds the issuer writes a receipt (the CD) offering a one-off interest payment plus repayment of the face value of the deposit at maturity. The CDs are negotiable and can be traded.

City Code for Takeovers: rules regulating merger and acquisition activity in the United Kingdom market. The code is administered by a takeover panel which is an independent body appointed by the Bank of England. Organizations that act in contravention of the code can find their listing on the Stock Exchange withdrawn and the case referred to the Financial Services Authority. The City Code is designed to ensure fair treatment of shareholders through the regulation of stake building.

Commercial paper: corporate 'IOUs' against borrowed funds. They are issued at a discount and repaid at their face value and no extra interest is paid. They are the short term equivalent of corporate bonds and can be asset backed or may be 'credit backed' where the issuing firm has a weak credit rating but can obtain credit support from another company. A CP is not normally traded but is usually held until maturity once issued.

Competition Commission: a statutory body in the United Kingdom with the task of ensuring that merger and acquisition activity is not against the public interest which is normally defined in terms of the likely impact of the proposal upon competition within the particular industry or sector concerned.

Contingency: this is the idea in valuation theory that significant business decisions are rarely 'closed' but give rise to future options for the business to pursue that may not be readily apparent at the point the decision is made.

Convexity: the difference in price calculated using the modified duration rather than equating the price of the bond to the discounted coupon payments and redemption value.

Correlation: a statistical measure of the extent to which to variables are related. Where variables are perfectly matched in their movement correlation is $+1$ and -1 when they perfectly negatively counter vary with one another. Zero correlation means that the two variables are completely unmatched.

Cost of capital: the rate of return (expressed as an annualized percentage rate that a company must offer to the market for a given source of capital (see also weighted average cost of capital).

Coupon: the fixed rate of interest paid on a bond at regular (usually annual or semi-annual) intervals.

Credit risk: (synonymous with default risk) the risk borne by a lender that the borrower will default either on interest payments, the repayment of the borrowing at the due date, or both.

Cum div: where a security is sold prior to the ex-div date such that the purchaser obtains full rights to the subsequent dividend or interest payment.

Currency future: an exchange traded forward contract for the sale or purchase of currency.

Debt Management Office: an executive agency of the UK Treasury responsible for the issue of government debt and the management of the auction system.

Default risk: see **credit risk**

Derivative security: a security whose value is derived from the value of some other financial security such as a share, bond, money market bill or foreign exchange.

Differentiability: the idea in valuation theory that the cash flows arising from a business decision can be separated from the other cash flows to the investor. Differentiability is a particular problem with highly entangled capital investments where it is difficult to isolate the cash flows of the project from those of the rest of the firm.

Differential return on capital employed: an accounting measure for the change in the firm's accounting profits (as reported) arising from a project divided by the change in the firm's total capital employed. This measure is evaluated in relation to the firm's existing return on capital employed.

Discounted payback index: the present value of a project's future cash flows divided by the capital outlay.

Discounted payback: the time taken for a firm to recover with its discounted cash flows the initial capital investment on a capital project.

Disintermediation: the removal of intermediaries such as banks and other financial institutions in the borrowing and lending process whereby borrowers issue securities in exchange for loan finance directly with investors.

Dividend cover: the ratio of earnings per share to dividend per share. Cover is related to the retention ratio (b) as follows:

$$b = 1 - \frac{1}{cover}$$

Dividend irrelevance hypothesis: this is the hypothesis that dividend policy is irrelevant in determining the value of the firm. If there is a perfect capital market the firm will be indifferent as to whether it raises finance for new investment either from the capital market or from retentions. The only thing that matters in determining the value of the firm is its ability to exploit positive Net Present Value investment projects.

Dividend valuation model: see **growth model**

Dividend yield: the ratio of dividend per share to price per share.

Duration (bonds): the average time taken to recover the cash flows on a bond including the repayment of capital on redemption.

Duration: the average time taken to recover the cash flows on an investment. The average is taken as the value weighted average of the number of the year (1 to n) in which the cash flows arise. In capital investment the duration can be calculated either using the firm's original outlay, or the present value of its future cash flows as the basis for the annual weighting.

Dynamic Delta hedging: the continuous adjustment of the balance between options and shares so as to ensure the maintenance of a risk a neutral position.

Eat or be eaten hypothesis: the theory based upon evidence that firms that make bids are less likely than others to attract attention from unwelcome predators in the corporate acquisitions market. The motivation behind the hypothesis is that there are a range of managerial incentives that encourage bidding behaviour as a method of avoiding attempted takeovers by others.

Economic Value Added (EVA®): a measure of the economic 'super' profit generated by a firm and is equal to the value of the firm's invested capital multiplied by its return spread. The return spread is defined as the difference between the Accounting Rate of Return and the firm's weighted average cost of capital. Alternatively, Economic Value Added can be defined as net operating profit after tax (NOPAT) less the value of a firm's invested capital multiplied by its weighted average cost of capital.

Efficient frontier: a limiting set of portfolios which offer the highest level of return for their given risk or the lowest risk for their given level of return.

Efficient market portfolio: a portfolio consisting of all tradeable risky assets in the global market which under the Markowitz/Tobin Separation Theorem will be held by all investors as their sole means of risky investment. The Efficient Market Portfolio is located at tangency between the capital market line and the efficient set.

Efficient markets hypothesis: the hypothesis that share prices respond instantly and without bias to new information such that an investor, with access to that information cannot expect to make a systematic return greater than that offered by the market for the level of risk to which they are exposed. The EMH is traditionally presented in three forms: weak form (w.r.t the information in past share prices), semi-strong form (w.r.t publicly available information) and strong form (w.r.t private information).

Equity risk premium: see **CAPM** the difference between the rate of return on a risk free investment and the expected return on holding the efficient market portfolio. The equity risk premium is difficult to observe from historical data because of biases including non-survivorship bias. Non-survivorship arises because securities within the market historically include those who subsequently succeeded and those who failed. Estimates of market return should include the failures as well as those who succeeded.

Equity share: a certificate or ownership of a fractional part of a business entity. Equity shares can be 'ordinary' or carry rights to dividends in preference to ordinary shareholders. Equity shares are not normally redeemable although 'redeemable preference shares' are sometimes issued.

Equivalent rate: a translation of a rate of return over a particular time period into a rate of return over another period such that if an initial sum invested for the shorter period is repeatedly reinvested over the longer period then the equivalent rate would be earned.

Eurobonds: debt denominated in any currency (dollars, yen, euro(s) etc.) which are traded on the international capital markets.

European option: an option that can be exercised only on the exercise date.

Expectations hypothesis: the hypothesis that the yield curve is a perfect reflection of expectations about future interest rates. A consequence of this hypothesis is that the period yield should be same irrespective of the term to maturity as an 'n' year bond can be replicated by a strip of $n \times 1$ year bonds or by a strip of bonds of intermediate term.

Fama and French's three factor model: a variant of the CAPM where firm size and exposure to distress are included as well as exposure to market risk. Early studies suggested that the three factor model had high reliability in estimating realized returns, however later studies have passed doubt on both the model's empirical success and its validity.

Financial appraisal profile: a managerial model of investment appraisal which uses indexing techniques to quantify the financial, strategic and risk implications of a given capital project.

Financial institution: companies such as banks, merchant banks, investment banks and other organizations offering financial services particularly in the arrangement and sponsoring of new security issues.

Financial risk: the alteration in the volatility of the residual earnings to the equity investor caused by an alteration in the firm's gearing and the resulting charge for interest is made to the firm's income above the line.

Fisher Effect: the proposition that real rates of interest are constant between countries which implies that there is a direct relationship between changes in nominal interest rates and inflation rates in different countries.

Fisher Formula: the relationship between real (r) and nominal interest rates (i) and the rate of inflation (h) is expressed through the following equation:

$$(1 + i) = (1 + h)(1 + r)$$

Fisher Hirshliefer Separation Theorem: in a perfect capital market under conditions of certainty the decision about the acceptability of a project is strictly independent of the way in which it is financed. Under such conditions all investors' marginal rate of time preference between current and future consumption is reduced to the market rate of interest.

FOREX: foreign exchange.

Forward agreement: an over-the-counter agreement to buy or sell an asset on a specified date at an agreed price (the forward price).

Forward Rate Agreements (FRAs): an agreement by the bank to enter into a notional loan or accept a deposit with a customer for a specified period of time and to settle with the customer the difference between the rate of interest agreed when the agreement is made and the rate prevailing when the notional loan/deposit is deemed to start.

Free cash flow to equity: operating cash flow less net interest and tax paid. The free cash flow to equity is potentially distributable to investors as dividend or can be retained in the form of net capital investment (capital investment less new capital introduced). In this book we define the free cash flow to equity as either before, or after, capital investment.

Future value: the projected value of a current cash sum, or a cash sum at some intermediate point in time, to a value at a specified future date. The future value is generated by compounding the current or intermediate cash flow(s) for the periods remaining until the required future date.

Future: an exchange traded forward agreement to buy or sell some underlying security at some future date for a currently agreed price.

FX swap: an agreement to swap currencies without a commitment to swap interest rate liabilities.

GEMMS: gilt edged market makers.

Geometric average: the 'nth' root of the product of n variables.

Geometric Brownian motion: this is a particular form of random walk where the step length is taken to the limit of the shortest time possible and the return generation process follows a log normal distribution.

Gilts edged security: bonds issued by the UK Government (sometimes referred to as Treasury bonds) which in the early days of this type of finance were represented by certificates with a fine gold leaf edge.

Goodwill (on acquisition): the surplus between the market value paid on acquisition of another company and the book, or fair value, of the company's net assets acquired.

Greeks: the first differential of the price of an option with the underlying variables in the Black and Scholes model. Of the Greeks the *Delta* value is particularly important as this expresses the rate of change of the option value with the price of the underlying. With knowledge of an option's *Delta* it is possible to create a combined position such that the risk in the underlying is eliminated by the potential payoffs on the option contract.

Growth model: a simple model derived from the general definition of return and assuming (i) continuous return generation, (ii) a flat term structure of equity returns and (iii) constant growth in dividends. The model equates the price of equity with dividend payout, the required rate of return by equity investors and the assumed growth rate. The growth rate can be set to be negative, zero or positive.

$$P_0 = \frac{D_0(1+g)}{r_e - g}$$

Hedging: taking positions in two or more securities which by their nature are designed to create perfectly counter varying returns. A short sale in a futures contract, for example, can offset the risk associated with a long position in an underlying asset. A perfect hedge is one where all chance of loss is eliminated.

Horizontal diversification: an acquisition of a competitor company or unrelated diversification by acquisition into another business line.

Hostile bid: bid to acquire another company that is opposed by the company's directors.

Hurdle rate: see **cost of capital**

Integration (with respect to acquisitions): acquisition of companies either in the supply chain (backward integration) or in the distribution chain (forward integration).

Implied volatility: given all the other inputs to the Black and Scholes option pricing model it is possible to determine the volatility of an underlying given that the price of the option is known. Implied volatility relies upon the validity of the model but many analysts regard this as a superior method of creating a forward estimate of volatility compared with estimation methods on the basis of past return data.

Initial margin: a deposit of cash or securities required by an exchange by parties to derivative agreements to underwrite any early losses that may be made on the position. Initial margin is about 20 per cent of the value of the position in the underlying.

Interest rate futures: these are notional securities traded on the futures markets whose prices depend upon prevailing interest rates. The value of the future is (100 – implied interest rate). Thus the greater the interest rate the lower the value of the future and vice versa.

Interest rate parity: the zero arbitrage condition relating the forward to the spot rate of exchange and relative interest rates in different economies. If interest rate parity does not hold 'covered interest arbitrage' is possible where by a combination of borrowing in one currency, depositing in another and a forward agreement to sell a profit can be made without risk.

Interest rate swaps: where two parties agree to swap their liabilities for interest rate payments on a given capital sum. This is usually, but not necessarily, a fixed for variable interest rate swap.

Intermediation/disintermediation: intermediation in a capital market involves the intervention of a bank or other financial institution between lenders and ultimate borrowers. Disintermediation is the process in the financial markets where companies like governments have sought debt finance directly from private and commercial lenders without recourse to the banking sector.

Internal Rate of Return: the rate of discount which gives a zero Net Present Value when applied to an investment's cash flows. The IRR assumes that all cash flows throughout the life of the project are reinvested at the IRR.

International Fisher Effect: if the Fisher Effect holds then changes in spot rate are directly related to changes in interest rate.

Intrinsic value: (of an option) the payoff if an option could be exercised immediately.

Kaplan Urwitz Model: the first of a series of multivariate models seeking to explain bond rating in terms of a range of observable market based or accounting measures.

Law of one price: securities presenting identical return distributions (simply: have identical return and risk) to investors should trade at the same price in perfectly competitive markets.

LIBID: London Inter-Bank Bid Rate. The effective lending rate in the interbank market representing the spread against LIBOR.

LIBOR: London Inter-Bank Offered Rate. The average overnight rate of interest offered by deposit accepting banks as compiled on a daily basis by the British Bankers Association. A LIBOR is quoted for sterling, dollar, yen, euro and other currency deposits.

LIFFE: London International Financial Futures Exchange.

Liquidity preference hypothesis: this reflects the supposition that investors prefer (other things being equal) short term investment to long term investment. As a result longer term bonds need to offer a higher rate of return (a liquidity premium) to compensate investors than shorter term bonds.

Log normal distribution: a distribution where the logarithm of the variable concerned (in our case price, or return) is normally distributed. The log normal distribution is appropriate where a series of multiplicative effects are expected such as is the case with return generation over time.

MAKENT© model: a resource based model of the asset structure of a firm which focuses upon prepotency and entanglement effects as the principal drivers of its value.

Managerial hubris hypothesis: the idea that management is overconfident in their ability to value a target company or indeed in their ability to manage a larger organization.

Marginal growth rate: this is the rate of return of a projects NPV to its outlay (the profitability index) calculated as an equivalent annual rate.

Marginal rate of time preference: the rate at which an individual is willing to substitute, at the margin, current consumption for future consumption through investment.

Market for corporate control: a theory first proposed by Henry Manne that there exists a market for managerial expertise and that mergers and acquisitions are a means by which a competitive market is able to purge weak or over-opportunistic management.

Market gearing: the ratio of total debt within a firm's capital structure at its current market value to the total market value of the firm (equity plus debt), or simply to the capitalized value of equity.

Market risk: driver of return risk in equities and other securities which is measurable at the level of the market. Changes in interest rates, taxation, foreign exchange rates and other macroeconomic variables as well as social tastes and preferences, for example, are all likely to influence the level of the returns on the efficient market portfolio (in theory) and hence count as contributors to market risk.

Market segmentation hypothesis: this is the idea that different types of investor prefer different maturities and that the yield curve reflects these differences.

Market to book ratio: the ratio of the market value of a firm (or on a per share basis, its share price) to its book value (or net assets divided by the number of shares in issue).

Markowitz/Tobin Separation Theorem: a deductive consequence from Markowitz Portfolio Theory with the addition of two assumptions: there is a perfect market in a risk free asset and all investors have common beliefs about the return distributions of all tradeable risk assets and the location of the efficient set. Under these conditions all investors will take a leveraged position in the tangency portfolio (the efficient market portfolio) and the risk free security congruent upon their risk preferences. The choice of risk investment is restricted to the efficient market portfolio and is separated from the choice about how to maximize their preference between return and risk.

Matching and netting: a process where interfirm indebtedness in different currencies are netted (with group companies) or matched (with trading partners) with the purpose of reducing the requirement for funds to move across international borders and suffer transaction costs on conversion.

Mean reversion: the tendency of stochastic variables to regress over time to their central value. Beta, for example, can be observed to have a mean reverting tendency where future betas are more likely to be closer to the market beta of one than current betas.

Merger waves: the accumulated evidence that merger and acquisition activity occurs in waves driven by some underlying structural characteristics of the corporate market.

Mezzanine debt: low grade debt issued by fast expanding businesses (often as a result of leveraged buyouts) which promises high rates of return and usually some form of equity participation through the attachment of warrants.

Minority interest: the share of the equity of an acquired company that is retained by shareholders who are not shareholders of the group company.

Modified duration: the duration of a bond divided by one plus its yield.

Modified Internal Rate of Return: the discount rate which equates the terminal or future value of a project's cash flows to the outlay assuming that the project cash flows are reinvested at the firm's hurdle rate or cost of capital.

Money market: the market for securities which normally have less than one year to maturity.

Monte Carlo simulation: a mathematical modelling process where random numbers are drawn from assumed distributions attaching to the variables within a given model. By repeated trials using random numbers the performance of the model can be examined under different assumptions about the nature of the underlying distributions.

Negotiable: when this relates to a financial security it means that the security concerned can be freely traded between different parties without loss of legal claim against the original issuer.

Net Present Value: the sum of all future cash flows discounted at the investor's required rate of return less the capital outlay. The Net Present Value, under conditions of perfect capital markets and using the money market rate of interest as the discount rate, yields the net increase in the investor's disposable wealth generated by the available investment opportunity. Under less than ideal conditions it, at best, represents the value added or lost by an investment opportunity.

NOPAT: net operating profit after tax.

Normal distribution: a statistical probability distribution which relates the probability (or strictly the probability density function (f)) to the values of a given variable (x_i). The normal distribution is perfectly central about the mean value of the variable concerned and is defined by just two variables: the mean of the distribution (μ) and its standard deviation (σ). The formula is of a guassian type:

$$f(x, \mu, \sigma) = \frac{1}{2\sqrt{2\pi}} e^{-\left(\frac{(x-\mu)^2}{2\sigma^2}\right)}$$

NYBOT: New York Board of Trade (the parent body for the New York options and futures exchange.

Ockham's (Occam's) Razor: the principle that a theory should be reduced to the fewest assumptions commensurate with its ability to explain and predict real phenomena. Where two theoretical explanations compete then the one with the fewest assumptions (often referred to as the simpler theory of the two) is the one that should be preferred.

Opportunity cost of capital: the rate of return a company must pay to the capital market in order to refinance the business in its current gearing ratio or, in a situation where the company has a surplus of capital, it is the saving in the rate of return the company would forego by not returning that capital to the market (in its current gearing ratio) by choosing an alternative investment opportunity for that capital. Where the capital markets are reasonably competitive there should be little difference in the 'replacement' and 'realizable' cost of capital.

Option: an agreement by one party to offer another the right to buy or sell an underlying security or asset at a currently agreed price at an agreed future date(s).

Options on Forward Rate Agreements (caps and floors): the bank as writer of the option agrees to cap the interest rate charged on a loan over a set period of time such that if the interest rate rises above the cap the difference in the rate is paid to the holder. If the interest rate does not reach the cap the holder does not have to reimburse the bank (as with the FRA). A floor is exactly the opposite where a minimum interest rate is set on a deposit.

Options on interest rate futures: options for the purchase or sale of IRFs at a specified future date.

Options on swaps (swaptions): where two counterparties enter into an option agreement to enter into an interest rate swap at some future date.

OTC: (over-the-counter) the term relating to private agreements between counterparties to buy or sell a security (normally, but not always, referring to derivatives).

Payback: the time required for a capital investment project to recover its initial outlay. Payback is measured in cash terms.

Pecking order hypothesis: this is the hypothesis that there is a natural progression in the way that manager will use the capital resources with the most preferred being retained earnings followed by debt followed by new equity issue.

Perfect capital market: this is a market characterized by unrestricted access to capital at the current market rate of return, perfect certainty, zero information costs and an absence of transactions costs and taxes.

Portfolio theory: after Markowitz a theory of investor behaviour under risk where investors are assumed to be rational, two parameter utility maximizers confronting a market of risky assets whose returns are uniquely described by the mean and standard deviation (volatility) of their returns.

Preference shares: equity shares issued with an entitlement to a fixed interest dividend payable (normally) at the directors' discretion but must be paid if an ordinary dividend is to be declared. Preference shares may be cumulative in that unpaid dividends are rolled forward; they may also be redeemable or convertible to ordinary shares at specified date(s).

Present value: the value of a future cash flow discounted using an appropriate discount rate to present day value.

Price/earnings (P/E) ratio: the ratio of a company's price per share divided by its earnings per share. This ratio is commonly used as a valuation metric by the multiple method.

Primary capital/money market: the market for the issue of new capital or money market securities by governments, corporates or other organizations.

Profitability index: the ratio of a project's Net Present Value to the capital outlay.

Prospectus: a document issued by a company proposing a new equity or other security issue. The document will contain, among other things, details of the issue, its purpose and a forecast of future performance.

Purchasing power parity: the theorem that changes in exchange rate are principally driven by differences in inflation rates and that the purchasing power of consumers in different economies should remain in equilibrium. PPP is based on the law of one price that identical baskets of consumer goods should command the same price in different economies.

Put option: an option to sell the underlying asset at the stated price on or before a given date to another party, the option 'writer'.

Put call parity: a formal relationship between the value of a European call and put option in the same underlying security. The difference between the value of a call and a put is equal to the difference between the current value of the underlying and the present value of the exercise price.

Rational: in an economic sense rational is commonly defined as a series of axioms (the 'Savage Axioms') that (i) individuals are personal utility maximizers where utility is taken as a subjective measure of a person's satisfaction with things, (ii) individuals can rank order their preferences and (iii) are consistent (transitive) in their rankings. What this means is that if A is preferred to B is preferred to C then C is not preferred to A.

Real option: an option attaching to the future cash flows derived from an investment in a capital asset by a firm. Real options include managerial discretion to delay, expand, withdraw, or redeploy resources within an investment project.

Repo agreements (repurchase agreements) and reverse repos: an agreement to sell a security at a given price with a simultaneous agreement with the purchaser to buy the security back at a given future date and price. A reverse repo is simply an agreement to purchase a security with a simultaneous agreement to resell.

Return: the financial reward expressed as a percentage of the opening price through holding a financial security over a set interval of time. Return will normally consist of two components: the dividend or interest yield and the capital gain.

Rights issue: an issue of new shares to existing shareholders in proportion to their current holding. The rights issue is made via an allotment letter which is normally negotiable if the investor declines to take the new shares.

Risk: the probability that a given peril will occur. With respect to financial return, risk is defined as the standard deviation of a security's or portfolio's return distribution where the returns are normally distributed.

Scenario planning: a general methodology which allows managers to speculate upon, analyze and prepare for a range of alternative futures.

Secondary capital/money market: the market for trading in existing securities.

Securitization: the process of converting claims upon an entity such as a government or a firm, or its assets, into negotiable certificates of entitlement which can be traded between individuals and where the holder at any point in time has the same rights as were held by the person to whom they were originally issued.

Senior debt: unsubordinated debt, i.e. debt which takes priority in the event of liquidation.

Spot curve: the interest rate required to discount future risk free cash flows arising at any given time.

Standard deviation: the second moment of a distribution and is the square root of the average squared deviations of the individual observations of X from the mean value.

Static trade-off theory: the idea that the cost of capital in the absence of taxes and default risk will be invariate with gearing. Taxes represent an opportunity, through the tax shield effect, to reduce the cost of capital, but this benefit is counterbalanced by the increasing return required to compensate for default risk. There is a trade-off between the two effects and hence a position where the cost of capital is optimized.

STRIPS: the separate trading of interest and principal. This is where (normally) government bonds are decomposed into a coupon element and a redemption element which are then traded separately in the market.

Swap: an agreement between two counterparties to swap a liability to interest payments or to swap an asset such as foreign currency.

Synergy: the concept, first introduced by Igor Ansoff, that mergers and acquisitions can create value that would not be available to either company independently. Synergy can be either: revenue, cost, or financially induced and is often used by management to justify mergers or acquisitions.

Technical analysis: the search for non-randomness with the movement of security prices such that systematic price predictions can be made. Technical analysis is contrary to the weak form of the efficient markets hypothesis.

Term to redemption: the period remaining before the bond issuer is required to make repayment of the capital sum to the current holder.

Tick: the smallest price movement on an exchange traded derivative contract. A tick is defined as the number of basis point movement in the value of the derivative times the unit of trading multiplied by the fraction of the year that the movement has occurred over.

Time value: this is the decline in the value of future cash flows to an investor because of the lapse of time. This time loss is caused by changes in the value of the currency (inflation/deflation) and risk attaching to the future returns as well as the liquidity preferences of the investor.

Time value: (of an option) the proportion of an option's value which is attributable to the time delay until the option can be exercised.

Tobin's Q: the ratio of the market capitalization of a firm to the replacement cost of its assets.

Transaction cost economics: The central premise of TCE is that markets and firms represent alternative means of coordinating production and the one which will be chosen is the one that minimizes the transaction costs of the exchange involved.

Treasury Bills: government 'IOUs' of usually of one or three months' maturity.

Value at risk: (VAR) the value which can be attached to the downside of a value or price distribution of known standard deviation and within a given confidence level.

Value at risk and related measures give an indication of the potential loss in monetary value which is likely to occur with a given level of confidence. The setting of the confidence level is necessary because in principle, if a price distribution is normally distributed for example, the downside loss is potentially infinite.

Value creation index: an index developed by the Cap-Gemini Centre for business innovation. The VCI uses a number of empirically determined metrics to estimate the undisclosed value of a firm.

Variation margin: further calls of cash or other securities from traders to underwrite any losses that may have accumulated against their position in a given derivative contract.

Venture capital: high risk finance for start-ups and other business ventures which is normally achieved through equity participation in the company concerned. Providers of venture capital are commonly backed by private equity finance.

Volatility: this is the measurement of the change in security price over time. It is normally calculated as the annualized standard deviation of the change in share price taken over time intervals (t). In finance it is the most common measure of risk.

Warrant: a long term call option to purchase equity in a company (usually) issued with debt to enhance its marketability.

Weighted average cost of capital: (in most situations) this is the firm's opportunity cost of capital. It measures the average return required by the firm's different classes of investor where the average is calculated using the proportions of each capital source calculated using their total market values.

Yield curve: the relationship between the yield that investors require upon risk-free bonds and the time to maturity (see also 'spot curve').

Yield: (with respect to bonds and other fixed interest securities) the discount rate which equates the present value of the future stream of coupon payments and redemption value with the current market value of the bond concerned.

Selected review activity and end of chapter questions

This section offers indicative solutions (numerical components only) to a range of questions throughout the book. More detailed answers to the selected and other questions in the book can be found on the web site.

Chapter 1:

Review Activity 1.1

date	share price	dividend	quarterly	return	(1 + r)	cumulative product
03/11/03	249.00		249.00			
28/11/03		2.07				
01/12/03	257.25					
02/01/04	240.41					
02/02/04	257.50		257.50	0.04245	1.04245	1.04245
01/03/04	245.75					
01/04/04	248.75					
04/05/04	249.00		249.00	−0.03301	0.96699	1.00804
01/06/04	266.25					
26/06/04		4.77				
01/07/04	254.75					
02/08/04	266.61		266.61	0.08988	1.08988	1.09864
01/09/04	285.88					
01/10/04	288.33					
01/11/04	297.89		297.89	0.11732	1.11732	1.22754
	average quarterly return =			0.05416		
	geometric average quarterly return =					0.05259
	equivalent annual return =			0.23489		0.22754

The geometric average return (monthly) is obtained as follows:

$$GAR = \sqrt[4]{1.22754} - 1 = 0.05259$$

Review Activity 1.2

Year	0	1
(i)		
Cash flow	−5 000	6 600
Discounted cash flow	−5 000	5 739
Present value	739	

Year	0	1	2
(ii)			
Cash flow	−5 000	2 400	4 200
Discounted cash flow	−5 000	2 087	3 176
Present value	263		

End of chapter question:

1 Calculation of future values

$$10\,000 \times 1.06^1 = 10\,600$$
$$10\,000 \times 1.06^5 = 13\,382$$
$$10\,000 \times 1.06^7 = 15\,036$$

2 Calculation of present values

$$\frac{50\,000}{1.1^6} = 28\,224$$

3 Equivalent annual return:

$$1.02^{12} - 1 = 0.2682 \equiv 26.82\%$$

4 Monthly and daily returns:

$$r_m = \sqrt[12]{1.24} - 1 = 0.01809 \equiv 18.09\%$$
$$r_d = \sqrt[365]{1.24} - 1 = 0.0005895 \equiv 0.05895\%$$

5 NPV calculation using an annuity

$$A\rceil^4_{0.06} = \frac{1 - \dfrac{1}{1.07^4}}{0.07} = 3.465$$
$$NPV = -16\,000 + 3.387 \times 5000 = 936$$

Chapter 2

Review Activity 2.2

	0	1	2	3	4
Capital investment	−34 000				
Incremental project cash flows		7 600	16 500	13 000	10 600
Net cash flow	−34 000	7 600	16 500	13 000	10 600
Discounted cash flow (8%)	−34 000	7 037	14 146	10 320	7 791
Net Present Value	5 294				

Review Activity 2.3

In this case the project cash flows would be insufficient to redeem the borrowing and the loan account with the bank would show a debit balance of £1101 at the end of the 4th year.

	0	1	2	3	4
Capital investment	−34 000				
Incremental project cash flows		7 600	16 500	13 000	10 600
Decommissioning costs					−4 000
Net cash flow	−34 000	7 600	16 500	13 000	6 600
Fred's borrowing carried forward	−36 354	−36 354	−32 026	−18 408	−7 065
Interest accumulated at 9%		−3 272	−2 882	−1 657	−636
Project repayment		7 600	16 500	13 000	6 600
Outstanding borrowing	−36 354	−32 026	−18 408	−7 065	−1 101

Review Activity 2.4

Finding the Internal Rate of Return

	0	1	2
Cash flows	−20 000	13 000	13 000
Internal Rate of Return	19.43%		

With this example the solution can be found using the quadratic formula:

$$x = \frac{-b \pm \sqrt{b^2 - 4ac}}{2a}$$

$$(1 + irr) = \frac{-13\,000 \pm \sqrt{13\,000^2 - 4 \times (-20\,000) \times 13\,000}}{2 \times -20\,000} = -0.5443 \text{ or } 1.1943$$

Thus the Internal Rate of Return is 19.43 per cent.

Review Activity 2.5

Finding the modified Internal Rate of Return

	0	1	2
Cash flows	−20 000	13 000	13 000
Future value of cash flows		14 040	13 000
Terminal value of future cash flows			27 040
Modified Internal Rate of Return	0.1628		

The modified Internal Rate of Return is calculated using:

$$MIRR = \sqrt[n]{\frac{\text{Terminal value of project cash flows}}{\text{investment outlay}}} - 1$$

$$MIRR = \sqrt[2]{\frac{27\,040}{20\,000}} - 1$$

$$MIRR = 16.28\%$$

Review Activity 2.6

Calculation of the Accounting Rate of Return

	0	1	2
Cash flows	−20 000	13 000	13 000
depreciation		−10 000	−10 000
contribution to operating profit		3 000	3 000
average profit	3 000		
average capital employed	10 000		
Accounting Rate of Retun	30%		

Review Activity 2.7

Calculation of payback and discounted payback

	0	1	2	
Cash flows	−20 000	13 000	13 000	
Cumulative cash flow	−20 000	−7 000	6 000	
Payback			1.54	years
Discounted cash flows	−20 000	12 037	11 145	
Cumulative discounted cash flow	−20 000	−7 963	3 182	
Discounted Payback			1.71	years

End of chapter questions

1

NOIDEA Ltd

	01-Jan 2004	31-Dec 2004	31-Dec 2005	31-Dec 2006	31-Dec 2007	31-Dec 2008	31-Dec 2009
Capital investment	860 000						
Expected scrap and resale							20 000
Annual depreciation (straight line)		(140 000)	(140 000)	(140 000)	(140 000)	(140 000)	(140 000)
Book Value	860 000	720 000	580 000	440 000	300 000	160 000	20 000
Preincurred design and development costs	(42 000)						
Sales revenue		520 000	650 000	600 000	600 000	500 000	350 000
Direct project operating costs		156 000	195 000	180 000	180 000	150 000	105 000
		364 000	455 000	420 000	420 000	350 000	245 000
Allocated company overheads		(117 000)	(146 250)	(135 000)	(135 000)	(112 500)	(78 750)
Depreciation		(140 000)	(140 000)	(140 000)	(140 000)	(140 000)	(140 000)
Annual project profit		107 000	168 750	145 000	145 000	97 500	26 250
Interest charge on capital invested		(51 600)	(43 200)	(34 800)	(26 400)	(18 000)	(9 600)
		55 400	125 550	110 200	118 600	79 500	16 650
Average project profit	84 317						
Less required return	86 000						
Average annual surplus/ (deficit)	(1 683)						
Project cash flow	−860 000						20 000
Operating cash flows		364 000	455 000	420 000	420 000	350 000	245 000
Cash flow	−860 000	364 000	455 000	420 000	420 000	350 000	265 000
Discounted cash flow	−860 000	330 909	376 033	315 552	286 866	217 322	149 586
Net Present Value	816 268						

(i) The items in red should be ignored.

(ii) The Net Present Value discounted at 10 per cent.

2

	0	1	2	3	4	5	6		
Value of land committed to project	–300 000	–315 000	–330 750	–347 288	–364 652	–382 884	–402 029		
Warehouse project – capital spend	–2 500 000								
Estimated break up value							294 123		
Estimated net cash savings		500 000	600 000	700 000	800 000	900 000	1 000 000	NPV	IRR
Warehouse project net cash flow	–2 500 000	500 000	600 000	700 000	800 000	900 000	1 294 123	£738 247	18.88%
Office block project – capital spend	–6 500 000								
Estimated break up value							764 719		
Annual rental income		1 000 000	1 200 000	1 800 000	2 200 000	2 400 000	2 400 000		
Warehouse project net cash flow	–6 500 000	1 000 000	1 200 000	1 800 000	2 200 000	2 400 000	3 164 719	£1 393 123	16.30%

Marginal growth rate:

Warehouse project

$$MGR = \left[\frac{738\,247 + 2\,500\,000}{2\,500\,000} \right]^{\frac{1}{6}} - 1 = 4.4067\%$$

$$MIRR = (1 + MGR)(1 + i) = 1.044067 \times 1.1 = 14.85\%$$

Office block project

$$MGR = \left[\frac{1\,393\,719 + 6\,500\,000}{6\,500\,000} \right]^{\frac{1}{6}} - 1 = 3.289\%$$

$$MIRR = (1 + MGR)(1 + i) = 1.03289 \times 1.1 = 13.62\%$$

Chapter 3

Review Activity 3.6

$$\beta_i = \frac{\rho_{i,m}\sigma_i}{\sigma_m}$$

$$(i)\ \beta_i = \frac{+1 \times 0.16}{0.18} = 0.89$$

$$(ii)\ \beta_i = \frac{0 \times 0.16}{0.18} = 0$$

$$(iii)\ \beta_i = \frac{-1 \times 0.16}{0.18} = -0.89$$

Review Activity 3.7

$$\beta_p = \frac{50}{164} \times 1.15 + \frac{24}{164} \times 0.98 + \frac{90}{164} \times 0.43$$

$$\beta_p = 0.73$$

The portfolio can be rebalanced by reducing the amount invested in security 3 and increasing the amount in security 1. A £10 000 substitution from 3 to 1 would give a portfolio beta of:

$$\beta_p = \frac{60}{164} \times 1.15 + \frac{24}{164} \times 0.98 + \frac{80}{164} \times 0.43$$

$$\beta_p = 0.77$$

On the basis that this substitution increased the beta by 0.05 this would imply that a further substitution of £46 000 will create a beta of close to one (in fact 0.98). However, this may overexpose the investor to security 1 and a rebalancing towards security 2 might be appropriate.

End of Chapter Questions

1   (a) The minimum risk portfolio is as shown with a standard deviation of 3.3 per cent
     (b) The efficient set is shown in green.

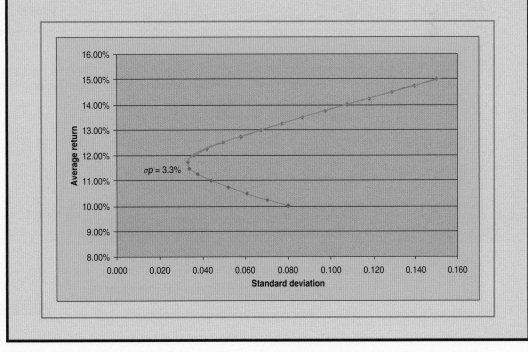

2 Calculation of the equity beta using the = LINEST function in Excel

BT	dividend	FTSE ASI	Ret(BT)	Ret(ASI)
202.25		2 492.84	−0.00369	0.03405
203.00		2 410.75	0.12671	0.06122
180.17	5.3	2 271.67	−0.06564	0.01928
198.50		2 228.70	0.12147	0.01443
177.00		2 197.00	−0.05851	−0.00471
188.00	3.2	2 207.40	0.06222	0.08862
180.00		2 027.70	−0.11535	0.02861
203.47		1 971.30	0.27792	0.13574
159.22		1 735.70	−0.18349	−0.08343
195.00	2.25	1 893.70	0.19909	0.05118
164.50	2	1 801.50	−0.33702	−0.20397
251.14		2 263.10	−0.10307	−0.11508
280.00		2 557.40	0.10641	0.01327
253.07		2 523.90	−0.25568	0.07836
340.00		2 340.50	−0.23937	−0.14208
447.00		2 728.12	−0.12353	0.00617
510.00		2 711.40	−0.09227	−0.09130
561.84		2 983.81	−0.20979	−0.01504
711.00		3 029.36	−0.17898	−0.00013
866.00		3 029.74	−0.25920	−0.02598
1169.00		3 110.56		
Average arithmetic return			−0.067	
Average Return (annualized)			−0.241	
		beta		**1.34692**

On the basis of the beta the company should be generating a return of 9.41 per cent per annum. The performance as shown is negative – this would suggest that the shares are overvalued in the market.

Chapter 4

Review Activity 4.2

	0	1	2
Cash flow on the bond	−90.15	5	105
Internal rate of return (yield)	10.73%		

Review Activity 4.3

	0	1	2	3	4	5	6	7	8
Cash flow to the investor	−101.37	2.5	2.5	2.5	2.5	2.5	2.5	2.5	102.5
Yield	2.31%								
Discounted value of the receipts		2.4435	2.3884	2.3344	2.2817	2.2302	2.1798	2.1306	85.3814
Proportion of the market value		0.0241	0.0236	0.0230	0.0225	0.0220	0.0215	0.0210	0.8423
Weighted value of the period number		0.0241	0.0471	0.0691	0.0900	0.1100	0.1290	0.1471	6.7382
Duration in periods	7.3547								
Duration in years	3.6773								

Review Activity 4.5

The semi-annual yield is 3.441 per cent (7 per cent annual) which gives a present value of the bond of £87.98.

Using the sensitivity of the bond value to yield as follows:

$$dV_0 = -\frac{4.575}{(1.045547)} \times £97.77 \times 0.01$$

$$dV_0 = -£4.28$$

A 1 percentage point change in yield would lead to a fall in price of £4.28. The actual yield drop is (7% − 4.5547%) which implies a fall in price of £10.46 i.e. to £87.31.

End of Chapter Questions

1 A bond issued at par will have the same coupon rate and yield. So the effective coupon rate is 5 per cent but the actual coupon rate should be 4.94 per cent (as 2.47 per cent in two annual instalments gives an effective annual rate of 5 per cent).

2 The table of bootstrapped yields derived from the bonds is given as follows:

Coupon rate (%)	Term to maturity	Market value	1	2	3	4	5	6	revised price
7	1 year	100	107						
7.5	2 years	104	7.5	107.5					96.99
5	3 years	100	5	5	105				90.82
5	4 years	100	5	5	5	105			86.49
4	5 years	96	4	4	4	4	104		81.90
6	6 years	106	6	6	6	6	6	106	80.12
		(1 + YLD)	1.0700	1.0528	1.0496	1.0497	1.0489	1.0478	
		(1 + YLD)^YR	1.0700	1.1084	1.1562	1.2140	1.2699	1.3230	
		YLD	0.0700	0.0528	0.0496	0.0497	0.0489	0.0478	

The spot curve is as follows

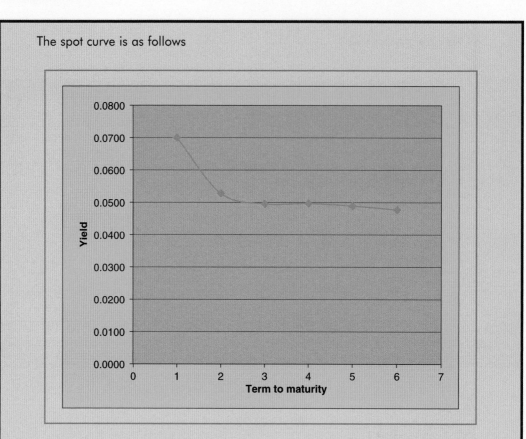

Chapter 5

Review Activity 5.1

$$r = \frac{d_0(1+g)}{p_0} + g$$

$$r = \frac{20(1.05)}{180} + 0.05$$

$$r = 10.53\%$$

Review Activity 5.2

$$\text{Cover} = \text{EPS/DPS}$$

$$\text{DPS} = 160/3 = 53.33\text{p}$$

$$\text{Retention ratio} = \frac{\text{EPS} - \text{DPS}}{\text{EPS}} = \frac{160 - 53.33}{160} = 0.67$$

Alternatively:

$$\text{Retention ratio} = 1 - \frac{1}{\text{cover}} = 1 - \frac{1}{3} = 0.67$$

Review Activity 5.7

Nominal Value	Coupon	Redemption	Market value	Term	Yield	Market cap	weight	w × YLD
145.00	0.05	2008	99.65	3	0.0513	144.49	0.1866	0.0096
160.00	0.06	2009	100.86	4	0.0526	161.38	0.2084	0.0110
240.00	0.07	2012	108.83	7	0.0545	261.19	0.3373	0.0184
80.00	0.06	2013	104.85	8	0.0553	83.88	0.1083	0.0060
110.00	0.07	2015	112.14	10	0.0540	123.35	0.1593	0.0086
						774.29	1.0000	0.0535

The average rate of return required by debt investors is 5.35 per cent.

The yield was established by setting up a formula as follows:

$$MV = A\frac{\overline{}^{Term}}{YLD} \times coupon \times 100 + \frac{100}{(1+YLD)^{term}}$$

and using the goal seek function in Excel the YLD was established that equalized the function to the stated market value.

End of chapter questions

1   A cover of 2.08 implies a retention ratio of 0.5192
    Assuming that the rate of growth is the rate of retention × Yield then:

$$r = \frac{YLD}{1-b-bYLD} = \frac{.0308}{1-0.5192-0.05192 \times .0308} = 6.63\%$$

If 6.63 per cent is the expected return on the market and the annualized one month T-Bill rate is 4.75 per cent this implies that the equity risk premium is (6.63% − 4.75%) = 1.88 per cent.

2   (i)   The regression analysis is as follows:

	Tops Group	FTSE ASI	y	x	yx	x2
Dec-05	202	2450	−0.121739	−0.004065	0.000495	0.000017
Nov-05	230	2460	0.045455	0.051282	0.002331	0.002630
Oct-05	220	2340	0.111111	−0.018868	−0.002096	0.000356
Sep-05	198	2385	0.042105	−0.002092	−0.000088	0.000004
Aug-05	190	2390	0.055556	0.083409	0.004634	0.006957
Jul-05	180	2206	−0.042553	−0.015179	0.000646	0.000230
Jun-05	188	2240	0.044444	0.022831	0.001015	0.000521
May-05	180	2190	−0.052632	0.068293	−0.003594	0.004664
Apr-05	190	2050	−0.103774	−0.023810	0.002471	0.000567
Mar-05	212	2100	0.087179	0.004785	0.000417	0.000023
Feb-05	195	2090	−0.005102	0.000000	0.000000	0.000000
Jan-05	196	2090				
			0.060051	0.166586	0.006229	0.015969

Solving the simultaneous equations with inputs as above gives a slope of 0.396 which is the beta coefficient.

(ii) The expected return using the beta above and the CAPM data is 5.89 per cent. The geometric monthly return is 0.0275 per cent which gives an annual return of 3.34 per cent. This suggests that this company is undervalued by the market.

3 First calculate the beta value:

$$\text{Firm's beta} = 0.95 \times 018/0.15 = 1.14$$

using the correlation coefficient of 0.95 and then the expected rate of return on equity using the Capital Asset Pricing Model

$$E(Ri) = 4\% + 1.14 \times 3.5\% = 7.90\%$$

Calculate the rate of return on government debt:

Government debt:

	0	1	2	3	4
Cash flow to the investor	−90	7	7	7	107
Yield	10.17%				

Yield = 10.17% (solve by linear interpolation or by using Excel = IRR function)

Add the credit risk premium to give a cost of debt capital = 11.17%

Effective (after tax cost of debt) = 7.82%

Finally the weighted average cost of capital is calculated as follows:

$$WACC = (1 - w_d)r_e + w_d r_d$$
$$WACC = (1 - .65) \times 0.079 + .65 \times 0.0782$$
$$WACC = 0.07848 \equiv 7.848\%$$

Chapter 6

Review Activity 6.1

$$\text{Market gearing ratio} = \frac{\text{Market value of debt}}{\text{Total market value of the firm}}$$

$$\text{Market gearing ratio} = \frac{TMV_d}{TMV_e + TMV_d}$$

$$Market\ gearing\ ratio = \frac{£2m \times 0.98}{1m \times 3.10 + £2m \times 0.98}$$

Market gearing ratio $= 0.39$

Review Activity 6.2

If the Modigliani Miller propositions 1 and 2 hold then the firm's weighted average cost of capital is the same as its pure equity cost of capital:

$$r_e = r'_e + (r'_e - r_d)\frac{MV_d}{MV_e}$$

$$r_e = 0.09 + (0.09 - 0.04) \times 0.5$$

$$r_e = 0.11.5 \equiv 115\ per\ cent$$

End of chapter questions

1

$$r_e = r'_e + (r'_e - r_d)\frac{MV_d}{MV_e}$$

$$r_e = 0.08 + (0.08 - 0.06) \times 0.5$$

$$r_e = 0.09 \equiv 9.0\ per\ cent$$

Market value of HI's equity:

$$MV_e = \frac{200\,000}{0.09} = £2.22\ million$$

2

$$r_e = r'_e + (1 - T)(r'_e - r_d)\frac{MV_d}{MV_e}$$

$$0.07 = r'_e + (1 - 0.35)(r'_e - 0.04) \times 0.4$$

$$r'_e = \frac{.07 + 0.0104}{1.26}$$

$$r'_e = 0.0638 \equiv 6.38\ per\ cent$$

3

$$\beta_a = (1 - w_d)\beta_e$$

$$\beta_a = (1 - 0.45)1.6$$

$$\beta_a = 0.88$$

$$\beta_a = (1 - w_d)\beta_e$$

$$0.88 = (1 - 0.6)\beta_e$$

$$\beta_e = 2.2$$

Chapter 7

Review Activity 7.1

DG05/01/14 Summary cash flow statement (sterling million)	0	1	2	3	4	5	6
Nominal project operating cash flow		0.830	0.890	0.905	0.913	0.949	0.775
Capital investment	−3.500						
	−3.500	0.830	0.890	0.905	0.913	0.949	0.775
Discounted cash flow at 5.88 per cent	−3.500	0.784	0.794	0.763	0.727	0.713	0.550
Net Present Value	0.831						

	0	1	2	3	4	5	6
Project real operating cash flow		0.814	0.855	0.853	0.844	0.860	0.688
Capital investment	−3.500						
	−3.500	0.814	0.855	0.853	0.844	0.860	0.688
Discounted cash flow at 8 per cent	−3.500	0.754	0.733	0.677	0.620	0.585	0.434
Net Present Value	0.303						

Compared with an NPV of 0.556 (see the text) the degree of overvaluation of this project given (i) is 27.5 per cent and the degree of undervaluation of the project given (ii) is 45.5 per cent.

Review Activity 7.2

Taking the original plan:

	Capital Outlay	Cum. Capital	NPV	IRR	PI
DG04/01/03	−5.333	−5.333	3.088	66.57%	0.5791
OG05/09/02	−12.000	−17.333	3.124	22.53%	0.2603
DG05/03/11	−3.650	−20.983	0.884	13.64%	0.2422
DG05/01/14	−3.500	−24.483	0.556	13.07%	0.1588
DG05/02/11	−1.517	−26.000	0.198	18.02%	0.1302
DG05/02/11	−2.493	−28.493	0.325	18.02%	0.1302
NM04/04/10	−4.000	−32.493	0.140	8.76%	0.0350
OG05/06/01	−19.100	−51.593	3.224	14.38%	0.1688
Capital Budget	**−26.000**		**7.850**	**22.55%**	**0.3019**

(a) Project DG05/0/11 requires £2.493 million for full scale investment. Given the assumptions of the model an extra £2 million would generate a return of 8 per cent plus a PI of 13.02 per cent. The maximum rate for short term borrowing would be 21.02 per cent.

(b) An additional £6 million would generate a PI as follows:

$$PI = \frac{2.493}{6} \times 13.02\% + \frac{3.507}{6} \times 3.5\% = 7.46 \text{ per cent}$$

Which suggests a maximum rate of 15.46 per cent.

(c) If £19 million is available then project OG05/06/01 could be accepted which generates a rate of return of 16.88 per cent giving a maximum borrowing rate of 24.88 per cent.

End of Chapter Questions

1

		0	1	2	3	4	5
Plant and equipment	30%	−550 000	−385 000	−269 500	−188 650	−132 055	−92 438.5
Sales revenue	40		436 800	476 986	510 852	547 122	585 968
Labour	0.5		−136 500	−149 058	−162 771	−177 746	−194 099
Shadow price			−76 000	−56 000			
Materials	10		−110 250	−121 551	−134 010	−144 931	−156 743
Project specific overheads	45 000		−45 900	−47 736	−49 645	−50 638	−51 651
Operating cash flows			68 150	102 641	164 425	173 806	183 474
Plant and equipment		−550 000					92 439
NCF		−550 000	68 150	102 641	164 425	173 806	275 913
Money cost of capital			1.0710	1.0920	1.0920	1.0710	1.0710
Compound factor			1.0710	1.1695	1.2771	1.3678	1.4649
Discount factor			0.9337	0.8550	0.7830	0.7311	0.6826
Dicounted cash flow		−550 000	63 632	87 762	128 746	127 069	188 347
NPV		45 557					
Cum cash flow		−550 000	−481 850	−379 209	−214 784	−40 978	234 935
Cum disc cash flow		−550 000	−486 368	−394 088	−250 463	−87 714	147 369
Internal Rate of Return	10.60%						
NPV/£ outlay	0.0828						
Payback	4.1485						
Discounted payback	4.3731						

Chapter 8

Review Activity 8.1

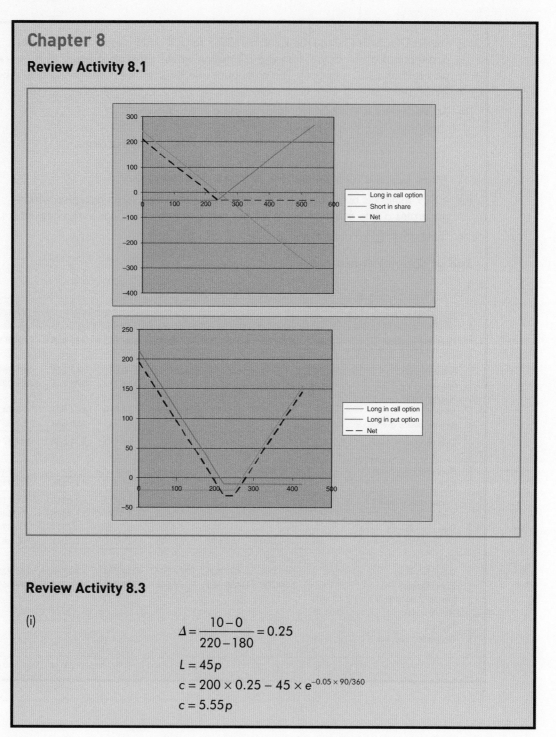

Review Activity 8.3

(i)

$$\Delta = \frac{10-0}{220-180} = 0.25$$

$$L = 45p$$

$$c = 200 \times 0.25 - 45 \times e^{-0.05 \times 90/360}$$

$$c = 5.55p$$

(ii)
$$\Delta = \frac{60 - 0}{250 - 150} = 0.6$$

$$L = 90p$$

$$c = 200 \times 0.6 - 90 \times e^{-0.05 \times 90/360}$$

$$c = 31.12p$$

(iii)
$$c = 200 \times 0.4 - 60 \times e^{-0.05 \times 180/360}$$

$$c = 21.48p$$

(iv)
$$c = 190 \times 0.4 - 60 \times e^{-0.05 \times 90/360}$$

$$c = 16.75p$$

(v)
$$c = 200 \times 0.4 - 60 \times e^{-0.08 \times 90/360}$$

$$c = 21.19p$$

Review Activity 8.4

A	B	C	D
	Black and Scholes Option		
1	**Pricing Model (Call)**		
2			
3	Current price	200.00	
4	Exercise price	210.00	
5	Risk free rate	0.05	
6	Time to exercise (days)	90	
7	Volatility	0.2000	
8			
9	d1	−0.19658	
10	d2	−0.31658	
11			
12	N(d1)	0.42208	
13	N(d2)	0.37578	
14			
15	call value	6.91	
16			

A	B	C	D
	Black and Scholes Option		
1	**Pricing Model (Put)**		
2			
3	Current price	200.00	
4	Exercise price	210.00	
5	Risk free rate	0.05	
6	Time to exercise (days)	90	
7	Volatility	0.2000	
8			
9	d1	−0.19658	
10	d2	−0.31658	
11			
12	N(−d1)	0.57792	
13	N(−d2)	0.62422	
14			
15	put value	13.16	
16			

Review Activity 8.6

A	B	C	D
	Black and Scholes Option		
1	**Pricing Model**		
2	**Cobham plc**		
3	Current price	1410.50	
4	Exercise price	1410.50	
5	Risk free rate	0.0475	
6	Time to exercise (days)	250	
7	Volatility	0.1380	
8			
9	d1	0.41320	
10	d2	0.27520	
11			
12	N(d1)	0.66027	
13	N(d2)	0.60842	
14			
15	call value	112.95	
16			

End of Chapter Questions

1

$$99\Delta - L = 9$$
$$81\Delta - L = 0$$
$$\Delta = \frac{9-0}{99-81} = 0.5$$
$$L = 40.5p$$
$$c = 90 \times 0.5 - 40.5 \times e^{-0.05 \times 90/360}$$
$$c = 5.00p$$

On the basis of this the purchase of 500 shares taking out a loan at 5 per cent of £405 would produce the same payoff as the option described. The cost of the replicating transaction would be £50 (i.e. options on 1000 shares at 5p each).

2

(i)

$$P_0 - PV(P_e) = c - p$$
$$204.5 - 200 \times e^{-0.05 \times \frac{90}{360}} = 22 - p$$
$$p = 15.02$$

Chapter 9

Review Activity 9.1

A	B	C	D
	Black and Scholes Option		
1	**Pricing Model**		
2			
3	Current price	70.00	
4	Exercise price	150.00	
5	Risk free rate	0.05	
6	Time to exercise (days)	750	
7	Volatility	0.3500	
8			
9	d1	−0.70666	
10	d2	−1.31288	
11			
12	N(d1)	0.23989	
13	N(d2)	0.09461	
14			
15	call value	4.58	
16			

Review Activity 9.3

A	B	C	D
1			
2	**Merton (1974) Structural** **Debt Model – value of debt**		
3			
3	Current asset value	674.19	
4	Value of outstanding debt	500.00	
5	Risk free rate	0.05	
6	Time to exercise (days)	1500	
7	Asset Volatility	0.2324	
8	PV of gearing (g)	0.5494135	
9			
10	h1	–1.33670	
11	h2	0.76744	
12			
13	N(h1)	0.09066	
14	N(h2)	0.77859	
15			
16	Market value of the debt	349.52	
17	Spread	0.00967506	

Entering the results as generated but raising the value of the outstanding debt to £500 million we obtain a likely spread of 97 basis points.

End of chapter questions

1

(i) The Net Present Value of the project can be determined using a modified annuity formula for a growing cash flow:

$$PV = CF\frac{(1+h)}{(1+i)} + CF\frac{(1+h)^2}{(1+i)^2} \cdots\cdots\cdots CF\frac{(1+h)^{10}}{(1+i)^{10}}$$

$$PV\frac{(1+i)}{(1+h)} = CF + CF\frac{(1+h)^1}{(1+i)^1} + \cdots\cdots\cdots CF\frac{(1+h)^9}{(1+i)^9}$$

Taking the first equation from the second and rearranging:

$$PV = CF\left\{\frac{1-\dfrac{(1+h)^{10}}{(1+i)^{10}}}{i-h}\right\}(1+h)$$

$$PV = 1.5\left\{\frac{1-\dfrac{(1.025)^{10}}{(1.08)^{10}}}{0.055}\right\}(1.025)$$

$$PV = 11.38$$

Where *h* is the inflation rate, *i* is the discount rate, *CF* is the real cash flow.

Given an outlay of £12 million this gives a Net Present Value of –£0.62

(ii) A minimum estimate for the value of delay is given by the Black and Scholes model:

A	B	C	D
	Black and Scholes Option		
1	**Pricing Model**		
2			
3	Current price	11.38	
4	Exercise price	12.00	
5	Risk free rate	0.05	
6	Time to exercise (days)	750	
7	Volatility	0.3000	
8			
9	d1	0.44639	
10	d2	–0.07323	
11			
12	N(d1)	0.67234	
13	N(d2)	0.47081	
14			
15	call value	2.79	
16			

(iii) Using a 12 time step model for an American call option the value of the real option is £2.79. This suggests that there is no value in early exercise.

American Call Option – price/value generation table

		0	1	2	3	4	5	6	7	8	9	10	11	12
$\sigma=$ 0.3000	0	11.38	13.22	15.36	17.85	20.74	24.09	27.99	32.52	37.78	43.90	51.00	59.26	68.84
$r=$ 0.0500	1	0.00	9.79	11.38	13.22	15.36	17.85	20.74	24.09	27.99	32.52	37.78	43.90	51.00
$\Delta t=$ 0.2500	2	0.00	0.00	8.43	9.79	11.38	13.22	15.36	17.85	20.74	24.09	27.99	32.52	37.78
$u=$ 1.1618	3	0.00	0.00	0.00	7.26	8.43	9.79	11.38	13.22	15.36	17.85	20.74	24.09	27.99
$d=$ 0.8607	4	0.00	0.00	0.00	0.00	6.25	7.26	8.43	9.79	11.38	13.22	15.36	17.85	20.74
$p=$ 0.5043	5	0.00	0.00	0.00	0.00	0.00	5.38	6.25	7.26	8.43	9.79	11.38	13.22	15.36
P_0 12.00	6	0.00	0.00	0.00	0.00	0.00	0.00	4.63	5.38	6.25	7.26	8.43	9.79	11.38
$v=$ 0.9876	7	0.00	0.00	0.00	0.00	0.00	0.00	0.00	3.98	4.63	5.38	6.25	7.26	8.43
	8	0.00	0.00	0.00	0.00	0.00	0.00	0.00	0.00	3.43	3.98	4.63	5.38	6.25
	9	0.00	0.00	0.00	0.00	0.00	0.00	0.00	0.00	0.00	2.95	3.43	3.98	4.63
	10	0.00	0.00	0.00	0.00	0.00	0.00	0.00	0.00	0.00	0.00	2.54	2.95	3.43
	11	0.00	0.00	0.00	0.00	0.00	0.00	0.00	0.00	0.00	0.00	0.00	2.19	2.54
	12	0.00	0.00	0.00	0.00	0.00	0.00	0.00	0.00	0.00	0.00	0.00	0.00	1.88

American Call Option – tree analysis

	0	1	2	3	4	5	6	7	8	9	10	11	12
0	2.79	3.96	5.52	7.52	10.05	13.15	16.87	21.25	26.37	32.34	39.30	47.40	56.84
1	1.10	1.67	2.48	3.61	5.14	7.15	9.70	12.84	16.58	20.96	26.08	32.05	39.00
2	0.34	0.56	0.89	1.39	2.15	3.23	4.74	6.76	9.36	12.53	16.29	20.67	25.78
3	0.08	0.14	0.23	0.40	0.67	1.10	1.77	2.80	4.30	6.36	9.03	12.24	15.99
4	0.01	0.02	0.04	0.07	0.13	0.24	0.44	0.77	1.35	2.30	3.81	6.00	8.74
5	0.00	0.00	0.00	0.01	0.01	0.03	0.05	0.10	0.21	0.42	0.83	1.67	3.36
6	0.00	0.00	0.00	0.00	0.00	0.00	0.00	0.00	0.00	0.00	0.00	0.00	0.00
7	0.00	0.00	0.00	0.00	0.00	0.00	0.00	0.00	0.00	0.00	0.00	0.00	0.00
8	0.00	0.00	0.00	0.00	0.00	0.00	0.00	0.00	0.00	0.00	0.00	0.00	0.00
9	0.00	0.00	0.00	0.00	0.00	0.00	0.00	0.00	0.00	0.00	0.00	0.00	0.00
10	0.00	0.00	0.00	0.00	0.00	0.00	0.00	0.00	0.00	0.00	0.00	0.00	0.00
11	0.00	0.00	0.00	0.00	0.00	0.00	0.00	0.00	0.00	0.00	0.00	0.00	0.00
12	0.00	0.00	0.00	0.00	0.00	0.00	0.00	0.00	0.00	0.00	0.00	0.00	0.00

2

	A	B	C
1		**Merton (1974) Structural Debt Model – call value**	
2			
3		**Current asset value**	**354.15**
4		**Asset Volatility**	**0.4477**
5			
6		Value of outstanding debt	150.00
7		Risk free rate	0.05
8		Time to exercise (days)	1250
9		Value of equity	250.0
10		Volatility of equity	0.6
11			
12		d1	1.60846
13		d2	0.60745
14			
15		N(d1)	0.94613
16		N(d2)	0.72822
17			
18		Value of the equity call on the firm's assets	250.00
19			
20		Actual equity – call	0.00
21		Equity less Ito estimate	0.00
22		**Squared total**	**0.00**
23			
24		**Value of debt**	104.15
25		**Spread**	0.022964

(i)   Current Asset Value and asset volatility as above

(ii) Value of the firm's debt is £104.15. Implied yield is 7.296 per cent (risk free rate plus spread)

(iii) The potential loss is given by the difference between the present value of the outstanding debt and its current market value:

$$Loss = Debt \times e^{-txR_F} - MV(D)$$

$$Loss = 150e^{-5 \times 0.05} - 104.15$$

$$Loss = 12.67$$

As a proportion of the value of the outstanding debt the potential loss is 10.85 per cent.

The risk free default probability is given by $(1 - N(d2)) = 1 - 0.72822 = 0.272$

This implies that for every £100, £27.20 is at risk. Given that likelihood of potential loss is £10.85 per £100, the recovery is as follows:

$$Recovery = \frac{0.272 - 0.1085}{0.272} = 0.6 \, (60\%)$$

Chapter 10

Review Activity 10.2

Sector average for the market to book ratio = 3.063

Value of Rolls Royce = £2307 million × 3.063 = £7066.34 million

This is equivalent to a share price of 414.50p per share given that there are 1704.77 million shares in issue.

Review Activity 10.3

Valuation model for finite time duration

$$p_0 = \frac{D_0 \left[1 - \dfrac{(1+g)^n}{(1+r_e)^n} \right] (1+g)}{(r_e - g)}$$

Using this formula the values and the proportion to the perpetuity model

$$p_0 = \frac{D_0(1+g)}{(r_e - g)}$$

can be found.

(i)   301.5 (43.1%)

(ii) 528.9 (75.6%)

(iii) 658.2 (94.0%)

Review Activity 10.5

Using the growth model based upon Free Cash Flow to Equity but setting growth equal to the firm's rate of return on equity invested rather than the cost of capital we have the formula:

$$p_0 = \frac{FCFE_0(net)(1 + b_c \times ROI)}{r_e - b_c \times ROI}$$

Setting the values into the model as shown in the chapter but solving for the return on investment given a price of 1404p we obtain a value of 6.6 per cent. This suggests that the company is not expected to generate the minimum required rate of return on its future investment of cash within the business. If we assume that the company is able to earn the minimum required rate of return on its investment then the firm's cost of capital (and its rate of return on investment) would be 9.42 per cent.

Review Activity 10.6

earnings forecast	annual growth	(1 + g)	accum (1 + g)
94.9			
100.8	0.06217	1.06217	1.06217
112.1	0.11210	1.11210	1.18124
120.1	0.07136	1.07136	1.26554
arithmetic average	0.08188		1.08166
geometric average			0.08166

End of chapter questions

2

Free cash flow to equity	£million	450
Rate of return on equity		0.08
Shares in issue		400
CAPEX	£million	260
Distributable cash per share	£	0.475
Retention ratio		0.578
Implied growth		0.046
Value of the equity per share	£	14.713

The retention ratio is taken as the CAPEX/FCFE which when multiplied by the current rate of return on equity gives a growth of 4.6 per cent. The growth model is then applied to obtain the value of each equity share.

1

		ape	financial services	Beaser
(i)	Ape Training			
	gearing	0.05	0.05	0.12
	gearing (tax adjusted)	0.0291	0.0291	0.0672
	equity beta		1.4000	1.6000
	asset beta	1.4481	1.3592	1.4925
	equity beta (Ape)	1.4915		
	Number of shares in issue	10 000 000		
	Expected return (equity cost of capital)	0.0972		
	Cost of debt capital	0.075		
	WACC (tax adjusted)	0.0946		

Equity cost of capital used for estimating required rate of return to equity WACC for estimating discount rate for internal, marginal investment.

(ii)	PE ratio (Beaser)	16.75
	EPS (Ape)	95
	Market value based on PE relatives	1591.25
	Ape retention ratio	0.58
	growth assuming equity cost of capital	0.06
	market value	1032
	Weighted growth	0.054
	Market value assuming 6%	976

Note the above spreadsheet solution follows the following steps for calculating the equity cost of capital.

The tax adjusted gearing is taken assuming £100 of equity in each case, the gearing ratio (quoted as debt/equity) gives the amount of debt and from that the tax adjusted version can be calculated (see Chapter 6).

Using the equity betas for the financial services sector and for Beaser the respective asset betas can be calculated and from that an asset beta for Ape assuming a one third/two thirds business mix. Using Ape's gearing ratio an equity beta can be estimated.

2

(i) The value of the first ten years' cash flow can be obtained using the finite growth model:

$$p_0 = \frac{D_0\left[1 - \dfrac{(1+g)^n}{(1+r_e)^n}\right](1+g)}{(r_e - g)}$$

Substituting the values from the question gives a present value of the future cash flows until year 10 of £1043.89.

At year 10 the cash flow will be:

$$CF_{10} = 85 \times (1.12)^{10} = £264.00 \; million$$

This as a perpetuity capitalized at 8 per cent is valued at £3300 which in present value terms gives £1528.54 million.

The combined value of the cash flows is therefore:

$$(1043.89 + 1528.54 + 90) = £2662.43 \; million$$

This assumes that the £90 million of cash reserves are distributable without detriment to the future cash flows of the business.

(ii) The valuation of the firm's first ten years of cash flow is achieved using the Merton (1974) structural debt model (as shown in Chapter 9).

The solver routine is applied to the equity value and the equity volatility which is easily achieved by entering the values as highlighted. We have assumed that the outstanding cash is an addition to the present value of the firm to give £1 110.37. Guess values for the value of equity and the volatility of equity of £1000 million and 25 per cent respectively were included in the spreadsheet. The spreadsheet before the solver routine is applied is as follows:

	A	B	C	D
1		**Merton (1974) Structural Debt Model – call value**		
2				
3		Current asset value	1133.88	
4		Asset Volatility	0.2000	
5		Value of outstanding debt	380.00	
6		Risk free rate	0.05	
7		Time to exercise (days)	2500	
8		**Value of equity**	**1000.0**	
9		**Volatility of equity**	**0.2500**	
10				
11				
12		d1	2.83534	
13		d2	2.20289	
14				
15		N(d1)	0.99771	
16		N(d2)	0.98620	
17				
18		Value of the equity call on the firm's assets	903.98	
19				
20		Actual equity – call	96.02	
21		Equity less Ito estimate of equity value	94.97	
22		**Squared total**	**18 238.78**	
23				
24		**Value of debt**	229.90	
25		**Spread**	0.05025444	

And after. . . .

A	B	C	D
1	**Merton (1974) Structural Debt Model – call value**		
2			
3	Current asset value	1133.88	
4	Asset Volatility	0.2000	
5	Value of outstanding debt	380.00	
6	Risk free rate	0.05	
7	Time to exercise (days)	2500	
8	**Value of equity**	**904.0**	
9	**Volatility of equity**	**0.2503**	
10			
11			
12	d1	2.83534	
13	d2	2.20289	
14			
15	N(d1)	0.99771	
16	N(d2)	0.98620	
17			
18	Value of the equity call on the firm's assets	903.98	
19			
20	Actual equity – call	0.00	
21	Equity less Ito estimate of equity value	0.00	
22	**Squared total**	**0.00**	
23			
24	**Value of debt**	229.90	
25	**Spread**	0.05025444	

This model reveals that the value of the equity claim against the cash flows for ten years is £903.98 million.

(iii) We can now calculate the value of the firm as follows:

Equity value of the firm = value of the first ten years' cash flow + value of the residual cash flows less the outstanding market value of the firm's debt:

$$\text{Equity value} = £1133.88 \text{ million} + £1528.54 \text{ million} - £229.90 \text{ million}$$
$$= £2432.52 \text{ million}$$

Chapter 11

Review Activity 11.2

The first step in testing the sensitivity of a model of this type is to derive a mathematical expression that measures the rate of change of CIV with the variables of concern to us. Here is the calculation for the CIV:

$$CIV = \frac{\Delta r_A (1-t)(1+g)}{WACC}$$

$$CIV = \frac{82.17(1-30\%)(1.03794)}{0.0687}$$

$$CIV = £869 \text{ million}$$

Let K be a constant:

$$K = \Delta r_A (1-t)$$
$$K = 82.17(1-30\%)$$
$$K = 57.52$$

Then:

$$CIV = \frac{K(1+g)}{WACC}$$

$$\frac{\partial CIV}{\partial WACC} = \frac{K(1+g)}{WACC^2}$$

$$\partial CIV = -\frac{K(1+g)}{WACC^2} \times \partial WACC$$

and

$$\partial CIV = -\frac{K}{WACC} \times \partial g$$

A 1 per cent increase in the weighted average cost of capital will decrease the CIV by:

$$\partial CIV = -\frac{K(1+g)}{WACC^2} \times \partial WACC$$

$$\partial CIV = -\frac{57.52(1.03794)}{0.0687^2} \times .01$$

$$\partial CIV = -126.5$$

A 1 per cent increase in the rate of growth will increase the CIV by:

$$\partial CIV = \frac{57.52}{0.0687} \times 0.01$$

$$\partial CIV = 8.37$$

This demonstrates the relative importance of the cost of capital in determining the value of a firm.

End of chapter questions

1

(i) The return spread is given by the following:

$$\Delta r_i = 41 - 0.15 \times 100 = 26$$

The CIV is calculated as follows:

$$CIV = \frac{26 \times (1 - 0.3)(1.04)}{0.08}$$

$$CIV = £236.6 \ million$$

Chapter 12

Review Activity 12.2

(i) Working sheets following a £150 million cash bid for 90 per cent of the equity.

	FA	Inv	St	Db	C	=	STL	LTL	OC	SPA	PLR
Friendly Grinders' Balance Sheet per acquisition	640		33	12	35		24	90	20	45	541
New Loan finance					150			150			
Purchase of RufDiamond plc		150			−150						
Friendly Grinders' Balance Sheet post acquisition	640	150	33	12	35		24	240	20	45	541

	FA	GW	St	Db	C	=	STL	LTL	OC	SPA	PLR	MI
Friendly Grinders' (parent) balance sheet	640	150	33	12	35		24	240	20	45	541	
RufDiamond balance sheet	90		12	30	8		25	10	40	40	25	
Transfer RufDiamond's equity												
90% to goodwill		−36							−36			
10% to minority interest										−4		4
Transfer RufDiamond's share premium account												
90% to goodwill		−36								−36		
10% to minority interest										−4		4
Transfer RufDiamond's profit and loss reserve												
90% to goodwill		−22.5									−22.5	
10% to minority interest											−2.5	2.5
Consolidated balance sheet	730	55.5	45	42	43		49	250	20	45	541	10.5

Group balance sheet

Friendly Grinders (group) plc
Balance Sheet at date of
  acquisition (£million)

Fixed Assets		730.0
Goodwill on acquisition		55.5
		785.5
Current assets:		
Stocks	45.0	
Debtors	42.0	
Cash	43.0	
	130.0	
Less short term liabilities	49.0	
		81.0
		866.5
Less long term liabilities		250.0
		616.5
Owner's Equity		
Share capital		20.0
Share premium account		45.0
Profit and loss reserve		541.0
		606.0
Minority interest		10.5
		616.5

(ii) Working sheets following an 80 million cash bid with shares for 80 per cent of the equity:

	FA	Inv	St	Db	C	=	STL	LTL	OC	SPA	PLR
Friendly Grinders' Balance Sheet per acquisition	640		33	12	35		24	90	20	45	541
New loan		80						80			
Purchase of RufDiamond plc issue of 6.5 million ordinary shares for 1100p											
6.5 million at 25p to issued share capital		1.6							1.6		
6.5 million at 1075p to the share premium account		69.9								69.9	
Friendly Grinders' Balance Sheet post acquisition	640.0	151.5	33.0	12.0	35.0		24.0	170.0	21.6	114.9	541.0

	FA	GW	St	Db	C	=	STL	LTL	OC	SPA	PLR	MI
Friendly Grinders' (parent) balance sheet	640	152	33	12	35		24	170	22	115	541	
RufDiamond balance sheet	90		12	30	8		25	10	40	40	25	
Transfer RufDiamond's equity												
90% to goodwill		−36							−36			
10% to minority interest									−4			4
Transfer RufDiamond's share premium account												
90% to goodwill		−36								−36		
10% to minority interest										−4		4
Transfer RufDiamond's profit and loss reserve												
90% to goodwill		−22.5									−22.5	
10% to minority interest											−2.5	2.5
Consolidated balance sheet	730	57	45	42	43		49	180	21.625	114.88	541	10.5

Group balance sheet:

Friendly Grinders (group) plc
Balance Sheet at date of acquisition (£million)

Fixed Assets		730.0
Goodwill on acquisition		57.0
		787.0
Current assets:		
Stocks	45.0	
Debtors	42.0	
Cash	43.0	
	130.0	
Less short term liabilities	49.0	
		81.0
		868.0
Less long term liabilities		180.0
		688.0
Owner's Equity		
Share capital		21.6
Share premium account		114.9
Profit and loss reserve		541.0
		677.5
Minority interest		10.5
		688.0

Review Activity 12.3

This is rather simple. The maximum that Friendly Grinders should pay is the potential value gain as a result of the acquisition. With an 80 per cent stake the Friendly Grinders' shareholders will gain £184 million and with a 100 per cent stake they gain £230 million. These are the maximum amounts that should be offered – any greater amount in either case and the shareholders will lose value.

End of Chapter Questions

1

(i) The cost of equity capital is derived from the Capital Asset Pricing Model but given this is an unquoted company a proxy must be taken for the company's beta and regeared to reflect the different financial risk exposure of FlyMe Ltd.

Ideally regearing beta requires an estimate of the market gearing for both companies. In the absence of that the book gearing can be used. However, the presence of corporation tax means that we need the values for both the debt and equity in BA.

$$BV(equity) = \frac{£3026.71m}{1.25} = £2421.4m$$

$$Gearing = \frac{BV(debt)}{BV(equity)}$$

$$BV(debt) = BV(equity) \times gearing$$

$$BV(debt) = 2421.4\,m \times 1.867 = £4520.75m$$

Using the formula for the asset beta where debt carries zero market risk:

$$\beta_A = \beta_e \times (1 - w_d)$$

where

$$w_d = \frac{BV_d \times (1-T)}{BV_e + BV_d \times (1-T)}$$

$$w_d = \frac{4520.75 \times (0.7)}{2421.4 + 4520.75 \times (0.7)}$$

$$w_d = 0.5665$$

$$\beta_A = 2.01 \times (1 - 0.5665)$$

$$\beta_A = 0.871$$

This is the asset beta for BA. We can now regear the beta to that for FlyMe as follows: Recalculate the tax adjusted gearing ratio for FlyMe Ltd

$$w_d = \frac{BV_d \times (1-T)}{BV_e + BV_d \times (1-T)}$$

$$w_d = \frac{150 \times (0.7)}{120 + 150 \times (0.7)}$$

$$w_d = 0.4667$$

$$\beta_e = \frac{\beta_a}{(1-w_d)}$$

$$\beta_e = \frac{0.871}{(1-.4667)}$$

$$\beta_e = 1.633$$

This is the estimated equity beta for FlyMe Ltd which when applied to the CAPM gives an expected rate of return as follows:

$$E(r_e) = R_F + \beta_e \times ERP$$
$$E(r_e) = 0.045 + 1.633 \times 0.035$$
$$E(r_e) = 0.045 + 1.633 \times 0.035$$
$$E(r_e) = 0.1022 (\equiv 10.22\%)$$

The equity cost of capital for FlyMe Ltd is therefore approximately 10.22 per cent.

(ii) For 2004 the FCFE is as follows:

$$FCFE = \text{operating cash flow} - \text{net interest paid} - \text{tax}$$
$$FCFE\ (\pounds m) = 210\,m + 1.5 - 4.1 = 207.4$$

In the current year £120.2 m was reinvested. This implies a retention ratio (b) of:

$$b = \frac{reinvestment}{FCFE}$$

$$b = \frac{120.2}{207.4}$$

$$b = 0.58$$

$$g = bxr_e$$

$$g = 0.58 \times 0.1022$$

$$g = 0.0592 (\equiv 5.92\%)$$

On the basis of this and given that the year 7 growth rate and forward will be 4 per cent. The pattern of growth we anticipate is therefore:

Year	1	2	3	4	5	6	7
Growth rate	5.92%	5.92%	5.92%	5.92%	5.92%	4.96%	4%

(iii) The valuation is straightforward. Using the free cash flow to equity net of reinvestment we have the free cash flow which is, in principle, distributable. We build a valuation model expanding this FCF through the next seven years. From year 7 forward the rate of growth is a perpetuity and we use the FCF analogue of the dividend growth model to estimate the value at year 7.

Step 1: take the growth rates as projected and estimate the future free cash flow to equity taking (£210m – £120.2m = £87.2m) as the starting point.

Step 2 discount these projected values at the cost of equity capital (10.22 per cent) to give a present value of £455.61m.

Step 3 using the formula:

$$V_e = \frac{FCFE_0(1+g)}{r_e - g}$$

Calculate the value of the growing perpetuity at the end of year 6 (note the timing of the year is important) using the expected FCFE in year 6. This gives a value at year 6 of £2040.20m.

Step 4: discount this at 10.22 per cent to give a present value of the residual term of £1137.92.

Step 5: add the two present values to give a valuation of the firm's equity at £1593.52 million.

Year	2006	2007	2008	2009	2010	2011	2012
Growth	5.92%	5.92%	5.92%	5.92%	5.92%	4.96%	4%
FCFE (2005) = £87.2m	92.36	97.83	103.62	109.76	116.25	122.02	
Discount at 10.22 per cent	83.80	80.53	77.39	74.37	71.47	68.06	
PV of year 1–6	455.61						
PV of perpetuity at 2011						2040.20	
PV of perpetuity at 2005	1137.92						
Present value of the firm's equity	1593.52						

Chapter 13

Review Activity 13.1

There are two rates: the higher is the rate at which a market maker will purchase the bill and the lower is the rate at which it will be sold. The lower rate is therefore the appropriate rate and the subscription value on new issue would be

$$subscription = \frac{50\,000}{(1 + 4.625\% \times \frac{90}{365})} = £49\,436.22$$

Review Activity 13.2

The risk exposure is to high interest rates. From the spot curves (a) suggests that the interest rate risk is on the downside and from (b) that the risk is on the upside. In the case of (a) the company would either do nothing or, if it was prepared to take the risk, sell an FRA to the bank, but in the case of (b) its exposure is upside and here it should seek to purchase an FRA to hedge the risk.

Review Activity 13.3

The current interest rate saving is 0.50 per cent to Jack and 0.25 per cent to Roger. This suggests that Jack should raise his new payment to Roger by 0.125 per cent. This can be achieved by lowering the fixed rate paid by Roger to 5.375 per cent or by increasing the variable rate paid by Jack to Base + 0.875 per cent (or by some intermediate solution).

End of Chapter Questions

1

The settlement from the bank (assuming a 360 day count) will be:

$$Settlement = \frac{(r_f - r_c) \times \frac{C}{365} \times Loan}{(1 + r_f \times \frac{C}{365})}$$

So in this case if the deposit is for (C) 90 days (three months) and the reference rate r_f is 3.9 per cent and the original contract rate r_c was 4.4 per cent. The difference is 0.5 per cent which is calculated on a three month basis:

$$Settlement = \frac{(.039 - .044) \times \frac{90}{360} \times 160\,000\,000}{(1 + .039 \times \frac{90}{360})}$$

Settlement = £198 069

The benefit of this agreement to the company is that the risk of a fall in interest rates will be hedged by the receipt of £198 069 which is the present value of the loss of interest over the three months of the anticipated deposit. However, the company will not gain from any future rise in interest rates.

2

There is a swap premium of 10 basis points:

Premium = (7.2% − 6.8%) − (LIBOR + 200 − LIBOR − 150)

Premium = 0.10

This relatively modest interest rate saving could be split by Ruskin paying LIBOR + 150 to Alfie and Alfie paying 6.75 per cent to Ruskin. This will reduce Alfie's potential fixed rate by 0.05 per cent (to 6.75 per cent) and Ruskin's potential variable rate by 5 basis points (to LIBOR + 195).

Chapter 14

Review Activity 14.1

(i)   dollar/yen (cross base/currency (base)) direct rate = 0.008453

dollar/sterling (cross base/currency (counter)) direct rate = 1.7224

yen/sterling cross rate = $0.008453 \times 1.7224^{-1} = 0.004907$ (indirect)

(ii) yen/SwFr direct rate = 90.1024

yen/Can$ direct rate = 100.8826

SwFr/Can$ = $90.1024 \times 100.8826^{-1} = 0.8932$ (indirect)

(iii) sterling/SwFr direct rate = 0.4422

sterling/dollar direct rate = 0.5806

SwFr/$ = $0.4422 \times 0.5806^{-1} = 0.7616$ (indirect)

End of chapter questions

1

The general formula for calculating a forward rate:

$$f_{\$/yen} = S_{\$/yen} \times \frac{(1+i_{yen}) \times \dfrac{days}{360}}{(1+i_{\$}) \times \dfrac{days}{360}}$$

$$f_{\$/yen} = 119.23 \times \frac{1.04000 \times \dfrac{90}{360}}{1.040525 \times \dfrac{90}{360}}$$

$$f_{\$/yen} = 119.21$$

This suggests that the yen is at a forward premium. For six months the calculation gives 119.19 and for one year 119.12.

2

This answer proceeds through a number of steps.

(i)   Calculate the project cash flows in Can$ at nominal by inflating using the Canadian inflation rate.

(ii) Calculate the post tax Canadian cash flow applying tax at 20 per cent.

(iii) Convert the UK post tax cash flow (remittable) at estimated future spot using the Purchasing Power Parity Fomula.

(iv) Calculate the additional UK tax by (a) doing a UK tax computation on the project and then deducting the Canadian tax (benefit or payable) using the expected future spot rate of exchange.

(v)   Deduct the additional tax payable to get a UK (nominal) post tax cash flow and then discount at 8 per cent:

	0	1	2	3	4	5	6
Project cash flow (real) – Can$	–6.600	2.000	2.000	2.000	2.000	2.000	
Project cash flows (nominal) – Can$	–6.600	2.040	2.081	2.122	2.165	2.208	
Benefit of capital allowance		1.320					
Tax on operating cash flows			–0.408	–0.416	–0.424	–0.433	–0.442
Project net cash flow (nominal) – Can$	–13.200	5.360	3.673	3.706	3.740	3.775	–0.442
Estimated future spot (PPP)	2.0079	2.0197	2.0316	2.0435	2.0556	2.0677	2.0798
Project net cash flow (nominal) – £	–6.574	2.654	1.808	1.814	1.820	1.826	–0.212
Additional UK tax	0.000	0.333	–0.096	–0.092	–0.087	–0.082	–0.078
Project cash flow (post tax) nominal	–6.574	2.986	1.712	1.722	1.733	1.743	–0.290
Discounted cash flow (8%)	–6.574	2.765	1.467	1.367	1.273	1.186	–0.183
Net Present Value	1.303						

	0	1	2	3	4	5	6
Tax calculation							
Project cash flows (nominal) – Can$	–6.600	2.000	2.000	2.000	2.000	2.000	
Convert at estimated spot	–3.287	0.990	0.984	0.979	0.973	0.967	
UK tax:							
Benefit of capital allowance		0.986					
Tax on operating cash flows			–0.297	–0.295	–0.294	–0.292	–0.290
Tax cash flow (sterling)	0.000	0.986	–0.297	–0.295	–0.294	–0.292	–0.290
Less Canadian Tax (converted at spot)	0.000	0.654	–0.201	–0.204	–0.207	–0.209	–0.212
Additional UK tax charge under DT agreement	0.000	0.333	–0.096	–0.092	–0.087	–0.082	–0.078

3

Using forward rates we can contract to buy sterling in three months at 1.7195 and buy euro(s) at 1.4421. The net euro(s) at the end will be:

$$Euros = \frac{12}{1.7195} \times 1.4421 = Euro\ 10\,064\,080$$

Conversion at spot would have given:

$$Euros = \frac{12}{1.7201} \times 1.4585 = Euro\ 10\,174\,990$$

The net loss over spot is €110 901 or £76 037